DICKENS STUDIES ANNUAL

Essays on Victorian Fiction

DICKENS STUDIES ANNUAL

Essays on Victorian Fiction

DICKENS STUDIES ANNUAL

Essays on Victorian Fiction

VOLUME
41

Edited by
Stanley Friedman, Edward Guiliano,
Anne Humpherys, Natalie McKnight, and Michael Timko

AMS PRESS, INC.
New York

Dickens Studies Annual
ISSN 0084–9812

Dickens Studies Annual: Essays on Victorian Fiction welcomes essay- and monograph-length contributions on Dickens and other Victorian novelists and on the history of aesthetics of Victorian fiction. All manuscripts should be double-spaced and should follow the documentation format described in the most recent *MLA Style Manual*. The author's name should appear only on a cover-page, not elsewhere in the essay. An editorial decision can usually be reached more quickly if two copies of the article are submitted, since outside readers are asked to evaluate each submission. If a manuscript is accepted for publication, the author will be asked to provide a 100- to 200-word abstract and also a CD-ROM containing the final version of the essay. The preferred editions for citations from Dickens's works are the Clarendon and the Norton Critical when available, otherwise the Oxford Illustrated or the Penguin. Since manuscripts are ordinarily not returned to their authors, no postage need be included.

Please send submissions to The Editors, *Dickens Studies Annual*, Ph.D. Program in English, The Graduate Center, CUNY, 365 Fifth Avenue, New York, NY 10016–4309. Please send inquiries concerning subscriptions and/or availability of earlier volumes to AMS Press, Inc., Brooklyn Navy Yard–Unit #221, 63 Flushing Ave., Brooklyn, NY 11205–1073, USA.

Dickens Studies Annual: Essays on Victorian Fiction is published in cooperation with Queens College and The Graduate Center, CUNY.

International Standard Book Number
Series ISBN-13: 978–0–404–18520–6
Series ISBN-10: 0–404–18520–7

Vol. 41 ISBN-13: 978–0–404–18941–9
Vol. 41 ISBN-10: 0–404–18941–5

All AMS books are printed on acid-free paper that meets the guidelines for performance and durability of the Committee on Production Guidelines for Book Longevity of the Council on Library Resources.

AMS PRESS, INC.
Brooklyn Navy Yard, 63 Flushing Avenue–Unit #221
Brooklyn, NY 11205–1073, USA
www.amspressinc.com

Manufactured in the United States of America

Contents

Preface

"Here's richness!" When that remarkable educator Wackford Squeers made this exclamation, he was not referring to Victorian fiction, but his words aptly describe it. The novels and stories of that era fuse the quotidian and the wondrous, interweave significant details and large, complex patterns, and combine the topical and the general. The submissions that we receive vary widely in approaches and purposes: one discussion may adduce specialized knowledge of the historical period to elucidate features in a narrative, while another essay may show how close attention to parts of a novel can illuminate selected aspects of Victorian daily life. A study may clarify by explaining cruxes or it may complicate our responses by disclosing previously overlooked inconsistencies and ambiguities. We believe that all of these endeavors, however, serve a primary goal of the humanities: study of the past helps further our understanding of the present.

We are especially grateful to the authors of essays submitted to us and also to our many outside readers, scholars whose informed reviews offer helpful guidance to us and to our contributors. The articles in this issue offer new insights into a number of subjects concerning Dickens and also into topics involving Wilkie Collins and Arthur Conan Doyle. In addition, we thank Cynthia Malone for her perceptive, valuable review essay examining Dickens studies appearing in 2008.

We have again been given generous assistance in practical matters by a number of academic administrators: President William P. Kelly, Provost Chase Robinson, Ph.D. Program in English Executive Officer Steven F. Kruger, and Nancy Silverman, Assistant Program Officer, Ph.D. Program in English, all of The Graduate Center, CUNY; and President James L. Muyskens, Dean of Arts and Humanities Tamara S. Evans, and Department of English Chair Nancy R. Comley, all of Queens College, CUNY.

We thank John O. Jordan, Director of The Dickens Project at the University of California, Santa Cruz; JoAnna Rottke, Project Coordinator for The Dickens Project; and Jon Michael Varese, the Project's Research Assistant and Web Administrator, for placing on the Project's website the tables of contents for volumes 1–27 of *DSA*, as well as abstracts for subsequent volumes. (These items are included in a link to *Dickens Studies Annual* on the Project's website, which can be reached at <http://dickens.ucsc.edu>.)

We sincerely appreciate the enthusiastic support of Gabriel Hornstein, President of AMS Press; the expert assistance of Jack Hopper, retired Editor-in-Chief at AMS Press; and the skills and foresight of David Ramm, Editor-in-Chief at AMS Press. We are also indebted to our editorial assistant, Brett Kawalerski, a Ph.D. candidate at The Graduate Center, CUNY, for reliably performing many important tasks.

—The Editors

Notes on Contributors

PHILIP V. ALLINGHAM, Chair of Undergraduate Studies in Education at Lakehead University, Thunder Bay, Ontario, Canada, has published widely on Dickens and Hardy in such journals as *Dickens Studies Annual, Dickens Quarterly, The Dickensian, The Thomas Hardy Year Book*, and *The Thomas Hardy Journal*. He is a contributing editor for George Landow's Victorian Web and a consultant for George Gorniak's *Dickens Magazine*. The present article is based on a paper that he gave at the "Dickens and Italy" Conference in Genoa in June 2007.

ANDREW BURKE is an assistant professor in the Department of English at the University of Winnipeg, where he teaches critical theory, cultural studies, and Victorian literature. His current project is on representations of modernity and modernization in contemporary British cinema, part of which is forthcoming in the journal *Screen*. He has also recently published articles in *Historical Materialism* and *English Studies in Canada*.

RODNEY STENNING EDGECOMBE lectures English literature at the University of Cape Town. He took his M.A. with distinction at Rhodes University, where he won the Royal Society of St. George Prize for English, and his Ph.D. at Trinity College, Cambridge, where he won the Members' Essay Prize. He also holds a Distinguished Teacher Award from UCT. He has published eleven books, the most recent being on Thomas Hood, and 308 articles on topics ranging from Shakespeare to nineteenth-century opera and ballet.

MICHAEL J. FLYNN is an assistant professor of English at the University of North Dakota. His work, which examines the strained relationship of Thackeray and Dickens and considers issues of intertextuality, fictional form, and the "dignity of literature" in early Victorian England, has previously appeared in *Notes and Queries, Dickens Studies Annual*, and the collection *Double Vision: Literary Palimpsests of the Eighteenth and Nineteenth Centuries*.

LAWRENCE FRANK is Emeritus Professor of English at the University of Oklahoma. He is the author of *Charles Dickens and the Romantic Self* (1984) and *Victorian Detective Fiction and the Nature of Evidence: The Scientific Investigations of Poe, Dickens, and Doyle* (2003), as well as various essays on Lewis Carroll, Charles Dickens, Arthur Conan Doyle, and Sigmund Freud. He is currently at work on a book that is tentatively titled "The Specter of Hamlet: Charles Dickens and the Darwinian Moment."

SARAH GATES earned her Ph.D. in English from Boston University. She is currently Associate Professor of English at St. Lawrence University, where she specializes in Victorian literature and culture, literary theory, gender studies, and the novel as a genre. She is the author of articles on George Eliot, Tennyson, and Dickens. This article is part of a larger project that explores Dickens's uses of intertextuality.

MELISSA VALISKA GREGORY is an associate professor of English at the University of Toledo specializing in nineteenth-century British literature. She has published on both poetry and the novel, and, recently, she has edited several versions of Dickens's collaborative Christmas numbers with Melisa Klimaszewski (Drake University) for Hesperus Press. She and Professor Klimaszewski are also currently working on an edited version of *The Lazy Tour of Two Idle Apprentices*.

LAUREN N. HOFFER is Lecturer in English at Vanderbilt University, where she recently completed her Ph.D. in English Literature. Her research specializations include Victorian literature and culture, the novel, and gender studies. She is currently at work on a book-length study of manipulative forms of sympathy and the paid female companion in the Victorian period.

Chair of the Department of English at the University of New Mexico, Professor GAIL TURLEY HOUSTON received her Ph.D. from UCLA in 1990. Her publications include *From Dickens to Dracula: Economics, Gothic, and Victorian Fiction* (Cambridge: Cambridge UP, 2005); *Royalties: The Queen and Victorian Writers* (Charlottesville: UP of Virginia, 1999); and *Consuming Fictions: Gender, Class, and Hunger in Dickens's Novels* (Carbondale: Southern Illinois UP, 1994). Having also written numerous articles on Victorian topics, she is currently completing a fourth manuscript on Victorian women writers and the idea of a female messiah.

LANYA LAMOURIA is an assistant professor at Missouri State University, where she teaches Victorian literature. Her contribution to *Dickens Studies Annual* is part of her current manuscript, an exploration of Victorian literary responses to the European revolutions of 1848. In 2009, she published an article on William North, a recently rediscovered Victorian novelist.

CYNTHIA NORTHCUTT MALONE is a professor of English at the College of Saint Benedict and Saint John's University. Her current research projects focus on Dickens and on the history and future of book publishing.

KATHERINE MONTWIELER teaches literature in the English Department of the University of North Carolina at Wilmington. Her publications include articles on the work of Maria Edgeworth, Letitia Elizabeth Landon, Elizabeth Barrett Browning, and Felicia Hemans. She is currently working on an essay on Shelley's *Frankenstein* and Duras's *Ourika* and a longer study on sensibility in nineteenth-century women's poetry.

JUDE V. NIXON is Professor of English and Dean of the School of Arts and Science at Salem State College, in Salem, Massachusetts. He is the author of *Gerard Manley Hopkins and His Contemporaries: Liddon, Newman, Darwin, and Pater* (1994), editor of *Victorian Religious Discourse: New Directions in Criticism* (2004), co-editor of volume 5, *The Sermons and Religious Writings*, of the eight-volume *Collected Works of Gerard Manley Hopkins* (OUP, 2010), and co-editor of volume 3, *Science, Religion, and Natural Theology*, of the eight-volume *Victorian Science and Literature* (Pickering & Chatto, 2010). His work has appeared in journals such as *Renascence, The Hopkins Quarterly, Carlyle Studies Annual, Dickens Studies Annual, Modern Philology, Victorian Studies, Victorian Poetry*, and *Texas Studies in Literature and Language*. He is a member of the editorial boards of *Victorian Poetry, The Hopkins Quarterly*, and *Dickens Studies Annual*.

TREY PHILPOTTS is Chair of the English Department at the University of Arkansas at Little Rock and the Review Editor for *Dickens Quarterly*. He has published *The Companion to Little Dorrit* (Helm, 2003) and is a contributor to *A Companion to Charles Dickens*, published by Blackwell in 2008. He has also published articles in *Dickens Quarterly, Dickens Studies Annual*, and *The Dickensian*. His most recent book, *The Companion to Dombey*, is scheduled to be published in 2011.

ROBYN WARHOL-DOWN is Arts and Humanities Distinguished Professor of English at the Ohio State University, where she is a core faculty member of Project Narrative. She is author of *Gendered Interventions: Narrative Discourse in the Victorian Novel* (1989) and *Having a Good Cry: Effeminate Feelings and Popular Forms* (1993) and co-editor, with Diane Price Herndl, of *Feminisms: An Anthology of Literary Criticism and Theory* (1991, 1997), as well as *Feminisms Redux* (2009). She has published essays in *Narrative, Style, Novel, Studies in English Literature, PMLA*, and other journals. A feminist narrative theorist, she has been working recently on the trope of narrative refusal in the nineteenth-century British novel. Parts of that longer project have been published in *The Henry James Quarterly* and *The Blackwell Companion to Narrative Theory*.

Theatrical Dance in Dickens

Rodney Stenning Edgecombe

This essay examines Dickens's presentation of social dance in various novels and sketches, and traces its comic heightening and stylization to Victorian ballet and pantomime. Dick Swiveller's behavior on the dance floor at the Wackleses' assembly, implausible as a social record, makes sense as a transcript of a coryphé's solo in a danse génerale, *while the equally implausible deftness and resilience in the performances of the market gardener in "Meditations in Monmouth Street" and Mr. Fezziwig in* A Christmas Carol *can be explained by the way young dancers impersonate unathletic people on the stage. The essay also examines the comic application of balletic mime to everyday life in "The Last Cab Driver."*

A large body of criticism has explored the impact of the legitimate theater on Dickens's fiction, some of it monitoring his debt to the comedy of humors ("Bobadil, indeed is almost the greatest of Jonson's creations. It is worth noting that Dickens knew and acted this character" [Sampson 299]), some the impact of Victorian melodrama as in, for example, the "heroic" diction of *Nicholas Nickleby* (MacKay 152), and some, more generally, tracing his habitual recourse to dramatic frames (Garis passim). Dickens also had a fondness for the musical stage, frequenting the opera, and acquiring a repertoire of effects and affects from that in turn. (How many English novelists can boast of dining with Auber and Scribe, doyens of the Opéra comique?) Even though, unlike Thackeray—one thinks of *La sonnambula* and *Fidelio* in *Vanity Fair*—Dickens remains tantalizingly vague about the particular operas that Edith Dombey attends in London or the Dorrits in Venice, this in no way signifies indifference to the form, for its influence far transcends the mere dropping of names. The magnificent monothematic proems of *Bleak House* and *Little Dorrit*, unparalleled elsewhere in Victorian fiction or drama, have kinship with the compressed atmospheric preludes, say, of *Lucia di Lammermoor* and *Lucrezia Borgia*, and also with the expansive but no less potent overtures to *Don Giovanni* and *Der Freischütz*. What is more, opera clearly inspired Dickens's use of leitmotiv, which was additionally enriched by his experience of Shakespearian image matrices. He would have known, for example, the majestic "statue" chords intercalated at points of *Don Giovanni* and would not have sneered either at "Home, Sweet Home," the humble "plug" (recurring theme) in Henry Bishop's *Clari*.

But while the operatic element manifests itself primarily in effects of pathos and drama, some of his comic effects derive from another theatrical influence, one that has received less attention. Clearly the ballet meant less to Dickens than the opera, but it has left its imprint on his fiction even so. As in the case of the operatic legacy, it declares itself in general issues of stylization rather than in the superficial naming of names. For example, even though Dickens hints at the luminous figure of Fanny Elssler when her namesake executes a minuet in the Marshalsea (*Little Dorrit* 72; bk 1, ch. 7), she never steps out of the narrative wings. By the same token, he also refuses to identify the balletic reach-me-downs in the repertoire of Fanny Dorrit's company, his artistic concerns centering on issues of why rather than what. For theatrical dance, no less than opera, trades in archetypes and humors, heightening the ordinary movements of humankind to a point where, like poetic meter, they become renderings of the originals—clearly based upon them, but alchemized to a point of transcendent generality. To that extent ballet parallels Dickens's own peculiar gift—one matched only by Shakespeare's—of distilling a convincing reality from otherwise implausible devices and materials. Both depend upon the heightenings and intensifications of "maniera," for just as ballet distorts the human form to make it more expressive, so does Dickens throughout his novels, even though his debt to theatrical dance relates largely to effects of comedy.

The maniera that makes possible his archetypal comic humors also enables his tragic ones, even though George Eliot mistakenly tried to divorce them: "he scarcely ever passes from the humorous and the external to the emotional and the tragic, without becoming as transcendent in his unreality as he was a moment before in his artistic truthfulness" (G. Eliot 98–99). If Dickens can be said to have transmogrified the demon king of Victorian pantomime into Quilp, then, as I shall argue below, he was equally likely to have transformed a trope of the Victorian ballet into the comedy of Dick Swiveller's extraordinary display at the Wackleses' dance. *Both* figures represent the "humorous and the external"—one dark, one light—and both are unreal, but *transcendently* so in a sense that Eliot never intended her epithet to signify. Dickens's operatic/pantomimic/balletic polarization of the humorous and the tragic offers each as the corollary of the other, entailing Little Nell in Quilp, as Cordelia is entailed in Edgar. What validates them is not that timid standard of encounterability called the plausible, but rather the vital performance per se. Virtuosity—and Dickens is the supreme virtuoso of the novel—is its own apodeictic reward, and has as slight a connection with documentary realism as a Paganini cadenza with the scrapings of a village fiddler or multiple pirouettes with a roistering country dance. Dickens's diagnosis of his performance as an actor applies a fortiori to his performance as a novelist: "As to the mere effect, of course I don't go on doing the thing so often without carefully observing myself and the people too in every little thing, and without (in consequence) greatly improving in it" (G. Eliot 144). His point of reference here is the mimetic stylization per se ("observing myself") not the raw materials that it has processed, and the same thing might be said of a danseuse watching her every move reflected in a studio mirror. Given, therefore, this stylistic substrate linking his narrative art with that of theatrical dance, it comes as no surprise to discover that the latter provided him with materials ready-made for his comic purposes.

While Dickens often treats dancing as a festive rite, he never gives it the symbolic value it enjoys in the finales of Shakespearian comedy, where the triumphant couples, set in ordered motion, signify "matrimonie— / A dignified and commodious sacrament" (T. S. Eliot 178). For the sacramental forging of social bonds, he prefers the table to the dance floor. It's not insignificant, therefore, that the socially defective Podsnaps invite some "friends of their souls" to a vacant carpet rather than a laden board—a symptom of their quid pro quo, contractual take on hospitality:

> There were still other friends of their souls who were not entitled to be asked to dinner, but had a claim to be invited to come and take a haunch of mutton vapour-bath at half-past nine. For the clearing off of these worthies, Mrs. Podsnap added a small and early evening to the dinner, and looked in at the music-shop to bespeak a well-conducted automaton to come and play quadrilles for a carpet dance.   (*Our Mutual Friend* 131; bk. 1, ch. 11)

The reason for this subordination of dancing to eating is not hard sought. Dickens had plentiful firsthand experience of banquets, but his knowledge of dance assemblies, given the vagaries of his childhood, seems to have been rather less extensive. In this essay, I shall argue that he compensated for this by drawing on the theatrical representations of these events.

It's impossible now to reconstruct the extent of Dickens's familiarity with Victorian ballet, but there are several indications that he was well acquainted with the art, among them the account of a dance rehearsal in *Little Dorrit*, and a letter to Georgina Hogarth proving that he had seen *Robert le diable* (and therefore the ballet of the spectral nuns). It records an encounter with the prince of Schleswig-Holstein,

> who sang a German song by the bye (in a raging bass voice) which I supposed to be Caspar in the Freischütz and Bertram in Robert, in partnership with some accursed invocation to the Evil One. —I was afterwards told that it was a gentle little anecdote concerning two soldiers.   (10:261)

Additional proof comes from "Night Walks," an essay in *The Uncommercial Traveller*, in which he visits an empty theater where Auber's *Muette de Portici* is being performed. This opera also features an extensive inset ballet (guaracca, bolero, and tarantella) and a mute heroine who communicates entirely by stylized signage, one source (no doubt of many) for his comic treatments of balletic mime:

> The ground at my feet where, when last there, I had seen the peasantry of Naples dancing among the vines, reckless of the burning mountain which threatened to overwhelm them, was now in possession of a strong serpent of engine-hose, watchfully lying in wait for the serpent Fire, and ready to fly at it if it showed its forked tongue.   (129)

And an oblique hint of ballet-going is lodged in "The New Year" (*Sketches by Boz*): "Prolonged approbation; above which the noise of the ladies dancing the Spanish dance among themselves, is distinctly audible" (223). The naively monolithic definite article (*"the* Spanish dance") points to a theatrical rather than a firsthand encounter with the phenomenon—and also shows, incidentally, that the women of the 1830s were less staid and timorous than those who succeeded them. The fandango, bolero, and seguidilla are nothing if not passionate and abandoned, and would certainly not have been taught to them by their dancing masters.

So these women seem to have let their hair down and are recreating (as best they can) the dances of *Ines de Castro*, staged at the King's Theatre in 1833. The vehemence of its Italian executants had startled the English public, and one hears, *avant la lettre*, the tones of Mr. Podsnap in one of the reviews: "At the last scene on Saturday night, he also seized his adversary Driego so strenuously, and tugged him so heartily by the hair, that we entertained very serious apprehensions for either wig or scalp. This is not English-like, and it only excites our ridicule" (qtd. in Guest, *Romantic Ballet* 54). We must recall, also, that Victorian ballet subsisted in and through a multitude of forms and vehicles. As Peter Schlicke points out, "within the plays [that Dickens saw for most of his life], actors were liable on the least provocation—or none at all—to burst into song, brandish swords, or group for a dance" (52). The

same scholar also provides unwitting testimony to the ballet's having permeated the circus too: he fails to point out in his list of equestrian spectacles
that *Nathalie ou la Laitière suisse* (1821) had in fact been a Taglioni vehicle:

> Thus, in the late 1820s clear up to the 1840s, Miss Woolford, billed as 'the
> sylph of the circle' and 'the first female equestrienne', appeared regularly in a
> solo performance called 'The Italian Flower-Girl', and floral motifs were often
> associated with other equestriennes as well. Miss Woolford also starred in a
> duet with Ducrow entitled 'The Swiss Maid and the Tyrolean Lover', in which
> they performed an 'equestrian ballet on two horses, at the same time, whilst
> the horses are at their swiftest speed, a rustic scene of the Mountain Shepherd
> and the Swiss Milk Maid'.
> (157–58)

As far as country dances go—dances that seem in Dickens's eyes to have
embodied the heartiness and high spirits of the age of Fielding (diminished
by the "respectability" of the usurping quadrille)—we can scan the ballets
that he might have seen at The King's (later Her Majesty's) Theatre from the
time of his clerkship onwards, and at least one title springs out—*La Noce du
village* (1823)—that might have offered a balletic rendering of the dance,
over and above the fact that corps work, as we shall see, almost always has a
"contre-danse" component. A further possibility is *The Romantic Amoureux*,
which Leigh Hunt saw at another theater in 1830, and which ended with a
"pell-mell dance" (*Dramatic Criticism* 246), as likely a description as any
for a country dance turned ballet.

It's not surprising that Dickens should have had to rely on these and other
theatrical spectacles to supplement his experience, for his formal education
at the Wellington House Academy offered precious little in the line of social
dance—"There was a fat little dancing-master who used to come in a gig,
and taught the more advanced among us hornpipes (as an accomplishment in
great social demand in after life)" (*Reprinted Pieces* 572). The wry parenthe-
sis attests to the fact that this was worse than useless, for the energetic
hornpipe offered no practice in deportment, and, being exclusively male,
provided no contact with the opposite sex. When Dickens reached the independence of his clerkship in 1827, the country dances that would later figure
in his fiction had fallen from grace in the city:

> However, Mr. Swiveller had Miss Sophy's hand for the first quadrille (country-
> dances being low, were utterly proscribed), and so gained the advantage over
> his rival, who sat despondingly in a corner and contemplated the glorious figure
> of the young lady as she moved through the mazy dance.
> (*The Old Curiosity Shop* 63–64; ch. 8)

The banishment of a perceivedly "low" dance points to the pretensions of
the Wackles sisters (there is a vindictive—not to say exterminatory—force

behind the adverb "utterly")—a note of cultural provincialism that Dickens would sound again and again, especially in his satire on Mr. Podsnap and his tribe. For, in fact, if only the Wackleses had known it, quadrilles themselves were old hat in 1836, and the English aristocracy, the tone-setters in such matters, had already moved on to the waltz. Even in the California of 1836, triple-time was "in"—"After the supper, the waltzing began, which was confined to a very few of the *gente de razon*, and was considered a high accomplishment, and a mark of aristocracy" (Dana 203)—and duple time "out," as witness the fact that that the fandango—Californian analogue of a "country dance"—had earlier been danced by the hoi polloi.

Byron had looked ahead to this change of fashion twenty-three years before, hymning the waltz at a point when it had become the rage of Europe, though much of England (provincial in its puritanism) looked on askance. He prefaced "The Waltz" with an introduction by a country gentleman,[1] who, on going to a ball chez the countess of Waltzaway, is denied any glimpse of "a country dance, or at most, cotillons, reels and all the old paces to the newest tunes" (146). From this we can deduce that even in 1813, long before the Wackles sisters pronounced it "low," the country dance had begun to lose "*ton*." This point is borne out by R. W. Zandvoort, who observes that while "the Country-dance continued to enjoy great popularity" throughout the eighteenth century, in

> polite circles it steadily grew more conventional, stilted and affected. At the same time the Longways form gained the upper hand to the exclusion of other kinds; as early as the ball days of Miss Burney's Evelina it was the only one danced at Assemblies. It was also the only form adopted in France and then introduced into England again; and these two circumstances account for the false etymology which, in spite of the New English Dictionary, has persisted down to our own day.   (306)

"Conventional, stilted and affected" though it might have become, the large number of dancers required to execute it created a semblance of rowdiness, something the "intimiste" quadrille was at pains to scale down. One senses from Byron's preface to "The Waltz" that Horace had actually been half-resigned to the fact that the country-dance *wouldn't* appear on the cards, while in the poem itself, it's banished quite roundly—one might almost say "exorcized"—when the poet, momentarily forgetting all about Horace, speaks *in propria persona*:

> Endearing Waltz!—to thy more melting tune
> Bow Irish jig and ancient rigadoon.
> Scotch reels avaunt! and country-dance forgo
> Your future claims to each fantastic toe!   (ll. 109–12)

Byron remembers his Father Grundy before long, however:

Say—would you make those beauties quite so cheap?
Hot from the hands promiscuously applied,
Round the slight waist, or down the glowing side,
Where were the rapture then to clasp the form
From this lewd grasp and lawless contact warm? (ll. 233–37)

What most shocked the English about the waltz was the fact that its dancers closed in on each other, unlike those in the precursive minuet, who had done nothing more indecorous than brush fingertips. Here Horace sounds like Mr. Podsnap, born out of time.

For one senses that the middle classes resented not only the waltz's intimate contact, but also its exorbitant spaciousness. Demanding expanses of polished parquet rather than a square of carpet, it was better served by the halls of Belgravia than the drawing rooms of Kensington, and this (hidden) economic factor also helped turn the quadrille into a badge of Podsnappery. The circumstances of Georgina's birthday dance explain its ascendant place in her world, for her parents' drawing room can accommodate it without disruption, and the carpet will baffle (in the sense both of thwarting and of muffling) any potential showiness on the part of the dancers. We can invoke the testimony of Irina Baronova in this regard: "It was hellish for doing *pirouettes* and *fouettés*, because one's toe shoes sank into the rug. I had to force each turn and concentrate on my balance" (64). Not only would the movements of the Podsnap guests have been braked by the pile, but any breaking out would have been dampened by the metronomic tick of the accompaniment. No possibility of "lawless contact warm" when the pulse of the dance is at the mercy of the "well-conducted automaton" who, by regulating music into soullessness, turns the affair into a celebration of "getting up at eight, shaving close at a quarter-past, breakfasting at nine, going to the City at ten, coming home at half-past five, and dining at seven" (129; I, ch. 11). The absence of "lawless contact" is also, no doubt, a prophylactic against blushes in the cheeks of the "Young Person" for whose sake the whole excruciating event has been engineered. Dance that has been drained of its spontaneity is dance travestied, and Georgina herself senses that its spirit, lost to the parlors of Stucconia, still animates the Mayday bacchanales of the London sweeps:

'About the chimney-sweeps?'
'Hush! Ma'll hear.'
'She can't hear from where she sits.'
'Don't you be too sure of that,' said Miss Podsnap in a lower voice. 'Well, what I mean is, that they seem to enjoy it.'
'And that perhaps you would have enjoyed it, if you had been one of them?'
Miss Podsnap nodded significantly.
'Then you don't enjoy it now?'

'How is it possible?' said Miss Podsnap. 'Oh it is such a dreadful thing! If
I had been wicked enough—and strong enough to kill anyone, it should be
my partner.'
   This was such an entirely new view of the Terpsichorean art as socially
practised, that Mrs Lammle looked at her young friend in some astonishment.
                                              (136–37; bk. 1, ch. 11)

At moments like these, Dickens becomes proto-Lawrencian, anticipating a
comparable passage in *Lady Chatterley's Lover*:

Standard Five girls were having a singing lesson, just finishing the la-me-doh-
la exercises and beginning a 'sweet children's song'. Anything more unlike
song, spontaneous song, would be impossible to imagine: a strange bawling
yell followed the outlines of a tune.   (qtd. in Leavis 74)

Podsnappery in motion could similarly be described as a strange bloodless
mincing to the outlines of a tune.
   The Wackleses, on the other hand, seem to have taken up the carpet for
their quadrilles, no doubt to their enduring regret, for this decision (as much
as anything else) allows Mr. Swiveller to make a spectacle of himself. (Proof
that carpets *were* taken up for this purpose comes from *Sketches by Boz*: ''We
know it is a quadrille party, because we saw some men taking up the front
drawing room carpet while we sat at breakfast this morning'' [222].) What's
more, the exposed wooden floor on which the Wackles's guests disport themselves has blended in Dickens's imagination with the stages of the King's
Theatre or of Drury Lane, and his reportage of a middle-class cotillion runs
into memories of the ballets staged at those venues. We need to remember
that the quadrille was a forerunner of the square dance, and not very different,
choreographically speaking, from the country-dances it displaced. What distinguished it was the patina of sophistication provided by its accompaniment—a medley of tunes from fashionable operas and ballets, in contrast to
the folk melodies (and tunes of the English baroque) associated with its
predecessor. The Wackles sisters would no doubt have felt as au courant with
the metropole, dancing to the strains, say, of the *Puritani* quadrilles of 1835
as Mrs. Podsnap to the *Faust* quadrilles of 1863. Because most of these
arrangements were painfully simple (their melodies often transposed into keys
within two fifths or fourths of C), and therefore suited to the least able pianist,
they (and the barrel organ) helped popularize operatic music in the days
before the gramophone. Aside from some ironic mock-quadrilles—Emanuel
Chabrier's *Tristan und Isolde* effort comes to mind—the kinds of melodies
that lent themselves to quadrillification were frankly popular, and were made
even more safe and accessible to the middle-class parlor by the unchanging
Gestalt of the form—*le pantalon*, *l'été*, *la poule*, and *la pastourelle*. (This

standardization should be born in mind in relation to Mrs. Podsnap's automaton at the piano, for it trimmed the lyric measures of Gounod or Verdi to a procrustean format.) In any event, we can be sure that all present at these quadrilles—Wackles sister or Podsnap parent—would have congratulated themselves on *not* hearing such "low" country-dance tunes as "Sir Roger de Coverley," and hummed along instead to the latest operatic "hits."

That crypto-theatrical fact almost certainly fuelled Dickens's imagination when he described Mr. Swiveller's performance, one that activates the gyrations of his very name:

> Nor was this the only start Mr. Swiveller had of the market-gardener; for, determining to show the family what quality of a man they trifled with, and influenced, perhaps, by his late libations, he performed such feats of agility and such spins and twirls as filled the company with astonishment, and in particular caused a very long gentleman who was dancing with a very short scholar, to stand quite transfixed with amazement.
> (*The Old Curiosity Shop* 63–64; ch. 8)

The floor patterns of quadrilles, as their name implies, were contained by a quadrangle, and required each of its four couples to advance by turn from its corners. Since these advances and returns were square-cut and the steps correspondingly clear-cut, the quadrille doesn't remotely deserve the adjective "mazy," even though the consciousness conferring it half belongs to the market gardener who "who sat despondingly in a corner and contemplated the glorious figure of the young lady as she moved through the mazy dance." But if maziness isn't a property of the domestic quadrille, it certainly is of its amplified avatars on the ballet stage. The complex threading and interleaving of a corps de ballet indicates that Dickens has transposed the dance out of the parlor and into the theater, and further proof of this displacement comes from Mr. Swiveller's comically improper (and improbable) self-display. His evolutions recall those of Joseph Mazilier, who danced *The Devil on Two Sticks* at the Drury Lane Theatre in 1836, or Jules Perrot, who, in that same year, but in the King's Theatre, executed a tarantella with Carlotta Grisi. Contemporary reviews of these dancers use the idiom that Dickens employs here.

Of Jules Perrot, for example, *The Morning Herald* had written that "his power of springing with facility from both or either of his legs singly [is] as great as if the limbs had all the qualities of Indian-rubber" (Guest, *Romantic Ballet* 47), while the same journal, writing about a pas de deux executed by Samengo and Brugnoli, remarked that

> the dancers, redoubling their marvellous exertion, quivering, cutting, interlacing, and glancing, conclude with one tremendous whirl of pirouette, during

which every limb performs peculiar evolutions of its own—the leg shaking or trilling—the arms poising and twining, and the body coiling itself with as many convolutions as would puzzle a Mussulman Fakir, or excite the envy of the dancing serpents of La Vaillant.   (49)

Common to all three passages is the sense of almost superhuman showiness, as far removed as it is possible to be from the country-dance familiar to the market-gardener. For, unlike its deft and athletic congeners north of the border, it was an altogether tame affair, as witness the condescending tone of this Scots commentator:

Minor *Kemkósy*, Setting or Footing Step. This is an easy familiar step, much used by the English in their country-dances. You have only to place the right foot behind the left, sink and hop upon it, then do the same with the left foot behind the right.   (Surenne vi)

In other words, many country-dances require only the mastery of the *coupé*, and while the quadrille was a shade more elaborate, it still belonged to the realm of the "easy familiar." But one would never have gathered as much from Mr. Swiveller's extravagance: "he performed such feats of agility and such spins and twirls as filled the company with astonishment, and in particular caused a very long gentleman who was dancing with a very short scholar, to stand quite transfixed with amazement." Quadrilles don't make provision for any kind of *pas seul*, let alone a *pas seul* as exuberant as this. A male might conceivably support his partner in a single turn, but if he himself were to "spin" (pirouette) and "twirl" (*tour chaîné*), he would have to leave go for the duration, a discourtesy not only to her but to the entire company, whose figures he would have interrupted. (Only in the social dance of the twentieth and twenty-first centuries, which has become increasingly uncoupled and individuated, is space made for Mr. Swiveller's kind of "riffing.")

This scene from *The Old Curiosity Shop* becomes plausible, then, only if we realize that it has been imagined in a context of theatrical dance, for ballet typically embeds *pas seul* in its *danses génerales* as a way of breaking their monotony. Even in its adaptation of social dance—the waltz, for example—strategic thinnings in the texture signal that an individual or a single couple is stepping forward for a solo. Think, for example, of the oboe passage in the *Valse génerale* of the Wilis (*Giselle*), when Moyna executes her *attitudes en pointe*, or the woodwind interlude in the Mazurka from *Swan Lake*. The title of the dancers to whom such solos are assigned—"coryphées"—says it all. They are seldom virtuosic, however, and Dickens has injected extra grotesquerie by making Dick Swiveller dance with the confidence and brilliance of a premier danseur—a Jules Perrot or Joseph Mazilier.

The author pretends to be uncertain as to whether the dazzling "riff" originates in drink ("influenced, perhaps, by his late libations"), so as to suggest that it does. That means that the general astonishment in the Wackles parlor must also trench on outrage, and that the brilliant dance may include some skids and barely recovered balances. Here Dickens carries into his social reportage another tradition of the ballet, namely, the drunken solo.[2] It figures in such works of the modern repertoire as Macmillan's *Manon*, and extends back to *Chanson à boire* in Delibes's *Coppélia*, and the *Chant bachique* in *Sylvia*, the *indications scéniques* of which—"*ses jambes faiblissent . . . tout tourne autour de lui*" (*Coppélia* 79–80) and "Orion que sa vie sauvage a retenu dans les forets ne connait pas l'usage du vin" (*Sylvia* 79)—indicate staggerings-about to music. And we can be fairly certain that there were also examples in the Victorian ballet and pantomime, and that Dickens was as familiar with them as with another chestnut of comic dance, the coupling of a tall with a short dancer[3]: "and in particular caused a very long gentleman who was dancing with a very short scholar, to stand quite transfixed with amazement." In brief, the novel has modulated at this point into a burlesque ballet, laced with its standard tropes and situations. Dickens was never one to let mere verisimilitude inhibit his invention.

By eclipsing a "market-gardener" in his quadrille-cum-*pas seul*, Mr. Swiveller has overturned the stereotypes of the languid "cit" and the vigorous bumpkin, one that goes back as far, at least, as the Restoration: "Lord, a country-gentlewoman's pleasure is the drudgery of a footpost; and she requires as much airing as her husband's horses" (Wycherley, *The Country Wife* 2.1, *Restoration Plays*, 96). Dickens also seems to imply that the market-gardener, being, like Hamlet, acquainted with "country matters," would have excelled in the "low" dances proscribed by the Wackles sisters—as opposed to the slick and modish urban dance that a Cockney clerk has turned to his advantage. But if he *is*, his lines were crossed, for country-dances have nothing to do with their name. It's in fact a corruption of "contre," and refers to the alignment of opposing rows of dancers. They were thus called contre-danses in France, and then misnamed "country" dances when later they recrossed the Channel. Indeed there is every reason to believe that the contre-danse, with its serried rows, helped shape the gestalt of the modern corps de ballet. Look how loose—not to say aleatoric—the groupings must have been that Pierre Beauchamp devised for his ballets in the seventeenth century—and this from the man who codified the five positions:

> To those who complimented him on the variety of his entrées, Beauchamp said that he had learned to compose the patterns for his ballets from the pigeons in his loft. He would go up there himself to give them their grain, and throw it to them. As the pigeons ran to the grain, the different patterns and varied groupings they formed gave him ideas for his dances. (Guest, *Paris Opera Ballet* 10)

Proof of the continuity between the "military" lines of the classical corps de ballet and those of country-dance is also afforded by this glimpse of tutu-ed Vauxhall figurantes going through motions that Dickens wittily construes both in terms of Keats's expressions "Flora and the country green" and "a long age in the deep-delved earth" ("Ode to a Nightingale"): "The sun shone upon the spangled dresses of the performers, and their evolutions were as about inspiring and appropriate as a country dance in a family vault" (*Sketches by Boz* 130).

But let's get back to Mr. Swiveller's market-gardener. If the quadrille from *The Old Curiosity Shop* becomes theatrical by accident of conventions that Dickens has imagined into it, the earliest of all his dance scenes was purpose-fully so. In "Meditations in Monmouth Street," one of the *Sketches by Boz*, the essayist stands in an old-clothes market, and, having deduced likely wear-ers from a jumble of shoes, sets them dancing:

> We had been looking on at this little pantomime with great satisfaction for some time, when, to our unspeakable astonishment, we perceived that the whole of the characters, including a numerous *corps de ballet* of boots and shoes in the background, into which we had been hastily thrusting as many feet as we could press into the service, were arranging themselves in order for dancing; and some music striking up at the moment, to it they went without delay. (81)

If Edward Costigan is right to claim that the "central situations and incidental episodes of some of the tales [in this collection] follow patterns that prevailed on the contemporary stage" (405), then we can argue a fortiori that this particular scene follows patterns even more literal than those prescribed by a Victorian *maître de danse*. Dickens's nonce collective noun—"a numerous *corps de ballet* of boots and shoes"—while it provides a mock-heroic foil for the homeliness of the footwear, also throws a proscenium arch over the spectacle, recalling the conventions and tropes by which social dance was rendered in the ballet. The market-gardener metonymized by the boots makes it clear that a country-dance is underway, even if some of its choreography has been heightened—as it often is by ballet's paraphrase of ethnic dance. The boleros and seguidillas in the ballets of the nineteenth-century choreographer Marius Petipa, are known—affectionately by balletomanes, contemptuously by aficionados of the real thing—as "St. Petersburg Spanish," so extensively have they been processed into a late classical idiom. And since the Victorian stage almost certainly made comparable adaptations to the country-dance, it's upon these that Dickens seems to have based his Disneyesque fantasia:

> It was perfectly delightful to witness the agility of the market gardener. Out went the boots, first on one side, then on the other, then cutting, then shuffling, then setting to the Denmark satins, then advancing, then retreating, then going round, and then repeating the whole of the evolutions again, without appearing to suffer in the least from the violence of the exercise.   (81)

Echt country-dances are communal affairs, and their focus diffused through the entire company lined up in opposing rows. In this one, however, Dickens trains a spotlight on the market-gardener to the virtual exclusion of all the others (he was do the same again for Mr. Fezziwig in *A Christmas Carol*). The dance thus turns into a showy *pas seul* à la Swiveller, complete with cabrioles ("cutting") and that systematic inversion of the first position (toe to toe, then heel to heel—"shuffle") that propels the dancer sideways in the hornpipe—a moment remembered from the Wellington House Academy, but entirely inappropriate to a country-dance. So we are dealing once again with a theatrical rendering (with all the attendant latitude and inauthenticities), renderings in which such moments were not only appropriate but de rigueur. A common or garden country-dance would make for dull watching, and limelit interludes like the market-gardener's were the birthright of the cory-phée and the privilege of the audience.

There are also other clues to the balletic provenance of this episode, not least the fact that the market gardener is grotesquely overweight: "There were his huge fat legs bulging over the tops, and fitting them too tight to admit of his tucking in the loops that he had pulled them on by" (80). Overweight people aren't nimble in real life, but on the ballet stage they can be, since more often than not they are impersonated by young men and women, agile and deft as befits their youth, who have been fattened up with wadding. The figure of Sancho Panza in Petipa's *Don Quixote* comes to mind in this regard, and so too some of the Biedermeier bourgeois guests in his *Casse Noisette*. It's clearly one of the reasons why, in Dickens's imagination, the market-gardener appears not to "suffer in the least from the violence of the exercise." Such wadding had likewise imparted majesty to the riding-master at Astley's, the topic of another "Sketch by Boz." His torso is as strikingly sculptural as Mr. Veneering's in *Our Mutual Friend* ("having this very evening set up the shirt-front of the young Antinous [in new worked cambric just come home]" [8; bk. 1, ch. 2]—which one suspects might also have more to do with quilting than with muscle tone):

> He is none of your second-rate riding-masters in nankeen dressing-gowns, with brown frogs, but the regular gentleman attendant on the principal riders, who always wear a military uniform with a table-cloth inside the breast of the coat, in which costume he forcibly reminds one of a fowl trussed for roasting.
>
> ("Astley's" 109)

Here Dickens frankly acknowledges the theatrical nature of the image, and the willing suspension of disbelief upon which the Herculean physique of the master depends:

> With the exception of Ducrow, who can scarcely be classed among them, who ever knew a rider at Astley's, or saw him but on horseback? Can our friend

in the military uniform, ever appear in threadbare attire, or descend to the comparatively unwadded costume of everyday life? Impossible! We cannot—we will not—believe it.   (111)

In the case of the market-gardener, the balletic context has been suppressed, however, and leaks in only around the edges. But leak it does, for legs as actually fat as those that Dickens imagines would *not* be equal to the figures they execute, nor could real hearts lodged in such fleshy frames bear the violence of the exercise without pain. What we are witnessing is a young danseur in outsized breeches filled with bombast, and with rouge on his face instead of a really apoplectic complexion.

Exactly the same contradiction obtains in the depiction of Mr. Fezziwig in a country-dance, for while the man himself is clearly overweight ("He rubbed his hands; adjusted his capacious waistcoat; laughed all over himself, from his shoes to his organ of benevolence; and called out in a comfortable, oily, fat, jovial voice" (*Christmas Stories* 34; Stave 2), he is as limber as his predecessor in the "Boz Sketch," and thinks nothing of executing cabrioles with an elevation and speed that make his perfect landings all the more remarkable. Such feats would be difficult for a burly man, and inconceivable for one in a capacious waistcoat. In both instances we are witnessing Dickens's version of Merrie England as framed by the Victorian stage, for we have by-passed the prim middle-class mincings of the Wackles Seminary and entered the (notional) world of Fielding, and of Sir Roger de Coverley himself—so much so, indeed, that we all but imagine Mr. Fezziwig's knitted Welsh wig, prompted by his festive-fuzzy-wiggy surname, to be an actual bagwig. The vignette starts in a bluff, rustic idiom ("a good stiff piece of work") that helps project a jovial "manly" frankness:

> Then old Fezziwig stood out to dance with Mrs Fezziwig. Top couple, too; with a good stiff piece of work cut out for them; three or four and twenty pair of partners; people who were not to be trifled with; people who *would* dance, and had no notion of walking.

Soon, though, Dickens has recourse to the theater, and recaps the Swiveller *pas seul*, though with only a hint of grotesquerie—the grotesque of stringy mutton bounding like little lambs as to a tabor's sound:

> But if they had been twice as many—ah, four times—old Fezziwig would have been a match for them, and so would Mrs Fezziwig. As to *her*, she was worthy to be his partner in every sense of the term. If that's not high praise, tell me higher, and I'll use it. A positive light appeared to issue from Fezziwig's calves. They shone in every part of the dance like moons. You couldn't have predicted, at any given time, what would have become of them next. And when old Fezziwig and Mrs Fezziwig had gone all through the dance; advance and retire,

both hands to your partner, bow and curtsey, corkscrew, thread-the-needles, and back again to your place; Fezziwig "cut"—cut so deftly, that he appeared to wink with his legs, and came upon this feet again without a stagger.

(35–36; Stave II)

This deft old man has matching topoi on the ballet stage—the clumsy old man, and, worse, the clumsy lecherous old man. And, if we return to the Monmouth Street fantasia, we will also find hints of gaslight and greasepaint in conduct of the list shoes:

Nor were the Denmark satins a bit behindhand, for they jumped and bounded about in all directions; and though they were neither so regular, nor so true to the time as the cloth boots, still, as they seemed to do it from the heart, and to enjoy it more, we candidly confess that we preferred their style of dancing to the other. But the old gentleman in the list shoes was the most amusing object in the whole party; for, besides his grotesque attempts to appear youthful, and amorous, which were sufficiently entertaining in themselves, the young fellow in the pumps managed so artfully that every time the old gentleman advanced to salute the lady in the cloth boots, he trod with his whole weight on the old fellow's toes, which made him roar with anguish, and rendered all the others like to die of laughing. (82)

The idea that gusto can cover a multitude of technical sins (as it does in the case of the Denmark satins) belongs more to a newspaper review of professional dancing than reportage on its society page. Dickens writes as if he had noticed a winning but coltish member in a corps de ballet—a Fanny Dorrit, perhaps—and has given her nonce embodiment in "the coquettish servant maid . . . who accepted [a market-gardener's] offer of a ride, just on this side of the Hammersmith suspension bridge"—a datum no doubt gathered on one of the author's walks through London. Like many journalists before and after him (men not particularly versed in the niceties of ballet technique), he is more impressed by her spontaneity and undisciplined elevation than by the correctness of her fellow dancers.

The *Autobiography* of Leigh Hunt postdates this "Sketch by Boz," but the value it sets upon freshness rather than accuracy is of a piece with the judgment Dickens passes on the Denmark satins:

French dancers, in spite of their high notions of the art and the severity of their studies (perhaps that is the reason), have no mind with their bodies. They are busts in barbers' shops, stuck upon legs full of vivacity. You wonder how any lower extremities so lively can leave such an absence of all expression in the upper. (*Autobiography* 362)

Further proof of the theatrical color of the Monmouth Street ballet comes from the improbable conduct of the "young fellow in the pumps" who treads "with his whole weight on the old fellow's toes, which made him roar with anguish, and rendered all the others like to die of laughing"—unbecoming, not say brutal, behavior at an actual gathering, but recognizable as an item from the ballet's limited repertoire of comic topoi. Without being able to cite chapter and verse from the ballets that Dickens would have known himself, we can confidently extrapolate similar moments in his theater-going from those incidents in the current repertoire where aspiring age and lechery are punished with crushed toes. The treatment meted out by Quiteria (Kitri) to Camacho (Gamache) and her father in Petipa's *Don Quixote* is a case in point, and so too the mockery of Wolfgang, the tutor in *Swan Lake*, who tries to dance with some young girls. Of course this kind of nastiness is bearable but tiresome in ballet—as no doubt it is bearable but tiresome in professional wrestling and animated cartoons—simply because the suffering is simulated. The author has drawn on a stage convention to inoculate the pain.

So entrenched had the image of the balletic country-dance become in Dickens's mind that even when he witnessed the exotic dances of African-Americans during his tour of the United States, he seems to have viewed them through its lens either on the spot or retrospectively, when processing his notes. As in the Wackleses' quadrille, and as in the shoe fantasia in *Sketches by Boz*, this dance vignette in *American Notes* relies on the (balletic) formula of energizing a dull *danse génerale* with an extravagant *pas seul*:

> But the dance commences. Every gentleman sets as long as he likes to the opposite lady, and the opposite lady to him, and are so long about it that the sport begins to languish, when suddenly the lively hero dashes in to the rescue.
>
> (91)

It's possible, though by no means certain, that Dickens means us to read into this languor a hint of cultural betrayal—of the displacement by prim western dance conventions of a livelier indigenous one. But whatever his intention, there can be no doubt that conforming boredom is banished by the irruption of a vigorous individual talent:

> Instantly the fiddler grins, and goes at it tooth and nail; there is a new energy in the tambourine; new laughter in the dancers; new smiles in the landlady; new confidence in the landlord; new brightness in the very candles.   (91)

The theatrical framework that Dickens employs to interpret the dance also declares itself in the notation of the movement:

> Single shuffle, double shuffle, cut and cross-cut; snapping his fingers, rolling his eyes, turning in his knees, presenting the backs of his legs in front, spinning about on his toes and heels like nothing but the man's fingers on the tambourine;

dancing with two left legs, two right legs, two wooden legs, two wire legs, two spring legs—all sorts of legs and no legs—what is this to him?   (91)

The dance begins decorously, its movements recognizable enough to invite the language of the classroom. Shuffles were familiar to Dickens from his schoolboy hornpipes, and cuts are what ballet calls cabrioles (one imagines that cross-cuts, listed, but not explained, by the *OED*, must be entrechats, a step in which the legs are not only brought together as in the cabriole, but also cross after touching). But then the enterprise develops into virtuoso grotesquerie that he can render only by adunata—"two left legs, two right legs"—for the movements have become too quick and (above all) too unorthodox—to permit any detailed transcription. There can be no doubt that Dickens was witnessing a stage in the evolution of the cakewalk which, if we were to guess choreographic outline from a succession of examples from Louis Gottschalk's "Bamboula: Danse de[s] negres," composed three years after *American Notes*, to one of the last in the line (Debussy's in *Coin des enfants*—1908), was marked by rapid tempi, displaced accents, and rhythmic reversals. Some of these quirks were already implicit in the refrain of the song "Jim Crow" which Dickens would have heard at the Surrey Theatre in 1836, and which leapt to mind on this occasion, when he wittily used a fake "blackface" minstrel as the touchstone of actual negritude: "he finishes by leaping gloriously on the bar-counter, and calling for something to drink, with the chuckle of a million counterfeit Jim Crows, in one inimitable sound!" (91). And it is in terms of that dubious theatrical experience that Dickens has also partly shaped this account of indigenous American dance.

Sometimes the theater context is more explicitly stated, as it is in *Little Dorrit*. Twelve years before Dickens began publishing his novel, Jules Perrot had staged a ballet at Her Majesty's Theatre entitled *Un Bal sous Louis XIV*. Ivor Guest has pointed out that its title "was explained by the following number—the *Menuet de la Cour* and the *Gavotte de Vestris*, danced by Elssler and Dumilâtre. This pair of dances, traditionally given together, had survived as a popular example of the style of the previous century. They had been arranged by Maximilien Gardel for the ballet *Ninette à la cour* in 1778 . . . " (Guest, *Jules Perrot* 95–96). It seems clear to me that this particular ballet provides the background for chapter 7 (bk. 1), for even though it figures in the lower case, without italics or inverted commas, and with an indefinite article, it isn't customary to characterize minuets as being "of the court." Dickens surely means us to acknowledge that Fanny Dorrit has, in a very short space of time, mastered a dance associated in the public mind with two leading ballerinas, one of them Fanny Elssler (her namesake): "Indeed the dancing-master was so proud of it, and so wishful to display it before he left, to a few select friends among the collegians, that at six o'clock on a certain fine morning, a minuet de la cour came off in the yard—the college-rooms being of too confined proportions for the purpose—in which so much ground was covered, and the steps were so conscientiously executed, that the dancing-master, having to play the kit besides, was thoroughly blown'' (72–73; bk 1, ch. 7).

Proof of the balletic origin of this surreal tableau can be sought in its largesse—the fact that it can't be executed in an ordinary domestic space—''college-rooms being of too confined proportions''—and requires either the ballroom of a stately home (where the minuet wouldn't have been danced for decades) or the wide space of a London stage, where, as Guest makes plain, nostalgic recreations of eighteenth-century dance forms were not uncommon. The theatrical connection is pursued in the novel when Dickens makes Fanny a professional dancer and gives us a glimpse of rehearsals in an ''unfashionable'' theater, presumably a kind more associated with pantomime (which featured much dancing) than with the ''legitimate'' ballets of Perrot and Lumley. Dickens wittily suggests that if Fanny *had* been a member of a more fashionable troupe, Mrs. Merdle would have had no objection to Mr. Sparkler's irregular liaison with her: ''Therefore when I heard that my son was supposed to be fascinated by a dancer, I knew what that usually meant in Society, and confided in her being a dancer at the Opera, where young men moving in Society are usually fascinated'' (240; 1, ch. 20). It is only on finding ''what the theatre was'' that she is ''much surprised and much distressed.''

Dickens's habit of conceiving dance scenes in theatrical terms is also attested by the unconscious anachronism in one of the Christmas stories, *The Perils of Certain English Prisoners*, which is set in 1744: ''When we had saluted and he and the lady had waltzed away'' (175). Ballet scores, no matter what the notional date of the action (the Gothic *Swan Lake* and *Raymonda*, the baroque *Sleeping Beauty*), invariably fall back on waltzes, and a memory of couples waltzing in eighteenth-century costume has probably led Dickens astray here. On other occasions, though, he uses the ballet quite purposely to create an absurd concordia discors. The simple act of hiring a cab turns into a theatrical spectacle in one of the *Sketches by Boz*:

> The getting into a cab is a very pretty and graceful process, which, when well performed, is essentially melodramatic. First, there is the expressive pantomime of every one of the eighteen cabmen on the stand, the moment you raise your eyes from the ground. Then there is your own pantomime in reply—quite a little ballet.   (''The Last Cab Driver, and the First Omnibus Cad'' 144)

The joke here centers on the application of ballet mime to an everyday event. Its impenetrability has long been a byword for puzzlement, since some of its gestures—those signifying the words ''mother'' and ''lake,'' for example—don't resemble their referents at all, and many ballet-goers discover that le lac des cygnes was created by Odette's weeping mother only after they've read their program notes.

And without such notes to hand, Leigh Hunt threw up his hands in mock despair after one particular visit to the theater: "The plots of ballets are seldom painfully clear; the violence of their nods of the head and other explanatory gestures is apt to be lost upon us: we wish extremely to comprehend the old father who tries to thump the mystery into us with his stick . . . but our endeavours are seldom repaid" (*Dramatic Criticism* 244). Ballet is bound by convention to forego speech; cab-drivers aren't, and the solemn trading of gestures becomes doubly amusing. Nor should we forget the deviously ambiguous mime of the oyster woman in "The Misplaced Attachment of Mr John Dounce":

> So the young lady sat down with Mr John Dounce, in a little red box with a green curtain, and took a small sip of the brandy and water, and a small look at Mr John Dounce, and then turned her head away, and went through various other serio-pantomimic fascinations, which forcibly reminded Mr John Dounce of the first time he courted his first wife.   (*Sketches by Boz* 245)

Classical ballet's congenital habit of allegory (in the courtly masque as well as in the later productions of the Sun King's court) eventually found its way into the Victorian pantomime divertissement, and this, along with eighteenth-century paintings and Augustan odes, seems to have been a primary vector for Dickens's knowledge of the mode, which he held in amused contempt. Here, for example, is his affectionate but exasperated account of a divertissement in a working-class theater:

> We began at half-past six with a pantomime—with a pantomime so long, that before it was over I felt as if I had been travelling for six weeks—going to India, say, by the Overland Mail. The Spirit of Liberty was the principal personage in the Introduction, and the Four Quarters of the World came out of the globe, glittering, and discoursed with the Spirit, who sang charmingly. We were delighted to understand that there was no liberty anywhere but among ourselves, and we highly applauded that agreeable fact. In an allegorical way, which did as well as any other way, we and the Spirit of Liberty got into a kingdom of Needles and Pins, and found them at war with a potentate who called to his aid their old arch enemy Rust, and who would have got the better of them if the Spirit of Liberty had not in the nick of time transformed the leaders into Clown, Pantaloon, Harlequin, Columbine, Harlequina, and a whole family of Sprites, consisting of a remarkably stout father and three spineless sons.
>   (32–33)

Tossed together in an absurd gallimaufry are the allegorical elements of ballet—the demotic Italian commedia del'arte and the courtly French—which also happen to be those of Victorian pantomime. We have only to look forward to such ballets as Manzotti's *Excelsior*, staged three decades later, to see that the old habit of signification remained as vigorous as ever, for this ballet is a psychomachia pitting "la luce" against "l'oscurantismo," and ensuring her victory not by the offices of "la libertà" (as in Dickens's pantomime) but of "la civiltà." Along the way, in frothy tutus, and executing the abstractly irrelevant steps of the *danse d'école*, we encounter "l'invenzione," "la concordia," "la costanza," "la fama," and "il valore"—the whole affair summed up (with Polonius-like thoroughness) as an "Azione coreografica, storica, allegorica e fantastica in due parti e undici quadri." Thus when we read in *Our Mutual Friend* that Britannia is "meditating one fine day (perhaps in the attitude in which she is represented on the copper coinage" (244; II, ch. 3), we can guess that Dickens also saw her so represented on the Victorian stage. And the mainstream ballet would ironically reabsorb the representation when Diaghilev mounted *The Triumph of Neptune* in 1926—homage to the sort of spectacle that Dickens both loved and derided. Here is how Hilda Munnings (a.k.a. Lydia Sokolova) recalls the occasion:

> The one which fitted me was a queer tight-fitting tunic falling to my thighs, done up with enormous Victorian hooks and eyes: it was entirely covered with pear-shaped coloured stones set in pewter, which caught the light and tinkled as a I danced, sending thousands of flashing rays across the footlights. With this costume, the heaviest ever worn to dance a hornpipe, I sported a Glengarry, tartan gaiters, a little dagger, and red shoes. To crown my pleasure they called me 'Britannia'.   (Sokolova 252–53)

These, then, are some of the ways in which the dance of the Victorian theater found its way into the novels of Dickens. In one of his speeches, he had claimed that every "good actor plays direct to every good author, and every writer of fiction, though he may not adopt the dramatic form, writes in effect for the stage" (262). He could, in his own case, have added an important rider—for the stage, and *of* the stage.

At first blush, the stylized conventions of ballet and opera would seem to disqualify them from executing Hamlet's mandate to the Player (3.2.22): "to hold, as 'twere the mirror up to nature." However, there is something specious about that definite article, especially since Hamlet, though sober and prosaic at this point of the play, has spoken, and will soon again be speaking, the recitative of blank verse. And indeed in his soliloquies he lifts language to a plane that is higher still—that of expressive, cadenced arioso. There can be no denying the multitudes of mirrors at an artist's disposal, multitudes that call for an indefinite article in the circumstances. Some mirrors reflect back precisely, others blurrily, and others again distort and rend even as they render. In practice, Shakespeare had recourse to all of them, marrying the masque—that compound opera ballet *avant la lettre*—with the legitimate theater to give birth to the expressive potential latent in such combinations. Dickens, Shakespeare's imaginative and stylistic equal in this regard, was likewise ready to enrich his art with all the forms and devices that the Victorian stage had put at his disposal. Not the least of these, as we have seen, was that of the dance.

NOTES

1. Horace's surname, Hornem, seems to hint the phrase "give 'em a horn[pipe]" as well as "gore 'em," and we will meet his avatar as a market-gardener in two of Dickens's dance sequences.
2. I have seen no detailed account of scenario that Adolphe Nourrit derived from Shakespeare in *La Tempête*, a ballet staged at the Paris Opera in 1834. There is a faint likelihood, though, that Caliban might have been assigned a drunken dance in that if the librettist deigned occasionally to nod at this source, and, if it did, one could add this ballet to those I list with known drunken solos.
3. A modern avatar is the *pas de deux* created by Wayne Sleep and Vergie Derman in Macmillan's *Elite Syncopations*.

WORKS CITED

Baronova, Irina. *Irina: Ballet, Life and Love*. Gainesville: UP of Florida, 2005.

Byron, George, Gordon, Lord. *Byron Poetical Works*. Ed. Frederick Page. Rev. John Jump. London: Oxford UP, 1970.

Costigan, Edward. "Drama and Everyday Life in *Sketches by Boz*." *RES* 27 (1976): 406–21

Dana, Richard Henry. *Two Years Before the Mast*. New York: Dodd, Mead, 1946.

Delibes, Léo. *Coppélia ou La Fille aux yeux d'émail: Ballet en 2 Actes et 3 Tableaux de MM. Ch. Nuitter et Saint-Léon. Musique de Léo Delibes. Partition reduite pour piano*. Paris: Henri Heugel, n.d.

———. *Sylvia ou La Nymphe de Diane. Ballet en 3 Actes et 5 Tableaux de M Jules Barbier et Baron de Reinach. Partition reduite pour piano*. Paris: Henri Heugel, n.d.

Dickens, Charles. American Notes and Pictures from Italy. Intro. Sacheverell Sitwell. London: Oxford UP, 1957.

———. *Christmas Stories*. Intro. Margaret Lane. London: Oxford UP, 1956.

———. *The Letters of Charles Dickens.* Ed. Madeline House, Graham Storey and Kathleen Tillotson. 12 vols. Oxford: Clarendon, 1965–2002.

———. *Little Dorrit.* Intro. Lionel Trilling. London: Oxford UP, 1953.

———. *The Old Curiosity Shop.* Intro. The Earl of Wicklow. London: Oxford UP, 1951.

———. *Our Mutual Friend.* Intro. E. Salter Davies. London: Oxford UP, 1952.

———. *Sketches by Boz and Other Early Papers 1833–39.* Ed. Michael Slater. London: J. M. Dent, 1994.

———. *The Speeches of Charles Dickens.* Ed. K. J. Fielding. Oxford: Clarendon P, 1960.

———. *The Uncommercial Traveller and Reprinted Pieces etc.* Intro. Leslie Staples. Oxford: Oxford UP, 1958.

Eliot, George. "Charles Dickens" in Wall, Stephen, ed. *Charles Dickens: A Critical Anthology.* Harmondsworth: Penguin, 1970.

Eliot, T. S. *The Complete Poems and Plays of T. S. Eliot.* London: Faber, 1969.

Garis, Robert. *The Dickens Theatre.* Oxford: Oxford UP, 1965.

Guest, Ivor. *Jules Perrot: Master of the Romantic Ballet.* London: Dance Books, 1984.

———. *The Paris Opera Ballet.* Alton, UK: Dance Books, 2006.

———. *The Romantic Ballet in England.* London: Phoenix House, 1954.

MacKay, Carol Hanbury. "The Melodramatic Impulse in *Nicholas Nickleby.*" *Dickens Quarterly* 5 (1998): 152–63.

Hollington, Michael. "The Dance of Death in Charles Dickens' *Dombey and Son.*" *Tanz und Tod in Kunst und Literatur.* Ed. Franz Link. Berlin: Duncker & Humblot, 1993. 201–11.

Hunt, Leigh. *The Autobiography of Leigh Hunt.* London: Smith, Elder, 1867.

———. *Leigh Hunt's Dramatic Criticism.* Ed. Lawrence Huston Houtchens and Carolyn Washburn Houtchens, 1949: Rpt. New York: Octagon Books, 1977.

Leavis, F. R. *D. H. Lawrence: Novelist.* 1955; Rpt. Harmondsworth: Penguin, 1964.

Sampson, George. *The Concise Cambridge History of English Literature.* Cambridge: Cambridge UP, 1949.

Shakespeare, William. *Hamlet.* Ed. Harold Jenkins. London: Methuen, 1982.

Schlicke, Peter. *Dickens and Popular Entertainment.* London: Allen & Unwin, 1985.

Sokolova, Lydia. *Dancing for Diaghilev: The Memoirs of Lydia Sokolova.* Ed. Richard Buckle. London: John Murray, 1960.

Surenne, J. T., ed. *The Dance Music of Scotland: A Collection of All the Best Reels and Strathspeys Both of the Highlands and the Lowlands for the Pianoforte.* Edinburgh: Wood, 1851.

Wycherley, William. *The Country Wife. Restoration Plays.* Ed. Sir Edmund Gosse, London: J. M. Dent, 1932.

Zandvoort, R. W. "Mr. Fezziwig's Ball." *Multiple Worlds, Multiple Words: Essays in Honour of Irène Simon.* Ed. Hena Maes-Jelinek, Pierre Michel, and Paulette Michel-Michot. Liège: English Department, University of Liège, n.d.; 303–09.

Mad Bulls and Dead Meat: Smithfield Market as Reality and Symbol

Trey Philpotts

This essay examines the richly symbolic space of Smithfield Market, and the related issue of the "mad bulls" that escaped from the drovers who were headed into and out of the market. Located at the very "heart" of London, Smithfield and its livestock represented a major obstruction in the way of arterial flow, the movement of traffic and goods through the streets, which signaled a healthy and well-functioning modern city. Its centrality—the fact that it was located very near the Bank of England and Lombard Street, as well as St. Bartholomew's Hospital, Newgate Prison, Christ's Hospital, and much else—also literalized a different metaphor, one of infection. The market was thought to produce tainted air and unwholesome meat, which was believed to cause a number of diseases, including cholera. As used by Dickens, Smithfield Market functions as a liminal space, and signals a transition into unfamiliar territory. The cacophony and confusion of Smithfield—brought to visibility by the problem of the mad bulls—also underscored its irredeemably public nature, and remind us that this was very much an unrestrained and pre-modern world, a world of beasts and human brutes.

In chapter 6 of *Dombey and Son*, Polly Toodle and Susan Nipper, along with their charges young Paul and Florence Dombey, are walking eastward along the New Road when they encounter Rob Toodle, who, they discover, is being harassed by "a ferocious young Butcher" and a group of young boys. In the ensuing confusion and immediately after Susan and the children are rescued from "a passing carriage," they hear cries of "Mad Bull!" The threat of being trampled by the mad bull frightens Florence, who screams and runs, eventually finding herself alone in the City (74). It is at this pivotal moment that Florence falls through a rabbit hole. She has left the safety of her home in the West End and the protection of her nurse, and her adventures in the world begin. The threat of the carriage and the mad bull leads to Florence's abduction by Mrs. Brown, her rescue by Walter, his introduction to Mr. Dombey, and many of the other plot developments in the novel. As he often does, Dickens has in mind a specific referent, in this case the accidents that occurred when oxen from Smithfield Market escaped from their drovers, and ran wild through the congested streets surrounding the market, frightening and sometimes trampling on passersby. Such alarming scenes were discussed and depicted in a wide range of places in the late 1840s and early 1850s, including *The Times*, *The Illustrated London News*, *Punch*, and in Dickens's own journal, *Household Words*.

The mad bull episodes brought to visibility, and made concrete, the main problems associated with Smithfield—the inhumanity of man to beast, the danger to pedestrians—and they underscored the incredible congestion in the area, which had resulted from the rapid growth of the city and the slow response of its municipal governing body, the Corporation of London, to this growth.[1] Smithfield had been a source of controversy since at least the eighteenth century, and the subject of parliamentary debate in the early nineteenth century. But it was at midcentury that the market came under especially intense parliamentary scrutiny,[2] with, in 1849, a Royal Commission recommending the market's removal to a more salubrious location. The contemporary engagement with the issue of the "mad bulls" and the market more generally—the so-called "Smithfield Nuisance"—made West Smithfield and its environs a particularly suggestive place, and, as such, highly useful to Dickens in *Oliver Twist*, *Nicholas Nickleby*, *Dombey and Son*, and *Great Expectations*. This article will explore the representation of the mad bulls at midcentury, and then consider the broader implications of Smithfield Market in Dickens's fiction.

First, a few facts. Smithfield Market was London's highly profitable and very crowded livestock and horse market. In one year alone, 1848, 236,975 cattle and 1,417,010 sheep were sold at Smithfield, worth a total of £6,594,977 (House of Commons Report of 1849; qtd. in *Report of Commissioners*, 1850, 11–12). Although livestock was sold on both Monday and Friday mornings, the big day for cattle sales was Monday, the day that most contemporary accounts describe and that Dickens invariably alludes to.[3] The livestock would be driven to Smithfield along country roads, often from hundreds of miles away, or transported by railway or steamship.[4] The cattle then would be held in temporary pens ("lairs") on streets near Smithfield until Sunday night, at which point they would be herded by torchlight into the southernmost part of the market. Sales began at first light on Monday morning. If the animals were sold, they would be sent to the slaughterhouses nearby;[5] if they were unsold, they would leave the market on Monday afternoon, along with carts, wagons, and other vehicles, and return to the neighboring lairs. It is on these trips out of the market, particularly on the way to the slaughterhouses, that most of the accidents occurred.

The cattle were subject to nightmarish conditions in the market, largely because of a crushing lack of space.[6] One particularly cruel and unnatural practice, the ring-drove, confused and enraged the cattle and was thought to contribute directly to the accidents in the street. Because of limited space, only about half of the cattle could be tied up, which meant that the remainder had to stand untethered in circles of about twenty each, known as "ringdroves." To keep the cattle in their proper positions, turned towards the center of the circle with their heads to the ground, the drovers would goad them on their flanks and strike them on their heads. If the cattle tried to move backwards, they would be subjected to further blows. Unfortunately, the cattle became "so perfectly disciplined" that when it was time for them to break from the circle, they had to be hit with additional blows, and in the process would often run terrified into other rings. "The breaking up of a ring-drove might have made a treat for Nero," Dickens and Wills remarked (124). "Their horns were torn off," a parliamentary reformer lamented. "At other times their hides were shockingly lacerated. In fact, beasts were at times so injured as to be scarcely fit to be cut up" (*Hansard* 107: 486). These bruised and beaten animals, driven into a frenzy, would often prove uncontrollable as they navigated the narrow and busily thronged streets surrounding Smithfield. "Many an 'unprotected female' was set into terrible commotion by the quadrupedal force," a contemporary observed, "many an animal lamed by the rude treatment it received; and many an angry word was uttered by those who thought it little too bad that our already over-crowded streets should be blocked up by these drovers" (Dodd 235–36).

The actual number of fatalities caused by the bulls was a point of contention at the time. During parliamentary debate in 1849, opponents of reform quoted the City coroner, who claimed to have discovered only two deaths "caused by the bullocks in the city of London" in the last seven years: "one, a little girl, named Mills, who was killed by a bullock in Lower Thames-street, in October, 1845; and the other, a little girl who met her death in a similar way in Bridge-street, Blackfriars, in October, 1846" (*Hansard* 107: 502). *The*

Times, on the other hand, attributed four separate mortal or near-mortal accidents to rampaging oxen on a single nightmarish day, November 24, 1846, about six weeks after Dickens had written the mad bull passage in *Dombey*:

> On Blackfriars-bridge, early yesterday morning, a young child named Elizabeth Drawbridge, whilst in the act of crossing the carriage-way, was knocked down by the ox proceeding towards Smithfield, and trampled upon and gored. She was conveyed in a hopeless condition to the residence of her parents. In the market, between 3 and 4 o'clock, a young married woman . . . named Tailor, was run against and knocked down by oxen. She sustained such injuries that her recovery is not expected. She was taken to St. Bartholomew's Hospital. Shortly afterwards, in the Blackfrairs-road, a child named Wade, crossing the road, was tossed by an ox coming from the market, endangering the child's life. Mary Ann Binical, a married woman, . . . was run over by no less than four beasts, and severely wounded.
>
> ("The Smithfield Nuisance," 25 November, p. 4)

A correspondent to *The Times*, writing about a week later (3 December), claimed, "Within the last twelvemonth I think it will be found that nearly as many persons, and those chiefly women and children, have suffered injury from this cause as from accidents on railways" (6). Another *Times* piece, "An Infuriated Ox," explained how "an ox of the Scotland breed, over-driven and excited, broke from its drove in the neighbourhood of Newport-market, and after causing great alarm and excitement in Long-acre and Great Queen-street, found its way into Lincoln's Inn-square" (8 August 1848). Attempts to stop the animal increased its fury: "In an instant the spectators were flying in every direction, barristers and butchers' boys mingling indiscriminately in their attempts to escape." The bull eventually gored one man and seriously injured several others. Although the number of actual fatalities might have been exaggerated for rhetorical effect, what is clear is that the incidents were treated as a near epidemic by the London press.

In this respect, *Punch* is typical. During late 1846, for instance, the magazine drew attention to a terrible accident on Lord Mayor's Day—which led to two young children being trampled—and then, in a follow-up piece, mocked City worthies for their characterization of such tragedies as "inevitable accident[s]" that should be "endured with the most Christian-like and uncomplaining resignation!" ("Smithfield Rights of Cattle" 11.209; "The Smithfield Abomination" 11.235). A third piece, accompanied by a large illustration, re-imagined the run-amuck bulls as participants in "The Smithfield Bull Fights": "From St. Bartholomew's Hospital to Blackfriar's Bridge, the road is enlivened three times a week with the playful gambols of a few bulls, and Chatham Place furnishes a sort of amphitheatre, which only requires a stand for spectators to give quite a Spanish air to the locality" (11.241; fig. 1). Another piece refigured these "bull fights" as military engagements and urged that the human toll "be published every week, and

PUNCH, OR THE LONDON CHARIVARI. 241

THE SMITHFIELD BULL FIGHTS.

It would really seem that there is a chance of the Spanish custom of Bull-fights being introduced into this country, for every Smithfield market-day one or more of the noble brutes may be found giving the public an elementary lesson in the exciting pastime. From St. Bartholomew's Hospital to Blackfriars Bridge, the road is enlivened three times a week with the playful gambols of a few bulls, and Chatham Place furnishes a sort of amphitheatre, which only requires a stand for spectators to give quite a Spanish air to the locality.

We recommend to the authorities that measures should be adopted for giving to the Bull performances all the benefit they can derive from the accessaries which are usual on similar occasions in the country where the Bull-fight is a part of the national amusement, as we expect it will become with us if the Smithfield arrangements are allowed to continue as at present. We do not see why the *picadores* ; while the policemen might be employed as *torreros*, with handkerchiefs affixed to the end of their truncheons, to brandish in the eyes of the bulls, and take off the attention of the animals from any *caballero* who may happen to be in jeopardy.

Fig. 1. "The Smithfield Bull Fights." *Punch* 11 (1846): 241. By permission of The Provost, Fellows and Scholars of The Queen's College Oxford.

pasted about the city'' (12.54). The most irreverent piece, though, is surely "The Bullfight of Smithfield Market,'' a poem, accompanied by an illustration (fig. 2). This piece contains the immortal lines,

> See there, see there, where high in the air nursemaid and nursling fly!
> Into a first floor window, see, where that old gent they shy!
> Now they [the Smithfield oxen] are bolting into parlours, now they're tumbling into cellars,
> To the great disgust and terror of the peaceable indwellers.   (12.151)

The rampaging bulls constituted a key element in Dickens's campaign against the abuses at Smithfield, which he waged in *Household Words* in the early 1850s.[7] In "The Heart of Mid-London'' (4 May 1850), for instance, Dickens and Wills describe a whole host of problems associated with Smithfield—the cruelty, the noise and confusion, the "bruised meat,'' the dangers of infection, and, towards the close of the piece, the mad bulls. The bulls enter the piece abruptly, as agents of chaos. Mr. Bovington, the well-intentioned livestock

Fig. 2. "The Bullfight of Smithfield." *Punch* 12 (1846): 151. By permission of The Provost, Fellows and Scholars of The Queen's College Oxford.

owner whose travails make up the bulk of the article, is about "to hazard a remark about abattoirs, when deafening cries again rose in the street: 'Mad bull! mad bull! mad bull!' resounded from the Smithfield-bars. 'Mad bull! mad bull!' was echoed from the uttermost ends of St. John Street." What follows next is a finely-balanced mix of comedy and terror:

> A fine black ox was tearing furiously along the pavement. Women were scream-
> ing and rushing into shops, children scrambling out of the road, men hiding
> themselves in doorways, boys in ecstacies of rapture, drovers as mad as the
> bull tearing after him [sic], sheep getting under the wheels of hackney-coaches,
> dogs half-choking themselves with worrying the wool off their backs, pigs
> obstinately connecting themselves with a hearse and funeral, other oxen looking
> into public-houses—everybody and everything disorganized, no sort of animal
> able to go where it wanted or was wanted; nothing in its right place; everything
> wrong everywhere; all the town in a brain fever because of this infernal market!

Realizing that this is his own "West Highlander," Mr. Bovington watches the bull flee from the market along St. John Street and, in the process, send "a nursemaid, a baby, and a baked potato-can" flying "into the air in opposite directions." In his pursuit of his bull, Mr. Bovington comes across additional victims—"two disabled apple-women, a fractured shop-front, an old man being put into a cab and taken to the hospital"—before finally tracing "the favourite of his herds into the back parlour in Liquorpond Street, into which he had violently intruded through a tripe-shop, and where he was being slaughtered for his own peace and for the safety of the neighbourhood" (121–25). With the details of the mad bulls established at length in "The Heart of Mid-London," and other contemporary accounts, *Household Words* was more concise and allusive in its subsequent attacks on Smithfield. In "Improving a Bull," published on 3 August 1850, a "highly respectable old lady" complains to a shopkeeper that a bull from Smithfield Market "run right at me, full butt, and so I grasped my umbrella with both hands and ran to where the shops was." To her complaints, the shopkeeper responds, "the outcry against Smithfield is very narrow-minded": "It don't consider shop-keepers. When a bull takes a line of street, it drives the people into the shops on either side, and they make purchases for fear of being gored" (Wills and Morley 450). This comment neatly joins two presiding concerns: the fear of mad bulls run amuck in the streets of London and the fear that the closing of Smithfield would result in a loss of income for the businesses in the vicinity of the market. Several months after this, on 8 February 1851, Frederick Knight Hunt described a woman who "is trying to cross her way to her work, just as an ox, driven and goaded all night, makes a grand tilt at his tormentors." "Her thin, poverty-stricken clothing," Hunt noted, "offers little resistance to the horn of the ox, and the blood shows that the blow took effect on her side" (457–58). And, on 8 March 1851, Ossian Macpherson remarked on a bull that, one morning in the City, "took such a fancy to pin me to the wall with his horns" (572). Such accounts were especially telling because they directly tied the mistreatment of the animals to the well-being of innocent bystanders, effectively enlarging the problem beyond the precincts of the market and thus having much the same polemical force as Carlyle's starving Irish widow, trailing contagion from the poorest quarters of London to the wealthiest.

It is perhaps inevitable, given their recurrent appearance in *Household Words*, that the bulls would make an impression on Dickens's fiction published in the late 1840s and early 1850s. In the case of *Dombey and Son*, the bulls appear twice. Once, as we have seen, towards the beginning of the book, during Polly Toodle's and Susan Nipper's (and hence Florence's) expedition into London. They also appear a second time, towards the conclusion, in H. K. Browne's final illustration—"Another Wedding"—which depicts the

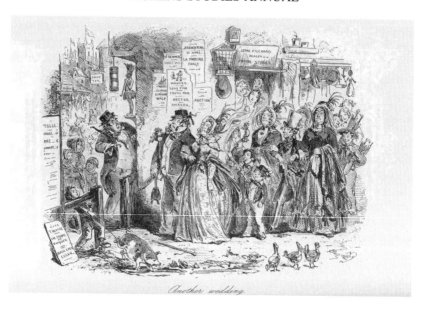

Fig. 3. H. K. Browne, "Another Wedding."

wedding procession of Mrs. Mac Stinger and Bunsby, Captain Cuttle's friend
(fig. 3). As characterized by Dickens, Bunsby is a "victim . . . meekly re-
signing himself" to the marriage ceremony, which is figured as "a procession
of sacrifice" heading to the "altar." To ensure that Bunsby will not escape,
Mrs. Mac Stinger has employed several close friends to watch his movements,
one of whom, Mrs. Bokum, "kept her eye steadily on the bridegroom, and . . .
on the alert to cut him off if he attempted escape." The "wretched man was
so secured by Mrs. Mac Stinger," Dickens writes, "that any effort at self-
preservation by flight was rendered futile" (ch. 60). On the whole, Browne's
illustration is an accurate rendering of the text. We have Cuttle turning a
corner and coming suddenly upon the procession; Bunsby, looking "distraught and melancholy"; "the young Mac Stingers in a body, exulting";
"Bunsby's boy, bearing umbrellas"; and so forth. What H. K. Browne adds
to the text are symbols that reinforce the idea of coercion and imprisonment.
Among other things, there are several caged birds over the procession; a sign
that reads, "Wanted. Some fine young men," directly over Bunsby's head;
and yet another sign, this advertising dramatic productions of *She Stoops to
Conquer* and *Black-Eyed Susan*, in the left foreground.[8]
    Of most relevance for present purposes is the left background of the illustra-
tion, which shows oxen and sheep being herded through the streets by a
drover, with a rod raised above his head, and the lower half of what seems

to be a woman (the figure is apparently wearing a dress), fleeing from the bulls. Browne depicts the most prominent bull looking askance at the marriage procession, with a glance that seems to betray both surprise and a certain amount of fear and bewilderment. Immediately behind the bulls is a butcher's shop, displaying the carcasses of several animals, including the head of a cow. There is a pig in the foreground, which may be headed to Smithfield Market as well, dragging a young boy into a bar on a tollgate.

As with the signs and the caged birds, the herded bulls and sheep are, of course, being used as symbols. They are being goaded to market, and to their eventual slaughter (represented by the carcasses hanging from butcher's shop in the background) by a drover[9] with a threatening stave, just as Bunsby is being goaded into marriage by Mrs. Mac Stinger and her watchful friends. The bulls are terrified and confused, as the "captive" mariner is "distraught and melancholy." "The first impulse" of both Captain Cuttle and Bunsby is "to run away," as it is with the bulls, who are about to trample a woman. Here, Browne cleverly picks up on a detail that was used earlier by Dickens, and exploits it for comic effect, as well as to reinforce motifs from the written description of the wedding ceremony. There is one significant difference between the bulls and Bunsby, however: unlike the cowed sailor, they still represent a threat to others, as is suggested by the inclusion of the fleeing woman, though their final end is in little doubt, as is evident by the hanging carcasses. It is unclear if Browne intended this as a subtle counterpoint to the text (suggesting the possibility that, if pushed far enough, Bunsby might eventually lash out) or if he simply cannot quite bring himself to domesticate fully the bulls, given their dangerous reality on the streets of London.

The bulls appear with greatest symbolic resonance, however, in *Bleak House*, written about two years after these *Household Word* pieces. As in *Dombey and Son*, "It is market-day" and again there are the mad bulls: "The blinded oxen, over-goaded, over-driven, never guided, run into wrong places and are beaten out; and plunge, red-eyed and foaming, at stone walls; and often sorely hurt the innocent and often sorely hurt themselves." It is these maddened bulls, the narrator says, that are "Very like Jo and his order; very, very like!" (237; ch. 16). The distinction between the bestial and the human, one of the defining characteristics of civilization, has all but disappeared. Jo is treated as a mere "creature" and, as such, has become one with the cattle and the other beasts that crowd the streets near his crossing: "To see the horses, dogs, and cattle, go by me, and to know that in ignorance I belong to them, and not to the superior beings in any shape, whose delicacy I offend!" (237; ch. 16). The abuse of bulls at Smithfield, which causes them to run amuck, injuring themselves and others, thus in *Bleak House* prefigures a larger concern with the abuse of human beings, an abuse with its own ramifying effects, including, in the case of Jo, the smallpox he contracts and passes to Esther Summerson.

The bulls are only one part of the "Smithfield Nuisance," however. It is the representative force of Smithfield that is most important and that returns us to *Dombey and Son,* and to a broader consideration of the meaning of the market for Dickens, as it also shows up in *Oliver Twist* and *Great Expectations.* To understand the evocative power of Smithfield, one must first understand its location. It is located in the so-called "liberties" of London, the district immediately outside the Roman wall that once surrounded the City, though still subject to the control of City authorities. Its "bars" or gates, which were located since the twelfth century on the north side of Smithfield, marked the boundary of the City and have served for hundreds of years as "control points for all travellers approaching the city" (Forshaw and Bergstrom 21). Smithfield thus occupied a transitional space: it was administratively part of the City, and yet just beyond its ancient boundary. And yet, despite this border position, it was the market's centrality that was inevitably mentioned in contemporary accounts. In 1847, for instance, Joseph Fletcher referred to Smithfield as "originally, as the name implies, an open field outside the town, but now inclosed in its very heart" (355–56). Another commentator compared it to the "central hold" of a spider, with "Narrow streets and swarming lanes" branching out on every side (Reach 121). The parliamentary commissioners remarked in 1849, "Smithfield is in the closest proximity to the centre of the business of the metropolis" (*Report of the Commissioners* 12). In fact, this identification of Smithfield with the "center" and "heart" of the City made it a useful synecdoche for the City itself, particularly for the most troubling and reactionary aspects of City administration, its opposition to the market's removal, and its pursuit of its own narrow interests. Significantly, the original instigator of the chaos caused by the mad bull in chapter 6 of *Dombey* is "a ferocious young Butcher," butchers having sided with the Corporation in opposing the removal of Smithfield.[10] The title of Dickens and Wills's piece for *Household Words*—"The Heart of Mid-London"—itself plays on the ambiguity of the market's centrality: that it is a symbol of London itself, the pulsing "heart" of the City, and that it is located in the congested and messy middle of things, at its very heart.[11]

This centrality enabled the salesmen and butchers to process their transactions speedily but also had a big disadvantage: "the position of the market in the centre of a dense population, surrounded by streets, and in the very focus of trade and traffic" made "the enlargement of its area expensive and difficult, . . . confines its approaches, and obstructs its thoroughfares; and produces the various inconveniences inseparable from the periodical congregation of a large number of cattle in the most frequented parts of an immense city" (*Report of the Commissioners* 13). As a contemporary observer remarked, "on great markets the neighbourhood is blocked up; with cattle which have reached to St. Sepulchre's church, situate at the corner of Skinner street, on the great thoroughfare leading from Holborn; and that on the 17th of December last, the cattle were standing in droves in Giltspur-street and on Snow-Hill'' (*Report of the Commissioners* 13). Of the seven approaches to the market, only one ''is of the minimum width required by the Building Act'' (13). Inevitably, as we have seen, forcing as many as 4,000 bullocks and thousands of sheep through such narrow passages, and then penning them in the limited spaces allotted, resulted in ''much cruelty'' and considerable danger. Smithfield and its livestock had become, in other words, a major obstruction in the way of arterial flow, the movement of traffic and goods though the streets, a movement that signaled a healthy and well-functioning city. If the ''streets of the city were the most visible signs of its progress or degeneration'' (16), as Linda Nead has suggested, then Smithfield was a major ''aneurism,'' undermining London's image of itself as modern and improving.

Smithfield's centrality—the sense that it was ''embedded in the heart of London'' (*Knight's Cyclopædia of London* 796)—also literalized a different metaphor, one of infection. The market and its slaughterhouses were only ''within a few minutes' walk'' of the core of the British commercial system—the Bank of England and Lombard Street. Even closer, within 220 yards, were ''placed the hospital of St. Bartholomew, the great gaol of Newgate, the Giltspur-street prison, the Central Criminal Court, the large chartered schools—Christ's hospital, and the Charter-house,'' ''in short, all those establishments from which it seems important to the public interests and to good order that a large market for cattle should be far removed'' (*Report of the Commissioners* 13; Horne 328). Here we might return to *Bleak House*. In chapter 32, Dickens's anonymous narrator remarks on the danger of infection associated with Smithfield and its nearby slaughterhouses: ''It is a close night . . . and there is a laggard mist a little way up in the air. It is a fine steaming night to turn the slaughter-houses, the unwholesome trades, the sewage, bad water, and burial grounds to account, and to give the Registrar of Deaths some extra business'' (466; ch. 32). The ''laggard mist'' and the ''fine steaming night'' that turn the unwholesome slaughterhouses and trades (among other things) to account refer to the miasmic clouds, or effluvia, which supposedly emanated from bodily exhalations and putrid organic matter, and which were thought to propagate infectious diseases such as cholera, typhus, influenza, and yellow fever. In early 1847, *Punch* cited Doctor Southwood Smith, a friend of Dickens's and one of the leading proponents of the miasmatic theory, who spoke ''of the effluvia—the mortal effluvia—arising from the garbage and filth of butchery, and doing the work of death in the lungs of the surrounding population'' (''Smithfield Martyrs.—Smithfield 'Salubrity' '' 12.116).

Dickens draws on the same association between bad meat and bad air in his most famous, and fullest, rendering of Smithfield, in *Oliver Twist*. The passage begins this way: "It was market-morning. The ground was covered, nearly ankle deep, with fifth and mire; and a thick steam perpetually rising from the reeking bodies of the cattle, and mingling with the fog, which seemed to rest upon the chimney-tops, hung heavily above" (136; ch. 21). Hanging "heavily" over Oliver, as he stands "amazed" before the market, is a cloud of infection and disease emanating from the "reeking bodies of the cattle." The "reek" reminds us that, to many mid-Victorian scientists, "all smell is disease," as Edwin Chadwick memorably put it (1846 testimony to parliamentary committee, qtd. in Johnson 114). In "A Monument of French Folly" (8 March 1851), Dickens describes the moral and physical corruption produced by Smithfield and its slaughterhouses, "the busiest . . . in London," in his view (553):

> you shall see the little children, inured to sights of brutality from their birth, trotting along the alleys, mingled with troops of horribly busy pigs, up to their ankles in blood . . . . Into the imperfect sewers of this overgrown city, you shall have the immense mass of corruption, engendered by these practices . . . to rise in poisonous gases, into your house at eight, when your children will most readily absorb them.   (534)

More was involved than just tainted air. According to Professor Richard Owen, of the Royal College of Surgeons, and a correspondent for *Household Words*, the constant driving of cattle produced "a state of fever," which reacted upon their blood and in turn injured "the character of [their] flesh," a condition made worse by "pain and terror," which harmed the quality of the meat (*Hansard* 107: 495). The unwholesome meat, in turn, was thought to cause a number of diseases, including cholera, but especially cancer. One of the leading parliamentary advocates for the removal of the market, Mr. Mackinnon, quoted Professor Owen at length in the House of Commons, and then cited the work of another investigator, Hector Gavin, the author of *Sanitary Ramblings* (1848). Mackinnon argued,

> the present system of selling and slaughtering cattle in the metropolis, and of making tripe and disposing of the offal, was most injurious to the health of the inhabitants. Dr. Gavin, one of the [parliamentary] witnesses, had stated that there was more sickness in the vicinity of Smithfield, arising from the stench and putrefaction of slaughtered animals, than in any other locality in that part of the metropolis.   (*Hansard* 107: 495–96)

Smithfield has other associations, of course, most notably its long and bloodied history as a place of human execution. This was where William Wallace was executed; where, during the Middle Ages and after, witches and heretics were burned, roasted, or boiled; and, during the reign of Mary Tudor, where over two hundred Protestants were put to death. In the words of contemporary

observers, Smithfield was said to stand prominent "Amongst places of sangui-
nary notoriety," to be "but another name for Protestant martyrdom," and to
have "been connected with many a sad tragedy—with many a blot upon our
history and our people" ("Annals and Antiquities of London" 685; Grant
172; Reach 123). The recurrent allusions to Smithfield's horrific history, in
so many contemporary accounts, and in Dickens's own *Child's History of
England*, suggest that the market had become both a loathsome reality and a
resonant symbol by the middle of the nineteenth century, "a doomed, but a
proper and consistent stronghold . . . of prejudice, ignorance, cupidity, and
stupidity," in the words of Mr. Bovington, the exasperated cattle-owner in
"The Heart of Mid-London" (123).

It is significant, I think, that Smithfield, as used by Dickens in *Oliver Twist*,
Dombey and Son, *Bleak House*, and *Great Expectations*, signals a transition,
what Robert Alter refers to, in a piece about Flaubert, as a "central *topos* of
the [realist] novel . . . the entrance of the protagonist into unfamiliar space"
(32). In *Dombey and Son*, as I have already suggested, Smithfield is where
Florence gets lost and taken prisoner by Mrs. Brown, who lives in the seedy
and disreputable neighborhood near the market, made up of "objectionable
localities," and "doubtful shops," such as "bladder blowers" and "horse
slaughterers," and "cat and rabbit fur dressers," according to a statement in
1851 by James Stevenson Bushman, member of the Royal College of Surgeons, and senior physician to the Metropolitan Free Hospital (qtd. in Joyce
79). Like the cattle and pigs at Smithfield, Florence is effectively "rendered"
for her byproducts, her hair and clothes, by a woman who herself lives off
recycled products—bones, rabbit skins, and "pure" (dog's dung)—made
available by the nearby market. Florence has moved from the safe, if loveless,
sanctuary of her father's home to the nightmarish openness of the bestial
and death-filled City, and Smithfield serves as the transitional space for this
movement. Indeed, it is this openness and permeability, what Dickens reads
in *Oliver Twist* as confusion, that was one of the identifying characteristics
of Smithfield. As Patrick Joyce points out, the market "was open, porous, a
place where on market day crowds of children could be seen running in and
out of the market cruelly taunting the animals" (83). Because there were few
physical boundaries, and little control or regulation, it was an essentially
liminal place, a place of commercial exchange, a place "where town and
country meet," as well as, most fundamentally, a place of life transformed
into death (Joyce 81–82). It is the maddened bulls, the bulls on their way to
their deaths in a crowded City, which betoken this openness and lack of
control. Of course, as is usually the case with Dickens, the openness of the
City also offers promise and opportunity, and suggests the possibility of
liberation, and is the place in which Florence will meet her future husband,
Walter Gay.

In *Oliver Twist*, Dickens again juxtaposes innocence, personified in this case by young Oliver, to the brutalities of the market. Although by the time he arrives at Smithfield, Oliver has actually been in London some time, he has been almost entirely indoors, as prisoner of Fagin and patient of Mr. Brownlow. But Smithfield *seems* like an introduction because so many of the street scenes that come before are rendered as indistinct, the result of "only a few hasty glances," which occur at night and on the fly. The one time Oliver does look outside, "nothing was to be descried" (179).

This all changes with Smithfield. In chapter 16, after he has left Brownlow's, and been recaptured by Sikes and Nancy, all three have to cross "a large open space; scattered about which, were pens for beasts: and other indications of a cattle-market" (97). At this exact point, while his characters are crossing Smithfield, Dickens has Sikes slacken his pace and speak to Nancy about the noise and clamor produced by Bartholomew Fair, which was held at Smithfield for three days each year, starting on September 3. The Fair, which was once the site of miracle and morality plays, and a market and cloth fair, developed over the centuries into a place of popular entertainment, featuring puppet plays, side show exhibits, wild beast shows, and a host of seedy characters, including conjurors, card-sharps, gamesters, charlatans who sold fraudulent medical remedies, and prostitutes, among many others. By the late-seventeenth century, Bartholomew Fair had acquired a reputation for seediness and by the early-nineteenth century had fallen into desuetude and disrepute. William Wordsworth, who visited the Fair in 1802, believed it was the home of "All out-o'-the-way, far-fetched, perverted things" (*The Prelude* 7.714); William Hone characterized it as "an annual scene of debauchery" in 1826 (*The Everyday Book* 1: 626), and Lord Brougham described it in 1843 as a "nuisance," "for the removal of which, time out of mind, the public had been clamorous" (*Hansard* 67.226). It was during Bartholomew Fair, Sikes tells Nancy, that he entered Newgate: "It was Barthlemy time when I was shopped, and there wasn't a penny trumpet in the fair, as I couldn't hear the squeaking on" (159). Here, Dickens uses Sikes to emphasize the extreme closeness of Smithfield to Newgate, located just down Giltspur Street, bringing together "pens for beasts," the chaos and clamor of the unsavory and squalid Bartholomew Fair, the immurement of prisoners in Newgate, and Oliver's own imprisonment by Sikes and Fagin. This scene sets the stage for the great description of Smithfield that follows a few chapters later. It is here, in this latter scene, that for the first time Oliver really stops and looks at the streets of London. It is early morning, and he is said to be "filled . . . with surprise and amazement" (136; ch. 21), as if he is startled by the sheer strangeness of the place. As with the earlier scene, it is the noise and clamor, its "discordant din," that is given the greatest emphasis: there is "whistling," "barking," "bellowing," "bleating," "grunting," "squeaking," "cries," "shouts, oaths, and quarreling," and so forth.[12] The "auricular organs have . . . to undergo a much more severe trial in Smithfield market," James Grant observed in 1842, "than they would in almost any other spot which could be mentioned in 'this great globe of ours' " (2: 179–80). One of the great social changes in the nineteenth century, Richard Sennett has argued, was a turn toward silence, "silence used as a protection of individual privacy" (343). The cacophony and confusion represented by Smithfield underscored its irredeemably public nature, the fact that, as Dickens said of English slaughterhouses, they were "most numerous in the most densely crowded places," as well as reminding us that this was very much an unrestrained, pre-modern world, a world of beasts and human brutes. In contrast, the modern meat markets and abattoirs at Poissey in France, which Dickens sees as positive models for reform, were much less public and visible, inasmuch as they were located in the suburbs of Paris, and much quieter. One of the most appealing qualities of the Parisian calf market was that, as Dickens noted, "There is little noise," adding that "The market for cattle [in Paris] is held as quietly as the market for calves" ("A Monument of French Folly" 556).

The other major appearance of Smithfield occurs in *Great Expectations*, and, again, it marks the protagonist's first real encounter with London, his entrance into "unfamiliar space." While waiting to meet Mr. Jaggers in Little Britain, "just out of Smithfield," Pip is advised to check out the nearby market: "So I came into Smithfield," he says, "and the shameful place, being all asmear with filth and fat and blood and foam, seemed to stick to me" (131). Here, the infection is both literal and figurative. This scene is paralleled, in the very next paragraph, by Pip's initial encounter with Newgate Prison, a place "where the gallows was kept, and also where people were publicly whipped," which Pip says "was horrible, and gave me a sickening idea of London" (131; ch. 20). Dickens is emphasizing Pip's guilt by associating him with the two places of imprisonment and slaughter, an association that is made clear in *Oliver Twist*, when Fagin asks, "What right have they to butcher me?" Dickens also draws on this association in one of the last pieces of journalism he ever published, "On an Amateur Beat" (27 February 1869). Here, he depicts Smithfield and the Old Bailey, the Central Criminal Court that condemned Fagin to death at Newgate, and which was itself located very near Smithfield Market, as twin evils expressive of a violently punitive past: "fire and faggot, condemned Hold, public hanging, whipping through the city at the cart-tail, pillory, branding-iron, and other beautiful ancestral landmarks, which rude hands have rooted up, without bringing the stars quite down upon us as yet" (382).

As this association between Newgate and Smithfield implies, it was more than Smithfield Market per se (the actual physical location of the market in

West Smithfield) that proved attractive to Dickens; it was the highly suggestive space in close proximity of the market, which included, as we have
seen, the Smithfield slaughterhouses, as well as St. Bartholomew's Hospital,
Newgate Prison, the Central Criminal Court, and the Charterhouse School.
This area brought together a range of institutions, "hospitals, churchyards,
workhouses, schools, infirmaries, refuges, dwellings, provision-shops, nurser-
ies, sick-beds," in Dickens's own words, which comprehended "every stage
and baiting-place in the journey from birth to death" ("A Monument of
French Folly" 554).

The suggestiveness of Smithfield and its environs, and its association with
Newgate Prison, is also evident in *Nicholas Nickleby*. Here, Smithfield is
introduced in relationship to Snow Hill, "an incommodious and even dangerous thoroughfare" (Burn 213), which is said to be "Near to the jail [Newgate
again], and by consequence to Smithfield, and the Compter" (the Giltspur
Street Compter, a City prison for debtors). Again, the area serves as an
introduction to the streets of London, this time for the reader (and, by implication, for Nicholas Nickleby, who has just arrived from Devonshire, with his
sister and mother, and who has just paid a visit to his uncle, Ralph Nickleby).
Dickens begins the passage, another highly wrought set-piece scene, with the
phrase "Snow Hill" followed by an exclamation mark:

> There, at the very core of London, in the heart of its business and animation,
> in the midst of a whirl of noise and motion: stemming as it were the giant
> currents of life that flow ceaselessly on from different quarters, and meet be-
> neath its walls: stands Newgate; and in that crowded street on which it frowns
> so darkly—within a few feet of the squalid tottering houses—upon the very
> spot on which the vendors of soup and fish and damaged fruit are now plying
> their trades—scores of human beings, amidst a roar of sounds to which even
> the tumult of a great city is as nothing, four, six, or eight strong men at a time,
> have been hurried violently and swiftly from the world, when the scene has
> been rendered frightful with excess of human life; when curious eyes have
> glared from casement and house-top, and wall and pillar; and when, in the mass
> of white and upturned faces, the dying wretch, in his all-comprehensive look of
> agony, has met not one—not one—that bore the impress of pity or compassion.
>
> Near to the jail, and by consequence near to Smithfield also, and the Compter,
> and the bustle and noise of the city; and just on that particular part of Snow
> Hill where omnibus horses going eastward seriously think of falling down on
> purpose, and where horses in hackney cabriolets going westward not unfre-
> quently fall by accident, is the coach-yard of the Saracen's Head Inn; its portal
> guarded by two Saracens' heads and shoulders, which it was once the pride
> and glory of the choice spirits of this metropolis to pull down at night, but
> which have for some time remained in undisturbed tranquillity; possibly because
> this species of humour is now confined to Saint James's parish, where door
> knockers are preferred as being more portable, and bell-wires esteemed as
> convenient toothpicks. Whether this be the reason or not, there they are, frown-
> ing upon you from each side of the gateway.   (29–30; ch. 4)

Here are a host of familiar motifs. We are again "at the very core of London, in the heart of its business and animation," though here it's Newgate that serves as the point of orientation. And, again, there is blockage at the heart, "stemming as it were the giant currents of life that flow ceaselessly on from different quarters." And clamorous noise: "a roar of sounds to which even the tumult of a great city is as nothing." And the omnipresence of death: "scores of human beings . . . have been hurried violently and swiftly from the world." And the association of place with nearby place, an association reinforced by the breathless quality of the passage, all setting the scene for the introduction of the Saracen's Head that immediately follows. Throughout the long passage, there is very much the sense of penetrating to a center. The fact that Smithfield is subordinated to Newgate, and then to the Saracen's Head, is less important than that this single space *is* a center, with a representative significance. Again, this is a highly compressed space, a compression that gives added force to the crowds and noise and a prevailing sense of chaos.

It may seem, from the above descriptions of Smithfield, that Dickens's use of the market was entirely negative. But, as I have suggested earlier, there was surely something very appealing about such a place for Dickens's insightful imagination. Put most simply, it gave something for it to catch on. Freedom, perfectly realized, has an anesthetic quality; it has the potential to dull the senses and deaden one's responsiveness. For all its noise and congestion, for all its violence and brutality, for all that it represented the past and everything Dickens detested, Smithfield was also a highly evocative place. It brought close the reality of London, in all its multiplicity and complexity. As Richard Sennett has pointed out, "resistance is a fundamental and necessary experience for the human body: through feeling resistance, the body is roused to take note of the world in which it lives" (310). It is this animating quality of resistance that Smithfield, at the very heart of the City, so richly embodied.

NOTES

1. *Knight's Cyclopædia of London* (1851) noted: "from 1740 to 1750 the population of the metropolis being about 670,000, there were sold at an average, during those ten years, about 74,000 cattle, and about 570,000 sheep. Between this period and 1831 the population increased about 218 per cent., and taking an average of three years ending with 1831, 156,000 cattle and 1,238,000 sheep were sold annually in Smithfield; being an increase of 110 per cent. on the cattle, and of 117 per cent. on the sheep, as compared with the numbers sold in 1740–50." Although the population of London had grown faster than the number of livestock sold, *Knight's Cyclopædia* observed that "the average weight of cattle is now about 640 lbs., and of sheep about 96 lbs.," as compared to "probably rather

too low'' an estimate from a century before, of 370 lbs. for cattle and 28 lbs. for sheep (796).

2. There were parliamentary inquiries in 1847, 1849, and 1850.

3. Monday was the day exclusively devoted to the sale of cattle, sheep, and swine. Fridays were reserved for the sale of donkeys, horses, vehicles, harness, whips, and other agricultural implements. On Tuesdays, Thursdays, and Saturdays, hay and straw were sold.

4. From "the north by Highgate Archway, and from the eastern counties by Whitechapel Road" (*Knight's Cyclopædia* 797).

5. Most of the 138 London slaughterhouses (in 1848) were located in Aldgate, a north-south thoroughfare, just east of Smithfield.

6. "Even with the utmost enlargement of Smithfield, the number of animals that could be accommodated at one time was not more than 4000 cattle and 25,000 sheep. When, therefore, five, six, or seven thousand cattle were present, the crushing and crowding were amply accounted for" (Dodd 239).

7. Besides the pieces mentioned in the text of this article, there were a number of other items in *Household Words* that discussed Smithfield and the related issue of slaughterhouses: e.g., Richard H. Horne, "The Cattle Road to Ruin," 1 (29 June 1850): 325–30; W. H. Wills, "Chips: From Mr. Thomas Bovington," 1 (13 July 1850): 377; W. H. Wills and John Docwra Parry, "Chips: Nice White Veal," 1 (10 August 1850): 467–68; W. H. Wills, "Torture in the Way of Business," 1 (14 September 1850): 587–88; and W. H. Wills, "Mr. Bovington on the New Cattle Market," 5 (17 July 1852): 422–23. These were part of an orchestrated attack on Smithfield. On 12 July 1850, Dickens asked Wills to gather additional information about "absurdities enunciated by this wiseacre" (a councilman named Henry Taylor), who had given "a most intolerably asinine Speech about Smithfield" in the Common Council, "absurdities" mocked in Dickens's piece, "The Lively Turtle" on 26 October 1850 (*Letters* 6: 129).

8. The latter play, which is alluded to earlier in *Dombey* (38; ch. 4), includes a sailor's vow of loyalty to his sweetheart immediately before he embarks on a voyage: "O Susan, Susan, lovely dear, / My vows shall ever true remain."

9. The scene takes place in Limehouse-Hole, which suggests the bulls are probably being driven *to* Smithfield Market from the docks nearby (presumably, they have been transported to London by ship).

10. "There was a combination between the butchers and the salesmasters to prevent the removal of the market, and that combination was most injurious to the public," according to one of the leading parliamentary reformers, Mr. Mackinnon (*Hansard* 107: 497).

11. Most obviously, of course, it puns on Walter Scott's *The Heart of Midlothian* (1818).

12. Cf. *Knight's Cyclopædia of London*: "The lowing of the oxen, the tremulous cries of the sheep, the barking of dogs, the rattling of sticks on the heads and bodies of the animals, the shouts of the drovers, and the flashing of the torches, present altogether a wild and terrific combination: and few, either of those who reside in the metropolis, or who visit it, have the resolution to witness the strange scene" (797).

WORKS CITED

Alter, Robert. *Imagined Cities: Urban Experience and the Language of the Novel.* New Haven: Yale UP, 2005.

"Annals and Antiquities of London." *Blackwood's Edinburgh Magazine* 60 (December 1846): 673–89.

Burn, Jacob Henry. *A Descriptive Catalogue of the London Traders, Tavern, and Coffee-House Tokens.* 2nd ed. Printed for the Use of the Members of the Corporation of the City of London, 1855.

Dickens, Charles. *Bleak House.* 1852–53. Ed. Stephen Gill. Oxford: Oxford UP, 1998.

———. *Dombey and Son.* 1846–48. Ed. Alan Horsman. Introduction and Notes by Dennis Walder. Oxford: Oxford UP, 2001.

———. *The Letters of Charles Dickens.* Pilgrim Edition. 12 vols. Oxford: Clarendon. 1965–2002.

———. "A Monument of French Folly." *Household Words* 2 (8 March 1851): 554–58.

———. *Nickolas Nickleby.* Ed. Paul Schlicke. Oxford: Oxford UP, 1990.

———. *Oliver Twist.* Ed. Kathleen Tillotson. Oxford: Clarendon, 1966.

———. "On an Amateur Beat." *The Uncommercial Traveller and Other Papers, 1859–70.* Ed. Michael Slater. Columbus, OH: Ohio State UP, 2000.

———, and W. H. Wills. "The Heart of Mid-London." *Household Words* 1 (4 May 1850): 121–25.

Dodd, George. *The Food of London: A Sketch.* London: Longman, Brown, Green, Longmans, 1856.

Donald, Diana. " 'Beastly Sights': The Treatment of Animals as a Moral Theme in Representations of London, *c.* 1820–1850." *Art History* 22 (November 1999): 514–44.

Fletcher, Joseph. "Statistical Account of the Markets of London. Read before the Statistical Society of London, 17th May, 1847." *Quarterly Journal of the Statistical Society of London* (November 1847).

Forshaw, Alec, and Theo Bergström. *Smithfield Past and Present.* London: Heinemann, 1980.

Grant, James. *Light and Shadows of London Life.* 2 vols. London: Saunders and Otley, 1842.

Hansard's Parliamentary Debates. 356 vols. London: T. C. Hansard, 1829–91.

Hone, William. *The Everyday Book or a Guide to the Year.* 2 vols. London: William Tegg, 1826.

Horne, Richard H. "The Cattle Road to Ruin." *Household Words* 1 (29 June 1850): 325–30.

Hunt, Frederick Knight. "Twenty-four Hours in a London Hospital." *Household Words* 2 (8 February 1851): 457–65.

Johnson, Steven. *The Ghost Map.* New York, Penguin, 2006.

Joyce, Patrick. *The Rule of Freedom: Liberalism and the Modern City.* London: Verso, 2003.

Knight's Cyclopædia of London. 1851. No. 34. London: Charles Knight, 1851.

Macpherson, Ossian. "Chips: The Smithfield Model of the Model Smithfield." *Household Words* 2 (8 March 1851): 572–73.

Nead, Lynda. *Victorian Babylon: People Streets and Images in Nineteenth-Century London.* New Haven: Yale UP, 2000.

Otter, Christopher. "Cleansing and Clarifying: Technology and Perception in Nineteenth-Century London." *Journal of British Studies* 43 (January 2004): 40–64.

Reach, Angus B. "John Bull and His Bullocks." *Douglas Jerrold's Shilling Magazine* 5 (January–June 1847): 119–23.

Report of the Commissioners Appointed to Make Inquiries Relating to Smithfield Market. London: W. Clowes, 1850.

Sennett, Richard. *Flesh and Stone: The Body and the City in Western Civilization.* New York: Norton, 1994.

"The Smithfield Abomination." *Punch* 11 (1846): 235.

"Smithfield Martyrs.—Smithfield 'Salubrity.' " *Punch* 12 (1847): 116.

"The Smithfield Nuisance." *The* [London] *Times* (25 November 1846).

"Smithfield Rights of Cattle." *Punch.* 11 (1846): 209.

Wills, W. H. and Henry Morley. "Improving A Bull." *Household Words* 1 (3 August 1850): 450–51.

Wordsworth, William. *Selected Poems and Prefaces.* Ed. Jack Stillinger. Boston, MA: Houghton Mifflin, 1965.

"What Might Have Been Is Not What Is": Dickens's Narrative Refusals

Robyn Warhol-Down

Looking at "narrative refusals" gives us a glimpse at a previously unrecognized facet of the complexities that form Dickens's style, allowing us to see differently what is there by turning our attention to what is marked as explicitly not-there. This essay outlines the pervasive uses of unnarration (when a narrator says he or she will not tell something) and disnarration (when a narrator tells something that did not happen in place of telling what did) in such Dickens novels as Great Expectations, Our Mutual Friend, *and* Dombey and Son, *then turns to an earlier work,* Nicholas Nickleby, *where narrative refusals are already incipient, though more rare than in middle and later Dickens. When narrative refusal is present in Dickens, the figure takes one of at least three different forms: negation of action or situation ("it was not . . . not . . . not"), misattribution of characters' feelings and agency to a fictitious "Nobody" (as in* Little Dorrit), *and subjunctive narration detailing what might have happened, but does not. I concentrate on negated and subjunctive disnarration of "what might have been" but "is not what is," to quote what R. Wilfer says about the counterfactual in* Our Mutual Friend.

Dickens's uniquely accretive style—with its repetitions and hyperboles, its enumerative descriptions and polysyllabic locutions—results in a delightful superfluity of telling. Ask me what makes Dickens wonderful, and I will quote you a passage from *Great Expectations* in which Pip retrospectively

---

Dickens Studies Annual, Volume 41, Copyright © 2010 by AMS Press, Inc. All rights reserved.

explains why he felt miserable at Christmas dinner: "Not because I was squeezed in at an acute angle of the table-cloth, with the table in my chest, and the Pumblechookian elbow in my eye, nor because I was not allowed to speak (I didn't want to speak), nor because I was regaled with the scaly tips of the drumsticks of the fowls, and with those obscure corners of pork of which the pig, when living, had had the least reason to be vain" (25; ch. 4). George Orwell attributed Dickens's distinctive style to his characteristic inclusion of "the *unnecessary detail*" (59, italics in original). "Everything is piled up and up," Orwell says, "detail on detail, embroidery on embroidery" (63; ch. 5), creating "that special Dickens atmosphere" (61; ch. 5). The superfluous details are unnecessary to moving the story forward; but they are, to be sure, crucial elements of Dickens's style. We can see examples here in the acute angle, the Pumblechookian elbow, and—not just the tips, but—the *scaly* tips of the drumsticks.

Perhaps less obvious in this passage than the unnecessary detail, but equally characteristic of Dickensian prose, is the elaborate series of negations. Pip brings up the angle, the elbow, and the scaly tips in the course of telling what was *not* making him miserable ("not because I was squeezed . . . nor because I was not allowed . . . nor because I was regaled" was Pip unhappy). Embedded in this series is yet another set of negations: for instance "I *was not* allowed to speak (I *didn't want* to speak)" and "those obscure corners of pork of which the pig, when living, *had had the least* reason to be vain." Behind all these negatives shimmers a potential diegetic world where children want to speak and are allowed to speak, where pigs have reason to be vain of the less obscure corners of their bodies, where being squeezed at the table or forbidden to talk or parsimoniously regaled with bad food are circumstances unusual enough to be the source of a child's discomfort. That is not, of course, the diegetic world Pip inhabits, nor is it a diegetic world present in any of Dickens's novels. "Ah, me!" R. Wilfer says to himself upon his first appearance in *Our Mutual Friend*, "what might have been is not what is!" (42; bk. 1, ch. 4). The rendition of what might have been and yet *is not* does form, however, much of the substance of Dickens's narrative prose. Direct narratorial references to some of the specifics of *what might have been and yet is not* are what I call "narrative refusals."

This essay comes out of my new project in narrative theory, a contribution, I hope, to the descriptive poetics of the nineteenth-century British novel. Like my previous work, "Narrative Refusals"—the longer project that inspires this investigation of Dickens's style— examines specific narrative gestures in the context of the cultural formation of subjectivity. My focus on this particular feature of novelistic style comes at a moment in literary-theoretical history when a contextualized neoformalism can, I believe, interest not only narrative theorists who never stopped caring about form, but also scholars of the nineteenth-century British novel redirecting their attention to "the secret of style," as D. A. Miller's 2003 book on Jane Austen calls it. Dickens's style, of course, is no secret, not even like Austen's an open secret, because everybody knows all about it. Everybody knows that Dickens's prose is uniquely recognizable as Dickensian; everybody knows that the writing in Dickens's later works is more complex than in his earlier ones. Looking at what I call "narrative refusals" gives us a glimpse at a previously unrecognized facet of the complexities that form Dickensian style, allowing us to see differently what is there by turning our attention to what is marked as explicitly *not-there*. I begin by laying out two modes of narrative refusal in Dickens's middle and later novels (with specific reference to *Great Expectations,* *Our Mutual Friend,* and *Dombey and Son*), then turn to an earlier work, *Nicholas Nickleby,* where narrative refusals are already incipient, though less common than in later Dickens. When narrative refusal is present in Dickens, the figure takes one of at least three different forms: negation of action or situation ("it was not . . . not . . . not"), misattribution of characters' feelings and agency to a fictitious "Nobody," and subjunctive narration detailing what might have happened, but does not. I will concentrate here on negated and subjunctive disnarration of "what might have been" but "is not what is."

In adopting the "not, not, not, but" sentence structure, Dickens participates in the domestication through the English novel of the classical forms John Milton borrowed for the epic effects of *Paradise Lost.* Milton's Adam uses the same rhetorical structure in speaking of Eve: "Her virtue, and the conscience of her worth,/ That would be wooed, and not unsought be won,/ Not obvious, not obtrusive, but retired;/ The more desirable" (511–12; Book VIII, lines 502–05). Adam's diction invokes the possibility of obviously and obtrusively virtuous women to contrast with Eve's unselfconscious perfection. Like Adam, Milton's fallen angels lean heavily on similar negations in the rhetoric of their debate, as when Moloch—who "rather than be less/ Cared not to be at all; with that care lost/ Went all his fear: of God, of hell, or worse,/ He recked not" (325; Book II, lines 47–50)—asserts "of wiles,/ More unexpert, I boast not: them let those/ Contrive who need, or when they need, not now" (325; Book II, lines 51–53) or Belial suggests that "Our supreme foe in time may much remit/ His anger; and perhaps, thus far removed,/ Not mind us not offending, satisfied/ With what is punished; whence these raging fires/ will slacken, if his breath stir not their flames" (330; Book II, lines 210–14), since, as Belial says, "our present lot appears/ for happy though but ill, for ill not worst,/ If we procure not to ourselves more woe" (330; Book II, lines 223–25). Transmitted from Milton and the classics through the mock-epic rhetoric of Pope and Fielding, the negative formations make their way into Dickens's prose by way of parody. As parody, they can account for much of the comic effect of the scene depicting Pip at the dinner table. The multiple negations invoke the epic mode, both illustrating and undercutting the misery Pip experiences at the hands of his family and Mr. Pumblechook. At the same time, just as they do in Milton, the negations point to particular possibilities that have been left out.

To be sure, an unimaginably large quantity of information is left out of all nineteenth-century fiction, considering everything that any novelist might have imagined or observed, but did not include in a particular text's story or discourse. Narrative elisions, suppressions, repressions, silences, gaps, omissions or lacunae: all of these invoke that which is ''unnarratable'' for any given text. Building on Gerald Prince's classic definition of the ''narratable,'' I have identified four types of unnarratability in prose fiction and film:

* subnarratable (what need not be told because it is too obvious or boring)
* supranarratable (what cannot be told because it is ineffable or inexpressible)
* antinarratable (what should not be told because of trauma or taboo)
* paranarratable (what would not be told because of literary convention).[1]

Thresholds of narratability vary from one genre to the next and, within the same genre, from one period to the next. Even within the genre of the Victorian realist novel, what is unnarratable for one author may fill up paragraphs for another. For instance, Trollope does not hesitate to mention the smallest gestures of body, face, and eye contact in scenes whose substance would be subnarratable (too boring or obvious) for even novelists as prolix as Thackeray or Dickens to mention. Always the text is finite, but that which isn't narrated is infinite. (Even an elaborate deconstructive reading intended to open out rather than close off meanings eventually reaches a boundary beyond which a particular text's utterances won't reach. Whatever else it may be, for example, *Little Dorrit* is not a novel about colonizing new planets in outer space.) So texts have limits. But there are no limits to the unnarratable.

If the unnarratable usually figures in fiction as a gap, silence, or elision, it can also motivate explicit narrative refusals of the kind that Pip makes in his description of the dinner table scene. Pip's childhood experience of abuse is antinarratable, too traumatic to recount in the genre of Victorian domestic fiction. When narrators enact this kind of narrative refusal, they point in the text to a particular subset of that which is being left out, thus explicitly marking something that is unnarratable. I have identified two distinct but related gestures of narrative refusal:

* unnarration: when the narrator indicates he or she can't or won't tell what happened.
* disnarration: when the narrator tells something that did not happen, in place of saying what did.

In contrast with that which is simply left out, the unnarrated and disnarrated aspects of a text become a vividly *present absence*, existing at a narrative level somewhere between the text and everything that is left out of it.[2] Unnarration—the kind of passage where a narrator will say "I won't go into details" or "words cannot express"—assumes knowledge on the part of the implied reader. Experience of life or of literary reading will help the reader fill in the blanks. Disnarration, by contrast, is more pedagogical. In the disnarrated passage—where the narrator evokes nostalgia ("something was there, but is no longer"), hopefulness ("something might be there, but is not yet"), or a sense of bare absence ("something never was and never will be there") —the implied reader receives a set of options to consider and ultimately to reject. The diegesis—or the virtual world created by the text—splits into multiple levels whenever disnarration occurs. Shadowing the imagined world of the novel, another diegesis lurks in the negated or subjunctive details mentioned in the disnarration. In his series of negations, for example, Pip's disnarration both invokes and masks the cognitive and emotional experience of trauma, leaving it for the moment unspoken somewhere in the space between the secondary, idyllic diegetic world implied by his negated examples (where children want to talk and are allowed to talk) and the imagined world represented in the comic text he speaks. That which is disnarrated is better left un-said.

In late and middle Dickens, disnarration becomes a dominant mode of narrative discourse, maybe even *the* dominant mode. Pip disnarrates the dinner-table scene when he brings into being that which is not (the alternative world where children might be happy) in place of telling details about that which is (his feelings about life at the forge). In revising and then re-revising the ending of *Great Expectations*, Dickens puts Pip through a paroxysm of disnarration, unbinding the novel's closure by negating and then double-negating the final action, rather than simply telling it. The draft ending leaves no doubt that Pip and Estella have parted forever, once they have greeted each other for the last time on a London street. The first revision moves their encounter to the ruined garden at Satis House, where Estella says they will "remain friends apart." In this version Pip—having taken Estella's hand and walked with her out of the garden—says he "saw the shadow of no parting from her" (484). As if this ending too unambiguously contradicted the first version by implying that Pip and Estella would become a permanent couple at the novel's end, Dickens re-revised it to complicate the disnarration with a further negation: "I saw no shadow of another parting from her" (507). Commentators may argue endlessly about whether "no shadow of another parting" means Pip anticipated that he and Estella would stay together and never part again, or whether it means this is their last parting and that Pip sees no reason to think they would meet again to part another time.[3] What makes the ambiguity irresolvable is Pip's narratorial negation of action: first he saw "the shadow of no parting," then "no shadow of another parting." By rendering the prediction negatively, Pip disnarrates the ending rather than telling us what did ultimately happen. I read the ending (as I do the similarly ambiguous end of Charlotte Brontë's *Villette*) to say that the narrator-protagonist remains forever single. Such an ending is, in 1860, unnarratable—specifically it is paranarratable, because it would eventually become not only acceptable, but conventional for realist novels to end in this way. If Dickens had faithfully followed Bulwer Lytton's advice and given *Great Expectations* an unambiguously "happy" ending, he would have been more radically pushing out the boundaries of the unnarratable in his genre. Even so, for a novelist as profoundly attached to his audience's pleasure and approval as Dickens was, the narrative refusal of closure is a startling choice.

The novel following *Great Expectations*, *Our Mutual Friend* sustains the same mode of negative disnarration from beginning to end. Like those in *Great Expectations*, disnarrations in *Our Mutual Friend* work to heighten a sense of absence. Like the last page of the previous novel, the first page of *Our Mutual Friend* leans heavily on negation, this time in the extradiegetic narrator's first description of Hexam:

> He had no net, hook or line, and he could not be a fisherman; his boat had no cushion for a sitter, no paint, no inscription, no appliance beyond a rusty boat-hook and a coil of rope, and he could not be a waterman; his boat was too crazy and too small to take in cargo for delivery, and he could not be a lighterman or river-carrier; there was no clue to what he looked for, but he looked for something, with a most intent and searching gaze.   (13; bk. 1, ch. 1)

This refusal to name Hexam's object is part of the opening scene's strategy for building the sense of "dread or horror" the narrator attributes to Hexam's daughter, Lizzie. It is therefore part of the machinery of suspense, and it operates throughout this novel built on a secret to emphasize the need for detection. But the disnarration also creates an alternate diegetic world, populated by industrious fishermen, cheerful passengers in brightly painted cushioned pleasure boats, busy cargo haulers, and helpful lightermen. Like the comfortable childhood Pip disnarrates, this world is entirely separate from Lizzie Hexam's experience—it is a present absence in the book.

Throughout *Our Mutual Friend*, the same explicit way of mentioning what is *not* there occurs repeatedly throughout the novel, even in scenes where suspense is not deployed:

> Not, however, towards the 'shops' where cunning artificers work on pearls and diamonds and gold and silver, making their hands so rich, that the enriched water in which they wash them is bought for the refiners;—not towards these does Mr. Wegg stump, but towards the poorer shops of small retail traders.
> (83; bk. 1, ch. 7)

[Mr. Venus] has no cravat on, and has opened his tumbled shirt-collar to work with the more ease. For the same reason he has no coat on: only a loose waistcoat over his yellow linen. His eyes are like the over-tried eyes of an engraver, but he is not that; his expression and stoop are like those of a shoe-maker, but he is not that.   (83; bk. 1, ch. 7)

As is well known to the wise in their generation, traffic in Shares is the one thing to have to do with in this world. Have no antecedents, no established character, no cultivation, no ideas, no manners; have Shares.
                (118; bk. 1, ch. 10)

It was not summer yet, but spring; and it was not gentle spring ethereally mild, as in Thomson's Seasons, but nipping spring with an easterly wind, as in Johnson's, Jackson's, Dickson's, Smith's, and Jones's Seasons.
                (147; bk. 1, ch. 12)

The voice of the falling water, like the voices of the sea and the wind, were as an outer memory to a contemplative listener; but not particularly so to Mr. Riderhood, who sat on one of the blunt wooden levers of his lock-gates, dozing. Wine must be got into a butt by some agency before it can be drawn out; and the wine of sentiment never having been got into Mr. Riderhood by any agency, nothing in nature tapped him.   (617; bk. 4, ch. 1)

[Eugene] looked at [Lizzie] with a real sentiment of remorseful tenderness and pity. It was not strong enough to impel him to sacrifice himself and spare her, but it was a strong emotion.   (675; bk. 4, ch. 6)

There was something in the attitude of [Lizzie's] whole figure as [Eugene] supported it, and she hung her head, which besought him to be merciful and not force her to disclose her heart. He was not merciful with her, and he made her do it.   (677–78; bk. 4, ch. 6)

[Charley] spoke as confidently, and with as entire an absence of any tell-tale colour in his cheek, as if there were no softening old time behind him. Not wonderful, for there *was* none in his hollow empty heart.   (693; bk. 4, ch. 7)

In each of these examples the disnarrated element is something more pleasant, more proper, more ideally desirable and comfortable than what is implicitly present in the text. The prosperous shops of the jewelers are absent, Mr. Venus's seedier establishment present; the respectable cravat and coat that Mr. Venus might have worn are absent, his ill-fitting waistcoat and stained linen present; the possibility that he might be an engraver or shoemaker is absent, the reality of his grim profession present. Young people wishing to make their way in the world might have antecedents, character, cultivation, ideas, manners—but no, they have Shares. Instead of warm summer or spring "ethereally mild," it is "nipping" cold spring; instead of being the season described by the poet Thomson, it is the weather experienced by the prosai-cally generic Johnsons, Jacksons, Dicksons, Smiths, and Joneses. Anyone else might contain the wine of sentiment, but Riderhood holds none; Eugene's sympathy for Lizzie might have moved him to spare her, but it is not adequately powerful; a better person than Charley might hold memories of old times in his heart, but Charley's is hollow and empty. In all the cases but one, the negation straightforwardly contradicts a positive possibility in order to assert a less ideal reality. In that one exceptional case, Dickens employs a double disnarration the more strongly to invoke the course Eugene ought to be taking with Lizzie, while emphasizing how far Eugene's actions stray from their more desirable opposite. The "whole attitude" of Lizzie's body begs him *not* to "force her to disclose her heart." "Disclose" is a negative locution for "reveal"; to "force her to disclose" is to do violence to her wish to be silent. Behind the disnarration of "not to force her to disclose" lies an image of Lizzie serenely unmolested, relieved by Eugene's imagined willingness to simply let her be quiet. He is, however, "not merciful," and so he makes her do it. Every disnarrated action in *Our Mutual Friend* has its corresponding positive action. It is as if the novelist is imagining a parallel diegetic world where the complications driving his novel's plot become moot, because the desires those complications continually thwart are all already realized. It is a shadow world, an alternate story that is not quite not-there. The disnarrations function here, as in *Great Expectations*, as a parody of the naïve view that would imagine this shadow world could be a possibility. If that shadow world is born of a naivety the parodic narrator scorns, it is also a world that is nonnarratable, where no conflict or complication would arise to motivate a story. In this respect, the disnarrations are spaces in which the narrator points to the narrative engines driving the text.

Dombey and Son, like *Our Mutual Friend*, also carries a shadow-narrative that flickers behind its main action. Like R. Wilfer, Dombey—finally repenting of his stony indifference to his daughter—"chiefly thought of what might have been, and what was not" (796). Of course, Wilfer—that loving father the narrator likes to call the "Cherub"—is aware of this discrepancy between the real and the potentially better from his very first appearance in the novel, while Dombey can see nothing beyond his own version of "what is" until he has lost everything. Whereas the narrator of *Our Mutual Friend* consistently invokes that other, more positive possible world through negations, the narrator of *Dombey and Son* couches disnarration in the subjunctive mode. Though both novels continually evoke what might have been and yet is not, *Dombey and Son*'s passages of subjunctive disnarration gesture toward a better possible world only at the novel's beginning, then shift to reinforce the novel's prevailing mood of despair. Early in the novel, the narrator raises the subjunctive possibility that Dombey might not have shut out his daughter Florence, had he been paying sufficient attention to her after her mother has died:

And, perhaps, unlearned as she was, [Polly] could have brought a dawning knowledge home to Mr. Dombey at that early day, which would not then have struck him in the end like lightning.   (40; ch. 3)

Had [Dombey] looked with greater interest and with a father's eye, he might have read in [Florence's] keen glance the impulses and fears that made her waver; the passionate desire to run clinging to him, crying, as she hid her face in his embrace, 'Oh father, try to love me! There's no one else!' the dread of a repulse; the fear of being too bold, and of offending him; the pitiable need in which she stood of some assurance and encouragement; and how her over-charged young heart was wandering to find some natural resting-place, for its sorrow and affection.   (42–43; ch. 3)

These subjunctive disnarrations, like the negations in *Our Mutual Friend* and in *Great Expectations*, bring to the surface of the text the specifics of a more positive version of "what might have been, and what was not." If he had been able to learn from Polly's example, or if he had been capable of reading Florence's fear of annoying him, Dombey would have realized the value of his daughter's attachment from the beginning, not just at the end. The disnarration invokes for the reader an alternate story where father and daughter recognize and console each other for the loss of wife and mother. Still, in this novel the shadow scene—the action that does not happen, but exists behind the action that does—is not a particularly cheerful alternative. The narrator brings in through the disnarration the spectacle of the child's wavering, crying, and clinging; her dread, her fear, her pitiable need, and her overcharged heart find their way into the text without Florence's having actually to enact them. The shadow-narratives brought forth by this and subsequent passages of disnarration come to rival the Dombey family's actual story for perversity and misery.

Neither do the hypothetical situations the narrator proposes as "better" than Dombey's actual relations with his daughter present anything like posi-tive alternatives to the diegetic action:

If every sorrowing tear [Florence] shed in [speaking of her father], had been a curse upon the head of him she never named or blamed, it would have been better for him, Walter thought, with awe, than to be renounced out of such a strength and might of love.   (753; ch. 49)

Oh, how much better than this that [Dombey] had loved her as he had his boy, and lost her as he had his boy, and laid them in their early grave together!
                    (906; ch. 59)

In the parallel potential story proposed here, Florence either curses her father when she renounces him, or else she dies young and beloved, like her brother Paul. Curses and early death would be better—Walter thinks and the narrator concurs—than that Florence should waste her affection on her insensible

father. Dombey's relations with Edith, his second wife, are identically hopeless, in both their narrated and disnarrated versions: "[Edith] had better have
been dead than laugh as she did, in reply, with her intent look fixed upon
[Mr. Dombey]. He had better have been dead, than sitting there, in his mag-
nificence, to hear her" (713; ch. 47). Better for them both to die than to laugh
and be laughed at with such disdain and indifference: in the "better" alternate
story behind the disnarration, both Dombey and Edith succumb to the murderous enmity between them.

   For that matter, Florence's father is so indifferent to her forgiveness and
sympathy that he is not just incapable of responding to them in the diegetic
world as presented. He is equally closed off in the possible world suggested
by the hypothetical passages of disnarration: "If [Dombey] could have heard
her voice in an adjoining room, he would not have gone to her. If he could
have seen her in the street, and she had done no more than look at him as she
had been used to look, he would have passed on with his old cold unforgiving
face . . . " (907; ch. 59). This is equally true of Dombey's relationship with
Edith, who from the beginning of their marriage defies his assumed power
over her.

> [Dombey] might have read in that one glance that nothing that his wealth could
> do, though it were increased ten thousand fold, could win him for its own sake,
> one look of softened recognition from the defiant woman, linked to him, but
> arrayed with her whole soul against him. He might have read in that one glance
> that even for its sordid and mercenary influence upon herself, [Edith] spurned it.
> (544–45; ch. 35).

Even if he had seen the loving girl on the hypothetical street, or recognized
the disdainful woman actually sitting before him, his situation would be
equally bleak. Up to the moment just before his epiphany, Dombey remains
even hypothetically incapable of connection with anyone other than his dead
son: "Here, thrown upon the bare boards, in the dead of night, he wept,
alone—a proud man, even then; who, if a kind hand could have been stretched
out, or a kind face could have looked in, would have risen up, and turned
away, and gone down to his cell" (908; ch. 59). In the alternate world invoked
by the subjunctive disnarration, Dombey's pride would keep him as isolated
as he is in the presenting story. "What might have been" for Dombey presents
no positive alternative. If the suddenness of his final reconciliation with
Florence seems to come without preparation, this is at least partly attributable
to the hopelessness of the parallel story the disnarration so consistently tells.

   Dombey and Son has its comical side, too, and its comic version of subjunctive disnarration. Repeatedly we are told that if Mrs. Blimber "could only
have seen Cicero in his retirement at Tusculum" she would have nothing
else to wish for. Never having seen Cicero, Mrs. Blimber has not achieved

the state of perfect satisfaction, but if she only *could* have, the novel would contain one character who is completely without unfulfilled desire. The joke is, of course, that she never *could* have seen Cicero in his retirement or in any other circumstances—and certainly, every time either she or the narrator expresses the wish that she had, the disnarrated image of how Mrs. Blimber might have actually benefited from the mere sight of Cicero becomes increasingly laughable.

Great Expectations, Our Mutual Friend, and *Dombey and Son* are all celebrated not just for the complexity of their plots, but also the complexity of their psychology. We take it for granted that the early (or early-middle?) novel *Nicholas Nickleby* is not complex in the same admirable way as the later work. It would be easy to say that *Nicholas Nickleby* (either the character or the novel) has no psychology—but then, no novel has a psychology, strictly speaking: psychology is an effect created through the narrative construction of interiority. Looking for narrative refusals in this earlier novel shows that Dickens is already working on the technology of structuring a subjectivity for the text. As in the later novels, *Nicholas Nickleby* employs the subjunctive mode of disnarration in its more seriously sentimental moments. Responding to her co-worker's question about whether she finds her black dress uncomfortably hot, Kate

> Might have said, that mourning was the coldest wear which mortals can assume; that it not only chills the breasts of those it clothes, but extending its influence to summer friends, freezes up their sources of good-will and kindness, and withering all the buds of promise they once so liberally put forth, leaves nothing but bared and rotten hearts exposed. (210; ch. 17)

That is, Kate might have told the truth by translating the seamstress's straightforward question into a metaphor comparing the effects on friends of a loved one's death to the killing actions of a winter frost. In the way that metaphor always imports visual images into a narrative text, this disnarration brings the imaginary frozen garden (and Kate's grief) for a moment into the foreground while allowing Kate in her behavior and even in her thoughts to be as polite and discreet as her Dickensian heroine status requires her to be. The disnarration also seems momentarily to invest Kate with a depth of consciousness she, as a character, does not possess. The narrator emphasizes this in a passage of subjunctive disnarration at the end of the same scene, after the haughty customers have insulted Kate: "Philosophy would have taught her that the degradation was on the side of those who had sunk so low as to display such passions habitually, and without cause; but she was too young for such consolation, and her honest feeling was hurt" (212; ch. 17). In both these instances the disnarration brings into the text, but not into the diegesis, narratorial wisdom that places Kate's limited emotional experience in relief against a deeper-seeming background.

In an extremely rare moment of sentimental reflection, Ralph Nickleby falls into a subjunctive reverie that briefly adds a depth-effect to his characterization:

> He thought of what his home might be if Kate were there; he placed her in the empty chair, looked upon her, heard her speak; he felt again upon his arm the gentle pressure of the trembling hand; he strewed his costly rooms with the hundred silent tokens of feminine presence and occupation; he came back again to the cold fireside and the silent dreary splendour; and in that one glimpse of a better nature, born as it was in selfish thoughts, the rich man felt himself friendless, childless, and alone.   (384; ch. 31)

Unlike the passages about Kate's mourning, this evocation of "what might have been but is not" is directly attributable to Ralph's consciousness, taking the form of an unvoiced direct discourse he is having with himself. The disnarrated images—the sound and sight of the young woman in the chair, the sensation of her hand on Ralph's arm, the "female touch" in the room's decoration and clutter—represent Ralph's own momentary sense of what might have been. Here Ralph is more than an early version of the *character type* Dickens will later develop into Dombey. His behavior and attitudes resemble Dombey's, to be sure, but more striking is the parallel between the ways the narrators of the two novels use subjunctive disnarration to structure the two characters' psychology. As the narrator remarks immediately after Ralph's musings, "A very slight circumstance was sufficient to banish such reflections from the mind of such a man" (384; ch. 31). Such reflections are also evidently banished from this text, as the narrator of *Nicholas Nickleby* refrains from disnarrating the potential reconciliations and recognitions that so strongly characterize the narrative refusals in *Dombey and Son*. Ralph's introduction into the text prefigures the negative disnarration so common in *Our Mutual Friend*, however:

> Mr. Ralph Nickleby was not, strictly speaking, what you would call a merchant: neither was he a banker, nor an attorney, nor a special pleader, nor a notary. He was certainly not a tradesman, and still less could he lay any claim to the title of a professional gentleman; for it would have been impossible to mention any recognized profession to which he belonged.   (21; ch. 2)

Like Gaffer Hexam, Ralph does not earn his living by any respectable means; like the list of boats that Hexam does not row, the inventory of professions Ralph does not practice stands as the positive—but for this story-world impossible—alternative. The list extends to some pretty improbable lengths: who would imagine Ralph to be a notary, for instance, or a special pleader (someone at the Inns of Court who takes the statements of parties in a suit)? The details of the disnarration sketch out a shadow world of ways to make a living, jobs that theoretically ought to be open to Nicholas as he begins to make his way in the world, but are not. The only professional connection he has is connected to no profession at all.

Negative and subjunctive disnarrations being part of the machinery for creating a shadow world repressed, as it were, from the main narrative, or for enhancing the effect of character depth, the narrator of *Nicholas Nickleby* has comparatively little use for them. Narrative refusal in this earlier novel more frequently takes the form of unnarration, in passages where the narrator explicitly says he will not or cannot tell what happened. Unnarration of the supranarratable—that which cannot be told because it is so ineffable as to defy language—is common in sentimental fiction before Dickens (I am thinking here of Susanna Rowson's *Charlotte Temple*, for example, where characters' emotions often exceed the narrator's claims to be able to represent the action). In *Nicholas Nickleby*, by contrast, unnarration is almost always a strategy for comic effect. To be sure, Nicholas's first glimpse of Madeline provokes a conventional claim for the supranarratable: "There are no words which can express, nothing with which can be compared, the perfect pallor, the clear transparent cold ghastly whiteness, of the beautiful face which turned towards him when he entered" (654; ch. 53). More characteristically, though, the narrator of *Nicholas Nickleby* claims incapacity in comical circumstances. For instance, when Tim Linkinwater sits down next to Miss La Creevy, making sure to show his "very comely feet" to advantage, the narrator remarks, "What in the world Tim was doing with his arm it is impossible to conjecture, but he knocked his elbow against that part of the window which was quite on the other side of Miss La Creevy; and it is clear that it could have no business there" (760; ch. 63). This narrator is as apt to *choose* not to tell details as to claim inability to tell. When Mr. Gride and his housekeeper form "a committee of ways and means" to discuss details for the reception of Mr. Gride's intended bride, the narrator declines to render their dialogue: "As they were, like some other committees, extremely dull and prolix in debate, this history may pursue the footsteps of Newman Noggs, thereby combining advantage with necessity; for it would have been necessary to do so under any circumstances, and necessity has no law as all the world know" (636; ch. 51). Their being "dull and prolix" makes the conversation subnarratable—it wouldn't be told because it is too boring. And while Nicholas—alone for the first time with his affianced Madeline—"had been engaged in a manner which every reader may imagine for himself or herself" (762; ch. 63), the action is subnarratable this time because it literally goes without saying.

Unnarration and disnarration can be understood as explicitly marking something like the unconscious of a text. It is not a collective unconscious, but rather a collection of specific possibilities and details the text presents in order to leave out, while not altogether forgetting, what I have been calling the "shadow narrative." When the shadow narrative emerges through narrative refusals, the "repressed" of the text returns, not quite not-there. My very favorite instance of the unnarratable in *Nicholas Nickleby*, however, is not marked by either unnarration or disnarration, though it stands out for me as the most vividly absent presence in the novel. I am referring to anything that is ever said, any speech that is ever made, by the Infant Phenomenon. Although in a solitary scene she "raised a loud cry" (366; ch. 29), she only has one single word ever attributed to her by direct discourse, indirect discourse, free indirect discourse, or any other narrative mode. Because she briefly speaks once, and she performs on stage—not without some talent—she clearly is not mute. In this novel that contains dozens of minor characters, all of whom have plenty to say for themselves, surely the Phenomenon's utterances are not subnarratable—very little goes without saying in this big, chatty book full of dialogue. What she might have said is unlikely either to be supranarratable—too ineffable for words; antinarratable—too traumatic or tabooed to be told; or paranarratable—too unconventional to fit into the hybrid picaresque/realist novel Dickens is writing. But she hardly says a thing. Although *Nicholas Nickleby*, in contrast to the later novels I have discussed, may appear to be a novel that represses nothing, and therefore has no unconscious, the Infant Phenomenon seems to carry the weight of the unnarratable on her youthful shoulders. We don't have to look too closely into her circumstances to understand where that weight comes from: plied with liquor to stunt her growth, forbidden for professional reasons to pass from childhood into puberty, the Phenomenon endures a form of child abuse so peculiar that Dickens treats it as comic spectacle. Her refusal of speech is necessary to making her situation funny. The text of *Nicholas Nickleby* does have an unconscious, and it makes a beginning toward the structuring of subjectivity for which the later novels are so celebrated.[4]

NOTES

1. See my "Neonarrative: How to Render the Unnarratable in Realist Fiction and Contemporary Film" in Phelan and Rabinowitz, eds., *The Blackwell Companion to Narrative Theory*.

2. Instances of narrative refusal share features in common with three distinct rhetorical figures (as defined by Richard Lanham): *occupatio* ("emphasizing a point by pointedly seeming to pass it over," 241), *litotes* ("denial of the contrary, understatement in order to intensify," 241), and *aporia* ("true or feigned doubt or deliberation about an issue," 240). In some cases unnarration or disnarration will combine effects of two or more of these figures. They are also related, though not identical to David Herman's "hypothetical focalization" (in which a narrator

or character produces "hypotheses . . . about what might have been seen or perceived—if only there were someone who could have adopted the requisite perspective on the situations and events at issue," 231) and Brian Richardson's
"denarration" ("in which a narrator denies significant aspects of her narrative
that had earlier been presented as given," 168).
3. Stanley Friedman makes a strong biographical case for reading the ending as an
affirmation that Pip and Estella will remain together.
4. I am grateful to participants in the 2006 Dickens Universe at the University of
California, Santa Cruz, for helpful suggestions on this paper. Helena Michie,
John Bowen, John Glavin, Matthew Kaiser, and Gerhard Joseph made especially
useful comments.

WORKS CITED

Dickens, Charles. *Dombey and Son*. 1848. Harmondsworth: Penguin, 2002.

———. *Great Expectations*. 1859–1860. Harmondsworth: Penguin, 2002.

———. *Nicholas Nickleby*. 1839. Harmondsworth: Penguin, 1999.

———. *Our Mutual Friend*. 1865. Harmondsworth: Penguin, 1998.

Friedman, Stanley. *Dickens's Fiction: Tapestries of Conscience*. New York: AMS
Press, 2003.

Herman, David. "Hypothetical Focalization." *Narrative* 2.3 (1994): 230–53.

Lanham, Richard. *Analyzing Prose*. 2nd edition. London: Continuum, 2003.

Miller, D. A. *Jane Austen, Or, The Secret of Style*. Princeton: Princeton UP, 2005.

Milton, John. *Paradise Lost. The Complete Poetry and Essential Prose of John Milton*.
Ed. William Kerrigan, John Rumrich, and Stephen M. Fallon. New York: Modern
Library, 2007.

Orwell, George. *Dickens, Dali, and Others: Studies in Popular Culture*. New York:
Reynal & Hitchcock, 1946.

Phelan, James and Peter Rabinowitz, eds. *The Blackwell Companion to Narrative
Theory*. Malden, MA and Oxford: Blackwell, 2005. 220–31.

Prince, Gerald. *A Dictionary of Narratology*. 2nd, rev. ed. Lincoln: University of
Nebraska Press, 2003.

Richardson, Brian. "De-narration in Fiction: Erasing the Story in Beckett and Others." *Narrative* 9.2 (2001): 16–75.

Purloined Pleasures: Dickens, Currency, and Copyright

Andrew Burke

*Stung by the hostile response to his comments on the issue of interna-
tional copyright during his speaking tour of America in 1842, Charles
Dickens fulminated in his letters about the losses he incurred due to
the widespread piracy of his work in the United States. In these letters,
and subsequently in* American Notes for General Circulation, *Dickens
represents America as a land of counterfeits and confidence tricksters,
and crafts an analogy between pirated texts and forged banknotes. I
argue that Dickenss distrust of American paper can be understood by
way of Slavoj Žižek's suggestion that nationalism rests on the resentment of the other's enjoyment. For Dickens, the American reader of
pirated texts was a thief in many senses. Piracy deprived authors of a
livelihood, but its shadow economy also undermined efforts to nurture
and sustain a national literature, both English and American. Dickens
marshaled these arguments in public, but in his private letters he is
consumed by the image of the American reader deriving excess, even
perverse, pleasure in reading illegally reproduced material. This paper
focuses on Dickens's fascination with these purloined pleasures, and
the way in which, for him, they compromised the wholesome enjoyment
of those readers who purchased the work legitimately.*

On the evening of February 8, 1842, Charles Dickens attended a banquet in
his honor in the city of Hartford, Connecticut. It was the day after his thirtieth
birthday, and he had landed in America less than a month before to great

Dickens Studies Annual, Volume 41, Copyright © 2010 by AMS Press, Inc. All
rights reserved.

fanfare and acclaim. His books were immensely popular in the United States, and he arrived on its shores triumphantly, lauded by his American hosts as the world's preeminent author. Following the conventional round of after-dinner toasts, Dickens took the podium to address the audience. A week earlier at a similar event in Boston, he had broached the issue of international copyright, largely without controversy. This topic was timely. Great Britain had passed a domestic Copyright Act in 1838, and further revisions to the act that would extend the duration of copyright from twenty-eight to forty-two years after an author's death were already underway and would become law in July of 1842. Dickens was an active participant in the campaign for the extension of domestic copyright, but he recognized that an act passed by a single nation was of limited use in an increasingly globalized publishing marketplace. The language of the British Copyright Act of 1838 effectively extended copyright protection to foreign authors whose books were published in the United Kingdom. Dickens, among others, felt that the United States had a moral obligation to reciprocate this gesture of legislative goodwill. Although he would later vigorously deny it, many at the time suggested Dickens travelled to America for the express purpose of pressuring the American government to sign an international copyright agreement with Great Britain. However, America was suffering through an economic depression and was therefore extremely reluctant to pass any bill that would compromise commerce, whether pirate or legitimate.

It was in these fraught historical circumstances that Dickens took the podium that night in Hartford. Bolstered by the positive reaction he received in Boston, he decided to pursue the issue of copyright. He began somewhat guardedly, informing his audience that he had "made a kind of compact with" himself that while in America he would never "omit an opportunity of referring to a topic" in which every author, on either side of the Atlantic, should have the greatest interest (Fielding 24). Dickens then begged leave to whisper into the ear of his American listeners two words: "International Copyright" (25). He followed this cautious opening with reference to comments made by one of his American hosts in Boston in support of an international agreement. Dickens recalls being profoundly moved when his American ally told the audience that, had there existed an international copyright agreement in the days of Sir Walter Scott, that great man "might not have sunk beneath the mighty pressure on his brain, but might have lived to add new creatures of his fancy to the crowd which swarm about you in your summer walks and gather round your winter evening hearths" (25). Dickens's paraphrase in this instance might be more eloquent than the original, as he invests it with his own passion for the issue. He augmented his fellow author's reference to Scott by drawing on memories of his trip to Abbotsford the year before. He conjured for his audience a scene of Scott on his deathbed, visited in his dying moments by the "ghosts of his imagination" (25). Squeezing all possible pathos from the scene, Dickens communicated to those gathered in his honor the image of Scott's characters assembled around their own creator:

> I pictured them, fresh from traversing the world, and hanging down their heads in sorrow and shame that, from all those lands into which they had carried gladness, instruction, and delight for millions, they had brought him not one friendly hand to raise him from that sad, sad bed. No, nor brought him from that land in which his own language was spoken, and in every house and hut of which his own books were read in his own tongue, one grateful dollar-piece to buy a garland for his grave.   (25)

In the absence of an international copyright agreement, these ghosts are forced to return home empty-handed from their travels throughout the world. America, Dickens implies, must bear the greatest portion of the blame. Scott was extraordinarily popular in the United States, yet he saw no profit from that popularity. Bankruptcy, ruin, and death were the consequences for Scott of America's refusal to submit to a binding international copyright agreement, and Dickens, in uncompromising terms, reminded his American audience of their complicity in the great man's demise.

While in public Dickens conjured the pathetic figure of poor Scott writing himself to death at Abbotsford in a futile effort to pay off his enormous debts, in his private correspondence he identifies himself as "the greatest loser by the existing Law, alive" (*Letters* 3: 76). Through the figure of the aggrieved author, Dickens connects one type of paper to another and imagines the literary marketplace in terms of its circulation. Notes are exchanged for novels at the point of purchase, but also in the form of royalties, which returns a different type of paper back to the author in exchange for that which he or she originally sent out. In his writings on America, Dickens highlights the breakdown in the proper circuit of exchange by presenting the pirated text in terms of the counterfeit note. The pirated text, he implies, is as potentially damaging to the literary economy as counterfeit notes are to the money economy. Paper, whether it takes the form of dollar bills or the literary commodity, must be backed by an issuing authority. Without this assurance, the notes are not merely inauthentic, but should be seen as wholly without value: commercial, moral, or aesthetic.

While other critics have looked at this episode and considered the role of nationalism in Dickens's response to America and his interventions in copyright debates, largely absent from this analysis is an examination of the degree to which Dickens's statements reveal the complex workings of nationalism itself.[1] In this article I want to go beyond diagnosing Dickens's nationalism as symptomatic of copyright squabbles between Britain and the United States to examine the role of pleasure in his reiterations of imperial Englishness and literary authority. The theories of Slavoj Žižek provide a helpful entry into my investigation. Dickens's extreme resentment in his letters from America is more than a personal or individuated example of hostility expressed by an author whose copyright has been violated and royalties lost. Rather, this resentment is part of a larger experience of nationalism conceived in Žižekian terms that sees the coherence of national identity bound to the ways in which enjoyment is organized, sanctioned, and protected. Nationalist fervor emerges most strongly when there is a feeling that some outside force threatens the way a nation organizes its pleasure in shared rituals, such as reading. When outsiders sully the purity of a national ritual, in this case by producing and circulating counterfeit or fraudulent texts integral to it, they threaten national enjoyment itself. I therefore want to reorient our gaze on Dickens's response to America to show how his personal agitation and irritation over the matter of copyright exemplifies a form of literary nationalism that connects pleasure and payment, economics and enjoyment. A theory of nationalism that takes into account the links between proprietary rights and fears of purloined pleasure is therefore necessary to explain the analogous relation between pirated texts and counterfeit money that caused such concern in Parliament and the press and also triggered Dickens's passionate reaction to threats to his livelihood and authority.[2]

In a letter to John Forster written from America, Dickens scorns the enjoyment the American reader derives from a counterfeit text. He presents the enjoyment in terms that stress its perversity. Reading a pirated text is an aberrant pleasure that has less to do with the content of the book than with the circumstances of its consumption:

> He has the Englishmen so regularly on the hip that his eye twinkles with slyness, cunning, and delight; and he chuckles over the humour of the page with an appreciation of it, quite inconsistent with, and apart from, its honest purchase. The raven hasn't more joy in eating a stolen piece of meat, than the American has in reading the English book which he gets for nothing.   (*Letters* 3: 232)

The fraudulence of the pirated text contaminates the experience of reading itself. That Dickens's disgust with this counterfeit enjoyment is conveyed in national terms indicates the international ramifications of the debate. Dickens resents the lost royalties, which are symbolic of his loss of status as the issuing authority of his books, but also takes exception to the very pleasure that American readers derive from reading pirated copies of his work. Such pleasure sullies the enjoyment for which his English readers must pay. Pleasure, Dickens implies, is made wholesome through the mechanisms of the market as governed by the rules of copyright. In the absence of an international copyright agreement, he imagines the proliferation of corrupt pleasures throughout America, spread by the circulation of pirated texts.

The unauthorized circulation of Dickensian texts in America distresses their author so thoroughly because it short-circuits ideas of genuine pleasure, legitimate appreciation, and legal exchange. Speaking in Hartford, Dickens contends that he takes great pleasure in the reception of his novels in America, but does not see this as a sufficient substitute for monetary recompense: "I do not see why fame, besides playing that delightful *reveille* for which she is so justly celebrated, should not blow out of her trumpet a few notes of a different kind from those with which she has hitherto contented herself" (Fielding 25). Dickens extends the metaphor into a musical register, and suggests that royalties for his work would be music to his ears, since whatever enjoyment he might derive from the widespread acclaim for his work is marred by the manner of its diffusion. He implies that the applause of his American supporters rings somewhat hollow when not backed by sound currency, banknotes that would represent a percentage of total sales.

Writing to Forster on February 24, Dickens remembers with pride that night in Hartford: "I wish you could have seen the faces that I saw, down both sides of the table at Hartford, when I began to talk about Scott. I wish you could have heard how I gave it out. My blood so boiled as I thought of the monstrous injustice that I felt as if I were twelve feet high when I thrust it down their throats" (*Letters* 3: 83). In a subsequent letter to his brother, he writes that when he delivered the speech he seemed in his own mind "to grow twenty feet high, and to swell out in proportion" (*Letters* 3: 230). Whatever Dickens's exaggerations (he grows from twelve to twenty feet in the two months separating the letters), there can be no doubt that he, in his own words, "gave it out" on the issue of international copyright. As Meredith L. McGill argues, Dickens manifests a kind of "superhuman rage" that is in itself monstrous in response to the monstrosity of the injustice he feels perpetrated against him by both American pirates and American legislators (78). McGill notes that in his letters Dickens savours the details of his daring in even raising the issue: "Part of the pleasure of this violent, retributory fantasy is that it is so out of keeping with the elaborate gentility of the occasion and with the American public's embrace of Dickens as a font of edifying sympathy" (77). The sheer force of Dickens's pleasure in savouring the exaggerated fantasy of himself looming above his American audience and forcing them to swallow the truth of their own inaction on the matter of copyright counterbalances the image of the American reader relishing the pirated text like so much stolen meat. But, ultimately, as McGill suggests, the fantasy points to Dickens's powerlessness: "Even inflated to twenty times its ordinary size, authorial outrage will prove no match for the clash of political principles, cultural values, and economic interests that converged around the issue of international copyright" (78). Reaction in the American press to his comments on copyright was swift and harsh. They accused Dickens of the worst kinds of mercenary behavior and avarice. He was stung by this severe reaction, but it served only to confirm for him the fundamental "scurrility" of the American press (*Letters* 3: 259).

Dickens vowed to Forster that he would continue his fight for a binding international agreement. Despite this promise, he was much more hesitant in broaching the topic in public after that night in Hartford. Upon his arrival in New York, Dickens perhaps realized the true extent of the controversy his comments had sparked. Even though no less a figure than Washington Irving made a toast to "International Copyright" on that night, Dickens himself alluded to it only in passing, and in a cautious and deferential manner. In an after-dinner speech delivered at a private engagement in Washington less than a month later, he avoided the subject altogether (Fielding 32–33). After the furor of the Hartford speech, Dickens transferred his energies to lobbying Congress in print and in private. Before he left America, crossing the border into a somewhat more copyright-friendly Canada at Niagara Falls, Dickens addressed an open letter to the editors of four major American newspapers.[3] In it, he reiterates in measured tones the arguments he had marshalled throughout his tour for the establishment of an international copyright agreement between the two countries. A petition signed by several literary luminaries, including Tennyson and Bulwer, accompanied Dickens's letter, as well as a message from Thomas Carlyle. Dickens implores the editors to read the latter as it speaks a "plain and manly Truth" on the subject and since Carlyle's sentiments are perfectly in accord with his own (*Letters* 3: 213).[4]

Given Dickens's active engagement with the issue of international copyright during his trip to America, it is somewhat curious that when he came to publish his *American Notes for General Circulation* in October of 1842, he chose to excise any reference to the topic. Certainly, the absence of the copyright issue gives fuller force to Dickens's anti-slavery arguments and his commendations of certain American institutions, such as factories and asylums. Yet the choice to leave it out entirely perhaps came down to a decision similar to the one that he seems to have made during the trip itself: to leave well enough alone because any further public engagement with the topic would hinder rather than help the copyright cause. Dickens chose to suppress the topic in the text that recounts his travels in America, yet it nevertheless makes itself felt through a series of metaphoric displacements and operates as a structuring absence. Dickens assiduously avoids the issue of pirated texts in his *American Notes*, only to address other types of piracy, counterfeit, and fraud. His extensive commentary on the American tendency toward honorifics, for instance, operates as a kind of analogy to piracy. Americans, he implies, always make themselves out to be something more than they really are, and this counterfeiting of identity both amuses and troubles him. Dickens would later satirize the inflation of character and rank in *Martin Chuzzlewit*

(1843–44). When Martin attends a party in New York, he observes, "There seemed to be no man there without a title" (234; ch. 16). He proceeds to catalogue the military men in the room: "there were no fewer than four majors present, two colonels, one general, and a captain, so that he could not help thinking how strongly officered the American militia must be; and wondering very much whether the officers commanded each other; or if they did not, where on earth the privates came from" (234; ch. 16).

Such satire betrays a deeper suspicion of things American, a suspicion that bubbles beneath the surface of *American Notes* and is linked to Dickens's frustrations regarding copyright. Things in America are never quite as they seem, and even the most seemingly respectable gentleman may be a confidence trickster. In his travelogue, as well as in the novel that draws on the same experiences in America, Dickens observes how the fabrication and inflation of identity undermines the trust and credit that should rightly be the basis of business transactions. Suspicion of those making the transactions is extended to include the means by which they are made. By the time Dickens arrived in 1842, America was renowned for fraudulent financial schemes and forged banknotes. The questionable status of American paper surfaces most compellingly in the work of Dickens's American contemporary, Edgar Allan Poe, whose "The Gold Bug" allegorically engages the most pressing financial question of its time: whether America should maintain a gold standard or give itself up to the uncertainty of paper currency. Poe inaugurates a series of efforts by American authors and artists to interrogate the representational capacity of paper money, using aesthetic representation as means to test the limits of fiduciary representations. As Kevin McLaughlin observes, Poe's tale appeared shortly after the financial panic of 1837 when, due in part to the failure of the Second National Bank, "counterfeiting entered a sort of golden age" ("Just Fooling" 47). At a time when even the most seemingly secure of financial institutions could collapse overnight, the ability of paper money to represent value was very much in question.[5] A visit to Wall Street prompts Dickens to remark,

> Many a rapid fortune has been made in this street, and many a no less rapid ruin. Some of these very merchants whom you see walking about here now, have locked up Money in their strong-boxes, like the man in Arabian Nights, and opening them again, have found nothing but withered leaves.
>
> (*American Notes* 92)

Fraudulent banks and creditors exploited the instability of chartered banks and the extreme volatility of paper currency by issuing notes that were soon discovered by those desperate enough to accept them to be utterly worthless. Therefore, it is perhaps not surprising that the counterfeit bill offers Dickens an analogue for his concerns about piracy. Both, he suggests, are paper perversions. In *American Notes*, as well as in *Martin Chuzzlewit*, Dickens expresses his frustration with the illegal republication of his novels by reference to this other sort of illegitimate reproduction that, like piracy, produces paper without value.

The very title of Dickens's text, *American Notes for General Circulation*, proposes this metaphorical substitution of bills for books and alludes to questions of legal tender. *Notes* refers first and foremost to Dickens's own writing, his recorded observations of America, but it also refers to banknotes, likewise susceptible to illegal reproduction. Dickens knew that this book, like all his others, would be extensively pirated in America, and that he would receive no recompense from the general circulation of the fraudulent copies. The connection between the two sorts of fraudulent note is made all the more clear by the epigraph he initially chose for the book but later withdrew. Dickens had wanted for the epigraph a quotation from an Old Bailey Report on counterfeit money: "In reply to a question from the Bench, the Solicitor for the Bank observed, that this kind of notes circulated the most extensively, in those parts of the world where they were stolen and forged" (*Letters* 3: 310). The proposed epigraph comments reflexively on the inevitable fate of the text to which it was to be appended. Dickens predicted that his *American Notes* would be extensively pirated in America within months of its official release, but could take no solace in the sales these pirated copies would have. Like counterfeit money, Dickens's texts were, to his mind, "stolen and forged" in the wilds of the American market. This may have ensured wide circulation, but the returns on that exchange were not of the right currency. His immense popularity in the United States rested on the open circulation of these pirated texts, but he regarded the admiration heaped on him during his American tour as scant recompense for the widespread piracy of what he regarded as his exclusive property. Cultural capital was a poor substitute for economic capital.

In *Imagined Communities*, Benedict Anderson argues that the idea of the nation itself is tied to the circulation of print commodities that bind an otherwise dispersed set of people together as a coherent group (32–36). Even though such a conception emphasizes the crucial role that novels, newspapers, and other printed matter play in the formation of the nation-state as an imagined community, the circulation of texts beyond the borders of the nation seems to present a different set of problems. On the issue of international copyright, Dickens frequently took recourse to nationalist arguments. He claimed that without an international copyright law to secure for English writers the benefit of overseas sales, British literature would suffer enormously. This shift in argument from the rights of the individual author to the need to protect a national literature may be, as Mary Poovey suggests, little more than a clever rhetorical move by Dickens to obscure his own financial interests in the matter, but it nevertheless forges a connection between the nation, its authors, and its national literature (113). The health of all three, Dickens maintained throughout the copyright debate, depends upon the protection of the rules governing the domestic and international circulation of books. Piracy so incensed Dickens because he perceived it as a violation of his rights, both as an author and an Englishman. Dickens sees the infringement of his authorial rights as an assault on the integrity of the nation itself, an effort to weaken the texture of its imagined community by compromising the industry and effort of its literary producers. He maintained that his fiction should have a world-wide readership, but he demanded that the novels return transformed into the royalties that would represent his sovereign control over his own literary production on a global scale and ensure his ongoing contribution to English literature. An international copyright agreement would ensure the transformation of one type of paper currency into another: books into bills, novels into notes.

Pirated texts, however, prevented these returns. Consequently, Dickens resented the American reader deriving pleasure that he felt was literally *at his expense*. This Dickensian resentment raises the spectre of a troubling kind of nationalist sentiment, one grounded in the disgust and revulsion generated by the difference of the other and triggered by the spectacle of his or her enjoyment. Žižek explains that nationalism is not reducible to any set of values or traditions that mark the limit of its inclusions, but rather that it is organized around that elusive entity called our way of life (201). Any attempt to define conclusively this way of life will fail because any enumeration of the rituals, events, and activities that constitute it never quite fully grasps what it really is. Žižek argues,

> The element which holds together a given community cannot be reduced to the point of symbolic identification: the bond linking together its members always implies a shared relationship toward a Thing, toward Enjoyment incarnated. This relationship toward the Thing, structured by means of fantasies, is what is at stake when we speak of the menace to our 'way of life' presented by the Other. (201)

The piracy of literary texts in America threatens Dickens's England not merely financially, but in challenging the underlying logic of what Norman Feltes calls "the commodity-text" (*Modes* 8): the idea that you pay for your reading pleasure. For Dickens, the financial transaction legitimizes the pleasure derived from the commodity as well as subsidizing and underwriting the activity that produces it. The enjoyment derived from the pirated text short-circuits this exchange of paper for pleasure. The notes, as it were, do not arrive at their proper destination. Having been diverted en route, they become part of a pirate's booty rather than being returned to the author as royalties.

Yet, whatever the disappointments of not securing his proper percentage, Dickens fixates on the illicit pleasure of the reader rather than the illegal activity of the pirate. Dickens's representation of the American reader taking pleasure in counterfeit texts troubles him so profoundly because of the sheer excess of readerly enjoyment. Denied the pleasure of royalties, Dickens sees his artistic labors transformed into the monstrous and excessive amusement of the American reader. This surplus enjoyment, described in terms that exceed any legitimate pleasure the text may normally produce, profoundly unsettles him. Consequently, what drives his arguments for an international copyright agreement is his revulsion with an excessive, and even perverse, American form of enjoyment that threatens to undermine not only legitimate forms of British commerce, but of amusement as well. Žižek argues that nationalism does not simply grow out of the differences between one national community and others, but from a resentment of the ways in which the others enjoyment is materialized in social activity:

> We always impute to the 'other' an excessive enjoyment: he wants to steal our enjoyment (by ruining our way of life) and/or has access to some secret, perverse enjoyment. In short, what really bothers us about the 'other' is the peculiar way he organizes his enjoyment, precisely the surplus, the 'excess' that pertains to this way: the smell of 'their' food, 'their' noisy songs and dances, 'their' strange manners, 'their' attitude to work. (203)

Dickens's resentment toward the American reader can be read in terms of what Žižek terms the theft of enjoyment (203). He is denied the pleasure of his royalties precisely because of the way the American reader organizes his or her enjoyment around the pirated text. To extend the Žižekian series, Dickens is bothered by "their" enjoyment of counterfeit texts that seem to be all the more enjoyed *because* they are pirated. Indeed, Dickens tells Forster in a letter from America that one of the major impediments to an international copyright agreement is "the national love [in America] of 'doing' a man in any bargain or matter of business" (*Letters* 3: 231). This passion for swindles, scams, and frauds diminishes the pleasures derived from books in and of themselves. Such pleasure is replaced, Dickens notes with disgust, by the thrill of the con: "I seriously believe that it is an essential part of the pleasure derived from the perusal of a popular English book, that the author gets nothing for it" (*Letters* 3: 231–32). Faced with the excessive enjoyment of the American other, Dickens must thoroughly condemn this form of gratification and characterize it as both inauthentic and unwholesome, a matter of bestial indulgence analogous to a raven scavenging stolen meat.

Dickens presents the grotesque enjoyment yielded by pirated texts as the obscene underside of the authentic delight afforded the reader of a copyrighted version. In this way, he accuses his American friends, whose refusal to pass an international copyright act makes them complicit with such illicit pleasures, of stealing enjoyment from the legitimate English audience and putting English literature itself in jeopardy. Dickens's frequent mobilization of a language of literary nationalism and authorial propriety barely masks his disgust with the American other and signals his desire to control both textual circulation and the forms of readerly gratification. But this resentment of American enjoyment perhaps betrays anxieties of a more domestic origin. Although the American reader seems parasitic on the legitimate reading pleasures of the English book-buying public, the degree of revulsion Dickens feels in relation to this foreign enjoyment seems somewhat disproportionate to the extent of the transgression. His sense of violation springs from what he perceives as an injustice, the violation of his rights as an author, but also suggests a more troubled relation to enjoyment itself, projected onto the American reader. Indeed, by identifying piracy as that which contaminates the purity of reading pleasure, Dickens reserves for legitimate purchase the purity and propriety of authentic enjoyment. This gesture perhaps masks a generalized anxiety about the circulation of texts as commodities and the legitimacy of those pleasures conveyed by them. Žižek's comments are again instructive in describing how nationalist sentiment, as articulated through the resentment of the other's enjoyment, displaces a nation's awkward relation to its own enjoyment:

> What we conceal by imputing to the Other the theft of enjoyment is the traumatic fact that *we never really possessed what was allegedly stolen from us.* . . . Every nationality has built its own mythology narrating how other nations deprive it of the vital part of enjoyment the possession of which would allow it to live fully. . . . What we gain by transposing the perception of inherent social antagonisms into the fascination with the Other. . . . is the fantasy-organization of desire. The Lacanian thesis that enjoyment is ultimately the enjoyment of the Other, i.e., enjoyment supposed, imputed to the Other, and that, conversely, the hatred of the Other's enjoyment is the hatred of one's own enjoyment, is perfectly exemplified by this logic of the 'theft of enjoyment.'
>
> (203–04, 206)

Dickens displaces worries about the legitimacy of the enjoyment that his writing might generate at home through his disgust with the American reader of pirated texts. Indeed, in the early 1840s, even though Dickens was firmly established as a writer and respected as one who had unique insight into the national character, the category of author itself did not yet bear the full mark of respectability. Dickens aimed to break free of the serialized marketplace and produce novels that did not circulate in periodicals alongside works that generated only the most fleeting and ephemeral pleasures. The novel represented for him a certain substantiality metaphorical for the durability and legitimacy of the enjoyment that it could generate.[6]

In counterposing the illicit enjoyment of the pirated text in America to the legitimate reading pleasure of his English reading public, Dickens relies on an idealized vision of the English publishing marketplace. Whether the enjoyment of the English reader in the early 1840s was as healthy and uncontaminated as Dickens purports is questionable. Indeed, Dickens himself makes every effort in this period to distinguish his own creations from those that offer less refined pleasures. Although the Copyright Act of 1838 governed the circulation of texts within Britain, and went far to establish the category of author as a legitimate and respectable profession, incessant market demands nevertheless compromised the authority of the position since writers were often forced into petty commodity production. Dickens's disgust, therefore, with the American reader of pirated texts is perhaps a symptom of the ongoing anxiety about the respectability of fiction-writing. Royalties are the mechanism by which authority over one's own creative production is confirmed, but the same market that establishes the author *as* an author is that which threatens to degrade and sully the category by making it merely one sort of commodity production among others. This vilification of the American reader of pirated texts serves to gentrify domestic reading pleasure, displacing worries about the legitimacy of writing and the respectability of authorship onto an external obstacle or block. Following Žižek, then, we may ask if the American reader steals from Dickens is that which he never had, the guarantee that his own reading public derives a pure and unsullied enjoyment from his work. His contempt for the American other's enjoyment is a sign that enjoyment itself, even when sanctioned by the author and governed within a domestic market, triggers a kind of anxiety since it troubles distinctions between legitimate and illicit pleasures.

Excessive, unmerited, or unauthorized enjoyment poses a threat to the integrity of a national literature, whether it occurs at home or abroad. The author of an unsigned article from *Blackwood's Magazine* in 1842, simply titled "The Copyright Question," echoes Dickens's comments in America that England needs a strong copyright law, not merely to protect the pecuniary interests of the author, but to protect the integrity of the national character as well.[7] The article addresses questions of taste and value that underlie the copyright debate. It argues that copyright law needs both spatial and temporal extension to ensure that serious works of literature continue to be produced (117–19). A consistent refrain in the domestic copyright debates of the era is the condemnation of the ephemeral pleasures of magazines and periodicals, which, it is assumed, can form no basis for a lasting national literature. Yet magazine writing is eminently attractive to authors who need to make money immediately and cannot wait, or do not wish to wait, for the long-term payoff of serious works that, in any case, would cease to yield returns after twenty-eight years. Even when legislation extended the term of copyright to forty-two years, authors worried that their work would not provide their children with the sort of substantial legacy they felt their literary labors merited.

According to the author of the *Blackwood's* article, the growth of the market itself threatens national literature since it generates demand for, and ensures a healthy rate of profit from, writing that does not long survive its publication: "it is the extension of the power of reading to the middle and working classes, that has, in great part, produced the present ephemeral character of our literature, and the incessant demand for works of excitement" (116). This excessive pleasure, derived as it is from ephemeral and insubstantial works, weakens the character of both the nation and its literature. Just as Dickens in his American speeches returns time and again to the demand for an international copyright agreement—ostensibly not so that he can benefit from the rewards for his own work, but for the good of both American and English literature—so too does the *Blackwood's* article pivot the copyright question away from private ownership to the issue of the national good: "Thus we have argued this great question of copyright upon its true ground—the national character, the national interests, the elevation and improvement of all classes" (121). In each case, authentic reading pleasure is reserved for those, either at home or abroad, who purchase authorized editions of books and those legitimate periodicals that do not traffic in the ephemeral pleasures of sensational material.

The "true ground" of the copyright question, then, is not the author's interest at all, but rather the national interest, tucked in between the need to maintain "the national character" and the presumably moral "improvement of all classes" (121). Such an argument derives from domestic debates about copyright and signals a distinct anxiety about the degradation of taste; international disputes over copyright seem at once a displacement and an extension of such concerns. The importance of literature to the processes of colonization is well documented in the work of Gauri Viswanathan, among others. In terms of Dickens's dispute with his American friends, it is not a matter of imperial expansion or colonial management, but the negotiation between sovereign states regarding the status of what may be anachronistically referred to as "intellectual property."[8] Nevertheless, the idea that British literature served a pedagogical and moral function structured the copyright debates between Great Britain and the United States. In paternalistic tones, British advocates for an international copyright agreement insisted that the Americans sign for their own moral and social good. Dickens argues that without an international copyright agreement, American writing will never flourish. Authors in the United States need to be protected from the widespread dissemination of pirated copies of British novels, such as those by Dickens himself, since the development of a truly American national literature depends upon American writers receiving due recompense for their authorial labors. Piracy floods the market with cheap (yet, Dickens implies, superior) British works. This is a process that has nipped the development of an American national literature in the bud. Again, in this argument, Dickens withstands accusations that he acts in his own interests (or even that he is motivated purely by patriotic or nationalist feeling) by framing the dilemma in terms of the greater national good of the United States. Although such a rhetorical move compels his American listeners to think of their own nation's growth and development, it does not fully obscure a measure of condescension, even disgust, in its suggestion that the Americans do not yet know how to regulate their literary pleasure. Dickens characterizes the circulation of pirated copies as a kind of expenditure that dissipates whatever youthful energies the nation may have. The result of such a frenetic and unregulated commercial energy is a kind of dual corruption. The objects circulated are in themselves corrupt, in the literary sense of being unauthorized and potentially riddled with all sorts of typographical and editorial errors. Furthermore, the manner of textual diffusion contaminates or infects the reader who succumbs to a sort of moral corruption of his or her own through reading the pirated, and potentially corrupt, text.

In the first of three speeches delivered before the House of Commons in 1838, Sergeant Thomas Noon Talfourd argues that only an international copyright agreement will ensure the circulation of uncorrupted texts throughout the American wilds:

> The great minds of our time have now an audience to impress far vaster than it entered into the minds of their predecessors to hope for; an audience increasing as population thickens in the cities of America, and spreads itself out through its diminishing wilds, who speak our language, and look on our old poets as their own immortal ancestry. And if this our Literature shall be theirs; if its diffusion shall follow the efforts of the stout heart and sturdy arm in their triumph over the obstacles of nature; if the woods stretching beyond their confines shall be haunted with visions of beauty which our poets have created; let those who thus are softening the ruggedness of young society have some present interest about which affection may gather, and at least let them be protected from those who would exhibit them mangled or corrupted to their transatlantic disciples.   (27–28)

Talfourd, to whom Dickens dedicated *The Pickwick Papers*, argues that literature, very much defined here as the vehicle for the efficient delivery of Arnoldian sweetness and light, needs to appear in its authorized form if investment in it is to yield its proper moral returns.

Copyright ensures that the text is enjoyed in its uncorrupted form and that the pleasure derived from it is similarly legitimate. The author who gains royalties from the sale of the work would, under an International Copyright Act, be redefined as an issuing authority whose sanction ensures that the benefit or pleasure derived from the work, whether overseas or at home, is a legitimate, legal transaction. As such, the author also guarantees the purity of both the text and the enjoyment derived from it. This transformed relation makes one type of paper currency, books, seem very similar to another, banknotes, in that the issuing authority guarantees the bearer of the note its value. Value in this case represents not merely the aesthetic integrity of the book and the commercial integrity of the transactions that govern its reproduction and distribution, but also the moral worth of the enjoyment that it brings. Given this, the international expansion of copyright stands in for a greater colonizing project, not merely that of imperial Britain, but of the logic of capital in general. Although it seems that culture tames the wilds of America, the book being the vehicle for the higher purposes of personal, national, and international cultivation, what really matters is that the form of the process that governs the reproduction and transaction of the authorized commodity becomes dominant.[9] Whatever the content of the book, the market demands that it be reproduced and disseminated in accordance with a commodity logic, even as it reserves for its author a place that suggests a certain measure of control and influence over its circulation. Copyright plays the key role, not simply in establishing the author as the issuing authority of the text, but in regulating its replication and exchange. This regulation, in turn, forms the criteria for what counts as legitimate enjoyment.

Given the troubling insubstantiality of paper, as well as its susceptibility to corruption, Dickens was perhaps justified in his suspicions of it, even if it was both the medium of his profession and the surest sign of his professional success. An incident during Dickens's return visit to America in 1867 demonstrates that he remained suspicious of paper currency in its American form for a long time after the controversial events of his 1842 visit. During this second visit, he repeatedly apologized for any offense he may have caused during his previous tour and steered well clear of the issue of copyright. In the intervening years, American publishers and authors had grown more confident in their calls for an international copyright agreement, drawing on the very same arguments Dickens had voiced in 1842.[10] Piracy was still pervasive, but not to the extent it had been twenty-five years earlier. And, even if it was not until the Chase Act of 1891 that the United States truly committed to a binding international copyright agreement, between Dickens's first and second visits the American government made a legitimate effort to discourage the circulation of counterfeit bills. Furthermore, in the intervening years, writing had been established as a respectable professional activity. Dickens himself was in great measure responsible for this gentrification of authorship. Although still caught in the circuits of commodity capitalism, literature had gained a kind of semi-autonomy, and even those who wrote novels, a form long tarnished by the uncertain moral status of the pleasures it offers, had attained a certain measure of social respectability. Within Great Britain and, to a much greater extent than in 1842, throughout the world, Dickens controlled the publication, republication, and circulation of his writings. This did not afford him complete control over the enjoyment of his texts, yet it did help consolidate his identity as England's greatest living author. The image of the excessive enjoyment of the American reader of pirated texts perhaps would no longer trigger such disgust, as it no longer suggested uncertain authority at home. Nevertheless, before he boarded ship to return to England, Dickens "insisted on changing bills for gold at a 40 percent discount" (Kappel and Patten 32). Although his worry about the fluctuating value of the American dollar in the aftermath of the Civil War may have motivated Dickens to bear the substantial loss, it is also perhaps a sign that, whatever changes there had been in both his personal and professional circumstances, and in domestic and international politics, he continued to suspect the authenticity of American notes some twenty-five years after he first published his own *American Notes*.

NOTES

1. Chris R. Vanden Bossche provides a thorough analysis of the copyright debates as they played out on a domestic level, focussing especially on how a perceived opposition between imaginative literature and useful knowledge structured the debates. Alexander Welsh and Gerhard Joseph consider the international ramifications of copyright reform in Great Britain and discuss Dickens's participation within the debates, both domestic and international, but do not explore the operations of pleasure in nationalist sentiment.

2. Juliet John draws the title of her recent article on *American Notes* from a comment Dickens makes in a letter from America: "The Nation is a body without a head" (qtd. in John 182). John argues that Dickens's enthusiasm for America and its populist energies quickly waned when he saw the form those energies can take: "everything that Dickens loathed about America—the press, the lack of an international copyright agreement, his lack of privacy, and (as he perceived them) bad manners—forced him to confront the possible reality of a mass culture he had thought he desired" (174). Not only did America sour Dickens on the idea of democratic populism, but it also, to extend John's argument, forced him to confront the ways in which the sullied pleasures of the pirated text compromised his own enjoyment as an author.

3. As Simon Nowell-Smith notes (25–26), the 1842 Copyright Act proved useless in Canada due to a loophole in the Customs Act, which allowed cheap American reprints into the Canada market. Despite this, Dickens reserves his vituperation for American piracy, and he presents crossing the border into Canada as a return to friendly soil governed by the sovereign laws of imperial Great Britain. For more on Canada, copyright, and the 1847 Foreign Reprints Act that granted Canada special rights to import American reprints rather than the vastly more expensive British colonial editions, see Barnes (138–52).

4. The petition signed by the eminent British authors is included as an appendix in *Letters* 3: 621–23. Also included is Carlyle's letter to Dickens, 3: 623–24.

5. For more on the importance of paper currency as a subject of nineteenth-century American literature and art, see Shell. McLaughlin's *Paperwork* contains an expanded reading of Poe, and also examines more broadly the representation and significance of paper in the nineteenth-century fiction (1–18).

6. For more on Dickens's efforts to break free from serialized publication in the hope of consolidating his position as a novelist rather than mere "writer of parts," see Kathryn Chittick (122–29). Yet, as Brantlinger points out, "the fiction question—that is, the questionable nature of novels and novel-reading—arises everywhere in nineteenth-century discourses about education and the uses and abuses of literacy" (19). Consequently, even as Dickens sought to transform himself from a mere writer of serials into a bona fide novelist, he had to struggle against representations of novel-reading as a degraded activity, thriving only because the growth of literacy had created a market for goods which traffic in unrefined pleasures.

7. In an anonymously published review of *American Notes*, James Spedding accused Dickens of travelling to America "as a kind of missionary in the cause of international copyright" (500). Dickens wrote the *Times* to defend himself against this attack, insisting that any such assertion was "destitute of any particle, aspect, or colouring of truth" (*Letters* 3: 423). For a detailed reading of this episode see Welsh (36–39).

8. Visawanathan demonstrates that the institutionalization of English literature as an object of study occurred first in India rather than in Great Britain, where the "classical curriculum still reigned supreme" (3). She argues that an English literary education served as a vehicle for imperial hegemony, providing the material through which the alleged superiority of the imperial nation is articulated and reinforced.

9. Caren Irr argues that the circulation of literary texts precedes the general expansion of capitalism during those historical moments when the system seeks out new markets or transforms already existing ones. As such, disputes over copyright function proleptically, and anticipate the conflicts that will arise when other commodities follow in their wake. Although Irr demonstrates how literary piracy is best understood in relation to the high-seas piracy that marked the growth and expansion of eighteenth-century capitalism, and connects this to more recent forms of copyright violation, she skips over Dickens in favor of other nineteenth-century examples. Nevertheless, Irr's argument that the literary commodity does not lag behind market expansion but advances ahead of it could profitably be expanded to include Dickens, since pirated versions of Dickens's texts circulated far more widely in America than the legitimate ones and did so well in advance of them.

10. For more on the political machinations that went into the formulation of an international copyright agreement in the closing decades of the nineteenth century, see Feltes's "International Copyright."

WORKS CITED

Anderson, Benedict. *Imagined Communities: Reflections on the Origin and Spread of Nationalism*. Rev. ed. London: Verso, 1991.

Arnold, Matthew. *Culture and Anarchy*. 1869. Ed. J. Dover Wilson. Cambridge: Cambridge UP, 1971.

Barnes, James J. *Authors, Publishers and Politicians: The Quest for an Anglo-American Copyright Agreement 1815–54*. London: Routledge and Kegan Paul, 1974.

Brantlinger, Patrick. *The Reading Lesson: The Threat of Mass Literacy in Nineteenth Century British Fiction*. Bloomington: Indiana UP, 1998.

Chittick, Kathryn. *Dickens and the 1830s*. Cambridge: Cambridge UP, 1990.

"The Copyright Question." *Blackwood's Magazine* 51 (1842): 107–21.

Dickens, Charles. *American Notes for General Circulation*. 1842. Ed. Patricia Ingham. London: Penguin, 2000.

———. *The Letters of Charles Dickens*. Vol. 3. Ed. Graham Storey and Madeleine House. Oxford: Clarendon Press, 1965.

———. *Martin Chuzzlewit*. 1843–44. Ed. Margaret Cardwell. Oxford: Oxford UP, 1988.

Feltes, N. N. "International Copyright: Structuring 'The Condition of Modernity' in British Publishing." *The Construction of Authorship: Textual Appropriation in Law and Literature*. Ed. Martha Woodmansee and Peter Jaszi. Durham: Duke UP, 1994. 271–80.

———. *Modes of Production of Victorian Novels*. Chicago: U of Chicago P, 1986.

Fielding, K. J., ed. *The Speeches of Charles Dickens*. Oxford: Clarendon, 1960.

Irr, Caren. "Literature as Proleptic Globalization, or a Prehistory of the New Intellectual Property." *South Atlantic Quarterly* 100.3 (Summer 2001): 773–802.

John, Juliet. " 'A body without a head': The Idea of Mass Culture in Dickens's *American Notes* (1842)." *Journal of Victorian Culture* 12.2 (Autumn 2007): 173–202.

Joseph, Gerhard. "Charles Dickens, International Copyright, and the Discretionary Silence of *Martin Chuzzlewit*." *The Construction of Authorship: Textual Appropriation in Law and Literature*. Ed. Martha Woodmansee and Peter Jaszi. Durham, NC: Duke UP, 1994. 259–70.

Kappel, Andrew J., and Robert L. Patten. "Dickens' Second American Reading Tour and His 'Utterly Worthless and Profitless' American Rights." *Dickens Studies Annual* 7 (1978): 1–33.

McGill, Meredith L. *American Literature and the Culture of Reprinting, 1834–1853.* Philadelphia: U of Pennsylvania P, 2002.

McLaughlin, Kevin. "Just Fooling: Paper, Money, Poe." *Differences* 11.1 (1999): 38–67.

———. *Paperwork: Fiction and Mass Mediacy in the Paper Age.* Philadelphia: U of Pennsylvania P, 2005.

Nowell-Smith, Simon. *International Copyright Law and The Publisher in the Reign of Queen Victoria.* Oxford: Clarendon, 1968.

Poovey, Mary. *Uneven Developments: The Ideological Work of Gender in Mid-Victorian England.* Chicago: U of Chicago P, 1988.

Shell, Marc. *Money, Language, and Thought: Literary and Philosophical Economies from the Medieval to the Modern Era.* Berkeley: U of California P, 1982.

[Spedding, James.] "Dickens's *American Notes.*" *Edinburgh Review* 76 (1843): 500–01.

Talfourd, Thomas Noon. *Three Speeches Delivered in the House of Commons in Favour of a Measure for an Extension of Copyright.* London: Edward Moxon, 1840.

Vanden Bossche, Chris R. "The Value of Literature: Representations of Print Culture in the Copyright Debate of 1837–1842." *Victorian Studies* 38.1 (Autumn 1994): 41–68.

Viswanathan, Gauri. *Masks of Conquest: Literary Study and British Rule in India.* New York: Columbia UP, 1989.

Welsh, Alexander. *From Copyright to Copperfield: The Identity of Dickens.* Cambridge: Harvard UP, 1987.

Žižek, Slavoj. *Tarrying with the Negative: Kant, Hegel, and the Critique of Ideology.* Durham, NC: Duke UP, 1993.

"[M]any jewels set in dirt":
Christology, *Pictures from Italy*,
and Pre-Raphaelite Art

Jude V. Nixon

This essay examines Dickens's growing interest in art beginning around 1844, an interest, it argues, that was informed largely by his Italian sojourn (July 1844 to June 1845). The trip provided Dickens the experience, insight, context, and critical eye by which to appraise art. Pictures from Italy, *along with letters written during Dickens's Italian journey, reveals expansive, insightful, and sustained reflections on art. It also offers an important window into Dickens's anti-Roman Catholic bigotry, fetishized in his attitude to Italy. Using John Everett Millais's* Christ in the House of His Parents *(1850), Dickens's review of it in* Household Words *(15 June 1850), and working backwards historically to* Pictures from Italy *(1846), this paper argues that Dickens's early views of the Pre-Raphaelites manifest a hostility to their Christology, exacerbated if not formed altogether in Italy. In Millais, it is not the picture of labor, the entire family involved in work, which troubled Dickens. What bothered him was the disorder and chaos of the place, the ordinariness or plainness of the representation, and the physical deformity of the figures. That the Holy Family would be depicted as working class was also disquieting. The essay contextualizes the Millais painting with John Rogers Herbert's* The Youth of Our Lord *(1847) and Holman Hunt's* The Shadow of Death *(1870–73) to show that all three paintings represent not only a radical shift in the tradition in art (realism and naturalism) but a shift also in the Christology.*

Dickens Studies Annual, Volume 41, Copyright © 2010 by AMS Press, Inc. All rights reserved.

The immense literary production in poetry, prose, and the novel in nineteenth-century England reveals in conspicuous contrast the relative neglect of the other arts. Music passed almost unnoticed, as did sculpture, with only Gilbert and Sullivan and the sculptor Sir William "Hamo" Thornycroft receiving notable acclaim.[1] Architecture was noticed in the revival of the Gothic, prompted in large measure by the writings of John Ruskin. Although the landscape art of John Constable, Frederick Walker, and Frederic Leighton was noteworthy, Turner attracted more attention. But it was the Pre-Raphaelites who took the art world of the nineteenth century by storm.[2] J. B. Bullen calls the bold challenge by Hunt, Millais, and Rossetti the "first avant-garde movement in British painting" (1), which revolved around representations of the human body: a sexuality bordering on pornography; a causal connection between angularity, physiognomy, facial expression, and morality; and questions about themes, subjects/objects, and theories of beauty. Pre-Raphaelitism became synonymous with scandal. Revolutionary, subversive, and secretive, it had all the signs of an underground movement. In its initial phase, Pre-Raphaelitism seemed "a particular kind of modern movement," which conveys "allegiance to the European 'primitives' of the period before Raphael," later finding expression in Fauvism and Cubism in France, and Die Brücke in Germany. "In each case the 'primitive' reference proposes a swerve away from the orderly flow of historical progress and cultural development in the modernised, industrialised Western world" (Prettejohn 18–19). The Pre-Raphaelites, according to Julie F. Codell, rejected "neoclassical standards of ideality, generality, and hierarchic order . . . in favor of the truth of specifics." Thus, the P.R.B., like Ruskin, "accepted the depiction of the grotesque in art" ("Expression" 281). Their very adoption of the clerical or occultish P.R.B. signature made them appear unconventional and iconoclastic.[3]

Dickens led the censure of the Pre-Raphaelites, with Millais the focus. His hostility must be viewed in the context of a presumed attack on the accepted Christology in their art, and his overall estimation of how Christ and Christianity were being re-presented. At issue especially was the way the Holy Family was presented as working-class and then not ennobled but depicted as deformed, dirty, and diseased. The Pre-Raphaelites wanted, after all, a fresh but imitative study of nature and the natural world. Dickens was also reacting to an equally sore subject to him—Anglo-Catholicism, Popery, what he was in the habit of calling Puseyism, the emergence of a Catholic, High-Church symbolist movement. His reaction was also xenophobic, perhaps even racist, for the Pre-Raphaelites "were burdened with all the associations of popery and foreignness that so repulsed the English. . . . That their names were foreign—Rossetti (Italian) and Millais (French)—from countries that were Roman Catholic, did not help their cause nor did the fact that they had formed a secret society" (Roberts 151). As far as Dickens was concerned,

Guido Fawkes was ready to implode the foundations of English Protestant art. The danger to Dickens was that Pre-Raphaelite art, given its Catholicity, was a form of nationalistic art attempting to return the nation to its Roman Catholic origin. My discussion concerns Dickens's growing interest in art beginning around 1844, an interest informed largely by his Italian sojourn. More important than Dickens's visits to the Royal Academy or friendship with Daniel Maclise and Sir David Wilkie was his trip to Italy (July 1844 to June 1845), which provided him the experience, insight, context, and critical eye by which to judge art. Italy exerted the same influence on Ford Madox Brown, the unofficial founder of the Pre-Raphaelites, whose art changed when he returned to England after seeing first-hand Italian art in 1845. What he experienced there, Brown admitted, "made a deep and, as it proved, lasting impression on me" (qtd. in Whiteley 10).

Pictures from Italy, along with letters written during Dickens's Italian journey, reveals expansive, insightful, and sustained reflections on art. Prior to that tour, Dickens did not possess the critical apparatus whereby to appraise great art, and admitted as much in *Pictures*, letters, and other writings.[4] His daughter, Kate Dickens Perugini, observed the surprising absence of art as plot/protagonist in his novels: "it seems almost strange that he should have neglected to place one of his prominent characters in the ready-made atmosphere of romance that is generally supposed to be the exclusive possession of an artist . . . nor does he appear ever to have been tempted to write of a comic painter, a needy painter, or a wicked, mysterious painter; indeed, on the subject of artists in general, he has been singularly silent" (I: 125).[5] Using John Everett Millais's *Christ in the House of His Parents* (1850), Dickens's review of it in *Household Words* (15 June 1850), and working backwards historically to *Pictures from Italy* (1846), I argue that Dickens's early views of the Pre-Raphaelites manifest a hostility to their Christology, a distaste exacerbated if not formed altogether in Italy. By contextualizing the Millais painting with John Rogers Herbert's *The Youth of Our Lord* (1847) and Holman Hunt's *The Shadow of Death* (1870–73), I seek to show that all three paintings represent not only a radical shift in the tradition in art (realism and naturalism) but a shift also in the Christology, both of which troubled Dickens.

Dickens's relationship with the Pre-Raphaelites remains vexed. Though highly respected, he was not accorded the same hagiographical veneration Carlyle and Ruskin received. Dickens and Millais viewed each other from a distance. They kept aware of each other's activities, and occasionally commented on each other's work, life, and public reputation. "The position of ourselves in relation to Dickens was a delicate one," Hunt observed. Following Dickens's assault on Millais, the Pre-Raphaelites found themselves strangely attracted to his novels. Dickens's friendship with Wilkie Collins, whose brother Charles was a member of the Pre-Raphaelites, helped to diffuse some lingering animosity. And a dinner at the Collinses' removed "all estrangement" and brought Dickens to appreciate "the power of Millais' genius and character." But subsequent comments made by Dickens once again "alienated the confidence of our circle from him" (Hunt 2: 185). Dickens, however, used his reputed business acumen to assist Hunt in placing *The Finding of the Savior in the Temple* (1854–60), which did much to heal the breach. It is generally thought that Millais's *Ophelia* (1851–52) was the source for Rosa Bud's recollection of her drowned mother in *The Mystery of Edwin Drood*: "Every fold and colour in the pretty summer dress, and even the long wet hair, with scattered petals of ruined flowers still clinging to it, as the dead young figure, in its sad, sad beauty lay upon the bed, were fixed indelibly in Rosa's recollection" (78).[6] But Millais's *Christ in the House of His Parents* troubled Dickens, whose Christ, created from his "own fancy," was very different; "the shock of seeing it so misrepresented . . . came upon him as a surprise and a pain, and without waiting to inquire of himself the real reason of his dislike to the work he wrote a very harsh and hasty criticism upon it" (Perugini I: 129). But Dickens knew exactly why he did not like the painting. His critique might have been harsh, but it was not hasty. Millais's painting was insufferable to Dickens, who had come to view Christianity and religious subjects through his own understanding of the Holy Family. His *Life of Our Lord* (1846–49), written one year before the Millais painting, declares this attitude of expressed "veneration for the life and lessons of our Saviour" (*Life* 4).

Many critics, like Perugini, have incorrectly deemed Dickens's reaction to Millais's painting an exaggeration. But Millais was merely the trigger for a representation of Christianity that disturbed Dickens, whose concept of Jesus was under systematic attack by proponents of Higher Criticism. Nowhere is this reaction more unambiguously expressed as in Dickens's 25 October 1864 letter to W. W. F. De Cerjat:

> As to the Church, my friend, I am sick of it. The spectacle presented by the indecent squabbles of priests of most denominations, and the exemplary unfairness and rancour with which they conduct their differences, utterly repel me. . . . How our sublime and so-different Christian religion is to be administered in the future, I cannot pretend to say, but that the Church's hand is at its own throat, I am fully convinced. Here, mere Popery—there, mere Methodism—as many forms of consignment to eternal damnation, as there are articles, and all in one forever quarreling body—*the Master of the New Testament put out of sight, and the rage and fury almost always turning on the letter of obscure parts of the old Testament which itself has been the subject of accommodation, adaptation, varying interpretation without end*—these things can not last. The Church that is to have its part in the coming Time must be a more Christian one, with less arbitrary pretensions and *a stronger hold upon the mantle of Our Saviour as He walked and talked upon this earth.*
>
> (*Letters* 10: 444; my emphasis)

Like his views on art, Dickens's Christology requires a separate and more detailed study.[7] I try merely to outline where such a study might go, beginning with *Life of Our Lord*, a text penned by Dickens for the religious instruction of his children and not initially intended for publication.[8] Other sources are his many comments on Christ in the correspondence, along with the way Christ, Christianity, and Christ-types are represented through characters in his novels, whether Little Nell, Tiny Tim, or Paul Dombey.[9]

Dickens's *Life* is an important voice in the most contentious religious debate of the nineteenth century, the argument over the Christology. He expresses uncompromising reverence for Jesus, the Holy Family, and the New Testament, "the best book that ever was or will be known in the world" (5). His preference for Luke's account is based on the physician/author's interest in the body and healing. Dickens's Jesus was "not a man" (*Life* 24) but a man of action: "Our Saviour did not sit down in this world and muse, but labored and did good" (*Letters* 6: 26). Dickens's own agenda for social change emerged from "the teaching of Our Saviour. . . . [M]y creed is the creed of Jesus Christ . . . and my deepest admiration and respect attend upon his life and teaching" (*Letters* 7: 629; 5: 45). Any treatment of Jesus, he believed, should elevate and idealize that life: "The most miserable, the most ugly, deformed, wretched creatures that live, will be bright Angels in Heaven if they are good here on earth" (*Life* 28). In a 24 December 1856 letter to Reverend Charles Davies, Dickens acknowledges unmitigated reverence for Christianity and the New Testament:

> There cannot be many men, I believe, who have a more humble veneration for the New Testament or a more profound conviction of its all-sufficiency than I have. If I am ever (as you tell me I am) mistaken on this subject, it is because I discountenance all obtrusive professions of, and trading in, Religion, as one of the main causes of real Christianity's having been retarded in this world; and because my observation of life induces me to hold in unspeakable dread and horror, those unseemly squabbles about the Letter, which drive the Spirit out of hundreds of thousands. (*Letters* 8: 24–445)

The declaration here is meant clearly for proponents of Higher Criticism, such as George Eliot, who translated Strauss's *Das Leben Jesu* (1846), the authors of *Essays and Reviews* (1860), Ernest Renan, author of *La Vie de Jésus* (1860), and John Colenso, who wrote *The Pentateuch and Book of Joshua Critical Examined* (1862). Casting an equally long shadow was Darwin's *On the Origin of Species* (1859), which, in calling for a reexamination of man's place in nature, also required a new interpretation of the biblical record.[10]

To Dickens, Mary's "pretty little boy" (*Life* 12), desecrated by Millais, was neither a boy nor pretty, and the artist's diseased Holy Family needed

Christ's healing touch.[11] The painting lacked the otherworldliness of art, which the Pre-Raphaelites, in their return to a kind of innocence pre-dating Raphael, rejected.[12] To them, the "great and glorious moments in the past must not be revered as remote, merely visionary and beyond our reach, but rather revived and brought down to a realistic, human level so that they can ennoble our humdrum lives" (*The Pre-Raphaelites* 3). Regarding the supernatural as being at home with the natural, and considering the miraculous of a piece with the ordinary, Pre-Raphaelite art moved to dispense with the received tradition in art, especially the tradition in religious art.[13] In Foucault's language, the Pre-Raphaelites wanted to push back "further and further the line of antecedents to reconstituting traditions ... disassociating the reassuring form of the identical" (12). Writing of this departure, Hunt states that "the first principle of Pre-Raphaelitism was to eschew all that was conventional in contemporary art" (2: 125), and to consider their goals part of a "reform movement" and the "general conversion we were attempting" (2: 164, 392). The Pre-Raphaelites were "self-declared agents of idealism and resistance, determined to reform and revivify the tired old standards of British art" (Mancoff 4). But theirs was a strange mix, an idealism wrapped up seamlessly in realism and naturalism.[14] The life of Christ, as Sue Zemka has pointed out, "became an important subgenre of the nineteenth century." Of a piece with it was a changing iconographic representation of Christ, along with a battle over "the perceived generational and gendered nature of religious authority" (101). The result of all of this was a Jesus stripped of all divinity and mystery, retaining only his historical facade. Millais's was one such recent reconfiguration, and a visual one at that.

No work by the Pre-Raphaelites created as much sensation as *Christ in the House of His Parents*, the second Pre-Raphaelite exhibition to go on display at the Royal Academy.[15] Shocking to the public was its ordinariness, naturalism, and realism, which came across as irreverence. Victorians were appalled by the way religious themes and sacred subjects were handled, as well as by the use, Herbert Sussman observes, "of a low, particularized style to treat formerly idealized Biblical material" (26). Barefoot peasants dressed in shabby, everyday garb, the Pre-Raphaelites' Holy Family was too familiar, too common. Evident here, says one reviewer, was "a kind of contempt for all pre-established ideas of beauty. It even seemed as if, in their resolution to copy literally the forms of Nature," the Pre-Raphaelites "took pleasure in seeking out such forms as would be called ugly or mean . . . they appeared to take delight in figures with heads phrenologically clumsy, faces strongly marked and irregular, and very pronounced ankles and knuckles" (Masson 203). Lacking iconic otherworldliness, the Holy Family did not appear all that holy. What distinguished the Pre-Raphaelites was "their audacity in presenting religious, historical, and legendary themes with brash, disrespectful

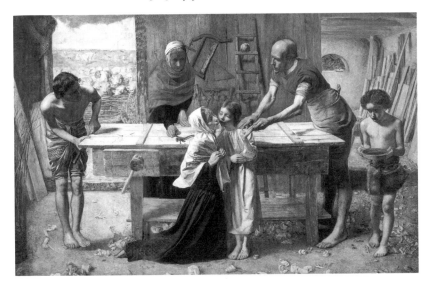

Fig. 1. John Everett Millais, *Christ in the House of His Parents* (1850). Tate, London/Art Resource, NY.

familiarity. Instead of treating the remote past with due awe, the rebels saw it in terms of modern life . . . . . To proper Victorians, such profanity was intolerable'' (*The Pre-Raphaelites* 2).

Christ in the House of His Parents (fig. 1) captures the crude workshop of the Holy Family. Wood shavings litter the floor, and tools of the trade and planks of wood overwhelm the cramped workplace. Clutter and dirt best describe the claustrophobic space, one absent the customary signifiers of cleanliness (as the broom, for example, in Herbert's *The Youth of Our Lord*). A frail and somewhat girlish-looking Jesus, an affront to Victorian ideals of manliness, receives comfort from an ordinary, even matronly, Mary, who, but for her symbolic blue dress and white habit, hardly resembles the Virgin Mother of great iconographic representations.[16] She gently kisses the boy, whose impaled left hand is offered up for attention. The symbolic nail lies harmless on the workbench, and blood from the wounded hand nearest the heart, prefiguring the blood shed on the cross, spills on to the left side of his dress and foot. (All are barefooted.) Typologically, the painting is nicely balanced. A kneeling Mary and the injured Child are the central figures in not one but two crucifixion scenes. Flanked on their sides are St. Anne and St. Joseph. And to their extremes are an apprentice and Saint John. St. Joseph examines the injury with one hand, his other still dutifully employed, and St. Anne reaches across the workbench to retrieve the instrument of harm. All eyes, however, are directed to the injured boy, including the boy John the

Baptist, dressed in sheepskin and carrying a bowl of water, symbols of his rustic lifestyle and later baptismal ministry. He darts a curious if furtive glance in the direction of the wounded Jesus, pretending not to have witnessed the injury, intuiting, perhaps, its symbolic importance.[17]

Mid-Victorian viewers of art, as Kate Flint has observed, wanted their favorite paintings to tell stories and, more importantly, to affirm narratives that help "to make sense of their lives" (197). Millais's *Christ in the House of His Parents* does that; but the story it tells was abhorrent to Victorians like Dickens because it did not lend the desired order, coherence, and beauty to their everyday lives. Dickens and other Victorian observers were troubled by the ordinariness and naturalness of the scene, its seeming baseness, and the ultra plain. *Blackwood's* could not imagine "anything more ugly, graceless and unpleasant . . . . Such a collection of splay feet, puffed joints and mis-shapen limbs was assuredly never before made within so small a compass" (qtd. in Sanders 71–72). To *The Times*, it was "plainly revolting":

> The attempt to associate the holy family with the meanest details of a carpenter's shop, with no conceivable omission of misery, of dirt, of even disease, all finished with the same loathsome minuteness, is disgusting; and with a surprising power of imitation, the picture serves to show how far mere imitation may fall short, by dryness and conceit, of all dignity and truth.
>
> (qtd. in Sanders 71–72)

I shall return later to this Victorian emphasis on dirt, the way it came to represent Victorian anxiety with contagion, and how the Millais painting evoked it. Dirt defines Dickens's Italian experience and describes Italy's base religious art. To Victorians, then, Millais's Holy Family was too human, making any attempt at veneration difficult.[18] The once imagined Early Christian Brotherhood, a name the Pre-Raphaelites had experimented with, might well have been a brotherhood, but it was not Christian enough for Dickens. It was not even Catholic enough for "detractors of our reform" (Hunt 2: 418) such as James Collison, who defected following the Millais exhibition, claiming that "as a sincere Catholic, I can no longer allow myself to be called a P.R.B. in the brotherhood sense of the term." He based this on a love and reverence for "God's faith" and "His holy Saints," which he felt were being dishonored and their merits debased, "if not absolutely to bring their sanctity into ridicule" (*P.R.B. Journal* 71). Collison points particularly to the Christology: "He had once humbled Himself to the form of man, that man might be clothed with, and know his love, His Divinity" (*P.R.B. Journal* 71).[19] While Pre-Raphaelite art had been recognized as the art of the Oxford Movement, *Christ in the House of His Parents* seems more in line with their detractors, whose campaign for a historical Jesus outweighed all claims to the divine. Still, the painting's religious message is symbolically/typologically informed.

In the background, a dove (symbol for the Holy Ghost) is perched on a ladder, and in a sheepfold overly attentive sheep (symbols of the Church) thrust themselves into the picture.

Dickens's "Old Lamps for New Ones" was the first salvo hurled at the painting. Dispatching it to Daniel Maclise on 30 May 1850, he framed his remarks not as a religious but as a social protest, wanting to suggest that the fault in the painting is the social message it conveys about labor, the total absence of all that is sublime and spiritual in labor—the Carlylean notion that labor lends order, coherence, and beauty to workers: "I feel perfectly sure that you will see nothing in it but what is fair public satire that opens very serious social considerations. If such things were allowed to sweep on, without some vigorous protest, three fourths of this Nation would be under the feet of Priests, in ten years" (*Letters* 6: 106–07).[20] What troubled Dickens about Millais's handling of religious subjects was the spectacle of "mere empty forms," as he calls them in *Pictures* (403), which contrasts with "the sublime simplicity of the New Testament and the general humanity to which our Saviour addressed it," including "the teachings of our great Master, and unostentatiously to lead the reader up to those great teachings as the great source of all moral goodness." "All my strongest illustrations," Dickens avows, "are derived from the New Testament: all my social abuses are shown as departures from its spirit; all my good people are humble, charitable, faithful, and forgiving. Over and over again, I claim them in express words as disciples of the Founder of our religion" (*Letters* 9: 556–57). His five Christmas Books were meant to illustrate that faith, which, he felt, cannot "be separated from the exemplification of the Christian virtues and the inculcation of the Christian precepts. In every one of those books there is an express text preached on, and the text is always taken from the lips of Christ" (*Letters* 9: 557).

Dickens's attack on Millais sought to check the spread of Popery and the accompanying "retrogressive" principle in Pre-Raphaelite art, which he had seen in the art of Catholic France and Italy, where the contraption of a cathedral clock, "the Virgin Mary—with a very blunt nose, like a hangman in Punch's Show," is made to represent the Annunciation and a little doll with wings Gabriel (*Letters* 4: 170).[21] Dickens's essay ridicules Pre-Raphaelite art, calling it an Aladdin cry of "Old Lamps for New Ones." It was, he felt, a complete fabrication of things associated with Raphael; there was nothing Pre- or Raphael in Pre-Raphaelite art.[22] Millais's painting was representative to him of a "perverse" age and one "very short of faith." Raphael and Titian, Dickens wrote satirically, were two feeble lamps "fed with a preposterous idea of Beauty—with a ridiculous power of etherealising, and exalting to the very Heaven of Heavens, what was most sublime and lovely in the

expression of the human face divine on earth.'' By way of a ''truly contemptible conceit,'' both Raphael and Titian were able to discover ''in poor humanity the fallen likeness of the angels of God,'' and to raise ''it up again to
their pure spiritual condition.'' In this way, ''Beauty came to be regarded as
one of its indispensable elements,'' and so ''Artists have continued until this
present nineteenth century, when it was reserved for some bold aspirants to
'put it down' '' (''Old Lamps'' 265).

Setting up as it were a ''dread Tribunal,'' the Pre-Raphaelites moved to
rid the world of all features linked to Raphael. Millais's Holy Family rejects
''all Post-Raphael ideas, all religious aspirations, all elevating thoughts; all
tender, awful, sorrowful, ennobling, sacred, graceful, or beautiful associations,'' and succumbs, instead, to ''the lowest depths of what is mean, odious,
repulsive, and revolting.'' Angered by the representation, Dickens refuses to
identify Millais's subjects, and deliberately misreads and misrepresents the
painting, even caricatures it; after all, Millais has mischaracterized the Holy
Family:

> You behold the interior of a carpenter's shop. In the foreground of that carpen-
> ter's shop is a hideous, wry-necked, blubbering, red-headed boy, in a bed-gown;
> who appears to have received a poke in the hand from the stick of another boy
> with whom he had been playing in an adjacent gutter, and to be holding it up
> for the contemplation of a kneeling woman, so horrible in her ugliness, that
> (supposing it were possible to exist for any human creature to exist for a moment with
> that dislocated throat) she would stand out from the rest of the company as a
> Monster, in the vilest cabaret in France, or the lowest gin-shop in England.
> Two almost naked carpenters, master and journeyman, worthy companions of
> this agreeable female, are working at their trade; a boy, with some small flavour
> of humanity in him, is entering with a vessel of water; and nobody is paying
> any attention to a snuffy old woman who seems to have mistaken that shop for
> the tobacconist's next door, and to be hopelessly waiting at the counter to be
> served with half an ounce of her favourite mixture. Whenever it is possible to
> express ugliness of feature, limb, or attitude, you have it expressed. Such men
> as the carpenters might be undressed in any hospital where dirty drunkards, in
> a high state of varicose veins, are received. Their very toes have walked out of
> St. Giles's.   (''Old Lamps'' 265–66)[23]

Expressed here is Dickens's image of the grotesque, degraded human beings
who populate *Pictures*. The word ''grotesque,'' along with its synonyms
''queer'' and ''goblin,'' show up routinely as descriptives for the repulsive
and unhygienic. In Dickens, cleanliness and dirt have become national attributes of Britain and Italy, Protestantism and Roman Catholicism, the Anglo
and the racialized other, respectively. The focus on Italy as Catholic and
other is meant to define Britishness and secure a national identity as something separate and different. Italy is a colonial frontier, represented in Dickens
as Africa and/or the Orient. Genovese women have their hair ''twisted up
into a knot on the top of her head, like a pad to carry loads on'' (*Pictures* 312).

In his Millais critique, Dickens repeatedly calls attention to history and the historical tradition in art. Rather than offer "reverence and homage to the faith in which we live and die," the painting assaults all aesthetic and religious taste. The wood shavings on the floor might be "faithful portraiture," and "admirably painted," but art demands "more than the faithful portraiture of shavings, or the skilful colouring of drapery." The work as a whole represents a "retrogressive principle" ("Old Lamps" 246). Masson captures well Dickens's sentiment: "the true painting of natural objects is but the grammar or language of art, and that, as the greatness of a poem consists, not in the grammatical correctness of the language, but in the power and beauty of the meaning, so the greatness of a painting depends on what there is in it that the painter has added out of his own mind" (219). Attracted as he was to the emerging microscopic science, Dickens welcomed accurate details in art; "the greatest and most enduring delight in those achievements of the pencil," he writes, "are truly great and grand, and worthy of their theme" (*Letters* 4: 283–84). But to him the truthful is not coeval to the beautiful, for there is more art and aesthetic taste than perfect craftsmanship. To Dickens, one has to be able to read nature well to discover its hidden truths. "Nature," he points out in an essay in *Household Words*, "never writes a bad hand. Her writing, as it may be read in the human countenance, is invariably legible, if we come at all trained to the reading of it" (qtd. in Flint 15). Dickens was critical of the excessive detail of the Millais piece, its too highly crafted, manneristic style. In fact, Hunt used the term "microscopic" to describe their painstaking search for accuracy of details (2: 433). What Dickens saw in Millais, to use Catherine Phillips's useful distinctions, were "facts in place of fancy, realism as a substitute for romance; thus historic compositions become archeological records, and landscape studies might serve to show geological strata" (163). Masson puts the argument this way: the Pre-Raphaelites "have treated as a mischievous fallacy the notion that this power of artistic invention, this painter's sway over Nature, is a thing to be taught in the schools, and have called attention to the fact that what is teachable in the art of painting, is the habit of patient observation and the power of correct imitation"; for them, "the prerequisite to invention in painting is the ability to paint" (220). Similarly, Dickens criticized the directionless, amateur artist Henry Gowan in *Little Dorrit*, who, like the Pre-Raphaelites, painted "perfect Claudes, perfect Cuyps, perfect phænomena" (224). To Dickens, base things must be idealized. Art, especially religious art, should elevate the ordinary, the common and commonplace, creating as it were occasions for the worshipful. Art should possess transcendent qualities, appealing to the mind, heart, and soul. Artistic craft and fidelity to details (what Ruskin describes as the Pre-Raphaelites' "fidelity to a certain order of truth") are insufficient, for a picture is a "sign and emblem," an appeal to the "mind and sentiment"

("Old Lamps" 246). As sign and emblem, *Christ in the House of His Parents* is defective, retrogressive.[24]

Dickens lampoons the P.R.B. signature, with its potential to spawn fringe brotherhoods, which the Pre-Raphaelites themselves had anticipated[25]: the Pre-Perspective Brotherhood, formed to subvert "all known rules and principles of perspective"; the Pre-Newtonian Brotherhood to protest the laws of gravity; the Pre-Galileo Brotherhood to forestall all revolutions around the sun; the Pre-Harvey Brotherhood to disavow the circulation of the blood and make as it were a pact with undertakers; the Pre-Gower and Pre-Chaucer-Brotherhood to return English to its archaic beginnings; and the Pre-Laurentius Brotherhood to abolish all but manuscript books. The Pre-Agincourt Brotherhood would "consign to oblivion Mozart, Beethoven, Handel, and every other such ridiculous reputation," even as the Pre-Henry-the-Seventh Brotherhood, established at the same time as its "twin brother," the Pre-Raphaelite Brotherhood, and sharing a similar love for "ugly religious caricatures (called mysteries)," and thus "thoroughly Pre-Raphaelite in its spirit," would wind the clock back on all social advances and return the nation to barbarism. In an age of development and progress, these brotherhoods are all "retrogressive." Epidemic, the Pre-Raphaelite Brotherhood is a disease that must be checked. Dickens wants to commemorate a holiday, appropriately April 1, "to amalgamate in a high festival," called "the Convocation of Eternal Bodies," the celebration of all these Brotherhoods ("Old Lamps" 248).

The painting that closely resembles *Christ in the House of His Parents*, though not stylistically, is John Rogers Herbert's *The Youth of Our Lord* (1847; fig. 2). Nowhere, as far as I can tell, does Dickens comment on the painting, which has all of the qualities of naturalistic art he admires. Herbert's boy Jesus is assisting in chores connected to the family's carpentry shop. All three figures in the painting are idealized, and have nothing of the foreignness and physiognomic oddities of Millais's figures. Joseph is busy at work sawing on a piece of wood, and a curious Mary stops her spinning at the wheel to ponder her son. The look recalls annunciation depictions of Mary. Jesus remains on the periphery, but Mary's deep, penetrating gaze draws a horizontal line from her eyes to his, bringing him into the center of the scene. In close proximity to Jesus is a water jar, symbolic of his later baptism, baptismal ministry, and Christ as the water of life. The other symbolic clues in Herbert's painting are subtly rendered. Next to Mary are two turtle-doves, one, like the dove in the Millais painting, perched not on a ladder but on a stool. Though crude, the shop is airy, hospitable, and organized. Its wide-open space is a reminder of Dickens's "love of open-air effect" (Perugini II: 164), which no doubt contributed to his censure of Millais's claustrophobic scene. Cleanliness, expansiveness, and yet a coziness define the workshop, and, in contrast

Fig. 2. John Rogers Herbert, *The Youth of Our Lord* (1847). Guild Hall Gallery, London.

to Millais's painting, Herbert's gives prominence to a broom. Its recent employment bears proof in the neat pile of wood shavings and pieces of wood collected at the center of the painting, symbolically defining the shop's atmosphere. The focus, clearly, is the shop, which is made to define Jesus' boyhood.[26]

The Pre-Raphaelites' Tractarian connections were not lost on many Victorians, including Ruskin, who immediately wanted to separate himself from them: "No one who has met with any of my writings will suspect me of desiring to encourage them in their Romanist and Tractarian tendencies" (8). Dickens also locates a Tractarian tie to Pre-Raphaelitism: "it is whispered that some other large educational Institutions in the neighbourhood of Oxford are nearly ready to pronounce in favour of it" ("Old Lamps" 266). The Pre-Raphaelites had an historical connection to Oxford, "closely connected with Oxford," as John Whiteley has shown.[27] Millais and Hunt painted their landscapes at Botley, Shotover, Godstow, and Port Meadow. The Pre-Raphaelites' models (especially those employed by Burne-Jones and William Morris, who worked on murals for the Oxford Debating Society) were perhaps "the kind of all-male fellowship fostered in Oxford . . . by John Henry Newman and his associates in the 'Tractarian' or 'Oxford Movement,' in which male mentorship and friendships were vital sources of religious as well as educational guidance" (Prettejohn 99).

Moreover, in a sense Millais's *Christ in the House of His Parents* had Oxford connections, Oxford Street, London. His carpenter's shop was located on Oxford Street, London, where he spent "nearly three weeks" at work on the painting.[28] "Sometimes he even slept there, in order to begin work early on the following morning. He studied and copied everything—tools, work table, shavings on the floor. Not least important was the artisan himself" (Fleming 57). Consistent with Pre-Raphaelite principles, the attempt was to get as close as possible to one's subject in order to observe and capture every detail, which introduced many inconveniences. "I was determined," Millais told Hunt, "to choose a real carpenter whose frame and muscles had been formed by the very exercise that had been the toil of the Virgin's husband" (Hunt 1: 202). The painting's title was Tractarian-informed. It was first called *The Carpenter's Shop*, but was exhibited without a title. Millais had chosen as the catalogue entry Zechariah 13: 6: "And one shall say unto him, What are these wounds in thy hands? Then shall he answer, Those with which I was wounded in the house of my friends." As Fleming has observed, "the passage has nothing to do with Jesus," but "with the response of someone accused of false prophecy because he has what may be a wound self-inflicted in a frenzied fit." Fleming detected in the passage a connection with E. B. Pusey, Regius Professor of History and leader of the Oxford Movement, "who saw the sentences as foreshadowing the crucifixion wound. This interpretation had some currency in Oxford, where Millais probably picked it up" (57). There were many other things that the Pre-Raphaelites picked up at Oxford, such as support from James Wyatt, patronage by the Tractarian sympathizer Thomas Combe, inspiration from Oxford sermons, commitment to the Union murals, and work on the chapel windows at St. Edmund Hall. Hunt, however, rejected the popular notion that theirs was an art calculated to endorse Tractarian propaganda. Pointing specifically to *The Light of the World*, he insisted that "The suspicion of certain thinkers that 'The Light of the World' was painted to support the Puseyite movement had no justification" (2: 411).[29] But with such Anglo-Catholic pieces as Hunt's *A Converted British Family Sheltering a Christian Missionary from the Persecution of the Druids* (1850) and Charles Collins's *Convent Thoughts* (1851), such Tractarian disavowal was unconvincing. .

    Dickens and the Pre-Raphaelites had more in common than his outrage would seem to indicate. One way of reading his harangue is to see it more as a declaration of intimacy than genuine hostility. For example, Hunt acknowledged the influence of *David Copperfield* on his *The Awakening Conscience* (1854) and later on Dante Gabriel's Rossetti's unfinished *Found*. Hunt had been reading the Dickens novel, which caused him to reflect on a picture "representing in actual life the manner in which the appeal of the spirit of heavenly love calls a soul to abandon a lower life." He was "deeply touched by the pathos" in *David Copperfield* and by the idea of "pity for the fallen'' when Peggotty went in search of the fallen Emily. Relatedly, Hunt "went about to different haunts of fallen girls to find a locality suitable for the scene of the old mariner's pursuing love. My object was not to illustrate any special incident in the book, but to take the suggestion of the loving seeker of the fallen girl coming upon the object of his search.'' The thought then led to a passage in Proverbs (25: 20): "As he that taketh away a garment in cold weather, so is he that singeth songs to a heavy heart.'' This, says Hunt, "led me to see how the companion of the girl's fall might himself be the unconscious utterer of a divine message'' (2: 429–30).

Dickens's censure of *Christ in the House of His Parents*, Hunt felt, transformed a storm into a hurricane, making "our enormity more shameful beyond artistic circles'' (1: 205). Dickens's remarks were religiously nuanced, directed to Popery and to the kind of religious art he had witnessed during his tour of Italy: "rich churches, drowsy Masses, curling incenses, tinkling bells, priests in bright vestments: pictures, tapers, laced altar cloths, crosses, images, and artificial flowers'' (*Pictures* 324). *Pictures from Italy* offers an important window into Dickens's anti-Roman Catholic bigotry, displayed in his attitude to Italy. Reading the travel narrative, one has to disentangle initial impressions from lasting ones, and both from nostalgia. The account raises the question of whether or not one can actually render a "true'' picture of a place, or whether impressions are the best one can offer, which may or may not conform to any existing reality. Dickens recognizes this dilemma, calling the travel narrative "Pictures,'' which implies the myriad and perspectival. Italy is not one picture but many. Mary Louise Pratt's *Imperial Eyes* offers useful approaches to *Pictures*. First, Pratt sees landscape as "estheticized'': it becomes a painting and then is described as such; "the esthetic *pleasure* of the sight singlehandedly constitutes the value and significance of the journey.'' Next, she finds a "*density of meaning*,'' in which landscape becomes "extremely rich in material and semantic substance.'' Finally, Pratt observes a "relation of *mastery* predicated between the seer and the seen'' (204).

Employing these strategies of perception, I argue that a useful way to read *Pictures* is by way of art criticism and criticism of art, for in this book travel is structured by or remembered as pictures. Dickens's favorite Italian sites, for example, are places of High Culture and High Art—Venice, Rome, and Florence. Conversely, the places he most dislikes are those where High Culture and High Art are presumably absent—Fondi and Naples. Dickens's imposed on Millais's *Christ in the House of His Parents* his antipathy to Roman Catholicism and disgust with Italian low art. It is not the picture of labor, the entire family involved in work, which troubled Dickens. What bothered him was the disorder and chaos of the place, the ordinariness or plainness of the representation, and the physical deformity of the figures. That the Holy Family would be depicted as working class was also disquieting.

In other words, what distressed Dickens was the fact that the holy was rendered one with the natural, the divine with the human, the way the image of "the Master of the New Testament" was rendered invisible, "put out of sight" (*Letters* 10: 444).

Pictures from Italy is an archaeology of Italy's Roman and Romish history. As slavery to Dickens was a social disease particularly American, so was Roman Catholicism to Italy. Thus, *American Notes* should be read alongside *Pictures from Italy*, for both travel narratives exemplify the same "retrogressive principle."[30] Dickens imposes on Italy a Euroimperialist gaze, employing the coordinates of "Redundancy, discontinuity, unreality" (Pratt 2). Time is a major trope. Dickens presents his visit not only as a stepping back into a primeval, even primitive past fraught with superstition, but also as a stepping out of time. Italy is a land where if time did not stand still, it was moving back retrogressively: "What a sad place Italy is! a country gone to sleep, and without a prospect of waking again" (*Letters* 4: 169). Italy's unreality carries the day. Dickens wants to believe and feel that Italy is still European even as his characterizations of it are not. One hardly gets the impression that Italy is part of the Continent, but, rather, a "colonial frontier," viewed from a "European expantionist perspective." Pre-modern, and reflective of Dickens's own ambivalence with the past, Italy is what Pratt would call a "contact zone," possessing the "temporal copresence of subjects previously separated by geographic and historical disjunctures, and whose trajectories now intersect." A "contact" or "anti-conquest" perspective, says Pratt, "treats the relations among colonizers and colonized, or travelers and 'travellers,' not in terms of separateness or apartheid, but in terms of copresence, interaction, interlocking understandings and practices, often within radically asymmetrical relations of power" (6–7).

Noteworthy are the countless ways Italy is viewed not from an Italian perspective but from a largely English, bourgeois one. The coordinates of Shakespeare, Keats, Byron, and Shelley are routinely located to forestall dislocation and disorientation. *Pictures* opens with *Midsummer Night's Dream*, and alludes to any number of other Shakespearean plays, among them *Macbeth, Hamlet, Merchant of Venice, Henry IV, Othello,* and *Romeo and Juliet*. This deployment of Shakespeare defines a poetics of allusion, "permeating as it does everything from the most covert to the most overt reference" (Gager 163).[31] For example, Dickens finds "nothing to connect [Verona] with the beautiful story" of *Romeo and Juliet* (*Letters* 4: 225). But he did find London in the deep blue Mediterranean sky, and was horrified to recognize similarities between Rome and London: "I swear, that keenly as I felt the seeming absurdity of the comparison, it was so like London, at that distance, that if you could have shown it me, in a glass, I should have taken it for nothing else" (364). Throughout *Pictures*, the Englishman as subject, which serves to "legitimate bourgeois authority and delegitimate peasant and subsistence lifeways" (Pratt 10), is never lost, forfeited, surrendered. There is never complete immersion within the experience. The bourgeois persists, whether in Dickens's sharing living quarters with a Spanish duke, or having dinner with the French consul general. Dickens employs Defoe to stage Italy, illustrating how immersed he himself had become in the colonial project of travel writing, of which *Pickwick Papers* and *Uncommercial Traveller* are his best examples. In *Pictures*, he can become Robinson Crusoe or Defoe's Complete English Gentleman, "European, male, secular, and lettered" (Pratt 30). Travels, explorations, and expeditions were all crucial to the Victorian imagination, much of it tied to the search for new knowledge and new frontiers. In the colonial enterprise, knowledge becomes linked to conquest. Historical figures like Mongo Park and Sir John Franklin, whom Dickens wrote about, are celebrated more for their heroic failures than successes.[32]

Dickens calls *Pictures from Italy* "a series of faint reflections—mere shadows in the water"—and sees his experiences in Italy as dreamlike states, "reminiscences," he calls them. To preserve those impressions, he turns to his private letters as "guarantee to the Reader that they were at least penned in the fullness of the subject, and with the liveliest impressions of novelty and freshness" (259–60). Despite its travel tropes and place names, *Pictures* belies a standard travel narrative, resisting the "stock" of extant travel histories. Dickens does admit reliance on Louis Simond's *A Tour in Italy and Sicily* (1828) and John Murray's celebrated *Handbook for Travellers in Central Italy* (1843). *Pictures* also pretends to be apolitical, avoiding "any grave examination into the government or misgovernment of any portion of the country" (259).[33] But whereas *Pictures* might be apolitical, it is not a-religious; in Italy, the two become wedded. Dickens's derides Jesuits as "black cats . . . slinking noiselessly about, in pairs" (296), "stealthy Jesuits creeping in and out" (369), and, like ravens, "sly and stealthy" and "croaking in answer to the [convent] bell" (427). Dickens is quite cognizant of the fact that *Pictures* can be taken as an attack on Popery, hence the disclaimer: "I hope I am not likely to be misunderstood by Professors of the Roman Catholic faith, on account of anything contained in these pages. . . . When I mention any exhibition that impressed me as absurd or disagreeable, I do not seek to connect it, or recognise it as necessarily connected with, any essentials of their creed" (260). But connect them he does. The Church at Rome was like an ancient architecture, a collapsing structure of "Broken aqueducts," "broken temples," "broken tombs," "an immense edifice, with no one point for the mind to rest upon" (367). At Bologna, he observes "brown piles of sacred buildings, with more birds flying in and out of chinks in the stone" (324). Italy and its churches are a dilapidated, disorganized mess tending toward anarchy. The chapter title "Doing as Rome Does" alludes not so subtly to Matthew Arnold's "Doing as One Likes," the very definition of anarchy. The Roman Church and Italy are marked by disease, filth, disorder, decay, and ruin, all symbolically brought together in the Jesuit House at Mora: "The stables, coach-houses, offices, were all empty, ruinous, all utterly deserted. Doors had lost their hinges, and were holding on by their latches; windows were broken, painted plaster had peeled off, and was lying about in clods" (287). Italy had become associated with dirt, disrepair, and disease, its art "representing some sickness or calamity" (273).

Dickens embarked on his tour of Italy on 2 July 1844, and arrived three weeks later. In the introduction to *Pictures*, "The Reader's Passport," he insists that while he is not "an earnest admirer of Painting and Sculpture," and has neither the skill or knowledge to "expatiate at any length on famous Paintings and Statues" (259), the picture he presents is nevertheless credible because fresh and spontaneous, not inventive or retrospective, "penned in the fulness of the subject, and with the liveliest impressions of novelty and freshness." He then adds his anti-Catholic disclaimer, before returning to the image of his travel narrative as "Pictures" and its analogy to "shadows in the water," which, if stirred too roughly, "mar the shadows." Dickens, in other words, does not want his "English audience" to view Italy less than "a noble country" (260) with a noble people albeit following a not-so-noble religion.

Thrust into a culture so different, his senses were immediately traumatized: "I never in my life was so dismayed! The wonderful novelty of everything, the unusual smells, the unaccountable filth . . . the disorderly jumbling of dirty houses, one upon the roof of another . . . and the disheartening dirt, discomfort, and decay." But these are early impressions which, Dickens discovers, often change on reflection: "I little thought, that day, that I should ever come to have an attachment for the very stones in the streets of Genoa, and to look back upon the city with affection as connected with many hours of happiness and quiet!" (283). Italy's squalor and filth—"the disheartening dirt, discomfort, and decay"—are of a piece with Roman Catholicism. Not even St. Peter's, mesmeric ("It looked immense in the distance, but distinctly and decidedly small, by comparison, on a near approach" [365]), escapes criticism: "It might be a Pantheon, or a Senate House, or a great architectural trophy, having no other object than an architectural triumph." But "it does not heighten the effect of the temple, as a work of art; and it is not expressive—to me at least—of its high purpose" (368). And so, too, the Roman Catholic clergy, exceeding all "varieties of sloth, deceit, and intellectual torpor" (296). Lacking vitality, Roman Catholicism is lethargic, hallucinogenic: "sitting in any of the churches towards evening, is like a mild dose of opium" (298).[34]

Dickens had traveled to Italy from Lyons, Avignon, and Marseilles, prominent French Roman Catholic regions where, for example, one cathedral looked "all grim, and swarthy, and mouldering, and cold" (269). A "whole town that is tumbled, anyhow, out of the sky," Lyons is a diseased city, as is pestilential Ferrara, "a city of the dead, without one solitary survivor" (270, 327). Dreamlike states, nausea, and claustrophobia characterize Dickens's journey through France and Italy. He retrospectively forges a connection between the two countries where religion, and in particular Roman Catholicism, dominates the social, political, cultural, and aesthetic landscape: "Thinking how strange it was, to find, in every stagnant town, this same Heart beating with the same monotonous pulsation, the centre of the same torpid, listless system" (320). In a clock tower at the cathedral in Lyons, he witnessed a "puppet of the Virgin Mary" and "The Angel Gabriel" (271). French religious frescoes, especially of the ubiquitous Madonna, are "abundant in Italy." In one woodcut, he saw again the very thing that appalled him in Millais: "a lady was having a toe amputated" (273). Dante was on Dickens's mind when he entered Italy. One of his first meteorological descriptions of Italy touches on the Italian sky and sea, an "awful, solemn, impenetrable blue" that yields "an absorbing, silent, deep, profound effect; . . . I can't help thinking it suggested the idea of Styx" (*Letters* 4: 159).

Connected to Lethe (and its companion stream Eunoë, "good memory"), Dante's sweet river of forgetfulness and tears (373, 409; see canto 28 of *The Purgatorio*), Rome also becomes purgatorial. At Ferrara, Dickens felt as though he had emerged out of Cocytus:

> the thrill I felt on seeing the accursed wall below, decayed and broken through, and the sun shining in through its gaping wounds, was like a sense of victory and triumph. . . . It cannot look more lovely to a blind man newly restored to sight, than to a traveller who sees it, calmly and majestically, treading down the darkness of that Infernal Well. . . . These heights [the hills above Marseilles] are a desirable retreat, for less picturesque reasons—as an escape from a compound of vile smells perpetually arising from a great harbour full of stagnant water.   (278).

Even Genoa, with its "bewildering phantasmagoria" (291), "beautiful confusion" (306), and "enchanting confusion"—a true picture of the sublime ("things that are picturesque, ugly, mean, magnificent, delightful, and offensive" [292])—could not escape Dantean associations; growth in a garden there appears infernal: "everything was green, gaunt, weedy, straggling, under-ground or over-ground, mildewy, damp, redolent of all sorts of slabby, clammy, creeping, and uncomfortable life" (290).

Genoa's plague of creatures—mosquitoes, flies, fleas, rats, lizards, scorpions, beetles, and frogs—came directly out of John's vision of the Apocalypse. Genoa is an Ichabod, where "one solitary firefly" becomes "the last little speck of the departed Glory of the house." The firefly's meandering is a quest for "the rest of the Glory" (*Pictures* 286, 290). Dante is not named until the end of *Pictures*, but his apocalyptic vision of Hell and Purgatory show up routinely. For example, Parma, "like streets in the city of the dead," one "never saw, or never will see, one ray of the sun" (385), bears the same Dantean feature: "The desolation and decay impress themselves on all the senses. The air has a moldering smell, and an earthy taste; any stray outer sounds that struggle in with some lost sunbeam, are muffled and heavy; and the worm, the maggot, and the rot have changed the surface of the wood beneath the touch. . . . If any Ghosts act plays, they act them on this ghostly stage" (320). But Dickens soon grew strangely accustomed to Genoa's preter-naturalness: "the flitting shapes and shadows of my dismal entering reverie gradually resolved themselves into familiar forms and substances" (290). Italy is "a land of contradictions" (*Letters* 4: 190), extreme beauty existing alongside glaring ugliness. The statement "Everything is in extremes" (*Letters* 4: 160), which describes southern France but was written from Italy, could well characterize Dickens's Italian experience. Dickens was also struck by Genoa's beauty, "its splendid theatre, terrace rising above terrace, garden above garden, palace above palace, height upon height," and its "stately harbour" (282–83); "never was anything so enchantingly graceful and full of beauty" (318).

Italy is topsy-turvy: "all fire goes up the chimney except the smoke" (326). The description of "grim Ferrara," "unreal and spectral," a "city of the dead, without one solitary survivor" (326–27), also seems constitutive of Italy, a "magic lantern" where something is "no sooner visible than, in its turn, it melted into something else" (329). Confusing to both sense and sensibility, Italy, throughout, possesses this mesmeric quality. Streets and building have a subterranean quality to them, "tremendous darkness of vast extent, half-buried in the earth and unexplorable" (385). Roman Catholicism, similarly, is a dark, unearthly, underworld religion—a religion of the cata-combs. Dickens's criticism of Italy was an attack on Catholicism and dis-ease, which to him went hand in hand. References to malaria spread through-out Dickens's Italian experience. His critique of Millais, according to J. B. Bullen, was directed to Pre-Raphaelite efforts to drag "the sacred subject into the gutter and the hospital" and to locate "the Divine in an ambience of disease and deformity." Here, interestingly, "the contemporary discourses of social degradation and pathology [were] being incorporated wholesale into art criticism as a means of devaluing Pre-Raphaelite art" (Bullen 42–44). Despite Dickens's disavowal of all artistic knowledge, believing himself un-qualified to remark on "the 'touch' of this or that master" (*Pictures* 346), suggesting that "High Art is out of my reach" (*Letters* 4: 283), *Pictures* drew out his views on art in ways he had not expressed previously. It comments on Correggio, Da Vinci, Titian, Van Dyke, Raphael, and others, all of whom manifest "tenderness and grace," "noble elevation, purity, and beauty." Canova's statutes left Dickens "beyond all reach of words" (394).

Italy's religious art, collapsing structures, anatomical disfigurement, and decaying religion become inseparable. Parma is a classic example. Its cathedral of rotting Correggios is surrounded by tombs and hidden altars. Dickens's description of its frescoes, "the Souls of Painters—perishing and fading away, like human forms," anticipates his critique of Millais, with its focus on decay and deformity: "This cathedral is odorous with the rotting of Correggio's frescoes in the Cupola. Heaven knows how beautiful they may have been at one time . . . ; but such a labyrinth of arms and legs: such heaps of shortened limbs, entangled and involved and jumbled together: no operative surgeon, gone mad, could imagine in his wildest delirium." Dantean, Parma is a "subterranean church" occupied by shades:

> From every one of these lurking-places, such a crowd of phantom-looking men and women, leading other men and women with twisted limbs or chattering jaws, or paralytic gestures, or idiotic heads, or some other sad infirmity, came hobbling out to beg, that if the ruined frescoes in the cathedral above, had been suddenly animated, and had retired to this lower church, they could hardly have made a greater confusion, or exhibited a more confounding display of arms and legs. (318–19)

Petrarch's Monument is also there, and in a gallery "remarkable pictures" are being copied by religious artists. The Farnese Palace, "a grand, old, gloomy theatre, mouldering away" (319), shares the same nexus of decay and dismemberment. Dickens's magic lantern nightmare, when he came across the Bridge of Sighs, anticipates the wood shavings in Millais's workshop: "carpenters, at work with plane and chisel in their shops, tossed the light shaving straight upon the water, where it lay like weed, or ebbed away before me in a tangled heap" (335). Millais, or Millais-type art criticism, where the closer one gets to the subject the more repulsive it becomes, is everywhere in *Pictures*: "The Italian face changes as the visitor approaches the city; its beauty becomes devilish" (367). Dickens would again find that "Much of the romance of the beautiful towns and villages on this beautiful road [the Cornice road to Genoa], disappears when they are entered" (312).

Art, Dickens maintains, must idealize rather than represent the truth of things, "resembling and refining upon nature, and presenting graceful combinations of forms and colour" (*Pictures* 346). When this quality is missing, as in Pre-Raphaelite art, art becomes perversely religious. Dickens's critique of the Holy Family in the church of the Ara Cœli mirrors his censure of Millais. He finds the painting "remarkable for the possession of a miraculous Bambíno, or wooden doll, representing the Infant Saviour. . . . The candles were on a kind of altar, and above it were two delectable figures, such as you would see at any English fair, representing the Holy Virgin, and Saint Joseph, as I suppose, bending in devotion over a wooden box, or coffer; which was shut.'' In this extravaganza, the little wooden Christ, ''in face very like General Tom Thumb, the American Dwarf,'' is paraded around the room and doted upon (*Pictures* 380–82). The procession—and Roman Catholicism to him is one long procession—soon takes to the road, and that same Bambíno parades the streets and domicile of invalids. To Dickens, this is vulgar Christianity and vulgar art—crude, distasteful, and common. Holy Week in Rome had the same circus-like quality; the Pope himself is ''perpetually carried up and down Saint Peter's like a glorious Guy Faux'' (*Letters* 4: 282).[35] For Dickens, as Edgar Johnson puts it, this was all ''a painted rigmarole, a humbug for which he could feel little except a contemptuous impatience . . . . The brilliant pageantry and processions of Rome, the colorful vestments, the incense, the elaborate symbolic rituals, all seem to him only a theatrical mummery'' (553, 562). Everywhere in Italy, Dickens confronts the vulgar, the bacchanal, the carnivalesque, the fanatical. Italy is a veritable ''toy shop of little objects'' (360) of cheap, contemptible Christian art. His description of it again anticipates his critique of Millais's workshop:

> There is seldom a figure on the cross, though there is sometimes a face; but they are remarkable for being garnished with little models in wood of every possible object that can be connected with the Saviour's death. The cock that crowed when Peter had denied his master thrice, is generally perched on the tip-top; and an ornithological phenomenon he always is. Under him is the inscription. Then, hung on the cross-beam, are the spear, the reed with the sponge of vinegar and water at the end, the coat without seam for which the soldiers cast lots, the dice-box with which they threw for it, the hammer that drove in the nails, the pincers that pulled them out, the ladder which was set against the cross, the crown of thorns, the instrument of flagellation, the lantern with which Mary went to the tomb—I suppose; I can think of no other—and the sword with which Peter smote the high priest's servant. (*Letters* 4: 290)[36]

This distaste for perverse art is again instanced in Dickens's remarks on Vatican art. Among its masterpieces is ''a considerable amount of rubbish,'' ''without any reference to its intrinsic merits'' (*Pictures* 392). Roman Catholicism and its representative art are all spectacle, spectacular, spectral.

Although unwilling to dispense with a ''natural perception of what is natural and true'' and ''such commonplace facts as the ordinary proportion of men's arms, and legs, and heads,'' Dickens remains bothered by Pre-Raphaelite realism which, despite its microscopic attention to details, is not truthful absent the worshipful: ''when I see a Jolly young Waterman representing a cherubim, or a Barclay and Perkins's Drayman depicted as an Evangelist, I see nothing to commend or admire in the performance, however great its reputed painter'' (*Pictures* 392). Pre-Raphaelite realism does not render ''the

true appreciation of the really great and transcendent works'' (393). Anticipating the emerging Darwinian metaphor of monsters and freaks, Dickens
calls such ''undeserving pictures'' ''intolerable abortions'' (393, 394), at
home with the ''monstrous union'' of Christian and pagan, a commonplace
in Rome, where ''the false faith and the true are fused'' (398). The Vatican
art of Titian, Raphael, Michelangelo, and Tintoretto epitomizes the sublime,
the awe-ful; but it also succumbs to the degenerative, when the transcendent
has too close an affinity to the common and commonplace:

> I cannot imagine, for example, how the resolute champion of undeserving pic-
> tures can soar to the amazing beauty of Titian's great picture of the Assumption
> of the Virgin at Venice; or how the man who is truly affected by the sublimity
> of that exquisite production, or who is truly sensible of the beauty of Tintoretto's
> great picture of the Assembly of the Blessed in the same place, can discern in
> Michael Angelo's Last Judgment, in the Sistine chapel, any general idea, or
> one pervading thought, in harmony with the stupendous subject. He who will
> contemplate Raphael's masterpiece, the Transfiguration, and will go away into
> another chamber of that same Vatican, and contemplate another design of Ra-
> phael, representing (in incredible caricature) the miraculous stopping of the
> great fire by Leo the Fourth—and who will say that he admires them both, as
> works of extraordinary genius—must, as I think, be wanting in his powers of
> perception in one of the two instances, and, probably, in the high and lofty
> one.   (393)

But Dickens's view of Italy vacillated, a sense of things he could not quite
arrest, whether Venice's and Rome's mystical qualities, Fondi's and Naples's
filth, or the false essentializing of Verona: ''You know Verona? You know
everything in Italy'' (*Letters* 4: 225). ''We like Italy more and more, every
day,'' he wrote on 20 November 1844 as he was to depart for Switzerland
and London. Dickens loved his dream city Venice, ''*the* wonder and the new
sensation of the world!'' He was charmed especially by its art, those ''silent
speaking faces of Titian and Tintoretto. . . . With your foot upon its stones,
its pictures before you, and its history in your mind, it is something past all
writing of or speaking of—almost past all thinking of.'' Venice possesses the
kind of sublime Dickens admired: ''Dreamy, beautiful, impossible, wicked,
shadowy, damnable. . . . I hardly think it possible to exaggerate its beauties,
its source of interest, its uncommon novelty and freshness.'' This dreamlike
state had come to describe Dickens's feelings about Venice, which he associates with the creative imagination, the pleasure dome of Coleridge's Kubla
Khan: ''The gorgeous and wonderful reality of Venice is beyond the fancy
of the wildest dreamer. Opium couldn't build such a place, and enchantment
couldn't shadow it forth in a vision'' (*Letters* 4: 217–20, 226). Although
Dickens had visited Modena, Parma, Bologna, Ferrara, Cremona, Florence,
Rome, Naples, and Palermo, Venice stood out as distinct, separate, singular,

incomparable. Naples "disappoints," and Rome surrenders some of its luster, feeling "no more my Rome" (*Letters* 4: 273, 257), but not exotic Venice: "The three days that I passed there, were like a Thousand and One Arabian Nights, wildly exaggerated a thousand and one times" (*Letters* 4: 238–38).

The enjoyable Venetian experience resulted largely from its art. Dickens had begun to separate in his thinking and aesthetic creed great art from base art, religious art from Catholic art, Italy's jewels from its dirt. Raphael, Titian, Tintoretto, and Correggio offered relief from base Catholic art. By 17 November 1844, and by his own admission, Dickens was "brim-full of cant about pictures," and sought to enlighten Forster on various schools and their (de-)merits: "I have never seen any praise of Titian's great picture of the Assumption of the Virgin at Venice, which soared half as high as the beautiful and amazing reality. It is perfection. Tintoretto's picture too, of the Assembly of the Blest . . . tending majestically and dutifully to Almighty God in the centre, is grand and noble in the extreme." What became clear to Dickens is the lack of inventiveness, freshness, and originality from artists who "painted monks and priests a vast deal too often," turning art into "a perfect night-mare." And so "pictures of tremendous power" often manifest not only defective anatomical rendering but also flawed imaginative composition, "heads quite below the story and the painter." Religious art must be idealized art, imaginative rather than imitative, not "portraits of monks I know at Genoa" showing up "in all the lame parts of strong paintings" (*Letters* 4: 220–21). The best religious art, Dickens felt, offers a sanctuary from Catholicism. His gallery visits with Raphael, Titian, Rubens, and Correggio ("Such tenderness and grace, such noble elevation, purity, and beauty") provided an escape from Popery and Papist art, and brought relief "from legions of whining friars and waxy holy families." On the other hand, the Pre-Raphaelite art of "whole orchestras of earthy angels" "persisted in reducing every mystery of our religion to some literal development in paint and canvas" (*Letters* 4: 277).[37] In seeking to naturalize Christianity, Pre-Raphaelite art robs it of mystery, the sublime, and the otherworldly.

Dickens's diatribe against the kind of religious art manifested in England had its source in Italy. Italy's religious art seeks as its models the average human on the street who stalks the area around the Church of Trínita del Monte near the Meloni's Hotel where Dickens lived, presenting themselves in "conventionally picturesque attitudes" (*Letters* 4: 280). Dickens satirizes these professional models, the Pastoral Model, the assassin Model, the haughty or scornful model, and the family model (Jesus, Mary, and Joseph). Regrettably, young artists "go on copying these people elaborately time after time and time out of mind, and find nothing fresh or suggestive in the actual world about them" (*Letters* 4: 281). When he first encountered these models, Dickens felt that he had seen them before. Returning to him as "perfect nightmares,'' they were the same images decorating the walls of the Royal Academy: ''a Jolly Young Waterman representing a cherubim, or a Barclay and Perkins's Drayman depicted as an Evangelist'' (*Letters* 4: 283). Dickens resented ''the Josephs surveying Nativities, from shiny backgrounds, in a state of considerable mystification,'' or ''the Saint Sebastians, of whom I wouldn't have a specimen on any terms, notwithstanding the extreme rarity of the subject'' (*Letters* 4: 283; see also *Pictures* 378–79). These observations reinforce his belief that the selection of models is based on caricature rather than character:

> many people select their models, much as the painters . . . select theirs; and that, whereas in the Royal Academy some evil old ruffian of a Dogstealer will annually be found embodying all the cardinal virtues, on account of his eye-lashes, or his chin, or his legs (thereby planting thorns of confusion in the breasts of the more observant students of nature), so, in the great social Exhibition, accessories are often accepted in lieu of the internal character.
>
> (*Little Dorrit* 164)

The Victorian assault on the naturalism/realism of the Pre-Raphaelites, led to no small degree by Dickens, clearly influenced the direction their art would take. ''[W]hether they choose the upward or downward path,'' Ruskin would write, ''may in no small degree depend upon the character of the criticism which their works have to sustain'' (8). Anticipating, perhaps, the Victorian assault, Collison left the movement and turned towards Rome. Dante Rossetti turned to secular and classical subjects. The brotherhood, school, or society, such as it was, literally fragmented; each went his own way.

But two decades later, Holman Hunt returned to Millais's carpenter's shop. In *The Shadow of Death* (earlier, *Shadow of the Cross* [1870–73]; fig. 3), Millais's boy Jesus is now a grown man. The circumstances surrounding the painting, rarely if ever told, are instructive. Hunt held an historical fascination with the life and person of Christ, especially the human and humble Christ that Mark, more than any of the other Gospel writers, depicted. For example, Hunt wanted to do a painting of Christ in the synagogue reading Isaiah to testify about the very messianic prophesies he was to fulfill. He even began a piece on *The Flight into Egypt* based on the Matthew account. And Hunt also, we know, did his famous *The Light of the World* and gave it a symbolic or allegorical interpretation unknown to most critics.[38] To paint *The Shadow of Death*, described as ''a jewel in a gorgeous setting'' (Hunt 2: 193), and to conform to the realism/naturalism of the Pre-Raphaelite and nineteenth-century landscape painters, Hunt wanted to be on the very scene. Desiring ''the robust out-of-door growth of native Pre-Raphaelitism,'' Hunt pursued the ''exact study of outdoor nature,'' ''working frankly on the canvas itself from Nature'' (2: 431–36). He wanted to paint in the very setting where

Fig. 3. William Holman Hunt, *The Shadow of Death* (1870–73). Manchester Art Gallery. British Library, HIP/Art Resource, NY.

Christ lived, and to seek out models native to the area. And so he traveled to Jerusalem and arranged an appropriate studio and setting: "I could not settle how to overcome the difficulties of arranging the details of my picture, until I had made it my business to visit many native carpenters at work, and had been over to Bethlehem, and searched out the traditional tools, fast being abandoned for those of European form. . . . Thus I could select the models for my picture from the inhabitants." One was "a timid woman [who] had hesitatingly posed for the Virgin opening the ivory chest," hesitatingly, because it was superstitiously rumored that the studio was haunted (2: 276). Hunt experienced some difficulty with his Jewish model for Mary. Her color became increasingly dark during the three years it took him to complete the painting. He was clearly mindful of British reception of a darkly complexioned Holy Family.

Hunt wanted to produce "a picture of Jesus engaged in His humbler duties, anterior to Messianic work" in order "to make the world realise more fully the value of His example in the perfection of His human life." He based it on an expression in Mark (6: 3): "Is not this the carpenter?" (2: 273). Hunt wanted to show Christ "day after day toiling like other men as the labourer 'who waiteth for his shadow,' uttering words which could only be interpreted as discouragement of [Mary's] immediate and temporal ambition for her Son and her Nation. Through all their fallen fortunes (like impoverished nobles) she would have retained the Magi's princely gifts." And so

> at the end of the day, when safe from intrusion, she would have joined her loved one at His toil, and opened the casket of her treasure to reassure herself that the gifts brought by the wise men were a reality, not the baseless fabric of a vision. She would see that there they lay, the golden crown, the royal sceptre, and censer for His enthronement. . . . Such were my imaginings, and I saw Him stepping over the plank at which He had been working, when the sun reached the horizon, and recognising that the end of the day's labour had come, stretching His weary frame to relieve the long-felt tension, while murmuring a prayer to His heavenly Father. The sun as this moment projected His shadow on the wall, and the tool-rack accentuated the resemblance to that of a crucified man. At the moment of the revival of His mother's trust the shadow attracted her over-anxious gaze, and awoke the presentiment of the anguish she was doomed to suffer. (2: 273–75)

Many Victorians, as well as the local religious authorities, disliked this representation of the Holy Family. Hunt's realism attracted some of the very same criticism Millais's did earlier. The Jerusalem observers were offended by its utter humanness and appalled by Hunt's Virgin Mary, who with "face hidden was denounced as a Protestant indignity to the Madonna." The religious authorities posted guards at the Jaffa Gate to prevent curious onlookers from viewing the painting. Hunt wanted to address their concerns, but settled on the painting as it had been done: "I had indeed tried many arrangements in order that the Virgin's face should be shown, but I had rejected all, from the conviction that nothing but the direct glance at the shadow gave the tragedy of the idea" (2: 307–8). In Jerusalem, Hunt observed, "the extreme Church party denounced it as blasphemous, altogether refusing to acknowledge that the record in St. Mark should be read as authority for representing Jesus Christ as Himself a carpenter'' (2: 310). The painting was meant to question prevailing assumptions of Christ in the context of the Higher-Critical debate concerning Christ's humanity. "This," Hunt declares, "was what I most desired, the dutiful humility of Christ's life thus carrying its deeper lesson" (2: 310). Dickens, Millais, and now Hunt were all pursuing different models of Christ. Even though Dickens acknowledged Christ's humanity, he wanted to focus on the exemplary model and on the divinity, on Christ as healer. Millais and Hunt, on the other hand, were much more attracted to Christ's humanness and humble background, on Christ as carpenter.

In a curious irony, the impulse that drove Dickens to serious contemplation about the true life of Christ was the same impetus that drove the Pre-Raphaelites. They, as well as he, wanted a simpler and supposedly nonsectarian Jesus, as they sought to recover, in Hunt's words, "much of the teachings of Christ's life . . . lost by history being overlaid with sacerdotal gloss" (2: 409). This desire is what drove Hunt to the East. Like other emerging accounts of the life of Christ, such as the one presented in *Essays and Reviews*, Hunt wanted to rid orthodoxy of its interpretive hegemony and to re-open the biblical text to accommodate new interpretive explorations, new frontiers of scholarship. Dickens's *Life*, which Georgina Hogarth describes as a "beautiful little New Testament which he wrote for his children" (5–6), was equally an attempt at another "History of Jesus Christ." Missing in contemporary accounts of the life of Christ, he felt, was the emphasis on Christ's goodness, kindness, and gentleness (11). Whereas Dickens wanted a sublime if exemplary Christ, Hunt and the Pre-Raphaelites sought a historical character but one who is more than historical—a sublime Jesus with foot firmly (perhaps too firmly) planted in nature and in historical time and place. Renan's *Vie de Jésus* (1860) did not trouble Hunt as it did Dickens, even when Hunt was warned that reading it would "entirely destroy my understanding of the history in the gospels." Hunt took up Renan's book in 1869 during his work in Jerusalem on *The Shadow of Death*. But, strangely, *Vie de Jésus* brought him around to a historical as well as a sublime Christ: "It was an exponent of the prevailing spirit of investigation, not only by comparison with records of the time, but also by reference to Eastern life as traced by a resident student in Syria." But Hunt faulted the book's "lack of imagination concerning the profundity and sublimity of the mind and purpose of Jesus" (2: 409), illustrating just how difficult it was for Hunt, the Pre-Raphaelites, and novelists to capture in art or literature any "true" account of the life of Christ. "To exercise original thought on sacred-story must, it seems, ever be a *challenge* to the world" (2: 409–10), Hunt concludes.[39]

In Hunt's cluttered workshop, Jesus pauses from sawing on a piece of wood to stretch his limbs. No mere relief from work, the stretch symbolically enacts the crucifixion posture. The shadow cast on the wall and Jesus' other-worldly gaze foreshadow the event of the cross by creating an image of the crucifixion. The anatomical features that so infuriated earlier critics remain, though here the image of Jesus appears neither sickly, deformed, nor working-class. "The sinewy bodily forms, emphasising each muscle and vein, repeat the physical specificity of Millais's earlier carpenters, and the wood shavings, so irritating to the critics of 1850, have proliferated" (Prettejohn 110). Observing *The Shadow of Death*, Gerard Manley Hopkins complained about the physiognomy of Christ, the drapery around him, the lighting, Hunt's use of color, and the excessive attention to realism that make the painting unnatural: "Also thin unmuscular but most realistic anatomy of arm and leg. Also type of figure not very pleasing—seems smaller from the waist down, head overlarge, and the feet not inscaped but with a scapeless look. . . . Face beautiful, sweet and human but not quite pleasing. . . . Shavings and all the texture too tufty and wooly. . . . The saws and other tools seemed over-blue. No inscape of composition whatever—not known and if it had been known it could scarcely bear up against such realism" (248).[40] Hopkins's close friend and physician, the Poet Laureate Robert Bridges, caught the spirit of Dickens's criticism and joined in the censure. He had seen some of Burne-Jones's pieces on exhibition, and felt that "the more one looks the less one admires." Remarking specifically on *The Angels of Creation—Sixth Day*, Bridges writes: "I never saw such badly drawn feet any where, his angels in the Creation have both gout and rickets. . . . Insanity is not as great an enemy to art as affectation and ill conceived mannerism" (236–37). But by then Pre-Raphaelite art had become the standard; "The avant-garde had modified the Academy" (Sussman 27). "Our position is greatly altered," Michael Rossetti observed in January 1853. "We have emerged from reckless abuse to a position of general and high recognition" (*P.R.B. Journal* 97). Attributing this new appreciation to Ruskin, David Masson notices that Pre-Raphaelitism was making inroads among artist themselves, artists "of high note and settled reputation" who show "more or less distinctly a touch of Pre-Raphaelite influence" (213). Hunt also pointed to the fact that Pre-Raphaelitism had become conventional and at peace with the literary and artistic establishment. Indeed, they had anticipated the spirit of the times, and were being patronized by mainstream Victorians, among them Tennyson, Thackeray, Gladstone, Ruskin, Browning, the Carlyles, and Thomas Combe.[41]

Dickens would not have known *The Shadow of Death*, which Hunt commenced in 1870, the year Dickens died, and exhibited in 1873. But Dickens and Hunt got to know each other well. Dickens offered Hunt extremely useful advice on *The Finding of the Savior in the Temple*, and *David Copperfield* inspired Hunt's *The Awakening Conscience*. Hunt also had become an extension of the Dickens family, joining Charles Collins's wedding party when he

married Dickens's younger daughter Kate in the summer of 1860. Dickens
would have been intrigued by Hunt's use of shadow, important as the concept
was to *Pictures* and coincident with the history of *Household Words*. One of
the magazine's names Dickens experimented with before settling on *Household Words* is *The Shadow*, an epistemic and philosophical concept, an impersonating, shaping spirit, "a kind of semi-omniscient, omnipresent, intangible
creature" (Forster 2: 79). *The Shadow* also applies to a geometrical theory
concerning light and optics, the ghostlike optical image, which, following
Newton, might be called *spectrum*.[42] To the Pre-Raphaelites, the shadow
concerned vision and perception, not "areas of reduced visibility or obscurity," as Prettejohn observes, but "the underlying principle . . . striving for
maximum visibility" (163). The word's pre-figuration, figuration, and multiple figuration ("mere," "shadow," and "water") that so intrigued Dickens
is precisely what Hunt intended. Hunt's shadow, no "mere" thing, is meant
not to mar but to make clear.[43]

Shadows in *Pictures from Italy* also pertain to dreams, and in particular
Dickens's "curious" Marian dream at Peschiere. A primer on dreams, *Pictures* opens with an allusion to Shakespeare's *Midsummer Night's Dream*
and later refers to "a dream within a dream" (385), the plot structure of
MND. But whereas *MND* contains a play within a play, *Pictures* includes a
dream within a dream. One entire chapter, "An Italian Dream," is devoted
to dreams, and Kubla Khan's "luxurious wonder of so rare a dream" is
recalled (335). Dickens's magic lantern, "A Rapid Diorama," concerns the
emerging science of photography, perception, the eye, and play of the imagination, all operating in that nebulous space between falling asleep and waking,
"in a sort of dream, and yet with the delightful sense of having awakened
from it" (279). Almost the same language describes Italy's streets and
churches, "so lovely, and yet so dead: so noisy, and yet so quiet: so obtrusive,
and yet so shy and lowering: so wide awake, and yet so fast asleep. . . . A
bewildering phantasmagoric, with all the inconsistency of a dream, and all
the pain and all the pleasure of an extravagant reality!" (293). To Dickens,
dreams, which call up events that occurred years earlier, only allegorically
relate to current events. This is the case with his Mary Hogarth dream, which,
recalling the episode behind Milton's "Methought I Saw," corroborates Dickens's view that people dream the same dreams. The dream deals with art
and Catholicism even as it speaks to the psychological nature of Dickens's
relationship with Mary:

> In an indistinct place, which was quite sublime in its indistinctness, I was visited
> by a Spirit. I could not make out the face, nor do I recollect that I desired to
> do so. It wore a blue drapery, as the Madonna might in a picture by Raphael;
> and bore no resemblance to any one I have known except in stature. I think
> (but I am not sure) that I recognized the voice. Anyway, I knew it was poor

Mary's spirit. I was not at all afraid, but in a great delight, so that I wept very much, and stretching out my arms to it called it "Dear." At this, I thought it recoiled; and I felt immediately, that not being of my gross nature, I ought not to have addressed it so familiarly. "Forgive me!" I said. "We poor living creatures are not able to express ourselves by looks and words. I have used the word most natural to *our* affections; and you know my heart." It was so full of compassion and sorrow for me—which I knew spiritually, for, as I have said, I didn't perceive its emotions by its face—that it cut me to the heart; and I said, sobbing, "Oh! give me some token that you have really visited me!"

(*Letters* 4: 196)

The apparition asks Dickens to make a wish. Not wanting to forfeit the vision, Dickens gives what he thinks is a selfless wish—the distress of Mary Hogarth (long dead) and his desire to have her released. The angel accedes to the request. Dickens poses a second question: "What is the True religion?" to which the apparition provides no answer. Fearing once more that he might lose contact with the ghost, Dickens offers this rejoinder:

"You think, as I do, that the Form of religion does not so greatly matter, if we try to do good?—or," I said, observing that it still hesitated, and was moved with the greatest compassion for me, "perhaps the Roman Catholic is the best? perhaps it makes one think of God oftener, and believe in him more steadily?" "For *you*," said the Spirit, full of such heavenly tenderness for me, that I felt as if in my heart would break; "for *you*, it is the best!" Then I awoke, with the tears running down my face, and myself in exactly the condition of the dream.   (*Letters* 4: 196–97)

Advancing his own dream interpretation, Dickens believes that the trigger was either his recent letter to Forster regarding the tragedy in his wife's family and the way it affected Dickens (the loss of Mary Hogarth in 1837, followed four years later by the death of her younger brother), or else the room in which he was staying. The room was used by a family to hold Mass, and before going to bed Dickens had been concentrating on a mark on the wall where a religious picture once hung. This caused him to wonder within himself "what the subject might have been, and what the face was like" (*Letters* 4: 196). He offers a third explanation for the dream. Before dropping off to sleep, he had been listening intently to the convent bells, which brought to mind Roman Catholic services.[44] Dickens interprets the dream in light of what Freud would later call wish-fulfillment—"the case of that wish being fulfilled by any agency in which I had no hand" (*Letters* 4: 197). Mindful of Keats (though in Keats's nightingale poem the church bells summoned him out of his dreamlike state back into reality), Dickens muses on whether it was a vision or a waking dream: "I wonder whether I should regard it as a dream, or an actual Vision" (*Letters* 4: 197). Dickens's Italian experience bears all of the qualities of a dream, with its retrospective ability to call up, albeit fragmentarily, deeply buried events, to create a kind of nebulous, shadowy state, to evoke awe and wonder amid great contradictions, and to reveal, mostly through similes and metaphors, things familiar and yet strange.

In Italy, Dickens developed his theory of art later worked out in *Pictures*. He valued art that used nature to illuminate a sublime idea and ideal. But he dismissed any aesthetic principle that attempted to perfect nature, making it an end in itself. The truth of nature, Dickens believes, resides in a certain transcendental quality. Returning to England and witnessing in Pre-Raphaelitism the art he had seen and abhorred, Dickens launched a savage attack, which included criticism of a Christology that questioned Christ's divinity. Dickens came away from Italy with the clear sense that his Italian experience would improve on reflection. And while it looked "as if the sun would never rise again, but looked its last, that night, upon a ruined world," the land and its people "may be, one day, raised up from these ashes" (*Pictures* 397, 433). Italy models the ravages of time. A dystopia, paralyzed and moribund, the country had reached apocalyptic closure, "the sunset of mankind" (Wells 31), "the extreme limit, the imminence of the *last*" (Derrida 20), the "end of the *Odyssey*, amidst the corpses" (Serres 252):

> What a sad place Italy is! a country gone to sleep, and without a prospect of waking again! I never shall forget, as long as I live, my first impression of it, as I drove through the streets of Genoa, after contemplating the splendid View of the town, for a full hour, through a telescope, from the deck of the steamboat. I thought that of all the mouldy, dreary, sleepy, dirty, lagging, halting, God-forgotten towns in the wide world, it surely must be the very uttermost superlative. It seemed as if one had reached the end of all things—as if there were no more progress, motion, advancement, or improvement of any kind beyond; but here the whole scheme had stopped centuries ago, never more to move on any more, but just lying down in the sun to bask there, 'till the Day of Judgment.
> (*Letters* 4: 169)

Dickens's departure held much regret, expressing a preference for Italy's preternatural dirt over Switzerland's paradisial cleanliness. The expression, "so many jewels set in dirt," captures Italy's "landscape of surpassing beauty steeped in the richest light" (*Pictures* 432) as well as its contrasting dirt and disrepair: "the beautiful Italian manners, the sweet language, and the quick recognition of a pleasant look or cheerful word. . . . Remembering them, I sigh for the dirt again: the brick floors, bare walls, unplaistered ceilings, and broken windows" (*Letters* 4: 322).

Dickens's obsession with dirt/dust contributed to his seeing much of it in Italy—"dust, dust, dust, everywhere" (*Pictures* 281). Italy's preternatural reality was too foreboding, too uncivil, for bourgeois Englishmen, its underbelly too visible, disclosing far too much of "the pain and pleasure of an extravagant reality" (*Pictures* 293). And the discussion, not merely about dirty Italy, was as much about Roman Catholicism and Catholic art, and how all of these coalesce in Pre-Raphaelite art. Dickens, like other Victorians, was obsessed with dirt/dust, and this occasioned *Our Mutual Friend* (1864–65), his novel on dirt.[45] The subject was the focus of a famous poem in *Household Words*, "King Dirt," subtitled "*A Song Adapted to a Slow Sanitary Movement.*" The poem points satirically to how central if revered dirt had become in the everyday lives of Victorians, celebrated for its power to wipe out whole populations of the poor, who "Drink from the dark and mantling pool." Several essays in *Household Words*, especially the ones by John Capper, deal with the way dirt/dust/waste might be recycled. Capper's "Important Rubbish" reflected on how things "thought worthless" can be reclaimed "to yield products the most valuable, results the most beautiful," how "hitherto refuse matter may be converted into really useful and valuable materials for the builder, the architect, and the decorator," and "how by a simple method, we may convert [an] ugly, useless clinker into a beautiful means of ornamentation" (377–78).[46] Dickens knew, as Henry Morley and W. H. Willis would point out in their essay on "Photography," that "dirt is a dear artifice" (55). Dickens was perhaps also mindful that "Heat is the great first agency employed by nature and by the philosopher in the decomposition and re-combination which produce some of the most beautiful and useful products" (Capper, "Rubbish" 377). When he talks of Italy as "many jewels set in dirt," Dickens is clearly alluding to how precious stones trapped in dirt are separated out, set apart, and assayed.

Italy remains, then, a land of dirt but also a jewel and wonder, where its people and their habits are all the more resplendent because they stand in seeming contrast to the land: "Give me the smiling face of the attendant, man or woman; the courteous manner; the amiable desire to please and to be pleased; the lighthearted, pleasant, simple air—so many jewels set in dirt—and I am there again to-morrow!" (*Pictures* 326). Italy is a land of great contrasts, its history marked by "siege, and war and might," along with "the triumphant growth of peaceful Arts and Sciences" (*Pictures* 432). Reflecting on his time in Italy, Dickens characterized the experience as "short of the miraculous," and resorted again to the image of the shadow, "the Shadow of the Bad Shadow" which passed for an instant, "escaping observation." He left Italy with an immense sense of loss and a heavy heart: "I can't forget Rome—and Albano—and Florence—and Perugia—and the walks uphill . . . and the queer Inns—and our happy company. I can't forget anything connected with it. I live in the Past now, in sober sadness" (*Letters* 4: 324–25). Wanting to represent art too naturally, to undertake what Hunt describes as "a stricter study of Nature" (1: 147), artists, Dickens felt, violated nature, "overstep[ping]" its "modesty" and presenting "no likeness to truth whatever" (Perugini II: 164). Dickens loved art, but had an even "greater love of nature," which he felt individual artists in their search for a particular kind of truth ironically violated (Perugini I: 130). Missing in Pre-Raphaelite art but present everywhere in Raphael was a kind of transcendental view of art, the "power of etherealizing, and exalting to the very Heavens, what was most sublime and lovely in the expression of the human face divine . . . raising it up again to their pure spiritual condition" ("Old Lamps" 265).

NOTES

1. Clapp-Itnyre maintains that despite its critical neglect, "music plays an *integral* part in the period's fiction." Victorian writers "embraced music so thoroughly in their novels" that any study of the literature is "incomplete without an examination of this 'other' aesthetic" (xv).

2. Early reviews of the Pre-Raphaelites treating them as avant-garde did not appear until it was known what the P.R.B. signature meant, Herbert Sussman finds. "Rather than bursting into and shattering the ranks of the art world like a true avant-garde, the Brotherhood, at least in this first exhibited painting [Rossetti's *The Girlhood of Mary Virgin*], was accorded its place in the formation." The avant-garde is something the Pre-Raphaelites brought upon themselves, "to see the works as an art of opposition" (Sussman 22–23). No other work so represented that departure as Millais's *Christ in the House of His Parents*, which, according to Michael Rossetti, ignited "a crusade against the P.R.B. The mystic letters with their signification have appeared in all kinds of papers. . . . But the designation is now so notorious that all concealment is at an end" (*P.R.B. Journal* 70).

3. The way members were selected, along with the formal rules, objectives, and protocols, made the P.R.B. appear more like an apostleship than a brotherhood or discipleship.

4. For example, Dickens remarked on 18 March 1845, "All this kind of High Art is out of my reach" (*Letters* 4: 283).

5. Kate Perugini ignores Henry Gowan in *Little Dorrit*. She believes that Dickens's aesthetic views did not develop until "he was able to travel and see for himself the pictures and statues of which he had only heard," and that his early art criticism, "written from a purely literary standpoint," gave way to a more refined and particular artistic vocabulary (I: 129, 130). His first journey to Italy, as Leonée Ormond also observes, "was the only time in his life when Dickens looked seriously at paintings for any substantial period of time, and, for this reason, it forms a water-shed in the history of his tastes" ("Old Masters" 133). Ordinarily hesitant to pontificate on art, Dickens loses all reticence in *Pictures*, "where he speaks very frankly on his likes and dislikes" (Perugini I: 129).

6. There is yet another Millais connection to *The Mystery of Edwin Drood*. Twelve of the fourteen illustrations were done by the young (26-year-old), aspiring artist/

illustrator and former Royal Academy student Luke Fildes (Charles Collins did the first two), who was introduced to Dickens by Millais, an admirer of Fildes's work. "I see Millais running to Charles Dickens," writes Vincent van Gogh, himself a Dickens admirer (qtd. in Cohen 221). It is believed that Fildes's watercolor of Dickens's office following the author's death, entitled *The Empty Chair*, influenced van Gogh's *Gauguin's Chair* (1888; see Cohen 226–28). Millais knew that Dickens would be "impressed with Fildes's moving scene," which Dickens himself "loved to depict in words" (Cohen 221). In a letter of 14 January 1870, Dickens acknowledges that the decision to hire Fildes was based on "the very earnest representations of Millais (and after having seen a great number of his drawings)" (*Letters* 12: 466). Kate Perugini recalled Fildes as having a "frank ingenious nature that has always endeared him to his friends. He had also a keen sense of humour, and my father found him so sympathetic that he looked forward with pleasure to his help" (II: 168–69). The Pre-Raphaelites' subjects were drawn largely from Dante, Shakespeare (their annual meeting was held on Shakespeare's supposed birthday, 23 April), Tennyson, Keats, and, to a lesser extent, Browning and Patmore.

7. Studies by Kate Perugini, Alastair Grieve, and Leonée Ormond merely chart the beginnings of any examination of Dickens and art. Ormond attributes Dickens's taste in art primarily to the friendship he forged with Sir David Wilkie in the late 1830s. Dickens's eulogy of Wilkie, however, is not the stuff of art criticism, but the description of an outlook on life and of an aesthetic credo similar to his own—the belief that art should possess dignity and beauty as it elevates the common and the commonplace. For treatments of Dickens's attitude to religion, and to Christianity in particular, see Cole, Larson, Zemka, and Walder.

8. For more on *Life of Our Lord* and its attempt to explore issues about the treatment of women and children, see Zemka.

9. Dickens's simple Christianity is perhaps best reflected in letters to his children, especially his 26? September 1868 letter to Plorn (Edward): "You will therefore understand the better that I now most solemnly impress upon you the truth and beauty of the Christian religion, as it came from Christ Himself, and the impossibility of your going far wrong if you humbly but heartily respect it" (*Letters* 12: 187–88). His 15 October 1868 letter to young Henry (Harry) reads similarly: "But I most strongly and affectionately impress upon you the priceless value of the New Testament, and the study of that book as the one unfailing guide in Life. Deeply respecting it, and bowing down before Our Saviour, as separated from the vain constructions and inventions of men, you cannot go very wrong and will always preserve at heart a true spirit of veneration and humility" (*Letters* 12: 201–02). These letters comment on the *Life of Our Lord.*

10. Dickens's *Life* added to this long list of nineteenth-century interpretations of the life of Christ. Dickens had much to say about *Essays and Reviews* (1860), the controversial series of tracts challenging biblical literalism. While he clearly took the side of those biblical literalists who opposed too strict an interpretation of revelation and literalism, Dickens accepted what he calls "timely suggestions" and a "very wise and necessary position" (*Letters* 10: 253). He cautioned, however, about the need for reverence in all of this, and complained in *Life* about

the "unspeakable dread and horror [of] these unseemly 'squabbles about the letter' " (5). For more on Dickens's response to *Essays and Reviews*, see *Letters* 9: 389, and for a treatment of *Essays and Reviews*, see Nixon, "Kill[ing] our Souls," and Altholz.

11. It is generally believed that Dickens's vitriolic response to the Millais painting had to do with the Victorians' attraction to theories of physiognomy, the belief that outward physical beauty was the manifestation of an inward spiritual beauty, "that facial configuration and expression revealed inner character.... [I]gnoring the dictates of physiognomy further compounded Millais's supposed sins.... [T]he facial and bodily configuration of Millais's Holy Family would not only indicate a lack of nobility but would indicate kinship with the working class.... Millais's picture not only outraged religious, political, and scientific beliefs, it also crossed class lines.... He, in effect, made the Holy Family look like a working-class family" (Roberts 152).

12. According to Hunt, Raphael was used "to mark the boundary line of progressive and decadent art; Pre-Machiavellian, Pre-Dantean, or Pre-Aretinesque would have been more appropriate names" (2: 437). Pre-Aretinesque is named after Pietro Aretino (1492–1556), Raphael's pupil and friend of Titian, whose portrait of Aretino is part of the Frick Collection.

13. According to Hunt, their objective was not to be "enslaved" by the existing traditions in art, "but in the fields of Nature and under the sky of Heaven frankly to picture her healthful beauty and strength.... Pre-Raphaelitism in its purity was the frank worship of Nature, kept in check by selection and directed by the spirit of imaginative purpose" (2: 452). For more on this and the Pre-Raphaelites working in what T. S. Eliot, in an essay in *The Sacred Wood* (1922), called "Tradition and the Individual Talent," see Hunt 2: 460.

14. According to Codell, "PRB naturalism was not only empirical, but also symbolic, and it implied a redirector of the epistemology and function of painting" ("Expression" 256).

15. Queen Victoria, it is said, asked to have the exhibition brought to her from the walls of the Royal Academy so that she could view it herself (*P.R.B. Journal* 71).

16. Carlyle had a somewhat similar reaction to Holman Hunt's *The Light of the World*, describing Hunt's Christ figure as "a puir, weak, girl-faced nonentity, bedecked in a fine silken sort of gown." He would rather have seen a man "toiling along in the hot sun . . . tired, hungry often and footsore.... His rough and patched clothes bedraggled and covered with dust" (qtd. in Hunt 1: 358).

17. William Michael Rossetti describes the painting this way: "Christ, having pricked his hand with a nail (in symbol of the nailing to the cross) is being anxiously examined by Joseph, who is pulling his hand backwards, while he, unheeding this, kisses the Virgin with his arm round her neck" (*P.R.B. Journal* 21).

18. The painting, however, drew much praise. The *Athenaeum*, for one, felt that the work displayed "much of that sacred mysticism inseparable from the works of the early masters and much of the tone of the poets of the same time" (qtd. in Prettejohn 46). The American response was equally laudable; see Susan P. Casteras (22–24). Dickens would have been equally appalled by Dante Gabriel Rossetti's *Ecce Ancilla Domini!* ("Behold, the handmaid of the Lord" [1850]).

The "golden glories" that ring Mary, Gabriel, and the dove would have received an equally pejorative "mildewed Glory" (*Letters* 4: 160).

19. The *P.R.B. Journal* is one account of the Brotherhood but, according to Holman Hunt, not an authorized account. William Michael Rossetti was made secretary to the Brotherhood, and so took it upon himself to narrate their history. Not wanting Michael's *P.R.B. Journal* to pass as "unquestioned history" (2: 434), Hunt's two-volume "History," *Pre-Raphaelitism and the Pre-Raphaelite Brotherhood*, seeks to emend Michael's account and to set the history of the group in another different context. Hunt finds his self-declared "more complete scrutiny of the course they pursued" entirely "necessary" (2: 421). He also wanted to correct Michaels's well-circulated claim that Dante Gabriel Rossetti was their leader. Hunt believed that the society was actually formed by Ford Madox Brown and that Hunt himself played an early role.

20. Dickens's hostility to Anglo-Catholicism is well documented. In an 11 November 1847 letter to Mrs. Sydney Smith, Dickens thanked her for the copy of her husband's *Sermons Preached at St. Paul's* (1846). Addressing the Sermon on Toleration, Dickens used such words as "the true Christian spirit shining," "enchanted," and "celestial light," language representing his otherwordly views of Christianity. He soon came to his distaste for Anglo-Catholicism. "There is," he writes, "not a word in the true and vigorous description of that preposterous abuse, Puseyism, that does not find an echo in my heart. I would that the church could better afford to lose such a servant, and the World such a Teacher, as the writer of this book. I cannot tell you how much I thank you for it" (*Letters* 5: 194). To spite his friend James White, whom Dickens urged to visit, and who was publicly averse to Anglo-Catholicism, Dickens vowed to "go over to Puseyism" (*Letters* 6: 30).

21. Millais's *The Annunciation* would also have appeared to Dickens as a work much inferior to Titian's *Assumption of the Virgin*.

22. One caricature engraving depicted a china dog being sniffed by a real dog, with Millais's picture in the background (*P.R.B. Journal* 87). In his 13 May 1851 *Times* review, Ruskin historicizes the movement predating Raphael as a return to realism "irrespective of any conventional rules of picture-making; and they have chosen their unfortunate though not inaccurate name because all artists did this before Raphael's time, and after Raphael's time did *not* this, but sought to paint fair pictures rather than represent stern facts" (9). The P.R.B. certainly saw the Ruskin review as favorable to their cause. It was encouraged by Patmore, a close friend of the Brotherhood. Ruskin had penned another favorable letter to *The Times*, but withheld it because, in Michael Rossetti's opinion, "it casts so strong a slur on all non-P.R.B. living painters" (*P.R.B. Journal* 96). Theirs was a "fondness for detail, and careful finish of the most minute objects," according to David Masson (204), who also saw the movement predating Raphael occupied by painters "faithfully copying what they found in Nature, and arriving at beauty and impressiveness through their implicit regard for truth" (201). According to Hunt, their "reform" encourages "allegiance to Nature, and to magnifying her teachings for further inspiration." It was never their attempt to refuse "admiration to Raphael" nor to his "elder contemporaries, Michael Angelo and Leonardo da

Vinci,'' nor did they "refuse whatever vital teaching there was in any ancient master or school'' (2: 491). Dickens's *Household Words* critique (1850), Masson's review in the *British Quarterly* (1852), and Ruskin's *Times* letter (1854) are seminal assessments of what Millais and the Pre-Raphaelites were attempting.

23. Dickens historically associated St. Giles's with disease and filth, which he found everywhere in Italy and its "infinite variety of deformed shapes'' (*Pictures* 295). In his early impressions of Genoa, he was struck by "The wonderful novelty of everything, the unusual smells, the unaccountable filth . . . the disorderly jumbling of dirty houses, one more close than any in St. Giles's or old Paris'' (283). He also saw St. Giles's in Naples: "It is not well to find Saint Giles's so repulsive, and the Porta Capuana so attractive.'' The rest of the comment is a fascinating comment on art's ability to capture the human condition (413).

24. For contemporary reviews of the work's reception, along with Dickens's censure, see Hunt 1: 204–20.

25. "When we agreed to use the letters P.R.B. as our insignia,'' Hunt writes, "we made each member solemnly promise to keep its meaning strictly secret, foreseeing the danger of offending the reigning powers of the time'' (1: 141).

26. On how the painting was received by critics, especially Catholic critics, see Roberts 153–54.

27. "The religious sentiment and symbolism of their first works owed much to the High Church Revival—the Oxford Movement. . . . Some of the Pre-Raphaelites' earliest and most important patrons lived in Oxford. . . . It was in the Oxford Union that their most important attempt at mural painting was made. Burne-Jones and Morris discovered Rossetti's art when they were undergraduates at Exeter College and the Aesthetic movement into which one strand of Pre-Raphaelitism developed, originated in Oxford'' (Whiteley 9; see also 24–25). See also Christian.

28. It is perhaps no irony that Dante Gabriel Rossetti's London studio was No. 72 Newman Street, where he painted *Ecce*. Ford Madox Brown also had his studio on Newman Street. It was also in that neighborhood that Hunt painted *The Light of the World*.

29. For more on this, see Prettejohn 243–45 and Roberts 155. According to Alastair Grieve, "Several of Millais's works, all post-dating *The Girlhood of Mary Virgin* [1849], can be related to contemporary High Church controversies.'' Speaking of the John the Baptist figure in *Christ in the House of His Parents*, Grieve suggests that the water John carries with the "intention of washing the wound of Christ can be related to the Tractarian emphasis on child baptism and regeneration through baptism.'' Grieve also observes other Tractarian connections in the painting, along with the Pre-Raphaelites' ties to Newman (294). On Dickens and the Pre-Raphaelites, see Sucksmith (159–63). That Keble College, Oxford, would be the recipient of Hunt's *The Light of the World* (1851) is yet another example of the subtle though generally unacknowledged ties between the Tractarians and the Pre-Raphaelites. (For the controversy surrounding the painting's location at Keble College, see Hunt 2: 410–16; see also notes on the "Transcription of Records Re Mrs Combe's Gifts and Bequests: Minutes of meetings of the Warden and Council of Keble College'' [Keble College Archives, shelf 35]). It is generally

believed that the painting was inspired by *David Copperfield*, and in turn inspired, Hunt tells us, Edwin Arnold's long poem, "The Light of the World" (1891; Hunt 2: 380).

30. Dickens, for example, subtly connected the two experiences (American and Italian) in a 9 May 1845 letter to Lady Blessington: "As to Vesuvius, it burns away, in my thoughts, besides the roaring waters of Niagara; and not a splash of the water extinguishes a spark of the fire; but there they go on rumbling and flaming, night and day, each in its fullest glory" (*Letters* 4: 303). The same association between Vesuvius and Niagara Falls is made in *Pictures*: "the region of Fire—an exhausted crater formed of great masses of gigantic cinders, like blocks of stone from some tremendous waterfall, burnt up" (420).

31. Linda Rozmovits, in her otherwise fine study of Shakespeare and the Victorians, ignores Dickens's seminal engagement of Shakespeare, even though her focus, admittedly, is late-Victorian literature. For Dickens's use of Shakespeare, see Arac, Hochberg, Poole, Smith, and Sawyer. The best and most thorough study of the influence is by Valerie Gager, who points out that "Dickens assimilated Shakespeare's plays and poems for his own creative purposes" (2). Gager believes that Shakespeare appears more frequently in Dickens than in any other Victorian: "The protean nature of allusion not only contributes to the levels of meaning to be found in Dickens's works but extends to all aspects of his writing including theme, plot, imagery, tone, foreshadowing, atmosphere, structure, and characterization" (145).

32. Dickens's classic parody of travel, *The Pickwick Papers* pokes fun at Victorian narratives of travel and the making of the scientific gentleman. This literature occasioned the adoption and possession of journals. In their introduction to Dickens's *Uncommercial Traveller*, Michael Slater and John Drew believe that *Uncommercial Traveller* "owes much to a great tradition in British essay-writing and travel-writing" (xv). Cotsell defines travel literature as "an account of a journey to somewhere less familiar and thus provides a strong sense of encountering unfamiliar facts. . . . Travel also presupposes some intention, some point of arrival or destination, and intentions can best be compared in terms of the intensity of the investment in arrival at a destination" (7).

33. On 9 March 1845, Dickens wrote to Forster: "None of the books [about Italy] are unaffected and true but Simond's, which charms me more and more by its boldness. . . . His notices of the leading pictures enchant me. They are so perfectly just and faithful." But while Dickens also admired Murray, he was less complimentary, perhaps because Murray catered too slavishly to popular tastes: "The Holy Week is in full force at this time; and hundreds of English people with hundreds of Murray's Guide Books and a corresponding number of Mrs. Starkes' [Mariana Starke, *Travels on the Continent* (1820), later *Travels in Europe* (1833)] in their hands are chattering in all the silent places" (*Letters* 4: 276, 282).

34. The only Roman Catholic divine Dickens singles out for admiration is Saint Carlo Borromeo, whose religion expressed itself in social reform: "A charitable doctor to the sick, a munificent friend to the poor, and this, not in any spirit of blind bigotry, but as the bold opponent of enormous abuses in the Romish church" (345).

35. This satire continued in the short story in *Uncommercial Traveller* on Italian art, "To Be Read at Dusk" (1852): "Then we looked round at all the pictures. . . . The Madonna and Bambino, San Francisco . . . Friars . . . Apostles, Doges, all my old acquaintances many times repeated" (628). I owe this to Ormond.

36. The cock in the painting is a familiar trope or symbol in Pre-Raphaelite art. In Dante Gabriel Rossetti's *The Girlhood of Mary*, a dove, ringed by a halo of fire, the so-called "golden glories," is perched on a branch outside. The dove returns in *Ecce Ancilla Domini!* though this time perched on a pedestal in the room. A similar dove is perched on a ladder in Millais's *Christ in the House of His Parents*, and two turtle-doves appear in Herbert's *The Youth of Our Lord*.

37. "What the Pre-Raphaelites asserted was, that all painters universally should cultivate the habit and possess the faculty of painting things with literal truth" (Masson 202).

38. Any "occult meaning in the details of my design," writes Hunt, "was not based upon ecclesiastical or archaic symbolism, but derived from obvious reflectiveness. My types were of natural figures . . . to express transcendental ideas. . . . The closed door was the obstinately shut mind, the weeds the cumber of daily neglect, the accumulated hindrances of sloth; the orchard the garden of delectable fruit for the dainty feast of the soul. The music of the still small voice was the summons to the sluggard to awaken and become zealous labourers under the Divine Master; the bat flitting about only in the darkness was a natural symbol of ignorance; the kingly and priestly dress of Christ, the sign of His reign over the body and the soul, to them who could give their allegiance to Him and acknowledge God's overrule. In making a night's scene, lit mainly by the lantern carried by Christ, I had followed metaphorical explanation in the Psalms, 'Thy word is a lamp unto my feet, and a light unto my path,' with also the accordant allusions by St. Paul to the sleeping soul, 'The night is far spent, the day is at hand.' The symbolism was designed to elucidate, not to mystify, truth" (1: 350–52).

39. Hunt shows how any number of Victorians, such as Carlyle, Thackeray, Ruskin, and followers of the extreme High Church and the liberal Broad Church used *The Light of the World* to debate the issue of a historical Christ (see 2: 409–10).

40. The wood shavings on the floor of both the Millais and Hunt paintings were clearly part of the works' appeal. In fact, when Hunt painted *The Shadow of Death*, curious observers wanted to touch the painting, especially the shavings, just to see if they were real.

41. Hunt believed that "had not the hue and cry against Pre-Raphaelitism been so blindly savage and general, such tardy patronage would not have been extended to our works" (2: 418).

42. For more on this, see Nixon, "[L]ost" 297.

43. Hunt's *The Light of the World* (1851) is yet another example of the Pre-Raphaelites' concern with illumination, vision, and perception. And so too *Pictures*, where vision, or seeing (sensory overload), is connected to the travel narrative on spectator culture and the traveler as voyeur. Millais was also concerned with this issue of vision, evident in at least two paintings he did on the subject—*The Blind Man* (1853) and *The Blind Girl* (1854–56).

44. This explanation is connected to another one of Dickens's Mary Hogarth dreams and the exchanges on dreams he had with Dr. Thomas Stone, whose essay on "Dreams" was making its way through *Household Words*: "Then, I was living in Italy, and it was All Souls' Night, and people were going about with Bells, calling on the Inhabitants to pray for the dead. —Which I have no doubt I had some sense of, in my sleep; and so flew back to the Dead" (*Letters* 6: 276–79). Stone's account incorporates many of Dickens's views on dreams, including his Italian dream and his Mary Hogarth recollection (Stone, "Dreams" 567–68). See also Stone's "Sleep" and "Somnambulism." The best discussions of Dickens and dreams is Catherine A. Bernard's "Dickens and Victorian Dream Theory" and Warrington Winters's "Dickens and the Psychology of Dreams." Regrettably, Winters overlooks Dickens's helpful accounts of dreams in *Pictures*, which, unlike the fiction, contains Dickens's own dream accounts and his attempts to make sense of them. Winters's idea that later in life Dickens would begin to use dreams as plots (1001–04) actually begins here in *Pictures*, with its own "dream within a dream" plot. Bernard is, of course, right when she claims that Dickens's many ideas on dreams "find much fuller expression in his novels." As she also notes, Dickens was unusual in this regard, for "dreams were not the standard ingredient of the Victorian novel" (206). Catherine Earnshaw's dream in *Wuthering Heights* seems the only other occasion where a dream features centrally to the novel's plot structure. But this too may be part of what Bernard sees as the Gothic plot and therefore not an exception. See also William G. Wall's "Mrs. Affery Flintwinch's Dreams: Reading and Remembering in *Little Dorrit*." In the novel, one is left to question the too-real dreams of Mrs. Flintwinch's, whether they are in fact dreams or that she simply calls things dreams that are not.
45. For a fascinating and informative study of dust in the nineteenth century, see Kate Flint (40–63).
46. See also Capper's "Waste." For studies on this reclamation of waste, what Capper calls "valuable rubbish" and how to make "rubbish a beautiful and useful adjunct to the arts" ("Rubbish" 378), see Metz and Steig.

WORKS CITED

Altholz, Josef L. *Anatomy of a Controversy: The Debate over "Essays Reviews 1860–1864."* Aldershot, England: Scolar Press, 1994.

Arac, Jonathan. "*Hamlet, Little Dorrit*, and the History of Character." *South Atlantic Quarterly* 87 (1988): 311–28.

Arnold, Matthew. *Culture and Anarchy.* Ed. R. H. Super. Ann Arbor: U of Mich. P, 1965.

Bernard, Catherine A. "Dickens and Victorian Dream Theory." *Victorian Science and Victorian Values: Literary Perspectives.* Eds. James Paradis and Thomas Postlewait. New York: New York Academy of Sciences, 1981. 197–216.

Bridges, Robert. *The Selected Letters of Robert Bridges*. Ed. Donald E. Stanford. Vol. 1. Newark: U of Delaware P, 1983.

Bullen, J. B. *The Pre-Raphaelite Body: Fear and Desire in Painting, Poetry, and Criticism*. Oxford: Clarendon, 1998.

Capper, John. "Important Rubbish." *Household Words*, 19 May 1855, 376–79.

———. "Waste." *Household Words*, 10 June 1854, 390–93.

Casteras, Susan P. *English Pre-Raphaelitism and Its Reception in America in the Nineteenth Century*. Rutherford, NJ: Fairleigh Dickinson UP, 1990.

Christian, John. *The Pre-Raphaelites in Oxford*. Oxford: Ashmolean, 1974.

Clapp-Itnyre, Alisa. *Angelic Airs, Subversive Songs: Music as Social Discourse in the Victorian Novel*. Athens: Ohio UP, 2002.

Codell, Julie F. "Empiricism, Naturalism and Science in Millais's Paintings." *John Everett Millais, Beyond the Pre-Raphaelite Brotherhood*. Ed. Debra N. Mancoff. Studies in British Art 7. New Haven: Yale UP, 2001. 119–47.

———. "Expression over Beauty: Facial Expression, Body Language, and Circumstantiality in the Paintings of the Pre-Raphaelite Brotherhood." *Victorian Studies* 29 (1986): 255–90.

Cohen, Jane R. *Charles Dickens and His Original Illustrators*. Columbus: Ohio State UP, 1980.

Cole, Natalie Bell. " 'Amen in a Wrong Place': Charles Dickens Imagines the Victorian Church." *Victorian Religious Discourse: New Directions in Criticism*. Ed. Jude V. Nixon. New York: Palgrave, 2004. 205–34.

Cotsell, Michael. "*The Pickwick Papers* and Travel: A Critical Diversion." *Dickens Quarterly* 3.1 (1986): 5–17.

Derrida, Jacques. "Of an Apocalyptic Tone Recently Adopted in Philosophy." *Oxford Literary Review* 6.2 (1984): 3–37.

Dickens, Charles. *American Notes and Pictures from Italy*. Oxford Illustrated Dickens. London: Oxford UP, 1957. Rpt. 1970.

———. *The Letters of Charles Dickens*. Eds. Graham Storey, Kathleen Tillotson, and Nina Burgis. 12 vols. Oxford: Clarendon, 1988.

———. *The Life of Our Lord*. New York: Simon and Schuster, 1934.

———. *Little Dorrit*. Oxford Illustrated Dickens. Vol. 12. New York: Oxford UP, 1953.

———. *The Mystery of Edwin Drood*. Oxford Illustrated Dickens. London: Oxford UP, 1956. Rpt. 1959.

———. "Old Lamps for New Ones." *Household Words*, 15 June 1850, 265–67.

———. "To Be Read at Dusk." *The Uncommercial Traveller and Reprinted Pieces.* Oxford Illustrated Dickens. London: Oxford UP, 1958. 621–34.

Fleming, G. H. *John Everett Millais: A Biography.* London: Constable, 1998.

Flint, Kate. *The Victorians and the Visual Imagination.* Cambridge: Cambridge UP, 2000.

Forster, John. *The Life of Charles Dickens.* Ed. Andrew Lang. 2 vols. London: Chapman & Hall, 1900.

Foucault, Michel. *The Archaeology of Knowledge.* New York: Pantheon, 1972.

Gager, Valerie L. *Shakespeare and Dickens: The Dynamics of Influence.* Cambridge: Cambridge UP, 1996.

Grieve, Alastair. "The Pre-Raphaelite Brotherhood and the Anglican High Church." *Burlington Magazine* 111 (1969): 294–95.

Hochberg, Shifra. "The Influence of *King Lear* on *Bleak House.*" *The Dickensian* 89.1 (1993): 45–49.

———. "Mrs. Sparsit's Corialanus Eyebrows and Dickensian Approach to Topicality." *The Dickensian* 87.1 (1991): 32–36.

Hopkins, Gerard Manley. *The Journal and Papers of Gerard Manley Hopkins.* Ed. Humphry House and Graham Storey. London: Oxford UP, 1959.

Hunt, William Holman. *Pre-Raphaelitism and the Pre-Raphaelite Brotherhood.* 2 vols. New York: Macmillan, 1905.

Johnson, Edgar. *Charles Dickens: His Tragedy and Triumph.* Vol. 1. New York: Simon and Schuster, 1952.

"King Dirt." *Household Words*, 27 March 1852, 31–32.

Larson, Janet. *Dickens and the Broken Scripture.* Athens: University of Georgia Press, 1985.

Mancoff, Debra N. "John Everett Millais: Caught Between the Myths." *John Everett Millais, Beyond the Pre-Raphaelite Brotherhood.* Ed. Debra N. Mancoff. Studies in British Art 7. New Haven: Yale UP, 2001. 3–19.

Masson, David. "Pre-Raphaelitism in Art and Literature." *British Quarterly Review* 16 (1852): 197–220.

Metz, Nancy A. "The Artistic Reclamation of Waste in *Our Mutual Friend.*" *Nineteenth-Century Fiction* 34 (1979): 59–72.

Morley, Henry, and W. H. Willis. "Photography." *Household Words*, 19 March 1853, 54–61.

Nixon, Jude V. "Kill[ing] Our Souls with Literalism: Reading *Essays and Reviews.*" *Victorian Religious Discourse: New Directions in Criticism.* New York: Palgrave, 2004. 51–81.

———. " '[L]ost in the vast worlds of wonder': Dickens and Science." *Dickens Studies Annual* 35 (2005): 267–333.

Ormond, Leonée. "Dickens and Painting: Contemporary Art." *The Dickensian* 80.1 (1984): 2–25.

———. "Dickens and Painting: The Old Masters." *The Dickensian* 79.13 (1983): 131–51.

Perugini, Kate. "Charles Dickens, As a Lover of Art and Artists.—I." *The Magazine of Art* (1903): 125–30.

———. "Charles Dickens, As a Lover of Art and Artists.—II." *The Magazine of Art* (1903): 164–69.

Phillips, Catherine. *Gerard Manley Hopkins and the Victorian Visual World.* New York: Oxford UP, 2007.

Poole, Adrian. "The Shadow of Lear's 'Houseless' in Dickens." *Shakespeare Survey* 53 (2000): 103–13.

Pratt, Mary Louise. *Imperial Eyes: Writing and Transculturation.* New York: Routledge, 1992.

The P.R.B. Journal: William Michael Rossetti's Diary of the Pre-Raphaelite Brotherhood, 1849–1853. Ed. William E. Fredeman. Oxford: Clarendon, 1975.

The Pre-Raphaelites. Trans. William P. Packer. New York: McCall, 1970.

Prettejohn, Elizabeth. *The Art of the Pre-Raphaelites.* Princeton: Princeton UP, 2000.

Roberts, Helene E. "Cardinal Wiseman, the Vatican, and the Pre-Raphaelites." *Pre-Raphaelite Art in Its European Context.* Ed. Susan P. Casteras and Alicia Craig Faxon. Madison, NJ: Fairleigh Dickinson UP, 1994. 143–59.

Rozmovits, Linda. *Shakespeare and the Politics of Culture in Late Victorian England.* Baltimore: Johns Hopkins UP, 1998.

Ruskin, John. "The Pre-Raphaelites." *The Times*, no. 20800, 13 May 1851, 8–9.

Sanders, Andrew. "Millais and Literature." *John Everett Millais, Beyond the Pre-Raphaelite Brotherhood.* Ed. Debra N. Mancoff. Studies in British Art 7. New Haven: Yale UP, 2001. 69–93.

Sawyer, Robert. *Victorian Appropriations of Shakespeare: George Eliot, A. C. Swinburne, Robert Browning, and Charles Dickens.* Madison, NJ: Fairleigh Dickinson UP, 2003.

Serres, Michel. *The Parasite*. Trans. Lawrence R. Schehr. Baltimore: Johns Hopkins UP, 1982.

Slater, Michael, and John Drew, ed. The *Uncommercial Traveller and Other Papers*, 1859–70. Columbus: Ohio State UP, 2000.

Smith, Grahame. " 'O Reason Not the Need': *King Lear, Hard Times*, and Utilitarian Values." *The Dickensian* 86.3 (1990): 164–70.

Steig, Michael. "Dickens' Excremental Vision." *Victorian Studies* 13 (1970): 339–54.

Stone, Thomas. "Dreams." *Household Words*, 8 March 1851, 566–72.

———. "Sleep." *Household Words*, 8 February 1851, 470–75.

———. "Somnambulism." *Household Words*, 3 May 1851, 132–38.

Sucksmith, Harvey Peter. "Dickens among the Pre-Raphaelites: Mr. Merdle and Holman Hunt's 'The Light of the World.' " *Dickensian* 72 (1976): 159–63.

Sussman, Herbert L. "The Language of Criticism: The Responses of Victorian Periodicals to the Pre-Raphaelite Brotherhood." *Victorian Periodicals Newsletter* 19 (1973): 21–29.

Walder, Dennis. *Dickens and Religion*. London: George Allen and Unwin, 1981.

Wall, William G. "Mrs. Affery Flintwinch's Dreams: Reading and Remembering in *Little Dorrit*." *Dickens Quarterly* 10.4 (1993): 202–06.

Wells, H. G. *The Time Machine*. 1895. Ed. Patrick Parrinder. New York: Penguin, 2005.

Whiteley, Jon. *Oxford and the Pre-Raphaelites*. Oxford: Ashmolean, 1989.

Winters, Warrington. "Dickens and the Psychology of Dreams." *PMLA* 63.3 (1948): 984–1006.

Zemka, Sue. *Victorian Testaments: The Bible, Christology, and Literary Authority in Early Nineteenth-Century British Culture*. Stanford: Stanford UP, 1997.

Charles "Carlo" Dickens In and Out of Italy in 1844: *The Chimes*

Philip V. Allingham

Residing in the Villa Bagnerello at Albaro, near Genoa, in the summer of 1844, Dickens began the not-so-grand portion of his year-long Italian Grand Tour. Despite the losses involved in prosecuting Peter Parley's Illuminated Library for pirating A Christmas Carol, *the young Dickens had regularly been called upon by his relatives—especially his father—for financial assistance. Moreover, having ground out so many full-length novels over the past eight years, Dickens must have been both exhausted and in need of emotional and artistic renewal. What he experienced is in part reflected in the prose he wrote in Italy: the novella* The Chimes *and the letters he later used as a source for the travelogue* Pictures from Italy. *These writings reflect his yearning for home and his sense of London as his defining context as a writer. As he attempted to master a new language while isolated in his lofty studies in his leased villas, separated from the Genoese by nationality, language, class, and culture, Dickens, to an extent, was practicing unwittingly the "solitary system" of recently constructed Pentonville Prison. Although Dickens's biographers from Forster to Ackroyd have considered the impact of that Italian sojourn upon the writer's social vision and particularly upon his Liberal attitudes towards the Italian states' national aspirations, little of a substantive nature has been offered in otherwise comprehensive analyses of the novella. The chimes that Dickens heard were Italian, but the train of thought this objective correlative set in motion was almost entirely English in terms of the plights of Meggy Veck, her fiancé Richard, the agricultural laborer Will Fern, and his niece Lilian,*

and the moral impostures of their heartless, self-important oppressors,
Alderman Cute and Sir Joseph Bowley. Having moved from the sleepy
suburb into a Renaissance palazzo in the heart of Genoa, Dickens saw
more clearly the "Condition of England" question, the ever-increasing
gulf between the indigent and the privileged. An informing context for
The Chimes *overlooked until now is the frescoes in the Villa Peschiere,*
particularly those in his study and bedroom, as inspiring both various
elements of his novella and his letter to Forster describing the book's
inception. Frescoes by Luca Cambiaso and his colleague Giovanni Bat-
tista Castello in particular influenced Dickens's vision and imagery.

Although only two of Dickens's works (and minor works at that), the travelogue *Pictures from Italy* and the second of the Christmas Books, *The Chimes*,
are directly connected with his initial trip to Italy, Charles Dickens learned
much during the course of his 1844–45 sojourn there, including the value of
family and leisure, and the individual's need for personal and social integration. He also learned a negative lesson, as it were: that, despite the perspective
he gained from writing about his society at a distance, he could channel his
creative energies most productively only if he were an immediate part of
what Wordsworth termed "That mighty heart," the pulsing social life of the
English metropolis, which embodied his themes and offered him an array of
real-life models for his character studies. "He craved for the London streets.
He so missed his long night-walks before beginning anything that he seemed
. . . dumbfounded without them" (Forster 1, 229). In short, hard on the heels
of his first American tour, through living abroad for a year he learned that
he could not be *both* an Englishman in Italy and a professional writer in
English. James Joyce could function effectively as an expatriate writer;
Charles Dickens could not, as his slight output from July 1844 through June
1845 testifies, *Pictures from Italy* being based largely on his correspondence
to Forster.

Living in Trieste, an out-of-the-way corner of a decadent empire, James
Joyce acquired an artistic detachment that enabled him to reflect dispassion-
ately on his Dublin childhood, adolescence, and early adulthood, and to see
more clearly the problems of his native land. In contrast, Dickens's residence
in Genoa and his subsequent travels throughout Italy confirmed for him the
necessity of artistic immersion in England. However, the Genoese idyll did
enable him to characterize at a personal level, in a brief but radical text, the
condition of England question, the 1840s issue of the unbridgeable gulf between the "two nations" (to borrow Disraeli's phrase in *Sibyl, or the Two
Nations* [1845]) of rich and poor. In Toby (Trotty) Veck, the quintessential
Common Man and innocuous protagonist of *The Chimes*, Dickens exemplifies

the defeatist, self-blaming attitude of the laboring classes during a period of social, economic, and political upheaval. A kind-hearted single-parent and indigent ticket-porter, Toby is a far cry from the childless "money man" Ebenezer Scrooge, the misanthropic curmudgeon who, as in the traditional pantomime, is transformed by his night's experiences with the Spirits into a model employer and philanthropist. Compared to the backdrop of *A Christmas Carol*, that of *The Chimes* is highly, at times even terrifyingly, realistic, and the momentary vision of the possible ramifications of Ignorance and Want becomes in the second novella "a caustic and abrasive analysis of social injustice" (Tarr 210). Whereas in the first Christmas Book, the miser Ebenezer Scrooge "is a product of past experiences" (Ford 439), an emotional oyster who has closed in upon himself to avoid the pain of rejection, Trotty Veck's gentle misanthropy is a byproduct of establishmentarian propaganda rather than a deep-seated conviction. The chimes that Dickens heard were probably those of a neighboring church convent in Genoa (Forster 1: 222), but the train of thought this objective correlative set in motion was almost entirely English in terms of the plights of Meggy Veck, her fiancé Richard, agricultural laborer Will Fern, and his niece Lilian, and the moral impostures of their heartless, self-important oppressors, Alderman Cute and Sir Joseph Bowley.

Dickens's emphasis on the need for a social life, a life outside the Utilitarian principles of commerce decried by his friend Thomas Carlyle as "the cash-nexus," is evident in his earliest "Sketches" such as "Seven Dials," of course, and therefore can hardly be attributed in *The Chimes: A Goblin Story of Some Bells That Rang an Old Year Out and a New Year In* (1844) to his having written the novella while living in Italy, that convivial land of extended family and extended dining hours. Dickens, in following up the popular success of the first Christmas Book, wrote a "powerful," "tender," yet "cheerful" novella as "a blow for the poor" ("*To* John Forster," 8 October 1844: *Letters* 4: 200), a blow aimed squarely at the Tory, land-owning, and commercially-oriented English establishment. However, his circumstances in Genoa, far from his familiar London haunts that had heretofore stimulated his creative processes, may at least be regarded as providing a context for the composition of the highly melodramatic (one might even say, given its highly emotional content, rhetorical style, and stock characters, "operatic") offering for Christmas 1844.[1] Another contextual element, as we shall see, was the Renaissance frescoes in Dickens's bedroom and study at the Villa Pallavicino delle Peschiere.

Dickens's contracting with his new publishers, Bradbury and Evans, to write a travel book and a second Christmas Book coincided with his plan to transport himself and his family to Genoa; after a period of adjustment to the foreign environment and its intense heat, he removed himself and his family from the relative isolation of what he terms, early in *Pictures from Italy*, his "Pink Jail"[2] in the sleepy suburb of Albaro, several miles from the city of Genoa proper and, as Peter Ackroyd notes, "swarming with fleas" (435). Determined to meet his publication commitments, he subsequently moved to the more refined, luxurious, and beautiful Villa Pallavicino delle Peschiere, located within Genoa's walls and offering a panorama of the city and its harbor. There, he quickly became caught up in the act of composition, working many hours each day from late September. In suburban Albaro, until his dialectal Italian was reasonably fluent,[3] he had remained somewhat alienated from the life of the Genovese about him; now, although his daily writing was undisturbed—for the Peschiere, as Forster notes, "stand[s] on a height aloof from the town, surrounded by its own gardens" (1: 222)—he was fully capable of participating in the daily life of Genoa. To this extensive Renaissance villa's *piano nobile* (main floor, with anterooms and grand sala), during the last week of September 1844, amidst a raging storm, as if making an operatic entrance, Dickens brought his family from the large but hardly palatial Villa Bagnerello, a playground for rats, flies, scorpions, and mosquitoes. Feeling close to the harbor at the Peschiere, he chose a magnificent, frescoed salon to the right or west of the splendidly decorated central sala as his study, and the left or eastern salon as his bedroom. In a letter to Samuel Rogers dated 1 September 1844, he described his new residence in suitably romantic terms as "splendidly situated, in the midst of beautiful gardens, and on the side of a steep hill" (*Letters* 4: 189). Even in September, the gardens surrounding the palazzo must have been aromatic with the "groves of camellias, and orange-trees" (*Letters* 4: 194) and lemon-trees as the fountains plashed and goldfish sported in the many ornamental ponds that gave the palazzo its name (Ackroyd 438; *Letters* 4: 173, 176–77).

Complementing the Michelangelo-esque frescoes in his study, the window of his new writing-place afforded him a splendid panorama of buildings and intensely blue water, with the beams of the lighthouse flashing five times every four minutes, beating out the time for the writer as the goblin bells do for Trotty Veck in the bell tower of the story. Both are thus made keenly aware of the passage of time from a height, a fresh perspective of a familiar scene for Trotty, an entirely new scene for his creator.

Adjoining the villa's grounds were a church and a hill upon which were held local festivals and dances of the sort that closes the novella, a celebration of communal life. Initially at Albaro, Dickens seems to have experienced writer's block, sensing that, in alienating himself from the teeming life of London, despite its high cost of living and its constant petitioners, he "had plucked [him]self out of [his] proper soil" (Forster 1: 229) and could not take root. His image is appropriate to a vine-growing landscape: without the nutrients of his native soil, the writer could not bear fruit—that is, generate the characters, situations, and conflicts that constitute a fictional text. Unused to his surroundings, he was still learning to speak the language through a tutor in thrice-weekly visits, and familiarizing himself with the country largely through the medium of a twenty-year-old poem (Samuel Rogers's *Italy*, published in 1826, and quoted by Dickens in his letter to the poet himself on 1 September). Early in August, Dickens alluded to his "feeble efforts . . . to acquire the language" (*Letters* 4: 170), but two weeks later he asserted to Forster that "He could ask in Italian for whatever he wanted in any shop or coffee-house, and could read it pretty well" (*Letters* 4: 182). Of course, such ability was hardly the same as complete fluency in the local dialect.

Isolated in his lofty chamber, separated from the denizens of Albaro by nationality, language, class, and culture, to an extent he was practicing unwittingly the "solitary system" of recently constructed Pentonville Prison. Having moved from the sleepy suburb, Dickens immediately became more aware of the noises of the vibrant city now surrounding him. The jangling of the bells from a nearby church steeple that he had pronounced "maddening" (?6 Oct. 1844 "*To* John Forster," *Letters* 4: 199), suddenly became an inspirational correlative when his creative subconscious connected the discordant sounds with one of Falstaff's lines from *2 Henry IV*: "We have heard THE CHIMES at midnight, Master Shallow!" (3. 1. 231).

This and nothing more he exuberantly wrote to Forster just a week after his arrival at the Peschiere, the numerous belfries of Genoa, particularly that adjacent to the villa, dissolving into the partly recalled and partly imagined bell tower of an old London church (*Letters* 4: 200). As Michael Slater remarks, the illustrations provided by Richard Doyle and Clarkson Stanfield, probably at Dickens's instigation, depict the belfry of St. Dunstan-in-the-West, Fleet Street, an edifice constructed upon the site of a medieval church that had been demolished in 1830, a building, moreover, that had a tower but "no steeple" (Slater, "Notes to *The Chimes*" 261).

Abandoning expensive London for an Italian sojourn, Dickens had chosen to make the northern state of Piedmont his and his family's destination in July 1844, partly perhaps because of his admiration for Joey Grimaldi's pantomime and Cavour's Liberalism, and his indignation at the much-reported governmental interception of Mazzini's correspondence in England. He may have settled upon Genoa as the base of his Italian travels, because, as Michael Hollington notes, Genoa was "the birthplace of Mazzini" (and therefore of the modern notion of "The People," and in particular of The Young Italy Movement, which advocated the creation of a single nation from the partitioned peninsula's many states) and "the most progressive and nationalistic region of a country whose most pressing concern was liberation from tyranny" (299). Liberal and national sympathies aside, Dickens's chief motivation in moving to northern Italy was probably to escape from the financial demands of his relatives and to spend a sabbatical in one of the least expensive parts of the Continent in order to reduce domestic expenses. Although his income was certainly not modest, Dickens felt his recently-won affluence threatened by his father's continual requests for financial assistance and imperiled by the financial reversals attendant upon his fruitless copyright lawsuit against the notoriously piratical publishing firm known as "Peter Parley's Illuminated Library" over the firm's theft of *A Christmas Carol.*

The "second *Christmas Carol*" that Dickens hammered out that October amidst the splendidly frescoed Italian palazzo's salas and salons is by turns, as David Parker comments in *Christmas and Charles Dickens*, witty, quibbling, intensely emotional, pathetic, pastoral, urban, sentimental, and (above all) "melodramatic" (237). Parker praises the novella's eloquent defence of the poor and its satirical directness in its lampooning the principles of political economy (advocated by the Utilitarians and epitomized by the newly-built Pentonville Prison) in the Malthusian statistician Filer, but criticizes its simplicity of narrative voice, its contrived plot, and its lack of thematic depth. Dickens, he contends, in attempting to apply a moral corrective to English society, has been swept away with his indignation at the authorities' callously ignoring the plight of the poor at the nadir of their economic distress, the Hungry Forties (238).

As for his first impressions of Genoa, Dickens reported to Forster "Everything is in extremes" (1, 217). Dickens, of course, had previously encountered and written extensively about poverty, and its associated lack of hygiene. In chapter 18 of *Oliver Twist*, for example, he had described the unhealthy environments to which the English poor were consigned as if blackened chimneys and gloomy back-garrets with rusty bars and mouldering shutters on their windows were the outward and visible signs of this class's moral corruption, meanness, and brutality. But in place of the black mists, mud, and slime of Whitechapel and the filth, neglect, and desolation of tottering house-fronts at Rotherhithe (chapter 50), in Genoa Dickens encountered excessive heat, high humidity, and swarms of insects alongside moldering frescoes and admirable architecture. Italian poverty, as he describes it in *Pictures from Italy*, is theatricalized and not at all associated with criminality and depraved conduct. Rats, creatures inspiring terror in *Oliver Twist*, are in Albaro's wine-making season the cause for a communal entertainment, the melodrama of the autumnal *festa* suggesting to Dickens a reenactment of Genoa's siege in the Napoleonic wars. And fleas, a great source of discomfiture heretofore in Dickens, and symbolic of the miseries of poverty, are in Albaro figures out of pantomime "who populate the coach-house to such an extent that," remarks Dickens, "I daily expect to see the carriage going off bodily, drawn by myriads of industrious fleas in harness" (*Pictures from Italy* 33). Although he finds the houses of the Genoese poor of that quarter as "dirty" and "straggling" as any in the Seven Dials slum in London (*SB* 71), in place of "squabbling" and "fighting" among the inhabitants he overhears vociferous but amicable greetings; "They are very good-tempered, obliging, and industrious" (*Pictures from Italy* 46). And, although hardly clean, they are family-oriented and generally devout, the most popular name being male and female forms of the city's patron, St. John the Baptist (*Pictures from Italy* 34).

Everywhere the buildings are painted inside and out with fresco, as if intended to be stage sets. As in the pantomime and melodrama, in Genoa's theater of daily life, in the narrow *vicos* and close dwellings, the people are "exceedingly animated and pantomimic" (Forster 1: 216). Everywhere he looked by day or night Dickens reveled in this theater of poverty because instead of the thievery of Fagin's gang and the potential for violence always lurking in the house-breaker, Bill Sykes, he found nothing but "deference, courtesy, more than civility" (220). Even in Genoa's slums, "there is nothing to be feared, I believe, from midnight walks in this part of Italy" (224).

This, then, is the benign image of poverty involving stable neighborhoods, rather than crime- and pestilence-ridden tenements, that Dickens recorded in his letters home to Forster. Distracted by the foreignness of the place and wearied by its heat, Dickens initially felt immobilized when it came to starting his second Christmas Book. He was mesmerized by the city's "strangest contrasts: things that are picturesque, ugly, mean, magnificent, delightful, and offensive, break upon the view at every turn" (*Pictures from Italy* 38). Despite the squalor and decay, he encounters none of the "guilt and misery of London" (*SB* 201) that he had observed so frequently from his earliest days in the mean streets of the English metropolis, whose poor in *Sketches by Boz* and *Oliver Twist*, in contrast to Genoa's, are physically deformed and spiritually warped, alcoholic, melancholic, and generally miserable. And this new experience of poverty without vice or cruelty is very much reflected in the working-class principals of *The Chimes*, named for the incessant ringing of the bells of churches and convents that Dickens heard so often during his residence in Genoa. Initially, gripped by what he proclaimed to be idleness, Dickens was, in fact, engaged in the pre-writing activities of intense observation and of learning the Genoese dialect.

The thirty-two-year-old Dickens possibly learned more about the essential humanity of the laboring poor by wandering the streets of Genoa, observing the general indigence and lack of hygiene on a daily basis, than he had from his night-time rambles through the slum districts of the English capital. In Genoa, he observed all levels of society, attending operas, and relishing popular performances of puppet theater in the streets. Since opera employs character comedy, patter, pathos, lyrical passages, musical accompaniment, and spectacular effect to achieve an emotional rather than an intellectual audience engagement, there may well be a connection between the theatrical entertainments that the Dickenses experienced while in Genoa and the mixed nature of *The Chimes*. Throughout August and September, "staggering upon the threshold" (*Letters* 4: 199) of active composition, the writer's imagination may well have been beguiled by plays such as an adaptation of Balzac's *Père Goriot* (Dickens in writing to Forster called it "The domestic Lear," *Letters* 4: 175) staged at Genoa's Teatro Carlo Felici: the miniature dramas seen in passing through the streets in innumerable puppet theaters, and the operas at Teatro Sant 'Agostino and Teatro Diurno (he specifically mentions in a 12 August 1844 letter to Thomas Mitton that he is using the box that belongs to Miss Coutts's representative, Charles Gibbs). The summer previous to undertaking *The Chimes* he had seen Dumas's 1836 play *Kean, ou Desordre et Genie* ridiculously mounted at Teatro Carlo Felice (*Letters* 4: 180); a ballet company from Milan, and fairy-tale puppet theater in which, as the editors of the *Pilgrim Letters* note, "the Marionetti [may be described] as a mixture of Punchinello and the opera" (*Letters* 4: 180 *n*.). In *Pictures from Italy*, he delights in ridiculing the puppet theater production about an incarcerated, exiled hero, "St. Helena, or the Death of Napoleon" (*Pictures from Italy* 52), fondly recalling how the Emperor's boots seemed to have a life of their own, as the chimes themselves do in the second Christmas Book.

Like the subgenre of the Newgate novel which Dickens helped to inaugurate in *Oliver Twist* in the previous decade (a work that he was revising for single-volume publication throughout the autumn of 1844), *The Chimes* combines Gothic and comic elements such as lampoon and caricature in a manner familiar to audiences of nineteenth-century English melodrama. His strong situations and sharply contrasting characters, so readily adaptable to the medium of the Victorian popular stage, are features that Dickens's earlier novels share with Italian opera, so there is no reason to think that he was especially influenced by the Italian operas he saw while resident in Genoa.

Let us, then, return to the influence that Genoa itself may have exerted upon Dickens. For him, a thorough urbanite, it was a return from exile. His letters suggest he could hardly wait to quit Albaro's relative seclusion and discomfort for the conveniently situated and far more aristocratic Villa Pallavicino delle Peschiere, so named because of its many garden fishponds and its sixteenth-century architect, Tobia Pallavicino. The mustard-yellow villa's brightly colored antique frescoes recall in their mythological subjects and pastoral landscapes those of Peruzzi's Villa Farnesina in Rome. Dickens, formerly lessee of much more modest residences, must have felt himself a true grandee in such surroundings, both as exotic as something out of *The Arabian Nights* and as capacious as an English royal residence. The resident of such a magnificent house with rooms as grand as those of "an enchanted place in an Eastern story" (*Pictures from Italy* 54), "in size and shape like those at Windsor-castle'' (Forster 1: 227), Dickens, looking out over the city, surely must have felt that he "had arrived." In his biography of Dickens, Peter Ackroyd remarks upon the degree to which the frescoed rooms of his Roman villa and of the rest of the city operated upon the writer's imagination:

> The frescoes on the walls of the public buildings, the gestures of the people, the very life of the streets, must have given him an unmistakable impression of some theatrical reality, the frescoes themselves looking uncannily like back-drops for the voluble and excited life of the inhabitants. It may well be that the stinking alleys reminded him of London, but this was London seen as a form of theatre. (435)

In *Pictures from Italy* and in his letters to Forster on which the travelogue drew, Dickens describes with obvious enthusiasm the scenes painted on his residence's walls and ceilings by Renaissance master Luca Cambiaso (1527–85) and his colleague Giovanni Battista Castello (1509–69, often called simply "*il Bergamasco*" from his birthplace) between 1558 and 1560, but as bright and fresh as if painted just prior to his moving in. The eastern or left-hand room (if one is facing south) immediately off the grand sala features Bergamasco's fresco of Phaeton, his chariot and horses, larger than life, "tumbling headlong down into the best bed" (*Letters* 4: 195; figs. 1A & 1B), in which Dickens and his wife slept. The eastern wall of the western or right-hand room, which he chose as his study, features "nymphs pursued by satyrs as large as life and as wicked" (*Letters* 4: 195)—actually, just one "nymph" (the female deity Diana) and one satyr (fig. 2). Dickens erroneously believed that these "paintings were designed by Michael Angelo" (*Letters* 4: 197), as if the name of this Renaissance giant of the visual and plastic arts conferred power on his residence, and hence on the lessee himself.

The Ovidian frescoes in "the two best bed-rooms" (Forster 1: 227) which on 30 September 1844 Dickens briefly but enthusiastically described to John Forster must be considered as part of the context of his composition of the second Christmas Book, *The Chimes*, which he had contracted to write for his new publishers, Bradbury and Evans, early in the previous May. Although Dickens, amidst the self-imposed quasi-isolation of the suburban butcher's villa at Albaro, had pondered what he might write, he had had little leisure for extended writing because his favorite child, Katey, had fallen seriously ill (perhaps from drinking unpasteurized milk in quantity) and had insisted that only her father should nurse her. What began in third week of July as a "sore throat" (*Letters* 4: 162) shortly developed into a seriously swollen neck which required constant attention, and her piercing cries (according to Lucinda Dickens-Hawksley) were hardly conducive to the peace of mind Dickens required to begin formulating his "second" *Carol*. The "illness of my pet little daughter," he reported to Count D'Orsay on 7 August, "[has]

Fig. 1a. Upper register of Giovanni Battista Castello ("il Bergamasco"), "The Fall of Phaeton" (c. 1560), Villa Pallavicino delle Peschiere, Genoa (personal photograph, June 2007).

Fig. 1b. Lower register of Giovanni Battista Castello ("il Bergamasco"), "The Fall of Phaeton" (c. 1560), Villa Pallavicino delle Peschiere, Genoa (personal photograph, June 2007).

sadly interfered with my good resolutions" (*Letters* 4: 166), even in terms of keeping regular correspondence. Fortunately, she was well on the road to recovery by the middle of August and was probably her old self weeks before the family began packing for their removal to the larger, far more prestigious villa within Genoa's walls. This suffering child may have become Meggy Veck's infant in Trotty's dream vision and, as clever and determined as her father, Katey may also have been the basis for the spiritual child-guide of *The Chimes*, Lilian Fern.

Whereas the frescoes in the Bagnerello are cheerful, amateurish, and colorful depictions of generalized nymphs and swains against sketchy pastoral backdrops, those in the Peschiere, the work of decorative masters of the High Renaissance, have both literary and local associations. In particular, Bergamasco's "The Fall of Phaeton" directly above the Dickenses' bed has a Ligurian as well as an Ovidian connection; visually, the urban and suburban landscape with towering mountains behind suggests the physical situation of Genoa itself, while narratively the cousin who deeply mourned the death of the imprudent Phaeton was Cycnus, "King of Liguria's province" (Ovid 67),

Fig. 2. Luca Cambiaso, ''Diana Wresting a Satyr'' (c. 1560), Villa Pallavicino delle Peschiere, Genoa (personal photograph, June 2007).

who, in the second book of the *Metamorphoses*, was transformed into a swan on the banks of the Po, not far from what is now Genoa.

Located in the *piano nobile*'s eastern bedroom, this Ovidian fresco, depicting the catastrophic careering of Phoebus's chariot out of its proper path, may be associated with dawn, its lighting a delicate shade of blue in the aerial perspective of the mountains in the background, with richer tones for the city walls and buildings in the foreground. In contrast, Cambiaso's "Diana Wrestling a Satyr" above the entrance inside the western bedroom has flesh tones and reds reminiscent of Titian's work, and consonant with the warm, late afternoon sunshine that would have spilled into the room over the rooftops of the city to the front and right. Both frescoes exemplify the issue of appropriate and inappropriate uses of power, with the Bergamasco picture implying the dire consequences of the misuse of power not only in the fate of the inverted youth at the top but of the peasants below who run from the scene, fearful that the remnants of the Sun's chariot will fall upon them. While Dickens's secondary characters, Alderman Cute and Sir Joseph Bowley, in *The Chimes* abuse their power, Dickens's sympathies lie with the working-class characters who feel powerless against the forces of the establishment, in particular with the story's sympathetic onlooker, Trotty Veck, who, as a spirit in the dream vision, cannot intervene to assist Lilian, Will, Meggy, and Richard. Like the Michelangelo-esque river deity in Bergamaso's "The Fall of Phaeton," Trotty is mere observer to the tragedy, although he is hardly as unmoved and detached emotionally. In the enforced passivity of the dream-vision Trotty watches in anguish as Will, poverty-stricken and unemployed, is unable to escape the catch-and-release cycle of the seasonally-employed, marginalized rural laborer. Despite working hard, Meggy and her alcoholic fiancé Richard cannot recover their wasted youth and love. And Lilian cannot escape her only means of livelihood, prostitution.

In Cambiaso's fresco above the study's lintel, the indignant goddess, an Italian form of the Greek Artemis identifiable by her "little crescent-shaped horns" (Rose 121), asserts her authority over her surly adversary as she prepares to deliver him a knock-out punch, vigorously resisting his attempted rape. We note that Dickens, perhaps subconsciously under the influence of this fresco (fig. 2), spoke of "making, in this little book, a great blow for the poor" ("*To* John Forster, [?13–14 October 1844]," *Letters* 4: 200), hoping that the second Christmas Book would, like the moon goddess in this picture, have "a grip upon the very throat" upon its opponents, the complacent, self-serving, upper-middle-class and aristocratic authorities who exploit or neglect the working poor. As he chose these phrases, he would have been writing to Forster at his desk at the window, just to the right of Cambiaso's fresco, one of the few in the villa both designed and executed by the maestro rather than his artistically inferior associate, Bergamasco. It is a masterpiece of pre-Baroque energy conveying a sense of the physical power and determination of the larger-than-life adversaries. In punishment for his hubris, his having squandered his god-given power and behaved without regard for the rest of humanity, Phaeton tumbles earthward, his father's chariot about to crush the fleeing peasants below. While the superb body of the noble youth in Bergamasco's picture sprawls across the upper register in a tragic free-fall, the almost triumphant Diana is employing both her muscular arms to vanquish the figure emblematic of unrestrained passion and license. The maestro depicts the heroic figures in violent emotion and swirling action with only the shadows of the wrestlers as backdrop. Bergamasco's tranquil pastoral scene—a Ligurian fishing village—on the bedroom's shutters (which hide a small altarpiece) would for Charles and Catherine Dickens have contrasted with the violence and drama of the scene above their headboard. In this bedroom, under the spell of the Renaissance frescoes, Dickens dreamed of Mary Hogarth, his deceased sister-in-law, wrapped in a blue drapery like some Raphael Madonna, perhaps emerging from the cupboard containing a Catholic altar directly at the foot of the bed and between the two south-facing windows.[4] For the arch-Protestant who detested all Catholic ceremonies and rituals as pagan violations of essential Christian teachings, her message to join the Roman church must have come as something of a shock, but may well be related to the communal life into which he was gradually being absorbed, if not to the altar hidden in the east bedroom of the Peschiere's *piano nobile*.

Amidst the crumbling desolation of alleyways and decaying churches, their exteriors bathed in a golden light, their interiors, dimly lit, haunted by past greatness and surrounded by the remnants of a bygone glory, but now cracked and peeling, Dickens in his magnificent study overcame his writer's block and conceived of a beggars' opera with virtuous rather than venial principals from the urban and rural underclasses of early Victorian England. In the *piano nobile* he would have noticed the many scenes depicting the chariot or wagon of Helios, as if the very walls and ceilings were constantly reminding him of the passage of time, and, by extension, the time that was running out on this projected second Christmas Book. Between bouts of busy writing he wandered the frescoed rooms and corridors of the Peschiere "as if he were in a vision" (Ackroyd 438) and looked down upon an Eden of fountains, terraced gardens, and groves of citrus trees, and to the sprawling city and port beyond. His spoken, dialectal Italian having become more proficient, he began to wander the city's streets, in his imagination all the while attending to the voices of time in the goblin bells of his story and the actual bells of the Genoese churches and convents below the Monte Faccio and the city walls, as described by him in "Genoa and Its Neighbourhood" (*Pictures from Italy* 54–55).

The last of the illustrations for *The Chimes* underscores Trotty's renewed conviction in the future of his daughter and of his class. The nightmare visions of the future according to St. Malthus are over: misled, as Kurata comments, by his inability to distinguish "between economic and moral superiority" (22), Trotty Veck has learned the folly of accepting the humbug of the upper-middle class toadies Alderman Cute and Filer as gospel truth. His discordant opinions about his own class's lack of morality have been delivered a corrective by the supernatural agency of the Chimes. The characters who appeared in his dream-vision suffering and dying are alive and well this New Year's Day, and Meggy and Richard will be able to marry one another as planned. Although he joins the neighborhood dance in his own peculiar gait, the fond father pairs off with Widow Chickenstalker as Richard pairs off with Meggy (fig. 3). Nevertheless, the social and spiritual or doctrinal reintegration of Trotty Veck lacks the humanitarian or altruistic dimension of Scrooge's conversion narrative: Trotty is not born again as a better man—but he is, like Dr. Manette in *A Tale of Two Cities* some fifteen years later, "recalled to life" and community by his suffering.

Despite what should be the exterior cold of a London winter, Trotty and his neighbors dance *alfresco*, "out of doors," as is evident by the bough of greenery that divides the text from the final illustration (fig. 3), just as Dickens had seen the locals doing near his second residence in Genoa. This is not a staid country dance of the "Sir Roger de Coverley" variety with which cinematic adapters often close productions of *A Christmas Carol*; in place of fiddlers or a pianoforte, a local street band of a Genovese character and under the direction of a markedly proletarian Jabez improvises to the cacophonous accompaniment of the rough wedding-music of marrow-bones and cleavers wielded by joyful friends of the young couple. Dickens contrasts this music with the dour and ominous voices of time, the ponderous Chimes of the church opposite: "not *the* Bells, but a portable collection, on a frame" ("Fourth Quarter") peal in honor of a wedding, full of bright promise for a future so different from the terrifyingly Malthusian dream. Whereas Ebenezer Scrooge, middle-class Utilitarian capitalist turned philanthropist, celebrates his regeneration with his nephew's family and then with his trusted employee, Trotty Veck, kindly ticket-porter still, celebrates the breaking of the spell at midnight, as the Chimes ring an old year out and a New Year in, exactly as the title page had foretold. Significantly, Dickens compels his middle-class readership to identify with a working-class protagonist; as Alexander Welsh notes,

> The alienated individual in this story is of a different social class from that of the author and readers. He is seen from the outside; his thoughts, especially his exaggerated class-consciousness—submissive to the general opinion that the poor must be born bad—are mostly bestowed upon him for the purposes of satire. But Dickens, building on the irony that Trotty Veck is more human than he himself knows, treats his hero sympathetically, even joyfully. (8)

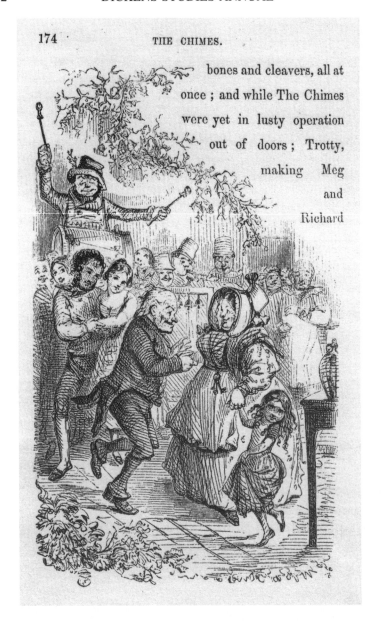

Fig. 3. John Leech, "The New Year's Dance," thirteenth illustration for
Charles Dickens's *The Chimes; or, A Goblin Story of Some Bells That Rang
an Old Year Out and a New Year In* (London: Chapman and Hall, 1845), 174.

Initially, Trotty had seemed a social isolate, attended only by his devoted daughter; however, by the novella's conclusion, he is revealed as a social lynchpin in a working-class neighborhood. Trotty's fellow London poor are neither vicious nor homeless. Whereas Trotty's dream had dramatized what Welsh terms the "theory of social causation" (10), that is, "that physical and social causes were responsible for moral ills; . . . that forces of hunger and cold and contempt, conditions of suffering and alienation, did bring about prostitution and death" (10), the New Year's dance reveals the denizens of these mean streets as connected to their village origins in a communal celebration; in other words, although they are supposedly a realistic facsimile of London's indigent, they behave as if they were Genoa's happy proletariat. Trotty's return to the present and the living is an affair not so much of the family as of the community. The working-class music of the street replaces the middle-class parlor games at the conclusion of *A Christmas Carol*, although both conclusions include social drinking. The street musicians and communal dance are not the only Italian touches, for Mrs. Chickenstalker supplies the equivalent of the smoking Bishop that Scrooge quaffs (in moderation) with Bob Cratchit at the counting house the day after Christmas—a hot flip "that steamed and smoked and reeked like a volcano" ("Fourth Quarter," p. 243 of the Penguin edition; p. 172 of the original).

The volcano, suggestive of powerful subterranean forces that cannot be repressed, is an objective correlative for deep-seated feelings that all human beings, no matter what their class or degree, share. Only months after completing *The Chimes*, Dickens, his considerable party (including six pack-horses), and twenty-two guides ascended the slopes of the great destroyer, Mt. Vesuvius, in severe winter weather. Perhaps this simile at the end of *The Chimes* reflects his anticipation of that climb, which was made on 21 February 1845, but which he had probably considered visiting as early as 7 August 1844, when he wrote to Count D'Orsay about his intention to visit Rome and Naples in February and to cross from "Mount Vesuvius, and Herculaneum and Pompeii, away into Sicily, to Mount Etna" (*Letters* 4: 177).

The letterpress text reinforces the sense of destiny fulfilled, of the "will" of Heaven enacted at last, as the determined denizen of the green world of Dorset, aptly named "Will Fern," discovers that Mrs. Chickenstalker is the friend of Lilian's mother for whom he had been searching when he first encountered Trotty on the street. The reader has a profound sense of recovery, for what was lost has been found—including Trotty's faith in The People and his hopes for his daughter's future happiness. Character, he realizes (and as Dickens wishes *us* to realize), is not solely determined by socioeconomic factors beyond the individual's control: in fact, benevolence and indignation may be exhibited more sincerely by the working poor than their social betters. Rich or poor, we all have the ability to make moral choices.

Engraver Linton's seventh plate and *Punch* caricaturist John Leech's fifth in the visual program contains or more properly squeezes out of the frame twenty-words of text, so that the narrative, auditory, and visual moments coincide precisely: the sound of

bones and cleavers, all at
once; and while The Chimes
were yet in lusty operation
out of doors; Trotty,
making Meg
and
Richard [the "second couple"].   (174–75 of the original text)

The second couple is a proper role for the traditional hero and heroine of romantic comedy, while the lead or central dancer would appropriately be Trotty, because his is the consciousness we have followed from the steps of Alderman Cute's townhouse to this celebratory moment. The presiding figure of the drummer, wielding his drumsticks, implies the unified, joyous response of the community at festival, as all figures in the frame move in unison to the rhythm he beats out. The sprig in his hat is consistent with the Christmas season, but the border between the dancers and the text, the decorated bough, is out of place or, more properly, out of time. It leads the eye from the drummer's crushed hat and drumsticks to the central dancers and so down to the knowing child, whose gaze is directed at the reader-viewer rather than at the figures in the frame.

Lilian, who in spirit form had served as Trotty's guide through the last sequence of his Dantesque vision, paralleling the vision afforded Scrooge by "The Last of the Spirits" in *A Christmas Carol* a year earlier, engages the reader-viewer directly at this moment, preparing the "consumer" of visual and narrative texts for the narrator's closing remarks. Paralleling the line of the bough are the heads of the young couple, whose fecundity and resilience the bough epitomizes, the older couple united in the dance, and the precocious child who dances on the right of the charmed circle. The movement of dancers and bough is the forward movement of the narrative that embraces present and future, taking us forward and then backward, into the present—a Shakespearean moment of *festa*, of celebration, which, like that of *As You Like It*, contains all ages and times but *not* all conditions and classes: the essence of Dickens's life and vision up to 1844, including his recent revising of *Oliver Twist*, his experiences in Genoa's streets and theaters, and, in particular, in the "Pink Jail," the less-than-grand and decidedly alienating Villa Bagnerello, well beyond the city of Genoa's walls, in semi-rural Albaro, and the luxurious, opulently frescoed Palazzo Peschiere within the walls and just a few minutes' walk from the city center and the magnificent Strada Nuova, the chief among those new, wide thoroughfares that Dickens christened "the Streets of the Palaces" (*Pictures from Italy* 39). Here, by virtue of his mastering the Genovese dialect of Italian, Dickens integrated himself into the social and cultural life of the community. No such integration or forging of "a common understanding between the classes" (Tarr 213), however, occurs in the final pages of *The Chimes*.

The "Condition of England" question, moreover, remains a matter of a failure at integration, of the Bowleys', and Cutes', not recognizing their common humanity with Trotty, Meggy, Richard, and Will Fern; these disparate social strata in Dickens's most radical fiction remain utterly alienated at the conclusion of *The Chimes*. As Marilyn J. Kurata notes, the modern reader is disappointed that, in the closing narratorial passage, "The affirmation of man's common humanity is articulated, not realized" (20). The reader is left with a sense of only partial closure since, although Dickens offers social and personal resolutions to the problems of Trotty, Meg, Richard, Will Fern, and Lilian, a happy ending emphasizing what Kurata terms the "spontaneous benevolence of Toby Veck and Mrs. Chickenstalker" (20), the Liberal author leaves the complacent "Friends of the People" (the Tories Bowley, Cute, and Filer) outside the charmed circle, unrepentant and still able to persecute Will Fern, and the broader issues of poverty, suicide, prostitution, oppression, and injustice unresolved.

NOTES

1. Indeed, the initial dramatic adaptation which appeared on the stage of the Adelphi, a working-class theater noted for melodrama, on 19 December 1844 has entirely the feel of a period melodrama in terms of its sympathetic presentation of its humble characters, its humor and its pathos. The plot, insofar as it deals with the impending marriage of Meggy Veck and Richard, may certainly be regarded as romantic, as is typical of early nineteenth-century melodrama, and involves a malevolent conspiracy (the persecution of Will Fern planned by Cute and Bowley). Moreover, the dramatists treat the contemporary issues of suicide, prostitution, and incendiarism sensationally, so that the Adelphi audience would have experienced the appropriately melodramatic emotions of indignation at the hypocrisy of Bowley (a character who, in the context of melodrama, should not be interpreted as well-meaning though ignorant), pity for the suffering Lilian and Meggy, and joy at the play's wedding dance, a conclusion which secures poetic justice for Trotty and the young couple, if not for the piece's pasteboard villains. The prostitute Lilian's "Magdalene-like death at Meg's feet" (Kurata 27) is at once socially realistic and melodramatically hyperbolic. Such stage directions as "*A loud scream is heard behind*" (4. 1, p. 16) and the musical accompaniment

specified by script at key moments are wholly consistent with staging practices in the minor theaters prior to the Licensing Act.

As Michael R. Booth points out, the nineteenth-century English melodrama of the domestic species and the novel shared a number of salient features: "sensation, spectacle, violence, true love, romantic fantasy, strong narrative, fine sentiment, rhetoric, courage, low comedy, domestic realism, home and family, eccentric characters, patriotic spirit and a happy ending" (35). All that seems missing from either the novella or dramatic adaptation of *The Chimes* is the patriotism; nevertheless, the book's realistic presentation of social ills, almost unprecedented in terms of contemporary literature, is wholly consistent with period melodrama, while the story's use of supernatural agency and spectacular effects is reminiscent of the pantomime.

Scripted by Gilbert Abbott à Beckett and Mark Lemon, *The Chimes* was staged with Dickens's active collaboration, which involved his supplying the adapters with "proof-sheets of the story in advance of the actual date of its publication" (Morley 203), and thereby enabling it to open only two days after the book's publication, in time for the Christmas bill at the Adelphi, a house noted for the domestic and middle-class oriented melodramas of J. B. Buckstone (1802–79).

Since this was also one of the two Christian holiday seasons associated with pantomime, it is noteworthy that one of the book's fairy tale-like illustrations, John Leech's "Sir Joseph Bowley's" (p. 55), utilizes side curtains in the upper register to accentuate the theatricality of the two scenes enacted at Sir Joseph's London mansion in the second quarter: "The illustration is framed by curtains pulled back at each side, and the artist has taken the same freedom as a dramatist. We accept the passage of time between scenes in a play and the transformation of characters in a pantomime" (Solberg 104). The Victorian pantomime, in its emphasis of the culminating transformation of the principal character, relied heavily for its effects on scene-changing apparatus, including a double system of flats and trap-doors. Leech's disposition of the characters and furnishings in both scenes in this seventh plate, moreover, suggests the shallow depth of a stage rather than a three-dimensional, realistic space.

2. Dickens uses this term, with capitals suggestive of a proper noun, in "Genoa and Its Neighbourhood" (*Pictures from Italy* 31). The fear of entrapment and alienation, of virtual imprisonment, that Dickens communicates again and again through a string of characters from Fagin and Bill Sikes in *Oliver Twist* through Dr. Manette in *A Tale of Two Cities* and Magwitch in *Great Expectations* probably has its origins in his father's imprisonment in the Marshalsea. Having lived a lonely existence as a child, then, Dickens was most concerned about the mental health issues involved in the supposedly progressive "panopticon" system he had seen at the "Solitary Prison" in Philadelphia: "In the outskirts, stands a great prison, called the Eastern Penitentiary: conducted on a plan peculiar to the state of Pennsylvania. The system here, is rigid, strict, and hopeless solitary confinement. I believe it, in its effects, to be cruel and wrong" (*American Notes*, ch. 7). Another such instance closer to home of incarceration organized on the Utilitarian principles was the recently constructed Pentonville Prison, as reported on the front page of *The Illustrated London News*, 7 January 1843.

3. In preparation for this extended stay abroad, Dickens and his wife had already taken lessons twice a week in Italian from an expatriate named Luigi Mariotti (Ackroyd 425), whom they had met on the voyage to America in January, 1842, aboard the *Britannia*. However, their mastering the local dialect probably proved difficult, as we may judge from the narrator's remarking in "The Italian Prisoner" (in *All the Year Round* 13 October 1860) that "provincial Italian [is] so difficult to understand" (*Uncommercial Traveller* 188). In Albaro, at least the Dickens family did not go without provisions from the local vendors because their cook quickly picked up the dialect, becoming much more proficient in spoken Genovese than anyone else in the household: "*She had so primed herself with* the names of all sorts of vegetables, meats, soups, fruits, and kitchen necessaries, *that she was able to order whatever was needful of the peasantry that were trotting in and out all day, basketed and barefooted*" (*Letters* 4: 175).

4. Whether Dickens actually dreamed of Mary in his first night at the Peschiere, by Forster's dating 23 September (one week prior to the letter from Dickens to Forster, 30 September 1844), or somewhat earlier, at the Bagnerello, remains a matter of conjecture. On 1 September 1844, Dickens wrote to Samuel Rogers that he had leased the Peschiere "for the next six months" (*Letters* 4, 189), but he specifically mentions to Thomas Mitton in a letter dated 12 August that he will "enter on the possession of, on the 1st. of October, and hold until the sixteenth of March, at 5 Guineas a week" (176), the rooms in the Peschiere being vacated early by "an English Colonel who is going away" (176). It is not beyond possibility that the colonel, whom Dickens describes as "a great Bozonian" (177) and therefore eager to accommodate the celebrated writer, might have vacated the premises several weeks in advance of the date upon which Dickens was originally expecting to move from Albaro, namely "on the first of October" ("*To* Count D'Orsay," 7 August 1844, *Letters*, 4: 167). Unfortunately, the accommodating English colonel has never been identified, and acquiring corroborating correspondence from that quarter has so far proven impossible for the editors of the Pilgrim Edition of the *Letters*.

WORKS CITED

A'Beckett, Gilbert A., and Mark Lemon. *The Chimes; or, Some Bells That Rang an Old Year Out and a New Year In.* A goblin drama, in four quarters. London: John Dicks, No. 819 (n. d.). Theatre Royal Adelphi, London: 18 December 1844. Lord Chamberlain's Add. MS. 42980 ff. 809–838. Licensed 18 December 1844. (Page reference is to the published text.)

Ackroyd, Peter. *Dickens.* London: Sinclair-Stevenson, 1990.

Allingham, Philip V. "Dramatic Adaptations of *The Christmas Books* of Charles Dickens: Texts and Contexts, 1844–1848." Diss. U of British Columbia, 1988.

Booth, Michael R. "Public Taste, the Playwright and the Law." Ed. Michael R. Booth, Richard Southern, Frederick and Lise-Lone Marker, and Robertson Davies. *The Revels History of Drama in English. Vol. 6: 1750–1880.* London: Methuen, 1975. 29–58.

"Christmas Day, 1860." *Harper's Weekly,* Vol. 4–No. 209. 29 December 1860: cover page.

Dickens, Charles. *The Chimes: A Goblin Story of Some Bells That Rang an Old Year Out and a New Year In. The Christmas Books.* 2 vols. Ed. Michael Slater. Harmondsworth: Penguin, 1971, rpt. 1978. 1: 137–252.

———. *The Chimes: or A Goblin Story of Some Bells That Rang an Old Year Out and a New Year In.* London: Chapman and Hall, 1845. (All page references are to this original text since the Penguin edition, by far the most accessible text for modern readers, has not always correctly given the original's relationship between the text and the illustration on the same page.)

———. *The Christmas Books of Charles Dickens.* Ed. Michael Slater. Harmondsworth: Penguin, 1981. Vol. 1: *A Christmas Carol.* 1–136; *The Chimes.* 137–255.

———. "The Italian Prisoner." No. 17 in *The Uncommercial Traveller. The Works of Charles Dickens in Thirty Volumes.* New York: Collier, n. d. [These essays were collected from other publications such as *Household Words* and *All the Year Round.*]. 28: 181–91.

———. *Oliver Twist.* Ed. Peter Fairclough. Intro. Angus Wilson. Harmondsworth: Penguin, 1972.

———. *Pictures from Italy.* Ed. Kate Flint. London: Penguin, 1998.

———. *The Letters of Charles Dickens. The Pilgrim Edition.* Ed. Madeline House, Graham Storey, and Kathleen Tillotson. Oxford: Clarendon, 1974 and 1977. Vols. 3 (1842–1843) and 4 (1844–1846).

———. *Sketches by Boz Illustrative of Every-day Life and Every-day People.* Intro. Thea Holme. Oxford: Oxford UP, 1987.

Dickens-Hawksley, Lucinda. "Katey and Italy." Unpublished lecture. Dickens, Victorian Culture, Italy. Conference in Genoa, Italy: 16 June 2007.

Ford, George H. "Dickens and the Voices of Time." *Nineteenth-Century Fiction* 24. 4 (March 1970): 428–48.

Forno, Ilaria. No. 100: "Villa Pallavicino delle Peschiere." *Genova Architectural Guide.* Ed. Lorenzo Capellini and Ennio Poleggi. Genova: Umberto Allemandi, 1998. 140.

Forster, John. *The Life of Charles Dickens.* 2 vols. London: Chapman and Hall, n. d.

Hollington, Michael. "Italy." *Oxford Reader's Companion to Dickens*. Ed. Paul Schlicke. Oxford: Oxford UP, 1999. 299–301.

Kaplan, Fred. *Dickens: A Biography*. New York: Morrow, 1988.

Kurata, Marilyn J. "Fantasy and Realsim: A Defense of *The Chimes*." *Dickens Studies Annual* 13 (1984): 19–34.

Morley, Malcolm. "Ring Up *The Chimes*." *Dickensian* 47 (1951): 202–06.

Ovid. *The Metamorphoses*, trans. Horace Gregory. New York: New American Library, 1960.

Parker, David. *Christmas and Charles Dickens*. New York: AMS, 2006.

"The Pentonville Prison." *The Illustrated London News*. 7 January 1843: 1–4.

"Review of *The Chimes*." Illustrated London News 21 December 1844: 395.

Rose, H. J. *A Handbook of Greek Mythology*. London: Methuen, 1983.

Rowell, George. *The Victorian Theatre 1792–1914: A Survey*. 2nd ed. London: Cambridge UP, 1978.

Slater, Michael. "Dickens (and Forster) At Work on *The Chimes*." *Dickens Studies Annual* 2 (1971): 106–40.

———. "Carlyle and Jerrold into Dickens: A Study of *The Chimes*." *Nineteenth-Century Fiction* 24 (1970): 506–26.

Solberg, Sarah A. " 'Text Dropped into the Woodcuts': Dickens' Christmas Books." *Dickens Studies Annual* 8 (1980): 103–18.

Tarr, Rodger L. "Dickens' Debt to Carlyle's 'Justice Metaphor' in *The Chimes*." *Nineteenth-Century Fiction* 27. 2 (Sept. 1972): 208–15.

Thomas, Deborah A. *Dickens and the Short Story*. Philadelphia: U of Pennsylvania P, 1982.

Wagenknecht, Edward. "Dickens at Work: *The Chimes*." *Dickens and the Scandalmongers*. Norman: U of Oklahoma P, 1965. 50–70.

Welsh, Alexander. "Time and the City in *The Chimes*." *Dickensian* 73 (1977): 8–17.

Pendennis, Copperfield, and the Debate on the "Dignity of Literature"

Michael J. Flynn

The "Dignity of Literature" controversy occurred in January 1850, when, having satirized men of letters in the middle of Pendennis, *William Makepeace Thackeray was excoriated by John Forster in the* Examiner *and defended himself in the* Morning Chronicle. *The exchange is usually read as a chastening defeat for Thackeray, who, having seen the harm he was doing his profession by depicting writers as not in earnest about their work, recanted in the second half of the novel. But the satire in* Pendennis, *like that in most of Thackeray's work, is primarily about snobbery, not earnestness, and reading the exchange with this in mind will reveal that Forster's actions in fact confirmed Thackeray's opinion that his fellow writers were snobs, and led to his strengthening that assertion in* Pendennis. *It will also show that* David Copperfield, *a novel about a writer's being cured of social pretensions, contains Dickens's rebuttal to Thackeray, an appendix of sorts to the "Dignity of Literature" debate. And finally, a full appreciation of the terms of that debate can help us recognize how deeply issues of snobbery and class status underlay some of the central issues of mid-nineteenth-century fiction—everything from Dickens's groundbreaking realism to Thackeray's penchant for loose baggy monsters.*

In 1851, David Masson began a joint review of *Pendennis* and *David Copperfield* with an observation that would become increasingly true over the next decade: "THACKERAY and DICKENS, Dickens and Thackeray—the

Dickens Studies Annual, Volume 41, Copyright © 2010 by AMS Press, Inc. All rights reserved.

two names now almost necessarily go together'' (57). *Vanity Fair*, serialized in 1847–48, had made William Makepeace Thackeray a household name, the second novelist of England. But he saw himself as more than a mere competitor of Charles Dickens; in matters of style, sensibility, and social status, he was assuming the role of a direct opponent. A letter to his mother, written in January 1848, reveals how fundamental this role was to Thackeray's understanding of his sudden lionization: ''There is no use denying the matter or blinking it now. I am become a sort of great man in my way—all but at the top of the tree: indeed there if the truth were known *and having a great fight up there with Dickens''* (*Letters* 2: 333; emphasis added).[1] If, as Thackeray felt, *Vanity Fair* had started such a fight, *Pendennis* was the advertising campaign that hyped the bout to the public. Reviewers constantly compared it and *Copperfield*,[2] and not merely because of the novels' contemporaneity. Rebecca Rodolff has shown, in a study of the *Weekly Chronicle*'s month-by-month reception of the two novels, that Victorians read them as being in dialogue or competition, that they expected a successful character or episode in one to elicit quickly an answer in the other.

Thackeray's letters reveal that Dickens's book certainly influenced his in at least a general way. *Pendennis* had begun its serial run in November 1848, and for five installments had told the tightly focused story of young Arthur Pendennis's foolish infatuation with Miss Fotheringay. Thackeray, however, seems to have lost his way thereafter; the sixth number, which takes Pen to Oxbridge, is meandering at best, and the seventh, which follows him home after he's been plucked, suggests that the author had as little sense of direction as his protagonist did. But the day that seventh number was published, 1 May 1849, also saw the release of the initial installment of *David Copperfield*. Thackeray's letter to Jane Brookfield of 4 May testifies to its effect upon him:

> Have you read Dickens?—O it is charming. Bravo Dickens. It has some of his very prettiest touches—those inimitable Dickens touches w[h] make such a great man of him. And the reading of the book has done another author a great deal of good. In the first place it pleases the other Author to see that Dickens who has long left off alluding to his the O A's works has been copying the O A, and greatly simplifying his style and foregoing the use of fine words. By this the public will be the gainer and David Copperfield will be improved by taking a lesson from Vanity Fair. Secondly, it has put me upon my mettle—for ah Madam all the mettle was out of me, and Ive been dreadfully & curiously cast down this month past—I say secondly it has put me on my mettle, and made me feel that I must do something.   (*Letters* 2: 531)

It's a puzzling but fascinating letter. No one has any idea precisely what lesson Dickens is supposed to have learnt from *Vanity Fair*; his style in *Copperfield* is not noticeably Thackerayan. No one has any idea what allusions to his own work Thackeray had previously spotted in Dickens's; Dickens's writings, public and private, refer to Thackeray relatively infrequently, and to his fiction even less often. It may be that in the first sentence of *David Copperfield*—"WHETHER I shall turn out to be the hero of my own life, or whether that station will be held by anybody else, these pages must show" (1)—Thackeray detected a reference to *Vanity Fair*, the "Novel without a Hero," and felt that Dickens had once again begun alluding to his works.[3] Whether or not Thackeray was right about *Copperfield*'s responding to his own fiction, however, the letter shows with absolute clarity that its author's sense of rivalry with Dickens had not diminished, and that Thackeray saw the first number of *David Copperfield* as a challenge to himself.

Just how deeply he felt that challenge is made clear by the obsessive repetitions of this letter which can be found in his other correspondence of the period. Thackeray told Mrs. Brookfield's husband that *Copperfield* "beats the yellow chap of this month [i.e., *Pendennis*, published, like all of Thackeray's serial novels, with yellow covers] hollow" (*Letters* 2: 533). To Lady Blessington he wrote that "My work shows my dullness I think—but on the other hand there is a fellow by the name of Dickens who is bringing out a rival publication and who has written beautifully"; after repeating his opinion that *Vanity Fair* had made Dickens a better stylist, he said, "I am glad of it. I hope it will put somebody on his mettle—somebody who has been careless of everything of late" (*Letters* 2: 535). And in "Mr. Brown's Letters to a Young Man about Town," one of the last series Thackeray ever wrote for *Punch*, Brown walks through the library of his club, sees a fellow clubman sleeping on one of the sofas, and asks, "What is he reading? Hah! 'Pendennis,' No. VII. Hum, let us pass on. Have you read 'David Copperfield,' by the way? How beautiful it is" (*Works* 6: 629). Thackeray, having ascended to the top of the tree with Dickens, was clearly embarrassed by what he perceived to be *Pendennis*'s inferiority to *Copperfield*, and felt he had to respond. Even if no further connections between the novels could be established, Dickens's work has to be seen as at least a direct spur to Thackeray's.

But further connections can be established, the most visible of them being what is generally known as the "Dignity of Literature" controversy, an acrimonious journalistic exchange between Thackeray and Dickens's best friend John Forster. This exchange was actually the second round in an ongoing quarrel between Thackeray on the one hand and Dickens, Forster, and a growing party of professional writers on the other; the first had occurred two-and-a-half years earlier, when Thackeray published the *Novels by Eminent Hands*, a series of parodies of contemporary authors. The *Novels* are an extension of *The Book of Snobs*: they imply that most early Victorian fiction was penned by lower-class Grub Street hacks who were less interested in writing good literature than in fallaciously portraying themselves as ornaments of high society. Dickens and Forster, who were devoting themselves to various projects designed to elevate the social reputation of Victorian men of letters, had been incensed by the series. Forster remarked to a mutual acquaintance that Thackeray was "false as hell"; having had the comment passed on to him, Thackeray cut Forster when they next met, refusing to shake his hand; the London post was snowed under with mutually recriminating letters until a public reconciliation was agreed upon a week later. The episode clearly rankled in the breasts of all involved, however. Seven months after the affair had been nominally settled, Dickens was still chiding his rival about the *Novels by Eminent Hands*, accusing the series of "depreciating or vulgarizing" Thackeray's fellow authors (*Letters* 5: 228), and arguing too that parody was an inherently lower-class form and that Thackeray had demeaned *himself* as well as his peers by dabbling in it.[4]

The rift between Thackeray and Forster was reopened in January 1850. The tenth and eleventh numbers of *Pendennis* take the novel's protagonist to London and introduce him into literary circles; the residents of those circles are satirized as deeply flawed inhabitants of Vanity Fair, as almost all of Thackeray's characters are. Forster, however, took especial exception to *Pendennis*'s portraits of literary men, seeing in them another affront to his and Dickens's efforts towards professionalism, and he publicly excoriated Thackeray for contributing to a national prejudice against men of letters. A heated debate about the dignity of literature ensued, and began the decades-long split of literary London into two camps—one consisting of self-professed gentlemanly writers who identified with Thackeray, the other of proud bohemian journalists who followed Dickens.

Biographers and critics have written a good deal about how the "Dignity of Literature" debate helped crystallize Dickens's and Forster's ideas about professionalization. But nothing's ever been said about the way in which it allowed Thackeray to continue the exposé of literary snobbery which he'd conducted in the *Novels by Eminent Hands*, or about how Forster's rhetoric in the debate served to validate *Pendennis*'s satirical portraits of literary men. Nor has it been adequately recognized that the conversation about snobbery contained in the "Dignity of Literature" debate was itself continued by *David Copperfield*. This is partly due to the fact that Dickens did not actively participate in the controversy, even though he was the unquestioned leader of the party whose views Forster was championing. Another reason is that it was Thackeray's depictions of literary snobbery in *Pendennis*, rather than his journalistic replies to Forster, to which Dickens most directly responded; since the depictions are generally unappreciated, it's only natural that the response has been, too. But it's a fact that David Copperfield shows no unmistakable signs of becoming a professional author until after the "Dignity of Literature" debate exploded in early 1850, and it's undeniable that once he does choose that career, he quickly becomes an author very unlike those whom Thackeray had been portraying in *Pendennis*. Dickens used David's literary career to show that professional authors were both middle-class and content with being middle-class.

The "Dignity of Literature" exchange thus prompted Thackeray and Dickens to use their fiction as well as their journalism to debate the social status of men of letters. It also prompted them to make claims about the social status of the literature those men of letters were producing. *David Copperfield* admits the existence of such things as lower-class writers and snobbish writers, but it contains and marginalizes them by suggesting that their work is not real literary composition but instead servile imitation or outright copying; we can see here the sequel to Dickens's statement during the "false as hell" fight that parody is the work of Grub Street hacks. Nor does *Copperfield* limit itself to class-coding the parodic mode—it goes on to contest the class status of realism. We never get to open the covers of the books David writes, but the novel suggests that the proper work for middle-class authors is realism, and by associating the work of lower-class imitators with forgery, it damns that work as, by definition, unrealistic. Because his novel does not actually describe David's writing, however, Dickens's claim on behalf of the bourgeoisie to the realistic mode had to be made obliquely. In *Pendennis*, Thackeray was feeling his way toward a more substantive counterclaim. Passages in that novel reveal him trying to prove that the structural principles of realism itself demanded that it be written not only by, but about, upper-class gentlemen, and the portrayal of Pen's literary career is as important to this effort to claim realism as Dickens's depiction of David's was to his. But perhaps we should start our examination of *Pendennis* and *Copperfield* by looking at the first result of Thackeray's writing a novel about a novelist: the "Dignity of Literature" controversy. That quarrel, after all, served to formalize the gap between gentlemanly and bourgeois writers and to publicize their mutual hostility; it thereby gave the Victorian instinct to class-code the age's literature an urgency it had not possessed in the years leading up to 1850.

I.

Despite Thackeray's protestations in May 1849 that *David Copperfield* had put him upon his mettle, he continued to have problems finding a direction for *Pendennis*; in the June number, Pen does nothing but saunter around Fairoaks and engage in a little halfhearted flirting with Blanche Amory. Near the end of the installment, it is decided that he should go to London and become a lawyer, but this doesn't mean that Thackeray had therefore settled on the future course of the novel; Pen doesn't actually leave for the metropolis until the end of the July number, and once he gets there, he neglects his legal studies just as he'd neglected his classical studies at Oxbridge. With only two weeks remaining before his deadline for the August installment, Thackeray was still writing to Jane Brookfield in the same vein he had two-and-a-half months earlier: "[I] am determined that Mr. Pendennis shan't dawdle any more, and that I'll do something to fetch up my languishing reputation, something uncommonly spirited, sarcastic, pathetic, humorous, it must be. Can you give me a hint or two? a guinea for a hint or two" *(Letters* 2: 565). But shortly thereafter he hit on an idea that, if not pathetic, was so spirited, sarcastic, and humorous, that it would reopen the breach with the Dickens camp that had been closed after the "false as hell" fight.

Thackeray decided to abandon his uninspired plan to make Pen a lawyer and instead steered him into another line of work, one he could treat with all the verve he'd displayed in *The Book of Snobs* and the *Novels by Eminent Hands*. Pen, an amateur poetaster from the beginning of the novel, had in the July number briefly entertained the idea of supporting himself with his writing during his studies for the bar (1: 272).[5] When, on the coach to London, he hears that Mr. Wagg, an acquaintance of his, is paid three hundred pounds a volume for his novels, Pen starts to calculate whether his own writing might not earn him five thousand a year (1: 280–81); he thinks it feasible, in other words, to use the odd moments he can spare from his legal studies to toss off five-and-a-half three-deckers every twelve months—a pace never approached even by G. P. R. James, who became a laughingstock in the 1840s because of the staggering frequency with which he produced historical novels. Literature, in Pen's opinion, does not require much effort, and certainly doesn't deserve to be considered a profession; it is, instead, the leisure activity of a gentleman, the trifling of a university-educated mind.

Pen's absurd calculations also show, however, that literature had the reputation of being wonderfully remunerative; he sees it as a commodity which goes to market at a price so far above its actual value as to make it appealing to a young gentleman a little short of pocket money. Such a commodity would be sure to attract more than its share of rogues, and describing rogues was what Thackeray was best at. So in the tenth and eleventh numbers of *Pendennis*, published in August and September 1849, Thackeray began introducing Pen into literary circles, and in portraying the residents of those circles, he once again undercut the image of the respectable professional author that Dickens, Forster, and their followers were trying so hard to establish.

Pen, for instance, only becomes a literary man himself after he squanders away the money his mother and sister have selflessly given him. He's encouraged to write for a living by his roommate George Warrington, who quite frankly admits that he had taken up the pen five years earlier for much the same reason. Warrington's account of himself supports Pen's impression that writing is basically a leisure activity, not the sort of thing that a man needs to do regularly: "When my purse is out, I go to work and fill it, and then lie idle like a serpent or an Indian, until I have digested the mass.''[6] And his reason for not telling Pen about his profession earlier is not calculated to raise that line of work in the young man's esteem: "I don't tell the world that I [write]. . . . I do not choose that questions should be asked: or, perhaps, I am an ass, and don't wish it to be said that George Warrington writes for bread" (1: 311–12). Yet Warrington is a gentleman at heart, *Pendennis*'s closest approach to a hero; it's the other writers in the novel, those Pen meets as Warrington conducts him through the literary world, who really drag the profession through the mire.

There are, for instance, Hoolan and Doolan, shabby Irish mercenaries perfectly willing to abuse each other in print, though in private life they are the best of friends. There are Hoolan's and Doolan's respective employers, the publishers Bacon and Bungay, who, "not having the least taste in poetry or in literature of any kind," rely on editors to make their creative decisions; Bacon's "professional gentleman" is tellingly named Mr. Hack (1: 313). There is Captain Shandon, whose genius can't overcome his improvidence, and who, confined to debtor's prison, drinks away all his income, not much caring that he's ruining his wife and children by doing so. And there is the party of authors who join Pen and Warrington for the dinner at Bungay's which finally convinces the former (who, on his arrival in London, had "believed fondly . . . in authors, reviewers, and editors of newspapers" [1: 280]) that "there are thousands of people in this town, who don't write books, who are, to the full, as clever and intellectual as people who do" (1: 346).

Thackeray's final comment on that dinner shows why he felt these portraits would "fetch up his languishing reputation":

> the literary personages with whom [Pen] had become acquainted had not said much, in the course of the night's conversation, that was worthy to be remembered or quoted. In fact, not one word about literature had been said during the whole course of the night:—and it may be whispered to those uninitiated people who are anxious to know the habits and make the acquaintance of men of letters, that there are no race of people who talk about books, or, perhaps, who read books, so little as literary men. (1: 346)

Thackeray was writing an insider's exposé of literary celebrity, an early form of tabloid journalism. *Pendennis* was widely read as a roman à clef, just as silver-fork novels had been in the previous decade: Wagg, the novelist who reportedly earns three hundred pounds a volume, is generally taken to be a caricature of Theodore Hook; Bacon and Bungay are Richard Bentley and Henry Colburn; Shandon is Thackeray's old acquaintance William Maginn; and most of the other literary characters have been "identified" as minor figures in early Victorian London's literary scene. It's hard to know how long Thackeray would have pursued this angle—he fell seriously ill in September, causing publication of *Pendennis* to be suspended for three months, and when he resumed writing, he took the novel in another direction—but this exposé, this literary gossip, was clearly his play to recapture his audience's attention.

As he might have expected, however, it also caught the attention of his fellow-writers, who saw it as another slight upon them, another denigration of their social status like the one committed in the *Novels by Eminent Hands*. The first complaint about Thackeray's depiction of literary men in *Pendennis* appeared on 3 January 1850, when the *Morning Chronicle* ran an editorial urging the government to discontinue literary pensions:

> One ill-bestowed pension acts like a prize in a lottery; and, although twelve hundred pounds a-year (the sum placed at the disposal of the Crown for the purpose) may be miserably inadequate as a regular provision for the needy sons and daughters of learning, it is quite sufficient to spread injurious and ill-founded notions regarding the claims of literary paupers upon the State. There is not the remotest risk that the supply of writers will ever fall below the demand in a country where education (superficial education, at all events) is so very generally diffused. In our opinion, Great Britain is already overstocked with authors of the middling and lower order; and the love of notoriety inherent in mankind, combined with the common distaste for continuous or unexciting labour, will always attract an undue number of recruits from other employments to literature. There may be no harm in this, so long as they can pay their way. For ourselves, we are disposed to regard the common craving after intellectual distinction, or literary fame, in men of rank and fortune, as a marked symptom of social progress. But why swell the stream or accelerate its flow by State bounties?   ("The death of Mr. P. F. Tytler . . . ")

Literature should be let alone, the editorialist argues, so that the laws of political economy can allow good writers to float and bad ones to sink. Literary pensions, by rewarding indigent authors, simply contribute to the low esteem in which men of letters were held in England. As does Thackeray, the *Chronicle* says offhandedly; in a brief digression, it accuses him of "fostering a baneful prejudice" against writers by satirizing them in *Pendennis*.

Two days later, Forster published a column about the "Encouragement of Literature by the State" in the *Examiner*. At first glance, the piece looks like a calm, reasoned rebuttal of the *Morning Chronicle*'s position; it argues that the principles of political economy do not apply to literature, and that even if they did, political economists had no qualms about the government's rewarding other professionals like soldiers, lawyers, clergymen, and diplomats, and so should have none about its recognizing writers. Underneath the column's placid surface, however, lies an anxiety that shows how closely the dignity of literature was connected with class in the minds of the Dickens party. When the *Chronicle* had mourned the glut in England of "authors of the middling and lower order," it had probably meant nothing more than that there was an abundance of poetasters, but Forster interprets the phrase as if it were a social slur; he snidely wonders if perhaps the *Chronicle* hadn't meant to say "'middling and lower order*s*,'" the insinuation being that the middle and lower classes were not the same thing and that writers were part of the former, not the latter. Forster also points out that the *Chronicle* applauds the "craving after intellectual distinction, or literary fame" when it is found in aristocrats but judges it a nuisance in anyone else, and he implies that the inconsistency is part of a devious plan to keep literature in the hands of the upper class. This accusation is absurd. Modern statistical studies have invariably found that literature had been a predominantly middle-class pursuit since the beginning of the eighteenth century,[7] but Forster, at the halfway point of the nineteenth, is acting as if the bourgeoisie had just gotten a foothold in the profession and was determined not to give it up. This conviction of holding a tenuous position, thoroughly unjustified though it is, makes it easier to understand why Forster reacted so virulently to what he saw as the *Chronicle*'s slights upon the social dignity of authors, and why he reacted just as virulently to Thackeray's.

For the only thing on which Forster and the *Morning Chronicle* could agree was that there was indeed a national prejudice against men of letters and that the tenth and eleventh numbers of *Pendennis* would exacerbate it. Forster's comments here, too, betray a terrible class anxiety. The novel's depiction of literary London, he opines,

> is a caricature such as Mr. Thackeray too often condescends to, and which might even have passed as the sarcastic suggestion of a useful truth (to wit, that there are quacks and imposters in the author's calling as well as in every other) if the writer had less frequently indulged a disposition to pay court to the non-literary class by disparaging his literary fellow-labourers.
>
>   ("Encouragement of Literature by the State")

The "non-literary class" which Thackeray is accused of "paying court" to is the aristocracy; *Vanity Fair* had gained him entrance into high society, and he moved in fashionable circles more often and more comfortably than any other major Victorian novelist. Many of Thackeray's fellow writers (especially those who, like Dickens and Forster, came from the very bottom of the lower class) were suspicious of his new social standing, and the cutting implication of Forster's article is that Thackeray's success in fashionable society since the publication of *Vanity Fair* was the result of his willingness to sell out his friends.

Thackeray, who'd recently recovered from the illness which had suspended the publication of *Pendennis*, responded to both of his critics on 12 January with "The Dignity of Literature," a letter to the editor of the *Morning Chronicle*. His basic defense against the charge of contributing to a national prejudice against writers is that he couldn't be doing anything of the kind, because that prejudice no longer existed:

> Does any man who has written a book worth reading—any poet, historian, novelist, man of science—lose reputation by his character for genius or for learning? Does he not, on the contrary, get friends, sympathy, applause— money, perhaps? . . . The literary profession is not held in disrepute; nobody wants to disparage it, no man loses his social rank, whatever it may be, by practising it. On the contrary; the pen gives a place in the world to men who had none before, a fair place, fairly achieved by their genius, as any other degree of eminence is by any other kind of merit. Literary men need not, as it seems to me, be in the least querulous about their position any more, or want the pity of anybody.   (*Works* 13: 630)

Thackeray was so convinced that the national prejudice against men of letters had disappeared that he frequently reiterated the contention during the next year or two. In the twelfth number of *Pendennis*, published just a few days before the "Dignity of Literature" controversy broke out, he'd had Pen's uncle, the aging Regency dandy, comment on how much more respectable writers were considered in the 1830s than they had been a decade or two earlier (1: 365); in the final number of the novel, published at the end of the year, Pen's acquaintance Mr. Bows notes the dramatic change in the social status of writers since the days of Samuel Johnson (2: 336); and at the end of his lectures on *The English Humourists of the Eighteenth Century*, delivered in 1851, Thackeray argued that the careers of the authors he'd discussed served to prove his point (106–08).

What Thackeray did not do, however, was agree with Forster's contention that writers should be considered professionals and treated with the respect that went along with that classification in mid-Victorian England. He says that a writer's work can earn him friends, sympathy, applause—even money, but he conspicuously leaves social standing off the list; when he mentions class status, it is only to say that a writer's work never causes him to *lose* it. We can see here one of the assumptions of Thackeray's essay: that social respectability is a function of a man's birth rather than his trade. Writing might not cause a man to lose his social rank, but neither, in Thackeray's mind, should it cause him to gain a greater one than he'd been born with; he would argue a few years later that "if they give honour [i.e., baronetcies] to English writers they should pick out gentlemen who write English," rather than any Tom, Dick, or Harry who happened to write a popular novel (*Letters* 3: 46). Forster and his friends might be successful writers, the implication is, but they hadn't been born into the professional or genteel classes, and so they had no right to ask the government to recognize them as professionals or gentlemen.

And, Thackeray insinuates, it's the latter status that Forster is really after; he suggests several times that what Forster wants is not professional respectability but a title, and he likens him to Pitt Crawley, the effeminate snob in *Vanity Fair* who keeps his court guide next to his Bible and "would have starved rather than have dined without a white neckcloth" (86). He also suggests that people who clamor after respectability do so because of their own insecurity:

> it seems to me that men of letters had best silently assume that they are as good as any other gentlemen. ... If I sit at your table, I suppose that I am my neighbour's equal, and that he is mine. If I begin straightway with a protest of "Sir, I am a literary man, but I would have you to know that I am as good as you," which of us is it that questions the dignity of the literary profession—my neighbour who would like to eat his soup in quiet, or the man of letters who commences the argument?   (*Works* 13: 632–33).

Forster protested the next week in the *Examiner* that he was not "aspiring to empty rank or inappropriate station" (" 'The Dignity of Literature' "), and he pointed out that though Thackeray had argued that abusing men of letters didn't appeal to any national prejudice, he hadn't denied that he had abused them terribly. Forster also repeated a cutting comparison of Thackeray with Henry Fielding which he had first made a year and a half earlier in a review of *Vanity Fair*, arguing that Fielding would never have satirized Parson Trulliber without providing Parson Adams as a counterweight, and that Thackeray's biggest flaw as a writer was his unrelieved scorn of humankind.

Thackeray did not reply—not in the periodical press, at any rate. But several authors, Michael Lund among them, have argued that *Pendennis*'s depictions of literary men undergo a quantum shift after January 1850. On 25 January, Lund reminds us, Thackeray admitted to Abraham Hayward that "the words in Pendennis are untenable be hanged to them" (*Letters* 2: 636), and starting with the thirteenth number of the novel, Lund argues, he began to atone for those words. The worst of the literary characters (Captain Shandon, for instance) quickly disappear from the story, and those that remain mend their idle ways: Pen settles down to steady, if uninspired, journalistic work rather than the sporadic bouts of scribbling Warrington had suggested, and Warrington himself becomes a model professional man, stepping up and filling in for Pen when the young tyro succumbs to a fever and becomes unable to complete his editorial duties. The difference is marked enough that Lund speaks of the "Dignity of Literature" controversy as something like a victory for the Forster and Dickens party, one that chastened Thackeray and reined in his unseemly levity.[8]

Such readings, in order to be convincing, have to misread *Pendennis* by examining it only through the lens which Forster provides us. Both he and the *Morning Chronicle* took especial offense to Thackeray's summation of Bungay's dinner party, to the passage about there being ''no race of people who talk about books, or, perhaps, who read books, so little as literary men.'' Their objection, in other words, was to the depiction of authors as mercenaries, men who wrote for the money but who had little real interest in what they did for a living. But that passage is in actuality a rather minor part of Thackeray's satire of men of letters, and Pen's becoming a more dedicated author in the second half of the novel is in reality a fairly minor concession to Forster. *Pendennis*'s literary characters are uninterested in their profession because the only thing they are in fact interested in is class; the middle of *Pendennis*, in other words, is, like the *Novels by Eminent Hands*, an unflinching look at literary snobbery. A failure to appreciate this will result in Thackeray's appearing more penitent than he really was (we have already noted that he reiterated his position on the dignity of literature the following year in *The English Humourists*, and he would publicly oppose Dickens's and Forster's attempts to professionalize literature throughout the early 1850s). It will also make Dickens's revaluation of Thackeray in *David Copperfield* almost impossible to see, because what Dickens most directly responds to there is Thackeray's conviction that English writers were snobs.

The satire of literary snobbery in *Pendennis* can be obscured by the fact that the novel is a review of snobbery generally: it starts, after all, with Major Pendennis sitting in his club, ostentatiously reading letters from aristocrats in front of one of his envious fellow clubmen; it describes for us the Major's brother, an apothecary whose life's ambition was to be thought a gentleman; and then it introduces us to Pen, who represses the knowledge that his father had ever worked in a surgery and carries himself as if he were royalty. The literary snobbery in the middle chapters of the novel can, understandably, blend into this backdrop, but overlooking it is a mistake. The very first literary man Pen encounters—Doolan, on the London coach—should alert us to what's in store. Doolan chats amiably with Pen during the long ride, but doesn't think anything special of him until they arrive in the metropolis and the young man is met by Harry Foker, an earl's grandson who wears white kid gloves and drives an elegant private cab; Doolan immediately revises his opinion of Pen and begins to feel ''a great respect'' for him (1: 281).

The effect of Pen's connections on literary men becomes a running joke once Thackeray introduces him into the world of London letters. His first appearance in print, for instance, is almost entirely a result of the fact that Bacon and Bungay are two of the most irredeemable snobs in all of Thackeray's work, and wage constant war to see which can publish the largest number of titled authors. Warrington, who is the younger son of a baronet himself, persuades Bacon to accept Pen's poem ''The Church Porch'' by exploiting this state of affairs:

Warrington knowing Bacon's weaknesses, acted upon them with great adroit-
ness in his friend's behalf. In the first place, he put on his hat to speak to
Bacon, and addressed him from the table on which he seated himself. Bacon
liked to be treated with rudeness by a gentleman, and used to pass it on to his
inferiors as boys pass the mark. "What! not know Mr. Pendennis, Mr. Bacon?"
Warrington said. "You can't live much in the world, or you would know him.
A man of property in the West, of one of the most ancient families in England,
related to half the nobility in the empire—he's cousin to Lord Pontypool—he
was one of the most distinguished men at Oxbridge; he dines at Gaunt House
every week."

"Law bless me, you don't say so, sir. Well—really—Law bless me now,"
said Mr. Bacon.

"I have just been showing Mr. Hack some of his verses, which he sat up
last night, at my request, to write; and Hack talks about giving him a copy of
the book . . . as payment for these verses. You don't suppose that such a man
as Mr. Arthur Pendennis gives up a dinner at Gaunt House for nothing? You
know, as well as anybody, that the men of fashion want to be paid."

"That they do, Mr. Warrington, sir," said the publisher . . . with a sigh.
"There was Lord Viscount Dodo, now; I gave his lordship a good bit of money
for his poems, and only sold eighty copies. [The Honourable Percy] Popjoy's
'Hadgincourt,' sir, fell dead."

"Well, then, I'll take my man over to Bungay," Warrington said, and rose
from the table. This threat was too much for Mr. Bacon, who was instantly
ready to accede to any reasonable proposal of Mr. Warrington's. (1: 316–17)

A few pages later, Warrington sells some of Pen's other work to Bungay
anyway, using precisely the same tactics with which he had wooed Bacon
(1: 326–27). The extent to which the two publishers are slaves to their snobbery can be seen by the fact that they sacrifice their profit margin to it.
Aristocrats do not make good writers in *Pendennis*; the only reason Bacon
needs Pen's poem at all is because Popjoy, Lord Falconet's eldest son, had
been commissioned to contribute a short lyric to a fashionable annual, and
instead produced drivel unprintable even in a publication which sold wholly
on the strength of its aristocratic contributors. Clearly, Bacon has had such
experiences before, and lost money because of them, but his business sense
is completely unable to conquer his snobbery.

The passage quoted above should also make it clear that Thackeray is not
satirizing literary men for simply being lower-class. Middle- and lower-class
men produce the vast majority of publishable writing in the novel (we quickly
learn that one such man ghost-writes a good portion of the work published
under Popjoy's name [1: 344]), and if Thackeray does laugh at them for not
liking to read or discuss literature, he never questions their ability to produce
it. A journalist named Archer, for instance, is praised by Warrington for his
professional ability and integrity, but is skewered by Thackeray for being a
compulsive liar who makes himself out to be the indispensable advisor to the
Duke of Wellington, the Marquis of Steyne, the Lord Chamberlain, and everyone else at court (1: 306–08). Captain Shandon is the closest thing in the

novel to a genius, but he fawns on Pen and Warrington when they visit him in the Fleet because he thinks them men of fashion, and attempts to entertain them with fictitious stories of his own adventures in the beau monde (1: 324).

The work such men produce, while done with wonderful facility, is every bit as pretentious as they are themselves. For instance, Shandon's prospectus for the *Pall Mall Gazette*, a new magazine he's starting for Bungay, boasts that the periodical will be "conducted by gentlemen of acknowledged reputation; men famous at the Universities . . . , known at the Clubs, and of the Society which they described" (1: 323)—but he plans to run it himself out of his cell in the Fleet Prison. The advertisement almost sounds like a sly parody, a ruse to sell a snobbish public the only thing it will buy, until we recall Bacon's complaints about how poorly aristocratic writing generally sold. When Shandon, a page or two later, starts to spin his yarns of high society for Pen and Warrington, it becomes perfectly clear that the absurd pretentiousness of the *Pall Mall Gazette* is designed to amuse its conductors and contributors rather than its readers; Pen, the indigent apothecary's son, had listened to the captain read the prospectus with a swelling heart, priding himself on being perfectly qualified to write for such a fashionable periodical. Thackeray is accusing literary men of exactly the same offense he had charged them with in *The Book of Snobs* and the *Novels by Eminent Hands*—of writing fashionable literature in an effort to be thought fashionable.

As for the dinner which finally shatters Pen's illusions about literary men, the narrator's derisive comment on which triggered the "Dignity of Literature" debate, it's as notable for what is in fact discussed around the table as for what isn't. Bungay invites as many aristocratic authors as he can, in the hope that their carriages will be seen by Bacon, who lives across the street; his other guests, those of a decidedly lower station, spend most of their time trying to look like they belong in such company. Mr. Wagg talks to Pen of his neighbors the Claverings and his distant relation Lady Rockminster, "not for Pen's ear so much as for the edification of the company, whom he was glad to inform that he paid visits to gentlemen's country seats, and was on intimate terms with the nobility" (1: 340); his rival Mr. Wenham informs one Miss Bunion that a duchess had enjoyed her last volume, which communication "quite put poor Wagg's dowager and baronet out of court, and placed Wenham beyond Wagg as a man of fashion" (1: 341); Bungay pretends that his wine has been bought from an alderman rather than from the local pub (1: 343); and so on. This, according to Thackeray, is what literary men do talk about while they're not talking about literature.

If, as we've seen, what Thackeray is satirizing in the middle numbers of *Pendennis* is not the social station of writers but their snobbish obsession with social station, then the "Dignity of Literature" debate needs to be reconsidered, because Forster's comments during it would have been much more likely to confirm Thackeray in his position than to prompt him to reconsider it. Forster's anxious objection to the *Morning Chronicle*'s lumping together the middling and lower orders, his angry accusation about Thackeray's flattering the non-literary class, and his clamoring for what Thackeray claimed were stars and garters, would all have made him look exactly like the literary snobs in *Pendennis*—would have been proof that Thackeray was not, in fact, filling his novel with distorted caricatures.

It should be no surprise, then, that while the work ethic of *Pendennis*'s literary men improves somewhat in the second, post-controversy, half of the novel, their snobbery doesn't abate a bit. Pen's increasing maturity can be seen in his gradual recognition of this snobbery, but there's no suggestion that he can continue to work in the profession without displaying it. His most notable work in the second half of the book is *Leaves from the Life-Book of Walter Lorraine*, an autobiographical novel based on his early infatuations with the Fotheringay and Blanche Amory, and drafted shortly after those affairs in an over-the-top Byronic style. When he decides to publish the manuscript, he has Warrington hawk it to Bacon and Bungay using precisely the same tactics with which he sold "The Church Porch," and with precisely the same success (2: 27–29). But Pen has to make a few revisions before the novel can actually go to press, the nature of which can be ascertained from a conversation he has with Blanche:

> she fell into a rhapsody about the book, about the snatches of poetry interspersed in it, about the two heroines, Leonora and Neæra; about the two heroes, Walter Lorraine and his rival the young Duke—"and what good company you introduce us to," said the young lady, archly, "*quel ton!* How much of your life have you passed at court, and are you a prime minister's son, Mr. Arthur?"
>
> Pen began to laugh—"It is as cheap for a novelist to create a Duke as to make a Baronet," he said. "Shall I tell you a secret, Miss Amory? I promoted all my characters at the request of the publisher. The young Duke was only a young Baron when the novel was first written; his false friend the Viscount, was a simple commoner, and so on with all the characters of the story."
>
> (2: 20)

The revisions to the original draft of *Walter Lorraine* may have been made at the request of the publisher, but we can see here that they do for Pen exactly what the *Pall Mall Gazette* was supposed to do for Shandon: they make him look as if he were a fixture in the most fashionable circles in London. They're so efficacious in this respect that even Blanche, who knows Pen's pedigree full well, begins to wonder if she's underestimated his social position. Pen laughs at the conclusions she draws from the book, but seems quite willing to let the vast majority of his readers make the same conclusion; he is playing a role much like the one Thackeray himself often assumes in his fiction, that of a critic who exposes hypocrisy, but who cheerfully practices it himself.[9] None of *Pendennis*'s other men of letters amends his snobbery even this much. When Archer reappears late in the novel, he drops names as egregiously and mendaciously as he did when we first met him (2: 193–95), and the last we hear of either Bacon or Bungay is the latter's agreeing to print Blanche's sentimental poems after she marries a French nobleman, and publishing them "with the Countess's coronet emblazoned on the Countess's work" (2: 371).

Thackeray's depiction of literature as a terribly snobbish profession is quite unchanged by the "Dignity of Literature" debate—as might be expected, considering that Forster's desperate clamoring for social respect would have done nothing to change Thackeray's mind on the matter. Nor is it likely that the controversy would have changed any reader's mind, since Forster's editorials never deny that literature is a hotbed of snobbery. Indeed, they do quite the opposite; the charge that Thackeray was abusing his fellow writers in an attempt to cater to the non-literary class is little more than Forster's turning the tables on Thackeray and calling *him* a literary snob. The "Dignity of Literature" debate is at its core two petty authors accusing one another of the same thing. If Forster's party were going to get what it wanted, it would have to put forward a more positive representation of a professional writer, a representation which negotiated issues of class status more constructively. It had to show the writer, that is, being cured of literary snobbery, rather than pointing it out in his fellows. Such a depiction is exactly what the second half of *David Copperfield* provides.

II.

The vexed question of the writer's relationship with the upper class was on Dickens's mind, just as it was on Thackeray's, in the years bracketing the composition of *Copperfield*. Dickens's engagement with the issue of literary snobbery, however, is less immediately apparent in his fiction than in his earnest political attempts to elevate writing into a profession—with all the class implications which that word carried in Victorian England—and a brief look at those attempts will help to highlight that issue in the novel. In the second half of 1847, with the "false as hell" fight fresh in his mind, Dickens had made an ineffectual attempt to form a Provident Union of Literature, Science, & Art, an association which would provide life insurance to literary men, and "shame the English Government, by giving as much every year to the reduced professors of Art, Literature, and Science, as the whole Civil List gives, on account of Great Britain" (*Letters* 5: 144–45). The second part of this scheme, the one proposing the distribution of pensions, clearly anticipates Forster's position in the "Dignity of Literature" exchange, but it came to nothing, which is why Forster was still bemoaning the government's failure to support men of letters two years later. The plan to unionize writers continued to occupy Dickens, however; he, Forster, and Edward Bulwer-Lytton began a campaign to establish the Guild of Literature and Art in late 1850, and spent much of 1851, the year after the "Dignity of Literature" exchange, working tirelessly to create an endowment for it. Though they succeeded in getting the Guild incorporated in 1854, legal restrictions prevented it from doing the kind of work Dickens had hoped it would achieve, and when he realized that this project, too, had been stillborn, he, Forster, and other members of their circle spent four fruitless years in the late 1850s trying to take control of the Royal Literary Fund and turn it into the type of institution they'd been unable to create from scratch.[10]

The Provident Union, the Guild, and the Royal Literary Fund were all primarily financial organizations. But the rhetoric which Dickens used when supporting them evokes the same class issues at stake in the "Dignity of Literature" exchange. He very carefully argued, for instance, that the Provident Union was designed not merely to distribute money to needy writers, but (unlike existing charities) to distribute its money in such a way that "it compromises the independence of no one recipient of it in the smallest degree" (*Letters* 5: 701). When Dickens began circulating advertisements for the Guild a few years later, he used precisely the same argumentative tactics: the new organization would, he claimed, "render such assistance to [Authors and Artists] as shall never compromise their independence" (*Letters* 6: 358n). Daniel Hack has demonstrated, in his study of the Guild, that the final prospectus repeats this language yet again (*Material Interests* 89).[11] And while Dickens's ostensible objection to the Royal Literary Fund was to its bureaucratic inefficiency (his attack on it is contemporaneous with *Little Dorrit*'s satire of the Circumlocution Office), the old insistence on the humiliating dependence which traditional charity forces on writers persists even there (Dilke, Dickens, and Forster 6–8). Hack argues that Dickens's insistence that the financial support distributed by the organizations he championed would not undermine the recipients' independence was an attempt to safeguard the respectability of the literary profession in a culture where receiving charity meant forfeiting all claims to social status. That is, the Provident Union, the Guild, and the reformed Royal Literary Fund would provide financial assistance to proud middle-class professionals, something government pensions, because of the degrading nature of their charity, were by definition unable to do.

"Independence," of course, is a relative term, and it's important to understand whom Dickens was trying to make writers independent of. The prospectus for the Guild, which explains the name Dickens, Forster, and Bulwer-Lytton chose for the organization, suggests an answer to that question:

It is . . . to express more emphatically the nature of an association which neither abrogates the disputable aims of an Academy, nor professes to bestow the humiliating charity of an Asylum, that it is intended, in accordance with the name given by old Saxon custom to societies in which the members of a class contributed to the benefit of each other, to call the Institution proposed

THE GUILD OF LITERATURE AND ART.   (*Letters* 6: 856)

It's not so much the independence of the individual that is being preserved here, as the independence of the class; by supporting one another, middle-class writers can avoid having to petition another class (and of course this means the upper class, in the person of government ministers or of individual benefactors) for patronage. Literary patronage was one of Dickens's bête noires; it was the patronage system, in his opinion, that led to the literary snobbery Thackeray and Forster were arguing about in the "Dignity of Literature" exchange. If his ostensible objection to the Royal Literary Fund was its inefficiency, for instance, the real reason for his dislike of it was its being more or less run by aristocrats (Dilke, Dickens, and Forster 15). It was bad enough that indigent writers had to appeal to such men, rather than to their fellow writers, when they applied to the Fund for aid. Worse was the fact that even the established and financially secure authors who were dues-paying members of the organization spent much of their time there fawning on their social superiors. Dickens's speech at the 1856 general meeting of the Fund could have come right out of *The Book of Snobs*:

let us remember what the Committee and their supporters asserted last year . . . that if you get £100 you are to spend £40 in management; and if you get £1000, of course you may spend £400 in giving the rest away. . . .
    It is in our fondness for being so stupendously genteel, by keeping up such a fashionable appearance, by giving way to the vulgar and common social vice of hanging on to great connexions at any price—that the money goes. . . . Why, sir, the very last distinguished writer of fiction whom you caught for your public dinner [this had been Thackeray], told you, in return for drinking his health, somewhere towards the small hours of the morning, that he felt like the servant in plush who is permitted to sweep the stage down, when there are no more great people to come on; and I myself, at a dinner some twelve years ago, felt like a sort of Rip Van Winkle reversed, who had gone to sleep backwards for a hundred years; and, waking, found that Literature instead of being emancipated, had to endure all manner of aristocratic patrons, and was lying at the feet of people who did nothing for it, instead of standing alone.
(*Speeches* 211–13)

Dickens, therefore, was just as aware of literary snobbery as was Thackeray. But he saw such snobbery as stemming from the organization of the Victorian marketplace, not as a constitutional flaw in the character of the writer. His efforts to form a literary union in the late 1840s and early 1850s can thus be seen as attempts to construct a positive representation of the professional writer freed from snobbery—precisely the sort of representation Forster had failed to provide in the "Dignity of Literature" debate.

The problem, as Daniel Hack has keenly pointed out, was that, given the state of British society at the time, it was virtually impossible to get such a union off the ground without the political and financial assistance of aristocratic patrons. Hack conjectures that Dickens's sensitivity to this fact may have led to the abandonment of the Provident Union scheme in 1847 (*Material Interests* 93), and he traces the ironic fall of the Guild of Literature and Art into just the kind of snobbery it sought to make obsolete. In planning the Guild, Dickens had proposed to supply its endowment through the proceeds from a series of amateur theatricals, but in order to stir up interest, he decided that they'd have to give the first performance at Devonshire House, with the queen and the prince regent in the audience. Dickens's letter to the Duke of Devonshire proposing the scheme is uncharacteristically apologetic, and suggests how sheepish he felt about compromising his principles:

> Sir Edward Bulwer Lytton and I, considering the matter in every possible light—with a view to the success of what our daily experience shews us to be so necessary—are agreed that the first representation of this comedy [Bulwer-Lytton's *Not So Bad as We Seem*] ought to be before Her Majesty and the Court; as the circumstance of its having been produced under such auspices, would have great weight with those who would form the staple of our after-audiences.   (*Letters* 6: 304)

Dickens tries to dissociate himself from snobbish fawning on the aristocracy and nobility—he's considered the matter "in every possible light" before settling on this course—but he eventually bowed to the necessity of doing so. Worse was to come. Hack notes that Bulwer-Lytton began to worry about whether their aristocratic host might not be offended by the play, which satirizes a self-satisfied duke, and records his panicked suggestions to Dickens that they may want to rewrite the piece; Hack also observes that Bulwer-Lytton's final version of the play (which contains a scene in which a Grub Street author sells a manuscript to the aforementioned duke) celebrates aristocratic patronage rather than demonizing it. Dickens, playing the role of one Lord Wilmot, found himself giving a speech in fulsome praise of the queen, who did in fact sit in the audience at the play's debut performance (*Material Interests* 94–99). And London newspapers recounted that performance in terms that would have made Bacon and Bungay envious. The *Illustrated London News*, for instance, cheerfully announced that "it is not our intention to enter upon a description of the play," and offered instead a roster of the titled luminaries who'd attended the event:

The play began at half-past nine—her Majesty, Prince Albert, and the Prince and Princess Royal of Prussia occupying the Royal box, a most beautiful structure erected for the occasion. The seats were filled by the most illustrious for rank and genius. There was the Duchess of Sutherland, a veritable Koh-i-noor; there was the "Iron Duke," in his best temper; there was Macaulay, Chevalier Bunsen [the Prussian ambassador], Van der Weyer [the Belgian ambassador]—themselves authors; in fact, all the highest representatives of the rank, beauty, and genius of this wonderful England, and her foreign Ambassadors.

("The Guild of Literature and Art")

Thackeray probably hit a raw nerve when he wrote to Forster following this performance, "I don't believe in the Guild of Literature I dont believe in the Theatrical scheme; I think *that* is against the dignity of our profession" (*Letters [Supplement]* 1: 417–18).

If Forster had failed, in the "Dignity of Literature" exchange, to provide a positive representation of the man of letters cured of snobbery, Dickens's professional activities in the years surrounding it were to meet the same fate. But for all his activity in that sphere, Dickens was not first and foremost a union organizer; he was a writer. And a fictional depiction of a professional writer would not be subject to the same pragmatic difficulties that were to plague Dickens's union schemes (difficulties which, admittedly, lay a year in the future at the time of the "Dignity of Literature" exchange, but which Hack suggests Dickens's keen business sense led him to foresee as early as 1847). So it should perhaps not be surprising that a few months after Thackeray and Forster had concluded their exchange in the periodical press, *David Copperfield* begins to give us exactly that portrait of the unsnobbish professional writer which Forster had failed to provide.

It's impossible to know for sure at what point in the composition of the book Dickens decided that its hero would become a novelist. There's no mention of that vocation in the serial title, *The Personal History, Adventures, Experience, & Observation of David Copperfield the Younger of Blunderstone Rookery (Which He Never Meant to Be Published on Any Account)*, and none of Dickens's number plans contains even an oblique allusion to the literary profession, before or after David enters it. A few scenes early in the novel do show that David has an innate talent for storytelling (the most important being his playing Scheherazade to Steerforth's sultan at Salem House, retelling the eighteenth-century novels he grew up with), but they don't lead in any direct fashion to David's career as an author. The first we hear of his plan to become a newspaper reporter is in the twelfth number, published in April 1850, and his first attempts at original work aren't described until two months later. David doesn't begin to write for a living, in other words, until after the "Dignity of Literature" debate had broken out in January.[12]

The thematic significance of David's becoming a writer suggests even more strongly than does its timing that Dickens had *Pendennis* in mind when he steered his protagonist towards a literary career. *David Copperfield*, though it sports a plethora of supporting characters and subplots, has a very simple and elegant dramatic structure. It is divided into halves, and has a two-part climax which bisects the book: the first part of that climax, Steerforth's seduction of Emily, comes exactly at the halfway point, the end of Number X; the second part, the news of Aunt Betsey's bankruptcy, comes one month later, at the close of Number XI. In the first half of the novel, David's search for his proper place in society (necessitated by that ultra-Victorian plot device, the death of the father) takes him in the direction of the upper class: his best friend is Steerforth, the aristocratic dilettante whom he thinks "noble" (84, 86, 253); the object of his affection is Dora, the future child-wife who is clearly not fit for a bourgeois existence; and his profession is the law, proctoring having been described to him as "the genteelest profession in the world" (331). David is, without realizing it, very much like the simpering fellow with the weak legs at Mr. Waterbrook's dinner party who boasts, "I'd rather at any time be knocked down by a man who had got Blood in him, than I'd be picked up by a man who hadn't" (320).

David is, of course, "knocked down" by Steerforth's treachery, and just how much he resembles the fellow with the weak legs is shown by the first sentence of the second half of the novel, where he admits that he loves Steerforth even more after his seduction of Emily than he had before it (388). But the episode does prompt him to reconsider his class sympathies—what Thackeray would call his snobbery—and his subsequent visit to Steerforth's mother, during which he informs her of her son's actions, impresses upon him the vast difference between his own mores and those of the gentility. His aunt's sudden bankruptcy then forces him to act on his new understanding, to exchange his genteel pretensions for the realities of a middle-class life. Steerforth is quickly replaced by Traddles, who models for David an earnest devotion to work; Dora eventually gives way to Agnes, the helpmate needed in a bourgeois household; and the law is abandoned for journalism and then for the writing of fiction.

David's career path, in other words, follows Pen's precisely. But Pen's foray into the literary world showed it to be just another booth in Vanity Fair; the snobbery which Thackeray felt was endemic to all members of British society is possessed in an even greater measure than usual by the writers we meet in the middle numbers of *Pendennis*. David's experience with literary life is quite different. Writing professionally is part of his rejection of aristocratic values, his adoption of the bourgeois work ethic, and his acceptance of his social station; he does not want stars and garters, as Thackeray thought Forster did, and he does not want to hobnob with dukes, as Forster grumbled about Thackeray's doing.

David's professionalization brings a significant—and related—change in his relationship with other writers, and here, too, we can see Dickens responding to the "Dignity of Literature" debate. We know that in Forster's eyes, what allowed Thackeray "to pay court to the non-literary class" was his willingness to disparage "his literary fellow-labourers"; loyalty to one group, for him, meant opposition to the other. The same thing is true in *David Copperfield*. Dickens may not have known in the early stages of his book that David would grow up to be a novelist, but the scenes in which he had his protagonist act as Steerforth's Scheherazade would later provide a useful contrast to Copperfield's mature professional ethics. When the young David happens to mention *Peregrine Pickle* on the playground of Salem House, Steerforth decrees that Copperfield shall entertain him with recitations of that story and any others that come to mind; for the remainder of the term, David, working from memory, obediently lulls Steerforth to sleep every night and rouses him every morning. This is an allegory of the patronage system which so thoroughly irritated Dickens. Steerforth, the aristocrat, dictates what and when the author will write; David, despite his "great pride and satisfaction" in being sponsored, is forced to admit that the arrangement puts him to no little "inconvenience" (79); the *Arabian Nights* imagery only serves to emphasize the inequity of the system, giving the patron even the power of life and death over the writer.[13] Most important, however, is the fact that by performing for his aristocratic patron, the writer offends against the other members of his profession. "What ravages I committed on my favorite authors in the course of my interpretation of them," the adult David says, "I am not in a condition to say, and should be very unwilling to know" (79–80); he may not have disparaged Smollett, exactly, but in the attempt to recite his works to Steerforth, he has done something akin to infringing on Smollett's copyright or authoring a parody of *Peregrine Pickle*. Dickens and Forster, as part of their campaign to elevate the social status of literature, had been working throughout the 1840s to eradicate both practices.

The adult David, the middle-class David, on the other hand, would be as little likely to commit such professional sins as would Dickens himself. The following passage, in which he passes judgment on his career, will illustrate this:

> I will only add, to what I have already written of my perseverance at this time of my life, and of a patient and continuous energy which then began to be matured within me, and which I know to be the strong part of my character, if it have any strength at all, that there, on looking back, I find the source of my success. I have been very fortunate in worldly matters; many men have worked much harder, and not succeeded half so well; but I never could have done what I have done, without the habits of punctuality, order, and diligence, without the determination to concentrate myself on one object at a time, no matter how

quickly its successor should come upon its heels, which I then formed. Heaven knows I write this, in no spirit of self-laudation. . . . My meaning simply is, that whatever I have tried to do in life, I have tried with all my heart to do well; that whatever I have devoted myself to, I have devoted myself to completely; that, in great aims and in small, I have always been thoroughly in earnest. I have never believed it possible that any natural or improved ability can claim immunity from the companionship of the steady, plain, hard-working qualities, and hope to gain its end. There is no such thing as such fulfilment on this earth. Some happy talent, and some fortunate opportunity, may form the two sides of the ladder on which some men mount, but the rounds of that ladder must be made of stuff to stand wear and tear; and there is no substitute for thorough-going, ardent, and sincere earnestness. Never to put one hand to anything, on which I could throw my whole self; *and never to affect depreciation of my work, whatever it was*; I find, now, to have been my golden rules.

(517–18; emphasis added)

Obviously this passage addresses one of the issues at stake in the "Dignity of Literature" debate: the indolence which Warrington had suggested made a literary career attractive, the "distaste for continuous or unexciting labour" which the *Morning Chronicle* had claimed was felt by most literary men. But the really interesting part of the paragraph is the phrase in the last sentence about David's not depreciating his work, a phrase which stands out because it has no obvious logical connection to the rest of the passage. The only explanation for that phrase's being there is that in David's mind—and, clearly, in Dickens's—the middle-class work ethic which is the paragraph's primary concern is indelibly linked to a respect for one's profession. If writers working within the patronage system generally commit ravages on their fellow authors, those writing in a professional environment, Dickens is arguing, take care that they never do so. The passage reads like a homily meant for Thackeray, whom Dickens had been chiding just two-and-a-half years earlier for "depreciating" his fellow authors in the *Novels by Eminent Hands*.

This echo in *David Copperfield* of the "false as hell" fight should alert us to another aspect of the novel's revaluation of Thackeray. Dickens had written a postscript to the "Dignity of Literature" debate by using David's history to argue that snobbish, indolent authors of the sort satirized in *Pendennis* belonged to an older system of literature which pitted men of letters against one another for the amusement of the upper class; he'd also intimated that the modern system of literature, by contrast, produced authors content with their social station, earnest men of letters devoted to professional solidarity. He'd supported Forster's position, in other words, and opposed Thackeray's. But Dickens also made sure that Thackeray would get the point by revisiting the issue at stake in the previous disagreement between the two men—parody—and working it into the model of the literary profession which he was constructing. The young David's ravaging of his favorite authors, after all, is a result of his trying to reproduce them, and for many Victorian writers (especially those who had not gone to university and been exposed there to the rich classical tradition of the parodic mode), imitation, parody, and plagiarism were more or less indistinguishable.[14] It should be no surprise, then, that *David Copperfield* depicts copying—an act which occurs frequently in the novel—as the work of snobbish lower-class writers, and in fact as the only work that such writers are able to produce; original composition is reserved for professional middle-class authors like the adult David.

David does continue his copying throughout his young adulthood, working, for instance, as Doctor Strong's amanuensis and as a parliamentary reporter for a morning paper, but such writing is nothing more than an apprenticeship which he needs to serve; it is not itself a productive middle-class activity. Even Traddles, the lower-middle-class man who finds life a pull, discovers that copying legal documents isn't enough to support him, and moves up to writing briefs and encyclopedia articles (345–46)—if not imaginative work, at least original. Mr. Dick, whose lunacy prevents him from completing his Memorial, is put to work copying legal texts at the same time that David begins his writing career, and supposedly for the same reason: to make money for the suddenly bankrupt family. But this is done more to humor him than out of any expectation that he can really help; Mr. Dick's dream of making Aunt Betsey rich with the odd shillings his copying earns him is gently laughed at as the delusion of a madman (451–52, 557).[15]

On the other hand, copying is the life's work of Uriah Heep, the charity-school boy who obsequiously fawns on his social superiors while plotting to supplant them. When we first meet Uriah, he is employed as Mr. Wickfield's clerk; one of the richer set pieces of the novel occurs when the young David peeks into the office to watch him at his business:

> Uriah . . . was at work at a desk in this room, which had a brass frame on the top to hang papers upon, and on which the writing he was making a copy of was then hanging. Though his face was towards me, I thought, for some time, the writing being between us, that he could not see me; but looking that way more attentively, it made me uncomfortable to observe that, every now and then, his sleepless eyes would come below the writing, like two red suns, and stealthily stare at me for I dare say a whole minute at a time, during which his pen went, or pretended to go, as cleverly as ever.　　　　　(189–90)

What separates David from Uriah, the hero from the villain, the middle-class man from the usurper, is a piece of original writing. That writing is an impediment to Uriah, who needs to find a way around it if he wants to look at David (note that the reverse does not hold true; David can tell that Uriah is facing him even with the writing hanging between them), and Uriah has to circumvent the impediment by looking below it, an indication that Dickens considers his copying a *sub*literary activity. The fact that Uriah's pen contin-ues to move while his eyes are on David is also significant; it suggests that copying could be inspired by a person as well as by a text. This was certainly true of the parody in the *Novels by Eminent Hands*, whose spleen was vented as much on the authors Thackeray targeted as on their fiction, and as we've seen, Dickens's verdict on the use of such parody was that it betrayed a lower-class hand slandering its social betters.[16]

Uriah's copying, of course, eventually leads to the most serious crime in the second half of the novel, his repeated forgery of Mr. Wickfield's signature on business documents. That crime certainly "ravages" Wickfield, the origi-nal author of the text being copied, physiologically and psychologically. But it also affects David; Uriah uses his forgeries to embezzle Aunt Betsey's money, and by doing so harms her ward, his enemy. This financial repercus-sion of copying again ties the activity to parody. Copyright law was one of Dickens's biggest professional concerns. Much has been written of his lob-bying for an international copyright agreement during and after his first trip to America in 1842. But Dickens also wanted better protection at home against imitations, adaptations, and parodies, and in 1844 had sued a two-penny weekly called *Parley's Illuminated Library* to recoup the losses he'd incurred due to its thinly-veiled plagiarism of *A Christmas Carol*. Copying and parody were, for him, forms of writing undertaken by lower-class writers at the expense—figuratively and literally—of middle-class ones, and Uriah's forgeries reflect that conviction.

David Copperfield's conflation of copying, parody, and forgery thus shows Dickens writing postscripts to both the "false as hell" fight and the "Dignity of Literature" debate. That conflation also suggests, however, that Dickens was opening up a third front in the fight he was waging with Thackeray over the class status of literature. Forgery is a kind of writing that raises issues of authenticity as well as originality—something not necessarily true of copy-ing—and a discussion of authenticity in fiction will invariably lead to a consideration of realism.

A straight copy of a written text is by definition less original than its source, but it is not necessarily less authentic; in the legal world, where most of *David Copperfield*'s copying takes place, a duplicate often has the same authority as the document it replicates. A forgery is altogether different; like a straight copy, it is unoriginal writing, but it is also inauthentic—unreal. This is true regardless of how well it reproduces its source text; in fact, a forgery which accurately copies its original is more effective than one which does so poorly, and must therefore be considered a more serious crime. That crime, we've seen, is given social overtones in *David Copperfield*; when Uriah forges Mr. Wickfield's name, it is with the intent of rising into the middle class and simultaneously reducing David to the lower class. Dickens's conflation of copying and forgery, and his assigning both forms of writing to the working class, thus produces a value system which privileges lower-class authors who embrace artificiality and frowns on those who attempt realism; the former make themselves visible and are therefore easily contained, while the latter blend in with middle-class culture and thereby gain the power to subvert it. Maintaining realism as a strictly bourgeois pursuit becomes an important part of maintaining class stability in England.

It should be no surprise, then, that as David matures into an original writer, he also, so far as we can tell, becomes a realistic one. His early storytelling—the sort that resulted in his ravaging his fellow authors—is wholly escapist. He retells *The Arabian Nights* and James Ridley's *Tales of the Genii* in addition to Smollett's novels, and does so during precisely those periods when he most wants to avoid the reality of his existence: his mother's marriage to Mr. Murdstone, his tenure at Salem House, and his employment in Murdstone and Grinby's warehouse. The adult David's judgment on this escapism is telling: "Whatever I had within me that was romantic and dreamy, was encouraged by so much story-telling in the dark; and in that respect the pursuit may not have been very profitable to me" (81). As David grows up and embraces his status as a middle-class man, he learns to accept and engage reality; since he is a middle-class novelist, we might expect that his fiction would reflect this.

It's impossible to know for sure, however, because we never get to see any of the books he produces. Critics have often remarked that, for a portrait of the artist as a young man, *David Copperfield* spends very little time portraying the young man as an artist. There are a few rousing credos, like the one in which David prides himself on never having affected depreciation of his work, but in general his literary career is glossed over very quickly: his "high repute" as a journalist and his coming out as a writer of fiction (535) are included in one of the impressionistic retrospects rather than related in a passage of full-blooded narration, and are there subordinated to his marriage with Dora; his "beginning in a small way to be known as a writer" (551) and his increasing success in that vocation (567) are both tersely described in parenthetical clauses. And, on two separate occasions, David vocally refuses to discuss his literary output on the grounds that his autobiography should be about his personal growth and progress, rather than his fiction (588–89, 723).

Because Dickens chooses not to show his protagonist writing realistic novels, he is in the end unable to cement his insinuation that realism is a middle-class art form. But the lacunae that hide David's books may, ironically, result from the very fact that they are so staunchly middle-class. As part of his response to *Pendennis*, after all, Dickens had endowed the adult David with an aggressively bourgeois work ethic—and had thereby run into a problem that puzzled many Victorian writers: how to represent literary labor as respectable middle-class work. Since *Pendennis* was also a portrait of an artist, Thackeray, too, had to struggle with the problem of depicting the work of writing. But though, like Dickens, Thackeray was interested in claiming realism as his own and in denying it to his rival, he was not constrained by the necessity of having to prove it a middle-class mode; Thackeray had always considered himself a gentleman by birth and breeding, and after the success of *Vanity Fair* gained him entrance into fashionable circles, he had found himself with the reputation of an upper-class novelist. And as he was writing *Pendennis*, Thackeray discovered in the difficulty of portraying literary labor a way to support his class's claim to realism—a way to ground such a claim, as Dickens had not, in the formal characteristics of the realistic mode itself.

III.

The preface to *Pendennis* is widely quoted by critics writing about the Grundyism of the Victorian age; Thackeray's complaint that "Since the author of Tom Jones was buried, no writer of fiction among us has been permitted to depict to his utmost power a MAN" is often cited as a prescient statement about the impossibility of achieving realism in fiction. But that sentence comes from the final paragraph of the preface, and if it is read in the light of what comes before, our appreciation of its meaning will change considerably. The preface begins with Thackeray's assuring the reader that, though *Pendennis* may well be a loose baggy monster, "it at least has the advantage of a certain truth and honesty, which a work more elaborate might lose" (1: xv). An account of the composition of the book then follows:

> Perhaps the lovers of "excitement" may care to know, that this book began with a very precise plan, which was entirely put aside. Ladies and gentlemen, you were to have been treated, and the writer's and the publishers' pocket benefitted, by the recital of the most active horrors. What more exciting than a ruffian (with many admirable virtues) in St. Giles's, visited constantly by a young lady from Belgravia? What more stirring than the contrasts of society? the mixture of slang and fashionable language? the escapes, the battles, the murders? . . .
>
> The "exciting" plan was laid aside (with a very honorable forbearance on the part of the publishers) because, on attempting it, I found that I failed from want of experience of my subject; and never having been intimate with any convict in my life, and the manners of ruffians and gaol-birds being quite unfamiliar to me, the idea of entering into competition with M. Eugène Sue was abandoned. To describe a real rascal, you must make him so horrible that he would be too hideous to show; and unless the painter paints him fairly, I hold he has no right to show him at all.

Even the gentlemen of our age—this is an attempt to describe one of them, no better nor worse than most educated men—even these we cannot show as they are, with the notorious foibles and selfishness of their lives and their education. Since the author of Tom Jones was buried, no writer of fiction among us has been permitted to depict to his utmost power a MAN. We must drape him, and give him a certain conventional simper. Society will not tolerate the Natural in our Art.   (1: xvi–xvii)

The chronological rhetoric of this passage—all the more important given that the composition history is a fiction concocted entirely for the purposes of the preface—has never been fully appreciated. Thackeray is describing a process of discarding a type of novel which cannot be realistic and settling on one which has at least the potential to be; he is describing a journey towards greater realism in fiction, not away from it. The reason the passage is crucial to our inquiry, however, is that it shows Thackeray accepting or rejecting the types of novels available to him at least partially on the basis of their formal characteristics, and assigning those characteristics to various social classes.

The subgenre which he dismisses is one created by Eugène Sue's *Les Mystères de Paris* and further popularized in England by G. W. M. Reynolds's *The Mysteries of London*. The penny dreadful, which is related to the Newgate novel which Thackeray had spent much of his career satirizing, was scorned for much the same reason—it was considered indelibly lower-class. Sue was, in Thackeray's opinion, a snob whose early novels of high society gave him away; in 1843 he'd observed that

Monsieur Sue has tried almost always, and, in "Mathilde," very nearly succeeded, in attaining a tone of *bonne compagnie*. But his respect for lacqueys, furniture, carpets, titles, *bouquets*, and such aristocratic appendages, is too great. He slips quietly over the carpet, and peers at the silk hangings, and looks at Lafleur handing about the tea-tray with too much awe for a gentleman. He is in a flutter in the midst of his marquesses and princes—happy, clever, smiling, but uneasy.   (*Works* 13: 385–86)

Les Mystères de Paris abandoned the pretense of respectability and told stories of lower-class life from a decidedly socialist point of view. The novels of Reynolds, who'd been swept up by French revolutionary politics in the 1830s and had become a leader of the militant wing of the Chartist movement in 1848, were just as radical; *The Mysteries of London* gave hundreds of thousands of working-class readers thrilling tales which contrasted the honest but miserable poor with members of a degenerate aristocracy.

One of Thackeray's reasons for dismissing this type of novel as unrealistic—that he is not personally familiar with convicts, ruffians, and jail-birds, and thus cannot write about them—is fairly straightforward, and may in fact sound familiar, since he had said the same thing of the same subgenre in the sixth chapter of *Vanity Fair* (52). But another reason—one having to do with the formal elements of that subgenre—is new. Thackeray associates the penny dreadful with "excitement," with "active horrors," with escapes, battles, and murders; it is a form defined by incident. For Thackeray, such novels are intrinsically unrealistic, the "elaborate" pains with which the plots of such books are worked up testifying to the writer's having overused his imagination and consequently failed to provide "a certain truth and honesty."

Novels structured around incident are also, in Thackeray's opinion, intrinsically lower-class. In 1843 he had reviewed Louis Reybaud's episodic novel *Jérôme Paturot*, and intimated that its hero's endless adventures reflected the class anxiety of the French; an English equivalent of Paturot, Thackeray scornfully opined, would have been satisfied with the social station he'd achieved at the end of the first volume, "but in 'the empire of the middle classes' matters are very differently arranged, and the *bonnetier de France peut aspirer à tout. . . .* [Paturot feels the need] to push forward towards the attainment of those dignities which the Revolution of July has put in his reach" (*Works* 13: 393). Incident, in other words, comes from lower-class characters'—and readers'—desperate desire to convince themselves that they belong to a higher class than they really do, and from their desperate search to attain that fancied status. Real upper-class readers had no need for constant stimulation, because they had no such class anxiety. Thackeray's early sense of this truth can be glimpsed in *Vanity Fair*, when he applauds his "gentle" readers for understanding that Amelia's story "does not deal in wonders" and contains no more thrilling incidents than Georgy's getting the measles (391); it's instructive that the major incidents in that novel, like Rawdon's confrontation with Lord Steyne, are instead part of the history of the social climber Becky. The preface to *Pendennis* reveals that time had only made Thackeray more certain that incident was irrevocably lower-class; once he decides he can't write about convicts, ruffians, and jailbirds realistically, he discards the plan for an exciting novel as a matter of course, never even entertaining the notion that a novel of incident could be written about the upper class.

Thackeray's review of *Jérôme Paturot* is especially interesting, however, because it associates the sort of exciting lower-class fiction he rejects in the preface to *Pendennis* with exactly the sort of fiction he was writing in the chapters of that novel which led to the "Dignity of Literature" controversy. Paturot's long and eventful career, the one Thackeray supposes designed for an insecure lower-class audience, begins in the literary marketplace:

> Like many an idle honest fellow who is good for nothing else, honest Paturot commences life as a literary man. And here, but that a man must not abuse his own trade, would be a fair opportunity for a tirade on the subject of literary

characters—those doomed poor fellows of this world whose pockets Fate has ordained shall be perpetually empty. Pray, all parents and guardians, that your darlings may not be born with literary tastes! If so endowed, make up your minds that they will be idle at school, and useless at college; if they have a profession, they will be sure to neglect it; if they have a fortune, they will be sure to spend it. How much money has all the literature of England in the Three per Cents? That is the question; and any bank-clerk could calculate accurately the advantage of any other calling over that of the pen. Is there any professional penman who has laid by five thousand pounds of his own earnings? Lawyers, doctors, and all other learned persons, save money; tradesmen and warriors save money; the Jew-boy who sells oranges at the coach-door, the burnt-umber Malay who sweeps crossings, save money; there is but Vates in the world who does not seem to know the art of growing rich, and, as a rule, leaves the world with as little coin about him as he had when he entered it.

So, when it is said that honest Paturot begins life by publishing certain volumes of poems, the rest is understood. You are sure he will come to the parish at the end of the third volume; that he will fail in all he undertakes; that he will not be more honest than his neighbours, but more idle and weak; that he will be a thriftless, vain, kind-hearted, irresolute, devil-may-care fellow, whose place is marked in this world; whom bankers sneer at, and tradesmen hold in utter discredit.

Jerome spends his patrimony, then, first, in eating, drinking, and making merry; secondly, in publishing four volumes of poems, four copies of which were sold; and he wondered to this day who bought them; and so, having got to the end of his paternal inheritance, he has to cast about for means of making a livelihood.   (*Works* 13: 388–89)

Paturot eventually returns to literature in the course of his search for that means: he becomes in turn the editor of a journal, a dramatic critic, an author of romances, and the editor of a newspaper, and by the end of the first volume has "gone through all the phases of literary quackery" (392). His goal, though, is not mere subsistence; it is, as Thackeray snidely puts it, "the attainment of those dignities which the Revolution of July has put in his reach." If his literary work does not lead to stars and garters, it's because literary work rarely does, not because Paturot doesn't long after them. His later career testifies to his snobbish social climbing: he joins the National Guard, hoping to be promoted to captain; not satisfied with that rank once he's achieved it, he works his way up to lieutenant colonel, and is invited to Louis Philippe's court at the Tuileries; his unbounded ambition helps him become a full colonel, a member of the Legion of Honor, a deputy, and almost a minister before he goes bankrupt and is forced to retire to the country. Everything he does, he does with the aim of rising above his proper social station; literature is simply the least successful of his schemes.

As early as 1843, then, Thackeray had coded literary activity as exciting and therefore lower-class. He'd also coded novels about literary activity as exciting and lower-class, as being designed to appeal to exactly the same social group that writing itself did. And yet in the middle numbers of *Pendennis* he was authoring just that sort of novel, and as a result he was accused of encouraging people afflicted with "the common distaste for continuous or unexciting labour" to swell the ranks of English literary paupers. After the success of *Vanity Fair*, Thackeray was enjoying a reputation as a writer of upper-class fiction; why, then, had he started dabbling in a form he'd coded low?

The answer probably lies in his not being on his mettle in the middle of 1849. When Thackeray had begun *Pendennis*, it had clearly been with the intention of writing a novel about a gentleman; Pen may not be the prince he fancies himself, but he lives a leisured existence on a country estate, and has plenty of aristocratic connections. As we've seen, though, Thackeray lost his way as the novel progressed, and, faced with a rival publication by Dickens which he clearly thought superior to his own book, he may have decided to adopt what he'd called a lower-class mode, the exciting novel about literary men, in order to win back readers. The preface to *Pendennis*, after all, shows that Thackeray associated the exciting mode with success in the marketplace; he suggests there that his initial plan for a novel of incident would have filled his and his publishers' pockets, and makes sure to note their "very honorable forbearance" at his decision to abandon that plan. Thackeray did not wholeheartedly adopt the mode he'd demonized in 1843, and instead assumed a characteristically dialogic tone which both indulged the lower-class interest in incident and literary gossip and satirized it for what it was. But in January 1850, Forster called him to task for portraying men of letters as lower-class, and though we've seen that this complaint missed the main thrust of Thackeray's satire, it had to have stung its target, who had already been accused of writing lower-class literature by Forster's chief following the "false as hell" fight, and who had now been caught employing what he knew was a lower-class subgenre. The abruptness with which Thackeray stopped depicting writers as penniless, drunken hacks after the "Dignity of Literature" controversy is a sign that he was returning to a more socially respectable mode. Though Thackeray had never considered writing a penny dreadful in the mode of Sue or Reynolds, his claim that he had in the preface of *Pendennis* probably reflects the fact that he had flirted with another lower-class form and been forced to abandon it.

With the February installment of his novel due in a matter of weeks, however, Thackeray was faced with a resumption of the problem that had originally led to the literary chapters of *Pendennis*: what to do with his hero. Pen was now an established professional writer; Thackeray could have had him leave off writing entirely, but the novel had just started to recover from a lack of direction, and having Pen change his profession again would have thrown it back into turmoil. Keeping Pen a writer while making his work habits somewhat more regular, on the other hand, would have served as a kind of *mea culpa*, the kind of concession to Forster and Dickens which Michael Lund spots and assigns too much emphasis.

But making Pen a "professional" writer of the sort Dickens and Forster thought respectable entailed its own problems. One of the attractions of the novel of incident, after all, was that it sold well; if Pen was to become a middle-class writer, the exciting elements that made lower-class fiction popular would have to be abandoned, and perhaps pretensions to popularity with them. Even before the "Dignity of Literature" exchange forced the issue, Thackeray had been wondering whether realistically portraying Pen's work as a writer would be any more exciting than depicting his legal studies; the twelfth number of *Pendennis*, the first written after Thackeray's convalescence from his illness, begins thus:

> LET us be allowed to pass over a few months of the history of Mr. Arthur Pendennis's lifetime, during the which, many events may have occurred which were more interesting and exciting to himself, than they would be likely to prove to the reader of his present memoirs. We left him, in his last chapter, regularly entered upon his business as a professional writer, or literary hack, as Mr. Warrington chooses to style himself and his friend; and we know how the life of any hack, legal or literary, in a curacy, or in a marching regiment, or at a merchant's desk, is dull of routine, and tedious of description. One day's labour resembles another much too closely.   (1: 353)

The difficulty of depicting literary labor as an active pursuit was felt by many Victorian artists. In 1865, for instance, Ford Madox Brown exhibited his panoramic painting *Work* (fig. 1). In tribute to Thomas Carlyle, whose "gospel of work" had been a formative influence on the Victorian consciousness, Brown depicted the Sage of Chelsea standing with Frederick Denison Maurice, Christian socialist and principal of the Working Men's College, along the right side of the canvas, looking approvingly at the scene. Yet Carlyle and Maurice do not themselves appear to be doing any work at all. Brown was so concerned about this problem that he felt he had to address it in the catalog of the exhibition, where he argued that the two intellectuals, while "seeming to be idle, work, and are the cause of well-ordained work and happiness in others" (qtd. in *The Pre-Raphaelites* 164). Dickens had to solve a similar problem during the composition of *David Copperfield*; it may be that David depicts his writing so sparingly because sitting at a desk with pen in hand is not very evocative for a man who has envisioned work as cutting down trees, breaking stones (444), and hammering iron (465).

Pendennis, too, reflects this Victorian anxiety about the legitimacy of literary work; Pen's belief that he can produce five-and-a-half three-volume novels a year shows how little effort he thinks writing really requires. The passage

Fig. 1. Ford Madox Brown, *Work*. © Manchester City Galleries.

in the twelfth number in which Thackeray declines to narrate Pen's literary labors also reflects the Victorian anxiety about the possibility of depicting literary work. But that passage argues that *no* variety of work (literary, legal, religious, military, or commercial) can be satisfactorily portrayed in fiction—not because such depictions are impossible, but because they're unmarketable. Who, after all, would want to read an intentionally "dull" and "tedious" novel?

Thackeray, then, faced a dilemma in January 1850. On the one hand, he could write lower-class fiction structured around exciting incidents and watch it sell well. But doing so had gotten him into trouble with Forster, and, as the preface to *Pendennis* shows, it was not really his sort of thing, since such fiction was by definition lacking "a certain truth and honesty." On the other hand, he could write middle-class fiction structured around routine work, which might appease Forster and at the same time come closer to the elusive goal of realism. But the very thing that would make such a novel realistic would deter anyone from reading it, and for a writer as obsessed with earning money as Thackeray was, purposely writing unmarketable fiction was no option at all. This impasse, however, helped him solve the problem of the class status of realism. Upper-class fiction was the only remaining variety that stood a chance of being realistic: not silver-fork fiction, which in Thackeray's mind was written by the lower class about the aristocracy to gratify lower-class tastes, but real gentlemanly fiction by, about, and reflecting the values of the English upper class—exactly what he had been trying to write when he first started *Pendennis*, and exactly what he'd just returned to writing in the twelfth number, which takes Pen back into fashionable society shortly after it declines to depict his professional labors.

Upper-class realism is, in fact, precisely what the preface of *Pendennis* claims that Thackeray has produced. That preface is a nuanced essay about the social status of realism, not a blanket statement about the impossibility of achieving it, and its cause-and-effect structure should prompt us to recognize that the author's grumbling about Mrs. Grundy is really a minor quibble. When Thackeray says that "Even the gentlemen of our age—this is an attempt to describe one of them, no better nor worse than most educated men—even these we cannot show as they are," the repetition of "even" should show that his frustration is not a result of upper-class fiction's being less realistic than other varieties. Such fiction is presented as having a better chance of being realistic than any other kind, and if Victorian mores didn't allow it to be quite as realistic as Thackeray would like, that was unfortunate, but not a make-or-break consideration. On a relative scale, upper-class fiction was the most realistic available to him, and Thackeray, more than most Victorian authors, was at peace with relativism.

It must be admitted that Thackeray hadn't yet decided what the structural principle of such fiction was, if it wasn't incident or routine; that was a question which would occupy him for the rest of his career. In the second half of *Pendennis*, he would explore the ways in which leisure could be such a principle, and become especially interested in the possibility of structuring a novel around the amorous pursuits of a leisured man. The fact that depicting such pursuits was precisely what Mrs. Grundy wouldn't allow him to do may account for the famous passage in the preface. Thackeray would conduct increasingly radical experiments in later novels; *The Newcomes*, for instance, tries to construct a plot based not on what the characters do, but on whom they know—social connections, of course, being one of the defining principles of upper-class life. But by early 1850, he was already responding to the "Dignity of Literature" exchange in a very sophisticated way, not just writing realistic literature and staking a claim to it on behalf of a particular social class, but actually offering some reasonable grounds for that claim's validity. Thackeray's rivalry with Dickens had indeed put him upon his mettle: far from simply sparking a novel for a number or two, it had pushed him to explore the deep-seated class ideologies that underlay his profession.

NOTES

1. References to Thackeray's "*Letters*" are to Gordon N. Ray's four-volume edition of 1945–46; references to "*Letters (Supplement)*" are to Edgar F. Harden's two-volume follow-up of 1994, which has the same title.

2. In addition to Masson's article, see, for instance, Samuel Phillips's "David Copperfield and Arthur Pendennis," the *Prospective Review*'s "*David Copperfield, and Pendennis,*" and the essay in David Lester Richardson's *Literary Recreations* entitled "Dickens's *David Copperfield* and Thackeray's *Pendennis.*"

3. Quotations from *David Copperfield* are from Nina Burgis's Clarendon edition, which takes as copy-text the first volume edition of the novel. The first edition was assembled from unsold copies of the serial numbers—the version of the work that put Thackeray upon his mettle.

4. See my article "Novels by Literary Snobs" for a full discussion of the class discourse buried in the *Novels by Eminent Hands* and the "false as hell" fight.

5. References to *Pendennis* are to Peter L. Shillingsburg's Thackeray edition, which presents as reading-text the first volume edition of the novel; as was the case with *David Copperfield*, this edition was assembled from copies of the serial numbers. Though Shillingsburg's text is a single volume, he chose to reproduce the first edition's division into two volumes, and thus begins pagination again after the thirty-ninth chapter. My citations thus contain both a volume number (which points to the first or second half of Shillingsburg's text) and a page.

6. Much later in the novel, Warrington reveals that he is married to and separated from an avaricious lower-class girl, and explains his indolence by saying that if he were to make a name or a fortune for himself, his vulgar wife would hunt him down in an effort to claim her share of it (2: 188). But this is a revisionist argument made possible by serial publication; there's absolutely no indication that Warrington is married in the tenth number of *Pendennis*—or for many months thereafter—and the idleness he so cheerfully admits to at that point is quite genuine.

7. Such studies were in their heyday in the 1960s. See, for example, Raymond Williams's *The Long Revolution* 234–37, Richard D. Altick's "The Sociology of Authorship" 393–95, D. F. Laurenson's "A Sociological Study of Authorship" 315–17, and Laurenson and Alan Swingewood's *The Sociology of Literature* 136–38.

8. See the third chapter of Lund's book *Reading Thackeray*, which reprints his article "Novels, Writers, and Readers in 1850." Craig Howes makes an argument similar to Lund's in "*Pendennis* and the Controversy on the 'Dignity of Literature.' "

9. It's also possible that Pen is not merely passively acquiescing in the snobbery of the literary profession. His claim that he'd raised the rank of his characters at the request of his publisher is part of one of Thackeray's ubiquitous continuity errors: the chapter after the one in which Pen discusses *Walter Lorraine* with Blanche is a flashback to Pen's finding the manuscript of the novel, reading it, and debating its worth with Warrington, and two sentences there suggest that the duke was in fact a duke, not a baron, in the original draft (2: 24). This may be an innocent slip, of course, but it may also be that after accusing Bacon and Bungay of literary snobbery in chapter 41, Thackeray wanted to show Pen guilty of the same vice in chapter 42, and so inadvertently reused a joke. Thackeray may also have known exactly what he was doing all along, in which case Pen's placing the responsibility for the novel's aristocratic characters on his publisher has to be read as an attempt

to cover himself after having been embarrassed by Blanche's penetrating comment.

10. The proposed prospectus (it was never published or circulated) for the Provident Union of Literature, Science, & Art can be found in *Letters* 5: 700–02, and the prospectus for the Guild of Literature and Art in *Letters* 6: 852–57. K. J. Fielding has written the fullest accounts of Dickens's tortuous campaign to reform the Royal Literary Fund.

11. The third chapter of Hack's book, which I draw on here, reprints and expands upon his article "Literary Paupers and Professional Authors: The Guild of Literature and Art."

12. Michael Lund concludes, as do I, that, given the timing of David's adopting literature as a profession, the move is a response to the "Dignity of Literature" controversy (*Reading Thackeray* 74–76). But because he thinks that Thackeray was chastened by Forster and that he abandoned his satire of literary men in the second half of *Pendennis*, Lund speaks of *Copperfield* as if it were cooperating with Thackeray's novel rather than providing an alternative to it.

   Mark Cronin also reads David's eventual choice of profession in relation to the "Dignity of Literature" debate. His article "The Rake, the Writer, and *The Stranger*" does see Dickens's portrait of the artist as opposed to Thackeray's, and so in some ways his argument anticipates mine. But, like Lund, Cronin understands the target of *Pendennis*'s satire to be the levity of writers rather than their snobbishness, and thus he overlooks the central aspect of Dickens's response to his rival.

   Richard Salmon is the most recent critic to read *David Copperfield* as an appendage to the "Dignity of Literature" exchange. His article "Professions of Labour" shares my contention that David is Dickens's "coded rejoinder" to Pen (37), and to prove that contention, he points to some of the same passages from *Copperfield* that I am about to discuss. But our arguments diverge widely after this shared assumption. Salmon's article is a Marxist reading of the ways in which the two novels represent the conditions of labor faced by the mid-century professional writer; it is most interested in comparing Pen and David with lower-class manual laborers alienated from their work. My argument is that, as in most of Thackeray's writing, the primary tension in *Pendennis* is between the middle class and the class above it, not below it—and that both the "Dignity of Literature" exchange and *David Copperfield* should be read with that tension in mind.

13. The scene also codes the patronized writer as feminine: David is Steerforth's sultana. Such coding is an important move in a novel where David's dependent status is signaled by his being rechristened "Trotwood" and nicknamed "Daisy" after his nonexistent sister. It's also notable because the rhetoric of professionalization employed by the Dickens and Forster party by definition excluded women, and resulted in the gradual marginalization of female authors during the second half of the nineteenth century.

14. See, for example, the thirty-eighth chapter of *Copperfield*, in which David teaches himself shorthand reporting—which is theoretically straight reproduction—by attempting to transcribe famous parliamentary speeches dictated to him by Traddles. Traddles's reading of these speeches—which should also, theoretically, be

straight reproduction—quickly turns into parody, as he waves his arms and thunders away at Aunt Betsey and Mr. Dick (who represent the government or opposition benches, as the situation warrants). Parody then slides into satire: Traddles's reading Tory speeches one minute and Whig speeches the next becomes a comment on the unprincipled nature of politicians; Mr. Dick's fear that he may be guilty of the awful things with which Traddles charges him becomes a caricature of what Dickens saw as Parliament's inflated sense of self-importance. And at the end of the scene, David finds that he is completely unable to read the notes he's taken—a telling judgment about the possibility of innocent reproduction (465–66).

For a nonfictional take on the issue, see H. M. Paull's book on *Literary Ethics*, which, though published in 1929, expresses a representative Victorian mindset on parody. The book moves from the worst literary felonies to less egregious misdemeanors, and makes parody contiguous with plagiarism, piracy, forgery, and theft.

15. It's also telling that Dora is kept busy making unnecessary copies of David's work, and that the activity is shown to be about as useful as her holding his spare pens while he writes (553). Traddles, too, eventually employs his wife as a copying-clerk (724), and while her work is depicted as more helpful than Dora's, it still doesn't qualify as a profession, or even a trade. Copying is the only writing women do in the novel, other than penning a letter here or there; we should remember again that attempts to professionalize literature marginalized female writers in Victorian England.

16. It's possible that Uriah's ubiquitous clammy hands, first mentioned a few pages later, are yet another part of the discourse on copying being developed here. Clammy palms are Victorian shorthand for masturbation, a fact often brought up in discussions of *David Copperfield*. It may be that Dickens is declaiming the work of those hands—copying or parody—as a self-gratifying and unproductive activity, in contrast to original writing like David's, which, according to Agnes, has the "power of doing good" (721).

WORKS CITED

Altick, Richard D. "The Sociology of Authorship: The Social Origins, Education, and Occupations of 1,100 British Writers, 1800–1935." *Bulletin of the New York Public Library* 66.6 (1962): 389–404.

Cronin, Mark. "The Rake, the Writer, and *The Stranger*: Textual Relations between *Pendennis* and *David Copperfield*." *Dickens Studies Annual* 24 (1996): 215–40.

"*David Copperfield*, and *Pendennis*." *Prospective Review* July 1851: 157–91.

"The death of Mr. P. F. Tytler . . ." *Morning Chronicle* 3 Jan. 1850: 4.

Dickens, Charles. *David Copperfield.* 1849–50. Ed. Nina Burgis. Oxford: Clarendon, 1981.

———. *The Letters of Charles Dickens.* Ed. Madeline House, Graham Storey, and Kathleen Tillotson. 12 vols. Oxford: Clarendon, 1965–2002.

———. *The Speeches of Charles Dickens.* Ed. K. J. Fielding. Oxford: Clarendon, 1960.

Dilke, Charles W., Charles Dickens, and John Forster. *The Case of the Reformers in the Literary Fund.* London: Bradbury, [1858].

[Fielding, K. J.] "Dickens and the Royal Literary Fund." *Times Literary Supplement* 15 Oct. 1954: 664; 22 Oct. 1954: 680.

———. "Dickens and the Royal Literary Fund—1858." *Review of English Studies* ns 6.24 (1955): 383–394.

Flynn, Michael J. "Novels by Literary Snobs: The Contentious Class-Coding of Thackerayan Parody." *Dickens Studies Annual* 36 (2005): 199–228.

[Forster, John.] " 'The Dignity of Literature.' " *Examiner* 19 Jan. 1850: 35.

[———.] "Encouragement of Literature by the State." *Examiner* 5 Jan. 1850: 2+.

"The Guild of Literature and Art." *Illustrated London News* 24 May 1851: 440.

Hack, Daniel. "Literary Paupers and Professional Authors: The Guild of Literature and Art." *SEL* 39.4 (1999): 691–713.

———. *The Material Interests of the Victorian Novel.* Charlottesville: U of Virginia P, 2005.

Howes, Craig. "*Pendennis* and the Controversy on the 'Dignity of Literature.' " *Nineteenth-Century Literature* 41.3 (1986): 269–98.

Laurenson, D. F. "A Sociological Study of Authorship." *British Journal of Sociology* 20.3 (1969): 311–25.

Laurenson, Diana, and Alan Swingewood. *The Sociology of Literature.* London: Mac-Gibbon, 1971.

Lund, Michael. "Novels, Writers, and Readers in 1850." *Victorian Periodicals Review* 17.1/2 (1984): 15–28.

———. *Reading Thackeray.* Detroit: Wayne State UP, 1988.

[Masson, David.] "*Pendennis* and *Copperfield*: Thackeray and Dickens." *North British Review* May 1851: 57–89.

Paull, H. M. *Literary Ethics: A Study in the Growth of the Literary Conscience.* New York: Dutton, 1929.

[Phillips, Samuel.] "David Copperfield and Arthur Pendennis." *Times* 11 June 1851: 8.

The Pre-Raphaelites. London: Tate, 1984.

Richardson, David Lester. *Literary Recreations: or Essays, Criticisms, and Poems, Chiefly Written in India.* Calcutta: Thacker, 1852.

Rodolff, Rebecca. "*The Weekly Chronicle*'s Month-by-Month Reception of *Pendennis* & *David Copperfield.*" *Victorian Periodicals Review* 14.3 (1981): 101–11.

Salmon, Richard. "Professions of Labour: *David Copperfield* and the 'Dignity of Literature.' " *Nineteenth-Century Contexts* 29.1 (2007): 35–52.

Thackeray, William Makepeace. *The English Humourists of the Eighteenth Century* and *Charity and Humour.* 1851 and 1853. Ed. Edgar F. Harden. Ann Arbor: U of Michigan P, 2007. *The Works of William Makepeace Thackeray.* Ed. Peter L. Shillingsburg. 9 vols. to date. 1989– .

———. *The History of Pendennis.* 1848–50. Ed. Peter L. Shillingsburg. New York: Garland, 1991. *The Works of William Makepeace Thackeray.* Ed. Peter L. Shillingsburg. 9 vols. to date. 1989– .

———. *The Letters and Private Papers of William Makepeace Thackeray.* Ed. Gordon N. Ray. 4 vols. Cambridge: Harvard UP, 1945–46.

———. *The Letters and Private Papers of William Makepeace Thackeray: A Supplement to Gordon N. Ray*, The Letters and Private Papers of William Makepeace Thackeray. Ed. Edgar F. Harden. 2 vols. New York: Garland, 1994.

———. *Vanity Fair.* 1847–48. Ed. Peter L. Shillingsburg. A Norton Critical Edition. New York: Norton, 1994.

———. *The Works of William Makepeace Thackeray, with Biographical Introductions by His Daughter, Anne Ritchie.* The Biographical Edition. 13 vols. London: Smith, 1898–99.

Williams, Raymond. *The Long Revolution.* New York: Columbia UP, 1961.

"She brings everything to a grindstone": Sympathy and the Paid Female Companion's Critical Work in *David Copperfield*

Lauren N. Hoffer

In David Copperfield, *Charles Dickens employs Rosa Dartle, Mrs. Steerforth's paid female companion, as an agent of his narrative. The companion in Victorian literature is an ambiguous figure whose status as a genteel insider and outsider within the domestic circle makes her a unique vehicle for the disclosure of important information the narrative cannot otherwise convey. Companions in the nineteenth century were hired to provide company, amusement, and, most important, a sympathetic ear for their mistresses' confidences. But, as Dickens and other Victorian writers show, this purchased sympathy-for-hire can be corrupted and distorted to serve the companion's own selfish aims. In* David Copperfield, *Rosa manipulates the sympathy she is expected to provide her mistress in order to expose and critique the Steerforth family's true history and dysfunction. However, ultimately, Rosa cannot help but to reveal her own dysfunction as well. A precursor of Henry James's* ficelle, *Rosa's critical work represents an alternative narrative that David must contend with and absorb as the companion provides a specific form of domestic knowledge he himself cannot access. Through Rosa Dartle, Dickens explores a darker side to sympathy as well as the diverse narrative functions the companion's distinctive position allows her to perform.*

Dickens Studies Annual, Volume 41, Copyright © 2010 by AMS Press, Inc. All rights reserved.

During his first visit to the Steerforth home, David Copperfield witnesses a curious exchange between his friend James Steerforth and Rosa Dartle, Mrs. Steerforth's paid female companion. Rosa initiates the conversation, feigning ignorance as she asks Steerforth about his views on class difference. While he lectures her on the "pretty wide separation between them and us" by detailing the supposed lack of refinement and feeling in the lower classes, Rosa appears to accept the lesson gratefully; however, her response is rife with judgment, highlighting the injustice in Steerforth's opinion of his social inferiors as "animals and clods." " 'Really!' said Miss Dartle. 'Well, I don't know, now, when I have been better pleased than to hear that. It's so consoling! It's such a delight to know that, when they suffer, they don't feel! Sometimes I have been quite uneasy for that sort of people; but now I shall just dismiss the idea of them, altogether. Live and learn.' " Rosa concludes her satirical but veiled rebuttal by emphasizing the interrogative method she has used to achieve this critique of Steerforth, all the while maintaining the appearance of sympathetic agreement: " 'I had my doubts, I confess, but now they're cleared up. I didn't know, and now I do know, and that shows the advantage of asking—don't it?' " (252–53; ch. 20). Rosa has drawn Steerforth out, revealing his prejudices to the reader and to David, by posing a loaded question to which she already knows the answers—both the just answer as well as the reply her interlocutor will supply. This scene demonstrates one of the many ways in which Charles Dickens uses Rosa—a figure who is at once outsider and insider within the domestic circle—to reveal and comment on the Steerforths' true natures.

Paid female companions such as Rosa Dartle were generally genteel or middle-class "redundant" women, either single or widowed. The role was one of the few available employment options for women of this social status in the Victorian era. Like governesses, companions usually found employment by posting or answering advertisements or through familial connections; in fact, many ladies, when their financial situations required that they find some form of genteel labor, served as companions to members of their extended families. While governesses suffered from the tedium of long hours with often unruly, disrespectful young children, the companion role involved close personal service with the mistress or older daughter of a household and interaction with a genteel family and its guests rather than the more isolating instruction of children. But this is not to say that the companion's lot was necessarily easier than that of the governess. Although usually of equal or only slightly lower-class position than their mistresses, companions were nevertheless often expected to act with servility and endure disrespect and a lack of consideration from their employers. Forced to work for their self-preservation despite their social status, and victimized by their personal situations as well as the stigma associated with being single, these women often suffered from the coarsening and demeaning effects of their sycophantic, dependent occupation.[1]

A companion's duties ranged from keeping her mistress company at home and abroad, amusing her and tending to her whims, to serving as chaperone whenever the mistress entertained men. Companions read to their mistresses, played music for them, ran errands; they acted as both lackey and confidant—a "friend" who was always at her employer's disposal as a sympathetic receptacle for blame and frustration, light-hearted gossip, or intimate conversation. The companion's chief social function was to act as a monitor for her mistress. The families of single and even married women often encouraged or compelled them to hire companions who in effect served to temper their independence while also protecting their chaste reputations. Thus, the occupation satisfied a cultural impulse to contain the mistress's autonomy as well. To fulfill these diverse and often contradictory requirements, a companion's qualifications included good breeding, an array of feminine accomplishments with which to entertain her mistress, and a capacity for loyalty, humility, and especially sympathy.

With the rise of the cult of domesticity in the nineteenth century, sympathy became the core of the ideological feminine ideal—a specifically female trait that could allow women to personify Sarah Stickney Ellis's call for "disinterested kindness" and to be the moral foundation of the home and nation. "As the centers of Victorian domestic life," Audrey Jaffe writes, "women were expected to defer their own desires and work toward the fulfillment of others', and the name given that generalized identification was frequently sympathy" (17). Perhaps these very cultural expectations were among the factors that necessitated the role of the paid female companion in the Victorian period. The companion could fulfill needs for attention, emotional connection, and control that these women were not able to obtain from their families or social circles. Employing a companion could permit a Victorian lady with enough disposable income the opportunity to *receive* sympathy, without the necessity of reciprocation. The companion's dependent position, then, magnified by the mistress's expectations of emotional availability and sympathy from her companion, left this figure vulnerable in a different, more acute way than employees in other occupations. Because this was an intimate relationship between two women, situated within the domestic sphere, neither the state's legislation on employer responsibility nor older codes of paternalism applied, and companions were at the mercy of whatever manipulation or mistreatment their mistresses might devise. Authors throughout Victorian fiction have considered how the power dynamics inherent in the employer-employee aspect of the mistress-companion relationship causes confusion in the female bond of reciprocity and obligation. Dickens, for example, portrays the ways in which a mistress can take advantage of the sympathy her companion is required to provide, in turn endangering her companion, in his depiction of Kate Nickleby and Mrs. Wititterly in *Nicholas Nickleby*. However, as several Victorian writers also prove, there are opportunities for manipulation of sympathy on the part of the companion as well.

As the paid friends of other women, companions were expected to enact the private virtues supposed to be organic to relationships between women in exchange for money or alternative forms of compensation such as room, board, and other material "gifts," but this economic aspect of the relationship was problematic. A sympathy that is in essence purchased like a commodity immediately loses its sense of being an altruistic emotional interaction. This, coupled with the mistress's expectations of an almost automatic sympathy-upon-demand, allows for the possibility of a manipulative, performed sympathy in that the potential for genuine sympathy is often already corrupt. Therefore, Victorian novelists could use the mistress-companion dynamic to explore a latent darker, destabilizing side to sympathy. The companions featured in many Victorian novels employ sympathy as an egocentric strategy for gaining transgressive power, social mobility, and even romantic attachments. William Makepeace Thackeray's Becky Sharp, for instance, epitomizes this paradigm of the self-serving companion who disingenuously exhibits the sympathy expected of her in order to manipulate her mistress and her mistress's family. While Kate Nickleby represents the model of ideal companion behavior, Dickens's other companions, Rosa Dartle in *David Copperfield*, Mrs. General in *Little Dorrit*, and even Esther Summerson in *Bleak House*, exploit their positions as companions to achieve their own goals. Through these companion characters, Dickens and other Victorian writers interrogate and deconstruct sympathy as a mode of human interaction while simultaneously experimenting with the opportunities this alternative form of sympathy allows for their narratives.

A kind of nodal point of sympathy in *David Copperfield*, Rosa relates to the characters she encounters—David, Mrs. Steerforth, and Emily—through her desire for James Steerforth. However, Rosa manipulates that sympathy, using it as a tool rather than an earnest, altruistic sentiment. Her close observations, affective expression, interrogative insinuations, and passionate reprimands work to expose as well as to judge those who cross her path. Rosa provides Dickens with an intricate mode of characterization, a subtle narrative method that reaches beyond what David as narrator can comfortably "tell." Rosa also functions as Dickens's arbiter, invoking judgment upon his characters' problematic attitudes and behaviors. In this way, the companion character models an act of criticism for Dickens's readers to emulate. She is an agent of the narrative.

In his 1908 preface to the New York edition of *The Portrait of a Lady*, Henry James writes, "The house of fiction has in short not one window, but a million—a number of possible windows not to be reckoned, rather; every one of which has been pierced, or is still pierceable, in its vast front, by the need of the individual vision and by the pressure of the individual will'' (45–46). In *David Copperfield*, Rosa's "individual vision" and her "individual will" to assert her own perspective provide an alternative, supplementary narrative to David's first-person narration. In James's formulation, she offers us another window into David's story. In fact, David describes how Rosa's visage "pass[ed] from window to window, like a wandering light, until it fixed itself in one, and watched us" (366; ch. 29). Rosa acts as an almost extratextual presence in the novel as she seems to see through both David as narrator and the narrative itself. She observes and analyzes her fellow characters from a position that is at once part of the story and seemingly removed from it—just as her companion position situates her within the plot as both an insider and an outsider in the Steerforth family. Like the reader or critic, Rosa often seems to view the action of the plot from the outside looking in, a technique which allows her a degree of distance from which she can achieve her narrative work within the frame of the novel.

Although a minor character and never an actual narrator like Esther Summerson, Rosa functions as a kind of narrative assistant for Dickens and for David. In this way, Dickens's companion is an example of what Henry James would call a *ficelle*. James offers his fullest articulation of his theory of the *ficelle* in the preface to *The Ambassadors* (1903). Borrowing from nineteenth-century French theater, James defines the *ficelle* as "the reader's friend," an "enrolled, a direct, aid to lucidity" (47). This figure is "enrolled" by the author, assigned the role of assisting the narrative in conveying its meaning. For James, creating a character whose function was to illuminate for the reader information that could not otherwise be conveyed was as necessary as it was artistically thrilling. He describes his use of Maria Gostrey as *ficelle* as an "artful expedient for mere consistency of form," a solution to the limitations of first-person narration, but he also viewed his *ficelles* as "the refinements and ecstasies of method"—a "clear source of enjoyment for the infatuated artist" (49). The *ficelle* was not only a tool to aid reader and author alike but also a kind of trick; as Julian Wolfreys and Harun Karim Thomas write, "James knew full well what dubieties were implied by ficelle in French. Ficelles were no innocent balls of yarn. Une ficelle is also a trick done on stage, a performed deception, a crime even; it's a trickster, a deceiver, a kind of criminal" (363). This alternative characterization of the *ficelle* also seems appropriate to Rosa, who performs her narrative work in an underhanded manner, feigning sympathy with her employers only to expose and then mercilessly critique their family secrets. Dickens's characterization of this companion in *David Copperfield* is deeply ambivalent; Rosa seems to draw other characters, as well as the reader, toward her and repulse them at the same time.

In the preface to *The Ambassadors*, James considers the constraints first-person narration places upon the author and his ability not only to convey certain information but also to keep the "form amusing while sticking so close to [the] central figure" of the narrative. Here, James even mentions *David Copperfield* as an example of a text which manages to grant its narrator/hero "the double privilege of subject and object" (46). James's solution, similar to that of Dickens before him, is to give his hero "a confidant or two" who can, through his or her interactions with a variety of characters, reveal that which the narrator/hero cannot.[2] As a companion, Rosa's primary purpose is to act as a confidante to her mistress, Mrs. Steerforth. By occupation she is expected to be at once servile and sympathetic not only to her mistress's every daily whim, but also to her secrets and emotions. An intimate observer and participant in the domestic scene, made a party to the private dynamics of the Steerforth family—a family in whom David is deeply interested—Rosa's companion position makes her the perfect candidate for the *ficelle* role. She knows things about the Steerforth family that David cannot access or refuses to see because of his attachment to James Steerforth. Her knowledge and power to convey that knowledge place her in direct narrative competition with David, but also, ultimately, work to assist him in telling his own story. Her intense bitterness in response to the suffering and betrayal she has experienced in the Steerforth home leads her to manipulate her position and the expectations of sympathy in an effort to avenge herself. Dickens creates for himself a narrative assistant who possesses both the access she needs to perform her function as well as a clear motivation that preserves what James called "consistency of form" (49).

I. Rosa Dartle's Critical Affect and Speech

Unlike David Copperfield, Rosa Dartle appears to have no "Personal History." During David's first sojourn at the Steerforth home, in chapter 20, Steerforth states, " 'She was the motherless child of a sort of cousin of my father's. He died one day. My mother, who was then a widow, brought her here to be company to her. She has a couple of thousand pounds of her own, and saves the interest of it every year, to add to the principal. There's the history of Miss Rosa Dartle for you' " (253). The brevity and commonality of this "history" position Rosa for the reader as the hapless, "redundant" woman turned genteel companion. Major life events such as her being orphaned are relayed with curt nonchalance—"he died one day"—and she is granted no significant identity beyond her dependent service in the Steerforth family. David is initially complicit in this subtle act of containing Rosa's character in stereotypes; upon meeting her, he concludes that "she was about thirty years of age, and that she wished to be married. She was a little dilapidated—like a house—with having been so long to let'' (251; ch. 20). Rosa takes up this metaphor of domesticity near the end of the Steerforth narrative when she describes herself, in terms of her relationship to her mistress and Steerforth, as " 'a mere disfigured piece of furniture between you both; having no eyes, no ears, no feelings, no remembrances' " (674; ch. 56). The double emphasis on the domestic in these two passages is significant. David assumes that as a single, dependent woman, Rosa's only desire can be to marry and, in this case, he is not incorrect. From Rosa's perspective, she is ensconced in the home (even in the home of her marital choice) but not in the sense that she should be. This space is not her own, and both Steerforth and David would like us to believe that she is little more than a nonentity there, an inanimate "piece of furniture." Even Rosa participates in this effacement of her importance to the text; her assertion that she has no eyes or feelings is, as I will show, a moment of irony for her as well as for Dickens. For, throughout *David Copperfield*, Rosa Dartle's character resists such attempts at containment.

Rosa's history is not obscured by or subsidiary to the Steerforths'; her history *is* that of the Steerforths, and she serves as the vehicle through which that common history is revealed. Rosa's careful exploitation of her station enables her to appear, for a time, as nothing more than a "dilapidated," powerless woman, dutifully fulfilling her role as sympathetic companion. But as her trajectory throughout the narrative leads her to an ever-increasing vocality and ascendancy, it becomes clear that Rosa's apparent sympathy is a manipulative tool she employs to gain access to and divulge her employers' faults. Rosa thus does and undoes sympathy at the same time. Like many of her fellow companion characters throughout Victorian literature, her performance of sympathy simultaneously makes possible its antithesis: her merciless exposure and critique of her employers.

Rosa's specialized language, conveyed not only through her intricate speech but likewise through the affective power of her appearance, both mirrors the Steerforths' flaws back to them and also passes judgment upon them. The Steerforths' story is written on Rosa Dartle's face for David, as well as for the reader, to "read." Throughout the novel, the companion's facial markers, specifically her eyes and scar, signify as words would, creating a language of feeling in her physical appearance; I will refer to this phenomenon as Rosa's "affective language." The companion uses this subtle form of communication as a means of circumventing her subservient position, which prevents her from using direct speech against her employers. Rosa speaks with her face through expressions and her scar, and these serve as a mode of interpretation and critique. From his first encounter with Rosa, David is disconcerted by the power of her mere presence in the Steerforth home.

He states that, in addition to Mrs. Steerforth, "There was a second lady in the dining-room, of a slight short figure, dark, and not agreeable to look at, but with some appearance of good looks too, who attracted my attention: perhaps because I had not expected to see her; perhaps because I found myself sitting opposite to her; perhaps because of something really remarkable in her." David cannot discern why she is so striking to him, despite his multiple attempts at defining her effect on him. Eventually, he locates the strength of her presence in her appearance: "She had black hair and eager black eyes, and was thin, . . . Her thinness seemed to be the effect of some wasting fire within her, which found a vent in her gaunt eyes" (251; ch. 20). For David, Rosa's emotion shapes her physical frame and becomes legible there; yet her body cannot delimit the smoldering within her, which leaks out from her eyes. As it becomes increasingly clear that Rosa "seemed to pervade the whole house," and that "the fire within" her was originally lit and is continually fanned by her mistress and Steerforth, David begins to keep a close watch on Rosa's face in an attempt to translate the meaning he finds there (366; ch. 29).

Yet Rosa is not content to sit idly by as David studies her eyes; she also expresses her version of the Steerforth narrative through close observation. In one revealing passage, David describes the way in which he and Rosa gaze at one another:

> what I particularly observed, before I had been half-an-hour in the house, was the close and attentive watch Miss Dartle kept upon me; and the lurking manner in which she seemed to compare my face with Steerforth's, and Steerforth's with mine, and to lie in wait for something to come out between the two. So surely as I looked towards her, did I see that eager visage, with its gaunt black eyes and searching brow, intent on mine; or passing suddenly from mine to Steerforth's; or comprehending both of us at once. In this lynx-like scrutiny she was so far from faltering when she saw I observed it, that at such a time she only fixed her piercing look upon me with a more intent expression still. Blameless as I was, and knew that I was, in reference to any wrong she could possibly suspect me of, I shrunk before her strange eyes, quite unable to endure their hungry luster.   (365; ch. 29)

Seeking to comprehend the relationship between the men, the companion mimics David's position as narrator by watching in order to "read" him; in her seemingly unobtrusive, "lurking manner," she "lie[s] in wait" for information to interpret. Rosa challenges David's narration first and foremost by adopting, and then conquering him with, his own specific mode of storytelling: observation. Pointing out that observation is central to David's narrative mode, Michael Greenstein writes, "The title of the second chapter, 'I Observe,' as well as the novel's full title (with its *Observations of David Copperfield*), calls for a tentative exegesis of modes of observation, points of view, or multiple perspectives" (75). However, when David returns her gaze, the true force of Rosa's surveillance is revealed. In this moment, David the character and David the narrator seem to coalesce as the protagonist struggles with the companion for narrative control.[3] Rosa understands more than David can as she meets David's eyes and seems to look through him and into the narrative itself. Dickens appears to endow his narrative assistant with the power of foresight here and throughout the novel; as Rosa studies David in an attempt to determine this newcomer's role in the Steerforth family drama, she seems to know he will play some crucial role in their futures. David recognizes her power in this moment: his reference to blame here, for example, echoes his later assertions that he is not responsible for Steerforth's elopement with Emily Peggotty. At the mercy of her power to see through and preempt the story he has set out to tell, David "shrunk before her strange eyes." While Rosa's gaze toward David is "far from faltering," David is "quite unable to endure" hers, and Rosa emerges as the more adept, and dangerous, storyteller in this scene.

David is discomfited by the lack of narrative control he has over Rosa's affective language because of what it reveals about the Steerforths and about himself as well. Rosa's eyes are not the only instrument through which she absorbs, interprets, and asserts information; David is equally captivated by the distinctive scar which "cut through her mouth, downward towards the chin" (251; ch. 20).[4] In response to David's questions concerning the mark, Steerforth again obscures the details of her past, focusing the narrative on himself rather than Rosa. We do not know what provoked Steerforth, only that it was no accident, as David at first assumes: " 'No. I was a young boy, and she exasperated me, and I threw a hammer at her. A promising young angel I must have been!' " (253; ch. 20). While this retelling all but erases Rosa from the incident, eliding any emotional reaction she might have had preceding or following the attack, the scar remains to function as a perpetuating sign of Rosa's affective life. As the revelation and constant reminder of Steerforth's rage, and Mrs. Steerforth's neglect, the scar acts as a visible history. The dysfunction the scar represents cannot be contained as a family secret to be hidden from view; instead, it is broadcast on the companion's face.

However, Rosa is no passive text to be written on and then read. Her scar is not a static indictment of the Steerforths, but a vehicle she can manipulate to signify their transgressions. In this way, she gleans power from her attack, transforming herself from victim to subtle aggressor—just as she maneuvers within her dependent companion position to achieve the power of the critic. As David notes, "It was not long before I observed that it was the most susceptible part of her face, and that, when she turned pale, that mark altered first, and became a dull, lead-coloured streak, lengthening out to its full extent, like a mark in invisible ink brought to the fire" (253; ch. 20). Rosa's scar is the "invisible ink" through which she, and Dickens, can articulate the Steerforth characters in ways that David cannot directly express—it is the subtle subtext beneath the story that David tells and the only way that David can see beyond his own biased perspective to expose the Steerforths for himself and his reader.

When David finds a portrait of Rosa hanging in his bedroom, his struggle with Rosa early in the novel becomes clear.[5] Threatened by the competitive narrative she represents, he wonders "peevishly why they couldn't put her anywhere else instead of quartering her on me." Unable to escape or control her, David attempts to master her and the information her affect divulges by symbolically repeating Steerforth's attack: "The painter hadn't made the scar, but I made it; and there it was, coming and going; now confined to the upper lip as I had seen it at dinner, and now showing the whole extent of the wound inflicted by the hammer, as I had seen it when she was passionate" (255; ch. 20). In an effort to manage Rosa's scar, David forms the mark himself so that it, like the rest of the novel, is more fully his own creation and so under his control. His strategy fails him, however. As he tries to "get rid of her" by going to sleep, he "could not forget that she was still there looking" (255; ch. 20). Although David, the focal character in the text, might sleep, in effect halting narrative time, Rosa remains active—always watching and always offering her interpretation of the story.

In his dreams, David even finds himself unable to speak (narrate) outside of Rosa's own distinctive speech patterns: "when I awoke in the night, I found that I was uneasily asking all sorts of people in my dreams whether it really was or not—without knowing what I meant" (255; ch. 20). In this scene, the companion threatens to overtake not only the narrative itself, but also the voice of the narrator, as David temporarily takes on Rosa's characteristic form of speech: asking questions to obtain crucial, often damaging information. According to James's definition, a *ficelle* figure is the "reader's friend," not the narrator's, and the battle being waged in these scenes proves that this is the case for Dickens's Rosa Dartle as well. Because he is narrating the story through the lens of his perceptions at the given time, David, at this stage in the novel, cannot accept Rosa's perspective as a complement to his own; rather, he struggles against the story she is trying to tell. David does not yet understand that he needs her knowledge in order to complete his depiction of the Steerforths and even his portrayal of himself. Regardless of David's wishes, Dickens's narrative agent proves too strong for the narrator. David clearly loses his initial battles with the companion, not only in person but even when she is nothing more than a portrait on the wall.[6]

The silent, narrative power of Rosa's eyes and scar allow her to be critical of David and the Steerforths while still retaining the appearance of submissive sympathy. Only David seems aware of the subtle signification inherent in

Rosa's countenance. However, Rosa's critique of the Steerforths and her impingement on David's narrative are not restricted to her expressive face. As Graham Storey writes, "her voice, her constant insinuation of her views, combined with a trick of questioning everything first, gives her a major impact" (62). Early in David's acquaintance with Mrs. Steerforth and her companion, Rosa employs an indirect mode of speech to reveal the Steerforths' flaws. Rosa habitually interjects herself into conversations through questioning others' assertions in order to attain information. Recalling one particular visit to the Steerforth home, David notes that while he conversed with Mrs. Steerforth "all day" about her son, "Miss Dartle was full of hints and mysterious questions, but took a great interest in all our proceedings there, and said, 'Was it really though?' and so forth, so often" (304; ch. 24). Rosa consistently presents her questions as motivated by curiosity, by an innocent desire "to know," through couching her critical inquiries in language such as " 'I ask because I always want to be informed, when I am ignorant' " and " 'Oh! I am glad to know that, because I always like to be put right when I am wrong' " (366; ch. 29). In this way, Rosa plays the role of the eager student, desperate to be enlightened and ready to be sympathetic to the speaker's views. However, she cannot fool David; he realizes that, despite her ostensibly ingenuous strategy, she always "got everything . . . she wanted to know" (304; ch. 24).

Rosa's furtive questions are a mode of questioning the beliefs and relationships of those around her. David acknowledges this when he states, "Her own views of every question, and her correction of everything that was said to which she was opposed, Miss Dartle insinuated in the same way: sometimes, I could not conceal from myself, with great power" (252; ch. 20).[7] Rosa's passive-aggressive form of interrogation allows her to address the Steerforths' views on herself and one another. Irritated by Rosa's circuitous form of speech, Mrs. Steerforth accuses her of being "mysterious" by refusing to "speak plainly, in [her] own natural manner." Rosa's docile but loaded response, " 'Now you must really bear with me, because I ask for information. We never know ourselves,' " reveals the audacity of Mrs. Steerforth's statement: the reason for the change in Rosa is no "mystery." This point is further emphasized when Mrs. Steerforth returns, " 'I remember,—and so must you, I think,—when your manner was different, Rosa; when it was not so guarded, and was more trustful.' " The companion responds by feigning an ignorance that only serves to mirror and thereby reveal the purposeful forgetfulness of her mistress: " 'Really? Less guarded and more trustful? How can I, imperceptibly, have changed, I wonder! Well, that's very odd! I must study to regain my former self' " (367–68; ch. 29). As Mary Ann O'Farrell notes, because she is "scarred, she *cannot* imperceptively have changed" (89). Both women know that Rosa has "changed" due to her experiences with Steerforth, his toying with her affections as well as his disfiguring attack on her face, and Rosa mimics Mrs. Steerforth's pretended ignorance as a way to call attention to its injustice. She does not, however, refrain from a parting gesture that will drive the point home: she asserts that she will "learn frankness" from Steerforth. David, positioned like the reader as a silent witness of this exchange, notes that "there was always some effect of sarcasm in what Rosa Dartle said, though it was said, as this was, in the most unconscious manner in the world" (368; ch. 29). This hint of criticism is subtle enough, and while David catches it, the Steerforths have no idea that the companion is anything but sympathetic with their views.[8] It is this intimate access, united with the freedom from suspicion that the companion's performance of sympathy allows, that situates the companion throughout Victorian fiction in the perfect position to function as an agent of the narrative.

Immediately following this exchange, Rosa again exhibits powers of foresight when she foreshadows the approaching rift between mother and son by questioning the pair about their relationship. As if in warning, Rosa inquires " 'whether people, who are alike in their moral constitution, are in greater danger than people not so circumstanced, supposing any serious cause of variance to arise between them, of being divided angrily and deeply?' " (368; ch. 29). Unaware that, in her initial delicacy, Rosa refers to them, Steerforth answers in the affirmative. Yet, once she makes her meaning clear, Mrs. Steerforth interjects that she and her son will never be divided because they know their "duty" to each other. Rosa's caustic reply functions as a shrewd rebuttal to her mistress's defensive response: " 'To be sure. *That* would prevent it? Why, of course it would. Ex-actly. Now, I am glad that I have been so foolish as to put the case, for it is so very good to know that your duty to each other would prevent it!' " (368; ch. 29). Dickens's phrasing here makes the companion's assessment of the Steerforths' joint lack of self-awareness and their resulting self-satisfaction clear. In this scene, Rosa has uncovered the roots of the mother and son's dysfunction, their likeness as well as their fixation on one another, and foreseen its destructive end. In addition, Rosa has once again preempted David's narrative as she interprets the Steerforths' relationship and future for the reader in a way that David cannot. Despite her efforts, neither the Steerforths nor David can heed her forewarning; like that of the *ficelle*, her interpretation is for the reader more than for the characters.

In these two scenes, Dickens establishes a rich, complex dynamic of sympathy and repulsion between his characters. Rosa's ambivalent relationship with the family allows her the ability to sympathize with her mistress and Steerforth, to understand their emotions and motivations, but it also simultaneously allows her to *undo* that sympathy in order to present the reader as well as David with a satire of the Steerforths' social pretension and familial dysfunction. Rosa warps sympathy so that it is useful to her and damaging to the recipient, rather than salutary. For the companion, sympathy becomes a means of both obtaining information and exploiting it. By employing Rosa as both vexed character within the narrative frame and as an alternative perspective on that same narrative, Dickens is able to deconstruct sympathy in order to show that it can be just as vicious as its opposite.

II. Rosa Dartle Exposed

When the Steerforth plot transforms into one of scandal, anger, and alienation, no character serves as an indicator of this shift more than Rosa Dartle. Upon learning that Steerforth has run away with Emily Peggotty, Rosa embarks on a new mode of communication with those around her. No longer signifying through her eyes and scar or suggestive inquiries, she unleashes the full power of her passionate nature in judgment on her mistress and Steerforth. Ultimately abandoning her performance of sympathy, Rosa makes her condemnatory position within the family known. In the latter part of the Steerforth sections, Dickens brings Rosa's affective and verbal language together to form a clear critique of Mrs. Steerforth and her son. However, Rosa's outbursts also begin to represent a loss of control over that critique and thus serve as a revelation of her own character as well.

Rosa's eyes and scar continue to inform David's articulation of the Steerforth narrative. When David brings news of Steerforth's actions with Emily to Mrs. Steerforth, Rosa initially performs the role of sympathetic companion. She "glided" to her station behind her mistress's chair, "touched her" and "tried to soothe her" (395, 398; ch. 32). Nevertheless, David notes that her "keen glance comprehended" them all, and once David and Mr. Peggotty have withdrawn, Rosa pursues them to the door of the Steerforth home. David describes how "Such a concentration of rage and scorn as darkened her face, and flashed in her jet-black eyes, I could not have thought compressible even into that face. The scar made by the hammer was, as usual in this excited state of her features, strongly marked. When the throbbing I had seen before, came into it as I looked at her, she absolutely lifted up her hand, and struck it" (399; ch. 32). Rosa's reaction clarifies for the reader the depths of Steerforth's transgression, an act which arises out of the very behavior Rosa criticizes throughout the novel. Rosa's predictions have come to fruition. As if to emphasize that her emotional reaction carries significance, Rosa strikes her scar, drawing David's attention to the condemnation written on her face. However, Rosa's self-flagellation in this scene also represents for David and the reader her own inward, jealous pain. Repeating Steerforth's original brutality, Rosa's action suggests that she views Steerforth's elopement as yet another act of violence against her.

This time, Rosa does not stop there; she complements her affective response with speech that is more direct and accusatory than anything she has uttered to this point in the novel. " 'Don't you know that they are both mad with their own self-will and pride?' " she asks David. As she continues to assail the Steerforths, asserting that James " 'has a false, corrupt heart, and is a traitor,' " Rosa's speech simultaneously exceeds both David's and the companion's control. David admits that the intensity of her response supersedes what he as narrator can describe: "The mere vehemence of her words can convey, I am sensible, but a weak impression of the passion by which she was possessed, and which made itself articulate in her whole figure" (399–400; ch. 32). But Rosa also betrays her own investment in Steerforth's actions in her loss of verbal control. David notes that as she speaks Rosa puts "her hand on her bosom, as if to prevent the storm that was raging there" (399; ch. 32). In this scene, Rosa not only provides her most explicit assessment of the Steerforths; she also fully emerges as a figure who is not solely a source of removed, interpretive perspective—not just the "writing on the wall"—but one who is mired in the very milieu she works to expose. For the first time in the novel, it is undeniably clear that, despite her intensive criticism of his shortcomings, Rosa Dartle is still in love with James Steerforth. While her previous performances of sympathy were a tool which allowed Rosa to collect information and criticize her employers without their knowledge, we learn here, once she has abandoned that technique, that it has also served as an apparatus of self-management for the companion. When she openly acts outside of the expectations of her companion position, it is as if she also loses control of her critical methods, inadvertently revealing something of her *own* character to the narrator and reader.

For a time, Rosa turns her critical attention toward Emily. Perhaps she is not yet ready to confront the Steerforths themselves or her own feelings for them directly in this new, more open manner, and so she uses Emily as a kind of detour for her emotion. Eager to form and then assert her own narrative of the woman who has captured " 'James Steerforth's fancy,' " however briefly, Rosa finds Emily in Martha's garret and confronts her. Throughout her attack on Steerforth's lover, Rosa emphasizes her need to *see* Emily: " 'I have come to look at you. . . . I have come to see, . . . I want to know what such a thing is like' " (604; ch. 50). Just as she observed the interaction between David and Steerforth earlier in the novel, Rosa has come to "read" Emily. In this scene, Rosa once again appears to transcend David's narrative powers: while he, likewise, "came here to see," David is unable to witness the exchange visually; for much of the episode, he can only hear what is said. Yet, in this moment, David shows that he has finally accepted the force of Rosa's affective language and learned to interpret its meaning in order to supplement his own narration. Although David cannot physically see the enraged companion, he states, "I saw the flashing black eyes, and the passion-wasted figure; and I saw the scar, with its white track cutting through her lips, quivering and throbbing as she spoke" as "if I had seen her standing in the light" (604; ch. 50). As in his encounter with the painting, David can "see" the significa-tion of Rosa's expression without literally standing before her. He under-stands her judgment upon Emily and the Steerforths alike, but, this time, he reports her response as a way of describing the full meaning of the scene for his reader. Rather than fight the competitive narrative she presents, he acknowledges it and assimilates it into his own depiction of the episode.

Although Rosa's mission, in keeping with her previous behavior, would seem to be to interpret Emily in order to reveal something about Steerforth's character, what emerges in this scene is a critique not of Steerforth or Emily, but of Rosa herself. David once again describes her struggle to contain herself in order to prevent the exposure of her personal investments: "Her lips were tightly compressed, as if she knew that she must keep a strong constraint upon herself" (605; ch. 50). But, as Rosa denies any commonality between herself and the fallen girl, she in effect proves the underlying sympathy between them, a point which Emily addresses directly when she states, " 'If you live in his home and know him, you know, perhaps, what his power with a weak, vain girl might be' " (606; ch. 50). When Rosa responds, " '*You* love him? *You*? . . . And tell that to *me*,' " she confirms Emily's assertion.[9] Having served as a mirror to the Steerforths' dysfunction throughout the narrative, Rosa cannot abide the reflection of *herself* in Emily: " 'I can't breathe freely in the air you breathe. I find it sickly' " (607). As she leaves Emily's presence, recommending that she "consecrate [her] existence to the recollection of James Steerforth's tenderness" or "die," Rosa has so exposed herself that the reader understands she simultaneously speaks to herself.

By the time Rosa learns of James's death in the final scene of the Steerforth plot, the companion can no longer contain her judgment of the family nor deny her own passion. Leaving all pretense of sympathy behind, Rosa lays bare her critical stance for her mistress, David, and the reader. At the begin-ning of the scene, Rosa and David at last achieve an understanding as the companion and the protagonist/narrator collude to communicate solely through reading one another's faces. David states, "From the first moment of her dark eyes resting on me, I saw she knew I was the bearer of evil tidings. The scar sprung into view that instant. She withdrew herself a step behind the chair, to keep her own face out of Mrs. Steerforth's observation; and scrutinized me with a piercing gaze that never faltered, never shrunk." Immediately, Rosa interprets the nature of David's arrival and, unwilling to include her mistress in this moment of exchange, she moves out of view. Shortly thereafter, David reveals his purpose: "I said, by the motion of my lips, to Rosa, 'Dead!' " (671; ch. 56). It is significant here that, although

David's lips form the word, he does not actually say it aloud. Instead, he literalizes Rosa's interpretive and critical role in the narrative by giving her a word to read upon his mouth—just as he has been "reading" the scar upon her mouth throughout the novel.

David privileges Rosa by revealing the news to her before her mistress, perhaps partly out of sympathy in his understanding of her feelings for Steerforth, but also, no doubt, so that she can assist him in gently informing Mrs. Steerforth. Yet, as Mrs. Steerforth grows alarmed and calls to her companion, David describes how Rosa "came, but with no sympathy or gentleness" (673; ch. 56). With all hope of a union with Steerforth destroyed, Rosa orders her employer to realize the role she has played in her household: " 'look at me! Moan, and groan, and look at me! Look here!' " The companion now demands that Mrs. Steerforth look at and interpret *her* in the same way she has observed her mistress throughout the novel. First, Rosa forces Mrs. Steerforth to acknowledge her scar, and, as she disallows her mistress's sublimation of all that the mark represents, she blames the mother for making her son what he was.[10] Next, Rosa finally reveals her true feelings for Steerforth, indicting Mrs. Steerforth for her dysfunction and the role it played in keeping her from the man she so desired: " 'Look at me, I say, proud mother of a proud false son! Moan for your nurture of him, moan for your corruption of him, moan for your loss of him, moan for mine!' " (673; ch. 56). While much of this information has been clear to David and the reader throughout, Rosa's skilled method of manipulative sympathy has kept Mrs. Steerforth from realizing Rosa's true motivation and goals. This scene marks the first time in which Rosa unveils her position as critic to her mistress. As she blames her employer for Steerforth's faults as well as for his estrangement from his mother and from herself, she also reveals the depths of her own obsession with James.

Ultimately, Rosa makes it clear that she will now withhold nothing and show no mercy: " 'I *will* speak to her. No power on earth should stop me, while I was standing here! Have I been silent all these years, and shall I not speak now? I loved him better than you ever loved him' " (673; ch. 56). As she unfolds the story of her youthful relationship with James and the reverberations it has had in her own life and that of the Steerforths, she exposes the whole of the Steerforths' history, as well as her own. Here, more than ever before, Rosa narrates the story that David cannot tell as she reveals the full chronicle of her courtship with Steerforth, Mrs. Steerforth's cruel disapproval, and Steerforth's eventual betrayal and abandonment. This, a kind of origin story of the family's current dynamics and dysfunction, is Rosa's ultimate advantage over David. It is the necessary background that he cannot provide without the companion, who is the only one willing to lay it bare for the reader. But, for the last time, Rosa also reveals her own faults, again allowing David and the reader to turn a critical eye on her as well.[11] In response to David's assertion that Steerforth, too, had his faults and that not all the blame lies with his mother, Rosa retorts: " 'Faults! . . . Who dares malign him? He had a soul worth millions of the friends to whom he stooped!' " (674; ch. 56). Denying that any responsibility for his wrongdoing lies with Steerforth, Rosa shows what she *cannot* interpret—she cannot fully see beyond her love. Restricted to blaming Emily, Mrs. Steerforth, and, finally, David, the companion is unable to overcome her devotion to James.

Rosa is incapable of reconciling her own criticism of Steerforth with her love for him and so she cannot move forward, even after his death. Instead, she reveals herself to be just like those she has attempted to expose throughout the novel; callous, stubborn, and obsessive, she is no different than her mistress or her former lover. Rosa is trapped in her critical role ad infinitum. Although she has proved an adept assistant, and even at times a worthy opponent, it is David who emerges as the superior storyteller in the novel. With Rosa's help, David is able to transcend his biases and emotions regarding Steerforth, whereas Rosa, in the end, cannot. However, Rosa's prowess as an agent of the narrative is ultimately acknowledged by David's very act of including her in his account in this way. After all, David narrates his story retrospectively; so while his younger self is challenged by the companion, the older, narrator David ultimately accepts Rosa's role by willingly including her (even her temporary advantage over him) when he tells his story. But perhaps David's honest inclusion of Rosa's character represents more than his recognition of her as a worthy adversary in his narrative; his choice to portray Rosa's critical work, especially his own struggles with her, suggests he might harbor some feelings of guilt concerning Emily's and Steerforth's—possibly even Rosa's—fates. Rosa is the only character in the narrative to implicate him in the disastrous affairs of the Steerforth family, and although he repeatedly refuses to admit any culpability, his decision to include that aspect of Rosa's critique implies that he acknowledges his own complicity on some level. Thus, while Rosa may be left to suffer in the diegesis, she is empowered in the narrative structure of the novel.

Throughout Rosa's tirade, Mrs. Steerforth sits in an unresponsive, almost catatonic state—she cannot speak, she cannot cry, but only moan for her loss under the revealing attack of her trusted attendant. In the end, we do not know if Rosa's confrontation with her mistress even reaches the stunned Mrs. Steerforth, and the companion has no choice but to take "the impassive figure in her arms, and, still on her knees, [weep] over it, kissing it, calling to it, rocking it to and fro upon her bosom like a child" (675; ch. 56). Despite the history between them, no longer a secret, companion and mistress are stuck with one another—perhaps, finally in a state of true sympathy as they mourn the loss of their common beloved. As David states before concluding the Steerforth plot, Mrs. Steerforth "was just the same, they told me; Miss Dartle never left her'' (675; ch. 56). Graham Storey has called this scene ''as melancholy as anything in Dickens,'' and, indeed, this is a sad fate for the hypercritical companion (85).

As James Steerforth tells David, '' 'I told you she took everything, herself included, to a grindstone, and sharpened it. She is an edge-tool' '' (370). Rosa Dartle indeed acts as a grindstone in *David Copperfield*, sharpening and bringing into focus obscured histories and deeper meanings beneath the surface of the text. Dickens utilizes the complex, ambiguous nature of the companion's position in society and in the domestic circle to create a figure who can provide an alternative to the narrator's perspective within the novel. However, Dickens does not reward his ''edge-tool''; instead, he seems to punish Rosa for executing exactly the work he formed her to do. The companion is left unfulfilled and static because, although her efforts on the interpretive level are necessary for Dickens and, in turn, for his readers, he cannot condone her problematic behavior on the level of the plot.

By exposing the Steerforths' dysfunction to David and his readers, Rosa can gain some vengeance for the way she has been treated, but Dickens cannot let this misuse of sympathy go unaddressed. In her critical work, Rosa betrays the Victorian standards for the companion position and womanhood alike through her manipulation and degradation of sympathy. Thus, as she reveals the transgressions of the Steerforths, she must also betray her own. While she succeeds in her critical work, her own exposé inevitably turns on her, and in the end, Dickens robs her of whatever pleasure her function may have afforded her. With Steerforth dead and her mistress in need of more care than ever, Rosa is trapped in her painful position indefinitely. Having laid bare her full critique, there is nothing left for her to do, we suspect, but *properly* fulfill her prescribed role as submissive, sympathetic companion.

Dickens employs Rosa as a critic in *David Copperfield*, but he also critiques her in return. He takes advantage of the companion and the work she can accomplish both as an agent of the narrative and as a means of examining the concept of sympathy. Through Rosa, Dickens deconstructs sympathy and illustrates that it can be a manipulative, egoistic, critical mode as well as an altruistic means of human interaction. In this sense, Rosa's form of sympathy stands in contrast to other manifestations of genuine sympathy throughout the novel, and those characters who practice a selfless, generous version of sympathy generally are rewarded. Although Rosa's use of her own malign form of sympathy becomes a narratological instrument for Dickens, he eventually turns on his own narrative device. Rosa acts as a critique of herself: Dickens's own commentary on the potential dangers of the companion's position and the manipulative modes of sympathy she can use to accomplish her self-serving goals. Thus, Dickens acknowledges, explores, and even seems to identity with the darker side of sympathy in *David Copperfield* but ultimately refuses to align himself with it.

In the Victorian era, some novelists began to interrogate the conventional view of sympathy as a force which forges bonds of sentimental understanding between individuals, underpinning social hierarchies and stability. A particularly acute site of sympathetic expectation and potential manipulation, the mistress-companion relationship allowed authors like Dickens, and others such as Wilkie Collins, Anthony Trollope, Charlotte Brontë, and William Makepeace Thackeray, to experiment with portrayals of sympathy as a self-serving, disruptive, but often revelatory mode of relating. As Dickens's use of Rosa shows, the companion figure's ambiguous placement in the home, coupled with her cultural characterization as a locus of sympathetic prowess, also allowed Victorian authors unique opportunities for disclosure in their narratives. A wide variety of novelists made effective use of this device. In *Lady Audley's Secret* and *Anne Hereford*, for instance, Mary Elizabeth Braddon and Ellen Wood portray their companion characters as covert detectives. Phoebe Marks and Charlotte Delves Penn use their companion positions, particularly their manipulation of sympathy with their mistresses and others, to uncover and distribute the secrets at the cores of their respective novels, offering a feminine alternative to the techniques of the burgeoning male detective figure in mid-century sensation fiction. Companion narrators such as Charlotte Brontë's Lucy Snowe in *Villette*, Esther Summerson in *Bleak House*, and Collins's Madame Pratolungo in *Poor Miss Finch*, are able to relay the private confidences of their mistresses and other exclusive information directly to their readers; while other companions, like Mrs. General in *Little Dorrit*, are used much more subtly as touchstones that can reveal or emphasize information about other characters in the narrative.

Throughout the plots of these novels and others like them, the presence of the companion in the home, as well as her ability to manipulate sympathy, represented the dangerous infiltration of the public, economic world into the domestic space and domestic relationships. The companion's double allegiance to the private and public spheres represents a significant threat to the sanctity of private knowledge within the domestic realm. Because companions are at once intimate members of the family circle as well as paid employees, they are capable of seeing and acting in both directions. Their position grants them access to secret, familial knowledge, but in the absence of any genuine investment in those they serve, their status as professional women simultaneously allows them the ability to circulate that knowledge beyond the boundaries of the household. In this way, although often little more than minor characters, companions come to play a crucial role in many nineteenth-century novels, enabling Victorian writers to address troubled contemporary issues as diverse as sympathy, gender roles, employment dynamics, homoeroticism, and narrative structure in their work. Yet, despite the unsettling power of this figure, the companion is often lost to historical and literary studies. She lingers, strangely enough, mainly in the Victorian novels we read today.

NOTES

1. The paucity of critical or historical work on the companion makes it necessary to turn to the Victorian governess, an analogous but distinct figure, for insight into the daily conditions of actual companions. My work on the companion has benefited from valuable studies on the governess by scholars such as Kathryn Hughes and Bronwyn Rivers.

2. W. J. Harvey delineates the *ficelle*'s "many functions": "he may become a transitional agent between protagonist and society; he may afford relief and contrast of the simplest kind. . . . he may allow us the pleasurable relaxation of recognizing the limited and familiar after our struggle with the involvements or complexities of the protagonist. In innumerable ways he may act as foil to the protagonist, creating what I have called the perspective of depth. By his misunderstanding and partial view he may focus the protagonist's dilemma more clearly. Alternatively, by a flash of insight or simply by being the spokesman of sober reality and common sense, he may illuminate the protagonist's blindness and folly. He may stand as a possible alternative to the protagonist, incarnating what the character might have been. . . . Or he may embody in a simpler form some analogue, positive or negative, to the hero's experience. . . . He may be the moral touchstone by which we judge the aberration of others; he may, by being simple and static, become the point of reference by which we measure change and growth elsewhere" (63).

3. Alex Woloch's work on the intersection of and competition among various characters' "character-space" within the "character-system" of a narrative is particularly relevant here.

4. Scholars have shown themselves to be just as interested in Rosa's scar as David. John Jordan and Harvey Sucksmith read the mark in terms of Steerforth's dysfunctional sexuality. While Jordan refers to the scar as "the mark of Steerforth's sexual violence on her" (69), Sucksmith asserts that "It has become a symbolic rape, expressing her deepest longings, her sense of humiliation and outrage, and her hatred" (29). In contrast, Barbara Black, who refers to the mark as "an image of female genitalia" (95), and Mary Ann O'Farrell, who calls it "vaginal and Medusan" (87), view the scar as a specifically feminine locus of power and sexuality. Rachel Ablow examines the scar from a different theoretical angle when she writes that Rosa's scar is like a novel: "the scar registers how Rosa feels, even as it also serves as a memento of the love affair that provides the most relevant context for those feelings. It thus provides observers with everything they need to understand her feelings and so presumably sympathize with them: like a novel, it reveals the content of her responses, their immediate cause, and the historical circumstances that have gone into producing them" (34).

5. The portrait of Rosa serves as a reminder that Rosa's employer regards her as a relation as well as a paid female companion, as was the case for many Victorian companions. Rosa's status as a part of the family amplifies her privileged access to the Steerforths' secrets as it simultaneously heightens the sense of betrayal inherent in her critical work. Despite this acknowledgement of Rosa's connection

to the Steerforths, the placement of the portrait, hidden away in a spare bedroom, duly reflects her status within the family circle.

6. Shortly after this scene, David admits that, if only for a moment, he felt himself "falling a little in love with" Rosa (304). Michael Léger reads this scene as "of no little significance" because immediately preceding this statement, David spends the day "talking with her about the man they *both* love." He continues, "In the Girardian paradigm, David falls 'a bit' in love with Dartle because of Steerforth's past love for her" (313). In terms of my argument, I interpret this scene first as representative of the power of the sympathetic identification between David and Rosa in their common love for Steerforth; their sympathy on this point becomes so clear here that David confuses his feelings for one with his feelings for the other. Second, David's fleeting infatuation is a response to Rosa's domination of him—just as he is attracted to Steerforth's power over him, so too does he find Rosa's narrative competition seductive.

7. Françoise Basch discusses how Rosa's character was believed to be based on one Mrs. Brown, "ex-governess, and intimate friend of Miss Burdett-Coutts." Basch reveals, "In his letters Dickens alludes to the taste for contradiction and the extreme susceptibility of the woman he called the 'general objector' " (149).

8. Mrs. Steerforth's recognition that Rosa speaks in a "mysterious" way proves that she does realize Rosa is doing *something* with her speech; nevertheless, Dickens at no time implies that Rosa's mistress attributes this abnormality to anything more than her companion's harmless eccentricity. Steerforth, however, seems aware that Rosa may be "dangerous" to him. This is most apparent when he tells David, " 'Confound the girl, I am half afraid of her. She's like a goblin to me' " (258). But, like his mother, Steerforth is never able to see through Rosa's pretense of sympathy with the family.

9. O'Farrell points out that Rosa's earlier statement to David and Mr. Peggotty, "I would have her branded on the face," and her various—but unconsummated—threats of physical violence in her encounter with Emily serve to elucidate the companion's implicit acknowledgment of sympathy between the two women. She writes, "Rosa Dartle's real cruelty toward Emily involves, despite itself, the mottled generosity of throwing a fit rather than a hammer, making a scene rather than a scar" (98).

10. Several modern critics, including Gwendolyn B. Needham, John R. Reed, Arthur A. Adrian, and Mary Anne Andrade, have agreed with Rosa's appraisal of Mrs. Steerforth's guilt.

11. Considering the impact the relationship has had on her life, Rosa describes her affair with James very succinctly in this scene. She explains, " 'I could sing to him, and talk to him, and show the ardour that I felt in all he did, and attain with labour to such knowledge as most interested him; and I attracted him. When he was freshest and truest, he loved me. Yes, he did! Many a time, when you were put off with a slight word, he has taken Me to his heart!' . . . I descended—as I might have known I should, but that he fascinated me with his boyish courtship—into a doll, a trifle for the occupation of an idle hour, to be dropped, and taken up, and trifled with, as the inconstant humour took him. When he grew weary, I grew weary. As his fancy died out, I would no more have tried to

strengthen any power I had, than I would have married him on his being forced to take me for his wife. We fell away from one another without a word. Perhaps you saw it, and were not sorry'' (674). Patricia Ingham interprets Rosa's assertion that she would not have forced James to marry her as an implicit admission of her sexual relationship with him (59). If we accept this reading, then Rosa's narrative here would be her most significant *self*-revelation in the novel: she reveals herself as a fallen woman.

WORKS CITED

Ablow, Rachel. *The Marriage of Minds: Reading Sympathy in the Victorian Marriage Plot*. Stanford: Stanford UP, 2007.

Adrian, Arthur A. *Dickens and the Parent-Child Relationship*. Athens: Ohio UP, 1984.

Andrade, Mary Anne. "Pollution of an Honest Home." *Dickens Quarterly* 5.2 (June 1988): 65–74.

Basch, Françoise. *Relative Creatures: Victorian Women in Society in the Novel*. New York: Schocken, 1974.

Black, Barbara. "A Sisterhood of Rage and Beauty: Dickens's Rosa Dartle, Miss Wade, and Madame Defarge." *Dickens Studies Annual* 26 (1998): 91–106.

Braddon, Mary Elizabeth. *Lady Audley's Secret*. Ed. David Skilton. New York: Oxford UP, 1998.

Brontë, Charlotte. *Villette*. Ed. Mark Lilly. New York: Penguin, 1979.

Collins, Wilkie. *Poor Miss Finch*. Cirencester: Echo Library, 2005.

Dickens, Charles. *Bleak House*. Ed. George Ford and Sylvère Monod. New York: Norton, 1977.

———. *David Copperfield*. Ed. Jerome H. Buckley. New York: Norton, 1990.

———. *Little Dorrit*. Ed. John Holloway. New York: Penguin, 1985.

———. *Nicholas Nickleby*. Ed. Mark Ford. New York: Penguin, 2003.

Ellis, Sarah Stickney. *The Women of England: Their Social Duties and Domestic Habits*. London: Fisher, 1839.

Greenstein, Michael. "Between Curtain and Caul: David Copperfield's Shining Transparencies." *Dickens Quarterly* 5.2 (June 1988): 75–81.

Harvey, W. J. *Character and the Novel*. Ithaca: Cornell UP, 1965.

Hughes, Kathryn. *The Victorian Governess*. London: Hambledon, 1993.

Ingham, Patricia. *Dickens, Women, and Language*. Toronto: U of Toronto P, 1992.

Jaffe, Audrey. *Scenes of Sympathy*. Ithaca: Cornell UP, 2000.

James, Henry. *The Ambassadors*. Ed. Harry Levin. New York: Penguin, 1986.

———. *The Portrait of a Lady*. Ed. Geoffrey Moore and Patricia Crick. New York: Penguin, 2003

Jordan, John O. ''The Social Sub-text of *David Copperfield*.'' *Dickens Studies Annual* 14 (1985): 61–92.

Léger, J. Michael. ''Triangulation and Homoeroticism in *David Copperfield*.'' *Victorian Literature and Culture* 23 (1995): 301–25.

Needham, Gwendolyn B. ''The Undisciplined Heart of David Copperfield.'' *Nineteenth-Century Fiction* 9.2 (September 1954): 81–107.

O'Farrell, Mary Ann. *Telling Complexions: The Nineteenth-Century English Novel and the Blush*. Durham: Duke UP, 1997.

Reed, John R. *Dickens and Thackeray: Punishment and Forgiveness*. Athens: Ohio UP, 1995.

Rivers, Bronwyn. *Women at Work in the Victorian Novel: The Question of Middle Class Women's Employment*. Lewiston: Edwin Mellen, 2005.

Storey, Graham. *David Copperfield: Interweaving Truth and Fiction*. Boston: Twayne, 1991.

Sucksmith, Harvey Peter. *The Narrative Art of Charles Dickens: The Rhetoric of Sympathy and Irony in His Novels*. Oxford: Clarendon, 1970.

Thackeray, William Makepeace. *Vanity Fair: A Novel Without a Hero*. New York: Modern Library, 2001.

Wolfreys, Julian, and Harun Karim Thomas. *Glossalalia: An Alphabet of Critical Keywords*. New York: Routledge, 2003.

Woloch, Alex. *The One vs. the Many: Minor Characters and the Space of the Protagonist in the Novel*. Princeton: Princeton UP, 2003.

Wood, Ellen. *Anne Hereford*. New York: Aegypan, 2006.

Dickens's Collaborative Genres

Melissa Valiska Gregory

Recent readings of Dickens's collaborative relationships tend to focus on the struggle for literary control between Dickens and his less famous colleagues. But when the question of genre is brought to bear on his collaborative writing, it becomes apparent that Dickens created new literary forms which permit for more complex authorial negotiations than scholars have acknowledged. Despite Dickens's dictatorial tendencies, the collaborative genres he developed over the course of his career often promote a model of authorship where power relationships are in flux, and this fluidity creates new opportunities for epistemological exploration and authorial self-definition. I explore two of Dickens's collaborative genres that appeared in Household Words *and* All the Year Round. *The first is the annual Christmas number; the second is the "excursion article," which revolved around holiday outings taken by Dickens and his staff. An investigation of these collaborative genres reveals that they refuse to conform neatly to hierarchical patterns of dominance and subordination, thus enriching our understanding of the many and varied kinds of creative partnerships that emerged between male writers during the Victorian period.*

Since there is hardly any aspect of Charles Dickens's career that literary scholars have not excavated with relish, it is somewhat surprising how little work exists on his collaborative writing. From Wordsworth and Coleridge in *Lyrical Ballads* (1798) to Katherine Bradley and Edith Cooper, who published their joint works under the pseudonym ''Michael Field,'' new studies of collaborative authorship invite us to reconfigure conventional categories of

Dickens Studies Annual, Volume 41, Copyright © 2010 by AMS Press, Inc. All rights reserved.

professional, social, and personal identity in the nineteenth century. Yet Anthea Trodd's articles on Dickens's Christmas numbers and Lillian Nayder's *Unequal Partners* (2002) comprise the most recent major scholarship on Dickens's collaborative endeavors.[1] This dearth runs counter to Dickens's own habit of inviting other artists into his creative world, a love of working "in company" (*Letters* 8: 256) that was manifested not only in his passion for the theater, but also in his role as both an editor and contributor to *Household Words* (1850–59) and *All the Year Round* (1859–70). Given his interest in what he called "composite" writing, why is Dickens's collaborative work so rarely brought to the table, even when it offers so many attractive fusion dishes? What does his collaborative writing—and our treatment of it—tell us not only about models of nineteenth-century authorship, but also about ourselves as literary scholars?

I am motivated to explore these and related questions by a desire to complicate the growing body of work on literary collaboration in the Victorian period. We have long since rejected the dated influence model of the master training the apprentice, opening the door for more complex interpretations of the authorial relationships occasioned by collaborative work. In Dickens's case, new readings have productively revised the overly benign view of his creative partnerships that originated in John Forster's biography and which persisted for almost a full century, and we have reached a more nuanced if less forgiving understanding of the uneven power dynamics at work. The most recent corrective is *Unequal Partners*, which explores Dickens's collaborative relationship with Wilkie Collins as an increasingly serious rivalry. Nayder persuasively argues that Dickens's need for authorial control damaged their friendship, causing an almost irreparable rift between the two men by the end of Dickens's life. But I suggest that when the question of genre is brought to bear on his collaborative writing, Dickens appears to have created new literary forms that permit for more authorial negotiation than Nayder and others have allowed—on the page if not always in the process. The scholarly emphasis on Dickens's efforts to establish his supremacy over the very authors that he invited to work with him obscures some of the intriguing tonal nuances, weird internal friction, and peculiar crossbreeding effects that animate his collaborative work and make it a dynamic reading experience.

In what follows, I explore some of Dickens's composite writing that refuses to conform neatly to hierarchical patterns of dominance and subordination, investigating the strange and sometimes unexpected textual energetics that emerge in his collaborative projects. I argue that despite Dickens's desire to be in charge, the collaborative genres that he developed over the course of his career often promote a model of authorship where power relationships are always in flux, and I suggest that this fluidity creates new opportunities for epistemological exploration and authorial self-definition. Examining these genres, of course, expands our view of Dickens, but it also enriches our understanding of how periodical writing—especially the oft-derided Victorian short story—may have operated as space for aesthetic experimentation in the nineteenth century. Dickens's collaborative writing inspired some of the most unusual generic moments of his career, and a closer investigation of these moments not only offers new ways for us to talk about models of authorship, but also suggests new contexts for more familiar forms of Victorian fiction, such as the novel.

I investigate two different collaborative genres that Dickens developed in *Household Words* and, later, in *All the Year Round*. The first is the annual Christmas number, created by Dickens in the wake of his five solo Christmas books. The second is a form of composite writing that I am calling the ''excursion article,'' playfully imaginative essays that revolve around holiday outings taken by Dickens and his staff. I have chosen these two genres because the contrast between them illuminates the impact of literary form on the authorial negotiations inevitably occasioned by collaborative writing as well as the reverse, the impact of authorial negotiations on literary form. Both savor the chaos and disorder that can arise from collaborative work, but the formal conventions of the Christmas numbers disable the more fluid exchange of authorial power that occurs in the excursion articles. I have also selected these two genres because they present models of creative partnership that facilitate our understanding of the role of the Victorian professional literary man. Both are equally invested in domesticating the act of professional literary partnership, the former bringing authors under Dickens's roof, the latter sending them out into the world as already bonded pairs. But the Christmas articles show Dickens enacting a more traditional masculine role—playing the part of leader or captain—while the excursion articles promote a model of literary partnership predicated on male friendship, exuberantly melding the domestic with the professional as the writers travel, eat, and work together. These latter pieces encourage us to recognize the ways in which male writers from this period portray themselves as drawing upon rather than disavowing the structures of domesticity for creative inspiration, openly affirming the importance of male intimacy to professional partnerships.

I. Dickens's Christmas Collaborations

I begin with Dickens's Christmas numbers, which might best be described as a conflicted genre. Published annually in *Household Words* and then *All the Year Round* between 1850 and 1867, the Christmas numbers are collections of short fiction and poetry written by Dickens, his friends, and various other authors. They flirt with the familiar Victorian genres of the medley, the miscellany, and the annual keepsake, yet they insist upon a formal and thematic wholeness to which those other genres never aspire. At first, Dickens merely devoted a special issue of *Household Words* to the theme of Christmas, but, only two years after founding the journal, he began to conceive of the Christmas numbers as more unified, viewing them as collections of stories that shared a particular time or place. He eventually began to introduce and conclude them with editorial frames of his own devising. With the Christmas number, then, Dickens created a genre that allowed him to accept the contributions of other writers while retaining control over the collaborative process and, later, over the initial setting and overall context of the narrative itself. Both Nayder and Trodd cite these annual productions as evidence of Dickens's dictatorial personality, his compulsive need to take charge of what might otherwise be a companionable process of shared writing. To be sure, Dickens dominated each Christmas issue from its inception to its final publication: the various contributors did not communicate among themselves, and Dickens was exclusively responsible for vetting all of the submissions, compiling them, and linking them together. I propose, however, that as a genre, the Christmas numbers are more equivocal on the nature of authorial power than the process that created them might lead one to expect. They are not as flexible or comically self-aware as the excursion articles I will discuss momentarily, but the end result is perhaps less wedded to the idea of hierarchy than Dickens intended. Indeed, I suggest that a close look at the formal conventions of these annual numbers reveals a vertiginous textual energetics of friction, dissonance, and rupture. The ordered sense of discipline that Dickens sought when compiling each number rarely registers within the actual pages themselves, and sometimes Dickens even works this fragmented aspect of the genre to his personal advantage.

What are the prominent features of this genre, and how does it resist Dickens's controlling editorial tendencies? First, the Christmas number cheerfully flaunts its own heterogeneity. It is a collaborative form whose conventions are paradoxically grounded in the divisions and differences between the contributions from the various authors. As a genre dependent on the idea of collected tales, the Christmas number accommodates an almost unlimited variety of literary forms, subjects, and themes. Drawing upon an older oral tradition, including fairy tales and Dickens's beloved *The Arabian Nights*, the individual tales within the Christmas numbers aim chiefly to charm, delight, and surprise—what Captain Ravender from *The Wreck of the Golden Mary* calls "Music and Adventure, two of the greatest gifts of Providence to mankind" (28).[2] Poetry rubs elbows with fiction, comedy with tragedy. The stories toggle from gothic to satire and from adventure to melodrama and everything in between at a hectic pace, offering a feast of genres (or a dog's breakfast, depending on your point of view).[3] Good stories follow bad ones, and vice versa.

In *The Wreck of the Golden Mary*, for instance, Harriet Parr's melancholy story of a dissipated young man hopelessly obsessed with his lovely cousin, which ends on a wistful note of formal Christian prayer, awkwardly bumps up against Percy Fitzgerald's rollicking adventure story of a ghostly pirate ship. Similarly, Adelaide Anne Procter's sentimental poem about a sailor who returns home after many years to discover that his wife has married someone else, written in the traditional accentual meter of the ballad, collides with the Rev. James White's tale of a drowned girl, a prose story written in Scots dialect. In *Doctor Marigold's Prescriptions*, Rosa Mulholland's melodramatic Irish folktale of unrequited love concludes with a hyperbolic double death as a man who has driven the woman he loves mad follows her over the side of a cliff. The next story in the collection, which begins in the very same column in the original version of *All the Year Round*, is Charles Collins's satiric sketch of a prissy and pedantic English puzzle master who writes riddles for a living. Mulholland's breathless finale—"A hoarse panting, a dire swinging to and fro; and then the rock was standing naked against the sky, no one was there, and Coll Dhu and Evleen Blake lay shattered far below" (48)—is thus followed by the puzzle master's bathetic meditation on the plight of anonymous writers everywhere. "Does any one know who gives the names to our streets?" he complains. "Does any one know who invents the mottoes which are inserted in the cracker papers, along with the sugarplums?—I don't envy him his intellectual faculties, by the by, and I suspect him to be the individual who translates the books of the foreign operas" (49). Such abrupt, stomach-clenching downshifts are the norm for the Christmas numbers rather than the exception. Reading one from beginning to end is a little like riding in a manual transmission car with someone who hasn't quite mastered the art of the stick. Jerky, a little annoying, but also a bit of a thrill, since you never know if or when the engine will drop out. The narrators of these tales further contribute to the grinding noise of the gears. They tend to feature secondary characters from novels who have finally been given the opportunity to take center stage—waiters, cheap jacks, barmaids, cooks, ghosts—and who clamor desperately for attention. Alex Woloch suggests that Dickens's minor characters are always threatening to swarm the weak protagonists of his novels. In the Christmas numbers, they are already running amuck.

Of course, all Victorian periodicals naturally mixed their genres. A diverse array of voices and texts was not only common, but also expected by readers, and it occurred even in those issues of *Household Words* and *All the Year Round* where Dickens tightened up tonal inconsistencies and differences through heavy editing and rewriting. But the Christmas numbers are different because they foreground their effort to achieve unity, promising a certain harmony among the internal stories despite their thematic and formal differences. Hence, the dominant metaphors of Dickens's frame tales often self-reflexively spotlight the violent energy required to force texts from multiple authors together into one space. Each new annual number reveals Dickens's attempt to impose some sort of coherence on the genre, and, at the same time, each Christmas number also points toward the difficulty of achieving this goal. Dickens suggestively portrays the tales as castaways from a violent shipwreck, for instance, or mysterious neighbors who may not be authorized to be there. Or, as in the case of the 1862 Christmas number *Somebody's Luggage*, he depicts the contributions from the other authors as tales discovered among someone's personal effects: hat boxes, boots, and shaving kits. By assigning the stories to various parts of the body, Dickens implies that the literary corpus has been violently hacked apart and sewn back together with the seams still showing. The obvious metaphor hovering in the background of this odd and sometimes grotesque genre is Frankenstein's monster, but Mary Shelley's creature demonstrates both a fluidity of motion and an afterlife that Dickens's Christmas numbers never achieved. With their abrupt, lurching motion, Dickens's Christmas numbers manage to elude the total control of their authoritative editor, but the formal structure of the genre—a collection of tales that must be assembled by someone else—prevents them from ever fully taking on a life of their own. Dickens had to reanimate them every year, a role that both appealed to and frustrated him. On one hand, he was often baffled and exasperated by the Christmas numbers' inconsistencies, complaining to William Henry Wills of the 1855 number that "[t]he way in which they don't fit . . . amazes me" (*Letters* 7: 753). He similarly lamented to Collins that the stories he had received from the other authors were "so disappointing and so impossible to be fitted together or got into the frame" (*Letters* 7: 762) that he had been forced to write an additional story himself. As Dickens's use of the word "fit" suggests, he expected the stories from the other contributors to be so suitable ("befitting") as to attain an almost physical congruity with his own writing. Hence, as Trodd observes, when Dickens chose the figure of the British Tar to narrate the nautically themed Christmas number of 1857, he was beginning to model for his authors the disciplined chain of command that he hoped to see at work in the number itself, an "ideal literary collaboration, comradely but hierarchical" ("Collaborating in Open Boats" 203). On the other hand, if Dickens wanted to be the captain of this genre, then it is worth asking why he sometimes sneaks aboard the boat unseen, taking advantage of the genre's lack of coherence to perform sporadic acts of self-effacement, as follows.

In the collections *Somebody's Luggage* and *Doctor Marigold's Prescriptions*, for instance, Dickens inserts extra tales that are remarkably anonymous. "His Brown Paper Parcel" and "To Be Taken with a Grain of Salt," respectively, allow Dickens to perform a somewhat unexpected creative vanishing act, even if the Christmas number as a whole confirms his public presence.

Any reader familiar with Dickens will quickly recognize him as the author of the frame tale for *Somebody's Luggage*, narrated by a verbose restaurant waiter with literary aspirations. But would they immediately identify "His Brown Paper Parcel," the seventh tale in that same Christmas number? To be sure, the telltale use of personification and rhythmic repetition appear as early as the third paragraph. The story itself, however, about a bitter and perpetually anonymous artist who sells his sidewalk drawings to men that then pass them off as their own, eschews the subjects, themes, and modes of representation that characterize the other Christmas frame tales and which brand them as Dickens's. Lacking in character development, sentiment, and, in truth, less funny than Dickens at his best, the story is easy to overlook. "To Be Taken With a Grain of Salt," in *Doctor Marigold's Prescriptions*, similarly evades immediate authorial identification, and even Dickens's own readers did not recognize it. This tale also engages the question of public recognition but spins it in a gothic direction, featuring the ghost of a murdered man who haunts the narrator in the hopes of finding justice for his untimely death. An unsigned review in *The Saturday Review* praises the title character of Doctor Marigold, validating Dickens's frame tale for its fine sentiment and Christmas spirit, but also remarks, with that periodical's customary ruthlessness, that the subsequent "stories of a Quakeress, of a detective policeman, and of a murdered man's ghost . . . are very poor and very stupid, and are only fit for perusal in a railway train at that critical period when all the daily papers have been exhausted, and no book or periodical of any kind is to be had within a hundred miles" (418).

While it is not at all surprising that the logic of collaboration would dictate an identity adjustment on the part of all involved, it is unexpected to see Dickens pass unnoticed in a crowd. Perhaps he was simply exhausted or found himself "writing down" when the other writers failed to rise to his literary standards. Perhaps he was playing a metafictional joke, daring his readers to identify him. Perhaps he knew that any author with a public persona must maintain creative reserves, withholding part of himself from his reading public. Or perhaps these stories served as places where he could work through his own conflicted feelings about collaboration, meditating on its drawbacks even as he activated its mechanisms. The plots of both tales ironically hinge on a longing for public acknowledgment. In "His Brown Paper Parcel," the artist who allows other people to take credit for his work even as he bitterly resents his lack of fame ultimately loses the girl he loves, and the final paragraph of the story describes him as a solitary figure who haunts the streets of London in order to erase his own drawings:

> And often as you have seen, do see, and will see, my Works, it's fifty thousand to one if you'll ever see me, unless, when the candles are burnt down and the

Commercial character is gone, you should happen to notice a neglected young man perseveringly rubbing out the last traces of the pictures, so that nobody can renew the same. That's me.   (91)

Here, the only prize for authorial anonymity is neglect, depression, isolation, and no public legacy to speak of, since the artist must rub out everything he has drawn. By contrast, "To Be Taken With A Grain of Salt" aligns its sympathies not with the man seeking (posthumous) recognition, but with the tormented narrator of the story, who is being used as the unwilling agent of the murdered man's ghost to expose and punish his murderer. The former story suggests that keeping your artistic identity a secret results in profound dissatisfaction, while the latter implies that the dynamics of public revelation can be coercive and even brutal. The tension between self-commodification and the desire for a private life appears in many of the Christmas numbers, perhaps most notably in *Doctor Marigold's Prescriptions*, where Dickens portrays himself in the title role as a Cheap Jack hawking junk from the back of his cart. As a bestselling author from relatively nondescript origins, Dickens was famously dogged by and defensive about his self-made status in a world where Victorian professional men were expected to reject commercial self-interest with a gentlemanly contempt even as they actively pursued vocations.[4]

Although Dickens's anonymous—or, maybe more accurately, unmarked—tales occur only infrequently, their presence within the larger context of the Christmas numbers suggests that at times Dickens embraced the conventions of his own collaborative genre, using its anonymity and tonal inconsistencies to negotiate with his own celebrity. The conventions—the clamoring crowd of additional genres and narrators—temporarily push the Dickens of *A Christmas Carol* (1843) to the margins, helping him to explore the limits of the bestselling author. Perhaps this explains why Dickens continued to publish the Christmas numbers for almost two decades. Of course, they were extremely profitable, but surely Dickens, one of the period's most inventive authors, could have developed other literary ways to trade on Christmas. His persistent return to the Christmas number suggests that for all his desire to captain the ship, he may also have appreciated being able to ride along unseen as a passenger. The genre potentially offers all of its contributors the opportunity to explore various aspects of their authorial personae and to maneuver creatively in new ways.

Ultimately, however, Dickens's inability to control the Christmas numbers led him to dissolve the very genre he created. Despite its potential formal and personal pleasures, Dickens, as the years wore on, continued to try to eliminate any confusion about his role as the leader of the project, expecting his writing to set the tone and then expressing dismay when it failed to do so. His frame tales increasingly mobilized themes and modes of representation—especially sentiment—that were more recognizably his with every year. Reviewers followed his lead, making it clear that the only parts of the Christmas numbers that they really cared about were Dickens's. For instance, in E. S. Dallas's review of *Doctor Marigold's Prescriptions* for *The Times*, he calls Dickens's frame tale "a masterly sketch," but notes that he will "not propose to speak" (415) of the other contributions at all—a typical lack of interest in the other contributors that Dickens apparently never regretted. Eventually, Dickens began to reprint his frame tales from the Christmas numbers independently, excising the contributions from the other authors altogether. He said that he had always set his sights on future reprints and that he intended for his work to stand alone all along, a claim that was certainly true for the later Christmas numbers but probably not for the earlier ones. He also began to conceive of his own frame narrators, such as Mrs. Lirriper or Doctor Marigold, as designed for his public readings, a performance that completely erased their original collaborative context. In short, the longer he published the Christmas numbers, the more he sought to free his own writing from its collaborative origins. Dickens used the defining convention of the genre, its identity as a diverse collection sewn together with editorial string, to rip out his own seams, excerpting his work from the whole. The very aspects of the Christmas numbers that make them unique reading experiences thus became their undoing, as everyone, including Dickens, began to see him as the true captain of the ship, endowed with the authority to eliminate those authors and texts that displeased him. Until lately, these excerpted Dickens-only versions of the Christmas numbers have been the only ones in print.

Dickens's deconstruction of his own genre, excising all voices but his, ensured the longevity of his contributions because he could now market the radically excerpted versions of the Christmas numbers as exclusively his own. His ruthless editing, essentially a complete dismantling of the original text, lends each Christmas number—now just a Christmas story by Dickens—a new formal and aesthetic coherence. Yet from our contemporary vantage point, it also obscures the genre's strangeness. Awkward, disconnected, at once awful and charming, the Christmas numbers, when read in their entirety, are like an alien visitor from the Victorian past. As Dickens himself knew, they are not always very good. Yet, as solo ventures, Dickens's own contributions to the Christmas numbers have long been relegated to the ranks of his minor literature, suggesting that ultimately they do not bring much to the table on their own, either. As a genre, the Christmas numbers derive their energy from the friction, difference, and competition among the different internal genres and narrative voices—an energy that is lost in the Dickens-only versions that restore the authorial hierarchy that the genre never quite achieved on the page. A fuller exploration of the Christmas numbers lies outside my scope here, but I hope that the above suggests the ways in which even relatively hierarchical collaborations can still create compelling authorial negotiations in print. In the Christmas numbers, hierarchy remains intact, but the genre itself invites the testing of its own boundaries.

II. The Excursion Articles

The excursion articles resist hierarchy more knowingly in both process and form. Like the Christmas numbers, the excursion articles were formally planned acts of literary collaboration. But they were created through a remarkably different creative process, and they achieve different effects. If the Christmas numbers were annual rituals that required a fair amount of advance planning, then the excursion articles, by contrast, occurred on a more spontaneous and flexible basis. Regular features of *Household Words*, these pieces revolved around cheerful expeditions taken by Dickens and various members of his office staff. According to Stone,

> [a]pparently an idea for an article would occur to Dickens or a member of his staff—how does a letter go through the post office? how are inmates in an insane asylum treated and what is it like to attend a Christmas party at such an institution? . . . how is paper made? . . . what is it like to go to the races? an exhibition? a cattle market? a police station?—and because of the nature of the subject, or because part of the article required special knowledge, or because Dickens lacked time to do the whole piece, or because he wanted company, or because his collaborator had thought of the subject and procured the en-trée—whatever the reason, it was decided in advance that the article would be a joint effort.   (*Uncollected Writings* 1: 46–47)

After visiting the subject of the article, Dickens and his co-writer would often dine out together and then return either to London or to a nearby inn to begin writing.[5] While the contributors to the Christmas numbers usually submitted their final products to Dickens on paper, creating a professional distance that permitted less authorial negotiation between Dickens and his contributors, the authors of the excursion articles actually wrote in physical proximity to each other, often sharing drafts on the scene or later at the office. They bonded as friends and partners over the course of the trip. In other words, the collaboration was much more immediate, often occurred in person, and depended on shared experience.

I am less interested in the biographical specifics of each excursion than in how this particular collaborative process—a shared outing that led to a professional product—created a set of formal conventions and themes that add up to a genre, and I am particularly concerned with what that genre says about the act of literary collaboration as it emerges through masculine partnership. Although many good examples of the excursion articles were collected and edited by Stone in 1968, they have been largely ignored, perhaps because even Stone tended to view them as unexceptional except for Dickens's contributions, when his "eye, voice, and sensibility suddenly enter and quicken an essay" (*Uncollected Writings* 1: 51) that was dying on the vine in the hands of a less skilled writer. Yet they invite a closer look as examples of mid-Victorian collaborative writing that is professionally motivated yet depends on (male) friendship. I suggest that, formally, the excursion articles use authorial friction as a narrative tactic, depending on transitional moments between authors to create narrative momentum. Thematically, I believe that the excursion articles are more prone to self-reflexivity, often suggestively settling on topics that feature bonding, melding, and merging (gold-refining, glass-making, and so forth) and trip-taking, echoing as if by design the nature of the final product: a new amalgam or destination.[6]

As self-reflexive meditations on collaboration, moreover, the excursion articles offer a complex representation of male partnership, a concern that sometimes enters into the Christmas numbers, particularly those that Dickens shared with Wilkie Collins, but which rarely structured the nature of the genre itself. Rosemarie Bodenheimer observes that "Dickens himself lived primarily in a world of men. . . . Both his professional and his leisure hours were centered on friendships or working relationships with other men. It is not surprising that relationships between men in his fiction are more fully charged with erotic energy and conflict than those between men and women" (91–92). It is also not surprising, then, that the excursion articles stage with great liveliness the personal and professional tensions that inevitably occur with masculine collaborative writing. But they also display a sense of humor that suggests a warm avowal of this creative method despite its potential inequities and challenges. Indeed, the trips the sparked the excursion narratives had the flavor of bachelor holidays, and the genre either implicitly or—as in the case of *The Lazy Tour*—explicitly portrays male collaboration as a comic same-sex honeymoon.

Unlike the Christmas numbers, where the contributions from the other authors buck in their traces, the excursion articles aim to create a more coherent final product. Rather than a series of interpolated tales bundled together with a flimsy piece of editorial string, they are published as single-authored articles or stories, usually written in first person. Like the Christmas numbers, they contain narrative ruptures that point toward the shifts between authors. But the genre works not to disguise the breaks between the collaborators but to integrate them into the narrative movement of the article, using moments of collaborative transition to introduce shifts in style and tone that

enable the progress of the narrative. In these pieces, the creative partnership—the act of fusing the two writers—manifests itself as an ongoing and
evolving process, one where internal tensions fuel progress, and the transitions between the writers become catalysts for movement.

Take, for instance, "A Paper-Mill," an article about the process of making
paper written by Dickens and Mark Lemon for the 31 August 1850 issue of
Household Words. In this article, Dickens, as always, kicks off the piece,
positioning himself as the leader and assigning himself the pleasures of the
fanciful introduction. He assigns Lemon the grunt work of describing the
actual mechanical processes of the paper-making itself. The piece opens with
the narrator on a holiday, taking a trip to Kent to visit a paper mill. As he
watches the process, the narrator (again, written initially by Dickens) transfers
his subjectivity to the paper he is describing, becoming not just a person
touring the paper mill, but the actual paper itself. At that very moment,
Dickens also transfers the article to Lemon, whose writing, according to Harry
Stone, begins with the clause, "I *am* rags":

> My conductor leads the way into another room. I am to go, as the rags go,
> regularly and systematically through the Mill. I am to suppose myself a bale
> of rags. I *am* rags.
>   Here, in another room, are some three-score women at little tables, each with
> an awful scythe-shaped knife standing erect upon it, and looking like the verita-
> ble tooth of time. I am distributed among these women, and worried into smaller
> shreds—torn cross-wise at the knives. Already I begin to lose something of my
> grosser nature.   (Stone, *Uncollected Writings* 1: 139–40)

From there, Lemon describes the process of bleaching the rags and grinding
them into a "rich, creamy, tempting, exalted gruel!" (1: 140) that is finally
rolled into sheets of paper. Lemon concludes his description of the process
in the voice of the paper, saying, "I am ready for work" (1: 141), at which
point Dickens, in the middle of the paragraph, picks up with a political critique
of the excise tax, one of his current hobbyhorses. The breaks between the two
authors, which register as tiny seismic quakes in this article, spark narrative
momentum as the transfer of authorial power ushers in new parts of the narrative.

But the transitions between Dickens and Lemon have other consequences
besides their formal narrative effects. "A Paper-Mill" might also be read as
a wry form of self-reflexive commentary on the nature of collaboration itself,
or as an exploration of each author's mutual implication in a process that
blurs the division of power between boss and employee and collapses the
boundaries between friend and professional partner. "A Paper-Mill" is one
of many excursion articles to imply that literary collaboration is an energetic
give-and-take, always shifting, sometimes tense, sometimes friendly, often

competitive but also mutually supportive. It turns professional moments into opportunities for play, and vice versa. Dickens's staff and friends took at least two paper-mill jaunts, and Dickens's correspondence indicates that the trips were viewed as fun. "I look forward to a right jocund day," Edmund Jerrold wrote to John Forster about a visit to a paper-mill in Maidenhead in 1850 (qtd. in Dickens, *Letters* 6: 148n). If collaborative labor renegotiates authorial identity, then what kind of claim to authority occurs in this transfer of power between Dickens and Lemon—a transfer occasioned by a convivial outing? The above transitional moment is obviously a power negotiation, but who winds up on top?

At the moment that he takes control of the piece, Lemon imagines himself transformed into the very paper itself—not just paper, but the "rags" that form the basis of the paper pulp. His metaphor equivocates between figuring his authorship as a kind of primordial soup—the source of all writing—and a supreme sacrifice, where he is emasculated by the awful scythe-wielding female factory workers, torn into pieces in order to be reconstituted as something new. On one hand, this moment could be read as an authorial wail of helplessness, as the transfer from one author to the other dehumanizes Lemon—"I am to suppose myself a bale of rags. I *am* rags"—by portraying him as the text to be written upon rather than the writer himself. On the other hand, its hyperbolic parody of masculine weakness—featuring knife-wielding women who resemble Carlyle's Maenads from *The French Revolution* (1842)—reads as both too knowing and too funny for such an interpretation to stick persuasively. Lemon perversely embraces his transformation into rags with too much enthusiasm to be read as oppressed, even if his remark at the same time slyly comments on what it might be like to write alongside and with the internationally celebrated Dickens. I would suggest that this small rupture in the piece, a bit of cheekiness on the part of both authors as Dickens sets up Lemon to be destroyed and Lemon makes a joke out of his own destruction, shifting the narrative perspective radically and abruptly, gestures toward a metacritique of collaboration. It characterizes the act of shared writing here as an intimate if playfully forced fusion that promotes the importance of Lemon's contribution—he portrays himself as the stuff of writing itself, its most primal materials—even as it demonstrates that he works in the service of someone else's genius. Instead of reacting against this idea, he takes it on wholeheartedly with self-deprecating humor. The excursion articles relish the authorial give-and-take, an exchange that is not always equitable but is nevertheless profitable both literally and aesthetically. These moments are more complex, equivocal, and subtle than the authorial friction of the Christmas articles because the writers themselves are so much more intimately connected and more aware of the final project's goals.

The excursion articles thus posit male creative relationships at the heart of their narrative energy, and it is to this subject that I will turn more fully with *The Lazy Tour of Two Idle Apprentices*, which brings this idea home with particular force. *The Lazy Tour* depicts masculine collaboration as an exhilarating and liberating experience that verges on hysteria and occasionally rises to the level of giddy terror. Written jointly with Dickens's favorite and perhaps most prominent collaborator, Wilkie Collins, *The Lazy Tour* was published in five chapter-length installments in *Household Words* in October of 1857. It features the bathetic misadventures of two men bent on a holiday escape—the ultimate excursion—from London and from their mistress, Lady Literature. In the tradition of William Hogarth, Dickens and Collins assign themselves allegorical names for their protagonists: Dickens plays the role of the restless Francis Goodchild, who (the title of the work notwithstanding) cannot tolerate being idle and must be busy, while Collins develops the part of the melancholy and much beleaguered Thomas Idle, whose true indolence contrasts with Goodchild's manic need to fill his idle time.[7] (Bodenheimer points out that this portrayal of "Dickens the fanatical worker, Collins the dreamy idler" [113] became a standard aspect of each author's self-dramatization whenever the two men collaborated.) The two men travel north from London to Doncaster for race day, and the five installments describe one travel mishap after another.

Today, *The Lazy Tour* exists in print mainly in abridged or excerpted form, and literary scholars tend to take one of two rather reductive approaches to it. The first singles out for attention the two gothic short stories embedded within the five-chapter work, utterly abandoning the rest of the narrative by the wayside. The second reads it as thinly veiled autobiography, a coded exercise in erotic longing that confirms the flushed beginning of Dickens's infatuation with the young actress Ellen Ternan. This latter approach is admittedly compelling. Based on a real-life tour taken by Dickens and Collins in the month before its publication, *The Lazy Tour* was composed during the period leading up to the dissolution of Dickens's marriage. He had become infatuated with Ternan only one month earlier during the public performances of his and Collins's melodrama *The Frozen Deep* (1857), and evidence suggests that at least part of his reason for touring Cumberland was to see her perform in a play in Doncaster.[8] When he returned, he built the wall that forever divided his bedroom space from his wife's. It is no surprise, then, that *The Lazy Tour*'s teasing references to Francis Goodchild's infatuation with "a pair of lilac-colored gloves" (89) or Dickens's gothic tale of a bride who dies at her husband's command are commonly read as evidence of this turbulent domestic period.

But as a trip taken by two writers that was designed to produce work for *Household Words*, *The Lazy Tour* might also productively be read as the apotheosis of the excursion article, a genre that depends on the sharing of authorial power between two men. The intercollated tales, meandering narrative, and structural breaks clearly echo the fraternal dynamics of the picaresque tradition that Dickens deployed years earlier in *The Pickwick Papers* (1836–37) and his other early work. It also forecasts the relationship between Eugene Wrayburn and Mortimer Lightwood in *Our Mutual Friend* (1864–65), but while Mortimer and Eugene obsessively fret over their "domestic virtues" (or lack thereof), Goodchild and Idle settle into the intimacies of their temporary bachelor lifestyle more effortlessly, repeatedly declaring the benefits of male bonding (all with precious little erotic tension). And, instead of rerouting the male rivalries and friendships toward conventional marriages, *The Lazy Tour* remains focused on the masculine relationship that drives the text from beginning to end. I would also suggest that, unlike the other excursion articles, *The Lazy Tour* gives much fuller expression to the kinds of energies derived from male collaboration, largely because that is precisely the kind of exercise it features: two writers journeying and writing together. Nayder reads this piece as a comment on labor, particularly the debate over Lancastrian slaves (112), but my interest is in its buoyant self-reflexivity. When read as a text that comments on the act of shared writing, *The Lazy Tour* shares the cheeky humor of the other excursion articles, yet, at its end, it also injects a wistful note of anticlimax and loss, suggesting that the hectic fun of same-sex male professional relationships cannot be sustained long-term. As a story that explores both the productive energy and the fragility of masculine partnership, it illuminates the complexity of Dickens's literary collaborations as psychologically fraught, yet also personally pleasurable.

The Lazy Tour uses the device of the excursion to explode the hierarchical authorial relationships of the Christmas tales, for it portrays both travelers in this tale as equally inept, catastrophically ill-equipped to undertake a journey. Although Collins, as the long-suffering Thomas Idle, portrays himself as grudgingly compelled into action by Dickens's/Goodchild's manic energy (much like Lemon in "A Paper-Mill"), Goodchild's fervent need to keep busy hardly makes him more authoritative; indeed, more often than not, it works against his efforts to take charge. No one captains the ship in this narrative. Interruptions and delays plague the outing from the outset, which begins with the two men intending to take a walking tour into the north yet finding themselves perversely lying in a field (Idle) or walking south (Goodchild). As the excitable Goodchild, Dickens bullies Idle; as the misanthropic Idle, Collins phlegmatically digs in his heels, accepting Goodchild's autocratic tendencies only up to a point. Indeed, for most of the trip, Dickens and Collins portray themselves as engaged in mutual harassment, at times occasioned by misguided efforts at solicitude and at other times brought on by their minor resentments of each other. Hence, Goodchild forces Idle up a local mountain where he twists his ankle, and Idle reciprocates by taking his sweet time recuperating in a backwater hotel in Allonby, driving Goodchild so wild with boredom that he bursts into heartfelt tears when Idle finally proposes that they leave. Goodchild tries to force Idle to attend the races, but Idle holds Goodchild hostage with a long irrational discourse on his objection to horses. Dickens and Collins's shared glee in their own mutual torture is both the source of the narrative's comedy and its emotional core. Their fraternal hazing keeps the loopy, slapstick antics of the farce in the foreground, but I suggest that it is precisely this sense of play that reveals the shared benefits of intimate creative partnership.

What are those benefits? A sense of emotional and creative balance, for one. Idle prevents Goodchild from flying off the rails, keeping him grounded by avowing a practical disinterest in his frenetic plans and sometimes adopting a patronizing resistance to his emotional highs and lows. When Goodchild tours a local mental asylum, for instance, he returns troubled by a particular patient who traces and counts out the fibers of his floor matting, and the memory of the man's obsessive behavior threatens to bring on an epistemological crisis about the possible futility of interpretation in a meaningless world. "I thought how all of us, God help us! in our different ways are poring over our bits of matting, blindly enough, and what confusions and mysteries we make in the pattern" (64), Goodchild laments, clearly gearing up for a (typically Dickensian) rant on the question of mystery and divine order. Idle, however, smacks him down. He not only rebukes Goodchild for turning their holiday into a professional affair but also abruptly changes the subject, "diverting the conversation to grouse, custards, and bride-cake" (64). Goodchild's immediate capitulation to Idle's redirection of the conversation suggests that he gratefully staves off his own crisis by following his partner's lead. Throughout *The Lazy Tour*, Idle stands as a bulwark against a chaotic world that threatens to overwhelm Goodchild, and, by the time they reach Doncaster, he is "the only individual in Doncaster who stands by the brink of the full-flowing race-stream, and is not swept away by it in common with all the rest of his species" (93). Perhaps it is worth noting that both Dickens and Collins construct the Goodchild/Idle relationship in this way. In the above instance, Dickens wrote the scene where Goodchild returns from the lunatic asylum, while Collins is the author of the portrait of Idle on the brink of the stream on race day.

In turn, Goodchild prevents Idle from complete inertia, keeping him moving despite himself and thus increasing his opportunities for self-knowledge and self-definition. Although Idle repeatedly and explicitly resists Goodchild's dragging him about the country, it becomes clear that being towed in his wake encourages Idle to construct his own identity, insofar as he conceives of himself as dramatically opposed to Goodchild, imagining his own subjectivity by way of cheerfully and openly negating the other author with whom he is partnered. The more that Goodchild makes him travel, the more Idle happily embraces his love of inactivity, discoursing at length on the virtues of laziness and misanthropy. This stance, impossible to maintain without Goodchild constantly tugging at his elbow, proves to be a creatively productive posture. Goodchild's bullying gives Collins, as Idle, the chance to explore a ruthlessly self-deprecating comic side. Collins's long description of how Idle learned to value laziness—he calls it a meditation occasioned by "The Episode of the Sprained Ankle"—rivals some of Dickens's best comic writing. Both writers obviously benefit personally and creatively from this relationship not because they always treat each other fairly or kindly, but because they do not. Their relationship is based on personal friction—a dynamic of pushing and pulling, bullying and resistance—that both men find mutually sustaining and, for all their complaining, enjoyable.

Indeed, the alliance between Goodchild and Idle approximates the dynamics of a married couple on holiday tour, perhaps a lengthy honeymoon where the duration of the trip makes room for newlywed bliss to give way to mutual bickering. At one point, Idle even proposes that the two men visit an inn "where they give you Bride-cake every day after dinner." (61). "Let us eat Bride-cake without the trouble of being married or of knowing anybody in that ridiculous dilemma" (61), he declares. Biographical implications of this remark aside (it could be interpreted as a comment either on Collins's bohemian attitude toward domestic relations or Dickens's troubled marriage, or both), Idle's distinction between the act of eating wedding cake and the state of marriage might be read as a metaphor for the literary collaboration producing *The Lazy Tour*. The two authors embrace the domestic intimacy of a wedding and honeymoon without having to suffer any of the legal, social, or sexual hassles of marriage, getting to eat their (Bride) cake and have it, too. Goodchild and Idle have adopted the domestic structures of husband and wife, but their relationship consists of a less hierarchical personal and creative exchange. Neither author comfortably adopts the stance of the traditional patriarch.

This idea may help to illuminate the condemnation of heterosexual relations and particularly marriage implicit in the two gothic tales of *The Lazy Tour*. Literary scholars have taken up both of these tales independently for close readings, usually in relation to the biographical context I mentioned earlier, but I suggest that they are best read in their original context, which reveals the profound contrast between the homosocial world of the excursion article and the heterosexual world of marriage. Collins, for instance, tells the story of a medical student, Lorn, who inexplicably wakes up after being dead only to discover that the woman he loves is in love with someone else. Lorn lives a lingering, unfruitful existence (lovelorn, of course), getting nowhere and doing nothing. Dickens tells the tale of a man who systematically terrorizes his ward for over a decade from the time she is ten years old, finally coercing her into marriage and then killing her in order to obtain her fortune. The narrator of this story is the ghost of the murderer himself, and his unexpected appearance induces Idle into a comatose state, leaving only a transfixed Goodchild to hear his story.

The focus on the narrator of Dickens's gothic tale not only points to a critique of heterosexual marriage, but also might be read as a self-reflexive indictment of the single author. Portrayed as a master storyteller, the ghost has a voice so powerful that it takes Goodchild hostage, fixing him immobile in his chair. But when the clock strikes two, the ghostly narrator suddenly splits into two identical versions of himself, "each, exactly like the other: each, addressing him at precisely one and the same instant" (78). These selves multiply on the hour: the man is two men at two o'clock, three at three, four at four, and so forth until he splits into twelve selves. Each self waits for midnight, when they collectively relive the man's (now their own) execution. This spontaneous doubling and redoubling amplifies the ghost's power—there are now two, three, four pairs of eyes holding Goodchild fast—but it also intensifies his wretchedness, as each one of the twelve selves brings him "[t]welve times my old power of suffering and agony" (79). Each self increases his desperate need to communicate his anguish—a torment brought on by relentless authorial amplification and reduplication. The ghost is not spinning out different versions of himself, but identical copies, like clones, as if to create his own personal echo chamber. When read within the context of the excursion article, Dickens's tale implies that the ghost's misery might have been alleviated if only he had a partner to share the authorial burden instead of the relentless reproduction of his own self. The contrast between the ghost's lonely plight and the shared circumstances of Goodchild and Idle emerges with real clarity at the tale's conclusion, when a terrified Goodchild scoops up the insensible Idle in his arms and rushes downstairs with him in an attempt to rescue him from the ghost's horrors, affirming their mutual bond by saving Idle from the literal spectre of bad marriage. Removing either one of these two tales from the whole text of The Lazy Tour may facilitate biographical or other readings of each author, but acknowledging their original context clarifies their role in the text's larger view of male collaboration as a creative activity that embraces the structures and certainly the emotional intimacy of marriage for male partners even while it implicitly censures the legal institution itself.

Yet the intrusive nature of the two gothic tales, which radically disrupts the Pickwickian slapstick of the two idle apprentices, also highlights the fragility of domestic relationships more generally, and this is where I would argue that The Lazy Tour not only advances a more coherent and explicit view of male collaboration, but also suggests its limitations. For the very thing that gives The Lazy Tour its hectic energy is also what threatens to destroy it altogether: the shifting power dynamics and authorial friction between the two male authors, neither of whom adopts an authoritative stance over the other or the enterprise as a whole. The text suggests that this more domestic mode of writing, which derives its power from the kind of creative and interpersonal tensions that arise between couples who are truly intimate with each other, and where each author must give over some creative mastery in the service of the larger enterprise, cannot last forever. This may account for the anticlimactic, elegiac tone of the final chapter of *The Lazy Tour*, which features the darker side of masculine camaraderie at Doncaster. Throughout race week, the predominantly male crowds gather for daily drinking and open quarreling in the streets, and Dickens describes the race crowds as lunatics, jackals, and hyenas. Neither idle apprentice knows what to do on the Doncaster scene, which seems inhospitable on every front. Goodchild develops a crush on an unknown woman with golden hair; Idle, in the meantime, refuses to step outdoors. At this moment, the friction between Goodchild and Idle transforms from a productive tension to a creative stalemate, and Dickens concludes the piece not with a sense of satisfaction or finality but with ambivalent post-war imagery:

> On Saturday afternoon, Mr. Goodchild walks out and looks at the Course. It is quite deserted; heaps of broken crockery and bottles are raised to its memory; and the correct cards and other fragments of paper are blowing about it, as the regulation little paper-books, carried by the French soldiers in their breasts, were seen, soon after the battle was fought, blowing idly about the plains of Waterloo.
>
> Where will these present idle leaves be blown by the idle winds, and where will the last of them be one day lost and forgotten? An idle question, and an idle thought; and with it Mr. Idle fitly makes his bow, and Mr. Goodchild his, and thus ends the Lazy Tour of Two Idle Apprentices. (99–100)

With Dickens's final words, the creative energy swirling around the male partnership dissipates and subsides. Knowing that someday their work will be forgotten, each author takes a separate bow, a lonely gesture that befits the scene of devastation that surrounds them. The trip, which began as an effort at creative rejuvenation and masculine bonding, ultimately yields nothing more than "idle leaves" blowing against a backdrop of urban ruin. Randomly distributed until they fall into obscurity, these leaves conclude the story not with the reunification of the two men but separation and—to borrow one of Dickens's favorite words—parting. The conclusion of *The Lazy Tour* thus gestures toward the painful problem of all the excursion articles: that within a journal designed to confirm the domestic ideal, collaborating with other men can ultimately lead only to loss. There is no narrative available to Dickens and his collaborators that will hold up the idle apprentices as a permanent model for domestic and professional relationships. Their collaborations can only be construed as holidays away from the traditional authorial masculine self: pleasurable and productive but ultimately only vacations, transient and impermanent. Hence, *The Lazy Tour* refuses to take the novel's route of endorsing a social integration of the self through marriage, but then it can imagine no satisfactory alternative, and instead winds up pointing toward the fragmented wastelands of modernism.

Literary scholars tend to enlist Dickens's short fiction in support of the broader thematic trends they see in his novels. While I recognize the formal and historical logic of this subordination, I hope that exploring some of Dickens's short fiction and journalism by way of its generic conventions persuasively suggests that it is worth occasionally giving this work the spotlight. To be sure, not all of Dickens's shorter work offers the rich reading experience of his novels, and I would not argue, for instance, to substitute in the critical imagination *The Lazy Tour*'s idle apprentices for *Our Mutual Friend*'s. Yet I would continue to suggest that reading the former merely as a warm-up exercise for the latter may obscure our understanding of the ways in which Dickens's journalistic collaborations were important opportunities for all of the authors involved to experiment with new kinds of authorial selves and the new genres that accommodated those selves. Even though *The Lazy Tour* suggests that literary collaboration cannot be sustained indefinitely, it could certainly occur repeatedly, and Dickens went back to both the Christmas numbers and the excursion articles throughout his career. This approach to Dickens's collaborative journalism necessitates a close look at the effects of individual short pieces, occasionally taking the time to zero in on articles like ''A Paper-Mill'' to see what really appears to be happening on the page—a mode of paying attention that I can best describe as *listening* more carefully without defaulting to a preexisting critical apparatus that might tell us how to read the authorial relations it explores in advance. It also involves attending to these texts as genres in their own right. Ultimately, I hope that a close look at the Christmas numbers and the excursion articles as representatives of Dickens's collaborative genres enhances our ability to see his journalism as more than the testing ground for his fiction. Rather, the Christmas numbers and excursion articles are an important counterpoint to more dominant forms of Victorian fiction, an experiment with literary forms, processes, and gender relations that converse with rather than merely service the novel.

NOTES

This essay began in an NEH summer seminar directed by John Bowen (York University) and hosted by the University of California at Santa Cruz in July 2004. I further developed my thoughts on Dickens's Christmas stories in a collaborative lecture at the Dickens Project at UCSC in 2007, which I delivered with my good friend and colleague Melisa Klimaszewski (Drake University). Melisa and I have also co-edited three of Dickens's collaborative Christmas numbers for Hesperus Press.

1. Presumably, the in-progress manuscript by Trodd and John Bowen, *Dickens, Collins, and Collaboration*, which was not available at the time of my writing this, will be an important addition to this list. Other scholarship exists on Dickens's minor fiction and short journalism, of course, but it tends to focus on its biographical implications or the way in which Dickens's "minor" work illuminates his "major" work, the novels. Nayder's book remains the only recent major effort to investigate not only the nature of Dickens's most important collaborative friendship, but also the creative results on the page.

2. See both Harry Stone (*Dickens and the Invisible World*) and Deborah Thomas on the origins of Dickens's short fiction and the Christmas stories in particular.

3. Of course, as Harold Orel points out, the genre of the short story itself was also somewhat ill-defined during this literary period, and many authors saw little difference between the short story and the sketch (2). But this generic looseness only enhances the frictional energy of the Christmas tales.

4. My thoughts here have been partly informed by scholarly work from the mid-1990s on self-renunciation and masculinity—perhaps most notably James Eli Adams's *Dandies and Desert Saints*, which argues that male writers of the Victorian period often used self-renunciation as a strategy for grounding their literary authority. But the kind of self-effacement under discussion here does not, I think, really count as self-discipline, and it certainly is not part of an ascetic regime, even if I would readily admit that for Dickens, Christmas is a time to explore the virtues of renouncing self-interest. Studies of masculine self-negation and literary authority, moreover, rarely take up the question of genre, and I propose that Dickens's Christmas numbers, which were both generically inventive and extremely popular, are a productive place at which to unite an investigation of those cultural issues with questions of form.

5. See Stone, *Uncollected Writings* 1: 47–48.

6. As Stone observes, Dickens called these manufacturing articles "process" articles: imaginative and idiosyncratic accounts of specific manufacturing processes (*Uncollected Writings* 1: 53). By calling these pieces "excursion articles," I am widening the parameters of Dickens's own definition to include all of the composite pieces that depended on trips, which emphasizes the method that produced these articles along with their subject matter.

7. See Hogarth's series *Industry and Idleness* (1747).

8. See Stone, *The Night Side of Dickens* 289ff.

WORKS CITED

Adams, James Eli. *Dandies and Desert Saints: Styles of Victorian Masculinity.* Ithaca: Cornell UP, 1995.

Bodenheimer, Rosemarie. *Knowing Dickens.* Ithaca: Cornell UP, 2007.

Collins, Philip, ed. *Dickens: The Critical Heritage.* New York: Barnes and Noble, 1971.

Dallas, E. S. Rev. of *Doctor Marigold's Prescriptions*, by Charles Dickens. *The Times of London* 6 December 1865: 6. Collins 415–16.

Dickens, Charles. *Doctor Marigold's Prescriptions*. 1865. Ed. Melissa Valiska Gregory and Melisa Klimaszewski. London: Hesperus, 2007.

———. *The Letters of Charles Dickens: The Pilgrim Edition*. Ed. Madeline House, Graham Storey, and Kathleen Tillotson. 12 vols. Oxford: Clarendon, 1965–2002.

———. *Somebody's Luggage*. 1862. Ed. Melissa Valiska Gregory and Melisa Klimaszewski. London: Hesperus, 2006.

———. *The Wreck of the Golden Mary*. 1857. Ed. Melissa Valiska Gregory and Melisa Klimaszewski. London: Hesperus, 2006.

Dickens, Charles, and Mark Lemon. "A Paper-Mill." 1850. Stone, *Uncollected Works* 1: 137–42.

Dickens, Charles, and Wilkie Collins. *The Lazy Tour of Two Idle Apprentices*. 1857. *The Works of Charles Dickens*. Vol. 25. New York: Collier, 1911.

Hogarth, William. *Industry and Idleness*. 1747.

Nayder, Lillian. *Unequal Partners: Charles Dickens, Wilkie Collins, and Victorian Authorship*. Ithaca: Cornell UP, 2002.

Orel, Harold. *The Victorian Short Story: Development and Triumph of a Literary Genre*. Cambridge: Cambridge UP, 1986.

Rev. of *Doctor Marigold's Prescriptions*. *Saturday Review* 16 December 1865: 763–64. Collins 416–18.

Stone, Harry. *Dickens and the Invisible World: Fairy Tales, Fantasy, and Novel-Making*. Bloomington: Indiana UP, 1979.

———. *The Night Side of Dickens: Cannibalism, Passion and Necessity*. Columbus: Ohio State UP, 1994.

———, ed. *Uncollected Writings from* Household Words. 2 vols. Bloomington: Indiana UP, 1968.

Thomas, Deborah. *Dickens and the Short Story*. Philadelphia: U of Pennsylvania P, 1982.

Trodd, Anthea. "Collaborating in Open Boats: Dickens, Collins, Franklin, and Bligh." *Victorian Studies* 42.2 (2000): 201–25.

———. "Messages in Bottles and Collins's Seafaring Man." *SEL: Studies in English Literature 1500–1900* 41.4 (2001): 751–64.

Woloch, Alex. *The One Versus the Many: Minor Characters and the Space of the Protagonist in the Novel*. Princeton: Princeton UP, 2003.

Reading, Sympathy, and the Bodies of *Bleak House*

Katherine Montwieler

Within Bleak House *Dickens suggests that reading is fundamentally based on the senses of hearing and seeing, and that to read accurately involves both the body and the mind, or, perception and apprehension. The novelist calls for a return to physicality—albeit a physicality mediated by language—to better see and hear others. More provocatively, Dickens proposes that novels can provide a corrective lens through which to view the world rather than that offered by the texts of more socially regulated institutions—religious, political, juridical—ostensibly concerned with the social good as well;* Bleak House *as primer reveals that empathy is rooted in our physical sensibility: if we learn to see, to listen, and to understand, then we become ideal readers, aware of our connections to others and the brevity of our lives. In this essay, I discuss several acts of misreading within* Bleak House, *followed by an analysis of a few traumatic moments within the text, and conclude with a look at the characters who serve as ideal readers and ethical role models. Novels can teach us to read—to understand, to see, to hear, and to feel—and thus to empathize, to act, and to live in the world.*

Bleak House is a novel about reading and writing: from Jarndyce and Jarndyce to Jo's illiteracy to Nemo's occupation as a copyist to the letters accusing Lady Dedlock of murder, Dickens weaves the subject of literacy throughout the text in ways both conspicuous and subtle. And long before J. Hillis Miller published his 1971 introduction to the novel that began, ''*Bleak House* is a

Dickens Studies Annual, Volume 41, Copyright © 2010 by AMS Press, Inc. All rights reserved.

237

document about the interpretation of documents'' (11), a harbinger of the storm of deconstructive approaches to the novel that has not yet abated, critics acknowledged *Bleak House* offers many different models of how to interpret and to decipher—to read—not only words, but also faces, bodies, history, legalities, and other textual matters. Guppy, Tulkinghorn, Bucket, and Esther, for example, are all characters who on at least one level struggle to understand the intricacies of various mysteries, both material and verbal.[1] Most critics to date have focused on the intellectual aspects of such interpretations—that is, the idea that one can uncover mysteries through analysis (not surprisingly given the nearly uncanny appropriateness of deconstructive and psychoanalytic theory to the novel); however, within *Bleak House* Dickens also suggests that reading is fundamentally based in the body, in the physical sensations associated with watching and listening to the world, and in so doing, he draws on the eighteenth-century literary tradition of sensibility.[2]

At the same time, however, the act of reading itself (conventionally understood as the transmission of ideas), Dickens implies, is suspect for two reasons: the first, because words are so often used by individuals and institutions to separate, to mask, or to oppress because they articulate differences rather than collective humanity, and the second, because we so often read for meaning, looking for the significance of words rather than looking at or listening to the words themselves—and in that act we fail to see or to hear that which is before us. As John J. Fenstermaker observes, ''misuse of language pervades each of the four public institutions Dickens indicts—Chancery (and the Law), Aristocracy (and Government), Religion, and organized Philanthropy—and the crucial private institution, the family'' (241).[3] Dickens goes so far as to imply that humanity's emphasis on words, particularly words that encourage us to read symbolically or metaphorically, has deadened our senses of hearing and sight.[4] In other words, our interpretive activity has gotten in the way of some more elemental comprehension. Dickens restores these physical senses—seeing and hearing—to preeminence in *Bleak House*—the senses, of course, on which the act of reading physically depends. He posits then that reading accurately involves both the body and the mind, or, perception, and apprehension.[5] *Bleak House* suggests, when we attend to the primacy of our bodies—and the bodies of those around us, which our senses encourage us to do, we become aware of our connections with others in a more material, tangible way than we do when we distance our understanding of events from our embodied experience of them, and we also realize how so much of what we perceive as differences are fictions, created by language, that disguise our physical similarities, most profoundly embodied in the experiences of birth and death.[6] At the same time, as Ann Cvetkovich observes of Victorian novels, ''it is important to attend to how the representation of local instances of suffering can both call attention to and obscure complex social relations, and can both inspire and displace social action'' (3).

Deconstructionists love *Bleak House* precisely because of Dickens's attention to words. But to read the novel only through deconstructive lenses runs
the risk of being blind to one aspect of great importance to Dickens: the
ethical workings of language. And in a time of rampant destabilization, disso-
ciation, and disaffection—if an accurate descriptor of Dickens's era then
perhaps of our own moment as well—understanding ways in which language
affects individual bodies is more needed than ever. As Judith Butler points
out, it's through "reiterative and citational practice [that] discourse produces
the effects that it names" (2). But at the same time that Dickens shows the
problems inherent in looking at the world symbolically or metaphorically, he
also uses the metaphor of reading—and the act itself—to show his audience
how to perceive the world. Reading, Dickens suggests, can be a redemptive
activity, if one learns to read the right way. And thus we arrive at a paradox
in approaching reading Dickens ethically in a postmodern age, for the novelist
suggests we need to return to our own physicality—albeit a physicality that
is always mediated by language—to better listen to, see, and hear others. And
in literature's very ability to affect physically its readers—to cause hearts to
flutter or pulses to race—it emphasizes not only its own power, but also the
real bodies of the people engaged in the process of reading.[7]

It's important to recognize, however, as Cvetkovich observes, that "affect
is not a pre-discursive entity, a fact that is often obscured by the construction
of affect or bodily sensations as natural" (24). Affect, in other words, is
learned and produced through reading—through looking, listening, and processing. If reading could turn into a narcissistic, isolating practice in Dickens's
time, it could also lead to a recognition of our existence as physical beings
within a larger earthly community, or, a first identity as, in J. Hillis Miller's
words, "members of one family" (12),[8] even if *pace* Butler, the construction
of bodies is "neither a single act nor a causal process . . . but is itself a
temporal process" (10). Dickens suggests, by recognizing our shared suffering and mortality—an insight that grows out of knowingly and intentionally
combining physical senses with cerebral processes—we can begin to alleviate
the pain of others.[9] Dickens's hope then is that through the inclusion of scenes
of suffering and paragons of good (and bad) readers, he can inspire his
audience to look, to listen, and to act—to help others—as well. Cvetkovich
observes that Victorian "novels propose individualist solutions to what are
in fact intransigent social problems" (10), but given the potential solitary
nature of the reading act, this is perhaps not altogether surprising. As Suzanne
Keen notes, "a society that insists on receiving immediate ethical and political
yields from the recreational reading of its citizens puts too great a burden on
both empathy and the novel" (168).

Dickens, however, takes on that challenge. In *Bleak House*, and specifically
through the characters of the diseased Jo, the scarred Esther, and the post-
stroke Sir Leicester, he emphasizes the importance of physicality, and in

particular, he suggests that we know the world first through our bodies. If that initial apprehension is balanced with intellectual understanding, we can come to a more enlightened, compassionate, and ethical way of living than that realized by the Mrs. Jellybys, Reverend Chadbands, and Mr. Skimpoles, talkers all whose chattering palaver belies their lack of human connection or bodily awareness. Both the medical doctor Allan Woodcourt and the shadowy John Jarndyce fall in love with Esther, particularly because of her relation to disease that offers readers a way to perceive, to appreciate, and therefore, finally, to alleviate the world's suffering. The novel thus teaches us how to recognize our humanity—one not based on the awareness of what distinguishes humans from other creatures—our systems, our reason, our structures (including linguistic)—but rather a humanity based on an awareness of our corporal nature, particularly, our mortality.[10]

While *Bleak House* therefore restores physicality to importance in a way that recalls the eighteenth-century novel, Dickens does not encourage us to read bodies allegorically—the way sensibility posits we should; instead he gently goads us to arrive at understanding through our bodies, contending that in their proximity to disease, to death, and to suffering—lies their beauty. For although words can obfuscate, obscure, and deceive, bodies reveal an alternative history that one cannot elide. More provocatively, Dickens suggests that by directing us towards the sights and sounds of human suffering, novels offer a new way to communicate precisely because they can provide a corrective lens through which to view the world, rather than the distorted vision proffered by the texts of more socially regulated institutions—religious, political, juridical—that were ostensibly concerned with ethics and the social good as well.[11]

Dickens thus uses his characters' bodies not so much to index their morality, but rather to expose their inherent (and hastening) mortality. The body may be a symbol of something else (and we need only think of the allegorical names he so clearly relishes), but it also manifests its history (birth and other experiences), its future (death), as well as its present, and, consequently, all of humanity's as well.[12] But, the novel shows, one can only recognize a common humanity if one perceives the world not through lenses that obscure our similarities by highlighting social class or religion or education (constructions based in human invention, articulated by language, and designed to separate), but through the acknowledgment of humans' existence as sentient beings.[13] And novels, apparently incongruously given their life within words, can teach this lesson.[14] I believe that Dickens is arguing here not simply for a phenomenology, but something more complex and difficult to articulate—perhaps described by Wendell Berry, who reminds us that language

is the most intimately physical of all the artistic means. We have it palpably in our mouths; it is our *langue*, our tongue. . . . Our language passes in at the eyes,

out at the mouth, in at the ears; the words are immersed and steeped in the
senses of the body before they make sense in the mind. They cannot make
sense in the mind until they have made sense in the body. [15]   (192)

When we recall both the sheer physical presence of Charles Dickens—the
energy he exhibited daily in his peripatetic adventures and in his vocal performances—as well as the wonderful and widespread Victorian practice of reading aloud, we see the insight proffered by a behemoth of a work totaling more
than 900 pages as less paradoxical than it might initially appear.

Words therefore can lead to isolation—whether through the creation of
laws or the act of reading alone—and yet they also instruct, soothe, and
connect; for letters, as well as bodies, reveal the imminence—and the inevita-
bility—of mortality; and novels in particular can model compassion for others
(although, as Claudette Kemper Columbus points out, "at the level of para-
grams [verbal bits] even [Dickens] could not have known how the linguistic
network opens his own emotional life" [609]). *Bleak House* as primer reveals
that empathy is rooted in our recognition of our physical sensibility and that
of others: if we learn to see, to listen, and to understand—to employ both
our senses and our intellectual skills—then we become ideal readers, aware
of our connections to others and of the brevity of our lives, and are moved
by the profound insight of our interdependence and our commonality to help
others in physical, emotional, meaningful ways as John Jarndyce, Allan
Woodcourt, and Esther Summerson do.[16] *Bleak House*'s anonymous narrator
asks, "What connexion can there have been between many people in the
innumerable histories of this world, who, from opposite sides of great gulfs,
have, nevertheless, been very curiously brought together?" (235; ch. 16), and
it is this connection that the novel illuminates and explores.

Throughout the novel, Dickens offers lessons in reading—disastrous examples and pattern models—and he also suggests that certain physical and
emotional traumas catalyze a change in characters from seeing in a limited
fashion to perceiving and understanding themselves and others more clearly.
To show how Dickens offers his readers an education, I first explore several
of the acts of misreading in the novel (which occur on the levels of perception
and comprehension), and then follow with an analysis of a few of the traumatic moments in the narrative, before concluding with a look at the characters who, in observing, assessing, and alleviating the suffering of others, serve
as ideal readers of the world and consequently empathetic, ethical role models.

Within the novel, there are at least two ways to misread a situation. The
first is simply not to see what lies around one; a literal myopia blinds people
to seemingly insignificant details. I will focus on three characters here: Mrs.
Jellyby, Sir Leicester Dedlock, and Esther Summerson.[17] An exceptionally
lively caricature, Mrs. Jellyby is so fixated on her "telescopic philanthropy"

that she cannot see her own children, her "handsome eyes [having] . . . a curious habit of seeming to look a long way off" (47; ch. 4), earning the bemusement of Jarndyce, the condemnation of Caddy, and the disapproval of Esther.[18] Mrs. Jellyby simply does not perceive the disaster around her, the squalor of her home, the potential danger to her children, or the hopelessness of her husband, though in her kind understated appraisal of the household to Jarndyce, Esther says, " 'We rather thought . . . that perhaps she was a little unmindful of her home' " (76; ch. 6). In letting the devastation of Mrs. Jellyby's housekeeping speak for itself, Dickens reveals the damage wrought by her failure to see the consequences of her blindness to the world around her as she immerses herself in her own missives, continuing her perpetual letter-writing campaign. Later, Dickens more subtly criticizes the character and her real-life coterie when he describes the starving Jo sitting down on "the door-step of the Society for the Propagation of the Gospel in Foreign Parts, and giv[ing] it a brush. . . . He admires the size of the edifice, and wonders what it's all about. He has no idea, poor wretch, of the spiritual destitution of a coral reef in the Pacific, or what it costs to look up the precious souls among the cocoa-nuts and bread-fruit" (237; ch. 16). Mrs. Jellyby—and those of her ilk—fail to help the people around them, perhaps because they simply cannot see—their own good intentions and belief in the abstract rhetoric of missionary Christianity ironically and unfortunately blind them to the suffering of their neighbors.

Like Mrs. Jellyby, Sir Leicester also retreats in language, fascinated by the annals of the aristocracy and his personal family history. The Dedlock family baronetage offers him in addition to entertainment, significance—a reason for being—as the anonymous narrator remarks,

> His family is as old as the hills, and infinitely more respectable. He has a general opinion that the world might get on without hills, but would be done up without Dedlocks. He would on the whole admit Nature to be a good idea (a little low, perhaps, when not enclosed with a park-fence), but an idea dependent for its execution on your great country families.   (18–19; ch. 2)

Consumed with his family legacy, always looking towards the past, Sir Leicester is unable to perceive the ennui of his wife and the emptiness of his existence. And just as he sees himself, so for his lawyer, Joshua Tulkinghorn, Sir Leicester is not an individual so much as a symbol of a family, of a name: " 'Sir Leicester and the baronetcy, Sir Leicester and Chesney Wold, Sir Leicester and his ancestors and his patrimony,' " according to Tulkinghorn, are " 'inseparable' " (608; ch. 41). Sir Leicester conceives of himself then—and encourages others to perceive him as well—not as a human, embodied individual living at a particular historical moment, but rather as a metonymic figure, a symbol not only of one particular family, but of the aristocratic class, and more generally the historical and current class system. Sir Leicester is blind to his own embodiment, the same way that Mrs. Jellyby is blind to her physical existence, and for most of the novel he is also blind to those around him—the despondent Lady Dedlock, the hapless Rosa, and the calculating Tulkinghorn.

If Sir Leicester and Mrs. Jellyby cannot discern the pending devastation around them and the effects of their own connivance, Esther Summerson is literally blinded, if only temporarily. Arguably the novel's protagonist, Esther becomes blind in the act of nursing Jo, the "street-crossing sweeper," whose bare existence is disregarded by nearly all.[19] Her compassion for Jo leads to her physically acting to save him. In this effort she is contrasted most noticeably with Harold Skimpole, John Jarndyce's sometime friend and adviser, who recommends casting the young boy off since he appears sick. Skimpole accurately observes and assesses Jo; but, unlike Esther, he is not moved to pity or succor but to self-preservation. Rather than moving away from the gravely ill child, Esther, however, chooses to move closer, and in so doing, she winds up falling extremely ill herself. From its incubation, the disease is not named but associated with silence, its effects and symptoms alluded to in hushed whispers. When Esther feels herself beginning to take ill, she asks her maid, Charley, whether the young woman is "strong enough to be told a secret," but Esther never speaks the mystery aloud. Nevertheless, Charley looks at her mistress and comprehends "the secret in [Esther's] face" (463; ch. 41).

The unnamed disease Esther acquires blinds her temporarily and leaves her permanently physically altered; according to some characters within the novel, some critics, and Esther herself, she is "disfigured." In that period of blindness that forever changes Esther, Dickens recalls Saul on the way to Damascus, but Esther compassionate before and after her illness, undergoes a more subtle psychological transformation than the disciple.[20] If her near-death experience—its severity manifest in her blindness and scarring—changes Esther emotionally as well as physically, it may be that she no longer struggles with the mysteries of her parentage. She moves from a kind of neurotic worrying about their identity and the choices they made to a subtle awareness that it is not her origins that matter so much as who she is now—manifest in how she lives and treats others—or, in Helena Michie's words, "she comes into being through illness, scarring, and deformity" (199). Esther's blindness moves her from struggling to comprehend the world around her and the historical mysteries created by its institutions to an acceptance of its uncertainties, suffering, and injustices—whether her own or others'. Esther's illness literalizes her earlier blindness, but, unlike Mrs. Jellyby, she emerges from it.

Esther's blindness is not only physical, but also metaphorical. She begins her portion of the novel with the famous words, "I know I am not clever," and in so doing, she establishes herself as one of literature's most frustrating narrators. To say "I know I am not clever" indicates, of course, either a degree of self-awareness or disingenuousness, or both.[21] For if Esther knows she is not clever, then she does know herself more clearly than those who do not admit to or are unaware of a similar lack of comprehension. I'd like to posit, though, that Esther really does not understand herself or the people around her at the novel's beginning. While she observes cruelty and its effects and (even at a young age) chooses to act compassionately towards nearly all she encounters, indicating a mature sensibility (although she is not particularly generous with Mrs. Jellyby or Mrs. Pardiggle), she still struggles to understand the mysteries of her own birth, and she still trusts language, in Saundra Young's words, as "fixed and serious. . . . as she strives for sincerity, mimesis, and explicit moral judgment" (68–69). And it is in her early belief in language's veracity and the order of systems that Esther is "not clever." She cannot unravel her origins or her relation to John Jarndyce, her guardian who takes an unusual interest in her, and it's for this reason that Esther narrates the novel. If she could understand her situation or merely accept it, she would have no story—no tension. Esther tells us early on, "I had never heard my mother spoken of. I had never heard of my papa either, but I felt more interested about my mama" (25; ch. 3), and shortly thereafter begs her godmother, " 'pray tell me something of her. . . . What did I do to her? How did I lose her? Why am I so different from other children, and why is it my fault?' " (26; ch. 3). Her godmother scolds her into silence, but this wonder impels Esther—and the reader, who, like Esther, is driven by curiosity, by the belief that mysteries can be revealed in language—throughout the novel. The adult looking back on her childhood notes that this recollection still brings her to tears.

Later, when Jarndyce offers her an opportunity to ask questions about her past, she denies herself the knowledge of her own history, replying, " 'I am quite sure that if there were anything I ought to know of or had any need to know, I should not have to ask you to tell it to me. If my whole reliance and confidence were not placed in you, I must have a hard heart indeed. I have nothing to ask you; nothing in the world' " (112; ch. 8). This willful ignorance rings untrue, partially because of her earlier pathetic pleading to have her curiosity satisfied, partially because of her submissive relationship to Jarndyce, and partially because of her own insistence on her contentedness. Had she really been content, there would be no need for Jarndyce to ask the question at all, and, in including the exchange, Dickens draws attention both to Esther's and the reader's unsatiated—and for the moment, unarticulated—curiosity. If Esther's blindness is metaphorical, however, we readers must also acknowledge it is portrayed physically and as such has profound effects upon her and those around her. Once we recognize that Dickens returns metaphors to a physical origin for a specific ethical reason, then we can perceive and acknowledge *Bleak House*'s project, through our own "ethical historicism," if you will, a lens that Dickens both models and points us towards.

Before she falls ill, Esther does not realize that some mysteries cannot be resolved—that an intellectual interpretation of a situation cannot clear up all confusion. Perhaps her discomfort with her origins leads her to an instinctive sympathy for others, an unconscious attempt to make meaning out of a life, which in social terms, has none. Esther intuitively acts out of love and compassion towards others, to physically relieve physical suffering (we might recall her embracing the young girls at the boarding school), and, in so doing, she reveals her silent awareness of the human community. Until she herself becomes "marked" or "disfigured," however, Esther is unable to extend the same acceptance towards herself or towards her parents—but still grapples with reading her own history the only way she knows how—in social terms. But her instinctive compassion—manifest in physical acts of kindness—points towards her eventual ability to synthesize both social codes and an unspoken human connection, even for her own family.

Esther's intuitive kindness is more fully developed in the first scene at the brick maker's when "Mrs. Pardiggle's brand of rigid institutionalized charity is shown to be utterly inadequate and inhuman, and is opposed by Esther's spontaneous, dignified gesture of covering the dead baby, one of the individual acts of responsibility and love that Joseph Fradin, in an oft-quoted article, argues the text advances as the only possibility of human happiness" (Kran 150).[22] When Esther still struggles to understand those connections in systematic terms—whether that is the law, religion, or social status—she becomes befuddled, for, in Jan Gordon's words, she sees herself as a "stain," and therefore "vulnerable to being *read* as a quasi-transparency, like the law, seen *through* to the meaning which [she] simultaneously represents and displaces" (Gordon's italics, 218). At the novel's beginning, Esther has not yet learned that those linguistic constructions—whether created by law or religion—exist only within the minds of human beings but not in any other extrinsic reality, and that the label "clever" exemplifies another such meaningless moniker as opposed to her own intuitive recognition that "touching implies a form of knowing" (Morris 693).

Esther's is not the only natal mystery within the novel. As Michael Ragussis notes, "the novel's ever-present stain, a sign of the disease of language, explains the convergence of discourse with intercourse, of inkstain with bloodstain" (265). In Dickens's England, the physical act of illegitimate childbirth, of course, immediately led mother and child to be labeled, sometimes institutionalized, and condemned by social codes and religious doctrines. But the act of labeling itself also points to its own limitation. If Esther Summerson and Honoria Dedlock show the possible tragic effects of social mores—how children can become orphans and unwed mothers can suffer a lifetime of shame and guilt—Mrs. Snagsby offers the reader relief and laughter at the same time that she approaches the subject of illegitimacy from another angle. And with the introduction of another orphan (and the likelihood of his "illegitimate" origins), Dickens underscores that the personal tragedies affecting Esther, Jo, and their families point to larger social causes.

As Cvetkovich claims, "the causes of female suffering are structural and only symptomatically take the form of affect such as hysteria, depression, anxiety, passion or despair" (111). In other words, the characters' conceptualization of their suffering—or that of others—indicates their own position within an ideological system that masks the greater forces at work. We see a similar personalization in Mrs. Snagsby who comes to her preposterous—and funny—conclusion after Jo's arrival at her house:

> Mrs Snagsby screws a watchful glance on [him]. . . . He looks at Mr Snagsby the moment he comes in. Aha! Why does he look at Mr Snagsby? Mr Snagsby looks at him. Why should he do that, but that Mrs Snagsby sees it all? Why else should that look pass between them; why else should Mr Snagsby be confused, and cough a signal cough behind his hand? It is as clear as crystal that Mr Snagsby is that boy's father.   (Dickens 376–77; ch. 25)

Convinced that her husband has sired Jo, Mrs. Snagsby spends much of her time in the novel following either man or boy in an attempt to catch them in some kind of compromising relation. Her analysis could not be more misguided; watching Mr. Snagsby act compassionately towards Jo, Mrs. Snagsby assumes that her husband must feel some kind of paternal responsibility for an illegitimate son. The conclusion she reaches reveals more about her own adherence to conventional codes and her own sensibility, including her tendency to doubt her marriage, her lack of compassion, and her prurience, than illuminating the connection between man and child, but she is correct in seeing tenderness—she just doesn't know how to interpret it—what it signifies. Looking at Mrs. Snagsby's situation—her misreading—next to Esther's—reveals the nineteenth-century preoccupation with illegitimacy; and Dickens suggests that, by focusing so much on the naming and codifying of sexual relations and their possible consequences, we not only forget but in effect become unable to realize the other kinds of relations that can exist among people, relations not named by the state or religious institutions.

Jo himself is one of those figures who catalyzes so much of the novel's action but remains somehow peripheral, perhaps because the young boy simply cannot be *seen* by so many of the characters (though once again, it seems striking that Lady Dedlock, Captain Hawdon, Allan Woodcourt—Esther's original and chosen family—all perceive and show kindness to the sweep).[23]

And while Jo, with his keen eye for detail and his ability to quickly navigate London's streets, sees so much, he is unable to process or to understand—lacking the analytical skills that would allow him to make sense of those observations according to conventional human institutions. We see this puzzling over and over again throughout the novel—when the police interrogate him after Hawdon's death, when Reverend Chadband quizzes him on the Bible and personal salvation, and perhaps most poignantly in the chambers of Tulkinghorn when he is confronted with Hortense wearing the clothes Lady Dedlock had earlier donned: " 'It is her and it an't her. It an't her hand, nor yet her rings, nor yet her woice. But that there is the wale, the bonnet, and the gownd, and they're wore the same way wot she wore 'em, and it's her heigth wot she wos, and she giv me a sov'ring and hooked it' " (336; ch. 22). Jo's acute attention to physical detail here does not accompany the intellect needed for real understanding to take place. If Mrs. Snagsby's wrong-headed analysis blinds her to reality, Jo can only see the particulars around him; he is unable to construct a larger narrative that makes sense of the situation. It's crucial that Dickens does not blame Jo for his ignorance; rather he suggests the systems—social, government, and religious—are at fault. The boy has the aptitude but no training. Distressed and bored during Reverend Chadband's harangue, according to Jo himself and the narrator,

> it's no good *his* trying to keep awake, for *he* won't know nothink. Though it may be, Jo, that there is a history so interesting and affecting . . . that if the Chadbands, removing their own persons from the light, would but show it thee in simple reverence, would but leave it unimproved, would but regard it as being eloquent enough without their modest aid—it might hold thee awake, and thou might learn from it yet!   (383; ch. 25)

If Dickens is alluding to the Bible here, he is also alluding to his own work and that of other novelists. Literature, Dickens shows and tells, can move, teach, inspire, and model, if its teachers do not get in the way of the lessons.

Just as confused as Jo or Mrs. Snagsby, though more unsettling, Krook, the unofficial Lord Chancellor of Chancery, also stands on the sidelines of the novel, pouring through his paper and garbage heap in an attempt to uncover a detail of significance in Jarndyce and Jarndyce. According to his young tenant, " 'it's a monomania with [Krook], to think he is possessed of documents' " (475; ch. 32). Krook sees the world around him; he, unlike so many, recognizes that trash may hold valuable secrets, and so he sifts through piles of documents, hair, and wax, searching for that which will render him powerful.[24] But, in Krook's illiteracy, Dickens establishes that the character cannot understand—cannot process—the significance of that which he finds.[25] As Weevle reveals to Guppy, Krook " 'can make all the letters separately, and he knows most of them separately when he sees them; he has got on that much, under me; but he can't put them together' " (472; ch. 32). As his drawing of the letters "Jarndyce" and "Bleak House" makes clear to Esther and the reader, Krook can copy, but he cannot comprehend, and "his futile attempts at literacy underscore the fragile, tenuous relationship between linguistic symbol and lexical meaning" (Schuster 167). So, like Jo, Krook possesses the physical power of observation, but he does not have the mental faculties to put them to good use. Perception and analysis are both necessary for interpreting the world—and words—accurately.

Perhaps then it's not surprising that Krook is at the heart of a mystery that simply cannot be described in language. No one within the novel witnesses his spontaneous combustion—instead they see only the evidence that remains afterwards—the smoking fat, the greasy walls, Krook's hat and shoes, and the mysterious behavior of the sinister Lady Jane, who stands snarling "at something on the ground, before the fire. There is very little fire left in the grate, but there is a smouldering suffocating vapor in the room, and a dark greasy coating on the walls and ceiling" (476; ch. 32). And while the police are eager to understand and to explain what happened, and the lawyers to find and control the evidence held by Krook, Dickens leaves his readers with a sense that their conclusions are merely interpretations, and probably inadequate ones at that. Krook's existence—amplified by the piles of stuff, of things that fill his Rag and Bottle shop—is so deeply physical that he combusts as if his sheer energy was too much for the world that tried to contain him, or, in D. A. Miller's words, "as though apocalyptic suddenness were the only conceivable way to put an end to Chancery's meanderings, violent spontaneity the only means to abridge its elaborate procedures, and mere combustion the only response to its accumulation of paperwork" (62), for, as the anonymous narrator relays,

> Call the death by any name Your Highness will, attribute it to whom you will, or say it might have been prevented how you will, it is the same death eternally—inborn, inbred, engendered in the corrupted humours of the vicious body itself, and that only—Spontaneous Combustion, and none other of all the deaths that can be died.   (479; ch. 32)

With Krook's life and death, then, Dickens shows the wondrous qualities of language to describe excess. Krook's physical presence and that of his home overwhelm Esther, the other characters, and the reader, but the moment of his death is not described; it remains a hole, or aporia in the text. The reader, like the detectives and the lawyers who file in, is met with a mystery that cannot be described—a death so intense it could not be witnessed—thus drawing attention to language's limitations.

Even so, if Dickens doesn't describe Krook's demise, he still names it, but refuses to name the disease that scars Esther and kills Jo. Critics have variously offered smallpox, typhus, and erysipelas as possibilities, but Dickens clearly deliberately leaves its name unarticulated.[26] Once again, readers are left with only the effects or remnants of what happened, the corpse of Jo, the marks on Esther's face, and the reaction of others to her. By not naming the disease, Dickens perhaps suggests that it's unknowable in language, or that its title doesn't really matter, although, according to Michael Gurney, Dickens's "descriptions of disease are frequently superior to the medical texts of his day. The illnesses are realistic and challenging enough that Dickensian diagnoses are often the subject of discussion in current medical journals" (80). But he leaves Esther's illness a mystery. Cvetkovich suggests a metaphorical interpretation: "constructed as the repository of secrets, the woman's body both reveals and conceals, making visible because it embodies them, otherwise invisible social determinations" (93), suggesting that the silence around Esther's body speaks to the silence of her origins, since it's rare of course within the novel that Esther is described physically at all.

The quiet surrounding Esther is most apparent when she falls sick. Her dream sequence when she first gets ill, her blindness, and her lack of description of herself all underscore the limits of language and rationality to explain what has happened to her. Esther relays of her disoriented state, "it seemed one long night, but I believe there were both nights and days in it—when I laboured up colossal staircases, ever striving to reach the top. . . . Dare I hint at that worse time when, strung together somewhere in great black space, there was a flaming necklace, or ring, or starry circle of some kind, of which *I* was one of the beads" (Dickens's emphasis; 513–14; ch. 35). The quotidian details of Esther's life disappear—replaced by a surreal script that links her human body with the heavens as a burning star (recalling Krook's death) or fiery piece of jewelry (evoking her mother). Esther's disorder and pain lead her to pray for some deathly release, but as if on cue, having hinted at the temptation of death and stillness, Esther returns to rationality, to her characteristic silence. "Perhaps the less I say of these experiences, the less tedious and the more intelligible I shall be [even though it] may be that if we knew of such strange afflictions, we might be better able to alleviate their intensity" (514; ch. 35).[27] Esther thus nods towards helping others understand her situation, but simply can't (or won't) narrate her experience, even if it were in their best interests. The trauma is too intense for her. And perhaps by leaving Esther's illness a mystery, Dickens ensures more sympathy for her from the reader—as if too graphic a description would threaten his intimacy with his audience.

This self-effacement, Helena Michie observes, is consistent with Esther's characterization from the novel's beginning: "Nowhere is Esther's narrative more informed by the paradox of erasure and assertion than in the discussion of her own physical appearance: her body and its desire. From the outset, the very structure of the first person narrative, the very possibility of a stable 'I,'

makes physical description, in the usual sense, problematic'' (203). Indeed
Esther's self-description paradoxically reveals not any kind of mimetic rendering of her body but that which she either does not know or does not wish
us to see. Esther reports on seeing herself for the first time after her illness,
"I was very much changed—O very, very much. At first, my face was so
strange to me, that I think I should have put my hands before it and started
back. . . . Very soon it became more familiar, and then I knew the extent of
the alteration in it better than I had done at first. It was not like I had expected;
but I had expected nothing definite'' (528; ch. 36). We know neither what
she expected nor what remains, though she says later on meeting Lady Dedlock, "I felt, through all my tumult of emotion, a burst of gratitude to the
providence of God that I was so changed as that I never could disgrace her
by any trace of likeness; as that nobody could ever now look at me, and look
at her, and remotely think of any near tie between us'' (535; ch. 36). What
we are left with—holding or seeing or comprehending—are the disease's
effects on the afflicted and those they encounter, though, as Michie notes, by
"refusing to show her face, [Esther] holds back the promise of meaning and
forces her spectator-readers into a symptomology of reading'' (206).

An expert at the art of withholding, Esther shortly after her encounter with
the mysterious disease, withholds her mother's letter of confession from her
readers. Although this action frustrates the reader seeking solutions to puzzles,
Esther, like Dickens, refuses to oblige.[28] Just as she earlier refuses to allow
her readers to know her disease, so Esther refuses to allow us to see Lady
Dedlock's letter and her reaction to it, the same way that she later refuses to
share her response to Lady Dedlock's corpse.[29] At these moments of psychic
and physical trauma, Esther retreats, leaving readers wondering. In some
ways then Esther acts as her aunt did. When offered an opportunity to explain
her history as described by her mother, Esther writes only, "So strangely did
I hold my place in this world, that, until within a short time back, I had never,
to my own mother's knowledge, breathed—had been buried—had never been
endowed with life—had never borne a name. . . . What more the letter told
me, needs not to be repeated here. It has its own times and places in my
story'' (539; ch. 36). But Esther never returns to those times and places
within *Bleak House*. Dona Budd suggests in a provocative reading that, like
Mrs. Bagnet, in deftly "suppressing her powers of language and releasing
them . . . Esther showcases her own virtue and both meets and challenges the
ideal of Victorian womanhood'' (199). While I value Budd's insight, I wonder
if something else may be at work in Esther's psyche, her "suspicion," in
Kran's words, that "language, as a systematic and social means of expression
is inadequate in its ability to convey the truth of the most basic and important
of human experiences'' (152). Simply put, some events or experiences, including her illness, recovery, the revelation of her origins, and her final
encounter with her mother's corpse, are too traumatic for Esther to articulate.

We see Sir Leicester Dedlock coming to a similar realization at the end of
the novel. Like Esther and Jo, he, too suffers an unnamed debilitating illness,
but one that falls on him with all the suddenness and efficiency of a severe
stroke. Once Sir Leicester learns his wife has had an illegitimate child, the
man who previously saw himself as a scion of family, nobility, and the
country itself, who "through most of the novel . . . talks with all the platitudes
of his class, and is linked with the Boodles and the Noodles" (Sampson 122)
changes to a nearly mute figure who learns, according to Budd, "that the
patriarchal voice and the aristocratic voice are essentially nonsense," and
who nonetheless displays his forgiveness for the woman he loves (211). His
change—like Esther's—can't be articulated in language—we can only see
the effects of it: "And even to the point of his sinking onto the ground,
oblivious of his suffering, he can yet pronounce her name with something
like distinctness in the midst of those intrusive sounds, in a tone of mourning
and compassion rather than reproach" (775; ch. 54). Left dumb in the wake
of the loss of his wife, nevertheless Sir Leicester is able to communicate—through tone, the written word, and the acts of leaving the curtains
open and the fire lit, metaphorical and material both,—"full forgiveness."
Speech fails him; his body does not. Cvetkovich observes that the Victorian
"discourse about affect represented marriage and the family as the product
of natural affective bonds" (6). But the "natural" love Sir Leicester and
Lady Dedlock share for each other is not manifest until the social ties have
broken. She leaves her husband out of shame and love for him; he mourns
for her, showing his love is not based on her social standing or their relationship as constructed by the state, but on her own person. Consequently, as
Cvetkovich observes, "the construction of affect as natural . . . also meant
that it might be uncontrollable; the discourse of affect thus includes the
apparently contradictory construction of affect as the source of both social
stability and social instability" (6). It is his surprising and generous mercy
that ennobles Sir Leicester, that makes him an unconventional hero in the
novel, a broken widower who realizes the fallibility of his earlier existence
and his newfound connection to others, manifest most clearly in his daily
walks with his new companion, George Rouncewell, and it is "infancy"—his
return to a prelingual state—that embodies this untried nobility.[30] Although
Sir Leicester's forgiveness of Honoria comes too late for her, it is not too
late for him—or for us—to acknowledge that nobility, law, and perhaps most
radically the institution of marriage itself are trivialities—merely names, or,
according to Ragussis, "only shadows . . . mere ghosts" (274)—in the face
of more profound unstated elemental human connections. It is through his
sympathy for Honoria that Sir Leicester becomes a new person—"a subject
[who] is produced, consolidated or redefined" (Ablow 2).

Sir Leicester, then, seems to realize that insight that John Jarndyce and
Allan Woodcourt possess all along: the recognition that they are connected

to all of humanity, in ways physical and symbolic, and that the body, in Berry's words *"characterizes* everything it touches. What it makes it races over with the marks of its pulses and breathings, its excitements, hesitations, flaws, and mistakes. On its good work, it leaves the marks of skill, care, and love persisting through hesitations, flaws, and mistakes" (italics Berry's, 193). Both authors realize that in those marks of suffering is a connection to humanity that is somehow beautiful. The first time we see John Jarndyce, he is not named, but offers the child Esther a savory pie and plum cake, with "sugar on the outside an inch thick" (32–33; ch. 3). We learn later that he is taking care of her financially, and it is in the combination of these two actions—a combination that he'll repeat again when she is an adult—the offering of food, alleviation of physical suffering, and a more abstract security that promises a kind of social sanctuary—that he shows his kindness.[31] Years later, Jarndyce again proffers Esther physical relief in the safety of his home, and proposes their marriage, a structure that will keep her protected from many of the difficulties that could face young women alone in the world,[32] the embodied manifestation of his attentive reading of the concrete and abstract worlds human must negotiate.

Allan Woodcourt, the other man taken with Esther, similarly helps the afflicted both physically and mentally. In their suffering, he sees their history, their potential, and their humanity. Looking at the body of Captain Hawdon, Woodcourt observes, " 'I recollect once thinking there was something in his manner, uncouth as it was, that denoted a fall in life' " (154; ch. 11), his ability to see and to understand articulated in his very introduction. As Pam Morris notes, "What is foregrounded in every representation of an interaction between . . . Allan Woodcourt with a character from the diseased world is bodily contact; compassionate knowledge, as opposed to telescopic perception, is embodied in intimate proximity" (694). We see this action most dramatically during Jo's death, when Woodcourt speaks with and holds the dying child, though it's intriguing that during this scene, like Esther's sickbed visions, Dickens uses explicit metaphors—not "realistic" language—to describe the experience: " 'Is there any light a comin?' 'It is coming fast, Jo.' Fast. The cart is shaken all to pieces, and the rugged road is very near its end. . . . The light is come upon the dark benighted way. Dead!' " (677; ch. 47). Jo's death climaxes in a metaphorical explosion of light, both recalling Krook's demise and Esther's nearly fatal dreams. With this turn to metaphor at the moment of death, Dickens again pulls back, drawing attention to the inadequacy of language to render the experience. And yet, even if the language use is always metaphorical, Woodcourt still uses it to soothe the dying child as he holds him close. Woodcourt's medical practice, particularly his bedside manner, embodies the connections between physical and mental health, and he "brings to the public domain of health the professional fusion of abstract with personal knowledge" (Morris 696).[33]

Neither Woodcourt nor Jarndyce shy away from suffering or disease. In fact, if anything, they appear to be attracted to it. I believe this is key to Dickens's project. Both Woodcourt and Jarndyce recognize that in people's suffering—in their mortality—lies a beauty, and this perception explains their continued, even intensified, feelings for Esther after her illness. Esther's disease indicates her mortality, and in the traces it leaves on her face, Jarndyce and Woodcourt see not deformity but a sign of life's brevity, and, consequently, its preciousness; yet the men see not only the metaphor of Esther's body—the sign of her (and humanity's) mortality—but also the specific body itself, which belongs to the compassionate, demurring woman they love.[34]

Esther recalls her opening speech and self-doubt at the novel's conclusion when in response to her husband's assurance ''that you are prettier than you ever were,'' she famously ends the book in the middle of a sentence:

> I did not know that; I am not certain that I know it now. But I know that my dearest little pets are very pretty, and that my darling is very beautiful, and that my husband is very handsome, and that my guardian has the brightest and most benevolent face that ever was seen; and that they can very well do without much beauty in me—even supposing—.   (918; ch. 67)

Critics have variously interpreted Esther's closing speech as indicative of her superficiality or her acceptance of a recognition of beauty's inconsequence.[35] Rather than engaging in those arguments, I suggest that in the sentence's inconclusive ambiguity, Esther articulates the realization of language's inadequacy to comprehend a situation fully, or, in D. A. Miller's words, ''a conspicuous recognition of all that must elude any [tidy conclusion]'' (97). Relieved by her acceptance of a kind of negative capability, Esther stops trying to interpret her looks or their significance the same way she earlier stopped struggling to understand the mysteries of her conception and birth according to any social order, because, according to J. Hillis Miller, ''there is the shade of suspicion that there may be no such centre, that all systems of interpretations may be fictions'' (32). Although her husband assures her of her ''prettiness,'' that quality no longer matters to Esther.

In other words, after Lady Dedlock has revealed herself as her mother and dies cold and alone, after Esther's own experience with her nameless disease, after John Jarndyce releases her from her engagement, leaving her free to marry Woodcourt and himself alone again in the world, after the death of Richard, and the recognition that Caddy's little girl will be deaf and dumb, Esther's conclusion, in LuAnn McCracken Fletcher's words, ''refuses to participate in the nineteenth-century fiction of authoritive interpretation; like a 'faulty' camera lens, it refuses to focus the events of the novel for us and, indeed, implicitly reminds us that our wish for such a focusing suggests our own complicity in the maintenance of a kind of Tulkinghornesque social authority'' (183).[36] The moment of discovering her mother's corpse crystallizes the disconnect between observation and comprehension for Esther. It is that final encounter with her origins, her loss, and her own mortality that brings Esther to an awareness of humanity's insignificance within the universe and our inability to control those happenings so basic—birth and death—whether through, law, religion, or language itself: ''I had not the least idea what it meant. I saw, but did not comprehend, the solemn and compassionate look in Mr Woodcourt's face. I saw, but did not comprehend, his touching the other on the breast to keep him back. I saw him stand uncovered in the bitter air, with a reverence for something. But my understanding for all this was gone'' (847; ch. 59).

At this moment, Esther learns that perhaps suffering in the world is without reason, but Dickens, unlike Esther, knows that one need not be mute before it. One instead can bear witness to suffering the way Dickens does throughout the novel, most poignantly, of course, with the death of Jo.[37] But if Dickens relies on metaphors to describe Jo's death, he uses understatement to describe Esther's finding Lady Dedlock's corpse: ''I lifted the heavy head, put the long dank hair aside, and turned the face. And, it was my mother, cold and dead'' (847; ch. 59). Simply bearing witness—observing and articulating—is powerful enough. And in that bearing witness we see the effects of human institutions—created in the imagination and articulated in language—that cruelly separate us, that allow us to live with indifference to others.[38] Reading—whether it's a literal text or the faces of the people around us—can divide or unite us, but attempting to control, to judge—to do anything other than to bear witness—is necessarily to lead with the limitations of the act, to lead with our own preconceptions rather than with genuine seeing or hearing, for, according to Ragussis, ''it is in the nature of language to present a mystery, actually to make a mystery, even a ghost story'' (275).

If we read the final sentence of *Bleak House* or, indeed, the whole novel for meaning, for a message, we lose the sound and the look of the sentence and the novel itself and its effect on us; but that effect, which, in fact, produces the act of questioning, which makes us wonder, which leads us out of ourselves—that effect, Dickens gambles, may lead us to an engagement with the world not based on already knowing—the way human institutions like the law, religion, the state operate—or even some human individuals—Mr. Tulkinghorn, Mrs. Jellyby, Mrs. Pardiggle—practice. It is a way of being that sees the brutality and hears the cries of suffering around us.[39] Dickens, of course, realizes that the novel is not ''real''—that as J. Hillis Miller argues, ''the power of the sign lies not in itself but what it indicates'' (16)—but I also believe Dickens is ''indicating'' the path towards a way of living.[40] Dickens knows language is removed from experience and yet writes believing the process somehow can be reversed, with the knowledge that language—if it is seen, heard, and comprehended—can affect a reader's perspective and life. William Reddy points out in his study, *The Navigation of Feeling*, that emotions are largely "the products of learning" (x). Dickens, I believe, would concur.[41] Novels can teach us to read—to understand, yes, but also to see, to hear, and to feel—and thus to empathize, to act, and to live in the world with a newfound awareness of and appreciation for those with whom we share existence.[42]

NOTES

1. For example, A. O. J. Cockshut writes, "the world of *Bleak House* is a world in which no problem is really faced, in which nothing is understood, in which the meanings of words has decayed" (127). For readings of the novel that follow Miller chronologically and thematically, see Cowles, Gordon, Marlow, Ousby, Ragussis, Schuster, Storor, and Tracy.
2. In her discussion of *Our Mutual Friend*, Ruth Tross offers a similar, apparently paradoxical, assessment when she observes, "Dickens could be said to argue for a mode of reading that is somehow more organic, that goes beyond the obstacle of the words to reach their underlying, almost non-textual meaning" (242).
3. Since so many others have successfully turned their critical faculties to the case that catalyzes the novel's action, in this essay I will not address Jarndyce and Jarndyce, which is an indecipherable muddle that no one can make sense of. Lawyers, accountants, involved parties, and spectators all attempt to understand the case, often dying while engaged in their pursuit, while "no two Chancery lawyers can talk about it for five minutes, without coming to a total disagreement as to all the premises" (14; ch. 1). Dickens is drawing readers' attention to the hypocrisies of the legal system—how it perpetuates itself and survives, if for no other reason than self-preservation—and he also underscores the banalities and the trivialities of its language. Legalese, the jargon of the system of the law, he argues, is a language that rather than shedding clarity or light on a situation—obscures and dims it, as referring to the Chancellor of the Court of Chancery as "mlud"—"introducing at the paragram level the deformation of language [and] the illiteracy of supposedly civilized people who cannot read what they do and who they are" indicates (Columbus 613). The language of the state then does not serve or help others; in fact it works to hide the truth from them, to create work for lawyers, judges, the Court of Chancery itself. But, notes the anonymous narrator, once "the laity" realize that the "coherent scheme" of the English law "is to make business for itself at [their] expense, surely . . . they will cease to grumble" (573; ch. 39). See Clarkson for a discussion of "the processes and effects of Chancery . . . as an allegory of the Derridean 'différance' of language" (125). See also Fenstermaker, Foor, Humphreys, and Ragussis, who all address language within *Bleak House*, and Brantlinger on the problem of literacy as "a threat to national security" (6).

4. At the same time, we need also remember how deftly and overtly Dickens employs figurative language, considering, for example, the name of Esther Summerson. In Carroll Clarkson's words, "the fact that the metaphor is so ostensibly defamiliarized (so blatantly 'laid bare'), points to the name's metafictional quality: Esther Summerson is a fictive construct whose being depends on the language which constitutes her, and it is precisely for this reason that her name can be so pertinent" (123). As Peter Ackroyd notes, Dickens "retained a very strong visual memory so that he could, as it were, effortlessly recall the visual details and elaboration of a scene without necessarily understanding its context or purpose. It is a rare and strange gift, currently believed by psychologists, to be related to obsession" (15). Within his novels, Dickens modifies the ideas expressed by Adam Smith in *The Theory of Moral Sentiments*, "[Our senses] never did, and never can, carry us beyond our own person, and it is by the imagination only that we can form any conception of what are [an individual's] sensations. . . . It is the impressions of our own senses only, not those of his, which our imaginations can copy. By the imagination we place ourselves in his situation, we conceive ourselves enduring all the same torments, we enter as it were into his body, and become in some measure the same person with him, and thence form some idea of his sensations, and even feel something which, though weaker in degree, is not altogether unlike them. His agonies, when they are thus brought home to ourselves, when we have thus adopted and made them our own, begin at last to affect us, and we then tremble and shudder at the thought of what he feels" (9).

5. Dickens's own remarkable eye for detail has been discussed by many, including Ackroyd and Burke. As Burke writes, "by rambling about the city and taking advantage of views provided by thoroughfares and courts, windows and doorways . . . the young Dickens developed a visual sense of how the physical structure of the city organized human relationships spatially and temporally, socially, and economically" (660).

6. See Brantlinger for a fascinating discussion of "two dramatically different sorts of reading"—"books 'written to make the world wiser' [and] criminal reading" in *Oliver Twist* (70).

7. Here I'd like to suggest that Dickens reestablishes sensibility's connection with morality. That is, learning through the senses can lead to empathy, and then to ethics. Here Dickens differs from that perspective described by Brantlinger of the sensation novel, "Beyond the innocent though absolutist eye of the realist author, narrator, and reader, . . . there is another, second way of seeing and therefore of reading. But that second way of seeing is neither self-evident nor safe. If it isn't exactly pornographic (at least, not in Victorian sensation fiction), neither is it the police. The detective and the pornographer, the victim and the villain, innocence and experience walk through the menacing, secretive front door of Audley Court together in collusion. . . . These patterns are not simply ways of expressing the universality of guilt; they also express the radical, regressive doubleness whereby the law-giving father gives way, if only momentarily, in some brief but shimmeringly traumatic primal-scene vision, beyond simple empiricism, to his obscene shadow" (162).

8. But, as Cvektovich observes of the sensation novel, it was decried as "deplorable because it reduces its readers to the conditions of animals who are driven by instincts" (20).

9. Dickens may here remind us of Rousseau, who, in David Marshall's words, suggests "that only sympathy, only the perception of resemblance that reveals what one has in common with others, will allow one to recognize others as fellow creatures rather than as monsters or giants or beasts or strangers; only the recognition of fellow feeling can save people from monsters: save them from turning others into monsters, save them from becoming monsters" (287–88).

10. Lauren Goodland offers another perspective on Dickens's humanitarian efforts: "Domesticity's personal relations were a bulwark against the atomization and mechanization of the social body, and a means to preserving individual autonomy. Thus Dickens connects Esther's motherly care for Charley and sisterly care for Caddy Jellyby, while likening Mrs. Pardiggle's wholesome 'benevolence' to 'a strait waistcoat.' Thus, on the very same grounds, he contrasts Woodcourt's compassionate 'habit . . . of speaking to the poor,' to Bucket's domineering officialism, and to the 'patronage' and 'condescension' of England's self-appointed philanthropic police" (542–43). David Storor suggests, however, that "Mr Bucket's grotesquely realised faculties of sight, sound, and smell are representative of the police's knowledge of the city. Thus what Dickens is articulating in the character of Mr Bucket is a new form of knowledge of society" (28). We can also turn to the reunion between Mrs. Rouncewell and George in the presence of Mrs. Bagnet. She "stands looking at [her son] . . . only her fluttering hands give utterance to her emotions. But they are very eloquent; very, very eloquent. Mrs Bagnet understands them. They speak of gratitude, of joy, of grief, of hope; of inextinguishable affection . . . and they speak in such a touching language that Mrs Bagnet's eyes brim up with tears, and they run glistening down her sun-browned face" (778; ch. 55). Saundra Young writes of the scene, Mrs. Rouncewell's "own inarticulate response is moving because it is exactly correct. If we feel the eloquence of the gesture [of Mrs. Rouncewell's fluttering hands], we feel it in spite of the words that describe it, in spite of our sophistication as readers" (82).

11. Ruth Tross observes that written words "are the only things that are ever real, and, as such, they seem to possess an ability not only to control but also to replace what they represent" (239). Jan Gordon offers an alternative interpretation: "the law is either *never fully present* in the lives of those it touches, or is thoroughly dissimulated in the form of spurious copies, which are the basis for a virtual industry dedicated to the representation, reproduction, and interpretation of antecedents by surrogates and pretenders" (italics Gordon's, 226).

12. J. Hillis Miller observes, "the novel must be understood according to correspondences within the text between one character and another, one scene and another, one figurative expression and another. . . . Once the reader has been alerted to look for such resemblances he discovers that the novel is a complex fabric of recurrences. . . . Every character serves as the emblem of other similar characters" (15).

13. Here we might turn to Tulkinghorn, who, in Arnold Kettle's words, "is the agent of an impersonal system more potent and more sinister than any expression of personal spite or hatred. . . . It is this very impersonality that makes Mr. Tulkinghorn so formidable. It is not his personal wickedness that Lady Dedlock is up against any more than it is the personal kindliness of the Lord Chancellor that determines the workings of the Court of Chancery. The sense of the Law as a force in itself, an independent business, self-perpetuating within its own closed circles of privilege and procedure, is basic to the meaning of *Bleak House*" (231–32).

14. David Cowles observes however that "Dickens's own worldview in the novel clearly depends on numerous systems: Christianity, patriarchy, class biases, nationalism, social convention, and so on. Consequently he uses the language of the very systems he criticizes—even as he attacks them" (161).

15. Laura Braunstein offers an alternative perspective in her analysis of Victorian detective fiction, which, as a genre, she suggests, "seems to validate subjective bodily knowledge (or reflexive readings of and writing on the body) on the level of the individual. On the other hand, the genre concedes that only objective bodily knowledge (or transitive readings of writings on the body) is legitimate. In evoking this polemical opposition, the genre suggests provisionally that we want to believe that what our bodies speak to us is true. However, we are caught in a world in which it is impossible to communicate such inside knowledge without resorting to language, which can only express such subjective understanding by transforming it into a readable text. . . . We cannot describe writing on the body without referring to it as something from which it is necessarily distinguished" (204).

16. Suzanne Keen posits that "broadcast strategic empathy calls upon every reader to feel with members of a group, by emphasizing common vulnerabilities and hopes through universalizing representations" (xiv).

17. There are other characters who cannot see: Mrs. Pardiggle, Richard Carstone, and Mrs. Barbary, for example, are also blind in some way to their own actions and their effects on others. Lady Dedlock, too, "supposes herself to be an inscrutable Being . . . yet every little star revolving about her, from her maid to the manager of the Italian Opera, knows her weaknesses, prejudices, follies, haughtinesses, and caprices" (21; ch. 2).

18. See Goodland for an alternative take on Mrs. Jellyby's misguided philanthropy.

19. It is telling that Captain Hawdon, Esther's birth-father, John Jarndyce, his surrogate, and Allan Woodcourt, the man she eventually marries, all see and reach out to Jo as well.

20. Cvetkovich writes, "the middle class woman's suffering often takes the form of psychic or emotional rather than physical pain. It gives rise to a politics of affect according to which the expression of emotion can be liberatory" (40).

21. Allison Case, for example, writes "a rhetorically canny Esther who deliberately and deceptively crafts these sympathy-winning moments is a far less attractive figure [than the inspiring image of self-effacing feminine goodness], and raises the question of just how far her canniness extends: are the numerous instances of her simultaneously reporting and modestly disclaiming other characters' praise

of her goodness similarly rhetorically self-conscious, for example?'' (315). See also Young.

22. Kran explores the significance of this event and the handkerchief itself in more detail: ''One might argue that the symbolic force of the handkerchief in the text is based on either metonymy or synecdoche as a signifier associated with Esther's charitable act, or as representing one in the series of such acts and gestures that define Esther's total character. However, since the covering of the dead baby with the handkerchief actually constitutes the charitable act, there exists a relationship of identity between the act and the signifier, hence a metaphoric relationship.'' Later he explains that the handkerchief ''as an irrefutable symbol of Esther's goodness . . . stands in defiance to the greater structures of society'' (151).

23. Judith Butler argues that the ''exclusionary matrix by which subjects are formed thus requires the simultaneous production of a domain of abject beings, those who are not yet 'subjects,' but who form the constitutive outside to the domain of the subject'' (3). Jo represents such a figure for most of the characters in *Bleak House*—as would Esther outside of the novel, her illegitimacy marking her as invisible.

24. Krook's illiteracy aligns him with Jo, another character who sees but cannot process. Of the latter, Dickens writes, ''It must be a strange state to be like Jo! To shuffle through the streets, unfamiliar with the shapes, and in utter darkness as to the meaning, of those mysterious symbols so abundant over the shops, and at the corners of streets, and on the doors, and in the windows! To see people read, and to see people write, and to see the postman deliver letters, and not to have the least idea of all that language—to be, every scrap of it, stone blind and dumb!'' (236; ch. 16). Ousby concludes, ''Jo's illiteracy makes him unable to detect any meaning of order in the surrounding world, let alone any benevolent relation to himself'' (387).

25. And here Krook is also aligned with his sister, Grandmother Smallweed, another character who cannot understand, though rather than copying with a pencil, she mimics in speech, always seemingly meaninglessly echoing the last phrase of the most recently uttered sentence.

26. See Gurney and West. Dickens himself was later diagnosed with erysipelas, ''sometimes known as 'St. Anthony's Fire' because of its connection with severe nervous affliction'' (Ackroyd 1001).

27. Ackroyd relates that in sympathy with his heroine, Dickens ''did manage to contract a very bad cold at the same time he was consigning Esther Summerson to smallpox'' (661).

28. We see this as well in the final ''resolution'' of Jarndyce and Jarndyce, which concludes not with any satisfying sense of closure but an articulation of its own meaninglessness, waste, and triviality.

29. The character of Lady Dedlock herself, as Cvetkovich points out, also suggests ''that the aristocracy's suppression of 'the natural feelings of the heart' can only lead to destruction'' (54).

30. Hortense calls Sir Leicester ''the poor infant'' as Mr. Bucket arrests her (774; ch. 54).

31. J. Hillis Miller observes that Esther and Jarndyce are examples of "A Christian humanism compounded of belief in 'the natural feeling of the heart' (55), in unselfish engagement in duty and industrious work, in spontaneous charity toward those immediately within one's circle, and of faith that Providence secretly governs all in this lower world" (30–31).

32. Clarkson asks "why should the possession of a proper name, and especially a family name, be so important for a sense of personal identity?" and answers the question, referring to Derrida, "The relations you bear towards your parents and family constitute a sense of origin and continuity and hence a sense of personal identity in terms of history and of a place in time. . . . Personal identity, like meaning itself, is not simply a self-presence" (128).

33. Dickens in his own life, according to Ackroyd, treated the ill and suffering in a similar fashion: "With the sick in particular he seems to have been singularly kind and tactful. He possessed, according to one who saw it, 'a curious life-giving power' so that his surplus energy, radiating through his brightness and optimism, seemed actually to help the curative process of those whom he visited" (535).

34. Marlow claims that Dickens "seems to create a living link between reference and referent that exceeds our understanding, muddling the distinctions between icon, index, and symbol and liberating the reader's mind from the iron dictates of conventional decoding of language" (190).

35. See, for example, Budd, Dever, Michie, Ousby, and Torgovnick.

36. Lynette Felber offers an alternative reading on the open-ended conclusion, noticing that "A finished sentence would close the novel and resolve the pattern earlier established, but Esther's final gesture as narrator, punctuating the ending of her story with a dash, *suspends* hierarchy—at once having the option of the last word and magnanimously refusing to speak and thus dominate, ending with the feminine but acknowledging the possibility of the Other" (italics Felber's, 18).

37. Young posits that "Dickens's increasing disbelief in the possibility of moving an audience by means of language provides some insight into the hysterical energy with which he threw himself into public readings: in public he could see women fainting; he could see language resulting in action if only in the most obvious way" (83).

38. Reading literature can profoundly benefit us, as the novel suggests, rather than endanger us, as "a form of leisure activity done instead of something else—a something that is almost always, as the 1890s opponents of libraries suggest, categorizable as mental improvement and therefore as a sort of work, albeit cultural or spiritual work" (Brantlinger 22).

39. Goodland observes that although Dickens in his private life was committed to various "reformatory institutions," in his fiction he "refrained from delegating the home's sanctified pastoral functions to the suspect space of the curative institution. . . . The only benevolent institution it figures is the home. . . . It is chiefly through overt hostility to women's organized philanthropy that Dickens expresses profound skepticism towards the curative institutions he privately helped to support" (543).

40. Ablow writes of Dickens's aesthetic, the goal "is to help us see ourselves in new ways: as endlessly improvable, limitlessly lovable, and as capable of enormously virtuous yet profitable acts of generosity" (21).

41. Keen provocatively counters, "fiction may evoke empathy in part because it *cannot* make direct demands for action" (106; emphasis Keen's).
42. *Bleak House*, thus, in Young's words, allows Dickens "to reveal language as artifice, to show the way eloquence can fail, and yet at the same time provide a fleeting—maybe even an accidental—glimpse of a possibility for eloquence" (83).

WORKS CITED

Ablow, Rachel. *The Marriage of Minds: Reading Sympathy in the Victorian Marriage Plot.* Stanford: Stanford UP, 2002.

Ackroyd, Peter. *Dickens.* New York: HarperCollins, 1990.

Berry, Wendell. *What Are People For? Essays.* San Francisco: North Point, 1990.

Brantlinger, Patrick. *The Reading Lesson: The Threat of Mass Literacy in Nineteenth-Century British Fiction.* Bloomington: Indiana UP, 1998.

Braunstein, Laura. "Strange Cases: Representing Epistemology in Victorian Detective Narratives." Diss. Northwestern University, 2000.

Budd, Dona. "Language Couples in *Bleak House.*" *Nineteenth-Century Literature* 49.2 (1994): 196–220.

Burke, Alan R. "The Strategy and Theme of Urban Observation in *Bleak House.*" *Studies in English Literature* 9.4 (1969): 659–76.

Butler, Judith. *Bodies that Matter: On the Discursive Limits of Sex.* London: Routledge, 1993.

Case, Alison. "Gender and History in Narrative Theory: The Problem of Retrospective Distance in *David Copperfield* and *Bleak House.*" *A Companion to Narrative Theory.* Ed. James Phelan and Peter J. Rabinowitz. Oxford: Blackwell, 2005. 312–21.

Clarkson, Carrol. "Alias and Alienation in *Bleak House:* Identity in Language." *Dickens Studies Annual* 23 (1994): 121–35.

Cockshut, A.O.J. *The Imagination of Charles Dickens.* New York: New York UP, 1962.

Columbus, Claudette Kemper. "The (Un)Lettered Ensemble: What Charley Does Not Learn about Writing in *Bleak House.*" *SEL* 28 (1988): 609–23.

Cowles, David L. "Methods of Inquiry, Modes of Evidence: Perception, Self-Deception, and Truth in *Bleak House.*" *Dickensian* 87 (1991): 153–63.

Cvetkovich, Ann. *Mixed Feelings: Feminism, Mass Culture, and Victorian Sensationalism*. New Brunswick, NJ: Rutgers UP, 1992.

Dever, Carolyn M. "Broken Mirror, Broken Words: Autobiography, Prosopopeia, and the Dead Mother in *Bleak House*." *Studies in the Novel* 27.1 (1991): 42–62.

Dickens, Charles. *Bleak House*. Ed. Stephen Gill. Oxford: Oxford UP, 1996.

Felber, Lynette. " 'Delightfully Irregular': Esther's Nascent écriture féminine in *Bleak House*." *Victorian Newsletter* 85 (1994): 13–20.

Fenstermaker, John J. "Language Abuse in *Bleak House*: The First Monthly Installment." *Victorian Literature and Society: Essays Presented to Richard D. Altick*. Ed. James R. Kincaid and Albert J. Kuhn. Columbus: Ohio State UP, 1984. 240–57.

Fletcher, LuAnn McCracken. "A Recipe for Perversion: The Feminine Narrative Challenge in *Bleak House*." *Dickens Studies Annual* 25 (1996): 67–89.

Foor, Sheila. *Dickens' Rhetoric*. New York: Peter Lang, 1993.

Fradin, Joseph I. "Will and Society in *Bleak House*." *Critical Essays on Charles Dickens's* Bleak House. Ed. Elliot L. Gilbert. Boston: G. K. Hall, 1989. 40–64.

Goodland, Lauren M.E. "Is There a Pastor in the *House*? Sanitary Reform, Professionalism, and Philanthropy in Dickens's Mid-Century Fiction." *Victorian Literature and Culture* (2003): 525–53.

Gordon, Jan. "Dickens and the Transformation of Nineteenth-Century Narratives of 'Legitimacy.' " *Dickens Studies Annual* 31 (2002): 203–63.

Gurney, Michael S. "Disease as Device: The Role of Smallpox in *Bleak House*." *Literature and Medicine* 9 (1990): 79–92.

Humphreys, Camilla. "Dickens's Use of Letters in *Bleak House*." *Dickens Quarterly* 6.2 (1989): 53–60.

Keen, Suzanne. *Empathy and the Novel*. Oxford: Oxford UP, 2007.

Kettle, Arthur. "Dickens and the Popular Tradition." *Marxists on Literature: An Anthology*. Ed David Craig. Harmondsworth: Penguin, 1975. 214–44.

Kran, Paul A. "Signification and Rhetoric in *Bleak House*." *Dickens Studies Annual* 26 (1997): 147–67.

Marlow, James E. "Towards a Dickens Poetic: Iconic and Indexical Elements in *Bleak House*." *Dickens Studies Annual* 30 (2001): 173–92.

Marshall, David. *The Surprising Effects of Sympathy: Marivaux, Diderot, Rousseau, and Mary Shelley*. Chicago: U Chicago P, 1988.

Michie, Helena. " 'Who is This in Pain?': Scarring, Disfigurement, and Female Identity in *Bleak House* and *Our Mutual Friend*." *Novel: A Forum on Fiction* 22.2 (1989): 199–212.

Miller, D. A. *The Novel and the Police*. Berkeley: U California P, 1988.

Miller, J. Hillis. "Introduction." *Bleak House*. Charles Dickens. Ed. Norman Page. Harmondsworth: Penguin, 1971. 11–34.

Morris, Pam. "*Bleak House* and the Struggle for the State Domain." *ELH* 68 (2001): 679–98.

Ousby, Ian. "The Broken Glass: Vision and Comprehension in *Bleak House*." *Nineteenth-Century Fiction* 29.4 (1975): 381–92.

Ragussis, Michael. "The Ghostly Signs of *Bleak House*." *Nineteenth-Century Fiction* 34.3 (1979): 253–80.

Reddy, William M. *The Navigation of Feeling: A Framework for the History of Emotions*. Cambridge: Cambridge UP, 2001.

Sampson, Edward. "The Problem of Communication in *Bleak House*." *Twenty-Seven to One: A Potpourri of Humanistic Material Presented to Dr. Donald Gale Stillman*. Ed. Bradford Broughton. Ogdensburg: Ryan Press, 1970. 121–25.

Schuster, Charles I. "Style and Meaning in *Bleak House*." *The Sphinx: A Magazine of Literature and Society* 4 (1989): 166–74.

Smith, Adam. *The Theory of Moral Sentiments*, ed. D.D. Raphael and A.L. Macfie. Oxford: Clarendon, 1976.

Storor, David. "Grotesque Storytelling: Dickens's Articulation of the 'Crisis of the Knowable Community in *Bleak House* and *Little Dorrit*." *Dickensian* 94 (Spring 1998): 25–41.

Torgovnick, Marianna. *Closure in the Novel*. Princeton: Princeton UP, 1981.

Tracy, Robert. "Reading and Misreading *Bleak House*." *Dickens Quarterly* 20 (2003): 166–71.

Tross, Ruth. "Dickens and the Crime of Literacy." *Dickens Quarterly* 21:4 (2004): 235–45.

West, Gilian. "*Bleak House*: Esther's Illness." *English Studies* 73:1 (1992): 30–34.

Young, Saundra K. "Uneasy Relations: Possibilities for Eloquence in *Bleak House*." *Dickens Studies Annual* 9 (1981): 67–85.

"Pretend[ing] a little": The Play of Musement in Dickens's *Little Dorrit*

Gail Turley Houston

Putting Dickens's Little Dorrit *in conversation with nineteenth-century philosophical precepts about the aesthetic, this article suggests that* Little Dorrit *illuminates and expands ideas about aesthetic "play" featured in Friedrich Schiller's publication of* On the Aesthetic Education of Man, *a work structured as a series of letters, that influenced Charles Sanders Peirce's later work on play and the "generals." If "The most important theory in the entire history" of thought regarding play is to be found in Friedrich Schiller's* On Aesthetic Education *(Elias 1: 106), this essay argues that* Little Dorrit's *brilliant representation of the aesthetics of play illustrates Dickens's sophisticated views on the subject. Dickens's substantive portrayals of "Altro," Mrs. General, and Amy's "musings" articulate what Schiller's abstract analysis of play and Peirce's conceptual work on the generals and musement can only theorize, that play is a superlative form of seriousness, leading to the highest levels of knowledge, love, and morality. The essay briefly summarizes Schiller's and Peirce's ideas as a prelude to analysis of Dickens's articulation of play illustrated in Amy Dorrit's Princess story and in contradistinction to Mrs. General's dangerous disciplinary work.*

If in *Little Dorrit* the prison serves as both an actual and symbolic structure, even minor characters reflect the functions of discipline and freedom. At the beginning of book 1 John Baptist Cavaletto acts as a forerunner to the Christ-like Amy, who, with her potent imagination, holds the key to psychic and spiritual freedom. I would argue that Mrs. General fulfills an equally important signifying purpose at the very beginning of book 2. Dickens's "tags" or catch phrases for these two characters are illustrative (Newsome 543). Baptist's "ALTRO" and General's "prunes and prisms," represent, respectively, Dickens's aesthetics, that is, his belief in the necessity for the procreative imagination ("ALTRO") to counter stupefyingly restrictive Victorian conventions ("prunes and prisms"). Relating Dickens's novel to nineteenth-century philosophical precepts about the aesthetic, I suggest that in its architectonic form and thematics *Little Dorrit* illuminates and expands ideas about aesthetic "play" featured in Friedrich Schiller's *On the Aesthetic Education of Man*, a work that influenced Charles Sanders Peirce's own later study of play and the "generals." If, as one scholar suggests, "The most important theory in the entire history" of thought regarding play is to be found in Schiller's *On the Aesthetic Education of Man* (Elias 1: 106), I would argue that *Little Dorrit*'s brilliant representation of the aesthetics of play illustrates Dickens's sophisticated understanding of the subject. Indeed, Dickens's substantive portrayals of "Altro," Mrs. General, and Amy's "musings" articulate what Schiller's abstract analysis of play and Peirce's conceptual work on the generals and musement can only theorize, that play is a superlative form of seriousness, leading to the highest levels of knowledge, love, and morality.

Scholarship on the aesthetics of *Little Dorrit* affirms Dickens's increasingly complex rendition of Victorian social, moral, and linguistic tensions. Focusing on the differences between "those who lie and those who live truthfully," Janice Carlisle argues that the nineteenth-century concern that novels were necessarily immoral *because* they were fictions falls apart when faced with the eponymous heroine of *Little Dorrit*, whose white lies and lies of omission allow her family to negotiate the social, psychological, and emotional stresses of modern life (Carlisle 198). Thus, shockingly, Dickens has it both ways: Amy is a liar *and* the moral center of the novel. Dickens's "understanding of fiction," then, "is comprehensive enough to include its moral ambiguities without allowing them to undercut its moral utility" (Carlisle 211). Focusing on the ambiguities produced by the novel's "frequent gaps," "rhetorical evasions," and "pointless plot," Dianne F. Sadoff turns to Roland Barthes to explain the Inimitable's aesthetic mishmash: *Little Dorrit* shows that the pleasure of narrative is *not* to be found in closure (discovering origins) but in the text's refusal to provide answers (Sadoff 243). Ultimately, then, narrative pleasure obtains in the fictionality itself, even in the recognition that " 'truth' " may be only a metaphor (243).

The metaphorical troping of Amy's erotic yearning is of chief concern to Nancy Aycock Metz. Examining the ways that the masculine imagination wrestles with and brackets Little Dorrit's aesthetic representations of the return of her repressed, "libidinal" desire, Metz suggests that the gap that is Amy's text sutures the male will to contain the imagination (234–35). Robert Higbie contends that for Dickens "Imagination" both "undercuts belief and helps it survive, though in a reduced, imaginary form" (175). As Higbie suggests, in the same way that Little Dorrit's tale of the Princess helps her to envision keeping Clennam's "bright" "shadow" in her memory, so too does imagination create "an image of the ideal that we can keep in our minds even though we cannot believe it can exist in reality" (175). I would suggest that while these are probing and insightful approaches to *Little Dorrit*, it is also important to concentrate analysis on Dickens's articulation of a philosophical concept of play in its own right, especially since the ludic is crucial to Amy's very serious resolution of the aesthetic, erotic, ethical, and social responsibilities facing her in an increasingly fragmented and meaningless world.

Published in 1804, Schiller's *Aesthetische Briefe* (*On the Aesthetic Education of Man*) was read by the teenage Peirce in the mid-to-late 1850s, around the same time *Little Dorrit* was ending its serial run. We know, too, that Schiller's book was widely read in England by the literati, including, Coleridge, Ruskin, Mill, and Carlyle (Introduction Schiller x1–cxcvi). We do not know if Dickens read Schiller, but the latter's ideas may have been mentioned to him by his friend Carlyle who wrote a biography of the German thinker. Further, because Dickens's son Charley edited Schiller's *Der Neffe als Onkel* (1854) and *Der Parasit oder die Kunst sein Glück zu machen* (1856) for English readers, and the 4 November 1854 issue of the *Athenaeum* mentioned its appreciation of his edition of *Neffe als Onkel*, Charley probably would have discussed this and other of Schiller's works with his proud father (Dickens, Letter to Arthur Ryland: 6 Dec. 1854, *Letters* 7: 478n). In addition, the editors of the Pilgrim Edition of Dickens's letters suggest that the Inimitable's friends may have taken him to see Schiller's play *Fiesco, or the Revolt of Genoa* for his birthday in February 1850 (*Letters* 6: 31n). In any case, Dickens, whether or not he read Schiller's work, was investigating his own theory of play in his novels, especially in *Hard Times*, which features fancy as the restorative force for a society embedded in Utilitarian facts—a theme central to Schiller's *On Aesthetic Education*. I believe that *Little Dorrit* presents Dickens's most sophisticated engagement with play as a mechanism that not only provides a liberating effect, but also leads to the highest levels of love and morality. An analysis of the views of "play" expressed earlier by Schiller (in esthetics), then by Dickens (in fiction), and later by Peirce (in semiotics) reveals interesting and illuminating parallels.

For Schiller, the mission of *On Aesthetic Education* is to heal the "wound upon modern man" resulting from three modern trends: the divisions of knowledge into multiple sealed off branches of science, the "increasingly complex machinery of State," and the "sever[ing]" of "the inner unity of human nature" (Letter 6: 6).[1] Schiller provides a dialectical answer to the problem. Human nature, he argues, has three impulses: "Stofftrieb," or the material drive towards change and multiplicity; "Formtrieb," or the need for abstract form, which is by its nature resistant to change; and the important third impulse, "Spieltrieb," or the play-drive, which harmonizes "Stofftrieb" and "Formtrieb" (Brent, 53–54 referring to Sebeok 1). Until the play-drive reconciles the sensuous and rational drives, they are in continual conflict, with the formal-drive exploring abstract Truth and the sense-drive "bind[ing] the ever-soaring spirit to the world of sense," causing enormous tension in the human psyche (Letter 12: 3, 4, 5; 14: 5). Until "Spieltrieb" harmonizes "Stofftrieb" with "Formtrieb," the human intellect is incapable of connecting phenomena, so that the self is unable to create a "chain" of thought. Schiller's description suggests that in this stage man is exhausted by "imperious" sensuous needs (Letter 24: 2).

Arguing that, "Man only plays when he is in the fullest sense of the word a human being," Schiller asserts that beauty is the only path to freedom (Letter 2: 5; 15: 9). But not only is the aesthetic necessary for making connections between self and other; the aesthetic-drive creates the ability to make any connections at all because the aesthetic-drive guides "Stofftrieb" to the ideal forms and leads "Formtrieb" to the terra firma of sensuous matter (Schiller, Letter 18: 1). Thus, the play-drive causes the rational-drive and the sense-drive to merge, thus reducing the passions that are so central to the sense drive while simultaneously "depriv[ing] reason" of its "moral compulsion" (Schiller, Letter 14: 5, 6).

The play-drive also has a triple manifestation: on the primal level, it seeks gratification of minimal material needs; its secondary manifestation is experienced as desire for material excess, while its highest manifestation is a desire for "aesthetic superfluity" (Wilkinson Commentary 291). Schiller distinguishes between "aesthetic semblance" and "logical semblance," the former equivalent to play that recognizes its separation from reality, the latter identical with deception because it substitutes itself for the truth (Schiller, Letter 24: 5). Deriding the fields of philosophy, science, and religion because they only offer logical semblances, the German thinker avers that the very "essence" of the aesthetic drive is "semblance" that always admits its disinterested reconstructions of nature (Schiller, Letter 26: 5).

As Wilkinson and Willoughby suggest, for Schiller the aesthetic is equal to all other fields, for it dominates them because it "inform[s] all other modes, whether of perception, knowledge, or communication, with a new quality without altering their essential character" (Schiller, Introduction 1). What is more, the play-drive has more power than any of the other drives to encourage human beings to create the highest moral and aesthetic quality of life (Schiller,

Introduction xxii). Schiller uses the trope of erotic love to depict how play leads to the most moral (''Formtrieb'') and least constrained (''Stofftrieb'') relationships. Arguing that lust can be stolen, but ''love must come as a gift,'' this Romantic philosopher claims that the male can never win the heart of his beloved by enforcing the desire of his senses upon the female—he can only attain her love through a habit of mind that rationally acknowledges her own sensuous and rational desires. In other words, the lover must ''be willing to concede freedom, because it is freedom he wishes to please'' (Schiller, Letter 27: 7). Schiller's representation of how the aesthetic drive makes love possible gives new meaning to the notion of fore-''play,'' for Schiller aligns this mutual realization of freedom with the highest form of ''taste'' in the aesthetic sense. As Wilkinson and Willoughby suggest, in Schiller's trope ''love is defined as the ability to 'play' with its two concomitants, attraction and esteem,'' ensuring that the senses inform and are informed by the rational drive (Schiller, Introduction xi).

In a long letter to Lady Welby, Charles Sanders Peirce writes, ''As to the word 'play,' the first book of philosophy I ever read . . . was Schiller's *Aesthetische Briefe* where he has so much to say about the Spiel-Trieb; and it made so much impression upon me as to have thoroughly soaked my notion of 'play,' to this day'' (23 Dec. 1908; qtd. in Wiener 401). After reading Schiller, Peirce realized that esthetics and logic should not be seen as separate fields of knowledge, but that ''logic needs the help of esthetics'' (197, 200; qtd. in Sebeok 1). Building his concepts of ''Pure Play'' and the ''Play of Musement'' upon Schiller's theory of the aesthetic drive, Peirce argues that play incorporates ''no purpose save that of casting aside all serious purpose'' (6: 458). As Peirce famously concludes, play takes ''the form of aesthetic contemplation, or that of distant castle-building (whether in Spain or within one's own moral training), or that of considering some wonder in one of the Universes, or some connection between two of the three, with speculation concerning its cause'' (6: 458). Peirce suggests only ''five to six per cent of one's waking time'' need be devoted to play to obtain its highest benefits (6: 458–59). In his elegant trope for the liminal process through which play works, Peirce writes, '' 'Enter your skiff of Musement, push off into the lake of thought, and leave the breath of heaven to swell your sail. With your eyes open, awake to what is about or within you, and open conversation with yourself; for such is all meditation' '' (6: 460–61). Like Schiller, Peirce also sees play as harmonizing disparate entities, including ideas, the real, and signs (6: 455; Sebeok 35).

I would suggest that Dickens's heroine Little Dorrit enacts complex aesthetic forms of play that allow her a highly ethical compassion and dignity in the face of unrequited love, family dysfunction, and societal breakdown. In book 1 chapter 24, Little Dorrit, imprisoned by the inability to speak her love to Arthur, creates a story for Maggy about a Princess and a tiny woman. At the end of the tale, Amy looks "musingly down into the dark valley of the prison" without experiencing complete despair, a transcendent moment in the text (1.24: 289). But, before examining Amy's narrative, we should remember John Baptist's use of the word "ALTRO," for it seems to be one way that Dickens limns the free play of the mind and acts as a prelude to all other such manifestations. At the start of the novel, Rigaud asks Baptist, "You knew from the first moment when you saw me here, that I was a gentleman?" The narrator then describes Baptist's one-word response, "AL-TRO," in this manner: "The word being, according to its Genoese emphasis, a confirmation, a contradiction, an assertion, a denial, a taunt, a compliment, a joke, and fifty other things, became in the present instance, with a significance beyond all power of written expression, our familiar English 'I believe you!' " (1.1: 23) Prior to this conversation, the two jailed men have been served vastly different meals, Rigaud's, a feast and Baptist's, a slice of bread. But Baptist's powerful imagination turns the ration of bread into a veritable banquet, while Rigaud's banquet seems unsatisfying. As Baptist explains to the astonished Rigaud, " 'I can cut my bread so—like a melon. Or so—like an omelette. Or so—like a fried fish. Or so—like a Lyons sausage' " (1.1:22).

Like Baptist, Amy creates her own secular miracles through play. Indeed, she rather boldly claims, " 'I could never have been of any use, if I had not pretended a little' " (1.14:170). For example, in the chapter "Little Dorrit's Party," there is no such thing as a party going on. Walking to Arthur Clennam's abode, she travels through the most squalid parts of London and sees the most downtrodden citizens of the British capital. Yet, though she acknowledges the stark reality, she does the same thing Baptist does with his mere slice of bread, fancying, for just five to six percent of her waking life, if you will, that going to Arthur's house is a "party" where Arthur dances with her after which she will go home to a residence that is "light and warm and beautiful" (1.1: 175). Thus she seems to meld her own sensual desires ("Stoftrieb") and longing for a universal ethical meaning ("Formtrieb"), actually causing love to happen at the same moment that she frees herself from the confines of prison and is hoping to free Arthur from his own constraining "Formtrieb." Approaching Arthur's door at midnight when he has arrived at the end of a long contemplative self-interrogation, he asks himself, "What have I found!" In a gentle epiphany, and without missing a beat, Amy's words "came as if they were an answer: 'Little Dorrit' " (1.13: 167). The passive and sober hero has not yet found a way to achieve freedom and form via the uses of play, but in the aesthetic mode, Amy does not, in Schiller's terms, seek to steal his lust. Rather, she waits to extend her love to him as a gift—when he is ready to find, through play, a way to achieve the highest and most liberated of loves.

I suggest that Little Dorrit's Princess story represents one of the greatest achievements of the Play of Musement in the novel. In a moment of deep distress, Amy, through the aesthetic-drive, is able to fulfill the practical and the sensuous, the rational and the moral, the personal and communal, the contingent and the constrained, through "musingly" conceiving and telling a story. In the tale there is a king who has "everything he could wish for," including "gold and silver, diamonds and rubies," and "riches of every kind" (1.24: 286). The king's daughter also has everything: in terms of "Stofftrieb," she is "the wisest and most beautiful Princess that ever was seen," while as to "Formtriebe," she comprehends her school lessons before "her master taught them to her" (1.24: 286). In contrast, in the same kingdom there lives a "poor little tiny woman, who lived all alone by herself" (1.24: 286). The Princess must pass the tiny woman's cottage everyday, and when she passes, she sees the tiny woman at her spinning wheel, "and she looked at the tiny woman, and the tiny woman looked at her" (1.24: 288). Maggy interjects at this point that the two are " 'Like trying to stare one another out' " (1.24: 288). Finally, the Princess decides to stop and visit the woman. One of the Princess's many qualities is that she "has the power of knowing secrets," and, thus, without any preliminaries, she uncannily asks the tiny woman, "Why do you keep it there?" Stunned by the Princess's mind-reading powers, the tiny woman kneels before her and asks her never to tell her secret. The Princess promises and then asks to see "it" (1.24: 288). What the tiny woman shows her in "a very secret place" is a "shadow" that is the remnant "of Some one who had gone by long before" and who had "gone on far away quite out of reach, never, never to come back." The shadow is "bright to look at" and the tiny woman is "proud of it with all her heart, as a great, great treasure" (1.24: 288). Again clairvoyantly, the Princess asks, "And you keep watch over this every day?" (1.24: 288) The tiny woman responds affirmatively and the Princess says, "Remind me why." Her diminutive alter ego replies that, "no one so good and kind had ever passed that way," and that was why she kept the shadow (1.24: 286).

The narrator, Little Dorrit, notes that no one "was the worse for" her keeping the shadow of the beloved, for he "Had gone on to those who were expecting them" (1.24: 288). At this point Maggy remarks that "Some one was a man," which Amy simply affirms. The Princess comments that when the little woman dies the shadow would then be discovered, and the tiny woman completes the thought, saying, "it would sink quietly into her own grave, and would never be found" (1.24: 288). The Princess decides to make a closer study of the tiny woman, thus passing by the cottage every day to stare at her and be stared at in return until one day the Princess notices that the tiny woman's spinning wheel has stopped and the tiny woman has died (1.24: 289). The Princess searches for the hidden shadow but finds that it is nowhere to be found, and thus she knows "that the tiny woman had told her the truth, and that it would never give anybody any trouble, and that it had sunk quietly into her own grave, and that she and it were at rest together" (1.24: 289). Amy ends the story plainly, murmuring, "That's all" (1.24: 289). Maggy asks her "Little Mother" if the tiny woman was old, and Little Dorrit replies, "I don't know. . . . But it would have been just the same if she had been ever so old' " (1.24: 289). Both are silent as they look through the prison window. At this point, Pancks, otherwise known to Amy as the "fortune-teller," comes through the prison gates, and Maggy inquires if he could tell the Princess's fortune. Little Dorrit, "looking musingly down into the dark valley of the prison, shook her head" and calmly explains that neither could he tell the tiny woman's fortune (1.24: 289).

Muted in its emotional sentiment, this story is difficult to decipher except that we know that it is a projection of Amy's unexpressed love for Arthur. In light of the work of Schiller and Peirce, I argue that Amy's aesthetic musings allow her sensual desires ("Stofftrieb") to find structure ("Formtrieb") in a fairytale that seems to come out of the generalized wisdom of the folk. This aesthetic form permits Little Dorrit to express her repressed passion and need for stark rationality without compromising her selfhood and integrity. The Princess story also literally has elements of "castle-building," which Peirce refers to as one of the modes of the Play of Musement. Since Amy's indulgence in musement is moderate, unlike her father's later outlandish building of castles in the air (2.18), she is able to achieve a balance between unconstrained erotic desire and conformity to rational restraint of her sensuality. Through the aesthetic creation of the Princess story, she does not humiliate herself as her father does when he builds castles in the air about marrying Mrs. General, nor does she lose the experience of feeling sensual desire for Arthur. Through narrative play, this subdued and ardent heroine can keep the "treasured shadow" without selfishly imposing her will upon the beloved while simultaneously expanding her love for him (1.24: 289). In fact, her self-discipline and freedom are never more intense than when she is telling the story of the Princess and the tiny woman. Further, it is a triumphant moral moment for Little Dorrit because she seeks freedom for the man she adores even if it means freeing him from loving her. Indeed, Amy's love for Arthur could easily act as a trope in Schiller's argument that "Spieltrieb" increases the lover's care for the beloved's sensual, rational, and aesthetic needs.

Peirce suggests that the Play of Musement "begins passively" but then "impression soon passes into attentive observation, observation into musing, musing into a lively give and take of communion between self and self" (6: 458–59). This insight is helpful for understanding the psychic trajectories of Amy's spare but complex tale. For one thing, the Princess and the tiny woman might represent a conversation going on between Amy's inner selves. That it is a dialogue between self and self is indicated by the fact that the Princess knows what the tiny woman is thinking before she speaks. For example, upon first meeting the tiny woman, the Princess knows her alter ego has a secret, and she asks the tiny woman to "Remind me why," suggesting that the answers are already part of her unconscious. Further, it might be said that the dialogue between self and self contains all three levels of Schiller's forms of play, that of instinctual desire, desire for material superfluity, and the drive for aesthetic superfluity. Thus, through the Princess, the financially distressed Little Dorrit, who often goes hungry in order to feed her father, fulfills a primal and extravagant desire to have "riches of every kind." Maggy joins that conversation to provide the surplus that not only meets instinctual hunger but supplies material superfluity, adding to Amy's general explanation of "plenty of everything" the specific example of "Hospitals with lots of Chicking" (1.24: 286). The tiny woman's expansive desire to hold onto her unrequited love is also allowed because it meets the aesthetic and moral requirement that the beloved retain his freedom. In addition, the higher level of aesthetic play is fulfilled not only through the literary form of the fairy tale that is linked to universal forms of the folk. The story obtains its organically pleasing form by merging three levels of play along with the resolution of the sensual and the rational. Before Amy begins the tale, she herself has been crying like the tiny woman because she believes she will never receive a surfeit of love from Arthur—a love that never lacks but that is always in the mode of superfluity. Maggy forces her friend to admit that she has been crying but somehow instinctively knows not to interrogate her about Arthur explicitly. Instead, Maggy asks for a story, exclaiming, " 'Now, Little Mother, let's have a good'un!' " Intuitively, Maggy wants a tale that is "Beyond all belief" but that also fulfills Amy's psychic, emotional, and moral needs in this time of crisis. The only mode that accomplishes and contains all those needs, as Schiller and Dickens realize, is that of aesthetic play, in this case in the form of a fairy tale.

The formal features of the narrative are a tribute to Dickens's ability to merge the need for emotional restraint and passionate expression. The story of the Princess and the tiny woman is, in fact, a "good'un!" (1.24: 286). Of course, Dickens was no enemy of the proverbial purple passage, as witness the sappy renditions of sentiment regarding Little Nell's demise, Bella Wilfer's accession to the role of Angel in the House, and Esther's resurrected good looks. The Inimitable's unrestrained apotheosis of so many of his heroines does not bode well for his characterization of Amy. But perhaps because he consciously depicts her as a character who has to "pretend a little," and because we actually see her do so a number of times in the novel, she is a more compelling aesthetic subject than, say, Sissy of *Hard Times*, who is also supposed to represent the healing powers of fancy or play. In his depiction of this scene, Dickens's own aesthetic sensibilities require that he leave the situation in fluid play, sparingly describing Amy's emotional excess and her desire to be true to her own ethics—to say nothing of her sanity—through musement. Amy's forbidding logic of despair is interspersed with Maggy's hilarious intuitions of material and psychic need, and neither Amy nor Dickens feels required to come to a rigid conclusion to the tale. Because of Dickens's aesthetic control, the reader, like Amy, gradually moves through the Princess's story from the mode of passive "impression" to "attentive observation," that leads to "musing," and finally the "communion between self and self" (see Peirce 6: 458–59). Beginning in emotional collapse, Amy ends the story "musingly," with "the sunset bright upon her" though she is "looking into the dark valley of the prison" (1.24: 289).[2] Because musement is necessarily open-ended, the conclusion of the fairy tale intimates that Amy's potential is not confined—there is a halo of sunlight surrounding her despite oncoming darkness.

In order to understand the importance of Amy's uses of play, Dickens puts forward Mrs. General as the epitome of living by an effete credo; as Amy's foil, she illustrates "how not to do it," if you will. But for Dickens she is a dangerous as well as comic figure because Mr. Dorrit would have her sense of discipline negate and ultimately erase Amy's play, ethics, and eroticism as Mrs. General attempts to turn Amy into a literal abstraction. Referring to Platonic abstractions or forms as the "generals," Peirce writes, "Nomenclature involves classification; and classification is true or false, and the generals to which it refers are either reals in the one case, or figments in the other" (Mayorga 257; Peirce 5: 454). In terms of the aesthetic theories of Peirce and Schiller, Mrs. General illustrates Schiller's "Formtrieb" gone amok and Peirce's generals gone AWOL. Certainly, to call Mrs. General an idealist of the Platonic kind would be ludicrous, except that Dickens intuits in her characterization the fraudulence and excesses of absolute adherence to either a thoroughgoing idealist or materialist stance. Conforming to social rather than ideal forms since social convention in the Victorian period has replaced the former with the latter, Mrs. General holds to the "generals" that are what Peirce calls unreal "figments." Thus, she also represents Schiller's notion of deception—in other words, his belief that "logical semblance" is equivalent to deception because it substitutes itself for the truth (Schiller, Letter 26: 5).

Mrs. General is, in fact, all semblance, and the deceptions and figments of her general language illustrate Schiller's key idea that "Formtrieb" by itself will lead to reification if it and the sense-drive are not harmonized by the aesthetic-drive. To speak of Mrs. General's sense-drive is to speak of something long since buried, for, believing that "A truly refined mind will seem to be ignorant of the existence of anything that is not perfectly proper, placid, and pleasant," she maintains that "Passion was to go to sleep" in her "presence" (2.5: 459; 2.2: 435). Furthermore, with eyes that have "nothing to express," Mrs. General is described as "emotionless" and without dreams (2.5: 456, 435). The narrative also makes us realize that though she seems committed to the sensuous because she is "A model of accurate dressing," nevertheless, she would not be able to feel the sensual pleasure of wearing beautiful clothing because she is at once a "Ghoule in gloves" and a "piece of machinery" (2.15: 586; 2.1: 422). As to the form drive, her idea of " 'form[ing] the mind' " was to make her charges see that "all persons of polite cultivation should see with other people's eyes, and never with their own" (2.2: 435, 433). Her credo is that "Nobody said what anything was, but everybody said what the Mrs. Generals, Mr. Eustace, or somebody else said it was" (2.7: 492). Having no sense of the aesthetic, Mrs. General, though she is perfectly mannerly, reveals a lack of taste constantly illustrated by her inability to love, her rigid constraint of human interaction, and her ghoulish intrusion upon any exhibition of authentic personhood.

Thus, though Mrs. General teaches "taste" in terms of cultural conventions, there is not an aesthetic bone in her formidable body. At one point, the narrator of *Little Dorrit* explicitly refers to her aesthetic deficiencies, observing that "she felt it necessary that the human imagination should be chilled into stone" (2.15: 584). To this lady general, a great city with respected art and culture is to be seen not for its intrinsic aesthetic value but because, " 'As a place much spoken of, it is necessary to see it' " (2.1: 422). Likewise, the chapter solely devoted to Mrs. General describes this glorified governess as a person who "drove the proprieties four-in-hand" with superb "decorum"—and Dickens certainly implies that this is not a declamation of decorum in the classical aesthetic sense (2.2: 432). Hence, descriptions of Mrs. General herself speak to her surface rather than any depth, aesthetic—in Schiller's terms—or otherwise. As Rodney Stenning Edgecombe suggests, "Mrs. General . . . is a sculptress who turns women into lifeless simulacra" (279). A "varnish[er]" who participates in "the formation of a surface," she has no substance to her (2.5: 464; 2.7: 492). In short, "having long ago formed her own surface to such perfection that it hid whatever was below (if anything)," she may be regarded as an idealist without an idea, a maintainer of forms who has no interest in Form (2.7: 486). And that is why Mr. Dorrit's greatest crime against his favorite daughter, Amy, is, perhaps, that he is so enamored of societal forms as to demand that she be varnished by Mrs. General, who seeks to transmogrify Little Dorrit's exquisite and temperate aesthetic need to pretend into obsessive laquered pretense.

Mr. Dorrit also desires that Amy learn Mrs. General's general language. Here again, Mrs. General's speech ("prunes and prisms") is the polar opposite of Baptist's "Altro" and Amy's Play of Musement. Like a demented deconstructionist unchained from meaning, Mrs. General is only interested in the surface of language (the signifier) and its appearance upon mouths. Requiring Amy to participate in the patter of " 'Papa, potatoes, poultry, prunes and prisms' " may make perfect alliterative sense, but when Mr. Dorrit tells Amy to " 'attend to' " these " 'precepts of Mrs. General' " the stark difference between Little Dorrit's musement and Mrs. General's general language could not be more telling or more comic (2.5: 58).

As Edgecombe observes, "the unreality of her world view," can be seen in her regular "erasures and skirtings" of language itself (283). Vereen Bell maintains that Mrs. General personifies Dickens's satiric skewering of "the mid-century, middle-class ethos," an intellectually effete general language even if it was brutally effective socially (178, 179). As the narrative famously intones, "Mrs. General had no opinions. Her way of forming a mind was to prevent it from forming opinions. She had a little circular set of mental grooves or rails on which she started little trains of other people's opinions, which never overtook one another, and never got anywhere" (2.2: 435). Having formed her own mind to have "no opinions," she "lock[s] up" all political, social, and ethical controversies by saying "they had no existence" (2.2: 435).

Mikhail Bakhtin is relevant to a discussion of Mrs. General, and it is particularly surprising that there has been no analysis of her name and her language using Bakhtin's concept of "general language." In his own analysis of the novel, Bakhtin chooses to focus on the rhetoric of the Barnacles. Jonathan Yovel describes Bakhtin's concept of "General language" as that form of communication that creates myths or narratives that give ideological meaning to a culture and which are often expressed through code words, such as the "Alamo," "Pearl-Harbor," and "September 11" (Yovel 15–16). If this general language "solidif[ies] collective identity," it also, as Bakhtin asserts, "gives expression to forces working toward . . . sociopolitical and cultural centralization" (Yovel 15–16, 21–22; Bakhtin 271). Unitary or general language ostensibly represents the unified value system of the culture in the same way that the generic Everyman was supposed to represent all people. Thus, general language stands in complete contrast to heteroglossia ("Altro"), Bakhtin's term for writing that includes multiple voices and plural ideological stances. Mr. Dorrit's wholesale submission to what Bakhtin refers to as general language is illustrated by his fawning manner to Mrs. General. As Bell remarks, Mr. Dorrit's "pursuit of Mrs. General has a sort of abstract, Gatsbyean rightness about it, for in wedding her he would be uniting himself with the epitome of all that is correct and admirable in Society" (183). But on Mr. Dorrit's deathbed the irony is that he no longer recognizes Mrs. General's surface, even though just hours before he had intended to ask her to marry him. His mind erased of general language, Mr. Dorrit "had not the faintest knowledge of her" (2.19: 622). It might be said that Mr. Dorrit's stuttering exhibits, in part, that he is an immigrant rather than a native speaker of his culture's general language and that had he wedded Mrs. General his knowledge of her and of general language would have been perfected in a varnishing sort of way.

It is only when Arthur finally turns from the general language that tells him that at his age (he is around forty) it is inappropriate to expect a fairy tale romance that he is able to experience the aesthetic drive. In the depths of crisis, when he is confined as a debtor in the same prison cell that housed Little Dorrit, he experiences the play-drive. Like Little Dorrit, who had created the Princess story in her hour of personal despair, he realizes that

> Looking back upon his own poor *story*, she was its *vanishing point*. Every thing in its perspective led to her innocent figure. He had traveled thousands of miles towards it; previous unquiet hopes and doubts had worked themselves out before it; it was the centre of the interest of his life; it was the termination of everything that was good and pleasant in it; beyond, there was nothing but mere waste and darkened sky." (2.27: 702; emphasis added)

Here, Arthur constructs his life as a "story" with Little Dorrit as the "centre of interest" and as a painting with Amy as its "vanishing point." Through "Spieltrieb" harmonizing his erotic desire ("Stofftrieb") and his desire for overarching meaning ("Formtrieb"), Arthur is now able to make sense of his life as a set of phenomena and of events that are connected to each other and form an organic and teleological whole.

Little Dorrit is brilliant in her refusal to force her love onto Clennam at this crucial moment when his love for her is just coalescing. She leaves a small symbol of her love, a "nosegay" of flowers, in his room in the prison and when he awakes, alone, the first thing his body notices is the scent of the flowers. "Dozing and dreaming," he "lift[s] his head for the purpose of inquiring into" the scent (2.29: 722). At this point, Peirce's notion that musement "begins passively" but then "impression soon passes into attentive observation, observation into musing, musing into a lively give and take of communion between self and self" is helpful (6:458–59). Arthur is passive and prone when he first smells Little's Dorrit's gift of flowers; then he begins to "inquire" into where the scent comes from. Next he "took them up and inhaled their fragrance, and he lifted them to his hot head, and he put them down and opened his parched hands to them, as cold hands are opened to receive the cheering of a fire" (2.29: 722). Fully turning himself over to them sensually, intellectually, and aesthetically, he finally wonders who had given them to him—and ultimately who had created or authored this moment. At this point, Little Dorrit quietly appears—when he has at last become attuned to her love. Indeed, rather mystically, just as she appears "One of the night-tunes was playing in the wind" (2.29: 723). Because he now sees her, through the aesthetic-drive, as the heroine of his story, Clennam also realizes what was true all along—that she was not a child in emotion or intellect. Rather, "She looked something more womanly than when she had gone away" (2.29: 724). And in this case, "She looked" refers both to Amy's playful powers of seeing as well as to her appearance.

Little Dorrit is perhaps one of Dickens's least insipid heroines. She has a quiet strength and authoritative intellect despite the author's demand that she be the self-sacrificing Angel in the House. I suggest that she is able to express her passionate desire and maintain her ethical integrity because Dickens has characterized her as capable of profound and temperate musement or aesthetic play. Schiller had previously explored this philosophical concept in extraordinary depth early in the nineteenth century in *On the Aesthetic Education of Man*, and Peirce carried it forward at the end of the century, while Dickens explores the dynamics of play at midcentury through fiction, perhaps the richest generic form for extrapolating such fluid and complex intellectual ideas. The brilliance of this rendition in *Little Dorrit* is compounded by Dickens's graphic representation of the "generals" in the character of the rigid disciplinarian Mrs. General, who stands in binary opposition to Little Dorrit, a character who, in the darkest and most confined of spaces, knows how to "pretend a little." Thus, at the end of the narrative, Amy herself becomes what Schiller described as an "aesthetic semblance." In other words, she goes down in its history as a triple-decker novel when the clerk at the church exclaims of her, " 'Her birth is what I call the first volume; she lay asleep, on this floor, with her pretty head on what I call the second volume; and she's now a-writing her little name as a bride in what I call the third volume' " (2.34: 785). That she will continue "a-writing" her story in the chaotic "roaring streets" of London is Dickens's final image of hope—and play—in *Little Dorrit* (2.34: 787).

NOTES

This essay could not have been written without the intensive discussions of Dickens's writing that occurred in a graduate seminar on Dickens in spring 2008 at the University of New Mexico. I also must thank my student Stacey Kikendall for her generous help.

1. Schiller's work on play is seen by Elias as a response to Kant's *Critique of Judgment* and to Rousseau's educational theories (Elias I: 105).
2. Peirce suggests that the best times for the Play of Musement to occur are at "dawn and the gloaming" (6: 458–59).

WORKS CITED

Bakhtin, Mikhail. "Discourse in the Novel." *The Dialogic Imagination: Four Essays.* Ed. Michael Holquist. Trans. Caryl Emerson. Austin: U of Texas P, 1981. 259–422.

Bell, Vereen M. "Mrs. General as Victorian England: Dickens's Image of His Time." *Nineteenth-Century Fiction* 20 (1965): 177–84.

Brent, Joseph. *Charles Sanders Peirce: A Life.* Bloomington: Indiana UP, 1993.

Cantens, Bernardo. "Overcoming the Evidentialist's Challenge: Peirce's Conjectures of Instinctive Reason and the Reality of God." *Transactions of the Charles S. Peirce Society* 40.4 (Fall 2004): 771–86.

Carlisle, Janice. "*Little Dorrit*: Necessary Fictions." *Studies in the Novel* 7.2 (Summer 1975): 195–214.

Carlyle, Thomas. *The Life of Friedrich Schiller, Comprehending an Examination of His Works.* 1825; New York: AMS, 1969.

Dickens, Charles. *The Letters of Charles Dickens.* Vol. 6: 1850–1852. The Pilgrim Edition. Ed. Graham Storey, Kathleen Tillotson, and Nina Burgis. Oxford: Clarendon, 1988.

———. *The Letters of Charles Dickens.* Vol. 7: 1853–1855. The Pilgrim Edition. Ed. Graham Storey, Kathleen Tillotson, and Angus Easson. Oxford: Clarendon, 1993.

———. *Little Dorrit.* Ed. Steven Wall and Helen Small. London: Penguin, 1998.

Edgecombe, Rodney Stenning. "Middle-Class Erasures: The Decreations of Mrs. General and Mr. Podsnap." *Studies in the Novel* 31.3 (Fall 1999): 279–95.

Elias, Julius A. *The Dictionary of the History of Ideas.* Electronic Text Center. U of Virginia Library. The Gale Group, 2003. http://etext.virginia.edu/cgi-local/DHI/dhi.cgi?id=dv1–17

Higbie, Robert. *Dickens and the Imagination.* Gainesville: UP of Florida, 1998.

Mayorga, Rosa. "Diamonds are a Pragmatist's Best Friend." *Transactions of the Charles S. Peirce Society* 41.2 (Spring 2005): 255–70.

Metz, Nancy Aycock. "The Blighted Tree and the Book of Fate: Female Models of Storytelling in *Little Dorrit.*" *Dickens Studies Annual* 18 (1989): 221–41.

Newsom, Robert. "Style of Dickens." *The Oxford Reader's Companion to Dickens.* Ed. Paul Schlicke. Oxford: Oxford UP, 1994. 540–45.

Peirce, Charles Sanders. *Collected Papers of Charles Sanders Peirce.* Vols. 1–6. Ed. C. Hartshone and P. Weiss. Vols. 7–8. Ed. A. Burks. Cambridge, MA: Harvard UP, 1931–1968.

Ridenhour, Jamieson. " 'In that Boney Light': The Bakhtinian Gothic of *Our Mutual Friend.*" *Dickens Quarterly* 22.3 (September 2005): 153–72.

Sadoff, Dianne F. "Storytelling and the Figure of the Father in *Little Dorrit.*" *PMLA* 95.2 (March 1980): 234–45.

Schiller, Friedrich. *On the Aesthetic Education of Man.* Ed. and Trans. Elizabeth M. Wilkinson and L. A. Willoughby. Oxford: Clarendon, 1967.

Sebeok, Thomas A. *The Play of Musement.* Bloomington: Indiana UP, 1981.

Smith, Grahame. "Dickens and Critical Theory." March 1998. "Charles Dickens and His Work" Conference. Middle East Technical University, Istanbul, Turkey. Victorian Web. Laurence Raw, British Studies Manager, The British Council, Turkey. http://www.victorianweb.org/authors/dickens/turkey/turlit09.html

Wiener, Philip P. *Values in a Universe of Chance: Selected Writings of Charles S. Peirce.* Stanford: Stanford UP, 1958.

Yovel, Jonathan. "Running Backs, Wolves, and other Fatalities: How Manipulations of Narrative Coherence in Legal Opinions Marginalize Violent Death." *Cardozo Studies in Law and Literature* 16:1 (Spring 2004): 127–59.

"Let me see if Philip can/ Be a little gentleman": Parenting and Class in *Struwwelpeter* and *Great Expectations*

Sarah Gates

This article suggests that "The Story of Fidgety Philip" in Heinrich Hoffmann's best-selling children's book Struwwelpeter *(1845) should be considered one of the sources fueling Herbert Pocket's objection to the name "Philip." Its opening lines, "Let me see if Philip can/Be a little gentleman," voice the novel's central obsession and thus invite us to consider* Struwwelpeter *as a significant intertext in* Great Expectations. Struwwelpeter *is an ambivalent text, for its desired result of civilizing children seems hollowed out by the negative portrait of parenting that emerges in it. Tracing the instabilities created by this ambivalence in* Struwwelpeter *reveals a corresponding ambivalence and perplexity in the novel's treatment of its fundamental themes (becoming a gentleman, raising children, raising gentlemen)—issues Dickens faced himself as the son of disappointing parents and the father of disappointing children.*

In *Great Expectations*, when young Pip sits down to his first dinner with Herbert Pocket, he asks Herbert to help him attain the gentlemanly polish his "expectations" demand of him: "I further mentioned that as I had been brought up a blacksmith in a country place, and knew very little of the ways of politeness, I would take it as a great kindness in him if he would give me a hint whenever he saw me at a loss or going wrong" (178; ch. 22), a task

---

Herbert fulfills with graceful humor as they dine.[1] The preliminary gesture of friendship that allows this intimacy is an agreement between the two of them to use their Christian names, a gesture that yields Herbert's first correction—his renaming of Pip:

> "I don't take to Philip," said he, smiling, "for it sounds like a moral boy out of the spelling-book, who was so lazy that he fell into a pond, or so fat that he couldn't see out of his eyes, or so avaricious that he locked up his cake till the mice ate it, or so determined to go a birds'-nesting that he got himself eaten by bears who lived handy in the neighborhood."   (178)

Editions of the novel with explanatory notes all point to the same source for Herbert's "moral boy out of the spelling-book," William F. Mavor's *The English Spelling Book Accompanied by a Progressive Series of Easy and Familiar Lessons* (1801). Edgar Rosenberg, editor of the Norton Critical Edition (1999) supplies the most detail on Mavor, "a prolific author of tourist guides, creator of a 'Universal Stenography,' and compiler of educational manuals," and on *The English Spelling Book* itself, "which combined improving stories for the young with spelling exercises of graduated length" and "had allegedly reached its thirty-second edition within twenty-five years—at about the time Herbert raised his objection" (140n1). Margaret Caldwell, editor of the Oxford World Classics edition (1994), supplies in her note these details from the tales themselves: "Among Mavor's stories are one of a fat boy who ate all day and could scarcely see out of his eyes, one of a girl whose secretly hidden cake was eaten by a mouse, and one of a boy who went birds'-nesting. His fate was less drastic: all his young birds died" (496n).

In terms of the spelling-book *cum* cautionary tale genre and in the general outlines of some of Herbert's examples, then, Mavor looks like the source. It also works well for the novel's interior chronology. It was a book that Dickens likely encountered himself as a child and therefore provides another detail that helps establish the events of the novel as a "past" distinct from the clearly "present" time of its narration.[2] However, the fit is still not perfect. As Rosenberg goes on to point out in the Norton footnote (and as Caldwell suggests in hers), "Mavor's cautionary tales end less catastrophically than Herbert's borrowed (but nearly identical) instances; nor have I come across any Philips among Mavor's juvenile delinquents" (140n1). I would add to these differences the point that however tedious or insipid Mavor's moralizing tales might have seemed to Herbert (and behind him, the young Dickens), they would hardly cause an emotional recoil strong enough to render Herbert unwilling to call his new best friend by his own name and to feel the necessity of renaming him "Handel" in order to seal or clinch a hoped for "harmoniousness" in their future relations (179; ch. 22).

I would like to suggest that Herbert alludes to a richer mix of sources than these footnotes have allowed. While the earlier best-selling Mavor provides a generic and chronological surface for the allusion, a more contemporary best-selling children's book of cautionary tales, Dr. Heinrich Hoffmann's *Struwwelpeter* (1845), first translated in England as *The English Stuwwelpeter* in 1848 and again as *Struwwelpeter* in 1855 (just as the younger Dickens children would be learning to read), supplies the kind of "catastrophic endings" that Mavor's stories lack.[3] The title *Struwwelpeter*, known in the U.S. as "Slovenly Peter" and in Great Britain as "Shock-headed Peter," refers to the appalling figure of the boy pictured on the cover of the book, who has refused to let his hair or fingernails be cut and who thus represents the impulsive and recalcitrant misbehavior the stories were supposed to warn its young readers against. In *Struwwelpeter* we find, for example, "The Story of Johnny Head-in-Air," who falls into the river and nearly drowns (like Herbert's boy who falls into a pond) while the fish "enjoy the fun and laughter" (25). We also find an exact inversion of Herbert's fat boy who can't see out of his eyes in "Augustus Who Would Not Have Any Soup." Augustus dies of starvation, having dwindled to a stick figure in the illustrations, the last one of which pictures a grave topped by a large tureen of the objectionable soup (19). On the page facing the dwindling Augustus, moreover, and thus in plain view while both stories would be read, sits the most famously horrifying illustration of the book: the graphic illustration of the tailor cutting off the thumb of Conrad, the "Little Suck-a-Thumb," gouts of blood and all (see fig.1). Looking with a Freudian eye, we might conclude that a psychological censoring of this picture of a "castration" might have induced Dickens's inversion and displacement of it, in Herbert's remarks, onto a boy who "can't see out of his eyes," a boy who dwindles into a boy who swells, a boy who refuses food into a boy who eats all day.

However, it is specifically the name "Philip" that triggers Herbert's recoil. While there are no Philips in Mavor (according to Edgar Rosenberg), there is certainly one in *Struwwelpeter*. "The Story of Fidgety Philip" specifically takes place at dinner, its lesson all about gentlemanly table manners. It begins:

> Let me see if Philip can
> Be a little gentleman;
> Let me see if he is able
> To sit still for once at table.   (20)

Of course, Fidgety Philip cannot "sit still for once at table." He tips his chair so far back that he falls, pulling the table cloth, dinner, and crockery onto himself in the process. Pip has no such catastrophe during his dinner with Herbert, but he is plenty "fidgety" nonetheless. Herbert gives him several

Fig. 1. Left: from "Die Geschichte vom Daumenlutscher" [The Story of Little Suck-a-Thumb]; right: from "Die Geschichte vom Suppen-Kaspar" ["The Story of Augustus Who Would Not Eat His Soup"]. *Der Struwwelpeter: oder lustige Geschichten und drollige Bilder* [*Struwwelpeter: or Merry Stories and Funny Pictures*].

"hints" as he "goes wrong" in the course of their dinner, hints which give readers a clear picture of Pip's untaught condition. He eats with his knife, tips his wineglass upside down on his nose to get the last drop, holds his fork overhand (thereby displaying "the attitude of opening oysters, on the part of the right elbow"), and tries to stuff his napkin into his water tumbler—all things Herbert corrects with the lightest possible touch, so that they "both laugh" and Pip "scarcely blushe[s]" (179; ch. 22).

The humor and especially the desire not to cause pain or embarrassment that Herbert demonstrates in this scene present a model of the gentlemanly politeness Pip hopes so anxiously to learn. Moreover, the gentlemanly lessons imparted as the scene proceeds are redoubled in the story of Compeyson's gentlemanly pretensions that Herbert narrates as they dine, the whole episode thus underscoring the central question of *Great Expectations* itself, a question voiced in those opening lines of "Fidgety Philip": "Let me see if Philip can/ Be a little gentleman." This direct hit on the novel's central nerve, as it were, invites us to consider *Struwwelpeter* as a minor but possibly significant intertext in *Great Expectations*. Both are ambivalent texts in that the desired result in each—of becoming a gentleman, of civilizing children—seems hollowed out or undermined by the portrait of parenting that emerges in them.

It might be useful, then, to take a closer look at *Struwwelpeter* and the ways it claims to "civilize" its young readers.

This infamous children's classic evoked and continues to evoke powerful responses since its original appearance in Frankfurt in 1845. Despite its enormous popularity, many critics in the period found it too radically subversive. Elisabeth Wesseling notes that "critics particularly found fault with his illustrations, which, they felt, were too *'fratzenhaft'* (frolicsome) and as such, made fun of adult authorities" (340), while Eva-Maria Metcalf quotes an even stronger critique: "we hereby denounce a children's story in front of the court of public opinon that has gained surprising popularity within a short period of time—the 'Struwwelpeter'—as a pamphlet of revolutionary propaganda. To you, German mothers, this word of warning: throw Struwwelpeter out of your homes whenever you find it" (210). This reading might have been reinforced by the uses to which it has been put, from that time forward, for social and political satire.[4] S. S. Prawer notes in his review of the 1984 *Der Struwwelpeter Polyglott* that

> Some nineteenth-century commentators sought political significance in the *Struwwelpeter* stories; they saw Shock-headed Peter as a German revolutionary, the Scissorsman as a censor, and Nikolas as the Czar of Russia—and Hoffmann himself gave colour to such speculations when he wrote political satires excoriating revolutionaries and reactionaries alike just after the 1848 uprisings.
>
> (1483)

It is worth noting, moreover, that Hoffmann's Frankfurt publisher was Zacharias Löwenthal of J. Rütten, who also published Marx and Engels's *Die heilige Familie oder Kritik der Kritischen Kritik*, and who was a member, as was Hoffmann, of the "Tutti Frutti," "a group of radical liberal democrats and socialists" (Savelsberg 181n2).

More recent scholars have also read it as a subversive text. Katrien Vloeberghs, for example, connects the *Struwwelpeter* characters to various types of trickster figures. J. D. Stahl notes that while the book has "undoubted cautionary and instructional content . . . [t]here is an undercurrent of anarchic energy running through this work that is not entirely contained by the moralistic frame" (171), an "energy" Elisabeth Wesseling locates especially in the visual "narrative" supplied by the pictures, a narrative that she says teaches a different "moral" from the verses: "a form of aesthetic education which gives children an idea of sublimation, which is something entirely different from repression" (341). Some readers apparently identify with this "undercurrent of anarchic energy" as well. J. D. Stahl recounts Clara Clemens's account of the book's appeal to her father, who was (like Hoffmann) "contemptuous about most of the genteel children's literature of his time" (169):

"There is an impious spirit of contrariness in the verses of this work that appealed to Father, suffering as he was from the blue Berlin mood of those first few weeks. He could sympathize with Kaspar ["Augustus" in the English versions], who wouldn't take his soup, because Father did not care for German soup either."   (Stahl 170)

Ralph Waldo Emerson's children also reportedly found the tales to be "rollicking good fun" (Knoepflmacher 89).

On the other hand, twentieth-century scholars of children's literature tended to consider it an egregious example of repressive patriarchal and bourgeois authoritarianism, potentially traumatizing to its young readers and thus unfit for their consumption. Jack Zipes elaborates a Marxist materialist analysis of the book's usefulness for "the indoctrination of children to the standards of a ruling class [while] also serving the market needs of the book industry"—just the reverse of the "revolutionary propagandist" readings of the 1840s ("Down with *Struwwelpeter*" 164). Thomas Freeman explores the ways in which the book could be psychologically damaging to its young readers and finds that the stories not only "play upon some of the worst fears which can torment a child," but also that they do not teach morality "for morality's sake." Rather, "we are told to behave—or else" (813). He reports the response of one defender of the book, who nevertheless supplies a typical reaction to it as a young reader: "She recalls that when she was little she used to quickly skip over the page with the skinny tailor and the big scissors with all the blood dripping down—and Conrad screaming. But she could never resist glancing at it either" (811). This response seems more typical of many twentieth-century readers as children, if the "reader reviews" of the book on amazon.com are any guide. It has even been made into a theatrical production by the Tiger Lillies, *Shockheaded Peter: A Junk Opera*, which Jack Zipes reviewed in 2000, and in which he claims "a book that was intended to mollify adults' bad consciences and produce guilt in children is transformed into a bitter, if not cynical, attack on complacent adults who believe we have grown more civilized in our attitudes toward children" (134).

The most recent studies of the book tend to explore the ways both the subversive and the authoritarian strands operate uneasily together in the stories, an approach that seems the most congenial to Hoffmann's spirit generally when we recall S. S. Prawer's remark that Hoffmann "wrote political satires excoriating revolutionaries and reactionaries alike just after the 1848 uprisings." U. C. Knoepflmacher finds that if we view it as both an example of cautionary literature and simultaneously as a critique of cautionary literature, we can begin to unpack what he calls, quoting a remark by Marina Warner, the tales' "unstable ironies" (90). In his essay, Knoepflmacher reads his own childhood experience of the book through his scholarly expertise in children's literature in order to reach a clearer understanding of the "leitmotif" running through the tales "of children who are hurt or mutilated by parental neglect" (98) and to show the ways that "Hoffmann really has it both ways":

> The mother of the thumb-sucker warns Konrad about the scissor-wielding monster who will invade the home she then promptly deserts; she does nothing to avert her child's imminent mutilation. Whose irresponsibility is being satirized? The text seems to mock both the compulsive, addictive child and the impotent parent who must rely on bogeymen to help her establish an order free of addiction.   (92)

When we read Hoffmann as thus "having it both ways," the double aims of all the tales—to critique the children *and* the parental critiquers of children—become much clearer. When "foolish Harriet" burns herself up playing with matches, "Mamma and Nurse" have gone out "And left her all alone at play" while "on the table close at hand,/A box of matches chanc'd to stand" (8). Moreoover, once Harriet burns up, the copious "tears" of the feline parental surrogates in the tale, which "ran down their cheeks so fast;/ They made a little pond at last" (9), look more like the crocodile variety upon closer observation. "If the cats are apparently able to call forth this much water," Elisabeth Wesseling points out, "why did they not do so before in order to quench the flames consuming poor Harriet?" More darkly suspicious still, Wesseling notes of the final illustration, Harriet's hair ribbons have somehow been rescued from the flames and now decorate the cats' tails (328). The parental surrogate in "The Story of Little Suck-a-Thumb," the sun face that decorates the door arch above Conrad, frowns in disgust while he sucks his thumb, and then grins down in great satisfaction over his miserable thumb-less condition in the last illustration (Wesseling 327). Viewed with this kind of lens, even that tureen of soup squatting on Augustus's grave has a sneakingly smug look about it, as though it had pursued him there and means to keep him there. These tales thus capture perfectly a sort of entrapment or temptation of the child with his or her own impulsiveness that is set up by the adults' absent-mindedness or stupidity, an incompetence that deepens into a sadistic "I told you so" when the child inevitably succumbs to the trap.

In fact, with a single exception (which I will discuss later), there are no positive examples of impulse control, safe behavior, or even common sense in *any* of the book's characters—child, adult, supernatural figure, or adult surrogate. As Joachim J. Savelsberg usefully concludes in his sociological study of *Struwwelpeter* and its socio-historical context, "the norms encouraged by the *Struwwelpeter* story are primarily disciplinary. Yet, while the primary norms appeal to civilized behavior, many of the secondary norms . . . are uncivilized" because "the control of civility itself remained uncontrolled" (195). The cautionary narratives are produced by those in need of cautionary narratives themselves. Even the mother hare in "The Story of the

Man that Went Out Shooting'' hurts "her own child, the little hare" when she shoots at the hunter (with his own gun), hits his wife's coffee cup instead, and causes the hot coffee to scald the little hare's nose. "Oh dear!" the little hare cries, "Such fun I do not understand" (16). She might well complain. How can the children learn civilized behavior when the teachers themselves exhibit such lack of control?

Bruno Bettelheim's assessment of the book's widely variable effects on different readers becomes helpful here as well. Bettelheim explains that variety with a fuller picture of children and parents in relationship to each other. In his analysis, reception of the book depends on the kind of parenting within which the child is living. If that context resembles the cruelty or neglect displayed by the adults in Conrad's, Harriet's, or Augustus's tales, those tales can enhance the anxieties they feel, whereas children whose home life does not resemble them will find its exaggerations and energies "rollicking good fun." As Freeman reports of Bettelheim, "he believes that if a child is already 'happy and well-adjusted' the long term effect of the *Struwwelpeter* will not be significant," although "if a child already has trouble dealing with his anxieties, the *Struwwelpeter* can reinforce them, though it does not create them" (816).

Which brings us back to Herbert Pocket. As we have seen, Herbert's civilizing of Pip's manners works better than the lessons in the moral "spelling-book" because he sets the right example in his own feeling and behavior. As he says himself during this lesson (quoting his own father): "no man who was not a true gentleman at heart, ever was, since the world began, a true gentleman in manner. He says, no varnish can hide the grain of the wood; and that the more varnish you put on, the more the grain will express itself" (181; ch. 22). How is it, then, that this model of the "gentleman at heart," whose varnish shows such a lovely grain, gives Pip the distinct impression that "he would never be very successful or rich. I don't know how this was. I became imbued with the notion on that first occasion before we sat down to dinner, but I cannot define by what means" (177–78; ch. 22)? And why would such a seemingly "happy and well-adjusted" son of such a seemingly wise and loving father object to Fidgety Philip's name so strongly?

The chapter itself leads us into an answer when it brings Pip and Herbert to Hammersmith so that Pip can meet his new tutor, Herbert's father—author of the above observations on "true gentlemen." Here Dickens reveals his own deeper, one might almost say "Bettelheimian," insight into Herbert's character and family, and one reason for his response to "Philip." What Pip finds when he arrives is a picture of paternal helplessness in the face of maternal neglect and the consequent endangerment of children that could come straight from the pages of *Struwwelpeter*. The first thing he hears is a direct echo of "Johnny Head-in-Air" and the moral boy who falls into the pond: " 'Master Alick and Miss Jane', cried one of the nurses to two of the children, 'if you go a bouncing up against them bushes you'll fall over into the river and be drownded and what'll your pa say then!' " (186; ch. 22). Meanwhile, Mrs. Pocket is so intent on her Debrett's that she fails to notice that her footstool, hidden under her dress, is tripping everyone—including the nurse who tries to hand the baby to her. At dinner, she has absently given the baby the nutcrackers to play with, and Pip reports, "I was made very uneasy in my mind by Mrs. Pocket's falling into a discussion with Drummle respecting two baronetcies, while she ate a sliced orange steeped in sugar and wine, and forgetting all about baby on her lap: who did most appalling things with the nutcrackers" (193; ch. 23). In response to all this and more, Mr. Pocket, for all his wisdom about "true gentlemen," can only "put his two hands into his disturbed hair, and appear to make an extraordinary effort to lift himself up by it" (192; ch. 23). Pip's summary of this household sounds equally like a summary of those in *Struwwelpeter*: "Mr. and Mrs. Pocket's children were not growing up or being brought up, but were tumbling up" (186; ch. 22).

We can see just such a portrait of parental incompetence, in fact, in the final illustration of "Fidgety Philip," in which father and mother gaze in idiotic astonishment at the suddenly empty table, mother through her lorgnette and father impotently stamping his foot with his hands *almost* pulling himself up by the hair (see fig. 2). No wonder, then, that Herbert objects. It was a childhood he himself lived through (perhaps "survived" would be more accurate) and seeks to put behind him as quickly and thoroughly as possible. Indeed, all his siblings, he reports, are similarly bent on escaping by getting themselves "matrimonially established" as soon as possible: "Little Alick in his frock coat has already made arrangements for his union with a suitable young person at Kew. And indeed, I think we are all engaged, except the baby" (251; ch. 30). He clearly points to social ambition as the cause of parental failure when he praises his own fiancée to Pip: "But what a blessing it is for the son of my father and mother to love a girl who has no relations, and who can never bother herself, or anybody else, about her family!" (375; ch. 46). The topsy-turvy dynamic in the Pocket household demonstrates, just as *Struwwelpeter* does, that "the control of civility itself [is] uncontrolled," and that the very social desires that fuel the Pocket parents guarantee their inability to socialize their children, who must "tumble up" and raise themselves.

This dynamic is treated lightly and with much humor in the portrayal of the Pockets, but in the stories of the more central characters, it is responsible for the most painful and lastingly destructive effects in the novel. We need go no farther than Herbert and Pip's gentlemanly lesson during that first dinner together to pick up this motif in its female—and far more consequential—dimension: the ruination of Estella's "heart" (and thus Pip's chances

Where is Philip, where is he?
Fairly cover'd up you see!
Cloth and all are lying on him;
He has pull'd down all upon him.
What a terrible to-do!
Dishes, glasses, snapt in two!
Here a knife, and there a fork!
Philip, this is cruel work.
Table all so bare, and ah!
Poor Papa, and poor Mamma
Look quite cross, and wonder how
They shall make their dinner now.

Fig. 2. From "Die Geschichte vom Zappel-Philipp" ["The Story of Fidgety Philip"]. *Der Struwwelpeter: oder lustige Geschichten und drollige Bilder* [*Struwwelpeter: or Merry Stories and Funny Pictures*].

for a fulfilled emotional life) in her "raising by [Miss Havisham's] hand." As Herbert corrects Pip's manners, it is Miss Havisham's history that he relates, the Hoffmann-esque dynamic thus replicating itself in the content of their conversation as it unfolds directly in the actions of the chapter. "Miss Havisham, you must know, was a spoilt child. Her mother died when she was a baby, and her father *denied her nothing*" (179–80, my emphasis). This father proves equally neglectful of his duty in his handling of Miss Havisham's half-brother Arthur, who consequently "turned out riotous, extravagant, undutiful—altogether bad" (180; ch. 22), a son who "with debts and . . . new madness," "wasted [his means] most fearfully' " (180). Miss Havisham is similarly "too haughty" and impulsive, wasting *her* means on Compeyson—just the kind of figure the world sends in to punish "riotous, extravagant, undutiful," "haughty" children. As in "The Dreadful Tale of Harriet and the Matches," parental neglect leaves the child to her own impulses with disastrous consequences: Miss Havisham's impulse-driven life ends, like Harriet's, in a conflagration, but not without first, and more importantly, replicating itself via her own fatally impulsive and selfish parenting, in the headstrong, "spoilt," and especially self-destructive Estella. When Estella becomes a young woman, she in turn defies her parent's wishes by repeating her willful action: "throwing herself away" on a match just as wasteful and unsuitable as the one with Compeyson.[5] The parallels among Miss Havisham's "feminist" revenge project, which deforms Estella's character; Magwitch's "gentlemanly" revenge project, which deforms Pip's; and the civilizing project, which relies on the humiliation, mutilation, or death of the children in *Struwwelpeter* should all be clear enough.

These connections are mostly child-centered ones, explaining the characters and family dynamics from the filial perspective in the novel, and therefore they highlight ways in which *Great Expectations* and *Struwwelpeter* shake hands, so to speak, over the child's miseries and failures in the wake of uncivilized parenting. And, indeed, creating a children's book that proceeds from the child's point of view, rather than the adult's, was precisely Hoffmann's aim, as the famous story of the book's genesis in Hoffmann's dissatisfaction with other children's books shows. (One suspects that if Mavor's book had been available in Frankfurt in 1844, it would have been found wanting as well.) Eva-Maria Metcalf specifies the two reforms Hoffmann introduced with his book, which she maintains are "fundamental for modern children's books": "child orientation (i.e., an eye to the psyche of the child reader) and high entertainment value (an eye to the desires of the child reader)" (202). The stories therefore have those highly dramatic, fairy-tale-like plots, and illustrations in which "sizes are determined by the importance and emotional value invested in the figures" (207) and which, Stahl explains, "focus on the child's imaginative relationship to the object pictured, whether that relationship be physical or mental" (167). As Hoffmann himself explained this emotional rather than literal proportionality in those "frolicsome" pictures, "You cannot teach a child's soul with the absolute truth, or with algebraic or geometrical propositions; instead, you will make it waste away miserably" (Metcalf 204).

But Hoffmann wanted to civilize the civilizers as well, an aim subtly revealed in the exception to the generally uncivilized behavior of adults and their surrogates in *Struwwelpeter*. In "The Story of Cruel Frederick" appears a picture of model adult civilization: the sweet-faced doctor who sits patiently, with legs crossed at the knees, by the bedside of "Cruel Frederick," whose cruelty had caused the dog to turn on him and bite his leg—a portrait, I am convinced, of pediatrician and psychologist Dr. Heinrich Hoffmann himself (see fig. 3). Hoffmann described the origins of some *Struwwelpeter* tales and illustrations in his own bedside methods for distracting and calming his small and frequently terrified patients, whose parents tended to use doctors as bogeymen to induce obedience:

> I would quickly take a notebook out of my pocket, tear a page out, draw with a pencil a small boy, and relate how this rascal doesn't let his hair and fingernails be cut. The hair grows, the fingernails become longer and longer, but he still refuses to let them be cut, and I draw hair and nails longer and longer, until nothing can be seen of the whole figure but a shock of hair and claws.
>
> (Sauer 221n23)

These tactics, Hoffmann points out, would "calm the little antagonist, dry his tears and allow the medical man to do his duty" (Sauer 221). In his practice, then, Hoffmann modeled not only the civilized control of impulses without using physical force, but did so by teaching the great effectiveness of sublimating those impulses with the creative imagination—something he clearly believed parents could learn as well as their children. That lesson is modeled precisely in this illustration, which ends the first story of the book, showing not only the doctor sitting so patiently, but the good effects of his tactics in Frederick's quiet (and safe) containment in his bed so that he can both get well and behave better—the only child in *Struwwelpeter* whose tale does not end with either emotional or physical disaster.

In *Great Expectations*, such modeling appears in Herbert, for his are the lessons that stick. They inspire the two actions Pip takes that make him into a "true gentleman at heart": his forgiveness and newborn love for Magwitch, which prove that he has broken with the paternal pattern *set* by Magwitch; and, of course, his silent purchase of Herbert's partnership in Clarriker and Co., which assures the success of both men as "gentlemen at heart" and as businessmen in the world. And yet, one way of reading the novel's closure is to notice that neither of them becomes a father himself. Herbert seems happily married to Clara and modestly successful with Clarriker, but no new brood of Pockets (either being raised or "tumbling up") is mentioned in the narration. Pip has not married and has only the oblique avuncularity of namesake: the new Pip, whose "happy and well-adjusted" condition is a correction of, rather than a product of, the elder Pip, and who is the son of Joe and Biddy, the two characters in the novel who have spent their lives completely innocent of "expectations" and social ambition. Successful parenting and

So Frederick had to go to bed;
His leg was very sore and red!
The Doctor came and shook his head,
And made a very great to-do,
And gave him nasty physic too.

But good dog Tray is happy now;
He has no time to say "bow-wow!"
He seats himself in Frederick's chair
And laughs to see the nice things there:
The soup he swallows, sup by sup, —
And eats the pies and puddings up.

Fig. 3. From "Die Geschichte vom bösen Friederich" ["The Story of Cruel Frederick"]. Der Struwwelpeter: oder lustige Geschichten und drollige Bilder [*Struwwelpeter: or Merry Stories and Funny Pictures*].

successful social climbing, the novel seems to conclude, must be mutually exclusive.

As well they might have seemed to the Dickens who was writing this novel. By 1860, he was enduring a moment when filial and paternal concerns ran against each other in intensely painful ways, as Grahame Smith describes. He was rereading *David Copperfield* in order not to repeat himself in *Great Expectations*, an experience that affected him, Smith quotes him as writing to Forster in 1860, "to a degree you would hardly believe," not only because of the power of the book itself but also because of the childhood memories of the blacking factory experience and the parental failure and betrayal leading to it that it stirred up (49). Reinforcing this pain was the exploratory research into the nightmarish conditions endured by children in poverty that he had been conducting as the "Uncommercial Traveller," research that resulted in "a sketch [that] provided 'the germ of the idea' for Dickens's novel" (Smith 43).

At the same time, his domestic situation was in turmoil from "the troubling marriage of a beloved daughter in the willed absence of her mother; . . . the death of a brother, the sale of the family home, and the destruction of 20 years of letters and papers" (Smith 51). One might add to this litany the recent departures of sons Sydney, Charley, and Walter to the navy, the East, and India, respectively, where they would accumulate debts, bankruptcies, and generally "become increasingly tiresome as their inadequacies became apparent" (Smith 44).[6] Peter Ackroyd wants to claim that Dickens is "part Pip and part Magwitch" (900), a persuasive argument regarding his ambivalence about being a self-made man, but I would add to this mix of ambivalent self-portraits the paternal one of hapless Matthew Pocket with his hands in his hair, helplessly watching his family go to pieces, despite all the gentlemanly wisdom and fatherly love he can offer them.[7] As Dickens himself wrote to his friend George Dolby some years later: "I can't get my hat on in consequence of the extent to which my hair stands on end at the costs and charges of these boys. Why was I ever a father!" (Adrian 276).

The self-irony of this portrait seems clear, but what does it tell us about the dialogue on parenting between Dickens and Hoffmann? Unfortunately, there is no record that I can find of Dickens's response to the book. It is not mentioned in letters, biographies, or even the memoirs of his children. (To be fair, none of them mentions Mavor, either.) Was Herbert's objection to "Fidgety Philip" not only an expression of filial rejection of bad parenting but also an objection by Dickens that the "how-to" message in *Struwwelpeter* for parents might be rather too simple? Or was Dickens coming to understand in these experiences with his older children, as Wesseling claims Hoffmann's illustrations demonstrate if we read them as a continuous *bildungsroman*, that children inevitably do some "tumbling up" no matter what adults do or say (339)?

Or perhaps my first reading of the published ending is too literal. We could say that the final narration *implies* a brood of Pockets growing up safely ensconced within Herbert and Clara's happiness, and even that it implies for

Pip a marriage and family following from that "shadow of no parting from her" (485; ch. 59). Or perhaps "plot" is the wrong place to look for the conclusions of this dialogue between texts—that "conclusions" are the wrong thing to look for. Perhaps Dickens was greeting Hoffmann's "unstable ironies" with ironies of his own, and in that worked and reworked final phrase—certainly the most unstable and destabilizing one in the text—Dickens's ambivalence and perplexity regarding his novel's fundamental questions about becoming a gentleman, raising children, and raising gentlemen come to the surface.

NOTES

1. Quotations come from the 1996 Penguin edition of *Great Expectations*, edited by Charlotte Mitchell.
2. Anny Sadrin estimates that Pip and Herbert would be about ten years older than Dickens himself. She notes other details to show the care with which Dickens establishes the temporal deviation between the narration and the action, such as references to "the king" (George III) rather than "the queen," the Bow Street Runners rather than the Metropolitan Police, and so forth.
3. Brian Alderson notes that the bibliographic study of editions and imitations of the book published by Reiner Rühle in 1999 contains 1,577 entries, "without counting many sub-entries such as eight variants, occupying four columns, for Julius Lütje's *Struwwel-Liese* (Hamburg ?1895)" and that, even with all these, "[Rühle] confesses to some frustration in his quest for examples from countries where children's books have been neglected in the national bibliographies" (415). Emer O'Sullivan recounts the publishing history of *Struwwelpeter* specifically in England, and notes that each of the two translations that were available by the time Dickens was writing *Great Expectations* went through many "editions, reprints, adaptations, and imitations," although the most "successful" of the two was the anonymously translated 1848 Volckmar edition (60). This is the version published by Dover now, and the version to which I will be referring in this essay.
4. David Blamires describes some of the British social and political satires that invoke or parody the *Struwwelpeter* tales, from serious digs at Nazi Germany to more "playful" parodies of, for example, university types or "the dangers and disruptiveness of the recently invented motor car" (46).
5. This nexus of daughterly willfulness, self-wasting in unsuitable marriage, and fire calls to mind Dickens's own favorite daughter, Kate, nicknamed "Lucifer Box" for her outspoken, hot-tempered character, who had just contracted her marriage to John Collins in 1858–a match that troubled Dickens so much that, as Kate reported, sister Mamie found him "with his head buried in her wedding dress, sobbing" (Ackroyd 876).
6. Arthur Adrian and Peter Ackroyd provide more detailed accounts of the failings of all Dickens's children—save Henry, who was "the one son . . . who did not

disappoint [him]'' (Adrian 289) and ''the most successful of the Dickens children'' (Ackroyd 878).

7. In her Introduction to the Clarendon edition of *Great Expectations*, in fact, Margaret Caldwell suggests the possibility that Herbert—in both his business interest and his character—was based on Dickens's own eldest son, Charley (xxvii), and that Dickens revised his portrayal of Mrs. Pocket, in some of the most drastic changes between manuscript and published versions (aside from the novel's ending), so that her failings as a mother came to resemble more closely his idea of wife Catherine's failings in that regard (xxviii–xxx).

WORKS CITED

Ackroyd, Peter. *Dickens*. New York: HarperCollins, 1990.

Adrian, Arthur A. " 'Why was I ever a father!' Charles Dickens as Father." *Victorian Literature and Society: Essays Presented to Richard D. Altick*. Ed. James R. Kincaid and Albert J. Kuhn. Columbus: Ohio UP, 1984. 276–99.

Alderson, Brian. Review of *Böse Kinder: Kommentierte Bibliographie von Struwwelpetriaden und Max und Moritziaden mit Biographischen Daten zu Verfassern und Illustratoren*. By Reiner Rühle. *The Library* 7.2.4 (2001): 415–16.

Blamires, David. "Social Satire in English *Struwwelpeter* Parodies." *The Princeton Library Chronicle* 62 (2000): 45–58.

Caldwell, Margaret. Introduction. *Great Expectations*. By Charles Dickens. Oxford: Clarendon, 1993. xiii–lxiii.

Dickens, Charles. *Great Expectations*. Ed. Margaret Caldwell. Oxford: Oxford UP, 1994.

———. *Great Expectations*. Ed. Charlotte Mitchell. London: Penguin, 1996.

———. *Great Expectations*. Ed. Edgar Rosenberg. New York: Norton, 1999.

———. *The Letters of Charles Dickens*. The Pilgrim Edition. Ed. Madeline House, Graham Storey, and Kathleen Tillotson. 12 vols. Oxford: Clarendon, 1965–2002.

Dickens, Charles, Jr. *Reminiscences of My Father*. New York: Haskell House, 1973. [Rpt. "Supplement to the Christmas Windsor." London: Ward, Lock, 1934.]

Dickens, Sir Henry F. *Memories of My Father*. London: Victor Gollancz, 1928.

Dickens, Mamie. *My Father as I Recall Him*. New York: Dutton, 1897.

Freeman, Thomas. "Heinrich Hoffmann's *Struwwelpeter*: An Inquiry into the Effects of Violence in Children's Literature." *Journal of Popular Culture* 10 (1977): 808–20.

Hoffmann, Heinrich. *Struwwelpeter.* New York: Dover, 1995.

Knoepflmacher, U. C. "Validating Defiance: From Heinrich Hoffmann to Mark Twain, Rudyard Kipling, and Maurice Sendak." *The Princeton University Library Chronicle* 61 (2000): 83–107.

Metcalf, Eva-Maria. "Civilizing Manners and Mocking Morality: Dr. Heinrich Hoffmann's *Struwwelpeter.*" *The Lion and the Unicorn* 20 (1996): 201–16.

O'Sullivan, Emer. " 'Any thing to me is sweeter . . . ': British Translations of Heinrich Hoffmann's *Struwwelpeter.*" *Princeton University Library Chronicle* 62 (2000): 59–71.

Prawer, S. S. "The Shock-headed One." *TLS* 21 (1984): 1483–84.

Sadrin, Anny. "A Chronology of *Great Expectations.*" *Great Expectations.* By Charles Dickens. Ed. Edgar Rosenberg. New York: Norton, 1999. 537–43.

Sauer, Walter. "A Classic Is Born: The 'Childhood' of *Struwwelpeter.*" *Papers of the Bibliographical Society* 97 (2003): 215–63.

Savelsberg, Joachim J. "*Struwwelpeter* at One Hundred and Fifty: Norms, Control, and Discipline in the Civilizing Process." *The Lion and the Unicorn* 20 (1996): 181–200.

Smith, Grahame. "Suppressing Narratives: Childhood and Empire in *The Uncommercial Traveller* and *Great Expectations.*" *Dickens and the Children of Empire.* Ed. Wendy Jacobson. New York: Palgrave, 2000. 43–53.

Stahl, J. D. "Mark Twain's 'Slovenly Peter' in the Context of Twain and German Culture." *The Lion and the Unicorn* 20 (1996): 166–80.

Storey, Gladys. *Dickens and Daughter.* London: Frederick Muller, 1939.

Vloeberghs, Katrien. "Trickster as Figure and Force: Ambivalence in Busch's and Hoffmann's Picture-Books." *German as a Foreign Language* 2 (2002): 57–65.

Wesseling, Elisabeth. "Visual Narrativity in the Picture Book: Heinrich Hoffmann's *Der Struwwelpeter.*" *Children's Literature in Education* 35 (2004): 319–45.

Zipes, Jack. "Down with *Heidi*, Down with *Struwwelpeter*, Three Cheers for the Revolution." *Children's Literature* 5 (1976): 162–80.

———. "The Perverse Delight of *Shockheaded Peter.*" *Theater* 30 (2000): 128–43.

The Revolution Is Dead! Long Live Sensation!: The Political History of *The Woman in White*

Lanya Lamouria

This article examines the importance of Europe's revolutionary history in Wilkie Collins's creation of the sensation genre. During his literary apprenticeship in the 1850s, Collins wrote a number of stories set during the first French Revolution. By the end of that decade, however, the young novelist began to question the literary relevance of this history. I argue that in The Woman in White *(1860), Collins undertakes the project of defining his relationship to the revolutionary past. On the one hand, Collins uses* The Woman in White *to announce that the era of political radicalism is dead, a victim of the failed European revolutions of 1848–49. On the other, he positions his new genre of domestic terror as a literary substitute for the now defunct politics of revolutionary terror. My argument depends on reading Collins's novel in its original context, alongside Dickens's* A Tale of Two Cities, *the book serialized immediately before Collins's in* All the Year Round.

The conversation halted on irregularly, between public affairs on one side and trifling private topics on the other. Politics, home and foreign, took their turn with the small household history of St. Crux: the leaders of the revolution which expelled Louis Philippe from the throne of France, marched side by side, in the dinner-table

> review, with Old Mazey [a servant] and the
> dogs. . . . [Magdalen Vanstone] heard nothing in
> the conversation of the slightest importance to
> the furtherance of her own design . . . . She
> struggled hard not to lose heart and hope. . . .
> They could hardly talk again tomorrow, they
> could hardly talk again the next day, of the
> French Revolution and the dogs.
>
> —Wilkie Collins, *No Name* 644–45

Magdalen Vanstone, heroine of Wilkie Collins's *No Name* (1862), overhears this conversation approximately four weeks after the outbreak of the February Revolt in Paris, the event that inaugurated the French Revolution of 1848 and catalyzed a wave of political upheavals that briefly toppled monarchies across Western and Central Europe. For observers on the Continent and in Britain, France's new revolution was an event of world historical proportions. One of the first book-length British accounts of the February Revolt, Walter Kelly's *Narrative of the French Revolution of 1848* (1848), described it as "wondrous," as "transcend[ent]," even as "preaeternatural" (1).[1] Magdalen's attitude, however, is casually dismissive at best. For her, France's latest political crisis is no more unusual, and hence no more worthy of attention, than the "small household history" of St. Crux's habitually disobedient dogs. Indeed, Collins's heroine (apparently speaking for Collins himself) sounds quite like the many European artists and intellectuals who, in the months and years following the mid-century revolutions, watched with perplexity and disgust as newly established democratic governments collapsed and reactionary regimes again took power.

Karl Marx offers what has become the most famous expression of radical disillusionment with the failures of 1848–49. In *The Eighteenth Brumaire of Louis Bonaparte* (1852), written after Napoleon III brought an end to France's Second Republic by declaring himself emperor, Marx criticizes the new political movement for mimicking the upheavals of 1789–1815—but without representing any kind of authentic class struggle. In his opening paragraph, he declares that France's latest revolution has restaged the epoch-making "tragedy" of 1789 as a vulgar "farce," a farce in which a mediocre Napoleon has risen to prominence by rallying the support not of a specific class but of the heterogeneous "scum" of society (15, 26).[2] It is certainly worth noting that Marx and Collins, like many of their contemporaries, register their disappointment with France's mid-century revolution in aesthetic terms.[3] Marx insists that 1848 is suited only for a low dramatic genre, "farce," while Collins suggests that it finds its home among the "trifling private topics" of domestic realism. But the novelist's point in offering this criticism is finally quite different from the political theorist's. In the short passage quoted above from *No Name*, Collins disparages the February Revolt not principally as a social or political act but as a subject for the modern writer. Even more striking, he self-consciously positions the fictional world of his novel—a novel focused on the wonderfully elaborate "designs," or plots, that Magdalen devises in her efforts to recover a lost inheritance—as an alternative source of narrative interest. The era of revolution is over, Collins's seems to say, but in its place, he offers us a literary substitute: sensation fiction.

In what follows, I explore how, in *The Woman in White* (1860), Collins elaborates this thesis that sensation fiction, the genre of domestic terror that he pioneered, functions as a kind of cultural compensation for a post-1848 world in which the compelling drama of revolution appears to have come to an end. My Part 1 begins by taking a step back. Turning to Collins's stories of the first French Revolution, pieces written during his literary apprenticeship in the 1850s, I demonstrate that this political history exemplified for him the experience of "everyday terror" that he later explored so successfully in his mature fiction. That Collins never wrote a full-length novel of 1789 is in fact something of a surprise, but the novel that he wrote instead, *The Woman in White*, helps us understand why he, a novelist with ambitions to create a fiction of modern life, could not undertake this project.

As I explain in Part 2, Collins uses *The Woman in White* to announce that Europe's long and vital revolutionary history is now a relic of the past. Returning his readers to the years 1849–52, he frames the novel's principal narrative with a subplot that recalls the defeat of revolutionary republicanism not only in France but also in Italy—a dual focus that makes sense when we remember that Collins wrote the novel as Victorians were celebrating the recent efforts of the Risorgimento to release Italy from the thrall of foreign rule. The exiled Italian radical Professor Pesca, a man deeply ashamed of his radical youth, and the former-radical-turned-reactionary-spy Count Fosco are apt symbols of the fate of revolutionary impulses in the modern world: they are anachronisms, reminders of a political fight that is now over. Collins does not, however, simply discard the revolutionary narrative that, since his earliest days as a writer, he had found so compelling. Instead, he recycles it, creating a new fiction in which revolutionary-style battles against oppression and injustice are waged by British players on a small-scale domestic stage. As we will see, Collins actually turns his British protagonist, the parvenu Walter Hartright, into a modern freedom fighter, a bourgeois heir of the Continent's revolutionary legacy. The novelist's appropriation of the revolutionary drama emerges with the greatest clarity when *The Woman in White* is read in its original context beside Charles Dickens's *A Tale of Two Cities* (1859), the novel serialized immediately before Collins's book in *All the Year Round*.

Part 3 of my article examines how Collins's novel deliberately reworks the narrative structures and thematic preoccupations of his literary mentor's celebrated novel of the first French Revolution. Although Collins clearly views sensation as a type of fiction that updates the revolutionary past for modern Britain, when we read him alongside the Victorian giant Dickens we can see evidence of the younger novelist's skepticism about the value of this project. Undercutting Dickens's efforts to invest France's revolutionary history with transcendent meaning, Collins presents sensation as fiction appropriate for a post-'48 era in which neither history nor literary narrative has much meaning left to deliver.

Although other critics have explored "the idea of revolution" in Collins's novels, this article is, to my knowledge, the first that recognizes and examines the central role of the political histories of 1789 and 1848–49 in his creative life.[4] In a sense, my analysis answers Albert Hutter's call for a scholarship more attuned to the historical dimension of Collins's art: "the more we know about the historical fabric of Collins's works, the more immediate and persuasive are the bases for their suspense" ("Fosco Lives!" 196). Knowing that Collins inserts his parvenu protagonist into a story of revolutionary intrigue certainly explains why the book was so exciting for Victorian readers. The novelist makes the enterprise of class-climbing look like a vital, heroic battle in which the striver must fight and vanquish aristocratic oppressors on his way to the top. My goal, however, is not to paint Collins as a writer who valorizes social striving or the broader ethos of middle-class professionalism or (that critical catch-all) liberal bourgeois ideology. To the contrary, I argue that Collins makes sensation fiction out of the remnants of the revolutionary narrative precisely because he views the post-'48 world as one that lacks a vital and authentic drama of its own.

Part 1: The Revolutionary Origins of Sensation

Collins's revision of the revolution narrative in *The Woman in White* is best approached by way of his fiction of the first French Revolution, fiction that he wrote during the early 1850s. The young writer first signaled his interest in 1789 by publishing a translation, in *Bentley's Miscellany*, of one of Honoré de Balzac's stories of the first French Revolution, "Midnight Mass: An Episode in the History of the Reign of Terror" (1852). He quickly followed this with a French Revolution story of his own, "Nine O'Clock," also in *Bentley's* (1852). The next year, his second piece of French Revolution fiction, "Gabriel's Marriage" (1853), appeared in *Household Words*. This story was in turn adapted as a play, *The Lighthouse*, in 1855, the year in which Dickens's journal published Collins's longest and final narrative set in revolutionary France, "Sister Rose." [5] (Collins reprinted both "Gabriel's Marriage" and "Sister Rose," under modified titles, in his first collection of stories, *After*

Dark [1856].) These pieces do not represent Collins's only narratives of revolution. His first novel, *Antonina: Or the Fall of Rome* (1850), suggests that the drama of revolution, the drama of social outsiders pitted against an oppressive authority, played a fundamental role in his writing life. The French Revolution stories deserve to be treated separately, however, because they demonstrate the importance of this particular political narrative in the genesis of Collins's brand of sensation fiction. It was Henry James who first observed that Collins created his new genre in part by domesticating the conventions of the Gothic tradition: "instead of terrors of Udolpho, we [are] treated to the terrors of the cheerful country-house and busy London lodgings" (123). Considering Collins's French Revolution fiction, we should modify this claim. In the stories, Collins identifies the Reign of Terror as the historical moment when some of the most characteristic and terrifying scenarios of the Gothic world—entire families subject to fatal violence, innocents unjustly imprisoned, an atmosphere thick with secrets and unfathomable plots—became, first, a political reality and, second, a mass experience capable of contaminating the sanctum of the ordinary family home. If we take Collins at his word, what we recognize is that Radcliffe's Gothic terrors find their way into his mature fiction only after taking a detour through revolutionary France.

It seems that Collins conceived of his very first piece of French Revolution fiction, "Nine O'Clock," as a vehicle for exploring the idea that the Reign of Terror turned the Gothic world of supernatural mystery and violence into historical reality. On its surface, the story is a highly conventional reworking of the "ancestral curse" theme that, Robert Mighall reminds us, was commonplace in Gothic literature (79). Collins's protagonist, an imprisoned Girondin leader known only as Duprat, relates "the strange chapter of [his] family history" on the night of June 30, 1793, the night before the first day of the Reign of Terror (92). Duprat knows that he will die at nine o'clock, he stoically announces to a friend imprisoned with him, because it is the doom of all men in his family—at least since his brother, a boy who dabbled in occult sciences, learned how to create his own doppelganger. What makes this *Frankenstein*-style narrative of miseducation, unholy creation, and family doom innovative is relatively simple: Collins imagines that the Terror is the ultimate agent of the Duprat family's extermination. True, Duprat's younger brother and father die from obscure maladies (after languishing, in typical Gothic fashion, in their ancient country estate), but the curse is only complete when Duprat himself expires in the maw of the guillotine. Collins's clever Gothic adaptation reminds us that the Terror made the extermination of entire family lines a political imperative. In this way, he uses the story to demonstrate that the Revolution turned elements of Gothic nightmare (here the ancestral curse) into features of real life.

Collins's remaining French Revolution stories, "Gabriel's Marriage" and "Sister Rose," build in more or less direct ways on the literary-historical proposition of ''Nine O'Clock''—that the French Revolution makes the Gothic real. In ''Gabriel's Marriage,'' Collins takes an additional imaginative step, suggesting that if Gothic violence becomes a political reality during the Revolution, then what looks supernatural might in fact mask revolutionary content. In the course of the story, Gabriel Sarzeau discovers that the ancestral curse apparently plaguing his family is in actuality a superstition manufactured to hide a real and terrifying act of revolutionary violence: his father, an impoverished fisherman, has robbed and stabbed a traveling gentleman (a man who revives, becomes a priest, and ultimately leads Brittany's Catholic resistance during the Reign of Terror). ''Sister Rose'' moves Collins's literary experiment with the history of the French Revolution further still, as it dispenses altogether with the supernatural and plunges into the Gothic-style experiences of oppression and violence that, as Collins had already established, were unleashed by the politics of the Terror. Here the villainous Charles Danville, head of Robespierre's secret police, subjects his vulnerable wife, Rose, and her brother, the self-sacrificing Louis Trudaine, to relentless persecution. Brother and sister are spied on, denounced as traitors, subjected to a sham trial, imprisoned, and, finally, doomed to die by the guillotine. Most noteworthy is the way ''Sister Rose'' anticipates the sensation genre's focus on terror experienced in the domestic sphere. Indeed, Collins makes a deliberate effort to imagine exactly how the Revolution became a feature of daily life. In one chapter, for instance, his narrator wonders how agents of the secret police could issue and receive death warrants ''with [the] unruffled calmness of official routine'' (*After Dark* 156). The narrator then includes a series of police records that explain, in detail, how Robespierre's spies have kept Rose and Trudaine ''under perpetual surveillance'' (*After Dark* 160). What we see emerging in ''Sister Rose'' are the contours of a sensational world in which everyday life is permeated not only by experiences of oppression and violence but by a suffocating psychological atmosphere of terror and suspicion.

What we do not see in these stories also deserves emphasis, however. We find almost no evidence to support the claim that Collins's imaginative investment in the revolutionary history of the Continent was fueled by a commitment to political radicalism. Although it is true that the young Collins contributed to the socialist newspaper *The Leader* and counted British radicals among his friends, neither his biography nor his writings give us reason to conclude that his radical sympathies ran deep.[6] Tim Dolin and Lucy Dougan describe his political posture in the 1850s as one of defiant liberalism. Collins, they write, was ''a liberal intent on living down the Toryism of his father and wary of the radicalism of some of his friends'' (11). Collins's French Revolution stories, which at once express sympathy for victims of oppression but simultaneously dramatize the excesses of the Terror, testify to this wariness, as does his most explicit comment on the politics of the French Revolution—a comment tucked into "The Poisoned Meal," one of his articles on famous French crimes. Concluding this account of a servant girl framed for murder in the years before the Revolution, Collins first encourages his readers to remember that "the hard case of oppression" he has just related explains why the political upheaval was "a necessity" (423). Finally, however, he laments the Revolution's "excesses," excesses that France "is still expiating" (423). In a sense, when Collins looked at the French Revolution, he (like many of the Gothic novelists whose work inspired him) saw a disturbing historical illustration of what Ronald Paulson has called "that constant potential for the simple inversion of the persecutor-persecuted relationship"—the ability of radicals to become tyrants (538). The villain of "Sister Rose," Danville, perfectly illustrates this type of inversion. A thoroughgoing political opportunist, Danville is willing to work for Robespierre during the Terror, but after Robespierre's fall, he reveals what he really wants: an aristocrat's title and absolute social power.

Characters like Danville strongly suggest that Collins's suspicion of political radicalism was grounded in a belief that it always devolves into absolutism. What I hope to show in my reading of *The Woman in White*, however, is that his literary treatment of radicalism is also shaped by his understanding of the mid-century revolutions, events that, in his view, showed that the revolutionary era was over—that revolutionary radicalism was a politics of the past. Even in the fiction I have just discussed, Collins wonders whether the revolutionary history he is trying to reinhabit is fully accessible to modern readers and writers. In "Gabriel's Marriage," Collins's narrator observes that old Brittany, the Brittany of "the troubled times of more than half a century ago," no longer exists, having been domesticated by "regular tourists" who trample down the countryside's atmospheric "brambles and weeds" (115). By the time Collins republishes this story and "Sister Rose" in *After Dark*, he actually holds the French revolutionary era at arm's length, using frame narratives to foreground the historical, cultural, and ideological distance of the stories from the contemporary Victorian world. In the prologue written for "Sister Rose," for example, we discover that the story is told by the elderly French Governess Mademoiselle Clairfait and, further, that her account is so "fragmentary and discursive," so often interrupted by "outbursts of passionate political declamation, on the extreme liberal side," that the narrator (the temporarily blind painter William Kerby) is forced to tell it "in [his] own way" (*After Dark* 117).

To some extent, Collins's project in *The Woman in White* is an extension of Kerby's in *After Dark*. Collins wants to tell a story of the French Revolution, a story animated by the harrowing experiences of oppression and violence that he probed in his early writing, but he knows that this history has become so remote that it can only be brought into modern fiction if he tells it "in his own way," as sensation fiction. We might well wonder why Collins waited until 1859, the year he began writing *The Woman in White*, to take on this project of updating the revolutionary narrative for modern Britain. My next sections examine the two cultural events of 1859 that turned the thoughts of Collins, and his readers, to the Continental revolutions of the past: first, the Risorgimento campaigns of 1859 and, second, Dickens's publication of *Tale of Two Cities*.

Part 2: Walter Hartright: Revolutionary Class Climber

Collins wrote *The Woman in White* between the summers of 1859 and 1860, and he no doubt created the Italian subplot to capitalize on the Victorian public's appetite not just for news but for poetry, plays, and novels related to the Risorgimento.[7] Although Italy's heroic battle for nationhood had long been a subject of debate in the Victorian press and a theme for Victorian writers, the years of 1859–60 marked the high point of Victorian Britain's real and imaginative engagement with Italian politics, thanks in no small part to the stunning successes of General Giuseppe Garibaldi, the man Lucy Riall has called the first political celebrity. In the months before Collins began writing his novel, Victorians were immersed in extensive coverage of the war of 1859. As Riall explains, it was "the most newsworthy event of the year" (185). Their enthusiasm for the Risorgimento and its military leader Garibaldi had only become more frenzied by the time Collins finished composing *The Woman in White* in July of 1860. By then, Garibaldi had launched another successful campaign, accomplishing the remarkable feat of routing Sicily's Bourbon forces with fewer than two thousand men. (Garibaldi's "Thousand" would next free Naples, an event that made possible the partial reunification of Italy under King Victor Emmanuel in 1861.)[8] The period during which Collins wrote and published *The Woman in White* thus consolidated the Risorgimento's status as a British political cause and Garibaldi's appeal as an English-style hero. While "Pro Italia" Committees raised money for the general's campaigns, outfitted his troops with English rifles, and enlisted Englishmen to join in the fight, Victorian writers celebrated his marvelous military achievements.[9]

It must be stressed, however, that if Collins capitalizes on the topicality of the Risorgimento in *The Woman in White*, he does so in an unusual way. Rather than celebrate the recent successes of Italy's heroic battle for freedom, as did a host of major, minor, and amateur Victorian writers, Collins returns in his novel to the period of 1849–52, the very years when the reactionary regime of Louis Napoleon, later Emperor Napoleon III (1851), dealt a death blow to republicanism in Italy and France. Consider the political events that took place during the time-span of Collins's narrative.[10] *The Woman in White* opens in the summer of 1849, when all of Europe learned that President Louis Napoleon had betrayed republicans at home and abroad by sending troops to topple the new Roman Republic and reestablish Papal rule. By the summer of 1850, when Sir Percival and his bride visit the French capital (after touring Rome and other sites of failed Italian revolutions), Louis Napoleon's government had passed a series of contentious and repressive laws, one of which effectively disenfranchised millions of voters. The novel approaches its conclusion in the summer of 1851, with Hartright's discovery of Count Fosco's body in the Paris Morgue. It was then that Louis Napoleon, at loggerheads with France's Legislative Assembly, likely began laying the foundation for his December 2, 1851 coup d'état, the event that crushed France's remaining opposition movement (thousands of radicals were arrested and deported) and, in turn, paved the way for the establishment of the Second Empire.[11] That Collins concludes the novel with the highly suggestive image of Count Fosco's giant corpse is no accident. It serves as a vivid reminder of these events. Although the Count is explicitly compared to Napoleon I (and so, by implication, to Napoleon III), he dies disguised as an anonymous French artisan, a social group that Victorians identified with the revolutionary class.[12] Fosco's body is thus a wonderfully condensed symbol of what I take to be one of the novel's key historical arguments: in the wake of the 1848–49, Continental radicalism is dead, the victim of the Bonapartist political reaction.

Collins supports this argument most directly by way of his cast of characters. *The Woman in White* is populated by former political radicals, men and women whose youthful revolutionary enthusiasm the novel treats as a product either of political immaturity or of political opportunism. Professor Pesca, a man whose small size serves of an index of his incomplete political development, explains that he joined one of Italy's infamous secret societies during the "over-zealous" years of a "younger time" (574). Pesca's desire to distance himself from his radical past is stressed early in the novel. According to Hartright, the Italian is a slavish Anglophile who wears English clothes, emulates English athleticism, apes English colloquialisms, and, most tellingly, admires England's venerable political structures. (Pesca confesses, on the eve of the Hartright's departure for Limmeridge, "it is the dream of my whole life to be Honourable Pesca, M.P.!" [21].) Although Pesca is a former-radical in earnest, other characters have embraced a revolutionary-style ideology for reasons of fashion or expediency. There is Fosco, a former member of the Brotherhood who has become a counter-revolutionary spy in the pay of the Austrian or French governments (or perhaps both).[13] And then there is Madame Fosco. According to Marion, this woman, now slavishly devoted to her autocratic husband, was, in the years before her marriage, an advocate of "the Rights of Women" (232). Even Sir Percival, a man who commits forgery in a desperate attempt to secure his status as an aristocrat, has a decidedly radical lineage. Marion reports that the Percival's father, Sir Felix, is known for "being little better than a revolutionist in politics and an infidel in religion" (456). It should come as no surprise that the only self-avowed radical in the novel is the elitist Mr. Fairlie. Although Fairlie abhors the common masses, especially their children, and likens his servants to pieces of furniture, he insists, "my own views are so extremely liberal that I think I am a Radical myself" (159). What Collins wants to say could hardly be clearer: there can be no real radical revolutionaries in the post-'48 Victorian world.

It is tempting to read this relentless critique of political radicalism as a sign that Collins simply rejects the revolutionary past and wholeheartedly embraces the present. Mighall's important recent thesis about Victorian Gothic fiction, a category which includes sensation fiction, seems especially relevant here. The Victorian Gothic, he asserts, "dwells in the historical past, or identifies 'pastness' in the present, to reinforce the distance between the enlightened now and the repressive or misguided then" (xvii). Applying this line of argument to *The Woman in White*, we might conclude that Collins rehearses the death-throes of Europe's revolutionary movement in order to celebrate the emergence of the enlightened liberal present, an era in which social change is the product not of mass violence but of individual social striving. The problem with this approach, however, is that Collins does not unambiguously celebrate modernity (whether it be considered in its political, social, cultural, or economic guises)—a point that Dolin and Dougan's recent reading of *Basil: A Story of Modern Life* (1852) expresses with admirable clarity. As they explain, "Collins makes it quite clear in *Basil* that the old order, unreformed, is . . . corrupt," but he also insists that the "vulgar new order" is ultimately no better (15). That *The Woman in White* provides a similar, double-pronged criticism of past and present is neatly illustrated by Collins's portraits of Old and New Welmingham. True, the town of Old Welmingham is an all-but-abandoned collection of dismantled and decaying ruins. But it is the "clean desolation" of New Welmingham, home of Mrs. Catherick and her banal brand of modern evil, that inspires deep feelings of repulsion, expressed in some of Hartright's most overblown rhetoric: "The deserts of Arabia are innocent of our civilized desolation; the ruins of Palestine are incapable of our modern gloom" (483). Passages such as these indicate that, for Collins, the modern world is no "enlightened now." Instead, it is plagued by a kind of emptiness, a lack of authentic or vital meaning that he thematizes most suggestively by way of the novel's large cast of dead, ill, or languishing British men.

It is precisely because Collins believes the modern world is lacking that he must make his new fiction by recycling the cultural remnants of a revolutionary drama whose political meaning is exhausted. At key moments in the novel, he in fact tells us that, although the era of revolution is now dead, the men who have been lucky enough to endure it have participated in a life-and-death struggle against injustice and oppression that moderns should envy. Collins gives us a glimpse of this vital past early in the narrative when Hartright observes that tiny Pesca, so desperate to forget his radical youth, nonetheless possesses a "heart[iness]" and "impulsive[ness]" that present-day Englishmen lack (14). Later, when Pesca confesses that he is a member of "The Brotherhood," a secret society dedicated to "the destruction of tyranny, and the assertion of the rights of the [Italian] people," the professor argues that what differentiates Englishmen and Italians is that Italians remember what it means to fight for their freedom:

> It is not for you to say—you Englishmen, who have conquered your freedom so long ago, that you have conveniently forgotten what blood you shed, and what extremities you proceeded to, in the conquering—it is not for *you* to say how far the worst of all exasperations may, or may not, carry the maddened men of an enslaved nation. The iron that has entered into our souls has gone too deep for *you* to find it. Leave the refugee alone! Laugh at him, distrust him, open your eyes in wonder at that secret self which smoulders in him, sometimes under the every-day respectability and tranquility of a man like me . . . but judge us not! In the time of your first Charles you might have done [Italian revolutionaries] justice; the long luxury of your own freedom has made you incapable of doing us justice now.   (575)

Admittedly, Pesca's picture of himself and the Brotherhood as compounds of iron resolve and fiery resentment runs counter to their characterization in the rest of the novel. (The Brother who apparently acts as the Count's assassin, for instance, is a "fearfully pale" man with a "long, delicate, nervous hand" who struggles to descend the stairs after telling Pesca of the traitor's death [622]). What Collins articulates by way of Pesca's outburst, I would argue, is not so much the "truth" about Italian nationalism as his own nostalgia for a world of supercharged political drama, the drama of oppressive tyrants and oppressed victims that he staged in his French Revolution fiction.

It is easiest to see how Collins draws on the political drama of revolution in *The Woman in White* by examining his protagonist Hartright. The novelist actually turns this class-climbing artist into a heroic man of action by giving him a radical's life story. Tamar Heller reminds us that, at the beginning of *The Woman in White*, the nominally middle-class drawing master is in fact experiencing a severe "crisis of class definition" (116). Although he is the child of a professional artist (a man who secured the family's status by dint of "prudence and self-denial"), Hartright has lost his paternal inheritance through "extravagance" and is now sinking toward a social position so marginal that he can only imagine it as a kind of death. "Out of health, out of spirits, and . . . out of money," the destitute artist feels that "the small pulse of the life within [him]" is "sinking . . . languidly and more languidly, with the sinking sun" (10). The novel's primal sensation scene—Hartright's encounter with Anne Catherick—only confirms his keen apprehension of his social powerlessness. Anne's appearance is "sensational" precisely because she is the artist's uncannily familiar-yet-unfamiliar doppelganger. Her suspicious social position ("What sort of woman she was . . . I altogether failed to guess") and explosive class resentment ("Not a man of rank and title. . . . Thank God!") seem both to awaken and confirm what we might call his burgeoning class consciousness ("I am only a drawing-master") (24, 28, 27).

It is not until Hartright arrives at Limmeridge, however, that his sense of his social marginality reaches a point of crisis. Even before the lovely heiress Laura "lure[s] [the drawing master] from the recollection of . . . [his] position," his aesthetic appreciation of the estate's "luxury and beauty," coupled with Fairlie's "haughty familiarity and impudent politeness," aggravates his raw feelings of class injury (55, 40, 47). Hartright is no class rebel at this stage in the narrative, though; he accepts his social inequality, leaving both Limmeridge and Laura to his social better, Sir Percival. The next time we meet our protagonist, he has in fact grown into his marginal class identity. When Mr. Gilmore runs into Hartright outside a London train station, the young man, no longer "neat and gentlemanlike," is unrecognizably "slovenly," plagued by "nervous spasm[s]" and an air of suspiciousness that underscore his now complete identification with the novel's primary figure of class resentment, Anne (155, 156).

According to Heller, Collins saves Hartright from this life of disabling class resentment by making a man of him, by distancing him from disempowered women such as Anne (and the revolutionary feelings of "disenfranchise[ment]" she evokes) and aligning him instead "with the masculine, and middle-class, discourse of professionalism" (127). In many ways, this argument makes sense. *The Woman in White* does chart the triumph of middle-class English masculinity. What Hartright gains during his adventure to Central America is precisely a new manliness: "I came back to face [my future], as a man should" (406). And he succeeds in exposing Sir Percival and Fosco's conspiracy by modeling a "prudence and self-denial" that would make his professional father proud. Suppressing all concerns for self in order to undertake the painstaking project of collecting evidence of the aristocrats' guilt, Hartright apparently proves that middle-class virtues can defeat even the most corrupt upper-class power.

But this is not the only class story Collins's novel tells. Indeed, I would argue that Hartright emerges as a classic hero, as a man of action who succeeds in vanquishing Sir Percival and the Count, because he looks and acts more like a political radical than a middle-class professional. Recall that after reuniting with Marion and Laura, Hartright's first move is to join the ranks of the urban working class. He rents an apartment in "a populous and a poor" London neighborhood and finds work "drawing and engraving on wood for the cheap periodicals" (an occupation favored by many a British radical) (412). Only after he has adopted the identity of an "obscure, unnoticed" lower-class city dweller, a member of the dangerous classes, does he take up his battle against "Rank and Power," a battle that pits him against figures who represent both the old and new enemies of the radical movement—Sir Percival and Fosco, respectively (412, 414). If we want to find a pattern for this new-and-improved Hartright, we in fact need to look no further than Pesca's speech about the Brotherhood, the speech containing Pesca's description of his idealized revolutionary self. It is Hartright, not Pesca, who is pushed to extremity during a battle for freedom (Laura's, in this case). It is Hartright who discovers, in the midst of his fight to overthrow the enemy-oppressors, that he possesses a secret, smoldering self (a real "man") hidden beneath his unremarkable social façade. Indeed, some of the more eccentric features of Hartright's biography—his rescue of the drowning Pesca and his self-imposed exile in Central America, where he survives "death by disease, death by Indians, [and] death by drowning" (406)—strongly suggest that Collins modeled his protagonist's story on the life of the most famous mid-century radical, Garibaldi. As Riall explains, the biographies of the general that became widely available in 1859 follow a "three-stage sequential narrative." The first part describes Garibaldi's "minor adventures as a young man," when he saved three people from drowning; part 2 turns to his years as a political exile and fighter in South America, a "perilous and character-forming journey" in which he survives countless battles, multiple shipwrecks, and general hardship; and part 3 builds to "the epic battle for Rome where [Garibaldi] fights the enemy, finds his destiny and redeems" Italy's identity and freedom (148). The parallels with Hartright's three-part narrative of early trials, Central American training, and final epic battle are so obvious that they need hardly be detailed. What does need to be emphasized is that the man who reenters and possesses Limmeridge in the novel's final pages has achieved his new position of social power and prestige by becoming a modern heir of the revolutionary legacy. I would add that Collins's merging of the parvenu and the revolutionary does more to challenge than to endorse the status quo. It takes no stretch of the imagination to see that the novel characterizes the enterprise of social striving as fraught with moral ambiguity. Two men die as the result of Hartright's revolutionary-style battle to win his way up in the world.

The point I am stressing here—that Collins did not write *The Woman in White* to celebrate the heroism inherent in the humdrum world of modern

bourgeois life—comes into sharpest focus when we read the novel in its
original literary context alongside Dickens's *Tale of Two Cities*. In part,
Collins treats Dickens's novel in the same way that he treats the history of
the Continental revolutions—as a story that is outmoded but whose general
narrative structures can be repurposed in the new fiction of domestic terror.
When we look closely at how *The Woman in White* adapts *Tale of Two Cities*,
however, we can see that the younger writer also expresses considerable
uncertainty about the literary significance of the genre of fiction he is creating.
Pointedly deflating Dickens's attempts to invest revolutionary history with
higher meaning, Collins emphasizes the emptiness of his book and of the
post-'48 world. In Collins's view, it is a world in which the vital moral drama
of the revolutionary past has played itself out.

Part 3: *A Tale of Two Cities* Revisited

The final installment of *A Tale of Two Cities* appeared alongside the opening
pages of *The Woman in White* in the number of *All the Year Round* for
November 23, 1859.[14] When Collins's first readers finished the melodramatic
closing scene of Sydney Carton's sacrifice and began to read of Hartright's
midnight encounter with Anne (a figure Heller has likened to Madame Defarge), they may well have experienced a sense of déjà vu.[15] In *The Woman
in White*, Collins most directly indicates his interest in revising *A Tale of Two
Cities* by featuring characters that function as Victorian analogues of Dickens's late eighteenth-century English and French cast. Where Dickens has Dr.
Manette, prisoner of France's corrupt ancien régime, Collins offers Professor
Pesca, a political exile of Italy's Risorgimento. Collins splits Dickens's aristocratic French villain, the Marquis St. Evrémonde, into two men, the English
Sir Percival and the Italian Count Fosco. Collins's evil baronet, however,
clearly follows in the evil marquis's footsteps. Both men commit crimes that
violate marriage and disrupt generational relations; both lock up the witnesses
who threaten to reveal their wrongdoings; and both receive retribution for
their crimes in the form of dramatic fires.[16] Most importantly, *The Woman
and White* features a male hero who encompasses Dickens's twin protagonists. The artist Hartright is at once a Carton-like social outsider who begins
the novel on the margins of respectability and, at the same time, a Charles
Darnay-like intellectual who aspires to better himself.

Even a brief perusal of the major plots and themes in *A Tale of Two Cities*
and *The Woman in White* demonstrates that Collins forges his new fiction by
self-consciously appropriating the narrative structures and preoccupations of
Dickens's French Revolution novel. Collins, for instance, follows Dickens in
constructing a plot that moves between the poles of incarceration and death,

on the one hand, and freedom and resurrection, on the other. *A Tale of Two Cities* opens with Manette's "resurrection" and Darnay's acquittal; it then recounts Darnay's trials and incarceration in France, finally building toward the hero's climactic resurrection. In *The Woman in White*, Collins self-consciously retreads this narrative path. The stories of Pesca's reanimation and Anne's escape serve as a thematic counterpoint to Laura's domestic incarceration and false death—the mystery that Hartright must solve in order to reestablish and resurrect Laura's identity in the novel's concluding movement. In constructing this plot, Collins, like Dickens, makes use of doubled characters (Dickens has Darnay and Carton; Collins, Anne and Laura) and explores the intersections between incarceration and insanity (Manette is virtually driven mad by his false imprisonment, while Anne's apparent madness allows Percival to lock her away in the mental asylum). Winifred Hughes observes that Collins's archetypal sensation novel established "disguise and mistaken identity, insanity, and the return of the dead alive" as key elements of the genre (268). Collins's creation of these conventions, however, depends on his deliberate recycling of *A Tale of Two Cities'* narrative of revolutionary history—a history that, in his view, came to an end at midcentury, a full decade before Dickens attempted to recall it to life.

Perhaps most importantly, Collins updates Dickens's revolutionary drama by moving terror out of the public realm and into the private domestic spaces of the home and the psyche (exactly as he did in his early French Revolution fiction). In Collins's post-revolutionary Victorian world, the dynamics of terror and suspicion have broken free from political foundations and, as a result, become the dominant mode of human relation, structuring one character's response to another and readers' reactions to the text. The novel's keynote of suspicion sounds in the novel's primal scene, in which Anne immediately acknowledges that her out-of-placeness is suspicious: "You don't suspect me of doing anything wrong, do you?" (25). From here forward, all is not right with virtually every character Hartright meets, even those with whom he finds himself allied. He views Marion, as every reader will recall, as a disturbing mix of woman and man, and Laura immediately suggests the idea of "something wanting" (53). For D. A. Miller, the pervasive atmosphere of suspicion in the novel involves characters and readers in the psychological dynamics of paranoia: "From trifles and common coincidences, [they] suspiciously infe[r] a complicated structure of persecution, an elaborately totalizing 'plot' " (195). But Collins's characters are not simply paranoids. The novelist explicitly represents them as persecuted subjects and oppressive tyrants caught up in a psychological version of the revolutionary drama. When Sir Percival believes that Anne has told Laura and Marion of his "Secret," he reacts as an aristocrat beset by fears of revolutionary conspiracies and willing to employ blunt force or espionage to discover the truth. "I'll have your secret out of you," he rages, "and I'll have it out of that sister of yours as well. There shall be no more plotting and whispering between you. Neither you nor she shall see each other again till you have confessed the truth. I'll have you watched" (299–300). Fosco may be the only true spy in the novel, but almost every other character becomes a virtual spy, skilled at ferreting out conspiracies, hatching counter-plots, denouncing enemies, and eliciting confessions. Hartright and Marion are only the most obvious examples.

It makes sense, at this point, to note that Collins's reworking of *Tale of Two Cities* can (and probably should) be read as a challenge to Dickens, the literary mentor who, in the words of Lilian Nayder, made the young Collins feel like "a resentful and exploited hand" (*Unequal Partners* 2). In *The Woman in White*, Collins does seem to be trying to best his master, to show him what a modern novel of revolutionary history ought to look like. I would emphasize, however, that in answering Dickens, Collins does far more than express his resentment. He also expresses considerable uncertainty about the value of the genre that he is pioneering, insisting that his post-'48 novel no longer holds the key for unlocking the higher meanings of history, violence, or death.

In the course of the novel, Collins makes this point by relentlessly deflating the prophetic mode that Dickens, following Thomas Carlyle, employs in an effort to wrest significance from the destructive violence of revolutionary history. Collins's revision of one of Dickens's dominant themes—resurrection—serves as a key instance of this diminishment of meaning. In the opening pages of *A Tale of Two Cities*, Dickens represents Lorry's mission to dig Manette out of his "grave" in Saint Antoine as an act that participates in the mystery and magic that surrounds the miracle of Christian resurrection. The atmosphere of secrecy, the cryptic messages, and the heady philosophizing of the opening chapters emphasize the existence of meanings beyond those that are superficially visible, meanings that can only be grasped through the highly charged language of metaphor, such as "RECALLED TO LIFE" (12; ch. 2). By the novel's concluding pages, Dickens has transformed the history of the first Revolution into a parable of Christian redemption, fashioning Carton as a Christ-figure whose act of sacrifice both salvages his wasted life and anticipates the Phoenix-like rebirth of France—the event that will bring to a close the violent history of the ancien régime and the Terror and reveal its unseen significance.

In *The Woman in White*, however, Collins ruthlessly demystifies the metaphorical language that surrounds resurrection in Dickens's French Revolution novel and, placing a materialist emphasis on the physical body, refuses to redeem death from meaninglessness. Thus when Hartright rescues Pesca from drowning, it is a decidedly secular event. The Italian is not recalled to life from a figurative grave but is literally resuscitated. Fosco's perverse use of the word "resurrection" makes the novel's deflation of the concept utterly explicit. As the Count explains in his masterly "confession," the plot to steal Lady Glyde's identity and inheritance involves "the resurrection of the woman who was dead in the person of the woman who was living" (610). Here "resurrection" no longer signifies a miraculous reanimation of one who is literally or figuratively dead. The word is instead a euphemism for a macabre act of substitution: a dead body is replaced by a live one. In the novel's closing pages, Collins offers his most pointed response to Dickens's theme by leaving readers with the tableau of an enormous corpse (Fosco's) that resists efforts at interpretation. Dickens had concluded *A Tale of Two Cities* with a marvelous act of narrative resurrection. In describing Carton's execution, Dickens's narrator replaces the image of his beheaded body with a record of words speculatively attributed to Carton, words which, allowing the guillotined man to speak from the grave, project his legacy into future generations. By contrast, the scene in which Hartright views Count Fosco's corpse showcases the sheer materiality of a body whose narrative is never finally known. (As Hartright reports, the Countess's memoir of her husband "throws no light whatever on the name that was really his own, or on the secret history of his life" [624].) I suggest that Collins uses this scene in part to announce that he believes the role of the writer has become sharply limited in the wake of 1848. Hutter has argued that, in *A Tale of Two Cities*, the figure of the resurrectionist becomes a double for Dickens, a novelist committed to disinterring the past and restoring its life and meaning ("The Novelist as Resurrectionist" 11).[17] In Collins's novel, however, the author's most obvious fictional counterpart is Fosco, and when it comes to death, the Count characterizes himself as what might be called a "preservationist." [18] He claims to have developed "a means of petrifying the body after death, so as to preserve it, as hard as marble, to the end of time" (220). Fosco cherishes no illusions about the existence of eternal souls or of another life beyond the here and now. If the radical materialist Fosco can be read as a figure for the novelist, then Collins characterizes himself as a post-'48 writer who can simply maintain the past in lifeless form. He cannot speak for the dead.

To a certain extent, the observation I am making about *The Woman in White* echoes an observation that Patrick Brantlinger has made about sensation fiction generally: the genre tends to diminish the truth claims of realistic fiction such as Dickens's (23). Brantlinger explains this tendency by arguing that sensation writers aim low. Designing their books to be "diverting and diversionary," they only "mimi[c]" the work of serious writers (23). By contrast, I propose that Collins deflates the artistic ambitions of realism because he believes that the failures of 1848–49 have closed the curtain on the vital moral drama of "good versus evil" that, as Peter Brooks has shown, animates the weightiest nineteenth-century fiction.[19] Although we cannot deny that Collins was a critic of radical politics, he also believed that revolutionaries had fought the good fight (recall Pesca's speech). It is for this reason that *The Woman in White* does not celebrate the end of the revolutionary era but, instead, feels its loss. Collins's fiction of the post-'48 world is a fiction in which meaning is liquidated. The "blank space" that Hartright finds in the church register, the blank that testifies to Sir Percival's crime, is an apt symbol of the emptiness at the heart of the novel (509).

Although Collins's Victorian readers largely overlooked this emptiness, they did register the writer's effort to construct a new fiction out of the wreckage of worn-out revolutionary narratives. Victorian reviewers, for instance, often disparaged the sensation school as a French import in which they caught a whiff of sexual and political transgression.[20] Later novelists indebted to the new genre even brought Collins's revolutionary subtext back to the surface, setting their stories of thrilling domestic intrigue in revolutionary France during the first Revolution.[21] That twentieth- and twenty-first century scholars have been slow to recognize Collins's preoccupation with Continental political history only points to a stubborn blind spot in our view of Victorian literature: we do not think of Victorians as Europeans and, as a result, are wary of reading Victorian texts in terms of nineteenth-century European history. This analysis of Collins should begin to show that, for many Victorian writers, political events on the Continent were powerful forces shaping the way they experienced and imagined modern Victorian life.

NOTES

1. Kelly's book was one of two British accounts of the French Revolution of 1848 published within weeks of the February Revolt. Kelly, a journalist, compiled his *Narrative* to capitalize on the "revolution mania" that seized the British public between February and June, 1848, when the June Insurrection brought an end to the revolution proper. During these months, coverage of events in France dominated the metropolitan dailies and weeklies, and articles on French politics were staples in light magazines as well as sober political reviews.
2. Peter Stallybrass and D. Sandy Petrey have written especially useful articles exploring how the rise of Louis Bonaparte challenged Marx's theory of class representation.
3. A *Times* article about the February Revolt shows just how commonplace it was for Victorians to use aesthetic categories when evaluating the new revolution. Drawing readers' attention to a revolutionary crowd, the *Times*'s Paris correspondent writes, "You will hence perceive that there is to-day the same mixture of the grave and the gay, of tragedy and farce, that a French assemblage (I will not call it a mob) always exhibits" ("Express from Paris" 8).

4. Tamar Heller's *Dead Secrets* offers the most extensive and important exploration of revolution in Collins's writings. Although Heller recognizes that the mid-century crises influenced Collins, her analysis treats revolution as a discursive category rather than a political event. She thus argues that, for Collins, revolution is a "*sign for* the outbreak of types of gender and class rebellion," as well as for "a drama about the male intellectual's often conflicted relationship to this rebellion" (italics added, 10). For my response to her reading of *The Woman in White*, see below.

5. For details on the original publication of "Nine O'Clock," "Gabriel's Marriage," and "Sister Rose," see Catherine Peters (112, 127, 150). Neither Peters nor Collins's bibliographer, Kirk Beetz, mentions "Midnight Mass," but *The Wellesley Index to Victorian Periodicals, 1824–1900* attributes it to Collins (4: 71). Although Collins does not indicate that "Midnight Mass" is an English translation of a Balzac story, it most certainly is. See Balzac's "An Episode during the Terror" (originally published in 1831). *The Lighthouse* was performed during Collins's life, but it was not—and still has not been—published. For more on *The Lighthouse*, see Peters (156) and Beetz's *Wilkie Collins: An Annotated Bibliography* (5).

6. See Beetz's "Wilkie Collins and *The Leader*" on Collins's contributions to the journal during the years 1851–56. According to Beetz, Collins was "evidently a socialist sympathizer" when he began working for the publication ("*The Leader*" 22). It is important to note, however, that the young writer's essays and reviews did not address politics and that he distanced himself from the publication's heterodox religious positions ("*The Leader*" 23–25). For more recent discussions of Collins and radicalism, see Dolin and Dougan, as well as Dolin's "Collin's Career and the Visual Arts" (esp. 18–20).

7. John Sutherland cites Collins's account of the composition of the novel: "I began this story on the 15th of August 1859. . . , and finished it on the 26th July 1860" (647).

8. France and Piedmont's war with Austria began in April of 1859 and lasted until Napoleon III arranged the Villafranca agreement on July 11, 1859. Garibaldi and his "Thousand" sailed for Sicily in May, 1860. He had conquered the island by July and was welcomed by the city of Naples in September. See Riall, chs. 6–8, for a detailed account of the complex history of the Risorgimento from 1859 through 1861.

9. Although Riall's biography offers the definitive account of Garibaldi's popularity throughout Europe during these years (see esp. ch. 7), Harry Rudman's classic study includes a more complete catalogue of the large body British writing on Garibaldi (see chs. 14–15). Maura O'Connor's chapter on Garibaldi is also worth noting. She stresses that the British admired Garibaldi because he "project[ed] . . . all of the virtuous characteristics they associated with the gentleman and the hero" (151).

10. For a chronology of events in the novel, see Sutherland 662–68.

11. For a brief account of political events in France, 1849–52, see Roger Price (esp. 42–50). Gordon Wright helps us understand the significance of the coup. He reports that, after two days of fighting, "several hundred protesters had been

killed and twenty-six thousand arrested, ten thousand of whom were subsequently transported to Algeria'' (140). See Thomas Forstenzer (esp. ch. 6) for detailed discussion of how the repressive measures taken after the coup represent a watershed in the French government's effort to suppress radical opposition.

12. Marion, for instance, insists that Count Fosco ''is a most remarkable likeness, on a large scale, of the Great Napoleon'' (*Woman* 218). The Count's resemblance to the French emperor is more than skin deep, however. Like both Napoleons, Fosco flirts with radicalism before revealing his true commitment to ''the rights of the aristocracy, and the sacred principles of Order'' (625). For evidence of the association of artisan-workers with revolutionary violence, see Dickens's *Tale of Two Cities*. Although the Defarges are shopkeepers, other revolutionaries include the mender of roads and the wood-sawyer. Dickens also associates the novel's principle symbol of radical violence, the ''grindstone,'' with skilled labor, noting that the revolutionaries have borrowed it from ''some neighbouring smithy, or other workshop'' (269; ch. 32).

13. Scholars disagree when it comes to the question of which imperial power employs the Count. Lillian Nayder, following Harvey Sucksmith, argues that the Italian has been sent by the Austrian government to spy on London's Italian exile community during the Great Exhibition (''Agents of Empire in *The Woman in White*'' 2). Hutter, however, claims that Fosco is in the pay of Napoleon III's France (''Fosco Lives!'' 218). The novel supports both interpretations. On the one hand, the Italian is a ''Count of the Holy Roman Empire''; on the other, he is associated with the Rubelles, French spies (*Woman* 598).

14. See Sutherland (645) for a discussion of the novel's publication history.

15. In a brief discussion of *The Woman in White* as a ''sequel'' to *A Tale of Two Cities*, Heller notes that ''Anne's 'wild' and animal-like hatred, the clenched fist she shakes 'passionately' in the air, transform her into an iconic figure for the revolutionary woman, of which Madame Defarge is but one example'' (121).

16. The two men's crimes are as follows: Percival has forged a record of his parents' union; the marquis, before inheriting his brother's title, had raped a pregnant woman after causing her husband's death and then had killed her brother. It is also worth noting that although the marquis is murdered long before his chateau is set on fire, Dickens clearly represents the apocalyptic blaze as punishment for the aristocrat's life of cruelty. As the building burns, the narrator observes that one of the stone faces decorating the building ''struggled out of the smoke again, as if it were the face of the cruel Marquis, burning at the stake and contending with the fire'' (*Tale* 241; ch. 29).

17. Hutter agrees that Dickens embraces the Christian concept of resurrection, but he also argues that the novelist uses Cruncher, the resurrection man, to explore a subversive understanding of the term: ''Cruncher shows us what Carton cannot see: the emptiness of death, the nothingness of dust'' (''The Novelist as Resurrectionist'' 19). In this respect, Dickens himself deflates the theme of resurrection.

18. In the novel, Fosco has worked as an author. The Count claims to have had a career as a novelist, writing ''preposterous romances, on the French model, for a second-rate Italian paper'' (256). The villain also makes a show of his literary talent when Hartright forces him to compose the confession.

19. According to Brooks, after the Enlightenment challenged "the explanatory and cohesive force of sacred myth," many writers turned to the melodramatic mode, with its emphasis on the moral drama of good and evil, in an effort " 'prove' the existence of a moral universe" (15–16, 20).
20. As Brantlinger reports, some reviewers, incensed by sensation writers' preoccupation with illegitimate passions, argued that sensation novels represented the "British equivalent of the suspect 'French novels' " (6). These complaints about the genre's questionable morality, as well as criticism of its alleged aesthetic failings, masked a clear political subtext. For instance, Margaret Oliphant reviles the sensation school first for its indulgence of "French excitement" and then for its flirtation with the French-identified political system of "Socialism" (111).
21. I have identified three such novels: Sarah Tyler's *Citoyenne Jacqueline; A Woman's Lot in the French Revolution* (1866), Margaret Robert's *The Atelier Du Lys, or, An Art Student in the Reign of Terror* (1876), and Mary Elizabeth Braddon's novel of the French Revolution of 1848, *Ishmael* (1884).

WORKS CITED

Balzac, Honoré de. "Un Épisode sous la Terreur." *La Comedie humaine*. Ed. Marcel Bouteron. v. 7. Paris: Gallimard, 1955.

Beetz, Kirk. *Wilkie Collins: An Annotated Bibliography, 1889–1976*. Metuchen: Scarecrow, 1978.

———. "Wilkie Collins and *The Leader*." *Victorian Periodical's Review* 15 (1982): 20–29.

Braddon, Mary Elizabeth. *Ishmael: A Novel*. London: John and Robert Maxwell, n.d.

Brantlinger, Patrick. "What Is 'Sensational' about the Sensation Novel?" *Nineteenth-Century Fiction* 37 (1982): 1–28.

Brooks, Peter. *The Melodramatic Imagination: Balzac, Henry James, Melodrama, and the Mode of Excess*. New Haven: Yale UP, 1976.

Collins, Wilkie. *After Dark*. 1856. New York: Collier, [1900]. 118–263.

———. *Antonina: or the Fall of Rome*. 1850. New York: Collier, [1900].

———. "Gabriel's Marriage." 1853. *Wilkie Collins: The Complete Shorter Fiction*. Ed. Julian Thompson. London: Robinson, 1995. 104–30.

———. "Midnight Mass: An Episode in the History of the Reign of Terror." *Bentley's Miscellany* 32 (1852): 629–38.

———. "Nine O'Clock!" 1852. *Wilkie Collins: The Complete Shorter Fiction*. Ed. Julian Thompson. London: Robinson, 1995. 90–101.

———. *No Name*. Ed. Virginia Blain. 1862. Oxford: Oxford UP, 1993.

———. "The Poisoned Meal." *My Miscellanies*. 1863. New York: Collier, [1900]. 371–423.

———. *The Woman in White*. 1860. Ed. Matthew Sweet. London: Penguin, 2003.

Dickens, Charles. *A Tale of Two Cities*. 1859. Ed. Richard Maxwell. London: Penguin, 2000.

Dolin, Tim. "Collins's Career and the Visual Arts." *The Cambridge Companion to Wilkie Collins*. Ed. Jenny Bourne Taylor. Cambridge: Cambridge UP, 2006. 7–22.

Dolin, Tim, and Lucy Dougan. "*Basil*, Art, and the Origins of Sensation Fiction. *Reality's Dark Light: The Sensational Wilkie Collins*. Ed. Maria Bachman and Don Cox. Knoxville: U of Tennessee P, 2003. 1–33.

"Express from Paris." *The Times* 24 Feb. 1848: 8.

Forstenzer, Thomas. *French Provincial Police and the Fall of the Second Republic: Social Fear and Counterrevolution*. Princeton: Princeton UP, 1981.

Heller, Tamar. *Dead Secrets: Wilkie Collins and the Female Gothic*. New Haven: Yale UP, 1992.

Hughes, Winifred. "The Sensation Novel." *A Companion to the Victorian Novel*. Ed. Patrick Brantlinger and William Thesing. London: Blackwell, 2002. 260–77.

Hutter, Albert. "Fosco Lives!" *Reality's Dark Light: The Sensational Wilkie Collins*. Ed. Maria Bachman and Don Cox. Knoxville: U of Tennessee P, 2003. 195–238.

———. "The Novelist as Resurrectionist: Dickens and the Dilemma of Death." *Dickens Studies Annual*. 12 (1983): 1–39.

James, Henry. "Miss Braddon." 1865. *Wilkie Collins: The Critical Heritage*. Ed. Norman Page. London: Routledge, 1974. 122–24.

Kelly, Walter. *Narrative of the French Revolution of 1848*. London: Chapman, 1848.

Marx, Karl. *The Eighteenth Brumaire of Louis Bonaparte*. 1852. New York: International, 1987.

Mighall, Robert. *A Geography of Victorian Gothic Fiction: Mapping History's Nightmares*. Oxford: Oxford UP, 1999.

Miller, D. A. "*Cage aux folles*: Sensation and Gender in Wilkie Collins's *The Woman in White*." *Speaking of Gender*. Ed. Elaine Showalter. New York: Routledge, 1989. 187–215.

Nayder, Lillian. "Agents of Empire in *The Woman in White*. *The Victorian Newsletter* 83 (1993): 1–7.

————. *Unequal Partners: Charles Dickens, Wilkie Collins, and Victorian Authorship*. Ithaca, NY: Cornell UP, 2002.

O'Connor, Maura. *The Romance of Italy and the English Political Imagination*. New York: St. Martin's, 1998.

Oliphant, Margaret. "Sensation Novels." 1862. *Wilkie Collins: The Critical Heritage*. Ed. Norman Page. London: Routledge, 1974. 122–24.

Paulson, Ronald. "Gothic Fiction and the French Revolution." *ELH* 48.3 (1981): 532–54.

Peters, Catherine. *The King of Inventors: A Life of Wilkie Collins*. Princeton: Princeton UP, 1991.

Petrey, D. Sandy. "Representing Revolution." Rev. of *Revolution and Repetition*, by Jeffrey Mehlman. *Diacritics* 9.2 (1979): 2–16.

Price, Richard, ed. *1848 in France*. Ithaca: Cornell UP, 1975.

Riall, Lucy. *Garibaldi: Invention of a Hero*. New Haven: Yale UP, 2007.

Robert, Margaret. *The Atelier Du Lys, or, An Art Student in the Reign of Terror*. London: Longmans, 1876.

Rudman, Harry. *Italian Nationalism and English Letter: Figures of the Risorgimento and Victorian Men of Letters*. New York: Columbia UP, 1940.

Stallybrass, Peter. "Marx and Heterogeneity: Thinking the Lumpenproletariat." Representations 31 (1990): 69–95.

Sutherland, John, ed. *The Woman in White*. Oxford: Oxford UP, 1998.

Tyler, Sarah. *Citoyenne Jacqueline; A Woman's Lot in the Great French Revolution*. London: Strahan, 1866.

The Wellesley Index to Victorian Periodicals, 1824–1900. 5 vols. 1966–1989. Ed. Walter Houghton. Vol. 4. Toronto: U of Toronto P, 1987.

Wright, Gordon. *France in Modern Times: From the Enlightenment to the Present*. New York: Norton, 1981.

Panoptical Delusions: British India in
The Sign of Four

Lawrence Frank

In The Sign of Four, *Arthur Conan Doyle responded to an imperial discourse that emerged in the writings of Thomas Babington Macaulay, Henry Maine, Alfred Lyall, John Seeley, and John Strachey, among others. In their books, Doyle encountered a characteristic argument and shared figures of speech indebted to Jeremy Bentham and to James Fitzjames Stephen: the Raj became, especially in Strachey's* India *(1888) a machine for panoptical surveillance. In various tales featuring Sherlock Holmes, Doyle proceeded to turn the arguments and the tropes of the apologists for the Raj against them. In* The Sign of Four, *a fleeting allusion to Millbank Penitentiary evokes the Panopticon and Agra Fort during the Great Mutiny, as described by Mark Thornhill in his account of the Mutiny. The novella transforms Agra Fort into an imperial edifice, established on panoptical principles, whose foundations are eroded by the greed that informed the imperial project in India from the start.*

> The regimen of a blockaded town should be cheerfully submitted to when high purposes require it, but is it the ideal perfection of human existence?
>
> —John Stuart Mill

Persuasion, indeed, is a kind of force. It consists
in showing a person the consequences of his actions. It is, in a word, force applied through
the mind.

—James Fitzjames Stephen

I.

It has become something of an orthodoxy among academic critics to read
Arthur Conan Doyle's Sherlock Holmes tales through a Foucauldian prism.
Following an earlier Marxist tradition, they argue that detective fiction as a
genre perpetuates a prevailing worldview, reinforcing the assumptions that
inform a society, in the instance of the novellas and stories in which Sherlock
Holmes appears, the society of late-Victorian and early twentieth-century
Britain founded upon the ideology of a liberal imperialism.[1]

For those critics writing in the vein of D. A. Miller's *The Novel and
the Police* (1988), Sherlock Holmes functions to restore social order as he
encounters the crimes and the mysteries that confront him. For others, he
acts as an agent of empire, rationalizing the British presence on the Indian
subcontinent and elsewhere in the colonial world.[2] One of the more sweeping
claims is made by Ronald R. Thomas for whom detective fiction becomes an
"accomplice" (10) of various institutions—the police, forensic science, the
legal system—that enforce the values of a late nineteenth-century economic
liberalism. In turning to Doyle's *A Study in Scarlet* (1887) and *The Sign of
Four* (1890), Thomas claims that "[t]he Sherlock Holmes stories of the late
1880s and 1890s . . . may be regarded as popular agents in forging that new
identity" of the "true Englishman" so necessary for Britain "to secure its
identity as the predestined ruler of a great global empire" (238–39).

But, in a recent appreciation of Doyle's Sherlock Holmes stories in *The
New York Review of Books*, the novelist Michael Chabon observes, "to read
Sherlock Holmes, regardless of his frequent service to Queen and Empire, as
a prop and agent of the dominant social order, to regard the function and
effect of the stories as characteristic of industrialized, imperialist, Darwinistic,
bourgeois, nineteenth-century Britain, the literary kin of *Bentham's panopticon* . . . misses the point." For Chabon, the stories in the *Strand Magazine*
do not "reinforce or validate the dominant social order but . . . transcend
it, . . . if only for the space of twenty pages." Chabon goes further, quoting
the conclusion to "The Cardboard Box" (1893), a story dealing with a bizarre
ménage a trois that ends in a grotesque double murder : " 'What is the
meaning of it, Watson?' said Holmes . . . 'What object is served by this circle
of misery and violence and fear? It must tend to some end, or *else our universe
is ruled by chance*, which is unthinkable. But what end? There is the great

standing perennial problem to which human reason is as far from an answer as ever' '' (Chabon 14–15, emphasis added).[3]

So much then, Michael Chabon suggests, for the argument that the Sherlock Holmes tales function only to discipline human subjectivity.[4] In fact, his words turn us elsewhere, away from the spell cast upon us by Holmes's pronouncements and deeds, to a reconsideration of Arthur Conan Doyle's artistry in his detective fiction. His well-documented ambivalence toward the character that had made him famous and rich touches upon a resentment of the way in which Holmes had obscured not only the seriousness of his historical novels, but the intellectual and imaginative presence of Wayne Booth's implied author hovering behind Dr. Watson's accounts. It is this "Doyle" who marshals a complex array of allusions that point to other texts to which the tales respond while Watson and even Holmes remain . . . silent.

Writing in *Through the Magic Door* (1907) of the authors, past and present, who were his "own favourites"(4), Doyle turned especially to Thomas Babington Macaulay (1800–1859), observing that his historical essays "seem[ed] entwined into his whole life"(6). He remarked upon those on "Milton, Machiavelli, Hallam, Southey, Bunyan, . . . Clive, Hastings, Chatham" as "nuclei for thought!"—particularly through Macaulay's "broad sweep of allusion"(7). Here, Doyle hinted at his own practice through which allusion would inform even the Sherlock Holmes tales. Throughout Holmes's various cases there appear allusions, often fleeting, that function in a Bakhtinian sense. Never "voiceless words that belong to no one[,] [e]ach word [each allusion] contains voices that are sometimes infinitely distant, unnamed, *almost* impersonal[,] . . . *almost* undetectable, and voices resounding nearby and simultaneously" (Bakhtin 124, emphasis added). As "nuclei for thought," such allusions become clues integrated into the detective plot, generating associations that both complement and resist the thrust of a narrative that seemingly drives to the requisite resolution.[5]

In the essay that follows, I shall turn to familiar figures—Jeremy Bentham (1748–1832), James Mill (1773–1836), John Stuart Mill (1806–1873), John Seeley (1834–1895)—as well as to those perhaps less familiar—James Fitzjames Stephen (1829–1894), John Strachey (1823–1907), and Mark Thornhill (1822–1900) among them—not to summarize their justifications of empire, but to identify a characteristic language and shared figures of speech to which Doyle offered a counter-narrative. In stories like "The Five Orange Pips" (1891) and "The Crooked Man" (1893), he enacted a critique of British imperialism that exposed the chasm between a professed idealism and the crimes to which the imperial project had led, the institution of slavery perhaps the most notorious of all. And, yet, Doyle's attitudes toward empire were never to be free of those contradictions, even enthusiasms, that continue to be so unsettling.[6]

Such a discussion provides the context in which to consider *The Sign of Four* as Sherlock Holmes and Dr. Watson, in their service to their client Mary Morstan, uncover the theft of a fabulous treasure and a murder at Agra Fort during the Great Mutiny of 1857–58. As Holmes and Watson negotiate the maze of events confronting them, the plot of the novella becomes organized around three sites: Pondicherry Lodge in Norwood, London; Millbank Penitentiary on the banks of the Thames (now the site of the Tate Gallery); and Agra Fort under siege during the Mutiny. Each site becomes a figurative nucleus of a complex set of allusions that demand the recovery of various texts and contexts that point to the Mutiny and, beyond, to British rule in India after 1858. The allusions, some of them ''almost undetectable'' (Bakhtin 124) work to subvert British claims to a moral superiority to the people of India and to a benevolence mandated by the historical imperative, stated in Comtean terms, to bring European institutions to the subcontinent. These claims were to be articulated sweepingly in John Strachey's *India* (1888), a book that inadvertently revealed the workings of a panoptical regime that, in spite of pretensions to the contrary, facilitated the designs of those who had come to India only to enrich themselves.[7]

II.

In *The Sign of Four*, the Great Mutiny figures as the signal event that Thomas Metcalf, in his *Ideologies of the Raj* (1994), describes as a ''searing trauma'' for the British people (43).[8] It led *The Economist* in its 26 September 1857 issue to pose a challenge to the nation. ''The Bright Side of the Picture'' referred to ''the crisis through which we are passing'' as a ''terrible catastrophe'' that had roused the British from complacency: ''our very Empire in the East has for a moment been shaken to its foundation.'' The situation required a ''new edifice'' that was to be built upon the ruins of the old. It was time ''to study thoroughly and to determine distinctly . . . the principles on which our entire government of Hindostan [*sic*] shall in future be conducted'':

> We must now decide . . . whether in [the] future India is to be governed *as a Colony or a Conquest*; . . . whether we are to rule our Asiatic subjects . . . as their natural and indefeasible superiors, by virtue of our higher civilisation, our purer religion, our sterner energies, our subtler intellect, our . . . indomitable will;—or whether . . . we are to regard the Hindoos [*sic*] and Mahometans [*sic*] as our equal fellow-citizens, fit to be entrusted with the functions of self-government.   (1061–62)

The response to the challenge posed only rhetorically in *The Economist* would appear in James Fitzjames Stephen's *Liberty, Equality, Fraternity* (1873/74).

From 1869 to 1872 Stephen served as legal member of the Supreme Council in Calcutta, working to complete Thomas Babington Macaulay's reform of the Indian legal code. On his return voyage to England in 1872, Stephen began to write *Liberty, Equality, Fraternity* in response to John Stuart Mill's *On Liberty* (1859) and *Utilitarianism* (1861).[9] But, as the first edition of 1873 and then the second edition of 1874 made clear, Stephen had in mind any number of Mill's writings, including *The Subjection of Women* (1869)—wrong "from the first sentence to the last"—and the posthumous *Autobiography* (1873), with its account of Mill's education, that Stephen saw as a threat to the "[l]egislators and the founders of great institutions"—like the Raj?—who must deny "individual choice as to [the exercise of] religious or moral principles" (188, 100).

With his sneering allusion to the motto of the French Revolution, Stephen produced an Anglo-Indian tract that rejected out of hand Mill's Romantic individualism with its celebration of a duty to self-development. Instead, he endorsed the pessimism of Thomas Hobbes's *Leviathan* (1651): "When Hobbes taught that the state of nature is a state of war, he threw an unpopular truth into a shape liable to be misunderstood; but can anyone seriously doubt that war and conflict are inevitable so long as men are what they are" (111). In Stephen's view most people "are so constructed that . . . there are and always will be in the world an enormous mass of bad and indifferent people—people who deliberately do all sorts of things which they ought not to do, and leave undone all sorts of things which they ought to do" (72).

The language echoing the "General Confession" from the Order for Evening Prayer signaled Stephen's acquiescence to the burdens of empire: "The only way by which it is practically possible to act upon [men and women] at all is by compulsion or restraint" (72). The stay against the anarchy that the British had claimed threatened India with the death of Aurangzeb in 1707 must be coercion exercised by "an efficient minority . . . [of] an indifferent and self-indulgent majority" (83). There was in Stephen's view no place for vacillation: the English in India "*were forced to become* the direct rulers of the whole country, and to provide it with a set of laws and institutions. They found . . . that it is impossible to lay down any principles of legislation at all unless you are prepared to say, I am right, and you are wrong, and your view shall give way to mine . . . one of us two must rule and the other must obey, and I mean to rule" (90, emphasis added).[10]

And rule the English would through the deployment, as Auguste Comte had suggested, of "temporal and spiritual powers . . . understood as two distinct agents by which mankind are to be governed, each of which is to have its own sphere of action" (Stephen 128). Stephen went on to explain the relation of the temporal and the spiritual, of force and persuasion: "They are alternative means of influencing mankind. . . . No one applies force when persuasion will do and no sensible person applies force till persuasion has failed. . . . Persuasion . . . is, in a word, force applied through the mind'' (129–30). With these words, Stephen acknowledged the need for an ideological rationale for the Raj that would serve the purposes of the rulers, that "efficient minority," even as it demanded the acceptance of the ruled.[11]

Such an ideology was to emerge in the last decades of the nineteenth century in the form of a story, as Thomas Metcalf argues, ordering India's "past into a coherent narrative, . . . creat[ing] a secure and usable past" (148). The narrative so shaped by men like Alfred Lyall (1835–1911), Henry Maine (1822–1888), and John Strachey—whose *India* was ready-to-hand as Arthur Conan Doyle turned to the writing of *The Sign of Four* in September 1889—was informed by a broadly Comtean view of human history.[12] In their writings these men, each of whom had served in India, shared the basic assumptions enunciated by E. B. Tylor in his *Primitive Culture* (1871) and, later, by John Seeley in his *Expansion of England* (1883). In *Primitive Culture*, Tylor wrote of the natural "laws" governing the "stages of [human] development or evolution." In discussing "the culture[s] of the lower races"— Indian culture, of course, among them—Tylor resorted to the evolutionary doctrine of survivals, treating so-called primitive societies as living fossils, in a state of arrested development, that exhibited obsolete stages of intellectual and social organization. It was the historical obligation of Europeans to preside over such societies. It was a heavy burden, but one to be borne: the "doctrine of development . . . will lead [men] . . . to continue the progressive work of past ages . . . where barbaric hordes groped blindly, cultured men can often move onward with clear view. It is . . . at times [a] painful . . . office . . . to expose the remains of crude old culture . . . and to mark these out for destruction" (1: 1, 11, 16–17; 2: 453).

In the Cambridge University lectures that became *The Expansion of England* (1883), John Seeley followed E. B. Tylor, turning to an evolutionary vocabulary to call for a history, unlike that of Thomas Babington Macaulay's *History of England* (1849–61), that should be scientific in its methodology, even as he made the now notorious aside, "We seem, as it were, to have conquered and peopled half the world in a fit of absence of mind" (Seeley 10). Seeley set out to rise "above the current of mere chronological narrative, to apply a fixed principle to the selection of facts, grouping them not by nearness in time, nor by their personal biographical connection, but by the internal affinity of causation" (115). Invoking Tylor's "uniform action of uniform causes" (Tylor 1: 1), Seeley nonetheless recognized certain contingent events driving the histories of empire, past and present, as they reveal "the laws of political *growth and change*" (275, emphasis added).

The important contingent event in British history, according to Seeley, was the defeat of the Spanish Armada: "if once we begin to think of England as a *living organism*, which in the Elizabethan age began a process of expansion . . . into Greater Britain," we "shall feel the need of a completely new set of divisions to mark the successive stages of the expansion" (142, emphasis added). Such stages occurred irrespective of the reigns of monarchs or the acts of great men. Instead, the laws of history drew the English after 1588 to "parts of the globe which were so empty that they offered an unbounded scope for new settlement" (55). The "Continent of America [that] was so roomy, so thinly peopled" (119), exerted a centripetal force drawing people out of Europe—and England.

In the case of India, Seeley could not resort to the convenient myth of the empty continent. For, in India, "the English nation is but an imperceptible drop in the ocean of an Asiatic population" (Seeley 54). Instead, he invoked another myth, that of the anarchy following the death of Aurangzeb in 1707. With the collapse of the Mughal Empire, a political vacuum occurred, drawing in the British against their will: Robert Clive (1725–1774) and Warren Hastings (1732–1818) found in India "a condition of anarchy [that] seems almost to have been chronic" (Seeley 226). So it was that "[o]ur acquisition of India was made blindly. Nothing great that has ever been done by Englishmen was done *so unintentionally, so accidentally, as the conquest of India*" (Seeley 207, emphasis added). Under such circumstances, Seeley would claim, "It is possible to hold that England would be better off now had she founded no such Empire at all. . . . But the abandonment of India is an idea which even those who believe that we shall one day be driven to it are not accustomed to contemplate. . . . There are some deeds which, though they had been better not done, cannot be undone" (224).[13]

Echoing the language of *Liberty, Equality, Fraternity*, Seeley offered an apologia for the "Empire in the East." The inexorable laws of political growth and change informed a narrative that pointed to a seeming "Providence . . . that [produced] this *fabric* so blindly piled up [that it] has a chance of becoming a part of the *permanent edifice of civilisation*, . . . the greatest of all [England's] achievements" (303, emphasis added). Impersonal, non-teleogical forces were at work on the Indian subcontinent where "nothing like what is strictly called a conquest took place": "certain traders inhabiting certain seaport towns in India, were induced, *almost forced*, in the anarchy caused by the fall of the Mogul Empire, to give themselves a military character and employ troops, . . . by means of [which] they acquired territory and at last almost all the territory of India" (240–41, emphasis added).

In justifying British rule in India and explaining away the Great Mutiny, Seeley repeated the claims of those who had preceded him in the eighteenth and nineteenth centuries: "On the whole then it may be said that India has never really been united so as to form one state except under the English" (260). The "history of the great Mutiny" must be properly understood: it was not "a mutiny caused by a nationality-movement spreading among the people and at last gaining the army." Rather, "[i]t began in the army and was regarded passively by the people" (267–68). However, "the moment a mutiny is . . . the expression of a universal feeling of nationality, at that moment all hope is at an end, as all desire ought to be at an end, of preserving our Empire" (271).

But for those who had served the Raj after the Mutiny, such a moment "when all hope is at an end" was never to be. In their various books Henry Maine, Alfred Lyall, and John Strachey created a narrative—James Fitzjames Stephen's embodiment of "force applied through the mind"?—that was part Comtean, part evolutionary, that many found compelling. In his emphatically titled *India*, John Strachey set out to provide a capstone to the figurative edifice that was the product of many hands. He offered a pastiche of paraphrases and quotations from Maine, John Seeley, and Lyall, moving toward the acceptance of the onerous burden of empire, observing that while "we are foreigners [in India], and although I suppose no foreign government was ever accepted with less repugnance than that with which the British Government is accepted in India, the fact remains that there never was a country, and never will be, in which the government of foreigners is really popular" (359).

Inevitably, Strachey invoked the racial slurs and stereotypes in existence long before the Mutiny, now sanctioned by a purportedly scientific account of Indian history. At the start he observed, "There was never, as Professor Seeley has shown, any conquest of India by the English, according to the ordinary sense of the word 'conquest' " (6). Following Seeley and Stephen, he defended "an absolute government . . . administered by a small body of foreigners far more advanced in civilisation than the people of the country itself" (263). Indian culture remained in a state of arrested development, as Henry Maine had argued in *Ancient Law* (1861), and as Alfred Lyall had repeated in his *Asiatic Studies* (1882): "India with its multiplicity of religions and tribes, and its variety of political groups, is the best *surviving specimen*, on a large scale, of the ancient work of history" (vi–vii, emphasis added). As a living fossil India became "a great continent in which there are no nationalities": "For nationality is, as *we* know, a thing of modern growth" (2, emphasis added). In the same manner Lyall wrote of Indian religions: in India "[w]e begin to feel the true religious atmosphere of past ages. . . . We see that the polytheism of India still flows from sources and assumes shapes similar to those which produced the beliefs and worships of præ-Christian Europe" (vii). From its condition of primitive polytheism, Lyall argued, Hindu India was to be guided through evolutionary stages by those initiates who understood that "[Auguste] Comte has noticed with his usual insight into the minds of primitive people the manner in which a religious belief adapts itself to . . . social and political needs; . . . As the state of society *improves*, the religious beliefs seem to develop themselves by *a sort of natural selection*'' (58–59, emphasis added).

In *India*, Strachey picked up on Alfred Lyall's dollop of Darwinism, quoting *Asiatic Studies:* ''The Hindu religion is [according to Lyall] 'a religious chaos[,] . . . a tangled jungle of disorderly superstitions, ghosts, and demons, demi-gods, and deified saints, household gods, local gods, universal gods' '' (207–08). It was a historical imperative to uproot this jungle, to domesticate a tangled bank. In the words of Henry Maine, the ''Village Community of India . . . is known to be of immense antiquity[,] . . . the least destructible institution of a society which never willingly surrenders . . . to innovation'' (216). Maine had encountered a vestigial form of social organization that was to be transformed, under British direction, by the introduction of ''the Law of Persons, . . . the Law of Property and of Inheritance, and . . . the Law of Contract'' (306).

Even with this Comtean narrative available to him, Strachey repeated the traditional slurs that had existed before the Mutiny, now even more appealing after it.[14] He wrote of ''Mohammedans [*sic*] . . . [as] more generally energetic than Hindus, . . . possess[ing] greater independence of character,'' while the ''effeminate Bengáli'' had failed to adapt to the advantages of an English education so generously provided to them (Strachey 224–25). In fact, ''the existence side by side of these hostile creeds is one of the strong points in our political position in India'' (225). Ever ''Stephen's disciple'' (Metcalf 58), Stachey echoed James Fitzjames Stephen and John Seeley: ''We cannot foresee the time in which the cessation of *our* rule would not be the signal for universal anarchy and ruin, and it is clear that the only hope for India is the long continuance of the *benevolent* but *strong* government of Englishmen'' (360, emphasis added).

In resisting the force of this received narrative, Arthur Conan Doyle in his Sherlock Holmes tales turned the language of the apologists for empire against them, sapping their Comtean account of its apparent power. In stories appearing in the *Strand Magazine* after the publication of *The Sign of Four*, Doyle returned to imperial themes, all the while challenging prevailing rationales for the Raj and for empire. Three years after the publication of *The Sign of Four* Doyle wrote of India during the Great Mutiny in ''The Crooked Man'' (July 1893), one of the stories constituting *The Memoirs of Sherlock Holmes* (1892–93). The events narrated by Dr. Watson take place ''a few months after [his] marriage'' to Mary Morstan (Doyle, ''Man'' 155). Holmes has been called upon to investigate the death of Colonel James Barclay, who has been found in the morning-room of his villa outside of Aldershot, ''lying . . . stone dead, in a pool of his own blood,'' his wife ''stretched insensible upon a couch'' (160). The corpse is distinguished not only by a gash in the back of the head, but by "the contortion of the Colonel's face": "It had set . . . into the most dreadful expression of fear and horror" (162). The circumstances are complicated by the fact that the door to the morning-room has been locked from the inside and that the servants have overheard the colonel and his wife, Nancy, in the midst of a "furious altercation" (160). Inevitably, suspicion falls upon Mrs. Barclay, who, throughout Watson's account, lies stricken by brain-fever, unable to speak for herself.

The description of the corpse and the circumstance of the locked door to the morning-room recall the discovery of the dead Bartholomew Sholto at Pondicherry Lodge, his "features [set] . . . in a horrible smile, a fixed and unnatural grin," behind the locked door to a room "fitted up as a chemical laboratory" (Doyle, *Sign* 37). The intrigue in *The Sign of Four*, like that in "The Crooked Man," points to the Great Mutiny. Imperial themes are present from the start, announced in the name of the Barclay villa. Lachine turns out to be a contraction of "la petite Chine," the trading-post north of Montreal, established by Sieur de la Salle. The name mocked La Salle in his quest "to reach China by way of the Ohio, supposing, from the reports of Indians, this river to flow into the Pacific" (*Encyclopædia Britannica*, 9th ed., 1875–89). Later, in exploring the Mississippi River valley and the coast of the Gulf of Mexico, within "the present limits of Texas," La Salle was killed by his own men near the Trinity River in 1687.

The name of the villa offers an ironic context for the story of Colonel Barclay. According to Holmes, at the time of his death Barclay commanded the Royal Mallows, "one of the most famous Irish regiments in the British Army," noted for its service "both in the Crimea and the Mutiny" (Doyle, "Man" 157). Barclay "started as a full private, was raised to commissioned rank for his bravery at the time of the Mutiny, and so lived to command the regiment in which he once carried a musket" (157). Yet in the midst of an exemplary career there are tell-tale signs. Others have noted that Barclay was "capable of considerable violence and vindictiveness," that he revealed "a dislike of being left alone, especially after dark." Susceptible to a "singular sort of depression," Barclay would himself observe that "the smile had often been struck from his mouth, as if by some invisible hand" (158).

Through his investigation into Barclay's death, Sherlock Holmes discovers that the hand of the past has reached out to fell the colonel, as it has in *The Sign of Four* in the murder of Bartholomew Sholto. In examining the villa and its premises, Holmes finds "traces of [a] mysterious individual" (Doyle, "Man" 163), an unidentified "third person" who had entered the morning-room through its opened French doors, having "crossed the lawn coming from the [adjacent] road" (162–63) as the colonel and his wife were quarreling. The person was accompanied by a "companion" whose footmarks Holmes has traced upon a "sheet of tissue paper" (163). Here, the story again harkens back to *The Sign of Four* and to the make-shift laboratory in which Holmes and Watson come upon "the impression of a wooden stump," evidence of the existence of a "wooden-legged man" (Doyle, *Sign* 40; ch. 6) whom they have yet to see. In the attic above the laboratory, they find other "foot-marks" (52) that indicate that the wooden-legged man, Jonathan Small, has a curious companion, who will prove to be Tonga, the Andaman Islander.

In "The Crooked Man," Holmes concludes that a third person, "accompanied by a strange animal, . . . either struck the Colonel, or . . . the Colonel fell down from sheer fright at the sight of him" (164), striking his head on the fireplace fender in the fall. This inference leads Holmes and Watson to the crooked man of the title who proceeds to tell his story. Before the Great Mutiny, Corporal Henry Wood was "the smartest man in the 117th Foot" (170). As a "harum-scarum, reckless lad," he vied with James Barclay for the love of Nancy Devoy, "the daughter of the colour-sergeant" who "held true to [him]" (170). In the midst of the Mutiny, Wood volunteered to alert the approaching British forces that the cantonment of Bhurtee was under siege and in need of relief. But, then, Sergeant Barclay betrayed him into the hands of the mutineers, initiating a thirty-year ordeal that transformed Wood into "a wretched cripple," reduced to making "a living by the conjuring tricks that [he] had learned" (171) in his years of wandering on the Indian subcontinent. It was upon this deformed figure, "crawling with a stick like a chimpanzee" (171), that Nancy Devoy, now Mrs. Barclay, has chanced on the night of her husband's death.

The intertwined tales of Nancy Devoy, James Barclay, and Henry Wood stand in contrast to a conventional account of the Mutiny like John William Kaye's three-volume *History of the Sepoy War* (1864–76). For Kaye the Mutiny was a national epic peopled by heroic exemplars of the British character: "The story of the Indian Rebellion of 1857 is, perhaps, the most signal illustration of our great national character ever yet recorded in the annals of our history. It was the vehement self-assertion of the Englishman that produced this conflagration; it was the same vehement self-exertion that enabled him, by God's blessing, to trample it out. . . . Because we were too English, the great crisis arose; but it was only because we were English that, when it arose, it did not utterly overwhelm us" (1: xii). Throughout his *Sepoy War* Kaye provided "a bundle of biographies" of "a few eminent men" of a certain rank who were to distinguish themselves, "the *individuality of the English leaders*" marking them off from "the Indian *Dead Level* which the [English] system had created" (1: xii–xiii, emphasis added).

John Kaye did not live to complete his epic tale; it was left to G. B. Malleson to complete it in his *History of the Indian Mutiny of 1857–1858* (1878–80). But in his interrupted account Kaye had remained true to his grand design. He concluded volume 3 with the retaking of Delhi in September 1857 and with the death of John Nicholson "in the prime of his life, amidst a great wail of the universal Camp" (3: 658). Nicholson was not alone: others shared in "great deeds of heroism" as "civil servants of the Company": "men not trained to arms or wearing any insignia of the military profession . . . bore noble witness to the courage and constancy of the national character" (3: 220). [15]

The tale told by Henry Wood points to the "deeds" of others that do not "[bear] noble witness to the courage and constancy of the national character," but to those sordid, personal impulses at work throughout the imperial venture. The system presided over by the East India Company had provided an arena in which the meanest of motives could be given full sway. In "The Crooked Man" this reality is suppressed. At the inquest into the death of Colonel Barclay, "the medical evidence showed conclusively that death was due to apoplexy" (173), dispelling any suspicions about the behavior of Mrs. Barclay. Henry Wood and Teddy, the mongoose that is his companion, return to the obscurity from which they have emerged: they cease to exist. The case proves to be "a simple [one] after all" (173), relieving Holmes of the obligation to make public the circumstances of Barclay's death: "there is no object in raking up this scandal against a dead man, foully as he has acted" (172).

But the private scandal of "The Crooked Man" that need not be bruited about points to the scandal of empire writ large that Arthur Conan Doyle had already addressed in "The Five Orange Pips" (November 1891), a story appearing in *The Adventures of Sherlock Holmes* (1891–92). Again, Dr. Watson's account follows hard upon the mystery of the Agra Treasure. In "the latter days of September"—in "[t]he year '87'"—shortly after his marriage, Watson finds himself "in [his] old quarters at Baker Street" while his "wife [is] on a visit to her aunt's" (Doyle, "Pips" 102–03). He observes, "All day the wind had screamed and the rain had beaten against the windows, so that even here in the heart of great hand-made London we were forced . . . to recognize the presence of those great elemental forces which shrieked at mankind through the bars of his civilization" (103).

With his muted allusion to King Lear "Contending with the fretful elements" (3.1.4), Watson prepares for the appearance of John Openshaw, whose "strange, wild story seem[s] to have come to us from amid the mad elements—blown in upon us like a sheet of seaweed in a gale" (Doyle, "Pips" 113–14). Openshaw tells of the mysterious deaths of his uncle, Elias Openshaw, and, then, of his father, Joseph. According to Openshaw, the uncle had emigrated to the United State, part of a "Continent . . . [that] was so roomy, so thinly peopled" (Seeley 119), where he "became a planter in Florida" (Doyle, "Pips" 105), later a combatant on the side of the Confederacy in the Civil War and, finally, a member of the Ku Klux Klan. He left the States in the late 1860s, returning to England to take up the life of a country gentleman in Sussex, only to receive years later a letter with the initials "K.K.K." and, in the envelope post-marked Pondicherry, India, "five little dried orange pips" (106) that signaled a threat of some sort. After Elias's mysterious death, his brother, Joseph inherited the estate, receiving yet another letter, accompanied again by five orange pips: he, too, died under curious circumstances from a fall into "one of the deep chalk-pits which abound in the neighbourhood" (110). Now John Openshaw has received a similar letter, ordering him to place certain papers on a sun-dial near the manor house on the estate that is now his. Holmes finally determines that the Openshaws have been shadowed by members of the Klan who want to retrieve incriminating documents that, ironically, had been destroyed by Elias years before. But Holmes grasps all of this too late. John Openshaw becomes yet another victim to the family nemesis, dying from a seemingly accidental fall from the Embankment near Waterloo Bridge.

"The Five Orange Pips" offers a meditation upon empire as Elias Openshaw's "sins have overtaken [him]" (106), even as they are visited upon a figurative son, the seemingly innocent John Openshaw. The title of the story may point to John Seeley, who, in *The Expansion of Empire*, wrote that "the State is capable of indefinite growth and expansion": "The ripe fruit dropping from the tree and giving rise to another tree may be natural, but so is the acorn spreading into the huge oak that has hundreds of branches and thousands of leaves" much as "England [had] expand[ed] into Greater Britain" (66). True to this figure of speech, Seeley would later turn to the French Physiocrat Jacques Turgot (1727–1781) who "compared colonies to fruit which hangs on the tree only till it is ripe": "And indeed it might seem natural to picture the aggregate of English communities rather as a family than as an individual. . . . Now we may call our Empire a family, but we must not . . . assume that it will . . . dissolv[e]" as "literal families" (296–97) are wont to do.

In resorting to this "image, provided it is regarded only as an image, and is not converted by sleight of hand into an argument" (296), Seeley had engaged in just such a "sleight of hand" as "The Five Orange Pips" revealed. Seeley had invoked the family tree that may well bear a bitter fruit. For the lands in the West Indies and the North American colonies had been cultivated by enslaved peoples on plantations that had been introduced there and later transplanted to the Indian subcontinent in various forms. The three Klansmen who haunt the Openshaw family travel on the sailing barque the *Lone Star*, that carries them to India, then to Dundee, Scotland, and lastly to Albert Dock in the East End. Their travels reenact a return to the metropole, to the center of empire. [16]

Further, the dried seeds of the story's title suggest the language tree of historical philology. In the *Encyclopædia Britannica* (9th ed.), the entry on the "Orange" not only traces "the diffusion of the orange [tree] . . . in comparatively recent historical periods" from the tropical zones of Asia and India, it reconstructs the history of the "European name of the orange[,][providing] sufficient evidence of its origin and of the line taken in its migration westward: [t]he Sanskrit designation *nagrungo*, becoming *narunjee* in Hindustani, and corrupted by the Arabs into *náranj* (Spanish *naranja*), passed by . . . transition into the Italian *arancia* . . . and the later Provençal *orange*.'' In the story Doyle subtly played with the speculations of Sir William Jones (1746–1794) on Sanskrit as the root of the Indo-European family tree of languages: the three Klansmen from Florida have returned to a place of origin that the Empire has revisited and conquered in an act of filial violation.[17]

In ''The Five Orange Pips,'' Sherlock Holmes fails to save John Openshaw. He is even frustrated in his attempt to deliver the Klansmen who have murdered the three Openshaws to authorities in Savannah, Georgia. He alerts them to the date that the *Lone Star*—with its allusion to the slave state of Texas—is to dock. But he finds that ''[t]here is ever a flaw, however, in the best laid of human plans'' (122). The ''equinoctial gales of that year'' intervene: ''We waited long for news of the *Lone Star* of Savannah, but none ever reached us. We did at last hear that somewhere far out in the Atlantic a shattered sternpost of a boat was seen swinging in the trough of a wave, with the letters 'L.S.' carved upon it'' (122). The bit of wreckage serves as a warning to those who confidently justify empire in narratives that claim to understand the laws of growth and development. With its ''great elemental forces'' that can be experienced ''even here in the heart'' of London (103), the universe is not a place of Comtean law, but a chaos indifferent to human presumption. The storm in the story truly ''blend[s] with the text'' (103) that Watson has been reading on the night of John Openshaw's appearance in Baker Street. He has been ''deep in one of Clark Russell's fine sea stories,'' but ''the howl of the gale from without'' has suggested *King Lear*, while the fate of the *Lone Star* that frustrates ''the best laid of human plans'' (122), even those of Sherlock Holmes, suggests *Macbeth* and ''a tale/Told by an idiot, full of sound and fury/Signifying nothing'' (5.5.26–28).[18]

III.

In the midst of the elemental indifference to human endeavors, the scandal of empire would persist, associated by many late-Victorians with events in the eighteenth century that led to the impeachment trial (1787–95) of Warren Hastings. For those who went out to India, before and after the Great Mutiny, James Mill's account of the trial in his six-volume *History of British India* (1817) would have been required reading, scathing in its criticism of Hasting's behavior as governor-general, yet reassuring in its defense of British rule in India.[19] In his *History*, Mill at once attacked Warren Hastings, the man, and various self-perpetuating oligarchies, including the Court of Directors of the East India Company, the House of Lords, the Judiciary, and the Crown. For Mill, Hastings embodied both "pecuniary corruption" and "[abuse] of the law" (5: 83, 231), always serving personal ends. Yet he did not argue for the end of British rule in India, but for its reform, appealing both to Evangelicals and Utilitarians as they pursued their programs on the subcontinent.[20]

Arthur Conan Doyle may not have known Mill's *History*, but in *Through the Magic Door* he wrote specifically of Macaulay's "two great Indian [essays], Clive and Warren Hastings" (15) that would ultimately guide him to see clearly the institutions that Macaulay and those writing after the Mutiny had set out to defend. Macaulay himself saw India through the prism of the *History of British India*, sharing with James Mill a contempt for a people and a culture that he did not understand. He went out to India in 1834 with "no knowledge of either Sanskrit or Arabic." But, following Mill's lead, Macaulay would write in his Education Minute of 1835 "that a single shelf of a good European library was worth the whole native literature of India and Arabia. . . . [W]hen we pass from works of imagination to works in which facts are recorded and general principles investigated, the superiority of the Europeans becomes absolutely immeasurable" (Macaulay, "Minute" 241).

Such Eurocentric prejudices informed Macaulay's essays on Robert Clive and Warren Hastings in which he proceeded to criticize, and to exonerate, the two as men of their time, acting in accord with the less scrupulous values of the day.[21] He would never criticize their larger achievements and, thus, the legitimacy of the British presence in India. He, nevertheless, acknowledged that in the eighteenth century, before The Regulating Act of 1783, "India House was a lottery-office, which invited everybody to take a chance, and held out ducal fortunes as the prizes destined for the lucky few" (Macaulay, *Essays* 2: 440). An "ungovernable impatience to be rich" (2: 440) was the ethos shared by Clive and Hastings. Yet, with all of his reservations about Clive as someone who "having done what, if not in itself evil, was yet of evil example" (2: 431), he saw Clive as a hero, the man who defeated the French in India and went on to victory at Plassey in 1757, securing Bengal and the Indian subcontinent for England: "a young man of five and twenty, who had been bred a book-keeper" (2: 406), avenged the horrors of the Black Hole, triumphed over Indian forces at Plassey and, thus, "decide[d] the fate of India" (2: 425–26). Clive, however, succumbed to "Oriental politics as a game in which nothing was unfair": "this man, in the other parts of his life an honorable English gentleman and a soldier, was no sooner matched against an Indian intriguer, than he became himself an Indian intriguer, and descended, without scruple, to falsehood, to hypocritical caresses, to the substitution of documents, and to the counterfeiting of hands" (2: 421). Yet, in his military exploits and administrative skills, Clive was to prepare for the nineteenth-century Raj. When he returned to India for the last time in 1765, "Bengal was [still] regarded as a place to which Englishmen were sent only to get rich, by any means, in the shortest possible time" (2: 463). Clive proceeded to make "dauntless and unsparing war on that gigantic system of oppression, extortion, and corruption" (2: 463). He had redeemed himself by guaranteeing *"the purity of our Eastern empire"* (2: 463, emphasis added).

If in his "Lord Clive" Macaulay set out to excuse Clive's deeds, he was to absolve Warren Hastings in a similar fashion, all in defense of "our Eastern empire." Hastings, too, went out to India as a writer for the East India Company with a desire to restore the family fortunes, eager to be rich: "He was not squeamish in pecuniary transactions; but he was neither sordid nor rapacious" (Macaulay, *Essays* 2: 561), even though he was involved in peddling contracts for the Company's opium monopoly. In his defense of Hastings, Macaulay was to invoke familiar prejudices about the Bengali people who were "feeble even to effeminacy" (2: 566). In responding to "those arts which are the natural defence of the weak[,] . . . more familiar to this subtle race than to . . . the Jew of the dark ages" (2: 567), Hastings acted in kind. As in the case of Clive, Macaulay equivocated: yes, Hastings overreached, but "[h]e was beset by rancorous and unprincipled enemies" (2: 588) even as he preserved the "Eastern empire" from yet another French threat during the war with the American colonies: "On a general review of the long administration of Hastings, it is impossible to deny that, against the great crimes by which it is blemished, we have to set off great public services" (2: 619), including his creation of a functioning bureaucracy: "whoever seriously considers what it is to construct . . . *the whole of a machine so vast and complex as a government*, will allow that what Hastings effected deserves high admiration" (2: 620, emphasis added).

Those who went out to India after the Great Mutiny may have mocked Macaulay's "two great Indian [essays], Clive and Warren Hastings" as old-fashioned and unscientific. But they were avid in their desire to join "a small band of strangers, who exercised boundless power over a great indigenous population" (Macaulay, *Essays* 2: 623). They even resorted, in the case of Alfred Lyall, to Macaulay's own words. In his *Asiatic Studies*, Lyall concluded with the observation "that England's prime function in India is . . . to superintend the tranquil elevation of the whole moral and intellectual standard" of the Indian people. A "modern empire" must become "*the best machine* . . . and *the most powerful engine* whereby one confessedly [?] superior race can control and lead other races left without nationality or a working social organization" (305–06, emphasis added).

It was this machine, this engine, that Doyle proceeded artfully to dismantle in *The Sign of Four*, perhaps with John Stuart Mill's *Auguste Comte and Positivism* (1865) in mind.[22] As one of Comte's "English disciples" (Stephen

127), Mill endorsed "M. Comte's general conception of history" with its "laws of progress" governing "the natural order of intellectual progress among mankind": "the determining fact in their [*sic*] intellectual history *must be the natural succession* of theories of the universe[,] . . . consist[ing] of three stages, the theological, the metaphysical, and the positive" (Mill 10: 322, 324, 317, emphasis added). Yet, in turning to "The Later Speculations of M. Comte," Mill wrote of the Comtean vision of society as a virtual "dictatorship (M. Comte's own word)": he proceeded to criticize any "*foundation* [that] organizes an elaborate system for the total suppression of all independent thought" (10: 351, emphasis added). His words suggested the figure of speech to which he had already turned: "The regimen of a blockaded town should be cheerfully submitted to when high purposes require it, but is it the ideal perfection of human existence? M. Comte sees none of these difficulties" (10: 337).[23]

Yet, in his *India*, John Strachey had represented the British government as if it were, indeed, Mill's "blockaded town" under siege: "In India, where an *absolute government* is administered by *a small body of foreigners* far more advanced . . . than the people of the country itself, the most essential condition of safety to *the rulers*, and of good government to *the people*, is that authority should be strong, and authority cannot be strong unless it is *concentrated*" (263, emphasis added). He went on to describe the government in Calcutta from which emanated civil and criminal laws fashioned by men like Macaulay and, more recently, James Fitzjames Stephen: "The Code of Criminal Procedure . . . is in force throughout British India. . . . Among all the laws of India there is no one more important than this, *which regulates the machinery* by which peace and order are maintained" (150–51, emphasis added).

In a situation in which it was difficult to find "properly qualified Natives" (Strachey 260) to serve in administrative capacities, it was "the example [set by] the irreproachable integrity of the Englishmen employed in the higher ranks of the public service" (262) that was to be the model for the Indians in various other posts. In each District of India, Calcutta was represented by the District Officer—sometimes "called the Magistrate and Collector, or Collector alone" (264)—who controlled the administrative machinery. Strachey quoted Sir William Hunter's "India" in *The Imperial Gazetteer of India* (2d ed., 1885–87): "The district officer . . . is a fiscal officer, . . . he is also a revenue and criminal judge, . . . representative of a paternal and not of a constitutional Government. Police, jails, education, municipalities, roads, sanitation, . . . are to him matters of daily concern. He is expected to make himself acquainted with every phase of the social lives of the natives, and with each natural aspect of the country" (264–65). Strachey's next observation was telling: "All this signifies, *not that he is expected to be omniscient*, but that the magistrate and collector is the principle officer of Government . . . through whom *all the orders and measures of the ruling power are issued* . . . and on whom the Government depends for information of *every serious matter that occurs*'' (265, emphasis added).[24]

The implications of *India*—even with the disclaimer that the district officer was not ''expected to be omniscient''—became clearer as Strachey turned to the various public works undertaken by an enlightened regime in the years after the Mutiny. Roads, irrigation canals, dikes, railways, and a modern telegraph system would end famine and lift India out of poverty, even as they conveniently made possible ''[t]he maintenance of [a] dominion that is essential to the interest of India herself'' (114).[25] In his enumeration of British achievements, Strachey pressed on: ''Every district has its gaol, and there are *central prisons in convenient situations*. There are few countries in Europe where the gaols are so well looked after. *A great Indian prison* is a model of cleanliness and good management'' (271, emphasis added). As the ''representative of a paternal and not of a constitutional Government,'' Strachey's district officer had become Jeremy Bentham's inspector, exercising the power of surveillance. For ''the fundamental advantages'' of Bentham's Panopticon involved ''the *apparent omnipresence* of [an] inspector (if divines will allow . . . the expression) combined with the extreme facility of his *real presence*'' (Bentham 4: 45).

It was, then, appropriate that in *Liberty, Equality, Fraternity*, James Fitzjames Stephen had acknowledged ''the immense practical importance'' of Bentham's ''speculations,'' sensing in the ''Panopticon; or, The Inspection-House'' a model for a regime that turned to ''[p]ersuasion . . . [as] a kind of force[,] . . . force applied through the mind'' (Stephen 229, 129–30). Bentham's penitentiary made available a ''new mode of obtaining power of mind over mind'': ''[s]uch is the engine'' by which to implement an ''inspection principle'' that was ''to make [prisoners] not only *suspect*, but be *assured*, that whatever they do is known, even though that should not be the case'' (Bentham 4: 39, 66). With such a perspective, in *India* John Strachey emphasized the increasing vigilance required of that ''young Englishman'' who had inherited from ''his forefathers . . . not only their physical courage, but the powers of independent judgment, the decision of character, the habits of thought . . . that are necessary for the government of men, and the discharge of the various duties of civilised life . . . which have given us our empire'' (358). But if such English qualities were to no avail, there was always the model prison, the resort to force should persuasion fail, capturing the true nature of the Raj.

It was the situation of the Raj as a panoptical institution under siege that emerges in *The Sign of Four* as Dr. Watson's account moves from Pondicherry Lodge, the detached villa of the dead Major Sholto, to a fleeting yet telling reference to Millbank Penitentiary, and on to Jonathan Small's description of Agra Fort: "a very queer place—the queerest place that ever [he] was in" (Doyle, *Sign* 99; ch. 12). The name of the Sholto villa proves to be ironic, a response to John Seeley who in recounting the British rise to dominance in India observed, "It several times happened that the war by which [the East India Company] acquired territory wore the appearance before the English public of a war between England and France" (Seeley 245–46). Even "[t]he attacks that were made on the Company in Parliament, the vote of censure moved against Lord Clive, the impeachment brought against Hastings . . . contributed to make our Indian wars *seem* national wars, and to identify the Company with *the English nation*" (246–47, emphasis added).

Seeley did not suggest that such an "appearance before the English public" was part of a concerted policy to obscure the actions of the Company in India. But, in *The Sign of Four*, this national agon is dismissed as a form of self-deception, a way to disguise imperial motives. In the novella Major Sholto has embraced the national myth for his own purposes. He has betrayed Jonathan Small and his Sikh confederates, whom he dismisses as "three black fellows" (Doyle, *Sign* 113), and even his fellow officer, Captain Morstan. Upon his return to England, he has purchased the villa that he names Pondicherry Lodge. It is not clear whether Major Sholto has used part of the Agra treasure or the "fortune" (114) left to him by an uncle to secure the villa. In either case, Sholto has hoarded the treasure in an attic room of the lodge. On his deathbed, he tells his twin sons of his betrayal of Captain Morstan and his daughter, Mary, acknowledging the "cursed greed which has been [his] besetting sin through life" (26). As he confesses that he has "concealed not only [Morstan's] body, but also the treasure," he sees the "bearded, hairy face" (28) of Jonathan Small at the bedroom window, is driven to convulsions, and dies.

In an attempt to deny the greed that has possessed him, Major Sholto has seized upon the name, Pondicherry, the site of a French trading station, a "factory," associated with Joseph Dupleix, Robert Clive's formidable adversary. Pondicherry changed hands several times until the British triumph over the French in the eighteenth century (see Seeley 245, 305). Sholto has named his villa after Pondicherry rather than after Plassey, where in 1857, one hundred years before the Mutiny, Clive defeated the Nabob of Bengal on a "day which was to decide the fate of India" (Macaulay, *Essays* 2: 425–26). Macaulay's words suggested a turning point in the imperial enterprise in India. However, like the British nation, Sholto has willfully obscured the motives of the East India Company and, finally, his own.[26]

The allusion to Pondicherry, steeped in ambiguities, introduces a sustained critique of British India, associated with various sites that, at first, appear not to be connected. This is particularly the case when Sherlock Holmes and Dr.

Watson, after investigating the murder scene, follow the creosote trail of Jonathan Small and Tonga. With the dog, Toby, as their improbable blood-hound, they are led to the home of Mordecai Smith on the banks of the Thames. Small has hired out Smith's steam-launch, the *Aurora*, in preparation for a flight down the Thames. At this point, with the trail now cold, Holmes and Watson take a wherry across the river just below Vauxhall bridge, to be landed near Millbank Penitentiary (Doyle, *Sign* 64; ch. 8), that was to be closed in 1890 and later was to become the site of the Tate Gallery.[27]

For those reading *The Sign of Four* in 1890, before Millbank Penitentiary was razed, other associations were possible, even inevitable. In Henry Mayhew and John Binny's *The Criminal Prisons of London* (1862), they could read the history of Millbank and its association with the Panopticon: "Millbank Prison is a modification of Jeremy Bentham's 'Panoptikon [*sic*], or Inspection House.' . . . Part of Bentham's system consisted in placing the prisoners under constant surveillance. From a room in the centre of the building, the governor, and anyone else who was admitted into the interior, were to see into all parts of the building at all periods of the day, while a reflecting apparatus was even to enable them to watch the prisoners in their cells at night" (Mayhew and Binny 235). Mayhew and Binny reminded their readers that Bentham had purchased the site at Millbank, planning to build a privately-run prison modeled on his Panopticon. But "Bentham's plan of constant and general inspection . . . 'was referred to a Parliamentary Committee . . . [and] finally rejected' " (235). Bentham, then, sold the site to the government and upon it a prison consisting of six pentagons, with a chapel at the center, was built. The first pentagon was opened in 1816, to house women inmates; the other five were completed in 1822: in the 1840s Millbank became a holding depôt for prisoners to be transported to Australasia.[28]

Victorian readers might also have known Arthur Griffiths's *Memorials of Millbank* either in the 1875 edition or in the "New edition" of 1884. In the *Memorials*, Griffiths returned to similar themes: "With [Millbank] one intimately associates the names of men like [John] Howard and Jeremy Bentham": in fact, "the present Millbank Penitentiary is often supposed to have grown out of [Bentham's] proposal" (Griffiths 1, 14). Griffiths, too, wrote of the "Panopticon, or the Inspection House," as a "scheme . . . so peculiar that it deserves to be described": Bentham's "model prison" was to create " 'a sentiment of a sort of invisible omnipresence' [that] was to pervade the whole place" (14, 16–17). As he proceeded, Griffiths noted that Millbank was once "the great *depôt* for convicts *en route* to the Antipodes" (2). An imperial perspective was to pervade his account, not altogether surprising for someone who had been born in Poona, India—the son of a lieutenant-colonel in the Royal Warwickshires—and who went on to serve in various outposts of the empire before turning to a career with the English convict prison

service, finally in the role of a prison inspector, all the while writing prolifi-
cally.[29]

In Griffiths's book, Millbank Penitentiary emerged as a metaphor for the
Indian subcontinent, its inmates identified with the native populace. Even the
description of its site as "a low marshy locality" beside "the great highway
of the Thames" (Griffiths 22, 25) would suggest the Asiatic scenes of Thomas
De Quincey's *Confessions of an English Opium-Eater* (1821/1822) and his
representations of an Asia of the imagination, the figurative Antipodes to all
things European.[30] Griffiths described the penitentiary as "a six-pointed star-
fort; built, say, against catapults and old-fashioned engines of war" (26).
Within, it was "as confusing as is the labyrinth . . . to those who enter without
such clues to guide them as are afforded by familiarity and long practice":
"There was one old warder who served for years at Millbank . . . who was
yet unable, to the last, to find his way about the premises. He carried with
him always a piece of chalk, with which he 'blazed' his path as the American
backwoodsman does the forest trees" (27).

The geographical analogy prepared for the transformation of Millbank into
British India, its inmates, male and female, always threatening the anarchy—"Pandemonium let loose" (Griffiths 93)—that the British so feared.
The "star-fort" became "[a] small colony apart from the great world; living
more than as neighbours, as one family almost—but not happily—under the
same roof" (54). Always, in spite of "continuous vigilant supervision,"
there were "exhortations to riot and *mutiny*" (98, emphasis added). The
implications of Griffiths's language led to an inevitable conclusion: "A
prison should be like a fortress in a state of siege: officers on duty, guards
posted, sentries always on the alert, everyone everywhere ready to meet any
difficulty or danger that may arise" (117). With the Great Mutiny in mind,
Griffiths proceeded to compare the female prisoners, the most dangerous of
all, to the rebellious Sepoys: they communicated their desire to riot by ex-
changing messages concealed in "bag[s] of white linen": such bags were
"akin somewhat to the mysterious *chuppaties*, which were the forerunner of
the Indian Mutiny" (123). For Griffiths, India remained a passive, feminine
world, always threatening to stir into violence against the masculine West.[31]

Finally, Griffiths identified Millbank Penitentiary with Agra Fort during
the Mutiny. In writing of the prison first as a "small colony," then as a
"fortress in a state of siege," he associated the prison with Agra under siege
in 1857: "like a ship at sea, [Millbank was] shut off from the public, and
concentrated on what was going on within its walls" (54). In this observation,
Griffiths appropriated language from John Kaye's *History of the Sepoy War*
in which the siege of Agra led to "a curious sort of . . . 'board-ship life' on
a gigantic scale, . . . with a few state rooms for families, and little side-cabins
or hutches for bachelors, and some open places, as cuddies or poop decks,
for common resort" (3: 405).

The labyrinthine, panoptical world of Millbank Penitentiary that in Griffiths's *Memorials* became a figurative India during the Mutiny explains the larger implications of Dr. Watson's passing reference to the penitentiary, even as it prepares for Jonathan Small's account of his Indian adventures. For Arthur Griffiths's allusion to Kaye's *Sepoy War* invoked an account of the Mutiny to which Small's "strange story" (Doyle, *Sign* 94) would provide a counter-narrative not only of the events of 1857–58, but of the Indian empire. In describing the "great deeds of heroism" performed by "men not trained to arms" (Kaye 3: 220), Kaye had included the death of John Russell Colvin, lieutenant-governor of the North-Western Provinces who, as an "eminent [man]" (1: xii), in his final moments during the siege of Agra Fort quoted . . . the *Aeneid* (3: 415–16). In casting himself as a figure out of Virgil's epic, Colvin stood in striking contrast to Arthur Conan Doyle's Jonathan Small, the unheralded "Worchestershire man, " in his own words, one of "a heap of Smalls[,] . . . all steady, chapel-going folk, small farmers, well known and respected over the countryside" (Doyle, *Sign* 96). As the black sheep of the family—"I got into a mess over a girl" (97)—Small joined the army of the Crown like other "harum-scarum, reckless lad[s]" (Doyle, "Man" 170) before him, seeking in India a new life. There he was to become a casualty of empire, losing a leg beneath the knee to a crocodile in the Ganges. "[I]nvalided . . . out of the Army," he would experience various moral injuries, first as an overseer of "coolies" (97) on an indigo plantation, later as part of the conspiracy that led to murder in the theft of the Agra treasure. Enjoying the prerogatives of race, he became part of the plantation system integral to the empire as a whole, a white man overseeing Indian peasants coerced into cultivating a crop that generated profits for the British textile industry.

As an alternative to John Kaye's *History of the Sepoy War*, Small's narrative, like that of Henry Wood in "The Crooked Man," offers a different representation of the Great Mutiny. Inevitably, Small repeats the racial slurs that appeared in James Mill's *History of British India*, in Macaulay's essays on Clive and Hastings: he even echoes John Kaye (and surely others) as he states that the "whole country was up like a swarm of bees . . . [in] a fight of the millions against the hundreds" (Doyle, *Sign* 99). But his description of Agra Fort—"a labyrinth of passages and corridors" with "a central guardhouse in the middle" (100)—emerged neither from Kaye's *Sepoy War*, nor from G. B. Malleson's continuation. Rather, Small's description of Agra Fort, "the queerest [place] that ever [he] was in" (99), alludes to Mark Thornhill's *Indian Mutiny* (1884).

Tellingly, the indigo plantation where Small served as an overseer "was at a place called Muttra, near the border of the North-west Provinces" (Doyle, *Sign* 98; ch.2): "a large city in Upper India . . . on the banks of the river Jumna, thirty-four miles from Agra" (Thornhill 1), at which Mark Thornhill was magistrate. In January 1857, Thornhill had come upon "four little cakes" (2), the *"chuppaties"* of Arthur Griffiths's *Memorials of Millbank*. Thornhill's ensuing narrative became a self-consciously Romantic one. Caught up in the tumult of events, Thornhill experienced his adventures as "a fairy tale," even as "a sort of waking dream" (48, 64). On his flight from Muttra to Agra, guiding to safety the brothers Seth, members of one of the wealthiest banking families in India, Thornhill found himself guarding a fabulous treasure, "stores of gold and silver[,] . . . necklaces of emeralds, each stone the size of a large marble, enormous pearls" (99). The "[m]idnight [r]ide" (136) from Muttra to Agra began under the light of the moon; then there were torrents of rain until the "clouds rose higher," revealing "a deep, dull, lurid glare": "It was the glow of some vast conflagration . . . Agra was in flames" (143). In this phantasmagoric realm, escaped prisoners materialized in the darkness: "Many of them were now unfettered; they passed us like phantoms. . . . There was the black gloom, the lurid glare, the phantoms, the clanking chains; and over us some of the awe of the shadow of death" (147–48). While John Kaye had written of the Mutiny as an epic, Thornhill saw it as a descent into Dante's Inferno or Milton's Hell: "The scene was that which poets and painters depict for the infernal regions" (148).

Within this highly-wrought account, there appeared nuanced observations rejecting the convenient myths that were the foundation of British rule in India. Thornhill dismissed the claim that Indian natives feared the conditions that had followed upon the death of Aurangzeb: "It was the belief of the Government, and also of the English generally, that the natives were attached to our rule; and . . . that, weary of the present anarchy, they longed for the re-establishment of order." However, during the Mutiny "[n]o one regretted the loss of our rule; . . . all classes enjoyed the confusion" (Thornhill 114). Thornhill understood the "animosity" of the Sepoys toward "the *machinery* by which we enforced our *severe taxation*, and maintained that *disciplined order* which had become so distasteful" (87, emphasis added). He acknowledged British misconceptions about India, with a theory of land tenure out of Henry Maine's *Ancient Law*: "land was made liable to sale in the same manner as other property . . . in the course of a generation, the greater portion of the soil had changed owners" (33). With the restoration of British rule in 1858, "there were displayed many of the best English characteristics, but also some of our qualities less praiseworthy. There was no retaliation, no revenge; but . . . there was that rigid adherence to rule, that want of sympathy with the feelings of the people which, though perhaps it makes our government successful, certainly prevents it from being loved" (326). Ultimately, Thornhill faced the unpleasant truth that others dismissed, "that vague discontent which is necessarily and invariably produced by the domination of an alien race, especially of a race whose habits, ideas, and sentiments differ widely from those of the people they rule" (332).[32]

In Thornhill's narrative, Arthur Conan Doyle could find both a meditation on empire and the germ of the mystery of the Agra treasure. For once the threat to those who had retreated into Agra Fort had passed, Thornhill and others settled "into a sort of life very like that on board ship during a long voyage" (Thornhill 219). After this obligatory allusion to Kaye's *Sepoy War* (perhaps even to the "New edition" of Arthur Griffiths's *Memorials of Millbank*), Thornhill returned to familiar themes: "We met like travellers in a fairy tale. . . . As we talked, our conversation, our surroundings seemed to lift us above . . . the dull routine of ordinary life, into a region of poetry and romance" (222). Beyond the walls of the fort, "we looked on the river": amid "the ruins of what once had been palaces . . . pure, white and glistening, rose the 'Taj' " (220).

Suggesting "the idea of life amid decay" (Thornhill 220), the Taj Mahal inspired further imaginings. With time on their hands the British explored the fort, coming upon "a succession of courtyards and pavilions," "circular towers" upon the walls, and various palaces, including "the Zenana of the Emperor Akbar," and a place "known among the English as the 'Palace Square'; by the natives it is termed 'The Pearl Zenana' " (210–11). The fort offered "*a very labyrinth* of courts, enclosures, gateways, open spaces, and detached buildings" beneath which existed "what appear[ed]" to be "a black void" (213, 212, emphasis added).

The British inmates of the fort were therefore to divert themselves with "the more interesting subjects of seeking for hidden treasure and the exploration of subterranean passages" (Thornhill 225). After all, "[t]he fort of Agra had once contained half the wealth of India": "It was conjured that in secret vaults under the ground, or in recesses of the thick walls, some of the ancient hoards might lie concealed" (226–27). They sought out hidden vaults, yet, "having reached the bottom, we found neither vault, passage, nor concealed entrance—only the bare earth on which the foundations [of the fort] rested" (228). Frustrated by whatever might lie beneath the stones and mortar, the British turned to ghost stories about "the great Emperor Akbar," who haunted " 'the fortress of the illustrious Company' " by screaming, so the story went, " 'The house is mine! mine!! mine!!!' " (235–36). For further diversion, there was the story of "the four English soldiers" and "the vault" from which the four disappeared: "The vaults were searched, but the soldiers were not discovered, nor any clue as to what had become of them" (228–29).

The mystery of the Agra treasure, including the murder committed by those who were to be known under "The sign of the four" (Doyle, *Sign* 28), has, then, its associations with Mark Thornhill's account of the Mutiny. Even his indirect commentary upon empire had its echoes in Doyle's novella. The "labyrinth of courts, enclosures, gateways, open spaces, and detached buildings" (Thornhill 213) reappeared in Jonathan Small's descriptions of "the old fort of Agra," particularly "the old quarter" that was "full of great deserted halls, and winding passages, and long corridors twisting in and out" (Doyle, *Sign* 99–100). Within this labyrinth the "earth floor had sunk in at one place, making a natural grave" (107) for the dead Achmet, while a hollow in a wall became the hiding place for the treasure for which he was murdered. The earthen floor of Small's account echoes Thornhill's reference to "the earthen floor on which the foundations [of Agra fort] rested" (Thornhill 228). In each instance, the bare earth forms a foundation for an imperial enterprise that is to pass away as surely as has the former Mughal empire. Agra and its fort become figurative, both for the subcontinent and the British enterprise in India.[33]

In his description of Agra fort, Small reveals the panoptical nature of the Raj as envisioned, particularly, by John Strachey in *India*. The fort "is enormous in size, . . . [b]ut the modern part is nothing like the size of the old quarter, where nobody goes" (Doyle, *Sign* 99). With its "deserted halls, and winding passages, and long corridors" (99), the fort suggests the puzzling nature of Indian society and Indian culture to the British who now rule it. Inevitably, Small's story evokes Macaulay writing of that "small band of strangers, who exercised boundless power over a great indigenous population" (Macaulay, *Essays* 2: 623), and Seeley acknowledging that "the English nation is but an imperceptible drop in the ocean of an Asiatic population" (54). The machinery of government in such a situation is crystallized as Small observes, "We were short-handed. . . . It was impossible for us, therefore, to station a strong guard at every one of the innumerable gates. What we did was to organize a *central guard-house in the middle of the fort*, and to leave each gate under the charge of *one white man* and two or three natives" (Doyle, *Sign* 100, emphasis added). He offers a vision of the Indian empire as espoused in *India*, with the "central guard-house" as a type of the Calcutta government working to maintain its control through those district officers who engaged in a form of surveillance promoted by Jeremy Bentham in his advocacy of the Panopticon as an "engine"—"[a] new mode of obtaining power of mind over mind" (Bentham 4: 39).

IV.

For John Seeley and John Strachey the engine of the Indian empire was to exist in perpetuity, devoted magnanimously to the governance of a people apparently incapable of governing themselves. But in his "authoritative *India*" (Metcalf 188), Strachey was to leave traces of those practices that compromised the historic mission to which he and others had committed themselves, perhaps insuring its ultimate failure. At one point, he produced

a "table show[ing] . . . the actual gross revenues of India for 1886–87'' (Strachey 73–74), as he proceeded to justify "the so-called land revenue" by
arguing that "[f]rom time immemorial the ruling power [in India] . . . has
been entitled to a share of the produce of every acre of land," a share that
under British rule was less than that of any preceding (and less enlightened?)
government (75, 78). But, in turning to the various crops whose cultivation
yielded the land revenue, Strachey's language betrayed him. Without comment, he moved from "the pulses, maize, indigo, and cotton" to the "tobacco,
opium, linseed, and mustard" (232–33) grown in various parts of the subcontinent. He conflated those staples that sustained life with the cotton and indigo
destined for the textile mills of England and with the opium produced for
sale to China. Later, he wrote of the railway system that transported a mobile
work force of contracted "labourers *required* by Assam for its tea-planta-
tions" (285, emphasis added).

In a stroke, Jonathan Small's brief career as overseer on an indigo plantation becomes significant: he is part of a plantation system, imported from the
West Indies, that had become the bane, particularly in Lower Bengal, of the
Indian peasant, the *ryot* coerced into cultivating indigo and the opium poppy.
Through the legal structures of Henry Maine's *Ancient Law* and late nineteenth-century liberalism, the *ryot* was introduced to yet another form of
slavery. In his observation that "former Governments [in India] hardly recog-
nised the existence of [private] property" (Strachey 80), Strachey revealed
how alien institutions had been arbitrarily imposed upon Maine's "village-
communities," compelling an illiterate peasantry to honor contracts (some
of them forged) whose meaning was foreign to them. Where legal coercion
failed, the white planters who operated the indigo plantations turned to European and native mercenaries who threatened the *ryots* with physical violence
or intimidated them by holding members of their families captive. Unfortunately, the district officers—whose "irreproachable integrity" (262) Strachey
praised—identified with the white planters, colluding with them in the exploitation of the *ryots*. It was this system of coercion that led to the "Blue
Mutiny" of 1860 and to the Indigo Commission report of November 1860,
in part leading to the demise of the indigo industry by 1861–1862.[34]

Yet the system was to be replicated in northern India, particularly in Assam,
in the tea plantations, often euphemistically referred to as "gardens," to
which coolies of various nationalities were transported by the very railway
system built through the revenues collected by the British government (Strachey 285, 235). In their determination to find alternatives to Chinese tea and
to reduce the drain on silver that the trade produced, the East India Company
and, then, the Crown had established yet another plantation system in which
familiar abuses were to occur, all in the name of "private enterprise" (235)
and the fiction of the coolie as someone freely contracting for his labor. The

tea-gardens were no more than versions of the earlier indigo plantations. The British appropriated lands that were once held communally, granting ownership to European planters during Lord Canning's time as Governor-General. As tea cultivation demanded ever more laborers after 1858, the European planters imported illiterate coolies from southern India and elsewhere in southeast Asia. The contractors who supplied the coolies delivered them to their destinations in wretched condition—indeed, many died in transit and the rest lived out their lives under horrible circumstances.[35]

The realities of the plantation system, past and present, were suppressed in *India* as Strachey celebrated "the great tea industry of India, which now supplie[d] nearly one half of the tea consumed in Great Britain" (235).[36] But, in enumerating the revenues upon which the Calcutta government relied, John Strachey would reveal the hypocrisy of British claims to enlightenment and benevolence. In classifying revenue sources for the years 1886–1887, Strachey listed under "Land revenue" the income from the opium monopoly in the hands of the Raj, constituting some eleven percent of all revenues (74). Originally, the opium monopoly had been established in the late eighteenth century in order to generate larger profits for the shareholders in the East India Company. But the contracts negotiated with those who managed the cultivation of the opium poppy became notorious for the corrupt practices in granting them, especially among those who went out to India to make their fortunes. In his account of the impeachment trial of Warren Hastings, James Mill quoted Edmund Burke's assault upon the "Peculation in India . . . [that] would . . . stalk abroad in noon-day, and act without disguise" (Mill 5: 127) as agents of the Company sold contracts to those who provided them with bribes. Yet, in attacking Warren Hastings for those practices that inevitably accompanied oligarchic rule, James Mill avoided the ethical implications of the opium trade with China.[37]

Later, of course, the opium trade was justified by the need for silver to pay for the Chinese tea that had become the British national drink. By the 1880s there was only one rationale for the opium monopoly, the reliance upon the revenues that it provided to the Raj. This fact provoked a response in the form of the Anglo-Oriental Society for the Suppression of the Opium Trade (1874). In *India*, John Strachey wrote with an uneasy awareness of those who objected to the government-sponsored trade in an addictive opiate that was thought to ravage its users.[38] He defended the "strict system of State monopoly" by which the government "lev[ied] a heavy duty on every chest of opium exported," observing, "I do not propose to discuss the vexed question of the morality of the system under which the Indian Government derives revenue from the consumption of opium in China" (Strachey 84.) Yet, he was compelled to state that "[i]t is a common but complete mistake to suppose that the prohibition of opium from India would have the result of putting a

stop to opium-smoking in China'' (85). Strachey went on in his defense of
the indefensible: "Excess in opium, as far as the individual consumer is
concerned, may probably be as bad as excess in alcohol; it cannot be worse,
and its effects upon his neighbours are comparatively harmless. Used in
moderation . . . there can be no reason to believe that opium is injurious''
(85–86). Moreover, where "the Chinese Government [once viewed] the
opium trade with dislike and desire[d] its abolition . . . it undoubtedly now
desires that the trade should flourish, because it derives from duties on Indian
opium a large and highly prized revenue'' (86). Strachey brazenly invoked
the Chefoo Convention (1885) by which the Chinese had been compelled to
acquiesce, yet again, to their own addiction to opium revenues, an addiction
shared by the British government in Calcutta: and, in *The Sign of Four*, an
addiction shared by Sherlock Holmes.[39]

In justifying the opium monopoly, Strachey had ironically laid bare the
foundations of the imperial edifice that *India* sought to shore up. He had
exposed the insubstantiality of British claims to a moral superiority to those
Indian subjects over whom he and others ruled. He had exposed the illusion
of the permanence of the Raj, an illusion that Mark Thornhill had already
dispelled in his account of the Mutiny: "In the course of a month, from the
frontiers of Bengal to those of the Punjab, our empire had melted away''
(Thornhill 123), while India in its perplexing variety simply . . . endured.

Thornhill's observation had been preceded by a remark on the onset of the
rainy season: "A day or two after the commencement of the rains . . . insects
appear in the millions—rather, I should say in the millions of millions, for
over the whole extent of Upper India one may be seen in every square foot.
For a few days they continue moving all the while continually. Then they
burrow beneath the surface, and for another year are seen no more''
(Thornhill 122–23). To this day Thornhill's words are disturbing, as if he
were associating the insects that materialized in the "millions of millions''
with the Indian people who, in Jonathan Small's account of the Mutiny, were
"up like a swarm of bees'': "It was a fight of the millions against the
hundreds'' (Doyle, *Sign* 99) who constituted that small band of strangers in
a teeming foreign land.

Thornhill's words dramatized how unstable was the figurative soil upon
which "our very Empire in the East'' rested, how uncertain the ground to
support the "foundation[s] . . . [of the] new edifice'' for which *The Economist*
had called in 1857. We return, then, to the three edifices around which *The
Sign of Four* is, in part, structured. There is, of course, Pondicherry Lodge
whose grounds are "cumbered'' by "the great rubbish heaps'' that lead Dr.
Watson to exclaim, "It looks as though all the moles in England had been
let loose in [them]'' (Doyle, *Sign* 34–35; ch. 3). The allusion to burrowing is
reinforced when Inspector Athelney Jones appears upon the murder scene to

announce, "Why, the house seems to be as full as a rabbit-warren!" (44), another indirect, but unsettling, reference to a fecund Indian subcontinent.

The events at Pondicherry Lodge anticipate the moment when Sherlock Holmes and Dr. Watson take the wherry across the Thames to be "landed near Millbank Penitentiary" (Doyle, *Sign* 64). Watson says no more, even as his words evoke Arthur Griffiths's "six-pointed star-fort" standing upon "a low marshy locality, with a soil that was treacherous and insecure": "It was well known that the soil at Millbank was of such a nature as to render the establishment of a solid edifice thereon a matter of great difficulty and expense." Always, the Thames worked away at the foundations, requiring the government over the years to rebuild "three of the pentagon towers" (Griffiths 26, 22, 28, 35). Later, in *The Sign of Four*, as Holmes and Watson pursue the *Aurora* "downstream" (84), beyond the tower of London, the West India Docks, and the Isle of Dogs, they enter "a clear reach of the river, with Barking Level upon one side and the melancholy Plumstead Marshes upon the other" (86). The Thames has become one with the Ganges, in which Jonathan Small lost his leg to a crocodile, and with the Jumna that flows past Agra and erodes the foundations of Agra Fort. At this moment there appears to Holmes and Watson a nightmarish visitant from the Orient of the European imagination: Tonga, the Andaman Islander, "a little black man—the smallest [Watson has] ever seen—with a great, misshapen head and a shock of tangled, dishevelled hair" (86). As Tonga, "the unhallowed dwarf with his hideous face" (87), turns to the blow-pipe with which he has killed Bartholomew Sholto at Pondicherry Lodge, both Holmes and Watson fire their revolvers. Tonga, "his venomous, menacing eyes [flashing] amid the white swirl of the waters," falls into the river: like the Agra treasure, his corpse lies "[s]omewhere in the dark ooze at the bottom of the Thames" (87–88).

Tonga, a living fossil out of E. B. Tylor's *Primitive Culture* and Alfred Lyall's *Asiatic Studies*, has been consigned to the depths of the past. Now, the *Aurora*, still carrying Jonathan Small, runs aground upon a "mud-bank" in the midst of "a wild and desolate place, where the moon glimmer[s] upon a wide expanse of marsh-land, with pools of stagnant water and beds of decaying vegetation" (Doyle, *Sign* 87). Here, Holmes and Watson have entered the landscape of Mark Thornhill's India. They are delivered into a phantasmagoric world in which Pondicherry Lodge and Millbank Penitentiary merge with Agra Fort—"of unknown antiquity" (Thornhill 208)—to constitute a composite structure suggesting the nature of the Raj in the past, in the present, in the future. As a panoptical edifice, Agra Fort only seems impregnable, enduring. Jonathan Small later observes that the Jumna "river washes along the front of the old fort, and so protects it" (Doyle, *Sign* 100; ch. 12). But Mark Thornhill, and Arthur Conan Doyle, knew better. As Thornhill observed, "The river Jumna runs beneath a bank" and has over the centuries "[raised] up great mounds—on one of them stands the Fort of Agra. . . . Seen from beneath, the building realises every idea of an enchanter's palace; below, an impregnable castle, above, the bowers of fairies" (208–09). But the "appearance of strength, once a reality, is now a delusion" (209), as the fort had become vulnerable to modern artillery fire.[40]

Throughout, *The Sign of Four* resists John Strachey's seemingly authoritative *India*, an example of "persuasion . . . as force applied through the mind" (Stephen 129–30). Jonathan Small's strange tale has exposed "the cursed greed, which has been . . . [the] besetting sin" (Doyle, *Sign* 26), not only of Major Sholto, Captain Morstan, and others (including Small), but of the imperial enterprise from the start with the creation of the East India Company in 1600. The novella uncannily echoes Macaulay's "Lord Clive"—"Bengal was regarded as a place to which Englishmen were sent only to get rich, by any means, in the shortest possible time" (*Essays* 2: 463)—as Abdullah Khan says to Small: "We only ask you to do that which your countrymen come to this land for. We ask you to be rich" (Doyle, *Sign* 102; ch. 2).[41]

Abdullah Khan's words subvert the Comtean narrative put forth by men like Henry Maine, Alfred Lyall, and John Strachey, exposing it as an elaborate self-delusion. With its "lofty towers, its summit crowned with pavilions of white marble, whose roofs and cupolas are overlaid with burnished gold" (Thornhill 209), Agra Fort would seem to be a Coleridgean "pleasure-dome" out of "Kubla Khan," decreed into existence by someone like the Mughal emperor Akbar, builder of the Taj Mahal. But beneath a "dome of pleasure" whose shadow "Float[s] midway on the waves," there is only a deserted palace in various stages of disrepair, abandoned by the Mughal emperors to Akbar's ghost who, according to legend, cries out, "The house is mine! mine!! mine!!!"[42]

NOTES

1. For earlier discussions of detective fiction from a Marxist perspective to which critics continue to refer, see Knight, and Porter.
2. See *Adventures of Sherlock Holmes* in which Rosemary Jann writes of the "detective's . . . ideological power to invent and enforce social conformity" (67). She concludes her discussion of Holmes by observing, "Much of the undeniable charm of the Holmes stories lies in their assumption of a world in which scientific investigation confirms rather than undermines traditional values. . . . The adventures of Sherlock Holmes will always retain their definitive place in detective fiction because they work their magic[,] . . . embracing crime, irrationality, and evil, in order ultimately to reassert justice, reason, and right" (125–26). In a more nuanced approach in *Detecting the Nation*, Caroline Reitz recognizes in

Doyle "a *liberal* critique of imperialism's 'things as they are' . . . detective fiction works toward public acceptance of authority and even solidifies [the] imperial position not because of a wholesale endorsement of power but because it reimagines authority as consistent with . . . milder liberal principles'' (67).

3. Apart from this observation by Holmes, there are stories, for example "The Blue Carbuncle'' (1892) in *The Adventures of Sherlock Holmes* and "The Abbey Grange'' (1904) in *The Return of Sherlock Holmes*, in which Holmes does not turn a culprit over to the authorities, abdicating his purported role as a restorer of social order.

4. See Foucault, "Panopticism,'' *Discipline and Punish* 195–228.

5. It remains necessary to resist the coercive power of detective fiction that seems to drive to resolution. Adena Rosmarin discusses genre "as pragmatic rather than *natural*, as defined rather than *found*, as used rather than described'': conceptions of genre "are designed to serve the explanatory purpose of critical thought, not the other way around'' (25, emphasis added). Also, see Ed Wiltse, who discusses serialization featuring throughout a single character like Holmes as a new genre that resists the expectations that detective fiction hypothetically arouses and satisfies.

6. Doyle's attitudes toward empire were contradictory and, to those of us living in a nominally post-colonial time, unsatisfactory. Various biographers have dealt with his vision of a union of English-speaking peoples including the United States, Canada, Australia, New Zealand, and . . . South Africa. In a letter to his mother, Mary Doyle, dated 11 October 1899, Arthur Conan Doyle wrote, "What *is* old Kruger trying to do. He must be fey. He was so anxious to preserve the independence of his country that he has taken only the steps which could possibly imperil it. I do think that during the last two months he has set us increasingly in the right'' (*Arthur Conan Doyle: A Life in Letters*, 425). In a letter dated 26 December 1899, Mary Doyle pointed to the motives of the British in South Africa: "Gold the root of all evil is found & diamond mines & riff-raff of the world swarms down. . . . My idea [is] that a ring of those men—Millionaires so many times over—have encouraged all the discontent'' (*Life in Letters* 435). Doyle, of course, volunteered his services as a physician and went out to South Africa, landing there in April 1900, returning to England in early August: see Lycett 259–80.

7. My remarks about allusion have been informed by John Hollander, who writes that "the text alluded to . . . is part of the portable library shared by the author and his ideal audience'': "The reader of texts, in order to overhear echoes, must have some kind of access to an earlier voice. . . . When such access is lost in a community of reading, what may have been an allusion may fade in prominence; and yet a scholarly recovery of the context would restore the allusion, by revealing an intent as well as by showing means'' (64, 65–66). Hollander's "portable library'' suggests how *Through the Magic Door* was Doyle's attempt to create "his ideal audience.'' Also, see Garrett Stewart, who observes that the "whodunit format of detective fiction becomes the quintessential narrative form'' (513) offering a *telos* and closure; yet, a close attention to "diction, syntax, punctuation, figuration'' (541)—of which allusion is a part—provides a way of resisting the seductions of plot.

8. Throughout the essay, I refer to *The Sign of the Four* with the more customary title, *The Sign of Four*.

9. See R. J. White, introduction, *Liberty, Equality, Fraternity* 1–18. Also, see Metcalf 56–59.

10. Throughout, my discussion has been influenced by Eric Stokes's indispensable *English Utilitarians and India*; for a review of Stephen, see Stokes 281–85. Also, see Metcalf 29–65, and Hutchins vii–xiv.

11. It is necessary here to recognize our debt to Edward Said's *Orientalism*: "the major component in European culture is precisely what made that culture hegemonic both in and outside Europe: the idea of European identity as a superior one in comparison with all the non-European peoples and cultures" (7).

12. See Green and Gibson 33–42; and Roden, Introduction, *The Sign of the Four* xii–xvii.

13. See Brantlinger 81–82; Colley 128–32; and Metcalf 52–65.

14. See Brantlinger 21–24, 80–81; and Metcalf 55–57, 217–19.

15. For a discussion of Kaye's *Sepoy War*, see Herbert 194–204.

16. For a recent discussion of the myth of a "Continent . . . [that] was so roomy, so thinly peopled," see Mann esp. 3–27; for a discussion of the plantation system and empire, see Walvin: "Who even *thought* of the potato, or of tobacco, as crops acquired from the Indian peoples of America? Yet in the tortuous transmission of exotic crops into the fabric of European life . . . lay a harsh and ruthless exercise of power and ascendancy" (115).

17. See Aarsleff 115–62; and Anthony 3–38.

18. Yumna Siddiqi discusses both "The Crooked Man" and *The Sign of Four* in which poor, discontented characters who "have been excluded from the spoils of Empire" return to threaten those who have enjoyed those spoils (238). She concludes by observing, "Doyle makes the coupling of good and bad returns from Empire palatable by superimposing a juridicial and ethical narrative of crime and detection" to "restor[e] the social balance . . . [the crime] . . . *never* brings that balance into question" (244, emphasis added).

19. See Dirks 7–36, and, on James Mill, 317–22. Sara Suleri writes of James Mill's *History* as "a textbook for British administrators training for the Indian civil service" (18).

20. For a book-length discussion of the impeachment trial, see Marshall: "Mill used his long chapter on Hasting's impeachment (vol. v, chap ii) as a vehicle for his own views on law reform, but it remains the most comprehensive discussion of the legal and constitutional issues raised by the trial" (67, n. 1). Marshall wrote, of course, before Dirks's *Scandal of Empire*.

21. For an account of Macaulay's early career, see Clive esp. 289–341, 342–99.

22. In *Memories and Adventures*, Doyle acknowledged his awareness of John Stuart Mill: "It is to be remembered that [in my youth] these were the years when Huxley, Tyndall, Darwin, Herbert Spencer and John Stuart Mill were our chief philosophers, and that even the man in the street felt the strong sweeping current of their thought" (26).

23. See Zastoupil 7–27, 167–68; and Pitts 123–62.

24. For a recent discussion of the brothers John Strachey and Richard Strachey (1817–1908), see Caine 17–50.

25. Mike Davis refers in passing to the Strachey brothers: see 28, 57. For his accounts of nineteenth-century famines in India, see "Skeletons at the Feast" 141–75, and "India: The Modernization of Poverty" 311–40.

26. Recently, Maya Jasanoff has returned to John Seeley's themes with an apparently nuanced, post-colonial perspective. Of Tipu Sultan, Seringapatam, and Mysore in 1799, she writes that "Mysore's long-standing ties with the French have been *undeservedly* sidelined by imperial historians . . . it was *precisely* such French-Indian alliances that turned British imperial policy in India toward open territorial conquest" (153, emphasis added).

27. See "Millbank Penitentiary" and "Tate Gallery," *London Encyclopædia*; and Collins 20–21, 150–51.

28. See *Oxford History of the Prison* 94–95, 134–35, 336–37.

29. See the entry for Griffiths in the *Oxford Dictionary of National Biography*, 2004 ed.

30. See Barrell 1–24.

31. See Metcalf 160–71, and Wurgaft 1–16, 130–44.

32. See Inden 137–40, 176–80, 183–85.

33. In his introduction to *The Sign of the Four*, Roden argues that Doyle would have learned about "Agra during the Mutiny" through his personal contacts with Sir William Muir (1819–1905), "the new Principal" of Edinburgh University, and with Alfred Wilks Drayson (1827–1901), Doyle's "patient, mentor, and sponsor" during his years in Southsea (xix, xviii). We do not, of course, have a record of their conversations. Neither in Drayson's *Experiences*, nor in Muir's *Agra in the Mutiny* is there a description of Agra Fort similar to Jonathan Small's in *The Sign of Four*. I am indebted to Hibbert for directing me to Thornhill's account.

34. See Kling 17–20, 78–83, 140–46, 220–21.

35. See Macfarlane and Macfarlane, "Tea Labour," *Empire of Tea* 202–24. Also, see Burnett, "Tea: The Cup that Cheers," *Liquid Pleasures* 49–69; Mintz 55–61, 70–73, 112–23; and Walvin, "The Cause of All Distress: Plantations," *Fruits of Empire* 132–54.

36. For the complex relationship between tea, sugar, and British imperialism, see Burnett 55–56, 188–89; Mintz 6–9, 108–14, 116–22.

37. See Wright, "Opium," *East-Indian Economic Problems* 106–89. Also, see M. Booth, "The Factory Traders," *Opium* 103–37. Marshall observes, "The Managers [of the impeachment proceedings] attacked Hastings" for his dealings in the opium trade for his own profit, "but little was said about the ethics of trading in opium" (172).

38. See Berridge and Edwards 106–65, 182–83; M. Booth 139–73; and Wright 106–65.

39. Frank Dikötter, Lars Laamann, and Zhou Xun argue that in China "habitual opium use did not have significant harmful effects on either health or longevity: moderate smoking could even be beneficial" (3). In *Opium and the People*, Berridge and Edwards observe that concerns about opium addiction were caused by anxiety over domestic use in Britain: see 195–205.

40. Throughout, my reading of *The Sign of Four* has diverged from that of Joseph McLaughlin in *Writing the Urban Jungle*. For McLaughlin the representation of London as a figurative jungle blurs the boundaries between the imperial periphery and the metropole. In that urban setting there occurs a figurative invasion, of exotic commodities and people, that must be dealt with. In the character of Sherlock Holmes the novella acts upon "a knowledge that knows no geographic or cultural boundaries": it is a panoptical knowledge, part of "an imperial network" at the heart of "the imperial metropolis" (65). Such knowledge can be brought to bear upon a situation that involves a "return of the colonial and imperial repressed" (55), perhaps dispelling it. McLaughlin's reading of *The Sign of Four* replicates the strategy central to D. A. Miller's *The Novel and the Police*.

41. Niall Ferguson seems to echo John Strachey on India: "At its apogee in the mid-nineteenth century, two features of the Indian and Colonial services are especially striking. . . . First, British administration was remarkably cheap and efficient. Secondly, it was remarkably non-venal. Its sins were generally sins of omission, not commission." He goes on to quote the "economic historian David Landes [who] recently drew up a list of measures which 'the ideal growth-and-development' government would adopt," among them to "secure rights of property," to "enforce rights of contract," to "provide stable government," and "to hold taxes down" (361–62). Like Strachey before him, Ferguson does not dwell upon the production of indigo, opium, or Assam tea, nor on the plantation system that it necessitated. Dirks observes, "When imperial history loses any sense of what empire meant to those who were colonized, it becomes complicit in the history of empire itself" (332). At one point he refers to Niall Ferguson: "For Ferguson, imperialism was the means for the inauguration and spread of global capitalism, and that was a very good thing indeed . . . but what economic value did all this have for cheap, underemployed Asian labor?" (334).

42. Apparently, imperial delusions are still with us. Robert W. Merry discusses the Eurocentric "Idea of Progress": "Implicit in [Eurocentrism] was the view that other cultures were inferior to the West, hence universal progress *required* that these inferior cultures embrace the Western Heritage. . . . the Idea of Progress, in various guises and varying degrees of intensity, has essentially conquered the consciousness of European civilization, becoming the animating concept of the *secular West*. It is embraced *unconsciously* by people who could hardly articulate the concept and who know nothing of its long, agonizing emergence. It is *assumed* as a given among intellectuals toiling in the academic groves of the West" (18–19, emphasis added). I quote Merry with Karl Polanyi (1886–1964) and Harvey in mind. Polanyi observed, "Economic liberalism was the organizing principle of a society engaged in creating a market system. . . . it evolved into a veritable faith in man's secular salvation through a self-regulating market" (135). Of India, he wrote, "The term 'exploitation' describes but ill a situation which became truly grave only *after* the East India Company's ruthless monopoly was abolished and *free trade* was introduced into India" (160, emphasis added). Harvey has recently written of neoliberal "experiment[s] carried out in the periphery [as] model[s] for the formulation of policies in the centre" (9), an observation that leads from *The Sign of Four* to those stories in which Sherlock Holmes confronts nineteenth-century liberalism in the metropole.

WORKS CITED

Aarsleff, Hans. *The Study of Language in England, 1780–1860*. Princeton: Princeton UP, 1967.

Anthony, David W. *The Horse, the Wheel and Language: How Bronze-Age Riders from the Eurasian Steppes Shaped the Modern World*. Princeton: Princeton UP, 2007.

Arthur Conan Doyle: A Life in Letters. Ed. Jon Lellenberg, Daniel Stashower, and Charles Foley. New York: Penguin, 2007.

Bakhtin, M. M. "The Problem of the Text in Linguistics, Philology, and the Human Sciences: An Experiment in Philosophical Analysis." *Speech Genres and Other Late Essays*. Trans. Vern W. McGee. Ed. Caryl Emerson and Michael Holquist. U of Texas P Slavic Ser. 8. Austin: U of Texas P, 1986. 103–31.

Barrell, John. *The Infection of Thomas De Quincey: A Psychopathology of Imperialism*. New Haven: Yale UP, 1991.

Bentham, Jeremy. "Panopticon, or, The Inspection-House: Containing the Idea of a New Principle of Construction Applicable to Any Sort of Establishment, in which Persons of Any Description are to be Kept under Inspection." *The Works of Jeremy Bentham*. Vol. 4. Ed. John Bowring. 1843. New York: Russell and Russell, 1962.

Berridge, Virginia, and Griffith Edwards. *Opium and the People: Opiate Use in Nineteenth–Century England*. New York: St. Martin's, 1981.

Booth, Martin. *Opium: A History*. London: Simon and Schuster, 1996.

Booth, Wayne. *The Rhetoric of Fiction*. Chicago: U of Chicago P, 1961.

Brantlinger, Patrick. *Rule of Darkness: British Literature and Imperialism, 1830–1914*. Ithaca, NY: Cornell UP, 1988.

"The Bright Side of the Picture." *The Economist* 26 Sept. 1857: 1061–62.

Burnett, John. *Liquid Pleasures: A Social History of Drinks in Modern Britain*. New York: Routledge, 1999.

Caine, Barbara. *Bombay to Bloomsbury: A Biography of the Strachey Family*. Oxford: Oxford UP, 2005.

Chabon, Michael. Rev. of *The New Annotated Sherlock Holmes*, vols. 1 and 2, ed. Leslie S. Klinger. *The New York Review of Books* 24 Feb. 2005: 14–17.

Clive, John. *Macaulay: The Shaping of the Historian*. New York: Knopf, 1973.

Coleridge, Ernest Hartley, ed. *The Complete Poetical Works of Samuel Taylor Coleridge*. 2 vols. Oxford: Clarendon, 1912.

Colley, Linda. *Britons: Forging the Nation, 1707–1837.* New Haven: Yale UP, 1992.

Collins, Philip. *Dickens and Crime.* 2d ed. Cambridge Studies in Criminology 17. London: Macmillan, 1965.

Davis, Mike. *Late Victorian Holocausts: El Niño Famines and the Making of the Third World.* New York: Verso, 2001.

De Quincey, Thomas. *Confessions of an English Opium-Eater together with Selections from the Autobiography of Thomas De Quincey.* Ed. Edward Sackville-West. London: Cresset, 1950.

Dikötter, Frank, Lars Laamann, and Zhou Xun. *Narcotic Culture: A History of Drugs in China.* Chicago: U of Chicago P, 2004.

Dirks, Nicholas B. *The Scandal of Empire: India and the Creation of Imperial Britain.* Cambridge: Harvard UP/Belknap, 2006.

Doyle, Arthur Conan. *The Adventures of Sherlock Holmes.* Ed. Richard Lancelyn Green. Oxford Sherlock Holmes. Ed. Owen Dudley Edwards. Oxford: Oxford UP, 1993.

———. *The Memoirs of Sherlock Holmes.* Ed. Christopher Roden. Oxford Sherlock Holmes. Ed. Owen Dudley Edwards. Oxford: Oxford UP, 1993.

———. *Memories and Adventures.* Boston: Little, Brown, 1924.

———. *The Return of Sherlock Holmes.* Ed. Richard Lancelyn Green. Oxford Sherlock Holmes. Ed. Owen Dudley Edwards. Oxford: Oxford UP, 1993.

———. *The Sign of the Four.* Ed. Christopher Roden. Oxford Sherlock Holmes. Ed. Owen Dudley Edwards. Oxford: Oxford UP, 1993.

———. *Through the Magic Door.* London: Smith, Elder, 1907.

Drayson, Alfred Wilks. *Experiences of a Woolwich Professor during Fifteen Years at the Royal Military Academy.* London: Chapman and Hall, 1886.

Ferguson, Niall. *Empire: The Rise and Demise of the British World Order and the Lessons for Global Power.* New York: Basic Books, 2003.

Foucault, Michel. *Discipline and Punish.* Trans. Alan Sheridan. New York: Pantheon, 1977.

Green, Richard Lancelyn, and John Michael Gibson, eds. *A Bibliography of A. Conan Doyle.* Soho Bibliographies 23. Oxford: Clarendon, 1983.

Griffiths, Arthur. *Memorials of Millbank and Chapters in Prison History.* New ed. London: Chapman and Hall, 1884.

"Griffiths, Arthur George Frederick." *Oxford Dictionary of National Biography,* 2004 ed.

Harvey, David. *A Brief History of Neoliberalism.* Oxford: Oxford UP, 2005.

Herbert, Christopher. *War of No Pity: The Indian Mutiny and Victorian Trauma.* Princeton: Princeton UP, 2008.

Hibbert, Christopher. *The Great Mutiny: India, 1857.* New York: Viking, 1978.

Hollander, John. *The Figure of Echo: A Mode of Allusion in Milton and After.* Berkeley: U of California P, 1981.

Hunter, William, ed. *The Imperial Gazetteer of India.* 14 vols. London: Trübner, 1885–87.

Hutchins, Francis G. *The Illusion of Permanence: British Imperialism in India.* Princeton: Princeton UP, 1967.

Inden, Ronald. *Imagining India.* Cambridge, MA: Basil Blackwell, 1990.

Jann, Rosemary. *The Adventures of Sherlock Holmes: Detecting Social Order.* Twayne's Masterwork Series 152. New York: Twayne, 1995.

Jasanoff, Maya. *Edge of Empire: Lives, Culture, and Conquest in the East, 1750–1850.* New York: Knopf, 2005.

Kaye, John William. *A History of the Sepoy War in India: 1857–1858.* 3 vols. London: W. H. Allen, 1864–76.

Kling, Blair B. *The Blue Mutiny: The Indigo Disturbances in Bengal, 1859–1862.* Philadelphia: U of Pennsylvania P, 1966.

Knight, Steven. *Form and Ideology in Crime Fiction.* Bloomington: Indiana UP, 1980.

"LaSalle, Robert Cavelier Sieur de." *Encyclopædia Britannica*, 9th ed., 1875–89.

Lellenberg, Jon, Daniel Stashower, and Charles Foley, eds. *Arthur Conan Doyle: A Life in Letters.* New York: Penguin, 2007.

The London Encyclopædia. Ed. Ben Weinreb and Christopher Hibbert. 1983. Bethesda, Md.: Adler and Adler, 1986.

Lyall, Sir Alfred C. *Asiatic Studies: Religious and Social.* London: John Murray, 1882.

Lycett, Andrew. *The Man Who Created Sherlock Holmes: The Life and Times of Sir Arthur Conan Doyle.* New York: Free Press, 2007.

Macaulay, Thomas Babington. *Critical, Historical, and Miscellaneous Essays and Poems.* 3 vols. Chicago: Donohue, Henneberry, [1885].

———. *The History of England from the Accession of James II.* 5 vols. London: Longman, 1849–61.

———. "Minute on Indian Education." *Selected Writings.* Ed. John Clive and Thomas Pinney. Chicago: U of Chicago P, 1972.

Macfarlane, Alan, and Iris Macfarlane. *The Empire of Tea: The Remarkable History of the Plant that Took over the World.* New York: Overlook, 2004.

Maine, Sir Henry Sumner. *Ancient Law: Its Connection with the Early History of Society and its Relation to Modern Ideas.* London: John Murray, 1861.

Malleson, G[eorge] B[ruce]. *History of the Indian Mutiny: 1857–1858. Commencing from the Close of the Second Volume of Sir John Kaye's History of the Sepoy War.* 3 vols. London: W. H. Allen, 1878–80.

Mann, Charles C. *1491: New Revelations of the Americas before Columbus.* New York: Knopf, 2005.

Marshall, P. J. *The Impeachment of Warren Hastings.* London: Oxford UP, 1965.

Mayhew, Henry, and John Binny. *The Criminal Prisons of London and Scenes of Prison Life.* 1862. New York: Augustus M. Kelley, 1968.

McLaughlin, Joseph, *Writing the Urban Jungle: Reading Empire in London from Doyle to Eliot.* Charlottesville: UP of Virginia, 2000.

Merry, Robert W. *Sands of Empire: Missionary Zeal, American Foreign Policy, and the Hazards of Global Ambition.* New York: Simon and Schuster, 2005.

Metcalf, Thomas. *Ideologies of the Raj.* New Cambridge History of India. Ed. Gordon Johnson. Cambridge: Cambridge UP, 1994.

Mill, James. *The History of British India.* 2d. ed. 6 vols. London: Baldwin, Craddock, and Joy, 1820.

Mill, John Stuart. *Auguste Comte and Positivism. Essays on Ethics, Religion and Society.* Vol. 10 of *Collected Works of John Stuart Mill.* Ed. J[ohn] M. Robson. Toronto: U of Toronto P, 1969.

Miller, D. A. *The Novel and the Police.* Berkeley: U of California Press, 1988.

Mintz, Sidney W. *Sweetness and Power: The Place of Sugar in Modern History.* New York: Viking Penguin, 1985.

Muir, Sir William. *Agra in the Mutiny and the Family Life of W. and E. H. Muir in the Fort, 1857.* London, 1896.

"Orange." *Encyclopædia Britannica,* 9th ed., 1875–89.

The Oxford History of the Prison: The Practice of Punishment in Western Society. Ed. Norval Morris and David J. Rothman. Oxford: Oxford UP, 1995.

Pitts, Jennifer. *A Turn to Empire: The Rise of Imperial Liberalism in Britain and France.* Princeton: Princeton UP, 2005.

Polanyi, Karl. *The Great Transformation.* New York: Farrar and Rinehart, 1944.

Porter, Dennis. *The Pursuit of Crime: Art and Ideology in Detective Fiction.* New Haven: Yale UP, 1981.

Reitz, Caroline. *Detecting the Nation: Fictions of Detection and the Imperial Venture.* Columbus: Ohio State UP, 2004.

Roden, Christopher. Introduction. *The Sign of the Four.* By Arthur Conan Doyle. Oxford Sherlock Holmes. Ed. Owen Dudley Edwards. Oxford: Oxford UP, 1993. xi–xli.

Rosmarin, Adena. *The Power of Genre.* Minneapolis: U of Minnesota P, 1985.

Said, Edward W. *Orientalism.* New York: Pantheon, 1978.

Seeley, Sir J[ohn]. *The Expansion of England: Two Courses of Lectures.* 2d. ed. London: Macmillan, 1921.

Shakespeare, William. *King Lear.* Ed. Kenneth Muir. Arden Shakespeare. Cambridge: Harvard UP, 1959.

———. *Macbeth.* Ed. Kenneth Muir. Arden Shakespeare. London: Methuen, 1951.

Siddiqi, Yumna. "The Cesspool of Empire: Sherlock Holmes and the Return of the Repressed." *Victorian Literature and Culture* 34 (2006): 233–47.

Stephen, James Fitzjames. *Liberty, Equality, Fraternity.* Ed. R. J. White. Cambridge: Cambridge UP, 1967.

Stewart, Garrett. "Dickens and the Narratography of Closure." *Critical Inquiry* 34 (2008): 509–42.

Stokes, Eric. *The English Utilitarians and India.* Oxford: Clarendon, 1959.

Strachey, Sir John. *India.* London: Kegan Paul, Trench, 1888.

Suleri, Sara. *The Rhetoric of English India.* Chicago: U of Chicago P, 1992.

Thomas, Ronald R. *Detective Fiction and the Rise of Forensic Science.* Cambridge Studies in Nineteenth-Century Literature and Culture 26. Cambridge: Cambridge UP, 1999.

Thornhill, Mark. *The Personal Adventures and Experiences of a Magistrate during the Rise, Progress, and Suppression of the Indian Mutiny.* London: John Murray, 1884.

Tylor, Edward B. *Primitive Culture: Researches into the Development of Mythology, Philosophy, Religion, Language, Art, and Custom.* 7th ed. 2 vols. in 1. New York: Brentano's, 1924.

Walvin, James. *Fruits of Empire: Exotic Produce and British Taste, 1660–1800.* New York: New York UP, 1997.

White, R. J. Introduction. *Liberty, Equality, Fraternity.* By James Fitzjames Stephen. Cambridge: Cambridge UP, 1967. 1–18.

Wiltse, Ed. " 'So Constant an Expectation': Sherlock Holmes and Seriality." *Narrative* 6 (1998): 105–22.

Wright, H. R. C. *East-Indian Economic Problems of the Age of Cornwallis and Raffles.* London: Luzac, 1961.

Wurgaft, Lewis D. *The Imperial Imagination: Magic and Myth in Kipling's India.* Middletown, CT: Wesleyan UP, 1983.

Zastoupil, Lynn. *John Stuart Mill and India.* Stanford: Stanford UP, 1994.

Recent Dickens Studies: 2008

Cynthia Northcutt Malone

Scholarship in Dickens continued to flourish in 2008. This essay examines articles, book chapters, and books; the bibliography that follows the essay demonstrates the vitality and breadth of Dickens studies. After considering two essay collections, I organize the review into nine distinct but related areas of focus: (1) biography; (2) home; (3) elsewhere; (4) children; (5) women; (6) commodity culture; (7) reading; (8) modes of representation; and (9) echoes. The essay highlights work I found particularly compelling, and it poses questions that scholarship might pursue in the future.

The year 2008 yielded plenty of scholarship on The Inimitable, some of it compelling, some provocative, some intriguing, and some bound to set readers' heads on fire. In this essay, I hope to provide an overview of the year's work, to highlight particular achievements, and to frame questions that scholars haven't yet addressed fully.

Two wide-ranging essay collections, one edited by David Paroissien and the other by Eileen Gilooly and Deirdre David, offer useful beginning points for surveying Dickens scholarship in 2008. I'll begin with those collections, and then I'll examine the remaining work by considering nine general areas of focus. I confess to planting my feet and shoving hard to get a few of the essays and books onto one of these nine shelves, and I recognize that some works might have been equally at home on a different shelf. Generally, though, the nine categories serve well:

Biography
Home
Elsewhere
Children
Women
Commodity Culture
Reading
Modes of Representation
Echoes

Essay Collections

Gathering together the work of thirty-six contributors, David Paroissien has constructed *A Companion to Charles Dickens* that offers helpful guidance to undergraduate readers of Dickens and offers insightful new essays to Dickens scholars. The volume opens with "Perspectives on the Life"; the second section examines "Literary/Cultural Contexts," and the third turns to "English History Contexts." Part IV, "The Fiction," features short essays on each of Dickens's novels, and Part V, "Reputation and Influence," sketches the trajectory of criticism from Dickens's time to ours. To keep this *Companion* from ballooning to monstrous size, Paroissien limited the scope and length of the contributions and lets each essay point to "References and Further Reading." The smart, succinct essays, along with the fine bibliographies, will make this a much-valued *Companion*.

Gillooly and David divide the essays in *Contemporary Dickens* into three sections: "Ethics and Narrative"; "Material Culture"; and "Contextual Reading." The volume performs crucial genealogical work: each contributor has situated central questions historically—in Victorian material culture, in the history of ideas, in the development of the English novel—and each contributor concludes by commenting on the contemporary resonance of crucial issues in Dickens's work. For example, in "Ethics and Narrative," George Levine examines the tensions between "secularity and religion" and "ethics and money," especially in *Little Dorrit* (31); in "Material Culture," Karen Chase and Michael Levenson explore "Green Dickens"; in "Contextual Reading," Deirdre David illuminates the portrayal of angry women in the "theater of rage" in *Little Dorrit* (246). Each essay in the volume deserves closer attention than I can devote to it here. Taken as a whole, this volume demonstrates powerfully the innumerable ways in which the Victorian constitutes the present.

Biography

No full-length biographies of Dickens appeared in 2008; in *Brief Lives: Charles Dickens*, however, Melissa Valiska Gregory and Melisa Klimaszewski supplement the excellent lengthy Dickens biographies with their intelligent "brief life." Tracing the main outline of Dickens's personal life and his development as a writer, this fine, succinct account will be enormously useful as a course text.

Several essays probed particular life events, drawing on newly discovered material or bringing scientific or medical expertise to the Dickens archive. Peter R. Lewis, a forensic engineer, examines the documentation of the Staplehurst crash and similar disasters. He provides a detailed account of the causes and consequences of the railroad accident. In "Charles Dickens: A Neglected Diagnosis," I. C. McManus, a professor of psychology and medical education, reviews the accounts of Dickens's symptoms during the last years of his life. He gives particular attention to an occasion mentioned in Forster's *Life* in which Dickens found himself able to read only halves of letters and suggests that "Dickens had a right parietal or parietal-temporal disorder" (98).

Possibilities of hugger-muggery in June of 1870 continue to intrigue Dickensians. In "Dickens's Death," David Parker returns to the question of whether Dickens suffered his fatal illness at Ellen Ternan's house in Peckham. Parker reviews in detail the "Peckham conjecture" and concludes that the correct answer "is almost certainly, no" (193). Robert Garnett considers "The Mysterious Mourner: Dickens's Funeral and Ellen Ternan." Since Dickens left explicit directions for his funeral and prohibited from attending anyone who had no strong tie, Garnett argues, Dickens would have wished Ellen Ternan to attend. The list of mourners includes thirteen names, but the *Times* account states that fourteen mourners attended. Garnett concludes that the fourteenth must be Ternan.

Scouring the archives, scholars continue to identify works by Dickens. Angus Easson, Margaret Brown, Leon Litvack, and Joan Dicks continue their indefatigable work, publishing new letters in "The Letters of Charles Dickens, Supplement IX" and "Supplement X"; Supplement IX includes some particularly sparkly letters. In "The Juvenilia of Charles Dickens: Romance and Reality," Christine Alexander surveys the works attributed and misattributed to the young Charles Dickens and catalogues the extant works: "six poems, written between the ages of eighteen and twenty; and three fragments of amateur theatrical work written when Dickens was about twenty or twenty-one" (9). John Drew reprints a review of *Poems by Thomas Hood* published in *The Daily News* on January 29, 1846, during Dickens's stint as editor. The closing paragraph of the review, Drew notes, suggests strongly that Dickens is its author; Drew links the terms of praise and gratitude in that closing paragraph with other documentation of Dickens's gratitude to Hood for his review of *Master Humphrey's Clock* to provide convincing evidence for this hypothesis.

Les Standiford, in *The Man Who Invented Christmas*, describes the circumstances surrounding Dickens's decision to write *A Christmas Carol*. The small book is more comprehensive and thoughtful than the title might suggest. It surveys Dickens's personal and professional life in the early 1840s, but it also ranges widely to provide accessible descriptions of social contexts, including the contemporary book-publishing and bookselling industries, the problem of book pirating in the U.S. and elsewhere, the economic depression, and the terrible condition of children in "ragged schools." (Whether the book benefits from its description of Christmas practices in the Puritan colonies and later in New England, or from a history of Christmas trees in the U.S., we may wonder.) This book will serve a general audience of readers who prize *A Christmas Carol* and seek to know more.

Home

Answering Dickens's call for a good spirit who would take the house-tops off, Julia Prewitt Brown peers inside the middle-class home. Brown's *The Bourgeois Interior* opens by locating the "bourgeois domestic ideal" in "seventeenth-century Holland and [in] Dutch genre painting" (8). Beginning from that premise, she proposes "that the longing expressed in novels is implicitly for an earlier, more stable middle class, and that this nostalgia is characteristically played out through the medium of the bourgeois interior" (11). In her chapter on Dickens, Brown attributes this nostalgia to the particular experiences of Dickens's life; exploring Dickens's efforts to create "the bourgeois domestic ideal both in his fiction and in his personal life" (14), Brown suggests that the childhood trauma that destroyed his experience of "home" and caused valued objects to disappear from his life may contribute to Dickens's attempts to realize the bourgeois ideal in multiple forms, ranging from Urania Cottage to the homes of his fictional characters. Like the women of Urania Cottage, Brown suggests, David Copperfield must shed the signs of his past in order to enter "the coveted space of the bourgeoisie" (69). She goes on to offer provocative readings of "things" in Satis House, Boffin's Bower, and the Meagles's home. This chapter raises intriguing questions that the brief sections can't address fully, so I hope that the lines of interpretation that Brown has begun here will prompt fuller analysis.

That larger and endlessly fascinating home in so much of Dickens's work, London, is the subject of Michelle Allen's splendid *Cleansing the City*. Early in the introduction, Allen quotes a passage from *Dombey and Son* that links "noxious particles" of "vitiated air" with its corollary, "moral pestilence." "From Dickens's striking representation of urban pollution," Allen contends, "we may infer a provisional generalization about the meanings of filth for the educated members of the middle class in mid-Victorian cities: the problem of filth was at once a physical danger . . . , a demoralizing influence, and a social threat," and all of these perils intensified anxiety about the "urban poor" (9). Allen's work offers a valuable supplement to earlier studies of sanitary reform; as she points out, scholars typically share the values and perceptions of sanitary reformers like Edwin Chadwick. In her perceptive and persuasive analysis of mid-Victorian responses to sanitary reform, Allen demonstrates the "very different, often antagonistic, visions of and responses to sanitary progress" (17).

Grounded in recent work in geography, Allen's chapter on *Our Mutual Friend*, "A More Expansive Reach: The Geography of the Thames in *Our Mutual Friend*," attends to the specific conditions of sanitation and filth in the Thames-side locations that figure in Dickens's novel. As she points out, "*Our Mutual Friend* began appearing in monthly serialization about the same time that construction of the [Thames] Embankment was first becoming visible," so that the novel emerged during a time of "public debate about the condition of the river" (87). The scenes along the river—from the dredging of dead bodies in London to dinner in Greenwich to earnest labor in a Thames-side village—demonstrate the complexity and the range of meanings of the Thames and, by extension, of London: "By emphasizing the topographic range and diversity of the river, Dickens creates an image of the metropolis as an aggregate of localities, each with its own identity and set of resources," but all "connected by the river" (114).

In *Dickens and the Unreal City*, Karl Ashley Smith reads Dickens's London through the modernist transmutation of that city in Eliot's *The Waste Land*. Smith's study "addresses factors of the city that dramatise both negative and positive effects upon the spiritual life of the individual character, as consonant with the issues raised in Dickens's more direct statements on religious belief and experience" and "shows how these religious concerns interact with other more immediate influences upon the representation of these phenomena of urban life to add up to an account of the city that serves a blend of spiritual, stylistic and political functions" (6). Beginning with a survey of Dickens's "more direct statements" about faith and scripture, Smith goes on to examine specific elements of London in Dickens's work, organizing the chapters around the "deadening" and "life-giving" effects of urban decay, dirt, detective work, the railway, the Thames, and the crowds. Given the ambition of his enterprise, it is perhaps not surprising that the recapitulation of the argument in the final chapter is inconclusive: Dickens's London "functions as a recurring symbol, composed of many smaller symbols each of which individually interacts with related images in overlapping discourses and previous literary genres, but greater than the sum of its parts'' (219).

Jeremy Tambling aims the critical beam of *Going Astray in Dickens* at the juncture, or disjuncture, between London as an urban space that one can investigate and map and the unknowable. "Reading Dickens in and on London," Tambling observes, "must respond to a double demand''; "[o]ne sees the space created in the novels as responding to London as a pre-given, social reality,'' he explains, while "[t]he other is intrigued by the possibility of finding other spaces, not mappable, in the given space of the city'' (7). Discovering those "other spaces, not mappable,'' requires following the map and wandering from it—going astray. Moving step by step through Dickens's London, from the city he inherited from eighteenth-century writers to his early sketches and through the chronological sequence of his writings, Tambling responds to the "double demand,'' offering detailed treatments (and photographs) of empirical London and deploying wide-ranging theoretical work to make visible and comprehensible the spaces in Dickens's London that resist mapping. By my lights, Tambling articulates the aims and significance of the book most fully in the epilogue; I recommend beginning there.

Both Leslie Simon and Valerie Kennedy examine Dickens's representation of the relationship between "home" and "abroad." In "Archives of the Interior,'' Simon draws parallels between the narratives of empire travel and *Pickwick*; as the adventure narratives of travelers in the empire represent the people, places, and objects they encounter in ways that reveal the norms and values of the travelers, so the Pickwick party sets out from home, "nominally exploring tracts of otherness and uncovering signs of difference'' but "continuously and persistently moves *inward*, exploring the narrative subject himself and revealing much more about the explorer than the explored'' (24).

Valerie Kennedy's two-part study of "Dickens and Savagery at Home and Abroad'' offers a scrupulous study of "savagery'' in Dickens's fiction and journalism and classifies the uses to which Dickens puts the notion of savagery. In his journalism, Kennedy notes, Dickens "frequently compares civilization and savagery, usually to the advantage of the former''; his sympathy for slaves and Native Americans in *American Notes* serves as an exception to his more typical derogatory treatment of non-Europeans, Kennedy argues, and his ironic use of "savagery'' to describe practices of British culture also functions as "a complicating factor'' in the dichotomy between European civilization and non-European savagery (217). In Dickens's fiction, "savagery is not only a characteristic of the English poor and of criminals, but of 'gentlemen' too'' (218). Two deep fears underlie Dickens's treatment of "savagery,'' according to Kennedy: "the fear that neglect, ignorance, and poverty will destroy the possibility of civilisation,'' and the related "fear about what he might have become had his childhood experience of poverty continued, and . . . his later awareness of his own potential for violence'' (218, 219).

Angelia Poon begins her chapter on Dickens in *Enacting Englishness* by examining the ways in which the figure of the savage illuminates the performance of Englishness in Dickens's journalism. Poon argues that Dickens charges himself with ''the task of defining the English subject in terms antithetical to the savage body'' (109). She moves on to an analysis of *The Mystery of Edwin Drood*, a novel that, in Poon's view, demonstrates the difficulty of policing the English body: ''In *The Mystery of Edwin Drood*, we are presented with an England infused by an undifferentiated colonial world and its associated elements of primitive exoticism, savage appetite, and erotic Orientalism'' (114). Operating in ''an England encroached upon and stained by empire,'' the characters in this novel ''show how difficult it is to regulate appetite . . . and hence the English body'' (115, 114). Certainly, Dickens's journalism and fiction repeatedly and provocatively juxtapose wild, unregulated savagery with an ideal of ordered, regulated Englishness. However, Poon's argument would benefit from attending more carefully, as Kennedy does, to Dickens's complex rhetorical uses of invective against savagery, especially as social criticism of the English.

Elsewhere

Dickens's visits to and writings about America drew considerable attention in 2008. According to Igor Webb, Dickens found himself in ''a world without authority'' when he visited America. That experience informs *Martin Chuzzlewit*, Webb argues in ''Charles Dickens in America,'' in ways that extend far beyond topical issues; while Dickens saw the ''ideal form of narration'' as ''a union of spontaneity and control, of planned composition and improvisation,'' he penned a novel that many readers have found to be incoherent and chaotic (77). Webb sees in Nadgett the spy a figure for the author. Recalling Dorothy Van Ghent's ''The Dickens World: A View from Todgers's,'' Webb suggests that Dickens functions in *Martin Chuzzlewit* like that busy spy, ''a rapt, amoral observer'' of an immensely complex world, drawing connections and making discoveries (91). But no discovery or connection will yield the authoritative meaning of the world seen from Todgers's. In Webb's view, ''[t]he authority of the novel . . . resides not in its plot or in its characters but as it were in itself, in its act of narration'' (91).

In ''Colonial Ghosts: Mimicking Dickens in America,'' Andrew Smith draws on both Freud's notion of the uncanny and Homi Bhabha's treatment of mimicry in the colonial context to raise intriguing questions about Dickens's uses of the Gothic in *American Notes*. When Dickens observes colonial institutions—the school for the blind and the prison, for example—he recognizes both familiarity and strangeness, so that his accounts reveal "a pervasive undertow of alienation and estrangement" rendering him "a national outsider" and, thus, "a writer who struggles to make sense of American idioms" (186). Perhaps Smith will develop these ideas in a longer piece that provides fuller textual support and demonstrates more convincingly the differences between Dickens's use of the Gothic in *American Notes* and in writings about Britain.

Joe Lockard and Daniel Hack examine Dickens's treatment of the peculiar institution. In *Watching Slavery: Witness Texts and Travel Report*, Lockard draws a distinction between witnessing slavery and watching slavery in nineteenth-century travel accounts: "Watching slavery was a passive act; observers watched, reported, and discussed slavery but did not act against it directly. Witnessing slavery involved both observing slavery and acting against it" (xxiv). The first chapter, on Dickens and Thackeray, explores "Charles Dickens' fulminations against slavery in *American Notes for General Circulation* and refusal to travel deep into slave territory during his lecture tours, in order to ask how his once-antislavery politics evolved into tacit support for the Southern cause during the Civil War" (xxxii). Grounding his analysis in clearly stated political and ethical positions, Lockard documents Dickens's strong antislavery position in *American Notes* and his "gradualist approach to emancipation" in the early 1850s. Lockard cites an article titled "North American Slavery" written with Henry Morley for *Household Words* in 1852 to show that "for Dickens and Morley an inexorable whitening of the Southern states and the institution's economic constriction would of necessity lead to slavery's abolition" (32). Both writers supported Liberian emigration, Lockard argues, as one means of "whitening" the South. When the American Civil War broke out, "Dickens' concern for the economic dependency of British textile workers on cheap Southern cotton eclipsed his humanitarian interest in slaves" (35). Dickens's identification with the interests of white English workers, along with the influence of Carlyle and Thackeray, offer an explanation of Dickens's shift from antislavery writings in *American Notes* to support of Governor Eyre's brutal suppression of the Jamaican rebellion.

Both Lockard and Hack note the ways in which *Bleak House*, especially Dickens's satire of Mrs. Jellyby and her Borrioboola-Gha project, calls on readers to turn from schemes to ease the suffering of distant people and to focus instead on easing suffering at home—in the domestic home and in Britain. As Hack demonstrates in "Close Reading at a Distance," "[a]ntebellum African Americans and abolitionists seized upon *Bleak House* and put it to work in a surprising number of ways" (729). Thus, while "*Bleak House* does not merely fail to imagine a community that includes Africans, African Americans, slaves, and people of color in general but rather consolidates the national community it does imagine by their exclusion,'' antislavery writers ''find in *Bleak House* a material and imaginative resource for their own efforts to tell the stories they want to tell and build the communities they seek to build'' (731). Hack examines the discourse surrounding Frederick Douglass's serial publication of *Bleak House* in *Douglass' Paper* and concludes that ''Douglass' persistence'' in publishing the novel despite its apparent unsuitability for an abolitionist paper ''stems not from inertia or inattention but rather a determination to enlist '*the universal favorite* of the people' in the cause, if necessary despite himself'' (738).

Hack then turns to Hannah Crafts's *The Bondwoman's Narrative*, published in 2002; as Hack points out, ''Crafts renovates the novel—in part, paradoxically, by deconstructing it,'' reversing the charge of elements in Dickens's work that most concerned antislavery groups (747). Hack makes a powerful argument not only about the African Americanization of *Bleak House* in an essay that demonstrates how much critical work is yet to be done in the area of reading, rereading, and rewriting across the Atlantic.

Larisa T. Castillo focuses on the treatment of natural rights, authorship, and inheritance in relation to copyright issues in her essay, ''Natural Authority in Charles Dickens's *Martin Chuzzlewit* and the Copyright Act of 1842.'' She begins by citing Dickens's 1868 postscript to *Martin Chuzzlewit*, an acknowledgment of the changes that took place in America between his first visit, in 1842, and his second. This postscript, she argues, functions as ''a last will and testament to the Americans''; but ''his more generous depiction of America is only secure if he, and his descendants, have power over the book—have copyright'' (463). His argument for copyright, Castillo shows, is founded in the idea of natural rights, yet the narrator of *Martin Chuzzlewit* destabilizes that idea: ''the fictional voice of his novel exposes the laws protecting the intellectual property of authors . . . to be nothing more than arbitrary, or fictive, constructions of individual right.'' Castillo argues that ''[t]his challenge to natural right ultimately works against Dickens's own interest by threatening all categories under investigation: inheritance, copyright, and authorship'' (439). Thus, the novel registers the deepest tensions at work in the mid-Victorian debates about intellectual property.

Both Logan Delano Browning and Nancy Aycock Metz focus on the contrasts between Dickens's *American Notes* and *Pictures from Italy*. In Browning's view, Dickens experienced disappointment throughout his American tour; measuring experience against expectations, Dickens was repeatedly disappointed. *American Notes* resounds with certainty in the truth of his perceptions, Browning argues in ''Changing *Notes* into *Pictures*''; Dickens ''incorporates verbatim a number of printed sources to prove that his own views are correct or to support the veracity of his descriptions'' (244). From the outset of *Pictures*, on the other hand, Dickens offers ''impressions,'' emphasizing their mutability, and he lets his imagination roam across the scenes he visits.

In "Italy: The Sequel," Metz contends that *Pictures* is Dickens's sequel to *American Notes*, the trip to Italy a project designed "as a kind of antidote to America" (37). Metz argues that Dickens "had no idea how deeply embedded in his thinking and being were traditional English values and rituals until he experience a culture organized around different principles and practices"; when he traveled to Italy, he approached the experience differently: "In the consciousness of a socially-aware man on the move, *Pictures from Italy* seems to say, two cultures can frame and illuminate each other—in the process enabling a more legible reading of the English way of life" (44).

Norbert Lennartz situates *Pictures from Italy* in the tradition of Smollett. In "Charles Dickens Abroad," Lennartz contends that Dickens's descriptions of France and Italy recall Smollett's vituperative responses to those countries in his 1766 *Travels through France and Italy*. Both *Pictures from Italy* and Smollett's *Travels* employ "the persona of the Splenetic Traveler"—Laurence Sterne's phrase—as they encounter the "other" of famous Continental cities. Lennartz might extend the study to these writers' depictions of urban and rural Britain: both in *Humphry Clinker* and in Dickens's writing, after all, descriptions of urban squalor, sloth and indolence, and artificiality feature the same terms of disgust and recoil as the descriptions of France and Italy in Smollett's *Travels* and Dickens's *Pictures*.

The Uncommercial Traveller's visit to the Paris Morgue is the subject of Britta Martens's "Death as Spectacle." Martens explores a parallel between Dickens's description of the morgue as a sensational spectacle in his *Uncommercial Traveller* and in Robert Browning's "Apparent Failure." Both Dickens and Browning represent the Paris Morgue through the perspective of a figure in the text: Dickens's traveler and Browning's speaker use the dramatic monologue. These figures are drawn to the spectacle of corpses on display at the morgue, and the texts register "a shocking realization of the morbidity that lies at the heart of the taste for the sensational" (243). According to Martens, both writers attempt to resolve the moral discomfort of this realization by deploying the same strategy: "projecting [that sensationalism] onto the foreign, working-class crowd" of oglers at the morgue "and claiming the moral high ground" (243).

Jen Hill looks to the geographical limits of the known world in *White Horizon: The Arctic in the Nineteenth-Century Imagination*. Hill argues that "the Arctic was a test limit for ideas the Romantics and Victorians had about themselves, a place in which they experimented with and made legible forms of identity and their attendant anxieties" (3). In the polar regions, then, "Britons could stage debates about domestic and imperial identities, far from British and colonial shores" (3). Hill documents the British fascination with the polar expeditions, and especially with the ways in which the narratives of expedition constructed British masculine identity. This ideological context frames the public debates about the fate of Sir John Franklin's 1844 expedition. If the men of Franklin's team resorted to cannibalism, as John Rae contended after interviews with the Inuit, what were the consequences for notions of British masculinity? In "Arctic Highlanders and Englishmen," Hill reads Dickens's responses to Rae in *Household Words* and Dickens's and Wilkie Collins's play, *The Frozen Deep*, as Dickens's denial of the possibility that a British polar explorer could cast off his deepest and noblest values, even in extremity. Those sections of the chapter are lively and convincing. The chapter demonstrates less successfully the claim Hill makes in the introduction "that Dickens's and Collins's interest in the (im)possibility of cannibalism by the Franklin expedition contributed directly to the development of the sensation genre of the late '50s and early '60s, to which reassertion of the stability of identity (racial, national, gendered) and the status of evidence was central" (26). That provocative claim demands fuller evidence than Hill's reading of a single text, Collins's *Poor Miss Finch*.

Children

Fat children, suffering children, orphaned children, wandering children, neglected children: scholarship in 2008 provided many insights into the inexhaustible subject of children in Dickens.

Sander L. Gilman traces the figure of the Fat Boy from *Pickwick Papers* through medical literature in "Desire and Obesity: Dickens, Endocrinology, Pulmonary Medicine, and Psychoanalysis." In *The Pickwick Papers*, Gilman contends, Dickens offers "an explicit critique of the prevailing assumptions concerning our ability to read the physiognomy of the obese as opposed to the merely corpulent" (38). Judged by these prevailing assumptions, Mr. Pickwick's pleasingly rounded body asserts masculinity. In the figure of Joe, Mr. Wardle's servant, Dickens subverts the stereotype of "the stupid fat man" (38) who desires only food (and sleep)—a fat not-really-man whose obesity cancels masculinity. At two points in the novel, Dickens demonstrates that Joe understands and experiences sexual desire; he observes scenes of seduction and makes strategic use of the power he gains through witnessing those scenes. In the medical literature from the nineteenth and twentieth centuries, Gilman shows, the meaning of the "Fat Boy" shifts markedly; Gilman argues convincingly that "Joe . . . became a case study of pathology that overrode Dickens's much more complex image of limitation and awareness" (45).

Tamara S. Wagner and Laurie Langbauer juxtapose Dickens's suffering children with figures of children in other writers' fiction. In " 'We have orphans [. . .] in stock': Crime and the Consumption of Sensational Children,'' Wagner contrasts the treatment of orphans in *Our Mutual Friend* and the figures of orphans in contemporary sensation novels: "The first half of the nineteenth century can be credited with establishing the sentimentalized child as an iconic literary figure; novels of what came to be known as 'the sensational sixties' were eager to convert it for sensationalized use" (202). In place of the innocent, suffering orphan, sensation novels offer children who are "presumed innocent" and then "revealed to be villains" or who serve as "instruments of revenge" (202). This reversal, Wagner argues, functioned as a means of "capitalizing on the age's sentimentalization of childhood" (203). *Our Mutual Friend* self-consciously raises the issue of orphans as stock-in-trade when the Boffins seek a new John Harmon; it also highlights the replacement of the sentimentalized child when the Orphan dies and the Boffins select Sloppy. As Wagner shows, Dickens complicates the representation of the orphan figure "first by evoking [orphans'] exchange value as a commercial venture through the novel form itself, and then by reinstating the value of a domestic refuge beyond the marketplace" (213).

In "Ethics and Theory: Suffering Children in Dickens, Dostoevsky, and Le Guin," Langbauer argues that these writers use spectacles of suffering children "to jar a world apathetic to such horror"; but the depiction of children in pain involves the writers "in an ethical impossibility, repeating what they critique in order to critique it" (89). In the case of *A Christmas Carol*, Scrooge cannot even recognize the figures of Ignorance and Want as children, and the process of ethical change must include the recognition of the suffering child, including his own childhood self. The suffering child in this tale, and in Dickens's work more generally, replays the traumatic experience of Dickens's childhood: "Children in his words become a poignant symbol of how our self-absorptions blind us to and let us use others" (94). But the act of depicting a child in pain raises the larger questions Langbauer addresses: "What does putting others on display, making them into symbols—especially when we call those symbols 'children'—tell us about the limits and the possibilities of narrative?" And how do we move from questions of representation to the framing of an ethical position? These urgent questions deserve thoughtful consideration, and I wished for a dialogue between Langbauer and Mary-Catherine Harrison (see below).

Little Nell's struggles are the focus of Lisa Hartsell Jackson's "Little Nell's Nightmare: Sexual Awakening and Insomnia in Dickens's *The Old Curiosity Shop*." A girl at the threshold of womanhood, the vulnerable Nell dies before she can "embrace the sexual awakening that is a necessary step in undertaking the role of the idealized Victorian wife and mother" (57). In Jackson's view, "[t]he secrets of sexuality and her continuous pursuit by a multitude of roguish characters have killed both Nell and her potential to grow into"

Victorian womanhood (57). Worn down by "wandering, insomnia, and fatigue," she cannot make that transition (44). Jackson's reading of Nell through the lens of psychological work on adolescence may not convince all readers to see Nell as "a uniquely assertive, brave heroine" instead of "a timid, sickly girl," but its emphasis on the repetition of her struggles yields useful insights.

Lynn Cain's *Dickens, Family, Authorship* examines patterns of parent-child relationships. In her foreword, Cain acknowledges the intellectual legacy of Gillian Beer: "As Beer . . . argued in *Darwin's Plots*, in a post-Freudian age it is impossible to live a life which is not charged with Freudian assumptions, patterns for apprehending experience and ways of perceiving relationships" (x). Indeed, Cain argues, psychoanalytic criticism yields rich readings of nineteenth-century novels "because psychoanalysis itself [was] anticipated in the very texts under critical examination" (xi). Drawing on the insights of Freud, Lacan, Kristeva, and others, Cain examines parent-child relationships in four of Dickens's novels, *Martin Chuzzlewit, Dombey and Son, David Copperfield*, and *Bleak House*. Cain sees these novels as explorations of "the four primary relationships between parent and child: father and son (*Martin Chuzzlewit*); father and daughter (*Dombey and Son*); mother and son (*David Copperfield*); and mother and daughter (*Bleak House*)" (1). Cain reads *Martin Chuzzlewit* and *Bleak House* as "parricidal," *Dombey and Son* and *David Copperfield* as "desiring" (x). While Cain sometimes treats the novels as allegories of psychoanalytic theory—so that Warren's blacking factory, for example, is taken to embody the "darkness of pre-symbolia and the blankness of identity with which [Dickens] associated it"—her readings often move beyond psychoanalytic theory to situate the novels in Victorian material culture.

Women

Dickens's relationships with and representations of women yielded some fine new studies. Jenny Hartley's *Charles Dickens and the House of Fallen Women* provides a vivid, absorbing account of Dickens's work with Urania Cottage from the earliest days of planning to 1858. Hartley argues that Dickens shifted attention from Urania Cottage "not because he was disillusioned or judged it a failure"—on the contrary, she contends, he was pleased with the results of the experiment—but because "Dickens was a dropper" (243). Hartley's study of Dickens's work with Angela Burdett-Coutts adds much to existing scholarship; she documents scrupulously Dickens's plans and hopes for, and reactions to, every facet of life at Urania Cottage. As she points out, biographical scholarship on Dickens has focused primarily on this project as a feature of "the extra-curricular Dickens, the side of him which is not writing fiction" (3). She demonstrates the significance of the Urania Cottage experience to the development of fictional characters and plot strands; as she points out, "[t]he Urania years were the years of *Dombey and Son*, *David Copperfield*, *Bleak House*, *Hard Times*, and *Little Dorrit*, some of the greatest novels Dickens (or indeed anyone) ever wrote" (3).

In chapter 11, "Using the Plot," Hartley demonstrates the ways in which the Urania Cottage women's life stories informed Dickens's fiction. "The orphan, servants and child-carers, the seamstresses, milliners and theatre girls, the prostitutes, tramps and petty thieves, the half-starved apprentices and the attempted suicides: they all gave him their voices and stories," so that "they insinuated themselves ever more deeply into his imagination" and, consequently, "[t]hey swarm through the fiction of the late forties and fifties" (157). Hartley follows the stories of some of these women, from life on the streets or in prison to their lives at Urania Cottage, to their eventual emigration. Following the trail of documents allows us glimpses of fascinating women like the "elegant ex-governess who had concealed a shoe under her shawl so she could throw it at the chief magistrate," a man who evidently lacked the finer reflexes of George W. Bush—since a witness, Felicia Skene, reported the ex-governess's "exquisite enjoyment of the moment, when she saw her muddy old shoe flying through the air to lodge on the magisterial cranium" (11).

Beginning from the premise that critics of Victorian novels have focused largely on the binary terms of domestic ideal and fallen woman, Jennifer Hedgecock sets out to complicate that dichotomy in *The Femme Fatale in Victorian Literature*. The typical fictional femme fatale, Hedgecock argues, "takes it upon herself to seduce men and become the source of their obsession" (60). Dickens's *David Copperfield* offers a variant on this type, however; while the femme fatale typically exercises power over men, Rosa Dartle's "female power derives from victimizing the powerless," especially Emily, "in order to protect her liminal role in the system" (51). Others might extend the argument by examining more fully the representation of Rosa Dartle and Mrs. Steerforth late in the novel, after Steerforth's death, and by examining the dynamics of power in Dickens's figures of embittered, unmarried women more generally (Miss Wade in *Little Dorrit*, for example).

In short essays, Rodney Stenning Edgecombe and Kimberlie L. Brown offer revised readings of female characters. In "The Heroine of Quiet Service in *Dombey and Son*," Edgecombe sees Harriet Carker as "a pioneering figure in the history of English fiction," a turn away from the romance heroine and "a voice in the wilderness for the advent of Little Dorrit" (87). Brown's essay, " 'When I Kissed Her Cheek': Theatrics of Sexuality and the Framed Gaze in Esther's Narration of *Bleak House*," argues that Esther's narrative ''manifests a subtext of sexuality that seduces characters and readers toward action on personal levels that ripple toward social reform'' (170). Gaining the capacity to ''express sensual aspects of one's being'' is the necessary condition for agency; both characters and readers, Brown contends, must achieve that capacity before they ''can enhance their communities and work toward overturning crippling institutions'' like those that stymie the lives of characters in *Bleak House.*

Commodity Culture

Given Dickens's incomparable power to animate things and objectify people, critical work on Dickens and commodity culture is bound to generate tantalizing readings. Catherine Waters opens her splendid *Commodity Culture in Dickens's Household Words* by highlighting ''the fluidity of relations between people and things'' that characterizes commodity culture (5). In the introduction, she situates her own work in the context of recent work in Victorian material culture. Noting that most critical studies of *Household Words* focus on Dickens's contributions, Waters considers the full scope of nonfiction articles and examines ''recurring themes'' of the journal: advertising; questions of authenticity; the flaneur; the ''process article,'' or ''industrial tourist tale''; foreign goods; and ''two areas of trade in which the journal showed a recurring interest: death and second-hand clothing'' (16–17). Every chapter demonstrates Waters's encyclopedic knowledge of *Household Words*, and the quotations that illustrate her points will prompt readers to dive into the journal. Moreover, the scholarship is exemplary: subtle, lucid, and insightful. Blazingly smart and full of delights, *Commodity Culture in Dickens's Household Words* makes a powerful contribution to studies of material culture in the mid-nineteenth century.

Waters's article, '' 'Fairy Palaces' and 'Wonderful Toys,' '' supplements the larger study: ''while Dickens's attack on industrialism in *Hard Times* has become well known, the factory tourist tales he published alongside it in *Household Words* reveal a more mixed response to the industrial developments of this day'' (228). Waters demonstrates that ambivalence by citing Martineau's ''aesthetic appreciation of the factory'' and her ''attempts to convey the wonders of automatic machinery and the increased production it permits,'' on the one hand, and noticing, on the other, the articles that emphasize the damaging effects of industrialization on the workers—reduction to machinery, injury, and death (228).

The relationship between human and machine is also central to Katherine Inglis's study of automata, ''Becoming Automatous: Automata in *The Old Curiosity Shop* and *Our Mutual Friend.*'' ''The automaton's presence in such different novels, written decades apart,'' Inglis asserts, ''is a marker both of its significance in Dickens's imagination and its continued currency in popular culture and the Victorian material imagination'' (32). Focusing on characters who, like Mr. Dolls in *Our Mutual Friend*, resemble automata, Inglis argues that ''to display an automatous affinity is to be diminished'' (32).

James Buzard turns his attention to Dickens's demonstrations of and anxieties about generative powers in ''Enumeration and Exhaustion: Taking Inventory in *The Old Curiosity Shop*.'' ''Inventory *proliferates*,'' Buzard observes; and *Pickwick* had testified to Dickens's powers of creative proliferation (20). But *The Old Curiosity Shop* registers Dickens's anxiety about inventive powers, according to Buzard; as events and characters proliferate, they also blur together. This ''compulsive failure to stay distinct from one another'' is evident particularly at the end of the novel: ''In seeming mockery of his celebrated fecundity and variety as a storyteller, Dickens turns and turns his crank and gives us a series of insufficiently distinguishable deformed or wounded old bachelors'' joined together by the life, and especially the death, of Little Nell (38). Buzard takes inventory and counts ten in the novel, not including the members of Master Humphrey's club.

The relationship between proliferation and scarcity is also the topic of Tara Moore's ''Starvation in Victorian Christmas Fiction.'' Noting at the outset the disturbing effects of starving figures in Christmas literature, Moore examines Christmas literature by Dickens, Mary Elizabeth Braddon, the Mayhew brothers, and others, and she identifies the centrality of both the starving and the overly indulged figures in these stories. Moore notes that the writers of Christmas literature urged benevolence—and conveyed the notion that ''[f]ood-wealth can be redistributed without undermining class relationships'' (501).

Like Moore, Annette Cozzi, Julie E. Fromer, and Natalie Kapetanios Meir explore representations of food and dining in relation to social class. As Cozzi observes in ''Men and Menus,'' ''[t]he image of the well-fed Englishman, weaned on beef and ale or bread and cheese, is such an integral part of the British national identity that the male counterpart to the personification of Britannia is the stout and hearty John Bull, so well-nourished that his waistcoat strains at the seams'' (14). While the specific discussions of the novels are marred at times by inaccuracies—for example, the statement that Abel Magwitch, rather than the stranger he sends as a messenger to Pip, stirs his rum-and-water with a file—Cozzi shows that *The Old Curiosity Shop*, *Great Expectations*, *David Copperfield*, and *Oliver Twist* demonstrate the ways in which ''stratifications of society are sustained by the codification of dining and the discrimination of food'' (35).

In the opening chapter of *A Necessary Luxury: Tea in Victorian England*, Fromer notes that few scholarly studies of tea have given it detailed attention in the Victorian period; generally speaking, Fromer says, ''Victorian scholars have relied on the iconographic power of tea to connote the domestic ideal without pausing to investigate the role of tea in Victorian fiction and culture" (2). Scholars interested in nineteenth-century material culture can learn much from Fromer's study of a commodity so ubiquitous as to become invisible. Dickens scholars will find much to add to the reading of *David Copperfield* that Fromer outlines in chapter 5, as the tea table is made to bear a very great weight in this reading. To shift the metaphor, the tea spout turns out to be an extremely tiny aperture through which to view the novel. Fromer leaves room for much more critical work on the functions of tea in Dickens's fiction.

Meir's essay, " 'What would you like for dinner?' " examines David Copperfield's difficulties involved in learning the rituals and conventions of dining. As Meir points out, *David Copperfield* was published at a time when cookery books, restaurant conduct books, and housekeeping books were quite popular; however, Meir argues, "Dickens delineates a conflict between two different ways of learning proper etiquette: a process that is associated with book learning and a method that is represented as either intuitive or beyond the narrative" (131). Both mimicry and published guides fail to offer the social ease David seeks in dining; David's attempt to copy Steerforth's manners is no more successful than Dora's study of the housekeeping book. Finally, Meir suggests that the novel posits the importance of relying on "instinctive conception of proper social behavior" (142).

The Dickensian meal is an act of imagination in Joris-Karl Huysmans's *Against Nature*, Paul Fox argues in "Dickens à la Carte." The aesthete Des Esseintes transforms English dishes into the perfect Dickensian meal by means of imaginative alchemy. Though Des Esseintes has read Dickens during an illness that has left him with little appetite, his "imaginative conception of himself as a Dickensian Londoner requires certain appetites, appetites that are self-fulfilling in their power to stimulate that imaginative conception" (71). In a French tavern, des Esseintes "eats oxtail soup and sups porter because that is what Dickens's Englishmen do" (71): "The dull reality of London, after such a vivid imaginative experience, could only be a disappointment, for the reality of life always is to the Decadent aesthete" (63). The Dickensian meal, for the aesthete, is not a collection of dishes but an act of imaginative consumption.

Reading

How Dickens read, how the Victorians read Dickens, how we read Dickens and his Victorian readers are questions that continue to prompt stimulating discussion. Alison Case and Harry Shaw offer *Reading the Nineteenth-Century Novel* to undergraduate readers new to this type of narrative. The slim volume begins by highlighting some of the "social and economic changes" that provoked anxieties evident in the nineteenth-century novel, including technological developments, urbanization, and class conflict. Arguing that "[n]ovels provided a crucial social forum" for examining urgent questions of the period, Case and Shaw focus on issues of narration: "We experience the characters and the setting, and we come to understand the larger significance of the novels, through our developing relationship with the voice or voices that tell us these stories" (6). Drawing on Genette, the introduction goes on to provide clear definitions of useful narratological terms.

The seventh chapter explores the dual narration of *Bleak House*, proceeding through sections on serial publication, "The Esther Problem," the functions of Chancery, Lady Dedlock's secret, and an analysis of a single monthly part. Case and Shaw make observations in these sections that would be valuable to many undergraduate readers, and—probably wisely—refrain from attempting an extended critical argument. They wind up the chapter with a conclusion that few *DSA* readers would contest: "there is perhaps one thing on which readers of Dickens can agree, namely that his narration [has] a kind of power we simply don't find anywhere else in the nineteenth-century novel" (136).

In a highly idiosyncratic discussion of Victorian literature, Philip Davis proposes to explain *Why Victorian Literature Still Matters*. Davis compares his approach to Victorian phrenology; he argues that "there is, so to speak, a Victorian bump, a place in the mind that makes the experience of Victorian literature always matter" (7). For Davis, this "bump" involves ambivalence, transition, and other "in-between" conditions; it involves themes like Morality and Toughness; and it involves a mode of writing, fictional realism (7). Davis goes on to identify his audience as "*the reader*, not 'the critic' or 'the student' or 'the scholar' as such" (14), and he adopts the rhetorical posture of experienced guide. At the most local level, his readings of passages from *Oliver Twist*, *A Tale of Two Cities*, *Bleak House*, and *David Copperfield* offer valuable insights. However, the book needs to grapple more fully with the terms "Victorian" and "literature." Reducing "Victorian" to tensions among categories, recurring themes, and the mode of realism elides vast numbers of works we would normally consider "Victorian literature" and completely unmoors the term "Victorian" from history (and so it is hardly surprising that Davis concludes the book with discussions of contemporary "neo-Victorian novels" [147]). Delivered as lectures within a curriculum, these discussions might be intriguing and stimulating. However, the important question Davis broaches, Why Victorian Literature Still Matters, deserves a much more coherent structure of argument in book form.

Daniel Pollack-Pelzner and Bert Hornback examine scenes of reading in *Our Mutual Friend*. In "Reading and Repeating *Our Mutual Friend*," Pollack-Pelzner summarizes the long critical tussle over Mr. Boffin's deception of Bella in order to demonstrate that the novel anticipates interpretive moves of the critics. As Pollack-Pelzner notes, critical work on *Our Mutual Friend* includes plenty of attention to the Boffin plot and to scenes of reading in this novel; in an ingenious and intelligent weaving together of these critical discussions, Pollack-Pelzner demonstrates that "readers should relax in the knowledge that however they respond, Dickens saw it coming" and inscribed those responses in the plots of the novel itself (272).

Like Pollack-Pelzner, Hornback focuses on the act of reading in *Our Mutual Friend*. His essay, "Mortimer Lightwood," gives particular emphasis to the reader's task of piecing together: "A good *reader* . . . looks at details and puts them together," Hornback states. "And Dickens, reading life, is fond of putting things together—and fond of characters who put things together": Venus, Mr. Inspector, Wegg, and others (251). (Hornback's essay slyly demands that the reader engage in piecing together; the absence of transitions forces the reader to articulate the argument with Venusian attention.) In Hornback's view, it is Mortimer Lightwood, "the main observer in the novel as well as its designated storyteller," who succeeds most fully in putting things together: "In the end, Mortimer's understanding—his putting everything together and making sense of it—lets the novel have its wonderful, social title, *Our Mutual Friend*" (259).

Nan Miller provides a fictional account of listening to Dickens read in "We Came to Hear Dickens." Miller introduces her fictional account of Dickens's reading in Boston on 2 December, 1867, by noting that "[a]n insider's play-by-play account of Dickens's 1842 American tour appeared in *The Atlantic Monthly* shortly after Dickens' death in 1870," but no parallel account exists for the 1867 tour: "one must stitch together bits and pieces from many different sources" (49). Miller's narrator is the fictional sister of George Putnam, Dickens's secretary on the 1842 tour. The stitched-together narrative includes observation by eyewitnesses and critical reviews, and it offers a glimpse of Dickens's preparation for and performance of this 1867 reading.

In two essays published in 2008, Matthew Rubery considers experiences of reading Dickens and hearing Dickens read. In "*Bleak House* in Real Time," Rubery sets aside the spatial metaphor of "close reading" in order to examine the temporal metaphor of "long reading," the term he uses to describe the experience of reading Dickens's novels as they were published serially (113). In "Play It Again, Sam Weller: New Digital Audiobooks and Old Ways of Reading," Rubery attends closely to the experience of hearing Dickens's fiction being read aloud in the Victorian period and in the contemporary Western world.

"*Bleak House* in Real Time" proposes a "thought experiment" that highlights some of the crucial differences between reading the three-volume novel and reading the serial installments. For example, the apparently endless Chancery suit would drag on month after month, and the reader of the *Bleak House* serial numbers would share with the recovering Esther the sense of temporal distance from the time before her illness (115). Rubery notes that life experiences during the months of reading installments of *Bleak House* might well give the reader the sense that he or she, like the characters of *Bleak House*, changed over the time of reading the novel.

In "Play It Again, Sam Weller," Rubery surveys some of the crucial similarities and differences between the Victorian practice of reading aloud and the increasingly common practice of listening to audio books. Rubery argues that "digital audio will turn more of us into listeners," but also that "this same technology will turn more of us into narrators" because digital recording technologies are so widely disseminated. As Rubery notes, both uses of digital audio can be valuable in literature courses: "one of the most consequential effects of the new digital audio has been to bring back old ways of reading, specifically the practice of reading aloud associated with the nineteenth-century parlour" (74). Thus, the audio book "restor[es] the easily overlooked dimension of aurality to a literature hitherto received almost entirely in visual terms" (74). These essays have much to offer, both to Dickens studies and to discussions of reading in the digital age. During a time of intense debate about the future of the book, we desperately need the kind of nuanced, historically grounded, textured analysis that Rubery provides.

Danielle Coriale investigates Dickens's struggle with book form in her essay, "*Sketches by Boz*, 'So Frail a Machine.' " Coriale takes her title from Dickens's description of *Sketches by Boz* as a hot-air balloon, a frail machine for the authorial voyage. While Dickens sought to impose formal coherence on the collection of sketches, Coriale argues, his "*Sketches* . . . would remain a stubbornly disjointed collection of journalistic pieces that never fully cohered or formed a larger narrative structure" (802). Coriale traces carefully Dickens's efforts to "impose a narrative structure on writing that was fundamentally resistant to it" (808).

Following Matthew Rubery's provocative comparisons between Victorian and twenty-first century reading practices, other scholars might use Coriale's work as a foundation for examining the relationship between reading particular sketches in newspapers and other periodicals, on the one hand, and in the collected *Sketches by Boz*, on the other; and the relationship between reading blog postings and published essays, on the one hand, and a "blook" or collection of writings, on the other. With access to powerful databases and search engines, we now have the means of collecting and editing material in ways that no Victorian reader (or writer) could imagine, and the new possibilities for gathering material raise new formal questions.

Laurence W. Mazzeno has read and digested the writings of innumerable Dickens critics; *The Dickens Industry*, Mazzeno's encyclopedic survey of

Dickens criticism from the nineteenth to the twenty-first century, will be indispensable to advanced undergraduates, graduate students, and scholars wading into the deep, wide waters of Dickens studies. Focusing on book-length studies, Mazzeno poses the central questions of his study: "How was Dickens perceived? How did perceptions change over time? What works were valued by the Victorians, by their children and grandchildren, and by the academic community and the general public throughout the twentieth century? What critical issues occupied the attention of those writing about Dickens during the past 170 years? And finally, what does criticism of Dickens tell us about his critics?" (1)

The chronological study highlights areas of focus and critical debate; it also hovers close to the ground it surveys, using the writers' own formulations of their arguments. Mazzeno's taxonomies of criticism function best in the chapters that cover criticism before 1980; as Mazzeno himself acknowledges, more recent criticism resists classification by theoretical approach or disciplinary focus. As a whole, though, this valuable book helps to trace lines of interrogation across the past century and a half and to situate the well-known critical controversies in the broad context of Dickens studies. (A brief testimony to Mazzeno's cogent summaries of Dickens criticism: though I was surrounded by towers of Industry while making my way through Mazzeno's book, I kept jotting down titles of books I haven't yet read.)

While Mazzeno considers the enormous breadth of Dickens criticism, Toru Sasaki trains his sights on a single essay. In "Edmund Wilson's 'The Two Scrooges' Reconsidered," Sasaki sets out "to scrutinize this celebrated essay once again, and bring its strength and weakness into sharper focus" (32). The scrutiny turns up inconsistencies and untenable assertions—some of which, as Sasaki notes, Philip Collins identified long ago. Surely Wilson's essay, as Sasaki notes, "is well worth re-reading, or worth taking issue with"; having taken those steps, Sasaki might broaden the scope of the analysis to show how taking issue with Wilson opens up new areas of discussion in Dickens studies.

Modes of Representation

Work on Dickens gave much attention to modes of representation, including scenes of writing, modes of narrative, textual representations of affective and sensory experience, illustration, and emerging forms like photography and telegraphy. Criticism focusing on representations of Dickens's work in film concludes this section.

Marie McAllister and Keith Easley examine the act of writing in *Great Expectations*. In " 'Sneaking You as Writes but One': A Note on Forgery and Identity in *Great Expectations*," McAllister takes the notion of writing in a single hand as a metaphor for moral goodness; unlike the forger who writes in "fifty hands," Pip's single hand marks his eventual "reconciliation with himself" (159). Keith Easley's "Self-Possession in *Great Expectations*" proposes a beyond-the-book reading of *Great Expectations*. Drawing on Bakhtin's work on authoring and heroes, Easley argues that Pip's narrative work enables the younger Pip to become a hero. Not only does Pip achieve self-possession, Easley contends, but he also offers that to Estella: "He offers her the written text of the novel itself, in which she can find knowledge of herself and of the ways in which she has been authored, and through which she may take responsibility for her own authoring of Pip" (180). Easley's treatment of the relationship between the narrating Pip and the younger Pip yields fine points, but the argument about Estella would perhaps demand yet another ending for the novel, one in which Pip hands over the manuscript to Estella.

Garrett Stewart has devised a powerful magnifying lens for analysis of writing, and he provides instructions for its use in "Dickens and the Narratography of Closure." Stewart defines "narratography" in relation to "narratology" at the opening of his essay: "Where narratology aspires to a science of transmedial procedures"—an analysis of narrative in prose fiction, cinema, graphic novel, or other media—"narratography settles upon the immanent workings of a given medium and, in probing the conditioning operations of a graphophonemic or photomechanical inscription, for instance, sets its sights in turn on formative constraints and discrepancies" (509). Stewart demonstrates the practice of narratography in an analysis of the final chapters of *Little Dorrit*. Not since the heyday of poststructuralist criticism, perhaps, has an essay peered so closely at the individual graphemes constituting the semantic and syntactic structures of a text. Stewart demonstrates the critical practices of "narratography" in conjunction with a range of methodologies (narratological, psychoanalytic, generic). He deploys these methodologies with astonishing agility, arresting and probing elements of the novel that readers barely register while the final chapters propel them along. The essay succeeds triumphantly in both of its aims, illuminating the knots and fissures that trouble the ending of this novel and proving the critical value of narratography.

Jason Marc Harris touches lightly, in passing, on Dickens's interest in and use of specific fictional modes in *Folklore and the Fantastic in Nineteenth-Century British Fiction*. Harris proposes to demonstrate "how the tension between folk metaphysics and rationalism produces the literary fantastic" and to show "that narrative and ideological negotiation with folklore was central to the canon, as well as popular in the margins of British literature" (viii). Cynthia Manson considers the particular tale of Sleeping Beauty in relation to *Great Expectations* in *The Fairy-Tale Literature of Charles Dickens, Christina Rossetti, and George MacDonald*. Manson argues that the story of Sleeping Beauty functions "as a paradigm for the divinely intended spiritual development of humanity. To Dickens, the awakening of the enchanted princess represents the human individual who becomes conscious of his or her spiritual equality with other members of flawed and vulnerable humanity, and who embraces available grace to act for the good of others." The emphasis on "spiritual equality" and on caring for others, Manson argues, counters the "Mid-Victorian focus on economic and social advancement and class distinctions" (39). Certainly, Manson's careful reading demonstrates persuasively the multiple and complex functions of the Sleeping Beauty tale. However, the larger claim seems less persuasive. Couldn't *Great Expectations* be read as an "awakening" from romance to realism?

In a comparative study of three novels set during the French Revolution, Gerhart Hoffmeister examines competing narrative modes. In "The French Revolution and Prose Fiction: Allegorization of History and Its Defeat by Romance," Hoffmeister compares German, British, and French fiction set in the time of the French Revolution: Freidrich Maximilian Klinger's *History of a German of the Most Recent Past;* Dickens's *A Tale of Two Cities*; and Victor Hugo's *Seventeen Ninety-Three*. All three, he concludes, deploy "internal distancing" from the historical events of the Revolution; and in all three, "the conventions of romance win over mere historical narrative" (19).

Greater attention to literary modes would refine the argument of Oliver Conolly and Bashshar Haydar in "Literature, Politics, and Character." Conolly and Haydar argue that "literature can suggest insights into character," but "there are prima facie reasons for thinking that it is not well placed to communicate political insights, and that if it attempts to do so, it will be at the expense of character" (100). To illustrate this point, they cite the example of *Hard Times*. In the view of Conolly and Haydar, a reader cannot focus on a specific character and, at the same time, read that character as an element of a political statement; indeed, they argue that "in no genre is it aesthetically advantageuous [sic] to have characters stand for certain social groups" (95). (What about allegory, one wonders?) The writers conclude that "Dickens's successful characterization . . . precludes the communication of a political viewpoint" (100). In order to make the argument convincingly, the authors need to define and historicize "literature"; they need to attend more closely to particular narrative modes; and they also need to acknowledge and historicize the values and reading practices that create this teeter-totter dynamic between "successful characterization" and "communication of a political viewpoint."

In "The Paradox of Fiction and the Ethics of Empathy: Reconceiving Dickens's Realism" Mary-Catherine Harrison offers a bracing and well-researched argument to the contrary. Reviewing the research on the relationship between reading fictional narrative and showing empathy, Harrison cites evidence that the practice of reading synedochically, generalizing from a particular character to a social group, is widespread; furthermore, research shows that empathetic responses to fictional characters can lead to shifts in attitudes toward particular social groups and to actions that aid people in those groups. Harrison turns to *Bleak House* to demonstrate the strategies Dickens employs to motivate readers to read, feel, and act: through the character of Harold Skimpole, who feels for the sweep in song and sends away the suffering Jo, Dickens warns readers about misplaced empathy divorced from ethical action. Through apostrophes to readers, urging them to act on behalf of the suffering children dying on London streets, Dickens seeks to direct empathy for fictional characters into action on behalf of living children.

Michael Irwin considers the shifts between sentimentality and black humor in Dickens's representation of suffering children. In "The Bright Side of Death: Dickens and Black Humour," Irwin considers in the moments in Dickens's writing when the death of a child evokes a snort from ordinary readers, not just from Oscar Wilde. As Irwin notes, "pity, even extravagant sentimentality, on the one hand, and murderous ferocity on the other" sometimes appear "only a hair's breadth apart"; he argues that the textual swing from one to the other "finds a match in Dickens's own abrupt shifts of mood and perspective" (31).

William Cohen, Christine Ferguson, and Carolyn Dever probe sensory and emotional perception and expression in Dickens. Cohen grounds his fiercely smart *Embodied: Victorian Literature and the Senses* in three twentieth-century "paradigms": Merleau-Ponty's model of vision as "cutaneous rubbing of surfaces"; Deleuze and Guittari's model of subjectivity as "provisional construction" whose "parts . . . carry onto or plug into other things, phenomena, and energies"; and Bataille's model of the "body's interior exploding outward" (22–23). Turning to Dickens, Cohen focuses on scenes of keyhole spying in *The Old Curiosity Shop* and *David Copperfield*, emphasizing "the physicality of perception" in these scenes: "Embodied acts of looking and listening in Dickens, especially as they are focused and localized by keyholes, are . . . proximate, intersubjective, and material; they have as much impact on the observer as on the observed, for the keyhole has openings in both directions" (31–32). While Cohen acknowledges Foucauldian and psychoanalytic readings of these scenes, his analyses move beyond those readings to demonstrate the "full-bodied" richness of Dickens's representations (35. In *The Old Curiosity Shop*, Cohen shows, keyhole-spying leads to consumption: "[t]he keyhole enacts continuity between perception and other forms of bodily ingestion" (35). When Peggotty speaks through the keyhole to Davey, imprisoned for biting, her "words go down his throat rather than into his ear," so that "language . . . becomes the tactile sensation of breath felt inside the body" (37). Cohen notes that the "language of absorption and ingestion sets the pattern for Copperfield's future expressions of intense feeling," whether he is "steeped in Dora" or disgusted by Uriah Heep.

In "Sensational Dependence: Prosthesis and Affect in Dickens and Braddon," Christine Ferguson deploys the insights of earlier work in disability studies to examine the "somatic epistemology of genre" in fiction of the 1860s, giving particular attention to Mary Elizabeth Braddon's sensation novel *The Trail of the Serpent* and Dickens's story "Doctor Marigold." Ferguson argues that both texts "work to transgress the popular somatic epistemologies of Victorian realist and affective writing alike"; in this way, they complicate the emphasis of realist fiction on vision and the emphasis of sensation fiction on feeling (8). Both texts figure "characters with communication disabilities," and both interrogate the assumed norms of communication, for both "represent reading as a physically labile process, normalize dependence, and imaginatively diversify the bodily sites and signs of sentience" (21).

Carolyn Dever explores "The Gamut of Emotions from A to B: *Nickleby*'s 'Histrionic Expedition.' " Melodrama, Dever notes, involves the full range of emotions, from the extremes of joy to the extremes of melancholy. In *Nicholas Nickleby*, she says, Dickens uses the "high emotional highs and low emotional lows" of melodrama "to signify emotional subtleties" (2). Situating the dynamics of relationships—especially family relationships—along the continuum between the polar extremes, Dickens "posits ambivalence . . . as the engine of affective synthesis, and the prime signifier of psychological complexity" (2). "To apply the concept of ambivalence to the Nickleby family is in some sense to shoot fish in a barrel," Dever concedes cheerfully, but the powerful hostility and affection of these characters illustrate her argument. Dever highlights Dickens's strategy of twinning figures, arguing that "the novel attributes oppositional emotional qualities to characters who serve as doubles or mirror images for one another"; this strategy sustains the tensions between familiar emotions—love and hate, despair and hope—and forestalls resolution (14).

In *The Secret Vice*, Diane Mason highlights the ways in which the medical and moral discourse of masturbation informs the depiction of characters in Dickens, especially Bradley Headstone and Eugene Wrayburn. Turning from *Our Mutual Friend* to *The Mystery of Edwin Drood*, she considers "the pathology and symptoms of opium addiction" in relation to "those of masturbation" (9). Every page of the study benefits from her extensive research and careful documentation. Now that Mason has demonstrated so scrupulously the parallels between these discourses, others might pursue the analysis of tensions between the medical, moral, religious, and other discourses in Dickens's late novels.

Both Sambudha Sen and James Reitter turn to modes of pictorial representation; both study the ways in which Hogarth's illustrations, in particular, inform Dickens's work. In "Hogarth, Egan, Dickens, and the Making of an Urban Aesthetic," Sen proposes a genealogy of Dickens's "urban aesthetic" that runs from William Hogarth through Pierce Egan to Dickens. He examines that genealogy through Hogarth's *Industry and Idleness*, Egan's "Life in London," and—by way of *Sketches by Boz—Oliver Twist*, arguing that "these works reproduced the metropolis along two contradictory trajectories, attempting to topographize the city, to bring its dark nooks and corners under surveillance while discursively cordoning off the world of the respectable from the unregenerate 'other' London" (84). For Sen, the tension between the "social extremes" in these representations of London is the central dynamic of the "urban aesthetic" (104).

Reitter opens "Dickens and Three Stages of Illustration Evolution" with an acknowledgment of Dickens's debt to Hogarth. He proceeds to examine the transition in modes of illustration across Dickens's novels from the caricatures of Cruikshank to the realistic drawings of Marcus Stone. "Where the visual artistry of George Cruikshank in *Oliver Twist* provided the reader with insight into characters and enhanced the narrative," Reitter argues, "Marcus Stone's work in Dickens's last novel was simply a reflection of the text" (35).

Jenny Uglow surveys Dickens's relationships with his illustrators in *Words and Pictures*, noting that "[t]here were over nine hundred original illustrations to Dickens's work over the years" (131). She argues that the illustrations, like the fiction, "became more serious and realistic as the years went by" and contends that "in the later novels the detail and imagery of Dickens's descriptions almost annihilated any chance of faithful illustration" (135). Phiz, according to Uglow, struggled with the task of conveying the "detail and imagery" of *Bleak House* and *Little Dorrit*, and a variety of tensions between Dickens and Browne led to the engagement of Marcus Stone and Luke Fildes for the three final novels. The work of Uglow and Reitter provides a foundation for further comparative work in the relationship between shifts in visual and narrative modes of representation across Dickens's career, situating that comparison within the shifting modes of visual representation and technologies of reproduction in nineteenth-century Britain.

Daniel Akiva Novak, too, studies the relationship between narrative and visual representation; however, Novak focuses not on illustration but on the emerging technology of photographic representation. *Realism, Photography, and Nineteenth-Century Fiction* begins by examining the Victorian discourses surrounding photography, especially the widespread practice of assembling composite photographs from parts of images. While Dickens called attention to the strange and unsettling notion of pieced-together images of human bodies, Novak argues that he also deployed similar strategies in his own fictional practice.

In a reading of *Little Dorrit*, Novak demonstrates parallels between remembering and re-membering in the thematics of plot, the representation of the body, and the activity of reading. At the level of plot, Dickens uses the inscription "DNF" to enjoin characters (and readers) to remember the past, to piece together suppressed stories into a coherent narrative. Dickens highlights the complexity of remembering, however, by marking the differences between the past that Mr. Clennam enjoins his wife to remember and the past Mrs. Clennam chooses to remember. In his representation of Mrs. Merdle as a spectacular body, Dickens uses synecdoche—referring to her as "The Bosom"—as a means of suggesting a coherent whole, yet the description of her oddly mixed parts vexes the idea of a coherent and unified body. Turning to Mr. Merdle, Novak demonstrates the problem of composition in the thematics of the plot: Mr. Merdle's forgeries function as "badly composed fictions" that break down catastrophically (85). Strategic forgetting, Novak asserts, creates the illusion of a whole at all of these levels, and at the level of the novel form: "the novel depends on the reader forgetting how disconnected moments of reading become a text with an organic totality" (76).

Richard Menke examines the relationship between fiction and another emerging technology, the telegraph, in *Telegraphic Realism: Victorian Fiction and Other Information Systems*. Menke describes his ambitious aim in this study of information technologies and Victorian fiction: "not only to explore one aspect of Victorian life as treated in novels, but ultimately to recognize nineteenth-century realism as part of a world of new media and industrialized information" (9). Victorian realism, Menke argues, "[purports] to provide not naively transparent representations of references in the outside world so much as a system of analogies within the text that, like a perspectival drawing, simulates the relationships writers found in the world" (26). Telegraphic realism focuses on the ways in which "[n]ew media and information systems suggested new possibilities for representing the real" (27).

Menke documents Dickens's fascination with emerging information and transportation systems, and he offers richly rewarding discussions of *A Tale of Two Cities* and "The Signal Man." As Menke demonstrates, Dickens opens *A Tale of Two Cities* with a scene in which communication across distance requires physical transportation of written messages—though "on a wet November night in 1775 there simply could have been no 'lumbering old mail-coach' making its way to Dover," for the Dover mail was established a decade later (111). The development of plot requires faster transmission of information; drawing on Carlyle's description of the optical telegraph in the French Revolution, Dickens constructs around Madame Defarge "an optical telegraph system" 126). By the end of the novel, Menke argues, the beheaded Sydney Carton serves as "a device for disembodied information"; like the "new information systems" of the nineteenth century, characterized by "speed, communication," and "the annihilation of space and time," "Sydney Carton overcomes the constraints of time, space, matter, and personality to become a channel for information" (132). Thus, "for the sake of realism" Dickens's "historical fiction now must historicize communication systems as part of the relationship between past and present" (105). In his discussion of Dickens's ghost story, "The Signal Man," Menke shows "how the tale suggests the disturbing psychic effects, and even the potential trauma, of modern information" (167). This story revolves around the signal man's vision of a ghostly apparition that foretells the means of his own death; in this way, the ghostly self of the signal man provides at once an optical telegraph of the death he has suffered and the death that the mortal self will suffer. "The Signal Man" thus "highlights the ghostliness of information freed from time, space, or matter" (172).

The affinity between Dickens's work and the later technology of cinema continues to prompt new film and television productions. Brian McFarlane compares old and new productions of *Great Expectations*, surveying stage, radio, television, and film adaptations. McFarlane opens *Charles Dickens' Great Expectations: A Close Study of the Relationship Between Text and Film* by focusing on formal features: the serial numbers; the three "stages" of Pip's expectations; and the pivot points of the plot. Drawing on Roland Barthes's description of "cardinal functions" in narrative, McFarlane identifies fifty-four of these pivot points or "major cardinal functions in *Great Expectations*, major in the sense that without any one of them the outcome might have been different" (9). As McFarlane notes in the introduction, the 1946 adaptation, directed by David Lean, is "a major focus of this book"; he defers the full discussion of Lean's film until the end. "Having written about it at length before, I wanted to see how it stood up to comparison with other, less well-known, less critically regarded versions," McFarlane states; furthermore, he explains, "I wanted readers to have in mind, before reading about it at length, the other kinds of treatment the novel has attracted, without their simply being seen as cowering in the long shadow of the Lean film" (vii).

Unfortunately, the Lean film refuses to wait quietly in its place at the end of the book. It functions as the standard of comparison throughout McFarlane's discussion of other adaptations: the 1986 mini-series, *Great Expectations: The Untold Story*; the 1981 and 1999 mini-series; and the 1934, 1975, and 1998 films. Cinematography, screenplays, performances—all are measured against elements of Lean's film, so that readers learn that the "colour" of the 1975 adaptation "adds nothing to the ghostly chiaroscuro of Lean's film" (101) or that Anne Bancroft's performance in the 1998 film does not have "the implacable bitterness that Martita Hunt brought to the Lean version" (123) long before McFarlane discusses Lean's film. Given McFarlane's understandable regard for David Lean's achievement, it would have made better sense to situate the discussion of the 1946 film at the beginning of the book.

Great Expectations is also the focus of Ana Moya and Gemma López's "'I'm a Wild Success': Postmodern Dickens/Victorian Cuarón." Alfonso Cuarón's adaptation of *Great Expectations*, argue Moya and López, is "a dialogical response to nineteenth-century cultural and ideological constructions of subjectivity" (174). Cuarón's film, set in North America in the 1980s, "revitalizes the Victorian text and makes it available to contemporary audiences," they contend; they compare the "feminized foster fathers," the "gangster types," the "jilted brides," and the "textual heroines" of these texts and conclude that "contemporary American society," as represented in Cuarón's film, "seems to both inherit and to a certain extent reaffirm cultural constructions of identity which can be traced back to early nineteenth-century Victorian society" (186). Ultimately, in their view, the juxtaposition of film and novel illuminates the ways in which both texts interrogate the notions of loss and success.

Echoes

The echoes of classical and biblical texts in Dickens attract the attention of Mark M. Hennelly, Jr., and Jennifer Gribble. In "Dickens's Daniel-Plato Complex: *Dombey* and *Bleak House*" Hennelly draws together two recurring allusions in Dickens's writing, the writing on the wall in the Book of Daniel and the shadows on the wall of Plato's cave. Both the cryptic words and the spectral shadows on the walls present problems of deciphering truth. This "Daniel-Plato complex," Hennelly argues, "performs a variety of significant roles" in *Dombey and Son* and in *Bleak House*, "particularly prefiguring the unforeseen destinies of characters and foreshadowing subtly interrelated tropes and themes" (122). These figures for the difficulty of deciphering truth, according to Hennelly, serve to "[challenge] Dickens's own readers to discover the mysteriously hidden 'interpretation thereof' in his fiction" (122).

Gribble argues in "The Bible in *Great Expectations*" that the parable of the prodigal son serves as an "interpretive key" to *Great Expectations* (232). She suggests that the three stages of Pip's expectations parallel the three parts of the parable: "the son's claiming of his inheritance, his leaving home for a spendthrift life in a far place, and his return and reconciliation with the father" (232). Both the echo of this parable and the treatment of the Bible more generally deserve the closer attention that Gribble provides. From the illegible Bibles at Mr. Wopsle's great-aunt's dreadful school to Pip's "sanctimonious reading of the Bible" to Magwitch, the novel, in Gribble's view, calls into question the nature of biblical authority. "[T]he authority this novel finds in its grand narrative depends on its cultural work as story," Gribble concludes, "trans-historical, morally educative, endlessly interpretable" (239).

The unearthing of the ancient past, Virginia Zimmerman shows in *Excavating Victorians*, allowed the Victorians to reconstruct the narrative of that past. Beginning with the Ricoeurian idea of the "trace," Zimmerman examines Victorian responses to the work of geologists and archeologists, focusing particularly on "the relationship between the individual life and the immensity of time" (4). The fossil record provoked anxiety about the survival of species; ancient ruins provoked anxiety about the survival of the nation and the empire; and reflection on "the immensity of time" provoked anxiety about the brevity of the individual life. Zimmerman argues that projects of excavation, literal and metaphorical, offered opportunities for constructing meaning. "[E]xcavation became a powerful epistemological trope for the Victorians: it brings together notions of time as spatial and of a person's ability to stand outside the layers of the past . . . to plumb the depths and produce narrative accounts of what is uncovered within the rock and dust," Zimmerman asserts; "[e]xcavation was a way of knowing and conquering the depth of time" (8). Zimmerman gives particular emphasis to the uniformitarian theory of change; because the geological and archeological records demonstrated the enormous effects of small changes over long periods of time, those records testified to the power of the brief, small individual life: "If the minute actions of a water drop could carve a canyon, then the seemingly insignificant actions of a man or woman might also have great effect" (19).

In the chapter entitled "Dickens among the Ruins," Zimmerman deploys this insight in her reading of *Little Dorrit*; exploring the projects of excavation and surveys of ruin in that novel, she concludes that "[t]the acceptance that the past is irrecoverable and that progress toward the future is dull and uniform is *Little Dorrit*'s happy ending" (161). The chapter moves on to an analysis of *Our Mutual Friend*, focusing on the significance of excavation, especially the excavation of the dust heaps, and articulation, in both senses: assembly of fragments and construction of narrative. The book itself assembles its insights into a well-crafted argument, situating every knucklebone with scrupulous care to advance a line of critical argument that began with Gillian Beer's *Darwin's Plots*.

Vincent Newey investigates the relationship between Dickens and the Romantic past in "Rival Cultures: Dickens and the Byronic Legacy." Newey argues that Dickens regarded "Byronic Romanticism" with "deep fascination" even as he had to "forfeit it in favour of an ethos of solid social virtues." Newey suggests that "we should think of connections as well as departures, and of continuities as well as breaks" when we consider Dickens and Byron (68). While Byronic Romanticism surely features among the strains of Romanticism that inform Dickens's work, other scholars will no doubt wish to continue debate about particular elements of the argument. Newey proposes, for example, that "Dickens inherits from Byron a sense of the spiritual bankruptcy of the English upper classes and their regime'' (68), but Dickens surely received that legacy more directly from any number of his novel-writing forebears.

In a variety of ways, Dickens's writings echo the workings of his own mind. In *Dickens and Creativity*, Barbara Hardy reads Dickens's letters, articles, and novels to find in these texts the traces of his own creative imagination. She opens *Dickens and Creativity* with a brief overview of Dickens's writing life, ''A Career and its Context''; she then moves chronologically through the prodigious work of the Sparkler, looking at moments in which Dickens describes explicitly the workings of his imagination; at ''creative self-reference'' in narrating voices of the early writings (40); and at first-person narrators in Dickens's novels. Hardy then turns her attention to a small crowd of weird and garrulous characters who offer a means of peering into the magnificent and capacious authorial imagination. Very little recent scholarship informs the book, but Hardy has done useful labor in collecting and classifying voices that attest to the whirrings of Dickensian imagination.

Kate Summerscale's book, *The Suspicions of Mr. Whicher*, follows the developments in a contemporary case that caught Dickens's imagination. Both Dickens and Wilkie Collins were fascinated by the murder of little Saville Kent at Road Hill House in 1860, and Kate Summerscale recounts the tale of the murder and the detective work of Detective-Inspector Jonathan Whicher in an engrossing work ''modeled on the country-house murder mystery, the form that the Road Hill case inspired'' (xiii). According to Summerscale, aspects of this case informed Collins's *The Moonstone* and Dickens's *The Mystery of Edwin Drood*. As she traces the history of this sensational case, Summerscale knits into the detective story the comments that Dickens and Collins made as the case unfolded and points out specific ways in which both writers adapted elements of the Road Hill murder in their fiction.

Jerome Meckier and Deborah A. Thomas trace the influence of Dickens on other writers. In ''*The Three Clerks* and *Rachel Ray*: Trollope's Revaluation of Dickens Continued,'' Meckier examines Trollope's efforts to take Dickens down a peg in *The Three Clerks* and in *Rachel Ray*. In *The Three Clerks*, Trollope castigates Dickens for ''demonizing outsiders like Bill Sikes''; in *Rachel Ray*, he employs a very different tactic: ''In a skillful, low-key revaluation of *Great Expectations*, Trollope laughs at Dickens more successfully than he chastises *Oliver Twist* in *The Three Clerks*'' (169). While Dickens inverted the fairy tale, Meckier argues, Trollope ''retells'' the Cinderella story and ''reassures readers . . . that it was still possible to attain one's heart's desire'' (169).

Thomas's '' 'Don't Let the Bastards Grind You Down': Echoes of *Hard Times* in *The Handmaid's Tale*'' focuses on three elements of *The Handmaid's*

Tale that echo elements of *Hard Times*: the exercise of mind control in the schoolroom; the suppression of proper names; and the victimization of young women by powerful men. As she notes, Atwood's study of Victorian literature makes it quite likely that she knows *Hard Times* well. While Thomas may have identified a strand of narrative influence, others may wish to widen the scope in order to discover how these narrative elements function in a larger tradition of social-problem novels and dystopian fiction.

With so much to admire, so many new questions to pursue, I close the survey of Dickens scholarship in 2008 and pass the baton. I've tried to give a comprehensive and useful overview of the year's work, but I will borrow here the words of Dickens himself in case I have missed (or misread) work: "If an apology be necessary, I hope you will accept my unaffected assurance that I am exceedingly sorry" (Letter to Douglas Jerrold, 10 Nov. 1836). And finally, I add my thanks to all the gifted scholars working on Dickens and to the editors of *DSA* for this extraordinary opportunity.

WORKS CITED

Alexander, Christine. "The Juvenilia of Charles Dickens: Romance and Reality." *Dickens Quarterly* 25.1 (March 2008): 3–22.

Allen, Michelle Elizabeth. *Cleansing the City: Sanitary Geographies in Victorian London.* Athens: Ohio UP, 2008.

Brown, Julia Prewitt. *The Bourgeois Interior.* Charlottesville: U of Virginia P, 2008.

Brown, Kimberlie L. " 'When I Kissed Her Cheek': Theatrics of Sexuality and the Framed Gaze in Esther's Narration of *Bleak House.*" *Dickens Studies Annual* 39 (2008): 149–76.

Browning, Logan Delano. "Changing Notes into Pictures: An American Frame for Dickens's Italy." *Dickens Quarterly* 25.4 (Dec. 2008): 241–49.

Buzard, James. "Enumeration and Exhaustion: Taking Inventory in *The Old Curiosity Shop.*" *Dickens Studies Annual* 39 (2008): 17–42.

Cain, Lynn. *Dickens, Family, Authorship: Psychoanalytic Perspectives on Kinship and Creativity.* Burlington, VT: Ashgate, 2008.

Case, Alison, and Harry Shaw. *Reading the Nineteenth-Century Novel: Austen to Eliot.* London: Blackwell, 2008.

Castillo, Larisa T. "Natural Authority in Charles Dickens's *Martin Chuzzlewit* and the Copyright Act of 1842." *Nineteenth-Century Literature,* 62.4 (Mar. 2008):435–64.

Cohen, William A. *Embodied: Victorian Literature and the Senses.* Minneapolis: U of Minnesota P, 2008.

Conolly, Oliver, and Bashshar Haydar. ''Literature, Politics, and Character.'' *Philosophy & Literature*, 32.1 (Apr. 2008): 87–101.

Coriale, Danielle. ''*Sketches by Boz*, 'So Frail A Machine.' '' *SEL* 48.4 (Autumn 2008): 801–12.

Cozzi, Annette. ''Men and Menus: Dickens and the Rise of the 'Ordinary' English Gentleman.'' *Edible Ideologies: Representing Food and Meaning.* Ed. Kathleen LeBesco and Peter Naccarato. Albany: SUNY P, 2008. 23–52.

Davis, Philip. *Why Victorian Literature Still Matters.* Malden, MA: Wiley-Blackwell, 2008.

Dever, Carolyn. ''The Gamut of Emotions from A to B: Nickleby's 'Histrionic Expedition'.'' *Dickens Studies Annual* 39 (2008): 1–16.

Drew, John. ''Dickens on 'Poor Hood': A New Article.'' *The Dickensian* 104.2 (Summer 2008): 111–22.

Easley, Keith. ''Self-Possession in *Great Expectations*.'' *Dickens Studies Annual* 39 (2008): 177–222.

Easson, Angus, Leon Litvack, Margaret Brown, and Joan Dicks, ''The Letters of Charles Dickens: Supplement IX.'' *The Dickensian* 104.2 (Summer 2008): 140–58.

———. ''The Letters of Charles Dickens: Supplement X.'' *The Dickensian* 104.3 (Winter 2008): 236–46.

Edgecombe, Rodney Stenning. ''The Heroine of Quiet Service in *Dombey and Son*.'' *Dickens Quarterly* 25.2 (June 2008): 73–89.

Ferguson, Christine. ''Sensational Dependence: Prosthesis and Affect in Dickens and Braddon.'' *Lit: Literature Interpretation Theory* 19.1 (Jan. 2008): 1–25.

Fox, Paul. ''Dickens à la Carte: Aesthetic Victualism and the Invigoration of the Artist in Huysmans's *Against Nature*.'' *Art and Life in Aestheticism: De-Humanizing and Re-Humanizing Art, the Artist, and the Artistic Receptor.* Ed. Kelly Comfort. New York: Macmillan, 2008.

Fromer, Julie E. *A Necessary Luxury: Tea in Victorian England.* Athens, OH: Ohio UP, 2008.

Garnett, Robert. ''The Mysterious Mourner: Dickens's Funeral and Ellen Ternan.'' *Dickens Quarterly* 25.2 (June 2008): 107–17.

Gillooly, Eileen, and Deirdre David. *Contemporary Dickens.* Columbus: Ohio State UP, 2008.

Gilman, Sander L. "Desire and Obesity: Dickens, Endocrinology, Pulmonary Medicine, and Psychoanalysis." *Psychoanalysis and Narrative Medicine*. Ed. Peter L. Rudnytsky and Rita Charon. Albany: SUNY P, 2008.

Gregory, Melissa Valiska, and Melisa Klimaszewski. *Brief Lives: Charles Dickens*. London: Hesperus, 2008.

Gribble, Jennifer. "The Bible in *Great Expectations*." *Dickens Quarterly* 25.4 (Dec. 2008): 232–40.

Hack, Daniel. "Close Reading at a Distance: The African Americanization of *Bleak House*." *Critical Inquiry* 34.4 (Summer 2008): 729–53.

Hardy, Barbara Nathan. *Dickens and Creativity*. London: Continuum, 2008.

Harris, Jason Marc. *Folklore and the Fantastic in Nineteenth-Century British Fiction*. Burlington, VT: Ashgate, 2008.

Harrison, Mary-Catherine. "The Paradox of Fiction and the Ethics of Empathy: Reconceiving Dickens's Realism." *Narrative* 16.3 (Oct. 2008): 256–78.

Hartley, Jenny. *Charles Dickens and the House of Fallen Women*. London: Methuen, 2008.

Hedgecock, Jennifer. *The Femme Fatale in Victorian Literature: The Danger and the Sexual Threat*. Youngstown, NY: Cambria, 2008.

Hennelly, Mark M., Jr. "Dickens's Daniel-Plato Complex: *Dombey* and *Bleak House*." *Dickens Studies Annual* 39 (2008): 97–126.

Hill, Jen. *White Horizon: The Arctic in the Nineteenth-Century British Imagination*. Albany: SUNY P, 2008.

Hoffmeister, Gerhart. "The French Revolution and Prose Fiction: Allegorization of History and Its Defeat by Romance." *Romantic Prose Fiction*. Ed. Gerald Gillespie, Manfred Engel, and Bernard Dieterle. Amsterdam: Benjamins Publishing, 2008. 1–21.

Hornback, Bert. "Mortimer Lightwood." *Dickens Studies Annual* 39 (2008): 249–60.

House, Madeline, and Graham Storey, eds. *The Letters of Charles Dickens*. Vol. 1. Oxford: Clarendon Press, 1965.

Inglis, Katherine. "Becoming Automatous: Automata in *The Old Curiosity Shop* and *Our Mutual Friend*." *19: Interdisciplinary Studies in the Long Nineteenth Century* 6 (April 2008): <http://www.19.bbk.ac.uk/issue6/papers/inglisaautomata.pdf>. 23 July 2008.

Irwin, Michael. "The Bright Side of Death: Dickens and Black Humour." *The Dickensian* 104.1 (Spring 2008): 22–31.

Jackson, Lisa Hartsell. "Little Nell's Nightmare: Sexual Awakening and Insomnia in Dickens's *The Old Curiosity Shop.*" *Dickens Studies Annual* 39 (2008): 43–58.

Kennedy, Valerie. "Dickens and Savagery at Home and Abroad—Part I." *The Dickensian* 104.2 (Summer 2008): 123–39.

———. "Dickens and Savagery at Home and Abroad—Part II." *The Dickensian* 104.3 (Winter 2008): 206–22.

Langbauer, Laurie. "Ethics and Theory: Suffering Children in Dickens, Dostoevsky, and LeGuin." *ELH* 75.1 (Spring 2008): 89–108.

Lennartz, Norbert. "Charles Dickens Abroad: The Victorian Smelfungus and the Genre of the Unsentimental Journey." *Dickens Quarterly* 25.3 (Sept. 2008): 145–61.

Lewis, Peter R. "Dickens and the Staplehurst Rail Crash, 9 June 1865": *The Dickensian* 104.3 (Winter 2008): 197–203.

Lockard, Joe. *Watching Slavery: Witness Texts and Travel Reports.* New York: Peter Lang, 2008.

Manson, Cynthia. *The Fairy-Tale Literature of Charles Dickens, Christina Rossetti, and George MacDonald: Antidotes to the Victorian Spiritual Crisis.* Lewiston, NY: Edwin Mellen, 2008.

Martens, Britta. "Death as Spectacle: The Paris Morgue in Dickens and Browning." *Dickens Studies Annual* 39 (2008): 223–49.

Mason, Diane. *The Secret Vice: Masturbation in Victorian Fiction and Medical Culture.* Manchester: Manchester UP, 2008.

Mazzeno, Laurence W. *The Dickens Industry: Critical Perspectives 1836–2005.* Rochester, NY: Camden House, 2008.

McAllister, Marie. " 'Sneaking You as Writes but One': A Note on Forgery and Identity in Great Expectations." *Explicator* 66.3 (Spring 2008): 158–60.

McFarlane, Brian. *Charles Dickens' Great Expectations: A Close Study of the Relationship Between Text and Film.* London: Methuen Drama, 2008.

McManus, I. C. "Charles Dickens: A Neglected Diagnosis." *Dickens Quarterly* 25.2 (June 2008): 98–108.

Meckier, Jerome. "*The Three Clerks* and *Rachel Ray*: Trollope's Revaluation of Dickens Continued." *Dickens Quarterly* 25.3 (Sept. 2008): 162–71.

Meir, Natalie Kapetanios. " 'What Would You Like For Dinner?' Dining and Narration in *David Copperfield.*" *Dickens Studies Annual* 39 (2008): 127–48.

Menke, Richard. *Telegraphic Realism: Victorian Fiction and Other Information Systems.* Stanford, CA: Stanford UP, 2008.

Metz, Nancy. "Italy: The Sequel." *Dickens Quarterly* 25.1 (March 2008): 37–45.

Miller, Nan. "We Came to Hear Dickens."*Modern Age* 50.1 (Winter 2008): 49–57.

Moore, Tara. "Starvation in Victorian Christmas Fiction." *Victorian Literature and Culture* 36.2 (Sept. 2008): 489–505.

Moya, Ana, and Gemma López. " 'I'm a Wild Success': Postmodern Dickens/Victorian Cuarón." *Dickens Quarterly* 25.3 (Sept. 2008): 172–89.

Newey, Vincent. "Rival Cultures: Dickens and the Byronic Legacy." *Romantic Echoes in the Victorian Era.* Ed. Andrew Radford and Mark Sandy. Burlington, VT: Ashgate, 2008.67–84.

Novak, Daniel Akiva. *Realism, Photography, and Nineteenth-Century Fiction.* Cambridge: Cambridge UP, 2008.

Parker, David. "Dickens's Death: The Peckham Conjecture." *Dickens Quarterly* 25.3 (Sept. 2008): 190–93.

Paroissien, David. *A Companion to Charles Dickens.* Malden, MA: Blackwell, 2008.

Pollack-Pelzner, Daniel. "Reading and Repeating *Our Mutual Friend.*" *Dickens Studies Annual* 39 (2008): 261–80.

Poon, Angela. *Enacting Englishness in the Victorian Period: Colonialism and the Politics of Performance.* Burlington, VT: Ashgate, 2008.

Reitter, James. "Dickens and Three Stages of Illustration Evolution." *Interdisciplinary Humanities* 25.1 (Spring 2008): 33–53.

Rubery, Matthew. "Play It Again, Sam Weller: New Digital Audiobooks and Old Ways of Reading." *Journal of Victorian Culture* 13.1 (Spring 2008): 58–79.

———. "*Bleak House* in Real Time." *English Language Notes* 46.1 (Spring/Summer 2008): 113–18

Sasaki, Toru. "Edmund Wilson's 'The Two Scrooges' Reconsidered." *The Dickensian* 104.1 (Spring 2008): 32–44.

Sen, Sambudha. "Hogarth, Egan, Dickens, and the Making of an Urban Aesthetic." *Representations* 103 (Summer 2008): 84–106.

Simon, Leslie. "Archives of the Interior: Exhibitions of Domesticity in *The Pickwick Papers.*" *Dickens Quarterly* 25.1 (March 2008): 23–36.

Smith, Andrew. "Colonial Ghosts: Mimicking Dickens in America." *Le Gothic: Influences and Appropriations in Europe and America.* Ed. Avril Horner and Sue Zlosnik. New York: Macmillan, 2008.

Smith, Karl Ashley. *Dickens and the Unreal City.* New York: Macmillan, 2008.

Standiford, Les. *The Man Who Invented Christmas: How Charles Dickens's A Christmas Carol Rescued His Career and Revived our Holiday Spirits.* New York: Crown, 2008.

Stewart, Garrett. "Dickens and the Narratography of Closure." *Critical Inquiry* 34.4 (Spring 2008): 504–42.

Summerscale, Kate. *The Suspicions of Mr. Whicher; or, The Murder at Road Hill House.* London: Bloomsbury, 2008.

Tambling, Jeremy. *Going Astray: Dickens and London.* Harlow, England: Pearson Longman, 2008.

Thomas, Deborah A. " 'Don't Let the Bastards Grind You Down': Echoes of *Hard Times* in *The Handmaid's Tale.*" *Dickens Quarterly* 25.2 (June 2008): 90–97.

Uglow, Jenny. *Words and Pictures: Writers, Artists and a Peculiarly British Tradition.* London: Faber and Faber, 2008.

Wagner, Tamara S. " 'We have orphans [. . .] in stock': Crime and the Consumption of Sensational Children." Ed. Dennis Denisoff. *Nineteenth-Century Childhood and Consumer Culture.* Burlington, VT: Ashgate, 2008.

Waters, Catherine. " 'Fairy Palaces' and 'Wonderful Toys': Machine Dreams in *Household Words.*" *Dickens Quarterly* 25.4 (Dec. 2008): 215–31.

———. *Commodity Culture in Dickens's Household Words: The Social Life of Goods.* Burlington, VT: Ashgate, 2008.

Webb, Igor. "Charles Dickens in America: The Writer and Reality." *Dickens Studies Annual* 39 (2008): 59–96.

Zimmerman, Virginia. *Excavating Victorians.* Albany: SUNY P, 2008.

.

INDEX

(Page numbers in italics represent illustrations)